Making Supply Chain Management Work

Design, Implementation, Partnerships, Technology, and Profits

THE AUERBACH
BEST PRACTICES SERIES

Broadband Networking
James Trulove, Editor
ISBN: 0-8493-9821-5

Business Continuity Planning
Ken Doughty, Editor
ISBN: 0-8493-0907-7

**The Complete Book
of Remote Access:
Connectivity and Security**
Victor Kasacavage, Editor
ISBN: 0-8493-1253-1

**Designing a Total
Data Solution:
Technology, Implementation,
and Deployment**
Roxanne E. Burkey and
Charles V. Breakfield, Editors
ISBN: 0-8493-0893-3

**High Performance Web
Databases: Design,
Development, and
Deployment**
Sanjiv Purba, Editor
ISBN: 0-8493-0882-8

**Making Supply Chain
Management Work**
James Ayers, Editor
ISBN: 0-8493-1273-6

**Financial Services
Information Systems**
Jessica Keyes, Editor
ISBN: 0-8493-9834-7

**Healthcare Information
Systems**
Phillip L. Davidson, Editor
ISBN: 0-8493-9963-7

**Multi-Operating System
Networking: Living with UNIX,
NetWare, and NT**
Raj Rajagopal, Editor
ISBN: 0-8493-9831-2

Network Design
Gilbert Held, Editor
ISBN: 0-8493-0859-3

Network Manager's Handbook
John Lusa, Editor
ISBN: 0-8493-9841-X

**New Directions in Internet
Management**
Sanjiv Purba, Editor
ISBN: 0-8493-1160-8

**New Directions in Project
Management**
Paul Tinnirello, Editor
ISBN: 0-8493-1190-X

**The Privacy Papers: Managing
Technology, Consumer,
Employee, and Legislative
Actions**
Rebecca Herold, Editor
ISBN: 0-8493-1248-5

Web-to-Host Connectivity
Lisa Lindgren and Anura Gurugé,
Editors
ISBN: 0-8493-0835-6

**Winning the Outsourcing
Game: Making the Best Deals
and Making Them Work**
Janet Butler, Editor
ISBN: 0-8493-0875-5

AUERBACH PUBLICATIONS

www.auerbach-publications.com
TO ORDER: Call: 1-800-272-7737 • Fax: 1-800-374-3401
E-mail: orders@crcpress.com

BEST PRACTICES SERIES

Making Supply Chain Management Work

Design, Implementation, Partnerships, Technology, and Profits

Editor

James B. Ayers

AUERBACH PUBLICATIONS

A CRC Press Company

Boca Raton   London   New York   Washington, D.C.

Library of Congress Cataloging-in-Publication Data

Making supply chain management work : design, implementation, partnerships, technology, and profits / James B. Ayers, editor
    p. cm. — (Best practices series)
    A collection of 57 articles compiled from Auerbach Publications' Knowledgebase.
    Includes bibliographical references and index.
    ISBN 0-8493-1273-6 (alk. paper)
    1. Business logistics—Data processing. 2. Industrial procurement—Data processing. 3. Business networks—Communication systems. 4. Industrial procurement—Computer network resources. 5. Electronic commerce. I. Ayers, James B. II. Best practices series (Boca Raton, Fla.)

HD38.5 .M35 2001
658.7—dc21
        2001052489

Visit the Auerbach Publications Web site at
www.auerbach-publications.com

© 2002 by CRC Press LLC
Auerbach is an imprint of CRC Press LLC

No claim to original U.S. Government works
International Standard Book Number 0-8493-1273-6
Library of Congress Card Number 2001052489
Printed in the United States of America 1 2 3 4 5 6 7 8 9 0
Printed on acid-free paper

Contributors

RITU AGARWAL, *Associate Professor, Management and Information Systems, College of Business, Florida State University, Tallahassee, Florida*

DOUG ALDRICH, *Vice President and Managing Director, Global Strategic Information Technology Practice, A.T. Kearney, Dallas, Texas*

THILINI ARIYACHANDRA, *Doctoral Student, Management Information Systems, Terry College of Business, University of Georgia, Athens, Georgia*

MARY AYALA-BUSH, *Principal, Computer Sciences Corporation, Waltham, Massachusetts*

JAMES B. AYERS, *Principal, CGR Management Consultants, Playa del Rey, California*

PAUL BAYES, *Professor of Accountancy, East Tennessee State University, Johnson City, Tennessee*

ALEX N. BEAVERS, JR., *Chief Executive Officer, Thomson Industries, Port Washington, New York*

MARK BILLS, *Managing Director, Strategic Technology Management, Inc., Lisle, Illinois*

BERNARD H. BOAR, *Director, Strategic Solutions, RCG Information Technology, East Brunswick, New Jersey*

D.P. CARDARELLI, *President and Chief Executive Officer, Agway, Inc., Syracuse, New York*

JOHN CARE, *Director, Technical Services, Yardley, Pennslyvania*

HOUSTON H. CARR, *Professor of Management, Auburn University, Auburn, Alabama*

KAZEM CHAHARBAGHI, *Faculty Member, Manufacturing Technology and Production Management, Cranfield University, Bedford, United Kingdom*

STEVEN CHAN, *IT Specialist, IBM Global Services*

LEI-DA CHEN, *Faculty Member, Northern Michigan Univerisity, Marquette, Michigan*

TIM CHRISTMANN, *Senior Consultant, Deloitte & Touche Consulting Group, Toronto, Ontario, Canada*

Contributors

ANDREW J. CZUCHRY, *AFG Industries Chair of Excellence, Business and Technology and Professor of Management, East Tennessee State University, Johnson City, Tennessee*

TIM R.V. DAVIS, *Professor of Strategic Management and International Business, Cleveland State University, Cleveland, Ohio*

L.R. DEJARNETT, *Managing Director, The Lamar Group, Ranchos Palos Verdes, California*

DAWNA TRAVIS DEWIRE, *Editor, Information Systems Management, and Faculty Member, Babson College, Wellesley, Massachusetts*

RIK DRUMMOND, *Chief Executive Officer, Drummond Group, Fort Worth, Texas*

RAINER FEURER, *Research Student, Cranfield University, Bedford, United Kingdom*

TYLER FRANK, *Doctoral Candidate, Manufacturing Management Program, The University of Toledo, Toledo, Ohio*

MARK N. FROLICK, *Ph.D., Associate Professor of Management Information Systems, University of Memphis, Memphis, Tennessee*

IDO GILEADI, *Senior Manager, Deloitte & Touche Consulting, Toronto, Ontario, Canada*

HAL H. GREEN, *Consultant, Setpoint, Inc., Houston, Texas*

CRAIG GUSTIN, *Principal, CGR Management Consultants, Playa del Rey, California*

PAUL HELD, *Consultant*

DOUGLAS B. HOYT, *Consultant and Writer, Hartsdale, New York*

BILL JEFFERY, *Vice President, A.T. Kearney, Chicago, Illinois*

BRIAN JEFFREY, *Managing Director, International Technology Group, Mountain View, California*

RICHARD L. JENSON, *Ph.D., CPA, Associate Professor of Accounting, Utah State University, Logan, Utah*

I. RICHARD JOHNSON, *Ph.D., CPA, Professor of Accounting, Utah State University, Logan, Utah*

JOHN JORDAN, *Ph.D., Principal, Consulting & Systems Integration, Computer Sciences Corporation, Waltham, Massachusetts*

JERRY KANTER, *Director, Center for Information Management Studies, Babson College, Wellesley, Massachusetts*

MARIE KARAKANIAN, *Senior Manager, Deloitte Consulting, Toronto, Ontario, Canada*

KARL KELTON, *Consultant*

KEITH KENNEDY, *Principal, CGR Management Consultants, Playa del Rey, California*

WILLIAM R. KING, *Professor of Business Administration, University of Pittsburgh, Pittsburgh, Pennsylvania*

WALTER KUKETZ, *Technical Lead, Performance and Engineering, Consulting & Systems Integration, Computer Sciences Corporation, Waltham, Massachusetts*

MIKE KWIATKOWSKI, *Information Systems and Management Consultant, Dallas, Texas*

RICHARD LEE, *Senior Consultant, Operations Reengineering, Deloitte & Touche Consulting Group, Toronto, Ontario, Canada*

WILLIAM F. LENIHAN, *Senior Manager, Deloitte & Touche Management Consulting, Stamford Connecticut*

MARSHA LEWIN, *President, Marsha D. Lewin Associates, Inc., Los Angeles, California*

YOGESH MALHOTRA, *Founder and Chief Knowledge Architect, @Brint.com, Ft. Lauderdale, Florida*

ERIC A. MARKS, *Director of Consulting, BrightRoad, Inc, Andover, Massachusetts*

ROBERT J. MATYSKA, JR., *Doctoral Student, Accounting Information Systems, Michigan State University, East Lansing, Michigan*

HOLMES MILLER, *Associate Professor of Business, Muhlenberg College, Allentown, Pennsylvania*

JIM MORRISON, *Principal, A.T. Kearney, Chicago, Illinois*

RAJAGOPAL PALANISWAMY, *Doctoral Candidate, Manufacturing Management Program, The University of Toledo, Toledo, Ohio*

YANNIS A. POLLALIS, *Syracuse University, Syracuse, New York*

G. PREM PREMKUMAR, *Associate Professor of Information Systems, College of Business, Iowa State University, Ames, Iowa*

R. KELLY RAINER, JR., *Privett Professor of Management, Auburn University, Auburn, Alabama*

MAHESH RAISINGHANI, *Director of Research, Center for Applied Technology and Faculty Member, University of Dallas, Dallas, Texas*

JOHN F. ROCKART, *Director, Center for Information Systems Research, Sloan School of Management, Massachusetts Institute of Technology, Cambridge, Massachusetts*

JEANNE W. ROSS, *Principal Research Scientist, Center for Information Systems Research, Sloan School of Management, Massachusetts Institute of Technology, Cambridge, Massachusetts*

RICHARD ROSS, *Principal. CSC Index, New York, New York*

JAMES E. SHOWALTER, *Consultant, Enterprise Computing, Automotive Industry Business Development, Sun Microsystems, Greenwood, Indiana*

ROBERT L. SLOAN, *Business Information Systems Architect, Nylon Business Unit, E.I. du Pont de Nemours & Co., Charlotte, North Carolina*

SCOTT STEPHENS, *Business Manager, Commercial Supply Chain Management, Command and Control Integration Systems, Lockheed Martin, Manassas, Virginia*

STEWART L. STOKES, JR., *National Practice Director, Behavioral Skills Management, PLATINUM Technology Solutions, Inc., Wellsley, Massachusetts*

DJOEN S. TAN, *The Netherlands*

MOHAN TANNIRU, *Professor, School of Management, Syracuse University, Syracuse, New York*

Contributors

MARIE TUMOLO, *California State University, Fullerton, California*

RAY WALKER, *Senior Consultant, Process Monitoring and Control (PM&C) MigrationProgram, ProcessControlInitiative, DuPontEngineering, Wilmington, Delaware*

JOHN WARGIN, *Manager, Strategic Consulting and Business Alignment Practice, Hewlett-Packard, Germany*

HUGH WATSON, *Professor of Management Information Systems, Terry College of Business, University of Georgia, Athens, Georgia*

MICHAEL WEBER, *Project Manager, Redesign and Implementation of Processes and IT Support, Hewlett-Packard, Germany*

MADELINE WEISS, *President, Weiss Associates, Inc., Bethesda, Maryland*

MARGARET L. WILLIAMS, *Senior Disbursements Controls Specialist, Federal Express, Memphis, Tennessee*

MAHMOUD M. YASIN, *Professor of Management, East Tennessee State University, Johnson City, Tennessee*

DALE YOUNG, *Associate Professor, Department of Decision Sciences and Management Information Systems, Miami University, Oxford, Ohio*

Dedication

To all those striving to improve their supply chains. My hope is this book will in some way ease the pain.

Contents

Contents

Contents

Acknowledgments

This book collects the wisdom of many contributors to Auerbach Publishers' *KnowledgeBase*. I thank these authors for their contributions. Also, my thanks go to Christian Kirkpatrick, Cherise Walker, and Rich O'Hanley for their help in sorting through their ample supply of wisdom.

Introduction

This book compiles articles related to the impact of information technology on supply chain management (SCM) practice. The source for the articles is Auerbach Publication's *Knowledgebase*. Auerbach is renowned for its focus on information technology issues. The Knowledgebase, however, contains many selections that extend beyond technical issues. All deal with practical aspects of systems implementation.

The combination of technology focus and practical general advice leads us to the title: *Making Supply Chain Management Work: Design, Implementation, Partnerships, Technology, and Profits*. We hope the selections will first and foremost help readers make new supply chain designs work. To do so, they must vault several hurdles. These include strategy alignment, acceptance by the organizations that must operate them, enabling technology implementation, and deployment of a profitable business model.

From time to time over the past ten years, I have contributed articles to Auerbach publications. Many of these articles have dealt with the supply chain and are included here. Some were chapters in my book, *The Handbook of Supply Chain Management*. This work was published by St. Lucie Press (like Auerbach, an imprint of CRC Press) and APICS.

To organize the selections, I have borrowed the structure I employed in the *Handbook of Supply Chain Management*. The book begins with a section called "Introduction to the Supply Chain." This contains selections to orient the reader to the topic of supply chain management (or SCM). The book then describes five management tasks that are changing because companies will increasingly compete as parts of supply chains rather than stand-alone entities. These five also follow the five themes in our book title.

- Task 1. Designing supply chain for strategic advantage
- Task 2. Implementing collaborative relationships within the organization
- Task 3. Forging supply chain partnerships with other organizations
- Task 4. Managing supply chain information
- Task 5. Making money from the supply chain

Doing well in all five is likely to be a prerequisite for success. This will require more from all managers, even more so for IS management.

In undertaking this effort, there was a fear of not finding enough material in the Auerbach *Knowledgebase* to cover each of the five tasks. Certainly, there would be ample material on Task 4. But what about the other tasks. As it turns out, there were selections for improving performance on all five tasks. Many chapters address more than one task. When this was the case, I tried to pick the best fit. However, I woud acknowledge that another classification could be just as valid.

Each chapter is also classified in one of three ways: as a tutorial, a tool, or a technology. Tutorial chapters explain some aspect of SCM or information technology. Chapters on tools offer methodologies for assessing or implementing information technology for better SCM. Technology chapters describe hardware, software, case studies, and implementation planning.

My experience is that information technology is a major factor in the success of any supply chain initiative. Unfortunately, IT comes into play in one or the other of two extreme modes. At one extreme, the entire effort centers on the IT effort. The technology is "front and center" driving the program. The project may even be run by the IS team with varying levels of user participation. Often, these projects fail for lack of operating team involvement. At the other extreme, supply chain changes are implemented at some distance from the IS functions. They involve too little in the way of changes to information systems, running the risk of failure because new processes are not "locked in" by changes to systems.

There must be a "happy medium" between these extremes. This implies balanced implementation of supply chain change, accompanied by an appropriate amount of information technology change. This will reduce the risk that poorly performing systems pose to efforts to improve the supply chain. It might also avoid wasting what one client referred to as "buckets of money" on ineffective systems.

It is this vision of the happy medium that drove me to propose this project to Auerbach. My chapter selection reflects this mission. Fortunately, other authors have articulated similar sentiments, and these are included here.

The book should serve two audiences. The first is the IT manager. The book gathers information technology articles on a focused topic — the supply chain — from a variety of sources. Thus, even a subscriber to one or more Auerbach publications will now have a specialized resource on the supply chain topic. The second audience includes nontechnical managers who need more knowledge on the appropriate application of technology for improving supply chains.

Section 1
Introduction to the Supply Chain

This section frames the management issues around information technology and the supply chain. Line managers in the supply chain and IS professionals who need an understanding of pitfalls they might face in supply chain change should find value here.

For the IT professional, the section presents chapters with a general management perspective. These should help those in the IS function to communicate with users on business terms and to better understand the business needs behind a technology effort.

Chapter 1
A Primer on Supply Chain Management

James B. Ayers

Understanding the supply chain is increasingly important to those involved in related process and systems improvement. This chapter outlines the basic concepts and purposes of the supply chain.

The definition of a supply chain can legitimately be broad or narrow, depending on the perspective of the "definer." The trend is to broaden the definition of the supply chain. One speaker at a recent conference sponsored by the Council of Logistics Management (CLM) described it broadly. We paraphrase, "The supply chain is as all that happens to a product from dirt to dust." The supply chain begins, in the speaker's view, with mining ores and growing crops, extracting raw material from Mother Earth. The chain goes on to a multitude of conversion and distribution processes that deliver the product to the end user. It ends with ultimate disposal — presumably back to Mother Earth somewhere.

DEFINING SUPPLY CHAIN MANAGEMENT

Defining terms is a start in clarifying the supply chain discussion. The natural beginning is a working definition of *supply chain*. The supply chain is more than the physical move of goods "from earth to earth." It is also information, money movement, and the creation and deployment of intellectual capital. We would summarize with the following definition:

> Supply chain: Life cycle processes supporting physical, information, financial, and knowledge flows for moving products and services from suppliers to end-users.

The following terms further break down the definition:

1. *Life cycle* refers to both the market life cycle and the usage life cycle. These are not the same for both durable goods and services. That computer, a product, and that 30-year mortgage, a service, must be supported long after newer products replace older ones. Many products may be sold in a time window that is relatively short com-

0-8493-1273-6/02/$0.00+$1.50
© 2002 by CRC Press LLC

pared with their useful lives. For this reason, the longevity of the seller and its reputation for product support are important factors in the purchasing decision. After-sales support can be the most lucrative service provided — outpacing the money made on the original sale.

2. *Physical, information, and financial* flows are frequently cited dimensions of the supply chain. The traditional viewpoint of supply chains as only physical distribution is too limiting. Less frequently mentioned is the role of *knowledge* input into supply chain processes. Knowledge is as important, if not more, as physical and other types of input. A good example is new product development. This supply chain process requires close coordination of intellectual input (the design) with physical input (components, prototypes, and the like). Today, added value in the form of intellectual capital is vital to marketing profitable goods and services.

3. *Services* also have supply chains. Production planning for the product development department, which produces designs, not products, can benefit from the same techniques used by product manufacturers. Federal Express operates a service business, but it is certainly also a complex supply chain. A software company is challenged to constantly improve its product through upgrades. Its process also is a supply chain.

The term "product" describes the basic product or service. The *extended product* includes the basic product or service, the supply chain that delivers it, plus other features and factors that go along with the product or service.

In many markets, there may be little difference in products. However, there can be great differences in extended products. Examples include the broadened choices users have for buying personal computers. They can purchase them in a store (like the laptop from a leading maker), over the Internet (like a heavily discounted "no-name" desktop version), or by telephone. The furniture industry offers another example of varied channels. We can buy assembled furniture at a neighborhood store or go to a warehouse operation such as Ikea and buy it unassembled.

Choice begins with a need for the basic product or service, but quickly moves to extended product factors such as delivery, service, and reputation. For many products, the supply chain design is perhaps the single most important extended product feature (see Exhibit 1).

Once we decide we need a car, decisions must be made. We must decide what type of car — factors associated with the physical "base product." Should the car be large or small? New or used? How many seats should it have? What should it cost?

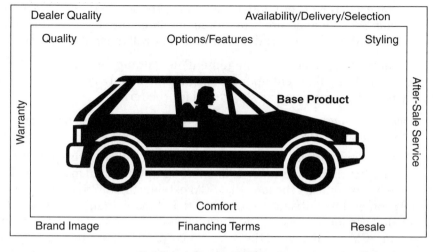

Exhibit 1. Extended Product

Having made these decisions, we still have decisions based on "extended product" features. These tend to be more subtle and intuitive. Exhibit 1 shows some "outside the box" factors we might consider. These include dealer quality, selection, brand image, support service, and resale. The supply chain enters into a number of these extended product factors. Exhibit 2 shows a few examples.

Many products that people buy or contemplate buying have similar customer dynamics. A poorly executed basic product will not succeed in the

Exhibit 2. Examples of Extended Product Factors

Dealer quality	Dealers for most auto companies are the distribution backbone. How they operate, their facilities, their reputations are key factors in the buying decision.
Availability/delivery/selection	Having the right model at the right time for the right buyer often means a sale. Supply chain cycle times and information systems improve the chances of being successful.
After-sale service/warranty	Many buyers look to this important support network when buying. For many, this service is the most lucrative.
Financing	Except for those who pay cash, the convenience and speed of this closely related service can make or break a deal.
Resale	Many outlets for resale will raise the market value. So will all the factors that contribute to the car's reputation.

marketplace. On the other hand, a well-done product does not necessarily ensure success. When competitors loom, it will be the basic product supplemented with extended product features that will most likely succeed.

The term "supply chain management" is gaining currency, implying there is something different about managing the supply chain. In fact, the acronym SCM, is employed as shorthand for the term.

> *Supply chain management:* Design, maintenance, and operation of supply chain processes for satisfaction of end-user needs.

SCM is a discipline worthy of a distinct identity. This identity puts it on a level with other disciplines such as finance, operations, and marketing. The above definition reflects the idea that SCM extends to both the supply chain formulation and its subsequent operation and maintenance. SCM creates new challenges for managers. Old missions must be achieved in new ways. In general, SCM is broadening the roles of many. We begin with a description of common supply chain viewpoints that exist in different companies.

SUPPLY CHAIN PARADIGMS

Supply chains and the tasks that go with SCM very much depend on the eyes of the beholder. Different companies and even managers in a single company have different viewpoints, or paradigms. And these are evolving rapidly. There is no right or wrong supply chain viewpoint. In fact, the view in one company probably should differ from the view in another. This is because their situations are surely different, and what makes one successful work for another. In addition, the right viewpoint is not static. As time moves on and competitive pressures shift, the need to change viewpoints will arise.

Below are descriptions of the generic paradigms and way to tie them together. They are described from the bottom up, from the narrowest to the broadest paradigm.

Functional Paradigm

The functional supply chain paradigm is what exists in most companies today. It is the "base" state. Companies that do not think in supply chain terms fit the functional paradigm. In this view, companies are composed of individual departments. Manufacturing company examples are procurement, operations, engineering, and distribution. Each department has, to a large degree, its own agenda. Oversight of links between departments is weak within the company. Between companies in the supply chain, this oversight is practically non-existent.

Performance evaluation in these companies is typically cost dominated. Procurement is measured on the purchase cost of material and material overhead rates. Manufacturing has measures such as direct labor productivity. Distribution effectiveness is measured on the percentage of selling price represented by distribution cost.

In the functional organization, strong department heads sponsor change. "Cross-talk" among departments is minimal, so most initiatives are local. They may or may not improve the supply chain as a whole. The actual impact on the total supply chain usually is not measured where the functional paradigm prevails.

Procurement Paradigm

Frequently, the move away from the functional paradigm begins with efforts to lower material cost. This viewpoint has given rise to the "supply" in supply chain. In many product-making organizations today, the cost of material is the major cost component. So, to paraphrase a famous bank robber, management goes "where the money is." When talking about the supply chain, these companies think of suppliers and procurement.

Service organizations also buy many goods and services. Many look for ways to consolidate their demand for support items such as office supplies, having realized they spend ample amounts. Many service organizations depend on other suppliers. For example, auto insurers have large networks of repair shops and adjusters. Healthcare is also an industry of networked providers; these include medical groups of doctors, hospitals, and insurers.

The cost of outside material and services makes this an attractive target for cost reduction. This brings on programs such as sourcing initiatives, supplier reduction programs, and vendor-managed inventory (VMI). In this paradigm, the procurement executive may take charge of the supply chain.

These efforts reach outside the company into the upstream supplier base. They include "partnering" with the supplier and shrinking the supplier base. Often, especially when the buyer dominates the seller, partnership talk focuses on price reductions. This usually shifts profits from one party to another in the chain without fundamental improvement.

Logistics and Transportation Paradigm

The idea of companies linked together has roots in the logistics field. Of course physical movement of products along stages in the supply chain is an important part of most national economies. The previously mentioned CLM (Council of Logistics Management) defines "logistics" as "that part of the supply chain process that plans, implements, and controls the efficient, effective flow and storage of goods, services, and related information from the point of origin to the point of consumption in order to meet customers' requirements." Note that the CLM includes both goods and services in its definition. It also addresses "customers' requirements" and the need to fulfill them.

In the logistics and transportation paradigm, when companies decide to anoint a supply chain executive, they will likely pick the distribution executive. In place of the supply chain term, these companies may turn to an alternative — the *demand* chain. This reflects attention paid to the outbound, rather than the inbound side, or supply side, of the business.

The logistics view often addresses the outbound, downstream side in much the same way the procurement viewpoint worked the inbound side. This is also a cost-reduction effort aimed at incremental improvements in profit. Typical activities include modeling warehouse, distribution center, and transportation networks to reduce cost.

Information Paradigm

The information paradigm seeks to improve the links both within the company and within the supply chain. New applications plus new ways of moving information around, make this an active area. Electronic data interchange (EDI) is an early example of ways to improve communications among companies. A barrier has been the lack of integrated software, both inside and outside the company. Efforts underway sponsored by organizations such as the Supply-Chain Council seek to standardize the definition of data elements and processes. This facilitates supply chain information sharing along the supply chain.

Dramatic results have come from the use of information to improve supply chain performance. A frequently cited example is Wal-Mart, which moves point-of-sale data back through its system to its suppliers. This reduces the need for forecasting in supply chain decision making.

One shortcoming associated with this paradigm is the lack of "process consciousness." Efforts to implement new systems often become all encompassing, absorbing time, staff, and money resources. The effort drives toward implementation of the technology, and not necessarily improvement in underlying processes.

Business Process Reengineering (BPR) Paradigm

Business process reengineering (BPR) efforts call for "radical" restructuring of processes to eliminate waste and improve quality. Such efforts take many forms. For example, new systems and reengineering are closely linked in many minds. "Six Sigma" is a quality initiative that's also a close cousin of BPR. Systems and technology designs should follow process design; this is the intent of BPR. Thus, the underlying process requirements, not the technology itself, are the dominant force behind the change. The technology becomes an "enabler."

Most BPR efforts are confined to one company; however, BPR across multiple members of the supply chain will become increasingly common.

Strategic Paradigm

Some view supply chain design as integral to their strategies for competing. For them, competing focuses not only on products but also on the operations that make up the "extended product." These operations put products into customers' hands. Within this viewpoint, supplier relations, logistics, and information systems support customer satisfaction. This, in turn, leads to increased market share and profit. Costs, while important, are secondary.

This paradigm has been discussed in depth.[1] All projects to implement a new supply chain or to change an existing one will affect an organization's ability to compete. This impact is better planned than left to chance.

EVIDENCE OF THE IMPACT

The business press, plus our own experiences as consumers, reinforces an important message. Supply chains in many industries are rapidly evolving. The following paragraphs contain examples — many of which may be familiar. Each situation reflects how the "extended product" which includes the supply chain, has become a competitive battleground. The discussion continues by describing the dangers of ignoring changes in the supply chain.

CASE STUDIES

Different industries and companies view supply chains and supply chain change in various ways. These changes reflect broad undercurrents and may not be seen by participants in the industry. These examples call attention to these undercurrents in a few selected industries, through the eyes of industry observers and commentators. This is "buzz." What they have to say points to the growing importance of supply chain management in the coming years. In the examples, we call this "spin."

Personal Computers

As this chapter was written, this is one of the most discussed and most commented on industries on the face of the planet. It holds lessons because of its speed of growth and the rapid evolution of supply chains used by competitors.

- *What observers say — the buzz.* The industry began as a high-growth, high-profit business with most sales coming from retail stores. However, the product itself evolved to where there are only minor differences between company offerings. In fact, much of the product innovation

11

effort centers on producing cheaper and cheaper machines. Making money by introducing ever-more sophisticated components (e.g., processors) has exhausted its potential for increasing sales dramatically. Consumers have found that lower-performing machines are "good enough." Practical day-to-day use requires much less. So knock-off processors and low-cost machines have penetrated the market.

One response has been the emergence of alternative supply chains. Dell sells directly over the telephone and through its Web site, thereby lowering overhead and improving cash flow by using supplier capital to finance its business. Existing channels make it difficult for other manufacturers to shift their supply chains. They fear alienation of their retail partners if they bypass them and go direct. But the pressure to have a direct outlet is irresistible. Internet sales are also growing. One software retailer, Egghead, closed its entire retail chain focused on software and started selling hardware on the Internet.

- *The supply chain spin.* These trends reflect the emerging dominance of supply chain design over product design. Personal computer components and software are readily available to all producers. Manufacturing is, in essence, an order-taking and final-assembly operation. Extended product activities, which are defined as part of the supply chain, have become the basis for competitive advantage. These features include customer support, the ability to customize, rapid response, purchasing clout, and operating economies.

Entertainment

This is an industry where knowledge is a primary input in the production process. The material content in the final product is trivial. A movie is something we buy from the video store for its entertainment value, not for the tape and plastic spool that comprise its package. The physical form of the product is a minor portion of the price we pay. Over 90 per cent of our dollar is for intellectual "components" arising from the creativity of artists, writers, directors, and producers.

One Company's Challenge. Rhino Entertainment undertook an overhaul of its supply chain. Rhino's specialty is re-release of popular music in a broad range of genres. Rhino uses the knowledge of its music experts to decide what "packages" will be successful in the marketplace. Rhino then gains permission to publish its selections from license holders. The licensers are various large and small music companies. Product managers for assigned markets decide how to promote the release in the marketplace.

Only after these steps are taken does the actual physical product take shape. This involves transferring recordings of the tracks (songs) from original sources, design of the packaging to attract buyers, and arranging production with a contract manufacturer. At Rhino, only a third of those involved in the process actually work on the physical aspects of the product. The remainder work with ideas, licensers, and the media. Only 20 percent of the customer's dollar goes to physical product; 80 percent goes to knowledge requirements.

The Rhino process produces about 15 releases each month. At the beginning of the project, the process took up to two years for any one release. An "uncontrollable" in the process was the time to get approvals from licensers. Although permissions were usually granted, there was frequently considerable delay in responding as requests for licenses queued up. This was considered, with much justification, as an "out-of-control" factor. Another factor in the extended lead-time was the lack of concurrent processes. Rhino's internal production tasks were serial, with none starting before the next one was complete.

The old process resulted in a loss of control over the timing of releases. This in turn hobbled financial planning and, more importantly, control over the timing of releases. Often, sales were tied to key events: Christmas music for Christmas is an obvious example; winning Academy Award tracks timed for release along with the Oscars is somewhat less obvious.

- *The supply chain spin.* Rhino is an example of a company whose product is far more knowledge than tangible product. However, efficient production requires the same management and coordination one must give to a complex physical product; thus, the domains of physical and intellectual products are not widely separated — if they are separated at all.
- *Adding value through brands.* Branding defines the collective view of a product. Brands are built on reputations among customers, product functionality, advertising and promotion, and awareness among potential buyers. A company's value will often greatly exceed its book value. Book value is a calculated value determined by accounting rules. These rules recognize tangible value in assets such brick-and-mortar and inventory; but the "market cap" or value place on the company by investors can greatly exceed book value. Much of this added value is due to brand value in an attractive market.
- *The buzz on brands.* Branding is a vital component in building shareholder value. The brand distinguishes the company and its products from a crowded competitive field. The importance of the brand increases in mature markets. In growth situations, there is often sufficient market for everyone. Having enough product may be the principal challenge. As capacity catches up with demand, the overall value of the brand becomes more and more important. Brand image evolves from product to extended product features. Brand value increasingly shifts from the physical product to other factors.

Exhibit 3. Supply Chain Operations that Contribute to Brand Image

Channels	Vans. This California shoe company caters to the youth market with skateboard parks and "hip" gear. It sells through retailers, its own stores, and factory outlets.
Hand-holding	Solar Turbines. This San Diego-based division of Caterpillar sells on-site power-generation equipment. It uses a "one-touch" repair guarantee to assure customers of uninterrupted service.
Free stuff	Free computers. Online services now compete for "eyeballs" by giving away the access tool, a personal computer.
Staying power	IBM. In its days of uncontested glory, decision makers could not miss by buying Big Blue.
Lots of product	Online booksellers. After Amazon's early market success, it and rival Barnes & Noble started competing on how many millions of titles they offer.
Cheap	"Category killers." Companies such as Staples and Home Depot use economies of scale to offer low price.
Roll-ups	U.S. Filter. This company actively acquired companies providing water equipment and services. When acquired for a premium, it was 15 times the size of its nearest competitor.

- *The supply chain spin.* The supply chain contributes greatly to brand image. Specific supply chain operations that contribute to brand image are shown in Exhibit 3.

Each example relies on the supply chain, at least in part, for its competitive edge. Vans uses its alternative channels to boost sales and off-load excess inventory. Solar has targeted a growing market for co-generation. This market, emerging from electric utility deregulation, involves placing small gas turbine generators at local operating sites. Customers are not accustomed to maintaining gas turbines; thus, Solar will provide this service as part of its "extended product."

Giving away computers is like giving away the razor to sell the blades. One cannot go on line without the computer. So the theory goes: give away the computer and gain a captive audience. IBM and the online booksellers compete on the breadth of their product. The IBM decision removed risk for buyers of large ticket systems. Booksellers are looking for product supply breadth as a competitive edge. This is after rivalry among online sellers has made the convenience and price no longer a point of differentiation.

The category killers and roll-ups have increased purchasing power. Making buys in large volume increases their clout with suppliers.

Health Care

In the United States, health care is an industry in turmoil. Much is due to the complexity of the supply chain, which includes medical service providers, insurance companies, employers, government regulators, and, of course, users of healthcare services. Most people do not pay directly for healthcare services. Private companies and the government pay, and the flow of money is a dominant factor in the turmoil. The industry accounts for 14 percent of the U.S. economy, but many payers feel they are not getting their money's worth. There are many anecdotes pointing out that the frequency of use has more to do with the available capacity than medical need. The disconnect between the buyers and users is blamed for building wasteful habits into industry management practices.

The industry contains supply chains of several types. There are professional services. These include physician and hospital services. There are highly lucrative pharmaceutical products, often developed at great expense. The industry also needs a plethora of support equipment ranging from sophisticated electronic testing equipment, to gloves used in patient treatment.

- *What observers say — the buzz.* Pressures on the industry have fostered innovation in the design of services and organizations. Most of the innovations have two themes. The first imperative is to get larger. This brings consolidation of individual physician practices and partnering between doctors and hospitals. The second imperative, supported by the first, is cost reduction. This includes many facets already encountered in other industries. Examples are variation reduction, overhauling processes, and upgrading management skills.
- *The supply chain spin.* The industry must find some flexible and efficient delivery "enterprise." This enterprise must have substantial capital behind it and be capable of efficient operations. This means effective management of a broad range of processes with diverse measures from medical outcomes to the cost of tissue paper. It is likely a trial-and-error process requiring persistence and patience. As evidenced by the number of physicians taking MBA courses, it also requires new skills.
- *SCM — defensive and offensive weapon.* There are many dangers in ignoring SCM as a discipline. The most serious is the loss of profitable customers. The supply chain in the Exhibit 4 illustrates this.

The chain shows the physical movement of products through a traditional network for a manufactured product. The flow begins with several suppliers. They send raw material to a factory. Other material that requires no conversion goes directly to warehouses that support customers. The factory outbound shipments supply a distribution center or regional warehouses. The distribution center and warehouses support customers.

However, these customers are not homogeneous. They divide into segments, and each segment has distinct requirements. These requirements may arise from differences in either the product itself or the extended

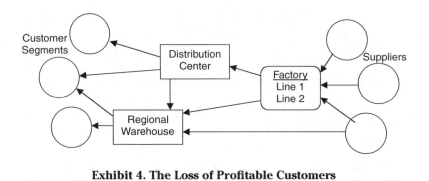

Exhibit 4. The Loss of Profitable Customers

product, including customer service, information, and technical assistance. Sometimes, companies fail to recognize these segments and their distinct requirements. This leads to a "one size fits all" supply chain design. In effect, the supply chain is a compromise based on the demands of different segments, and no segment is served as well as it should be.

The threat arises when a competitor perceives the service shortfall. That competitor detects an opportunity and structures a focused supply chain based on the needs of an attractive segment. The result is shown in Exhibit 5.

The consequence is loss of a customer segment. Very often, this segment is the most profitable. This is because the competitor does his homework not only on the supply chain features needed to serve the segment, but also on the economics of delivering those features. This process may occur over long periods of time and be seen as erosion of market share. More often, it can be dramatic — executed by an upstart company from outside the industry.

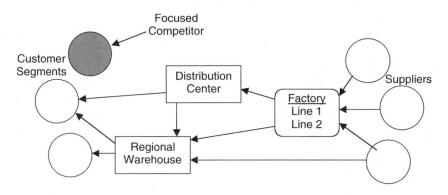

Exhibit 5. Competitor's Focused Supply Chain

This threat is also an opportunity. SCM enables one's own enterprise to "pick off" entrenched competitors, so SCM is both a defensive and offensive weapon. Managers with responsibility for supply chain decisions — and that includes many in most organizations — should prepare to meet both the challenges and opportunities that will surely find them.

Notes

1. Ayers, Jim, Supply Chain Strategies, *Information Strategy: The Executive's Journal*, Winter, 1999 (15/2), pp. 3-10.

Chapter 2
Electronic Commerce
Rik Drummond

Electronic commerce — the way businesses will do business in the future. Why use paper when things can be done easier and better without it? E-mail, EDI, electronic funds transfers, credit card transactions, electronic banking of all kinds, and all the thrills of electronic shopping are becoming available from the comfort of home, office, or car. Finance and banking are now available to even the novice home computer user. Where will it stop and what is in store? Will the Internet change the way we live or just the way we shop? This section looks at where and how electronic commerce is used, and even though many types of electronic commerce payment vehicles exist, it will focus on the credit card because it is currently the best documented.

THE BASICS OF ELECTRONIC COMMERCE

The question of how electronic commerce (EC) fits with e-mail and EDI frequently comes up in EC-related conversations. It is best defined in the following vignette. Joe, in front of a large audience, was leading a discussion that kept attempting to define what electronic commerce is and is not. Holding up a piece of blank paper, Joe said, "The best way to define electronic commerce is to picture doing business without this," as he crumpled the paper and tossed it into the waste can.

The definition of electronic commerce is doing business without using paper. Electronic commerce is not EDI, it is not e-mail, it is not Web browsers — it is all of these and more. It is electronic mail, Web servers, workflow systems, process changes and reengineering, EDI, Internet, video on demand, and voice messaging — electronic commerce is not using paper. Not using paper reduces errors in communications, speeds information flow, reduces mailing costs, increases opportunity costs, and helps make business processes more effective.

Because EC affects so many areas — all the ways companies do business — a broad set of disciplines must be harnessed to cover EC. This includes such disciplines as process reengineering, communications, databases, and applications (e.g., Web and e-mail clients).

This chapter covers several of these areas: EC interchange participants, EC interchange categories, EC human interface requirements, EC bandwidth and connectivity requirements, and electronic payment technologies.

ELECTRONIC COMMERCE INTERCHANGE PARTICIPANTS

Different participants in the EC product chain have different requirements and roles. Each industry has its own slightly different model. The following model is sufficient for these purposes. From the creation of a product to its purchase, five participants are involved in the process. They are:

Supplier → Manufacturer → Distributor → Merchant → Consumer

Supplier. The supplier produces raw material components used by the manufacturer to make the end product. Examples include a fuel injection system supplier for an auto manufacturer, or a paper supplier for a daily newspaper. The supplier-manufacturer relationship is recursive in that a supplier may also be a manufacturer for another supplier. Whether they are considered a supplier or a manufacturer depends on whether they produce the end product or not. The fuel injection company is a supplier if the fuel injection system is sold as part of the car, and a manufacturer if it is sold directly to the consumer.

Manufacturer. The manufacturer is an entity that produces an end product (e.g., cars, trucks, Monopoly games, auto fuel, paper, or Barbie dolls). Each offers a final consumer-ready product. They are often categorized as being part of the textile, automotive, transportation, grocery, petrochemical, or steel industries.

Distributor. The distributor takes the product made by the manufacturer and delivers it to the merchant or consumer. Mobil Oil produces automotive fuel and distributes it through outlets it owns or franchises called gas stations or marts. Ford manufactures cars and distributes them through Ford dealerships. At times, the distributor is also the end merchant, as in the case of the gas stations. At other times, it may be a middleman who moves the product from the manufacturer to the merchant, and has nothing to do with the final sale.

Making things even more complex, distributors use shippers, which may be partial or full load shippers, rail, sea, air, truck, pipelines, or others to get the product to the appropriate destination point. The area of transportation is so paper-intensive and complex that this is the area where the need for reduction of paper was first recognized. Transportation is where EDI first started, with an organization called Transportation Data Coordination Committee (TDCC) in the late 1960s. Even though EC is not EDI, EDI was the first to address the problem, and is arguably the grandfather of EC.

Merchant. The merchant is the organization that sells the product to the end consumer. The product is usually a physical entity (e.g., jeans, or computer software on a CD-ROM). For these purposes, it is not a service like telephone long-distance or AOL. The merchant who has contact with the consumer is the one who helps the consumer choose the product, explains product limitations, and sets consumer expectations. Merchants and the manufacturer are the ones the consumer blames if there is a problem, or goes to for help.

Consumer. The consumer is the one who consumes and uses the product — the end of the product chain and the reason the product is even manufactured in the first place.

In most industries over the last 25 years, EDI has helped reduce the paper used to negotiate, deliver, buy, and sell the product between the first parties in the supply chain. EDI was used to reduce paper between the supplier and the manufacturer, between the manufacturer and the distributor, and, in large retail or merchandising organizations (e.g., JCPenny or Wal-Mart), between the distributor and the merchant. What has been missing is the reduction in paper between the consumer and the merchant. Technologies that support EC between the merchant and the consumer have just fallen into place with the advent of Web technology.

SIMPLIFIED ELECTRONIC COMMERCE PARTICIPANTS

To keep things as simple as possible, it is helpful to assume that only three participants are in the supply chain by combining the manufacturer, the distributor, and the supplier. From a consumer viewpoint, the automotive industry fits this model. Thousands of suppliers send subcomponents to the manufacturer (e.g., General Motors), who assembles it and then sells it to the consumer.

Each of these manufacturers, merchants, and consumers interrelate and exchange at least four types of information in the relationship. Two types of relationships exist, each with different needs and requirements: manufacturer-merchant and merchant-consumer. These relationships exist to support the buying and selling of a product or service. Four basic process categories involved in these relationships will be described, as shown in Exhibit 1. This chapter will then go into further detail on the exchange of electronic value. The four categories of exchanges between participants are:

1. Negotiating the product and relationships
2. Order fulfillment, shipping, and delivery of the product, physically or electronically
3. Paying — exchanging the value

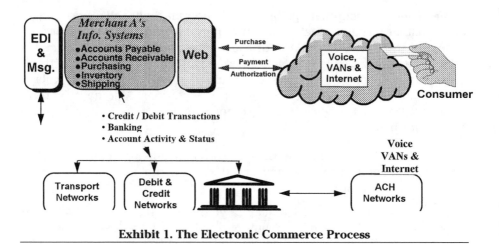

Exhibit 1. The Electronic Commerce Process

4. The ordering process — exchanging the paperwork (e.g., PO, invoices, and shipping notices)

Category One: Negotiating the Product and Relationships

This category encompasses processes necessary to establish the business relationship — in the EDI world that would be the trading partner agreement. This category would normally not cover the merchant-consumer exchange because the relationship is not an ongoing, frequent, or consistent one. The processes in this category are used to establish initial and ongoing relationships. These processes are not used for sporadic, unpredictable, unplanned purchases and exchanges like those often found in the consumer-merchant exchange.

This category will often use electronic messaging, paper mail, and voice to establish the relationship, negotiate the deals, and confirm the purchase price and terms for the relationship. Predominantly, this area would use electronic mail and not Web servers in the manufacturer-merchant relationship.

Category Two: Order Fulfillment, Shipping, and Delivery of the Product (Physically or Electronically)

Delivering the product electronically has to do with actually shipping the product electronically. In lieu of the transporters used in Star Trek, category two is only workable for products that start as electronic in nature. Examples include online magazines, software, music, video, books, and online services (e.g., AOL). Translation services — physical items (e.g., cars, clothes, and groceries) are also in this category. The delivery of these items would be supported by electronic paperwork and electronic purchase, but themselves are not electronic in nature. A new example of electronic products is *Encyclopedia Britannica.* For a yearly fee, it is no longer necessary to buy the set of books. The *Encyclopedia Britannica* may be accessed online through a Web server.

This category, the delivery of products electronically, uses both e-mail and Web clients and servers. Electronic products will probably be retrieved primarily through Web servers. For example, a subscriber orders a video by accessing the merchant on the Web and starts the download (i.e., delivery) of the movie *Red Tide* online.

Category Three: Paying (Exchanging the Value)

Delivering the value electronically covers the exchange of credit, debit, E-cash, and other payment types electronically. This is the area holding back consumer-merchant EC — it is the mechanism where the consumer purchases electronically.

Different value transfer needs and technologies exist. The oldest is electronic funds transfer between banks — the automated clearinghouse. Another example is the use of voice or the digital network to convey the consumer's credit card or debit card information to the merchant. Automated teller machines (ATMs) are changing the way banks do business, and overtaking ATMs are smart cards. New standards are being developed (e.g., secure electronic transactions, or SET by MasterCard and Visa), which will directly support consumer-merchant exchanges though existing monetary exchange vehicles (e.g., the credit card).

Category three will be electronic messaging and Web servers. Merchant-consumer exchanges will be using Web servers to exchange value and pay for products; the networks run by banks and credit card clearinghouses will, however, still exchange bulk reconciliation data and value exchanges (i.e., EFT) and EDI by the messaging structure. At the heart of the merchant-consumer relationship problem is an unsecure and bandwidth-limited network.

Category Four: The Ordering Process (Exchanging the Paperwork)

Delivering supporting documentation electronically is the historic EDI. This is the transmittal and receipt of purchase orders, invoices, shipping notices, credit information, and college enrollment information between participating parties electronically. This has historically been supported by the large value-added networks that often, but not always, handle the transmission between companies. This is where EC started 30 years ago. Much of what was learned during these manufacturer-to-merchant implementations is transferable to the merchant-to-consumer portions of EC.

The ordering process is currently messaging, but it is already moving to a more interactive focus. EDI is not going away any time soon, and will remain the primary means to conduct business-to-business exchanges, in the same way that electronic funds transfer will remain the way the banks reconcile value exchanges. Both of these are ultimately electronic messaging.

EDI is not the only technology needed for EC, but it is a primary one. Several infrastructure issues are holding back the full-scale implementation of EC. In very general terms, they are: the end-user device, the bandwidth and connectivity availability, and security and protection issues.

EC TECHNOLOGY ISSUES

Connecting the Consumer's Device

One of the major issues in EC is how to connect the consumer's device to the EC network. Glitz attracts users, and graphical user interfaces, or GUIs — visual graphic-based exchanges (e.g., the Web or multimedia-based e-mail) — deliver that glitz. ISDN is probably not a valid option over the long term. It is an old technology filling a short-term gap until other lower-cost, higher-bandwidth options come into production. There will probably be some sort of a hybrid option for the foreseeable future for most consumers.

Two options are available for wiring the consumer's device with sufficient bandwidth: create new ways to use the existing media (e.g., twisted pair or coax entering homes), or run new transmission media to the user's home. The latter is much too expensive and manpower-intensive, in that it requires that $300 to $500 per connection be invested up front just to install new wire or fiber from an existing junction box to the home. Some industry experts estimate it would take $120 billion to rewire U.S. homes to support the high-bandwidth needs. The price does not include other infrastructure costs that are attributable to upgrading the backbone infrastructure.

This may not slow the expansion of EC in the manufacturer-merchant area, however, where major savings will be realized just on the reduction of paper and information cycle times. The further automation of paperwork exchange between organizations is normally not a high-bandwidth requirement, as it is the case for exchange of graphical, video, and other types of products online.

Bandwidth and Connectivity Requirements for EC

Three infrastructure requirements must be addressed for EC to be implemented widely for both consumer and business-to-business communications: security, the ease of reaching others (i.e., interconnectivity), and the size-volume of the exchange. Negotiations, product delivery, value exchange, and paperwork exchange have different security, connectivity, and exchange size needs. This is referred to as the *manufacturer-merchant exchange* (see Exhibit 2).

Exhibit 2. Manufacturer-Merchant Exchange

| | Manufacturer-Merchant Exchange | | |
Exchange type	Security requirement	Exchanges size	Interconnectivity
Negotiating the product and relationships	High	Small to medium	Low
Product delivery	Low	Low	Low
Payment — exchanging the value	Low to high	Low	Low
Paperwork exchange	Low to high	Low	Low

Interconnectivity needs pertain to the number of parties who are capable of intercommunicating, and are relatively low in the manufacturer-merchant infrastructure. A limited number of trading partners are typically in this arena and the relationships are often planned. This is not always the case and will be less so in the future, but it is true now.

Exchange size is not as important in the manufacturer-merchant relationship as it is in the merchant-consumer relationship, because the amount of information exchanged per dialog is often low. These objects are dense, and are often textual and filled with large amounts of data required to support the exchange — not deliver the product. They are often in the hundreds or thousands of bytes — not millions. With the case of the product data and the product delivery, the size can be very large (millions of bytes) if the exchange is an engineering or integrated circuit drawing. This is different than the *merchant-consumer relationship* needs for EC, as shown in Exhibit 3.

In the manufacturer-merchant exchange, the connectivity requirements were relatively low, while in the merchant-consumer exchange, the connectivity requirements are high. For EC to work on the merchant-consumer side, many consumers must be able to get to many merchants in an ad-hoc manner to conduct shopping exchanges. In the supplier-merchant exchange, the communication is less ad hoc and more planned. Pervasive

Exhibit 3. Merchant-Consumer Exchange

| | Merchant-Consumer Exchange | | |
Exchange type	Security requirement	Exchanges size	Connectivity requirement
Negotiating the product	Low	Low	High
Product delivery	Low	Low to high	High
Payment — exchanging the value	High	Low	High
Paperwork exchange	Low to high	Low	High

supplier-merchant interconnect needs are not as high as in the merchant-consumer area.

In the case of a manufacturer-merchant exchange, high bandwidth among a few players in a planned, non-ad hoc loop will often solve the needs of the exchange, while in the case of merchant-consumer exchange, high bandwidth among the entire consumer and merchant universe would solve the needs. The supplier-merchant exchange requires a more limited connectivity, while the merchant-consumer exchange by definition requires broad connectivity across a large heterogeneous population. In the future, both will require high connectivity and high bandwidth; but for now, the merchant-consumer interchange, in all but a few cases, does not require high bandwidth. The exchange requires high connectivity penetration.

The Internet currently offers high connectivity, at low to medium bandwidth for the consumer. In Exhibit 3, the only place in the exchange size that requires high speed is that of product delivery. The delivery of things like movies, digital voice, and complex multimedia documentation are important, but are not precluded by bandwidth limitations.

Human Interface Requirements and Needs

What is so exciting about EC in the advent of the World Wide Web? Because EDI is already making major contributions between companies, what will the Web offer?

Corporations buy and sell in bulk, which fits the electronic messaging communications methodology well. Most consumers do not buy in bulk, however, and do not make a large amount of repeat purchases of the same thing. Consumers often window shop, which is exactly what is offered by the Web. The user decides when to shop, where to shop, and how often to shop — frequently without notice — just like going to the mall.

Electronic messaging is often called an example of a *push technology,* and the Web or database queries examples of *pull technology.* In a push technology, the user receive things when the originator wishes, as in the case of broadcast TV, postal mail, or radio. A pull technology is one in which the recipient decides when to retrieve the information, as in the case of the Web, video rentals, audio tapes, or video movies-on-demand.

People use both methods to effectively work and accomplish tasks. An office worker may be notified of the need to approve a purchase requisition by e-mail, at which time the worker accesses a database to actually read the supporting data and approve the requisition. Or a consumer is notified of a sale by broadcast radio, and then purchases the product by means of the pull technology of the Web. In implementing EC programs, it is important to remember to implement both technologies, and not make the user attempt to work with only a pull technology when they also need a push.

Exhibit 4. Electronic Commerce Status

Description	Status	Who/What
Ubiquitous communications infrastructure	In place	Internet/VANs
Uniform address space	In place	Internet IP
Protected exchange of electronic value	Partially in place	Banks, credit cards
Reduced cost and complexity of interface devices	Partially in place	TV, Internet terminals
Ubiquitous medium-speed wire to the consumer's device	In place	Dial-in modem
Ubiquitous high-speed wire to the consumer's device	2000+	Coax, twisted pair, satellite
User-friendly push-and-pull technologies	Partially in place	E-mail, Web
Reduced cost to participate in consumer EC	Ever?	Not clear

ELECTRONIC COMMERCE TECHNOLOGIES

Several items affect EC implementation, either as attractors or detractors. These items, their status, and who or what is needed are depicted in Exhibit 4. The items affect EC implementation in the following ways:

- Ubiquitous communications infrastructure is required to support the consumer access to the merchant. Every household must be able to access the merchant by way of the communications backbone.
- Uniform address space is the reason that the Web has taken hold so quickly. It is not the user interfaces on the Web clients; it is not the links between servers (hyperlinks); it is not the graphics — it is the uniform address space offered by the IP network that allows functions to be easily accessible (IP addresses).
- The protected exchange of value, or money, over the Internet is not hard for a limited group of participants. They are able to manage and coordinate the encryption keys. The banks were doing this without encryption keys for years. As the consumer becomes active, it is no longer a limited number of participants — it is hundreds of millions. How are the encryption keys that form the basis for signature and encryption for the value transfers managed? This area is just now being solved.
- Reduced cost and complexity of the interface device is very important. Currently, the large majority of those using the Internet are college educated and have PCs, UNIX workstations, or Macintoshes. These are not low cost for most people, and are not easy to support. The interface device must become simpler and lower in cost. As in the cellular phone industry, it must be given away as part of the purchase if hundreds of millions of people will be online.

27

- The wire to the consumer's device heavily affects the amount of functional ability, ease of use, and the type of product the end user can receive over the network. This wire is the last 50 to 100 feet — the run to the residence. Until satellite or cable television is cost-effective to the residence, this will be a major limiting factor.
- The high-speed wire solution is the same as what is required for medium-speed wire.
- User-friendly push-pull technologies are essential. The Web is a fairly user-friendly technology for those who are computer literate. It is difficult for those who are not; just as Microsoft Windows is not always user-friendly for those who do not have a computer background. The Web is a start; however, it is a long way from being simple enough for the hundreds of millions to use.
- A reduced cost to participate is necessary to facilitate the merchant-to-consumer EC interaction. This means it should be around the cost of a telephone (e.g., $10 per month, not $20 to $40 per month).

MERCHANT-CONSUMER ELECTRONIC PURCHASE PAYMENT PROCESS

As discussed earlier, the exchange of payment information in a secure manner in the merchant-consumer relationship is the last requirement for full-scale EC. A consumer can browse and window shop the Web servers for products using current technology; however, they cannot safely pay for it on the Internet without encryption technology. Protection requirements, each depending on encryption, have been identified as follows:

- Provide ease in identifying valid credit, debit, check, and cash type accounts
- Preclude interception
- Ensure that payment information is not alterable without being identifiable
- Ensure that the transaction has as much anonymity as possible
- Detect and prevent fake storefronts from masquerading and collecting credit and debit card account information.

Both MasterCard and Visa are leading the effort to implement the standard payment information exchange of EC. They are both working with others, including Microsoft, Checkfree, IBM, Netscape, GTE, and CyberCash. The merchant-consumer electronic payment exchange process is composed of two areas that must be addressed in concert before things become workable: processes and technologies. This includes: payment processes, encryption used in EC, electronic signatures, public/private key encryption, and certificates.

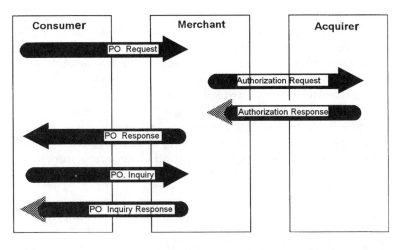

Exhibit 5. Merchant-Consumer Purchase and Payment Process

Payment Processes

Payment processes fall into several categories: establishing means to readily identify merchants, consumers, and banks, issuing certificates necessary for validating electronic signatures, and establishing the actual payment process. The payment process will be discussed later, and the first two categories will be addressed as the discussion weaves through the technologies.

The MasterCard and Visa consortium published the Secure Electronic Transactions (SET) specification in February 1996. They have spent much time defining the processes and technology, and their document will be used as a basis for the following discussion. Because the SET document is several hundred pages, many areas will be abbreviated here to simplify and consolidate.

Merchant-Consumer Purchase and Payment Process. Two types of processes must be supported for merchant-consumer EC: one based on e-mail and the other using the Web's capabilities, both offline and online. E-mail-based ordering will support offline shopping; this shopping uses catalogs or CD-ROMs to browse for products and then initiates an order by sending an e-mail message. The interaction between the consumer (who has a credit card) and the merchant, supported by a third-party credit card verification entity, and the acquirer bank is shown in Exhibit 5.

The consumer issues an e-mail request to the merchant; the e-mail is a purchase order (PO). The merchant responds with a PO response. Embedded in the PO from the consumer are credit card and digital signature information, in addition to the product and quantity requested. The credit card and digital signature information is passed on to the acquirer or bank for verification of the credit card numbers, account availability, and digital signature. The merchant never sees the actual credit card information. They are only told whether it is valid or not. The merchant sends the encrypted user's card information on to the acquirer for verification in an authorization request message, and is returned an authorization response that completes the transaction. The user may at some later time query the merchant for status of the order by issuing a PO inquiry message. The credit card and digital signature information are contained in a special package that will be discussed in the technical basis for this exchange.

Online, Web processing may be somewhat of a different process than e-mail because the user is already attached to the Web site in an interactive session. Because of this, the request sequence is somewhat different from the e-mail offline transactions. For example, because the consumer is already attached to the server and is assumed to have identified the product online, a PO request is not necessary.

It can be assumed that the price and terms of the purchase have already been agreed on. The consumer, or cardholder, starts by issuing an initial message to the merchant. The message contains the consumer's credit card information. The merchant responds with an invoice message that contains, among other things, the electronic signature identifying the merchant to the consumer and what is being ordered or purchased. The consumer then responds with a purchase order that includes the consumer's signature, certificate, and payment instructions. The consumer's payment information is passed on to the acquiring bank for verification. (The payment information is not revealed to the merchant. The merchant does not know the card number of the consumer transaction.) After the acquiring bank verifies the consumer's information, the merchant receives a purchase order response with the authorization code, the acquirer's signature, and authorization.

Encryption's Use in Electronic Commerce

Often, two types of encryption schemes are used in an attempt to maintain the privacy of the data being transmitted. The first is a symmetric scheme that uses only one key — a key both parties must possess to encrypt and decrypt the data. The one most often used is the Data Encryption Standard (DES), which has been used by the U.S. government for years. The other encryption scheme is the public/private key scheme, whose best known example is RSA encryption. Each has its positives and negatives and because of these, each adds a unique capability for information protection.

Data Encryption Standard. DES, the *symmetric* scheme, is used to encrypt large amounts of data. It is very effective and efficient at encrypting and decrypting data. Both parties, however, must know the same key — which means it is only usable between two parties that possess the key. The key must remain secure or other parties can decrypt the data sequence.

The DES scheme works very well with online encryption where two cryptographic devices, one on each end, exchange protected data. It does not work well for more spurious uses unless there is some way to distribute the key for this transmission, along with the transmission, in a protected manner so that only the intended destination is able to get the key and decrypt the transmission. This is where the public/private key encryption scheme comes into play.

Data can be encrypted with the DES algorithm. Then, the DES key, with the public key of the key-pair, is encrypted and sent to the destination, which recovers the key and decrypts the DES data stream. More on how the public/private key scheme works is included in the following sections.

Electronic Signatures

Credit card transactions must be signed to identify and confirm the entry initiating the purchase and resulting transaction. What is a signature? When a customer signs a check, it means the check is from the customer and the amount on the check is correct. Signing indicates that the piece of paper (i.e., the check) is from the customer and should be honored as from the customer. The same is true in the electronic world. However, there is a problem. Unlike the paper check, which is not easy to tamper with (e.g., change amounts or names without being discovered), electronic documents are easily modified without it being evident. If a customer signs a general electronic document, how is it known that the document is not subsequently changed, and how is it known what the signature applies to? Where does the document start and end?

To take care of this unique electronic document problem, the hash algorithm was introduced, which indicates to which document the signature applies. The document — the electronic check — is fed into an algorithm, which takes all the bytes of the document and computes a unique bit sequence from those document bytes. The bit sequence is designed so that if any part of the original document is changed, the bit sequence is changed. By applying the same algorithm at the receiving end, the receiver can tell whether the signed document is valid or not valid. The hash-produced bit sequence is then encrypted using the source's private key. The private key uniquely identifies the source, and the hash verifies that the document received is the same as the one signed. Both the hash algorithm and the public/private key pair are required to produce an electronic signature.

Public/Private Key Encryption

The encryption scheme these electronic transactions depend on is of a category of schemes called *nonsymmetric* or public/private key schemes. What is unique about these schemes is that each user is identified with one to many sets of unique key pairs. One pair can be for encryption and one pair for signature — one pair for can be personal and one for business. A key pair is very unique in that one half of the pair, the public, may be widely published without giving away the contents of the private half. What this means is that if some trusted third party (e.g., government, post office, MasterCard, Visa, or American Express) generates the keys for a known, verified entity, and publishes the public key widely, the entity may be easily identified. Before describing how they are identified, it is important to understand how the keys work together.

Certificates

Certificates are used to tie the user's identity to the public key in a way that does not allow tampering and is protected. It is the method used to distribute the public part of a key-pair with the user identities. X.509 certificates are the predominant means for doing this at this time. The latest version is from the 1993 X.500 standards and is the basis for the MasterCard signature methodology. In the X.500 world, these will be kept in the directory. In the initial phases of the MasterCard implementation, it is assumed that a directory may not always be available, and that the communicating entity must include the certificate with the signature so that the signature may be verified. This may happen in a completely secure manner and without loss of protection. This will become evident when the certificate creation and structure is discussed.

A certificate is composed of at least the elements in the following list. MasterCard has added a few additional fields to the certificate, as others will also do over time. The X.509 certificate contains:

$$CA(A) = CA\{V,AI,CA,UCA,A,UA,AP,TA\}$$

where:

- CA(A) is the certificate or user A produced by certificate authority CA
- V is the version of the certificate
- AI is the identifier of the algorithm used to sign the certificate — the CA's algorithm
- UCA is the X.500 type distinguished name of the CA
- A is user A distinguished identifier in X.500 format (in the case of the MasterCard use, it is an alias known only to the issuing bank)
- UA is a list of algorithms for A's public keys
- AP is a list of A's public keys
- TA is beginning and ending dates for which the certificate is valid

The public/private key pair is generated, and the identity of the user confirmed to the appropriate level for the use of the certificate. Is some cases, the user may have to show birth certificates and fingerprints, while in others much less identification will be required. In this case, for credit card use, the identity will probably be just an address, name, and signature. These will be sufficient to generate the public/private key pair, and tie the name to the published key.

The certificate is constructed in the following manner: A customer is sent the private key on disk or in a smart card. The public key may or may not be sent to the customer — either way is fine and it makes little difference. The customer's X.500 distinguished name is issued by the credit card bank, assigned a certificate serial number, and given a valid time frame for the certificate. All of these are appended together with the distinguished name of the CA. These are run through a hashing algorithm so that they cannot be changed, and the hash is appended to the rest of the data after being encrypted by the private key of the CA. The certificate is built and is then either given to the issuee or put in a directory for worldwide access.

Because of the construction of the certificate, the issuer is known without a doubt. They used their private key to sign it. It was not tampered with, because the entire string was hashed and the consumer's public key is known to be authentic because it is in an unaltered certificate from a verifiable certificate authority. In this case, the information signed by public key A for consumer A is valid for a credit card transaction.

SUMMARY

Electronic commerce is not just one process — by definition, it must cover all business relationships, those between consumers and business, and those between businesses. The large spread of EC indicates different needs and requirements. Some areas (e.g., electronic product exchange) may require large amounts of bandwidth, while others (e.g., the exchange of paperwork) may require much less bandwidth to be effective. Other applications (e.g., consumer shopping) require the ability to connect to a large number of sites and businesses over and above the need for sufficient bandwidth. This was solved when the Internet became available for wide-scale use.

The last item that must be addressed is the security of information exchanges, which the payment processes and technologies being driven by MasterCard and Visa will address. They are both based on public key cryptographic systems. These systems allow uniquely identified entities to ensure privacy on information exchanges. Two things will continue to reduce the speed of the EC expansion: high costs of the end-user device (i.e., currently the PC) and the inability to solve the ubiquitous higher bandwidth requirements.

Chapter 3
Is Supply Chain Management the Same as ERP?

James B. Ayers

Innovation in the supply chain puts new demands on information systems and the people who develop and manage them. Making information systems work to improve supply chains is an important SCM skill. But, putting technology ahead of strategic design and operational requirements is a frequent shortcoming. Consequently much effort is wasted or even counterproductive.

Systems issues present some monumental challenges to senior managers. The reasons are many. Senior managers "may not have a clue" about their needs for systems, the capabilities of information technologies, or how to implement the technology. They have only a hazy awareness of how computers work and what infrastructure capability like networks provides. Consequently, these managers are often at the mercy of their technical departments and software marketers. Or, their lack of knowledge leads to indecision.

Another influential factor is the constant barrage of stories of computer projects run amuck. Many war stories recount foul-ups costing tens of millions. In fact, some companies implement high-cost systems only to "unplug" them when they don't work. *The Wall Street Journal* recounted a flurry of such horror stories brought to light through lawsuits and visible corporate miscues.[1] Among the incidents reported in a single article were the following:

- Whirlpool, the appliance maker, having troubles shipping product due to high demand and conversion to SAP software
- W.L. Gore & Associates, the water-resistant fabric maker, suing Peoplesoft, Deloitte Consulting, and others over a botched installation of new systems

- A quickly implemented SAP ERP system keeping candymaker Hershey from delivering its products to meet the peak Halloween demand — despite having plenty of inventory
- Allied Waste Management, a service company, pulling the plug after spending $45 million on a $250 million SAP system

Of course, many organizations have completed large systems projects with better success than that described above. And often the fault is as much that of the craftsmen as it is of the tools.

The examples cite the application category called ERP. ERP systems automate "back office" operations. The back office consists of the many transactions fundamental to the business. Examples are personnel records, booking sales, and ordering materials. In the late 1990s, the need to address "Y2K" risks motivated many of these efforts. Older "legacy" systems built around the needs of individual departments were not ready for the new millennium.

We predict the next "drivers" for systems improvements will be getting strategic value out of systems to improve the supply chain. Those who have implemented new systems will look for ways to capitalize on their investments and exploit technology for competitive reasons. Frequently cited examples include E-commerce capability, electronic links along the supply chain, reducing inventory, exploiting databases for customer information, and otherwise increasing the role of technology in customer interfaces.

This chapter describes the wide and fragmented supply chain information landscape. We do it lightly, acknowledging that there are multiple sources for more detailed information. This is also a landscape with "blurry" boundaries between categories of applications. Hardly a week passes when we do not hear about a new acronym or "revolutionary" tool in the domain of supply chain systems. Unless one closely follows the technology, he or she can be excused for being confused. Describing each and every application category would require more space than we have available. So we will confine our descriptions to what we believe are the major categories.

SUPPLY CHAIN APPLICATIONS

The Council of Logistics Management (CLM), in conjunction with Andersen Consulting, maintains an "inventory" of supply chain applications. Its list of software in a CD format describes over 1200 application packages.[2] To find the right fit for his or her business, the user can select from the many categories shown in Exhibit 1.

Typically, any listed package will include several of the functions shown in Exhibit 1. Indeed, some packages claim to have them all. Herein lies a problem. One has to decide which features are most important to his or her business. He or she then has to decide how well each candidate pack-

Exhibit 1. CLM Software Categories

Order processing	Stock/pallet location	Vehicle maintenance
Inventory control	Labor performance	Physical distribution system modeling
Inventory planning and forecasting	Material handling	Electronic data interchange
Distribution requirements planning	Transportation analysis	Warehouse management
Materials requirements planning	Traffic routing and scheduling	Promotions and deals
Purchasing	Freight rate maintenance and audit	Other functions

age supports the need. Packages will undoubtedly be stronger or weaker in an area. If you need a great traffic routing and scheduling capability, for example, you will have to look closely at what each candidate package that provides this function. Some claiming to possess the functionality may, in fact, have it, but do it poorly.

When presented with a "short list" of candidate packages for implementation, we find that some clients — knowing there is an abundance of options — are uneasy with only a few alternatives. They realize that a software package selection could be a commitment for a decade or more. There is a suspicion that there might be a better solution out there beyond the short list presented. If the project does not go well, the selection team will shoulder the blame. To cover one's risk, they may believe, one must rummage through all 1200, or at least several hundred, to make sure the "right" choice is made. Of course, evaluating a single package is a time-consuming job, taking from one to three weeks for a diligent review. Imagine doing this for hundreds.

When it comes to the supply chain, this list — as comprehensive as it seems to be — is far from complete! Additional categories used by software suppliers, many of which have coalesced with the rise of SCM. They include SCM itself (Supply Chain Management), ERP (Enterprise Resource Planning), CRM (Customer Relationship Management), PDM (Product Data Management), CRP (Capacity Requirements Planning), MES (Manufacturing Execution Systems), and APS (Advanced Planning and Scheduling).

Also, one must consider the possibility of what are called "bolt-ons." These are combinations of packages to cover a user's requirements. They are often developed when two cooperating package purveyors "integrate" their offerings. For example, the Hershey example above included ERP (by SAP AG of Germany), APS (by Manugistics, Inc., of the United States), and CRM (by Siebel Systems of the United States) applications. Another party, IBM, managed the effort. A trend is the consolidation of bolt-on package functionality — in the Hershey case, the CRM and APS — into core ERP systems.

In addition to applications, supply chain systems include the means of communicating among partners. Many supply chain partners, for example, use Electronic Data Interchange, or EDI. The Internet is the emerging technology of choice, and packages are in varying states of "Internet-readiness." Another application category of software is EAI (Enterprise Application Integration) or "middleware." This category enables different applications to "talk to each other." This can be important both inside an organization and in managing a supply chain. Deploying middleware can bypass or delay investments in new applications.

We have indicated that understanding the benefits and risks of technology is a challenge for many. One would hope that system marketers would be helpful in this regard. Unfortunately, so called "solution providers" seldom emphasize clarity in their communications.

One might be excused if he or she concludes that this industry tends toward hyperbole. These companies have a large investment in product development, and each sale increases the return on that investment. So claims are often extraordinary. Descriptions of the results are vaguely worded superlatives replete with fuzzy multisyllable terms, like "transformation" or "integration."

However, there is no doubt that systems solve real problems. The claims made by Company A in Exhibit 2 are very similar to those made for TQM and JIT just a few years ago. In fact, the changes needed to achieve the benefits probably require both the software and nonsoftware disciplines to gain the most from the system. Often, the preparation for the system is as important as the system itself. Cleaning up the data is a necessary prerequisite to successful system use. Company B reflects a trend among many software suppliers — that of combining forces to offer a "new" product from two or more old ones. Some computer publications caution that many of these alliances are marketing ploys; buyers beware![3]

Exhibit 2. Claims by Information Technology Providers

	Source	Excerpt
A	ERP system marketer	"[Company] offers integrated Flow Manufacturing that enables dramatic benefits such as a 90 per cent reduction in cycle time, 50-90 per cent reduction in inventory and a dollar for dollar increase in working capital. These are all available with a low risk transition strategy"
B	Two software companies	"[Company 1] and [Company 2] have extended their relationship to offer customers a closed loop supply chain solution."
C	E-commerce provider	"[Company] is the leading provider of electronic commerce solutions that dynamically link buying and supplying organizations into real-time trading communities."
D	Supply chain software provider	"[Company] unveiled [product name], a new approach for demand-driven fulfillment that enables companies to anticipate and meet customer delivery expectations the first time, every time."
E	System integrator	"[Company] is a leader in industrial strength, e-business solutions for system and application response performance."
F	ERP systems provider	[Product name] allows people to harness the power of the Internet to work smarter, better and faster by optimizing supply chains, managing strategic relationships, reducing time to market, sharing virtual information, and increasing productivity and shareholder value."
G	Consulting firm	"[Company's] insight into the global consumer products complex from consumer to retailer to supplier, helps companies develop and implement winning strategies. The firm's thought leadership among retailers and consumer products companies has led to the transformation of entire industry sectors."
H	IT consulting firm	"[Company] is one of the most successful and fastest-growing IT consulting firms nationwide. [Company] is differentiated by its tradition of unsurpassed technology expertise; its strong track record of delivering; and its experienced, enthusiastic people — the best in the business."

References

1. Boudette, Neal E., Europe's SAP scrambles to stem big glitches, *The Wall Street Journal,* November 4, 1999, p. A25.
2. Haverly, Richard C. and Whelan, James F., *Logistics Software: 1998 Edition, Volume 1,* Council of Logistics Management. (Compact Disc format)
3. Slater, Derek, The ties that bolt, *CIO Magazine,* April 15, 1999.

Chapter 4
E-Factory Technology Solution Sets

Alex N. Beavers, Jr.

As technology and process trends accelerate the introduction of new technologies into the E-factory, decision-making about which software and hardware suppliers to use becomes more complex. Over the last half of the last decade there was a raging debate associated with information technology strategies as to whether a company should use a single software provider for all its business application and control needs, or whether there should be a "best-of-breed" approach. The rapidly growing enterprise resource planning (ERP) companies such as SAP and Oracle were of course advocating the single supplier enterprise approach. However, the reality was that the enterprise systems were hardly up to performing all the functions in a company, especially not for the E-factory. As a result, using a best-of-breed solution set is often the best approach to the E-factory. Thus, the "solution set" for an e-factory will likely consist of multiple suppliers.

The software and hardware companies serving the E-business and the E-factory marketplace are changing their products on a continual basis to better serve the market needs. As a result, the target set of solution candidates is not easily identified. The purpose of this chapter is to identify the leading, newest solution set providers in each of the solution set categories. While these lists will likely change as technology and application experience evolve, they do provide a starting point for an E-factory roadmap project.

DEFINITION OF A SOLUTION SET

E-factory solution sets are evolving from several directions. Very specialized software companies have been formed and have rapidly evolved over the last few years. They have been serving distinctive needs in separate areas in the factory as islands of automation were installed throughout the factory. Many of these small software companies have since been acquired by larger systems integration and hardware companies.

Manufacturing equipment companies that were started to serve specific process automation needs have now evolved to the point where they are trying to serve the needs of an integrated factory floor system. Process hardware companies are typically more concerned about getting the physics right in their manufacturing equipment and including only enough software to allow a human operator of the machine to be able to set up and operate the machine correctly. The technical evolution in the E-factory now requires that this equipment operate in a factory computer network and communicate with systems at higher control levels.

Systems integration companies, which initially began by providing the technical experts required to build interfaces between the different software packages and machine controllers that were necessary for a factory to operate electronically, have also begun to acquire software companies and offer solution sets for the E-factory market.

There is no off-the-shelf solution set that fits all, yet. ERP companies have advertised that they offer all the solution components that a manufacturing enterprise needs, but they do not, as yet, address the E-factory. There are supply chain management software companies that are rapidly bringing new product features to market to address the business-to-consumer and business-to-business market needs, but they too do not yet address the total E-factory. However, these products are rapidly evolving and it is important to be able to evaluate them when developing an E-factory roadmap.

Solution set refers to a set of software and hardware components that provides the E-factory capability. These components might come from different software and systems suppliers or be provided by one supplier. The solution set must be able to execute, facilitate, and accelerate the internal business processes and the operational scenarios that define the way an E-factory should work. These components must also support and execute the interfaces with the other internal and external processes that exist in the E-factory.

THE COMPONENTS OF A SOLUTION SET

The components of a solution set consist of hardware and software products whose operations cover all levels of the E-factory control hierarchy and both the vertical and horizontal dimensions in the supply chain.

The control levels are important because they provide a means of identifying what types of control are required, where they should be applied,

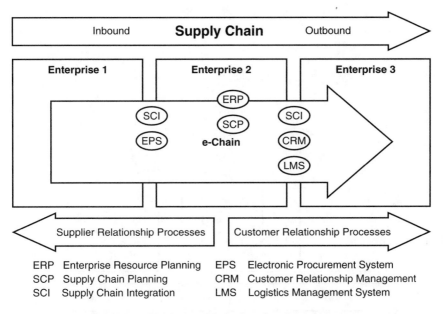

ERP	Enterprise Resource Planning	EPS	Electronic Procurement System
SCP	Supply Chain Planning	CRM	Customer Relationship Management
SCI	Supply Chain Integration	LMS	Logistics Management System

Exhibit 1. Horizontal Solution Set Components

and how they should be implemented. The control levels of the E-factory hierarchy include:

- Factory level
- Line level
- Cell level
- Machine level
- Unit level

The horizontal components of an E-factory solution set address the electronic supply chain, or "E-chain," requirements. They address the external business issues for the E-factory. Building on enterprise and supply chain models, the horizontal E-chain is illustrated in Exhibit 1. The horizontal components include:

1. Customer relationship management (CRM)
2. Supply chain planning (SCP)
3. Electronic procurement system (EPS)
4. Supply chain integration (SCI)
5. Logistics management system (LMS)

The vertical components of an E-factory solution set address the requirements that are created by the need to support the internal process requirements and the interfaces to the E-chain solutions that different customers and suppliers might have. The enterprise and supply chain model

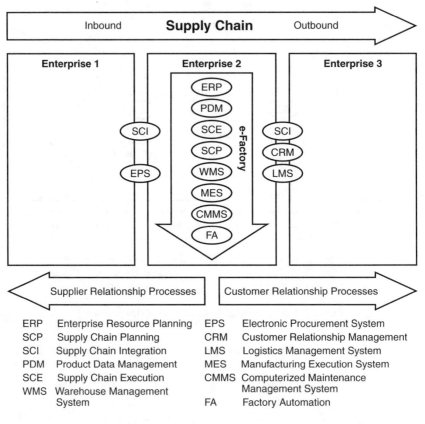

ERP	Enterprise Resource Planning	EPS	Electronic Procurement System
SCP	Supply Chain Planning	CRM	Customer Relationship Management
SCI	Supply Chain Integration	LMS	Logistics Management System
PDM	Product Data Management	MES	Manufacturing Execution System
SCE	Supply Chain Execution	CMMS	Computerized Maintenance
WMS	Warehouse Management		Management System
	System	FA	Factory Automation

Exhibit 2. Vertical Solution Set Components

extended to illustrate vertical solution set components is illustrated in Exhibit 2. The vertical components include the following:

1. Enterprise resource planning system (ERP)
2. Supply chain execution system (SCE)
3. Manufacturing execution system (MES)
4. Warehouse management system (WMS)
5. Factory automation system (FAS)
6. Factory floor control system (FCS)
7. Computerized maintenance management system (CMMS)
8. Product data management (PDM)

HORIZONTAL SOLUTION SET COMPONENTS

Each of the horizontal solution set component categories is described in the following.

Customer Relationship Management

Customer relationship management (CRM) is a term that has evolved to describe an entire industry of software vendors that serve the specific purpose of addressing the selling and marketing functions in a business enterprise. The functions typically included in CRM applications include:

- Salesforce automation
- Call center management
- Customer profile management
- On-line product catalogs
- Data mining
- Product configuration
- Proposal generation
- Proposal management
- Order entry
- Order status management

These functions are provided in separate software packages and in integrated packages. Highlighted in Exhibit 3 are the overlaps that exist between these different functional areas.

Salesforce automation (SFA) refers to those capabilities associated with keeping track of customers, the frequency of customer contacts, the scheduling of customer contacts, tracking and reporting on the status of sales opportunities, tracking and reporting on the sales success of each salesperson, and salesforce expense reporting.

Call center management (CCM) software performs a variety of functions necessary to automate and facilitate the activities of a call center. Companies that have a need to provide real-time information to their customers are using both on-line computer technology via the Internet and "on-line" human response via the telephone. Despite the innovation and improvement of computer technology over the last few years, the flexibility and psychological reward of having a person to talk to has not be supplanted. As a result, many companies are using a combination of computer technology and people to provide a comprehensive capability to answer telephone calls from their customers.

To be effective, a call center requires a variety of software. Automated answering and routing software is now available from private branch exchange (PBX) vendors. This is the software that provides the "push 1 if you want to make new reservations, push 2 if you want to check on your air miles" type of responses with which most of us are familiar. Customer and product information database software is also necessary for a call center. The people answering the phone calls must be able to answer fundamental questions about products, pricing, and the status of a customer's account.

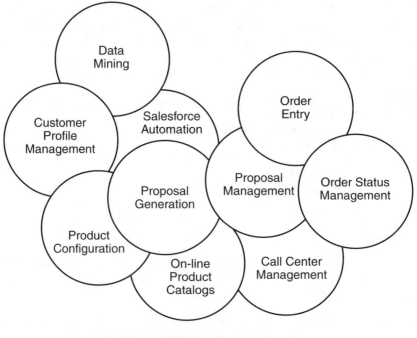

Exhibit 3. CRM Application Overlaps

These database systems are necessary for both the Internet on-line functionality and the call center functionality. A third type of software capability is the tracking of the performance of the people and the technology operating in the call center in terms of calls answered successfully, number of transfers required during a call, time a caller had to wait, etc. Call center management software provides these types of features as well as many of the other features described above.

Customer profile management refers to those capabilities associated with keeping track of customer purchases, complaints, preferences, personal information, response to direct selling techniques, and level of satisfaction achieved.

On-line and real-time product and service catalogs refers to making it possible for the salesperson directly or for the customer directly to be able to access a catalog that describes the products and services available from the selling company. This catalog can also include the appropriate prices and instructional information that can help a customer decide which product might be the best for a particular application.

Data mining software provides the capability to analyze a database of information or in some cases a continuous flow of information to identify key trends, relationships, and behavior of individuals and groups. This software a few years ago was touted as a fantastic breakthrough in marketing because it had the promise of providing "scientific" insight into how people's shopping behavior indicated what they might buy in the future. The concept is to apply advanced statistical analysis to very large databases of shopping activities and customer demographics to imply relationships between products and current customers. Thus, a person who goes to a grocery store to buy disposable diapers for a child and who pays for the item using a grocery store discount card becomes a database record. The record would include their name, address, telephone number, an estimate of their annual income, the number of times they buy diapers, other baby products they might buy, etc. At some point in time, this information would be processed by a data mining software package that would put the person's name and address into different mailing lists that advertisers of baby-related products, vacation package retailers, and others would use to begin sending catalogs and direct selling activities.

Proposal generation refers to those capabilities associated with generating a proposal to reflect the needs of the customer. This capability should include the ability to configure a proposal from a set of predetermined subsets of activities in the same way that one might create a meal and therefore the price of a meal from a menu.

Proposal management refers to the status tracking of a proposal once it is submitted to a customer for decision. Proposals are in many ways like fresh fruit in that they tend to diminish in quality with time until after a certain point they expire and are no longer viable.

Order entry is the creation of an order once a proposal has been accepted by a customer. This has traditionally not been part of the customer relationship management set of functions but it is becoming more so now that on-line purchasing is becoming more acceptable.

Order status management is the management and reporting of the status of a customer order. For build-to-order businesses, this function is quite important because it allows customers to track and understand the progress of their order. For ship-from-stock businesses, order status management is necessary as a real-time performance indicator of the quality of their order fulfillment service.

The leading multi-purpose CRM providers include the following companies.

- Siebel Systems, Inc.
- Oracle Corp.
- PeopleSoft, Inc. (Vantive)
- Trilogy Software, Inc.
- Nortel Networks Corp. (Clarify)

- Baan Co.
- Davox Corp.
- Aspect Communications, Inc.
- Astea International, Inc.

Supply Chain Planning

Supply chain planning (SCP) for a manufacturing company generally refers to long-range planning of the design and operation of the supply chain to which the company belongs. Supply chain design refers to the number of plants, the capacity of the plants, transportation modes, outsourcing options, the number and type of suppliers, the types of contracts with the suppliers, the number of warehouses and distribution centers, and the flexibility in assignment of each component in the supply chain. Supply chain operation refers to the number of shifts in each plant, decision rules for shipments and transportation, replenishment rates, and cycle times of each component in the supply chain.

Very long-range or strategic supply chain planning is done only infrequently, either on an ad hoc basis or on a regular or annualized planning basis. The ad hoc basis can be driven by events such as new product developments, consolidation of merged business units, or financial crisis. The regular or annualized basis is often part of a regular strategic planning schedule. As part of the longer-term perspective, supply chain planning tends to be focused on the structure of the supply chain and the simulation of different operational strategies. For the E-factory, this perspective becomes very critical because all new supply chain designs must be able to perform within the short cycle times and with the flexibility being required by the marketplace.

Short-term supply chain planning is done on a more frequent basis, which could be quarterly, monthly or weekly. The E-factory environment is forcing supply chain planning to be done even more frequently. At some point, what is called supply chain planning becomes identical to supply chain execution. Short-term supply chain planning focuses on activities that are more operational or low-level, such as multi-plant production scheduling.

A key part of supply chain planning is the search for the optimum plan. Optimization includes deciding on the location, size, and the number of plants, distribution centers, and suppliers that provide the best performance for the supply chain. Of course, performance must be defined as part of the supply chain planning process. Supply chain planning also includes sourcing and deployment strategies for each plant, each distribution center, and each customer. It also models the flow of goods through the supply chain network.

Developing a supply chain plan for one product is an interesting mathematical and management challenge. Expanding the plan to include multiple products makes the mathematical challenge exponentially greater. Expanding the plan to include multiple plants takes the mathematical challenge to an even greater level of complexity.

The leading supply chain planning companies include the following.

- i2 Technologies, Inc.
- SAP AG
- Manugistics Group, Inc.
- Aspen Technology, Inc.
- Baan Co.
- LPA Software, Inc.
- Logility, Inc.
- SynQuest, Inc.
- PeopleSoft, Inc.
- ILOG, Inc.
- Intentia International

Electronic Procurement System

When the operations of a manufacturing company are analyzed from a supply chain perspective, the basic question that results is how much value is being added by the manufacturing company to the goods and services that it purchases to produce a product that is sold to its customers. For many industries, the amount of purchased goods and services used directly in the manufacture of a final product runs in the range of 60 percent to 90 percent of the final manufactured cost of the product. In gross terms, the cost of purchased goods and services can run in the range of 25 percent to 50 percent of total revenue. From this follows the obvious observation that any decrease in the cost of purchased materials is amplified in the increase in net income because it falls to the bottom line directly. For example, if the cost of purchased goods and services is 80 percent of the cost of the manufactured goods and if the company sells the product so that it has a 50 percent gross margin, then the cost of purchased goods and services is 40 percent of revenue. If the cost of purchased goods and services is reduced by 5 percent, then that savings (which is 2 percent of revenue) drops directly to the bottom. If this example company was achieving 10 percent of revenue after tax earnings before, then the earnings would increase to 12 percent. Thus, the 5 percent decrease in purchase costs translates into a 20 percent increase in earnings. This is the dream that all CEOs have when they hear about the promise of electronic procurement systems. And some vendors and consultants promise 20 percent reductions in purchased material costs, which translates into net income percentage increases that are too exciting even for dreams. For some companies in slow growth industries, cost reduction of purchased goods is the only strategic option they have to show profit increases. The concept of using software to improve the earnings of a company, which has been promised before by virtually every new wave of business software developed, is almost too good to be true.

There is some substance, however, to the potential value of electronic procurement systems (EPS) to assist in the reduction of purchasing costs. The benefit comes primarily from two sources. First, the procurement business process in most companies today is inefficient in terms of the execution of purchase decisions and transactions, and wasteful in terms of matching purchasing needs with purchasing reality. EPS can reduce the transaction cost of the procurement business process. Second, there is now a body of knowledge and best practices on how to minimize the cost of purchased materials by combining purchasing requirements to buy at larger volume levels and by designing cost out of products by working more closely with suppliers during product development projects. EPS can help make better decisions about cost by searching through electronic catalogs for the lowest cost components that offer the same functionality (i.e., comparison shopping).

There are several ways for companies to execute purchasing decisions, including:

- Buy at an auction
- Buy from a distributor
- Buy from retail stores or shopping centers
- Buy from a supply chain partner

EPS can support all of these forums. They can also assist in deciding from which forum to purchase goods and services.

The basic elements that form an EPS are simple.

- All potential suppliers product catalogs are electronic and on-line.
- All terms and conditions (shipping quantities, prices, freight costs, warranty, etc.) in all purchase agreements between company and suppliers are on-line.
- All purchase requests, ordering, status checking, and receiving activities are an on-line and available to everyone that makes the final decisions.
- All settlement of purchase transactions are electronic.

The result is that all the inefficiencies in time and labor that come from having people in functionally specialized departments performing the purchase request form processing, shopping, buying, and settlement activities can be eliminated with automation. However, the cost of the procurement process (i.e., the cost of the people, facilities, and equipment employed within the procurement process) is small in comparison to the cost of the purchased materials. If purchased material is 40 percent of revenue, the cost of the purchasing department is 0.4 percent of revenue. The big cost saving is not going to come from the replacement of manual processes by automated processes. If fact, the cost of the automated process in terms of software and hardware costs could exceed the cost of the manual processes being replaced.

In addition, the new contractual relationships between supplier and customer that must be negotiated in light of the new E-business world will require a new, enlightened perspective on business processes, both internal and external, and on how supply chain partners will operate. This will require more talent and energy than the traditional types of buy/sell contract terms and conditions. Thus, the cost of establishing a contractual relationship may increase, especially if the new relationship requires suppliers to have a certain level of E-business capability to support the supply chain relationship being negotiated.

Then there is the issue of getting all product catalogs on-line. The suppliers can invest in putting their catalogs in electronic form rather than in paper form. In fact, with the tools that most companies are using today for electronic publishing, getting product catalogs on-line can be done as part of a multi-media product catalog strategy. The question then becomes one of standards and interfaces. The more standards and interfaces that a company has to support, the more cost incurred.

The real promise and benefit in electronic procurement is in reducing the cost of purchased materials through better decision-making. EPS can make a major contribution to this with the proper understanding of how a procurement decision process works and how it should be automated or supported.

There are two general types of procurement activities in most manufacturing companies: those for direct manufacturing and that for maintenance, repair, and operations (MRO). Effort has been focused on purchasing of goods for direct manufacturing from many quarters. MRP, PDM, ERP, and SCM packages are all designed to make the material planning and procurement processes more responsive to corporate needs. The introduction of the external business process concepts and supporting software have helped as well.

MRO buying is a relatively new area of opportunity and is the area that has received the most attention from electronic procurement software companies that have started up over the last five years and the companies that are buying their products. MRO includes everything from replacement tooling in a manufacturing facility to copier paper in the human resources office. In fact, MRO buying is a significantly more important function in service industries because there is no manufacturing material being purchased. MRO buying in the financial, insurance, education, government, and entertainment industries consumes larger percentages of the revenue than in manufacturing companies, and there has historically been less money invested in improving the procurement process in those industries. Thus, there are many new opportunities in MRO.

Specialized Web sites called e-markets and vertical portals have been created where people with similar business interests and needs can trade and talk business-to-business (B-to-B) on a round-the-clock basis. Suppliers, ranging from office products vendors to very specialized producers of raw materials or manufacturing components, have opened Internet stores and B-to-B marketplaces that post their catalogs and offer other client services.

A 70-year-old distribution company, W.W. Grainger, took its various 220,000 products to the Internet. At Grainger.com, a company can establish a corporate account, authorize purchasing agents with specific capabilities, review the status of accounts and shipments at any time, and receive one consolidated bill. Grainger's newest site, OrderZone.com, streamlines customers' purchasing processes across multiple suppliers. Office product vendor Staples has started up StaplesLink.com, a site that lets corporations open accounts and receive discounts on orders. US Office Products, will sell you everything from paper clips to coffee machine services, as well as consolidate your accounts.

Another innovation is online services that route purchase requests to appropriate managers for approval based on policies, provide customized online catalogs, and generate reports to help you track spending and negotiate volume discounts. Electronic and online procurement systems can have customized links to accounting, project management, and other resources. The enterprise system never has to touch the Internet, so internal security can be very tight.

The area of E-procurement is evolving rapidly. Ariba and Grainger are collaborating on specialized features written in Commerce XML (CXML) to automate the handling of supplier content. The suppliers receive orders by e-mail, fax, or electronic document exchange and settle accounts by electronic links through banks. In the most basic form, buyers need only an Internet connection, a browser, and a password to browse the combined material.

In its ultimate form, an E-market can become part of an enterprise's supply chain management system. Companies using ERP systems, such as those from Baan, J.D. Edwards, Oracle, PeopleSoft, or SAP, to control production, inventory, and accounting can benefit from using special E-market ordering programs tied to their ERP systems. Supply chain management, integrated with ERP, provides an automated way to order materials and settle accounts. It also supplies performance data on order fulfillment times, rejects, and other statistics that can give procurement professionals an objective way to measure vendors and the confidence to lower inventories and optimize production schedules.

The leading EPS vendors include:

- Ariba
- CommerceOne
- Trilogy Software
- i2 Technologies

Supply Chain Integration

One of the rapidly evolving horizontal applications in the E-factory is the area of integration between the internal and external business processes. This area is known under several names (e.g., enterprise application integration (EAI) or cross-applications), but the term "supply chain integration" (SCI) will be used herein. This area includes generic software services for security management, protocol management, data mapping, and software connector modules that let internal process software communicate with external process software.

Most of the SCI software packages are designed to use technologies and standards that incorporate one of the following: XML as a data-interchange format, Enterprise JavaBeans as a server architecture, CORBA or DCOM as programmatic methods for processes to call each other, message queuing systems to let systems communicate asynchronously, and transaction monitors to ensure that operations complete properly.

There are various types of supply chain integration. Typically they are application-to-application integration and customer-to-business integration. SCI software provides data transformation, mapping, workflow technologies, graphical tools to display data as seen by various applications such as ERP systems, transaction monitors, and databases. XML is fast becoming the unifier among integrated systems. XML is also the basis for SOAP (Simple Object Access Protocol), a new way for processes on different systems to communicate using standard, open protocols. SOAP could greatly simplify interoperability among systems because of the openness and simplicity of XML. SOAP is a communications protocol, not a description of the data in an E-business system. The fact that SOAP can run over any transport protocol (e.g., HTTP, SMPT, or message queuing) means that any two SOAP programs can communicate without another layer of middleware.

CORBA/IIOP and DCOM are the two main protocols for object communication across networks, including the Internet. These are low-level programming concepts, but often dictate compatibility between applications in a complex system. DCOM is used for Windows-based applications, and CORBA is found on many platforms. Because both have wide support in the market, one finds that many EAI systems, including those from Bridges for Islands and Saga Software, support both.

Not all calls between programs need an immediate response. Message queuing is a long-established technique that lets programs call each other using connections over which responses are not necessarily immediate — Internet connections, for example. Message queues deal with these calls asynchronously and can resend them if necessary. Message queues are an excellent means of connecting disparate systems, especially across the Internet.

The leading software vendors include the following.

- Applix
- Coral Sea Software
- Maconomy International Software
- IMAJ
- BroadVision
- QAS
- Saratoga Systems
- Silknet
- CrossWorlds
- FileNET
- Extricity

Logistics Management

Logistics management is the management of the warehousing, storage, transportation, and material tracking activities. The general area of logistics management has actually evolved independently from each of these specific areas and is merging into a unified solution set component. The trends in the E-factory are causing fundamental changes in the way logistics is managed and in the way companies think about logistics in their strategic structure.

At the highest level, every E-factory must be concerned with logistics management because of the need to ensure that the physical delivery portion of the order fulfillment process is successfully completed. As a minimum, information about material tracking, scheduling, and delivery confirmation is important to the E-factory. This information might come from an external process because the physical logistics operations have been outsourced or from an internal process because physical logistics operations are part of the e-factory core competency.

At the lowest level, the logistics process must be constructed to ensure that goods are stored, warehoused, picked, packed, shipped, and delivered as efficiently and as rapidly as possible. Volume and speed are critical parameters in determining success in a logistics process. As a result, full-service logistics companies have emerged so that they can offer the efficiencies of scale in logistics management to both large and small E-factory enterprises.

The leading logistics management software companies include:

- Manugistics, Inc.
- TRW, Inc.
- J.D. Edwards & Co.
- McHugh Software International
- Manhattan Associates, Inc.
- EXE Technologies, Inc.
- Optum, Inc.
- Catalyst International, Inc.

VERTICAL COMPONENTS

Enterprise Resources Planning Systems

During the past decade, no single software industry segment received more visibility, experienced more growth, was sought after more by customers, was stimulated by more experts and non-experts, and caused more confusion than that of enterprise resource planning (ERP) systems. What started out in the decade as the arrival of a promising new business system concept that employed the latest in mainframe computer technology ended up as a millennium bug solution fad that was being touted by the news media, high government officials, and the mainstream press.

In reality, ERP systems were a logical evolution in the business systems industry during the last ten years because there was a need for a business to integrate its operations using networked computers rather than a single mainframe with a myriad of terminals hardwired to it. However, the theory that a single software system could provide every functionality needed by a manufacturing company and also provide major productivity improvements just from the sheer force of technology was, in fact, difficult to accomplish. The implementation effort required to "configure" a generic ERP system and implement it in companies with multiple plants, legacy systems, established databases, and business processes in need of improvement often approaches or exceeds the effort required to build a custom system from a library of application modules or objects that are custom developed or designed for standard application.

The other problem with ERP implementations has been that of every major new system conversion: change management. The changes caused by the introduction of new system technology posed major new problems that had never been seen before. There were many reasons; but one of the biggest reasons was that the new ERP technology was designed to be used by virtually everyone in the company to record and report all the transactions and activities in the company. Thus, the change of systems technology was compounded by the fact that many employees who had not had to deal with computers as part of their workday life suddenly had to depend on them for every major action they took. It has taken some companies years to overcome the disruptions in operations due to the introduction of ERP.

All that having been said, the reality is that the concept and practice of enterprise solutions is here to stay. One of the key issues is whether the enterprise "solutions" should be monolithic from one supplier or best-of-breed from several suppliers.

Despite the actual track record — which is not one of total success — enterprise software products have evolved and improved and do represent an alternative or choice for many aspects of the E-factory requirements. While the term "enterprise" is a misnomer because these software systems do not provide all requirements for an enterprise, it does represent a significant genre of software packages. The leading enterprise providers are as follows.

- SAP
- Oracle
- Baan
- J.D. Edwards
- PeopleSoft

These leading ERP suppliers are continuing to invest heavily in expanding and improving their products to make them easier to integrate into a diverse solution set environment.

Supply Chain Execution Systems

Supply chain execution systems for manufacturing generally refer to systems that execute the transactions necessary for the supply chain to operate successfully. Supply chain execution systems include warehouse management, transportation management, logistics management, and distribution management systems.

The E-factory-based supply chain must respond to the needs of the Internet economy. The E-factory must be quicker, smarter, more flexible, and be able to process everything from an individual production unit to containers and truckloads. Supply chain execution systems are therefore rapidly evolving to support these needs. As a result, there is a blurring of the supply chain planning and supply chain execution systems packages.

Prior to E-business, manufacturers would have to plan to ship truckloads of pre-built product through retailers to corporate accounts. Now, manufacturers use distribution centers for custom configuring, assembling, and shipping smaller, even individual, orders. As a result, manufacturers must sell more individual orders to make the same revenue once generated from fewer but larger orders.

New companies are being formed which provide software and Internet-based services that are completely changing how manufacturers view their business and manage transportation. Manufacturing companies can now get everything they need from a software package, an Internet exchange, or an outsourcing company. Benefits include the ability to measure a carrier's performance and gain control over maverick transportation spending by negotiating volume service agreements.

Successful LX portals will offer transportation management software, provide visibility to shipments, and supply connectivity and supply chain event management to coordinate the activities of an entire trading community.

Leading supply chain execution system vendors include:

- Interactive Business Systems AB
- J.D. Edwards & Co.
- McHugh Software International
- Manhattan Associates, Inc.
- EXE Technologies, Inc.
- Optum, Inc.
- TRW, Inc.
- Catalyst International, Inc.
- Provia Software, Inc.
- Descartes Systems, Inc.
- Swisslog Management AG
- STS, Inc.
- HK Systems, Inc.
- Vastera
- Industri-Matematik International Corp.

Manufacturing Execution Systems

Toward the end of the 1980s, several experiments were conducted in the automotive, aerospace, and consumer goods industries in automating a manufacturing environment using custom-developed computer software. The results were promising enough to create a market for a general-purpose system that would monitor and control the activities and equipment in a manufacturing process. As a result, the term "manufacturing execution system" (MES) was coined in the early 1990s. It was created to define the software evolving at that time, which included a variety of functionality that associated with the control, monitoring, and reporting of factory floor processes. As with everything software, the functionality over the last ten years has expanded dramatically and now overlaps with other categories of E-factory software. A list of functionalities that are considered part of the MES category follows.

1. Operations monitoring
   a. Monitoring and tracking
   b. Product and workflow management
   c. Performance analysis
   d. Production reporting
   e. Cost accounting
   f. Labor tracking
   g. Finite scheduling
   h. Schedule dispatch
   i. Maintenance management
2. Manufacturing process engineering tools
   a. Process simulation
   b. Process engineering development tools
   c. Process planning (CAPP)
   d. Electronic document management
3. Quality management
   a. Quality documentation
   b. Audit and defect tracking
   c. Supplier management
   d. Statistical process control
   e. Inspection and test
   f. Laboratory information management systems
   g. Statistical analysis
   h. Cost of quality
4. Process control
   a. Supervisory control
   b. Cell control
   c. Man–machine interface
   d. Data acquisition control
   e. Historian and archive
   f. Recipe management
   g. Numerical control
   h. Operator support
   i. Data collection

The leading MES software suppliers include:

- Emerson Electric (Intellution)
- Invensys (WonderWare)
- Brooks Automation (FASTech)
- Applied Materials (Consilium)
- Hilco Technologies
- Real World Technologies
- POMS, Inc.
- USDATA

Warehouse Management Systems

A key part of the E-factory is the rapid and efficient control and movement of the material that is purchased and created by the manufacturing process. Finished goods warehouses have employed material handling automation for many years. As supply chain cycle times shrink, the size of shipped lots shrink, and the mix of items in an order becomes more diverse, the complexity of managing a warehouse increases to the point where the control can only be done by a powerful computer software system. Warehouse management systems were brought to market during the past ten years. The features offered in warehouse management systems include the following.

1. Quality control
2. Reporting
3. Returns
4. Transportation management
5. Order tracking
6. Fulfillment notifications
7. Receiving
8. Storage
9. Order selection
10. Loading
11. Shipping
12. Inventory arrangement

The leading warehouse management systems suppliers include the following.

- EXE Technologies, Inc.
- Catalyst International, Inc.
- JDA Software Group, Inc.
- Manhattan Associates, Inc.
- McHugh Software International
- Optum, Inc.
- TRW, Inc.

Factory Automation Systems

Factory automation systems (FAS) refer to the various hardware and software components, equipment, and systems that form the actual link between the material, processes, and information in a production line. Such items include:

1. Programmable logic control (PLC)
2. Robotics
3. Material handling systems
4. Cell controllers
5. Computerized numerical control
6. Intelligent valves
7. Actuators

The leading suppliers of factory automation systems include:

- ABB Industrial Automation
- Siemens Energy & Automation, Inc.
- Invensys plc
- Fisher-Rosemount Systems
- Honeywell
- Rockwell Automation
- Yokogawa Electric Corp.
- Cutler-Hammer
- GE Fanuc Automation Corp.
- Schneider Automation, Inc.

Factory Floor Control

Factory floor control systems (FCS) originated with the need to control high-volume, process-intensive production runs in industries such as chemicals, food, pharmaceutics, and automotive. The advent of E-business brings with it the requirements of having lower volume, more frequently changed, higher quality, build-to-order production processes. This puts more pressure on factory FCS to be able to facilitate and execute the actions required to have such capability.

Trends in process control include: (1) componentization of software that enables capabilities to be tailored and flexible; (2) predictive tools that permit real-time process optimization; (3) shrinking production cycle times that spur interest in process automation; and (4) E-business flexibility that demands plant floor visibility.

With optimization and connectivity to suppliers and customers as goals, factory floor control software is bringing to the table more sophisticated modeling capabilities and predictive tools, as well as enhanced data analysis and more robust management of infrastructure and production. As a result, companies are seeing improvements in information flow, asset management, operational flexibility, process efficiency and reliability, and throughput. Improvements are both initially high, in the capital investment phase and in the long term, as productivity and quality improvements reduce expenses.

While important, savings alone will not persuade a company to invest in process execution and control software. The software must also be easy to use. Ease of use is important for two reasons. First, there is a shortage of IT professionals, and qualified consultants are expensive. Second, IT professionals have been trained to use off-the-shelf office applications and do not have the time or patience for complex installation sequences and long learning curves. Products will have to be much more plug-and-play than process industries have seen in the past.

For users in traditional and new markets, the availability of modeling tools is increasing the appeal of factory FCS. As optimization has grown in importance, plant modeling has become a desirable feature. Six Sigma quality programs have clearly proven the need for quantitative analysis. Six Sigma quality means 3.4 defects per million opportunities. To achieve these high quality goals, significantly more accurate and reliable data is required for analysis.

The top ten suppliers for factory automation include the following.

- Honeywell
- Fisher-Rosemount Systems
- Invensys plc
- Rockwell Automation
- GE Fanuc Automation Corp.
- ABB Industrial Automation
- Aspen Technology Inc.
- GSE Systems, Inc.
- Nematron Corp.
- USData Corp.

Maintenance Management Systems

Computerized maintenance management systems (CMMS) or the newer term of "Enterprise Asset Management" (EAM) systems refers to the software that provides the management and control over the utilization, repair, and tracking of the equipment used in a manufacturing facility. Maintenance management software can extend equipment life; reduce downtime, repair costs, and capital investment; increase productivity; and improve product consistency.

The history of CMMS goes back many years to the earliest days of computer usage in manufacturing. The functions required in managing the maintenance for a large factory have always included:

1. Inventory management of the equipment to be maintained
2. Tracking of the scheduled and unscheduled maintenance performed
3. Maintaining and creating a database of suppliers of repair parts and services
4. Purchasing repair parts and services
5. Monitoring equipment availability and performance status

Stand-alone computers have always been used to store and manage the above information. New requirements for which there are available capabilities include:

1. Condition-based maintenance
2. Real-time equipment performance monitoring
3. Remotely managed maintenance schedules
4. Remote diagnostics analysis
5. Real-time online purchasing of repair parts and services

In addition to the software available, virtually all EAM software vendors have begun to offer or are working on on-line hosted models, which many view as more affordable and easier to implement. Other in-demand features include ease of use, real-time communication, and portability. Using these types of systems workers rely on wireless handheld devices to access work order assignments e-mailed from the program. Upon completion of a task, the worker reports back, detailing time spent and corrective actions taken. This input can be tracked to provide a snapshot of work in progress.

The leading maintenance management systems include:

- Indus International, Inc.
- PSDI
- Datastream Systems, Inc.
- Invensys plc
- Meridium, Inc.
- Mincom, Ltd.
- Fluor Daniel, Inc.
- Ivara Corp

Product Data Management Systems

Product data management (PDM) systems have evolved from the need to create, store, distribute, update, reuse, and glean information from data associated with the design and manufacture of products. These tools accomplish this by managing workflow as well as data. The primary objective of PDM systems is to increase the productivity and efficiency of the product realization process. However, additional objectives are being added as the needs of the E-factory grow.

The objectives and expected benefits of PDM include:

1. Classification control
2. Product structure
3. Workflow management
4. Work history management
5. Improved design productivity
6. Safeguarded data integrity
7. Intellectual property management
8. Product structure management
9. Change management
10. Configuration control
11. Automatic data release
12. Electronic sign-off procedures
13. Revisions
14. Audit trail of changes
15. Collaborative product realization

Collaborative product realization is one of the fastest growing new requirements and promises for PDM. Because of enterprise fission and supply chain fusion, the need for and the opportunity for intensive collaboration across enterprise boundaries are increasing. The key features of PDM that have been under development and enhancement for the past 20 years are now available on-line and in real-time. As a result, collaboration in the E-factory environment is one of the essential ingredients going forward.

Collaboration through PDM, also called collaborative product commerce (CPC), pays multiple rewards. Engineers are often conservative in their approach to problem-solving for no other reason than the time penalties for exploring alternative solutions are so high. PDM opens up the creative process by keeping track of all the documents and test results. This minimizes design rework and mistakes, reduces the risk of failure by sharing the risk with others, makes data available to the right people fast, and encourages team problem-solving and collaborative idea generation.

Leading PDM vendors include:

- SDRC
- PTC
- Documentum, Inc.
- MatrixOne, Inc.
- Unigraphics Solutions, Inc.
- Enovia Corp. (Dassault Systems)
- Eigner + Partner AG
- Agile Software Corp.
- SmarTeam, Inc.
- Auto-Trol Technology Corp.

SUMMARY

The E-factory environment is now served by hundreds of software and hardware products that represent a rich and diverse portfolio of solution components from which a solution set can be selected. The task of selecting a solution set depends on first understanding the business process needs, matching the capabilities of the candidate solution components to those needs, and then selecting the best set of components based on a well-defined set of performance criteria. This chapter has introduced the variety of solution components available on the market and where they serve key business process needs.

Chapter 5
Hot Information Technology Issues

Jerry Kanter

ISSUE 1: THE VALUE CHAIN IS BACK

The concept of the value chain is alive and well, but it now comes with a new definition of what constitutes the chain and an added sense of integration with a proper blend of outsourcing and insourcing. The value chain is not a new concept, as Michael Porter emphasized its importance in 1985.[1] Understanding the fundamental processes a product goes through from raw material, to manufacturing, to inventory, and then to the ultimate buyer was clearly delineated in Porter's concept of competitive advantage. Porter also recognized the importance of the supporting functions such as accounting and human resources. However, the playing field has been significantly widened with the value chain enablement provided by today's technology.

Certainly, the internal business processes must be connected and integrated in an expeditious fashion. Computer systems must track the processes and provide management with the data and information needed to optimize the value chain, ensuring that the right combination of products and services reaches the customer. This is no mean task and has provided an opportunity for the so-called enterprise resource planning (ERP) vendors to carve out a most profitable business niche. (As an aside, this author has always thought that the term "ERP" is a confusing appellation for what companies like SAP, Baan, Peoplesoft, and the rest purport to do — that is, to automate the value chain via information systems.) Many companies have indeed automated the value chain over the years. However, the dramatic changes in technology, such as the introduction of the client/server concept, data warehousing and data mining, and the Internet with its inherent capabilities in being able to communicate not only within the organization but outside as well, have changed the playing field. Other factors that have put a new wrinkle on the value chain are the significant increases in mergers and acquisitions and the resultant need to extend a common value chain across the changing organizational boundaries.

Probably the most significant change has been the opportunity to connect and extend the value chain to include outside vendors, business partners, and customers. This presents an entirely new dimension, but it may well be the key to competitive advantage, keeping in mind that competitive advantage is the ultimate objective of value chain automation. Managing inventories that one cannot see or does not own may seem a challenging task, but that is where much of the action lies. Two examples include Wal-Mart, which allows its suppliers to directly stock Wal-Mart stores, and Federal Express, which allows customers to link to its internal system for tracking deliveries.

To facilitate the above, a new breed of vendor — the application solutions provider (ASP) — has emerged. ASPs complement the supply chain vendors by building linked applications that provide specific product and industry specialization. For example, Reebok has teamed with SAP to develop a comprehensive add-on application aimed at the footwear and apparel industry. Further specialization may still be necessary, but considerably less with the use of the appropriate ASP product.

In its August 1998 issue, *CIO* magazine selected 100 companies for what it termed "Value Chain Excellence."[2] It was impressive that 28 judges were used in the process, and that the companies selected were judged on overall profitability as well as having a positive approach to optimizing the value chain. State Street Corporation was the opening example with their Internet-based security processing system called Global Horizon. It is a single global architecture that serves its own operations in 21 countries and its customers in 80 countries. It operates the same, whether one deals in dollars, guilders, or yen, and is an excellent example of extending the value chain.

Companies are looking to systems like SAP as a way of standardizing the value chain across the organization: creating a single standard while trashing old systems, extracting and reformulating old data into new formats, and changing the way data is extracted and used is a monumental job. Many companies have tried with mixed results. Success requires a total company commitment, cross-functional teams of business and IT people, and an ability to work with outside consultants and vendors. It also demands a sizable multiple-year investment. The benefits are there, but to obtain them often requires a radical change in the way companies are accustomed to implementing systems that have a major impact both internally and externally.

Once the decision to use a system like SAP or Baan is made, the decision and degree to which the use of consultants or outside contractors must be made. The decision requires a careful and realistic look at inside capabilities, the style and culture of the company, and the time and dollar commitments one is able to make. As mentioned, Boston Scientific outsourced a good portion of its installation of SAP to Andersen Consulting, while GTE did the job completely on their own without outside assistance. In this regard, GTE appears to be in the minority. The point being made is that revisits to the value chain require a careful analysis of multiple factors on the part of the CIO and the enterprise operations manager. This entire area is definitely a hot issue and will remain so in the years ahead.

ISSUE 2: IT INFRASTRUCTURE

Infrastructure is becoming the limiting or "gating" factor in everything we do and has new meaning in the world of alliances, mergers, and the integration of functions. Infrastructure can be likened to the building of a house. It provides for the electricity, the water, the heating, the foundation, and the walls that create the floor plan, rooms, and facilities. The architect and builder must take all of this into account when designing a house with future expansion in mind. Without proper attention, expansion, will be difficult, expensive and time-consuming. The parallel holds for the IT infrastructure designer. A series of events have made this a critical and difficult undertaking. Here are several situations that have caused severe problems for companies facing inevitable business and technology changes.

A marketing system built over several years centered around the customer where a database of customers and customer prospects was available to sales and marketing people via a desktop interface. It was deemed essential to include inventory balances by product and location so that sales personnel could respond immediately as to availability. However, it was discovered that the manufacturing and inventory people had developed their own desktop interface, which was incompatible with the marketing system. Major changes involving time and money were necessary to integrate the two systems.

A large banking and financial institution acquired a bank chain that had serious financial problems. One of the principal reasons for the acquisition was the belief that the bank's information systems functions could be incorporated into the host's IT operations. Considerable cost savings as well as an improved service level were anticipated. Two years later, the acquired bank's systems remained in operation with scant integration and economies of scale. The large institution finally realized that it had built up a complex infrastructure over many years and it was not possible to do any adapting. Major surgery was required.

These stories are repeated over and over as companies have come to realize that it is not trivial to add rooms and functions to an edifice built on an inflexible infrastructure.

The problem is heightened by the proliferation of desktop hardware and software — particularly the latter. The costs have become staggering.

While Moore's law states that technology doubles in power every 18 months with no increase in price, this can be misleading. The total cost of ownership has steadily risen as Moore's law focuses on hardware, not software, and the costs of operating the desktop. There is something called hidden cost — the productive time people spend talking to the Help Desk and their peers in getting the systems to operate. It has been estimated by a number of reliable researchers that the hidden cost can be two and a half times the known hardware and software costs. Lack of common, easy-to-use, and flexible software, geared to the new users who often are intermittent users and have lower technical skills than the dedicated users, are real roadblocks.

Suffice it to say, developing a standardized integrated infrastructure has become a vital element, particularly in the world of mergers and acquisitions and in the world of connectivity with workstations on just about every desk and reaching out to more people every day.

ISSUE 3: ELECTRONIC COMMERCE

The new electronic commerce (E-commerce) way of conducting business is changing company strategy and the competitive marketplace. It covers both tangible and intangible products and provides a new look at the combination of the two. E-commerce and the Internet together represent the driving force in today's economy. There is much that is real going on and probably more in the category of fun and games. In a speech, IT veteran and industry guru William Zachman opened by stating that, metaphorically, the Internet and E-commerce boom bring back the image of an old western town in the 1800s gold rush days when word got around that "there was gold in them thar hills."[3] In nearly no time at all, a sleepy little hamlet turned into a mining boom town. Real estate prices soared and would-be miners rushed in, hoping to become rich. Levi Strauss opened a shop selling denim to miners. Saloons, gambling dens, and brothels appeared and flourished. A railroad line was built to the town and investors backed everything enthusiastically, throwing money at all of it.

E-commerce bears a lot of the "gold in them thar hills" syndrome as it remains difficult to predict who mines or will eventually mine the gold. There is no question that the Internet is a bonanza, not to mention the intranet and extranet. The number of Internet users is debatable, but most agree that close to 100 millon people are connected or will be by the year 2000. The numbers soar every month. But, of course, just a fraction of the usage can be classified as E-commerce. It is important to remember that the fundamentals of the value chain described above still apply. It is still a brick and mortar business and shipping, packaging, pricing, and inventory control remain relevant. It works better when the product is information — bits as opposed to atoms — but even in these instances, the value chain must be considered. There are many start-up companies that are using the Internet to communicate, advertise, provide information via search engines, and assist individuals and companies in setting up attractive Web sites. These companies represent the periphery and there is "gold" there; but there has to be "real gold" as well at the end of the tunnel — the products and services ordered by the customer.

One company that has struck gold is the classic Amazon.com, which has become an all-familiar Web site. Indeed, Amazon is selling information but in the form of tangible books that one orders, pays for by credit card, and receives from a book warehouse. The value chain has been established so that inventory is identified and accumulated, and elements like inventory location, inventory renewal, physical order delivery, and customer billing are provided to complete the E-commerce cycle. This author uses Amazon.com to locate and order books, and the system works.

Like any new technology, the first issue is to ask the question, "Where does it fit in relation to the company's strategy?" The optimal use depends on the industry, the competitive positioning, and the particular niche the company is targeting in the marketplace. A manufacturer will look at E-commerce a bit differently than a retailer or a catalog company. However, there is no question that the Internet will dramatically change the way business is conducted for all but a few. The Internet really brings to light the metaphor of Marshall McLuhan's "global village." There *is* "gold in them thar hills."

ISSUE 4: KNOWLEDGE MANAGEMENT

Arguably, the issue of knowledge management is the most all-encompassing one these days. The concept is based on the computerization, not only of explicit information — products sold, inventory data, market survey statistics and the like — but the computerization and sharing of information that heretofore has been stored in the brains of a few strategic-thinking executives, so-called tacit information.

In his book, *Intellectual Capital: The New Wealth of Organizations,*[4] Thomas Stewart divides intellectual capital into (1) human capital, (2) structural capital, and (3) customer capital. One is likely familiar with structural capital, which relies heavily on technology and includes databases, data warehouses, data networks (the Internet), data mining software, groupware, and the like. Structural capital includes physical functions that have developed within the company, like the production line or customer support processes. Customer capital is the value of the relationship to the people with whom the company does business. Human capital is the least understood and resides in the minds of the company work force, not in company manuals, files, and databases. Human capital can be explicit; that is, a manager explains the thought processes used to analyze what the next generation of products should be and why they will have a positive impact on profits. But much of the human capital is implicit or tacit; that is, it is difficult to see, fully explain, or understand. Real corporate breakthroughs often emanate from these "flashes of brilliance," or whatever they are termed. A formative goal is to identify tacit knowledge and to make it as explicit as possible so that it can be used by others.

Knowledge management can be viewed as turning data (raw material) into information (finished goods) and from there into knowledge (actionable finished goods). The implication is that knowledge gives one the power to act, to make decisions that are value producing to the company. It is usually the tacit information that actually drives the transformation. The goal should be to discover the managers and workers who possess the proven tacit knowledge, and to then work with them to determine the combination of information they use and the thought processes they go through to turn that information into knowledge (value).

Consulting companies have taken a leadership position in knowledge management as their business is, in reality, selling knowledge to their customers. As an example, a true competitive advantage is that of a consultant conducting business with an insurance company in Sydney, Australia, that has the collective knowledge of the consultant company's experience in dealing with insurance companies around the world, and in such a way that the consultant's knowledge can be effectively utilized.

An important prerequisite for developing such capability is that the company's performance system reward the sharing of knowledge. This is an important and often overlooked element. In large consulting organizations, a variety of reward systems have been established. In some, it is a key part of an individual's performance appraisal. The question of how well the individual shares information about client work is placed in the appraisal form and given significant weight.

Articles and conferences on knowledge management abound, and often the reaction to such a blitz is that the subject matter is, in reality, a fad and will fade quickly. This author does not believe this to be the case. The principles of knowledge management — the concept of discovering the tacit knowledge within employees' minds that has proven to be successful, making that knowledge accessible to others throughout the organization, and using advanced technology to accomplish this — will remain a sound and successful business practice.

ISSUE 5: ALIGNING IT STRATEGY WITH BUSINESS STRATEGY

Alignment has always been a priority IT issue, but quick business changes and rapid economic reversals make this a continuing process rather than a long-term focus as in previous planning efforts. Flexibility and adaptability are essential, and this infers a closer IT/business strategy than ever before.

There has been an evolution in IT planning. Formerly, IT management would come together to develop a three- to five-year plan, the result of which would be a huge tome that was put on the shelf and created a warm corporate feeling. Key business managers would review the document but had little part in its development. As has been stated, rapidly changing business conditions require constant attention to planning. It is no longer a one-time event; it is a continuing process with participation from the business as well as the IT side.

In an article in the *Harvard Business Review,* Bensaou and Earl studied 20 leading companies in Japan, focusing on how they manage IT.[5] Research found that IT planning is not considered a separate activity and that Japanese executives would never consider developing a special IT strategy. Japanese companies preferred what they termed strategic instinct rather than strategic alignment, the former concentrating on meeting operational goals and supporting major business initiatives. This seems to be more in line with responding to the volatile business conditions that exist and will intensify in the coming years. Traditional long-term IT planning may just not be responsive enough.

A good example of a successful planning and business linking process was accomplished at GTE Government Systems Corporation in Boston, Massachusetts.[6] A high-level steering committee comprised of IT managers and business managers met quarterly and continues to do so after four years. The methodology and contents of the plan were significant, but the key to success was the support and backing of operating management and the participation of business management as well as IT management. Planning was viewed as an ongoing process. Business goals were discussed at the early meetings and agreement was reached on the six important business objectives. Application initiatives were ranked based on their importance in achieving business goals. With this established, technology initiatives were prioritized based on their impact in achieving the business goals. Then, projects were selected and a project plan produced with detailed project descriptions, cost and schedules, statement of projected benefits, and project milestones.

Studies of other companies indicate that satisfaction with the planning process seems to be based on the relationship between IT and the business managers. First, it begins with a mutual understanding of each other's job and the particular demands. Second, each individual possesses or is prepared to obtain an understanding of the other person's perspective on the problem at hand. Good relationships flow from a sense of being on the same team, a sense of sharing not only the problems but also the successes. The most commonly stated attribute contributing to a good relationship and to successful planning is constant communication between the IT manager, the business manager, and their respective staffs. Mutual trust is mandatory.

One line manager put it well, in such a way so as to define what is meant by aligning IT strategy with business strategy: "Working this closely with IT does not make me feel left out as it did in the past. We have come to understand what IT has been trying to tell us, and they have come to perceive what the business problems are and why we are trying to resolve them."

Notes

1. Porter, Michael E., *Competitive Advantage,* Free Press, New York, 1985.
2. Annual CIO — 100 Value Chain Excellence, *CIO,* August 1998.
3. Zachman, William, President, Canopus Research, Zachman Web site, "13 Industry Predictions," 1997.
4. Stewart, Thomas A., *Intellectual Capital: The New Wealth of Organizations,* Thomas A. Stewart, 1996.
5. Bensaou, M. and Michael Earl, The Right Mind Set for Managing Information Technology, *Harvard Business Review,* September/October 1998.
6. Cale, Edward G., Jr. and Jerry Kanter, Aligning Information Systems and Business Strategy — A Case Study, *The Journal of Information Technology Management,* Number 1, 1998.

Chapter 6

Information Darwinism: The Impact of the Internet on Global Manufacturing

Eric A. Marks

Anthropologists have long been familiar with what Stephen Jay Gould calls "punctuated equilibrium." The theory of punctuated equilibrium challenged the long-standing idea that evolution was a long, slow, gradual process resulting in the manifestation of changes in all living species based on natural selection acting on their respective gene pools over geological time. Punctuated equilibrium postulates long periods of stability with very little change marked by the sudden introduction of rapid change based on discontinuities caused by dramatic environmental shifts, mutations acting on the gene pool, and other similar forces. These radical changes spark selection of traits and attributes of populations in a dramatic fashion, far faster than the gradual evolutionary changes originally postulated by Charles Darwin. The point is that punctuated equilibrium is characterized by very rapid evolutionary change. In geological time, this would have taken place over millions of years, minimally hundreds of thousands of years; but as you know, this is a very very short time in evolutionary terms.

Punctuated equilibrium can be seen everywhere in today's business environment. With the introduction of the Internet, the already frenetic pace of business has been ratcheted up further! We now refer to Internet speed or Web speed as the current benchmark. What does this mean? Well, for business it means that every move a company makes, or doesn't make as the case may be, exposes it to new competitors, and new threats, as well as new customers and new markets. The changes are real and maddeningly

0-8493-1273-6/02/$0.00+$1.50

sudden for management teams who are already busy struggling with the rigors of today's business environment.

Wasn't it was just yesterday that we finished our Y2K remediation, and contingency planning, completed our ERP system implementations and rented those big generators? Aren't we done yet? Can we take a break now? Well, the answer is "no," and by the way, there is no finish line. There will be winners, and there will be losers. Which will you or your organization be? How will organizations adapt to the changing business landscape in the face of rapid change, shifting markets, globalization, staffing shortfalls, technological obsolescence, and more?

Well, I believe that information is the key. The ability of global manufacturers to harness information firmwide in every operation, to harvest knowledge and turn it into competitive advantage, will be the primary adaptive mechanism for firms intending to win in the new millennium. Information technology is a central theme of any modern business strategy today. Firms that don't subscribe to this view will not be around in the long term. This leads to the core concept of this chapter — "Information Darwinism." I believe that firms that invest in IT as a strategic resource for the future will survive. Those that do not will perish. Furthermore, executives who drive investing in IT as one of their primary strategic levers will thrive. Those who do not will be deselected.

The ability of firms to harvest information and drive their business based on information will separate the winners from the losers in the new economy. Strategic use of IT will be a key adaptive mechanism for all firms in the coming years, but especially so for global manufacturers.

In this sense, IT is analogous to culture for human beings. Physically, humans haven't changed much over the last million years or so. Two million years ago, *Homo erectus* had domesticated fire, used language to communicate, and crafted weapons. Five hundred thousand years ago, *Homo sapiens* emerged. This species was distinguished by the ability to create technology, as demonstrated by increased innovation and progressive sophistication in tool-making. 90,000 years ago, *Homo sapiens,* our immediate ancestors, emerged. Again, physically, we have not changed significantly over these time frames. However, we have continued to adapt, acclimate, and thrive in our environment, and to interact with other cultures, and adapt to new climates and new geographies. This is because as a species we have learned, through cultural adaptation as opposed to physical adaptation, to survive in varying geographies and climates, and to respond to unforeseen changes in the conditions around us.

Culture in humans can be likened to information technology for corporations. These are "software-like" adaptive mechanisms that allow for flexible responses to unforeseen changes. They allow responses in timeframes that are much faster — for example, Web speed — than geologic and evolutionary time fences, which are measured in hundreds of thousands of years, even millions of years. We don't use terms such as epoch, era, or Pleistocene to describe recent business trends, although we do refer to some companies as dinosaurs.

For manufacturers, there is compelling evidence for investing in IT as a means of adapting to the new economy. Manufacturers have typically been considered IT laggards in terms of spending as a percentage of revenue. Manufacturers on average spend 1.7 to 2.0 percent of gross revenues on IT, as opposed to what are typically considered the information-intensive industries (e.g. banking, financial services, and others). However, things are changing, and there are good reasons to believe that many manufacturers do understand the types of IT investments required by the new economy.

These manufacturers understand what the Internet opportunity means for their operations, for managing their supply chains, for their marketing and sales processes, and for their customer care processes. These are exceptional firms that saw what was coming and acted early. They are reaping first-mover benefits from having jumped into the Internet early and passionately. Firms that come to mind include Dell and Cisco, among others. And of course, there are plenty out there that don't get it. Look for them to go the way of the dinosaurs unless they act quickly.

In today's E-business environment, IT investing has been spurred on by the need to explore selling over the Web. Whether it is business-to-business (B2B), or business-to-consumer (B2C), IT spending in support of newly developed E-business initiatives has been proceeding at a frenzied pace. In fact, most IT management won't allow spending if there isn't some connection to that "E" preceding some other word such as procurement, logistics, commerce, and a bevy of others. But this is a new phenomenon, and we've only seen the beginning, the tip of the iceberg so to speak.

Corporations are just beginning to "walk upright," if you will, in their incipient responses to the Internet opportunity (or challenge) facing them. Evolutionarily speaking, we have seen the environment change, conferring sudden advantage upon certain companies, (e.g., dot-coms and others), and now we are seeing the old guard respond as best they can. Their adaptive calculus may allow them to respond in time, or it may not. Adapt or die, as my friend Dick Morley likes to say.

Look at the recent announcements by GM, Ford, and DaimlerChrysler in establishing trading exchanges for the automotive market. Have you seen some of the numbers for these trademarts?

The latest, in which GM, Ford, and Daimler-Chrysler will all conduct parts procurement in a single automotive trading exchange, is unbelievable. We're talking about moving $240 billion of spending annually through this trading community. By the way, that is only from the Big Three. When we add the purchasing volume represented by the other members of the trading exchange, it adds another $250 billion! So, roughly $500 billion will flow through this Web-based business.

This exchange will eventually be an independent firm. It will have a potential market cap ranging from $30 to $100 billion according to some analysts. And now add in annual revenues of roughly $7 billion from transaction fees, advertising, and the like, and now you've got a story. Oh, and don't forget about the savings for the firms in transaction costs. Ford alone was projecting annual savings of $8 billion in procurement prices, plus another $1 billion from reduced overhead, paperwork, and other efficiencies each year. We're talking about savings of roughly 25 percent of the retail price of a car through streamlining suppliers and distribution using the Web.

We're talking about big business here with these trading exchanges, and we've only seen the beginning. Wait until this really begins to unfold. We'd all better strap ourselves in and hang on for a wild ride.

But now, let me dial back to the not-so-distant past. Not so long ago when I worked for a large system integration firm in Detroit, I was fortunate to be involved in selling document management solutions to our customers. At the time — I'm talking about 1993 or 1994 — we had a very clever idea. We were putting various forms of documentation online in a document repository. We were using authoring tools to create hyperlinks for ease of content navigation using HTML, as well as full-text indexing to allow keyword searches.

To make all this happen, we developed a simple browser to perform the navigation functions for us. We of course didn't know much about the Web back then.

Does this sound familiar to anyone? Interestingly, we had a difficult time selling this solution to our customers. Why do you suppose that was the case? What was wrong with our business model? What was wrong with the technology at the time? What was missing that prevented us from making this solution a home run?

Well, timing was surely a factor. At the time, security was very important to the firm, so nobody was allowed outside of the corporate systems to access the incipient Internet. Several forms of justification were required, as well as upgrades to the desktop computing platforms to allow access to the Internet. In addition, the World Wide Web hadn't yet exploded into what it is now, so there was no outside push for access to this new and exciting world of ideas, information, and thought exchange. And although

Mosaic was around, none of us really knew much about a small start-up called Netscape or a gentleman named Marc Andreesen.

From a solution perspective, we were selling what we thought was quite a compelling value proposition: access to information by internal customers to help perform their jobs more efficiently. We considered ourselves a services company then, so we would bundle all of the hardware, software, and services together for a fixed price and then provide content management and authoring services on a per-transaction basis. Our solution was clearly in line with our corporate strategy! So, why didn't we make hundreds of millions of dollars from this solution that so closely resembles the Internet of today?

Well, I don't know the answer, but I have a suspicion. I believe the failure to propel our browser-based content navigation solution into history boils down to at least two components: vision and scope. We didn't have the vision for how these technologies were being positioned for the Internet at that time by Netscape among others. Had we understood a bit more of the possibilities, we could have painted quite a vision for our customers about how these tools and technologies would revolutionize the way business would be conducted in the very near future.

Regarding scope, Internet standards and technologies allow almost limitless scope and reach into new markets, new geographies, new ways of conducting business, and new ways of creating value. There are endless possibilities — as opposed to being anchored in today's realities, which are to a large extent derived from the paradigms of the past. These are the things that we didn't understand in our early Internet-based system back then. As I mentioned, at the time our company wouldn't even allow access to the Internet without several layers of approval because of security and other "internal control" reasons. Of course, that firm recently had several of its leaders, including its CEO, deselected because they didn't quite get it, if you know what I mean. You've heard the expression about companies getting "Amazoned"? Well, these executives got "Darwined"!

Let's discuss the business impact of the Internet.

- How will companies respond to global demand for products and services? How will multicurrency issues, language and cultural issues be addressed? Companies are just now, as I said, walking upright in their quest to conduct B2C and B2B business models over the Internet. All of these questions have to be answered.
- Another question: Can traditional manufacturers become so-called E-tailers? Do they have the core competencies such as customer support, catalog selling skills, and shipping order quantities of one versus large quantities like they're used to? Will channel conflict ever be re-

solved, or will there be massive upheaval of the traditional means of selling and moving goods and services to customers?

- Getting back to the automotive trade exchanges, can the Big Three successfully transition to a business model where they are generating large percentages of revenue through services, such as online access to the Internet from within the very vehicles they sell? Ford has announced this in its E-business plans. And we thought using cell phones while driving was dangerous. Can they really concentrate the buyers and sellers of automotive supplies in their trade mart and drive the savings they are targeting as well as the revenue from transaction fees, advertising, and so on? E-GM has moved its headquarters to a Silicon Valley location to tap into the talent pool as well as ideas on how these types of ventures are supposed to work. Can they succeed? Is it too late? Can Mark Hogan, a car guy, become the Internet guru for GM? For that matter, can a contact lens salesman sell cars either?

- The Internet has engendered a slew of new types of companies, new types of businesses, and, of course, new threats to the established order. Charles Fine of MIT calls these start-ups the "fruit flies" of business, because they are so fast and so agile. Their business models are all about speed to market and quickness to capitalize on new ideas. Their very survival is built on speed. Stay tuned as we watch how business changes in dramatic new ways, and how various companies respond to the changes within their particular industries. Again, using evolutionary metaphors, how will different companies adapt themselves in response to these environmental conditions?

But now, to the central issue: How will the Internet affect global manufacturing? Let's look at a few key areas to paint a vision of how it might look, given that the Internet will continue to evolve and change the way we fundamentally conduct manufacturing today.

Let's first examine the impact of the Internet on information technology (IT) strategy.

- Finally, E-business and the Internet have exposed that previous IT management goals were not necessarily market- or customer-oriented goals. They were about internal controls, accounting functions, cost containment, and reporting. For manufacturers to succeed today, their IT strategies have to become more market focused, not inward focused. IT must be engaged as a business partner to help drive top-line revenue opportunities, and support the marketing and sales efforts of firms, product development, and manufacturing. By considering the Internet as a new means of developing alternative revenue streams, old-line manufacturers may turn their IT organizations into profit centers rather than overhead.

- IT strategies of the future will be based on themes such as reaching out to new customers and new markets. IT will play an increasingly critical role in market development, customer retention, and all aspects of product development, manufacturing, order fulfillment, logistics, and distribution.
- IT will be a key for reintroducing your customers to the business processes that were originally supposed to support them — and I mean the real customers, not the corporate finance gods and the standards police, among others.
- IT must be used to reinstitute the enterprise agility that some ERP-centric architectures have removed in recent years. By this, I mean Web-wrapping the already legacy ERP applications with customer-facing and eminently flexible Web-based architectures, not the rigid architectures of the past.
- For example, in some cases, manufacturers are bypassing ERP by linking order entry systems directly to manufacturing execution systems, with ERP being relegated to invoicing and related financial functions. This is a recent trend but one to watch.
- A key point: the ERP system implementations did provide benefits that corporations are not yet taking advantage of: they did push companies toward common business process and common systems. Now, they may not be the right processes for today's environment, but they are at least a foundation from which firms can springboard to more Web-centric, customer-focused E-business processes.
- The Internet has also caused what I refer to as architectural inversion; plants are managed closer to the customers than ever before with Web technologies and Internet access. It also introduces the notion of the customers as schedulers. Who is really running your plants today? If you are truly being responsive to the marketplace with your manufacturing strategy, then your customers are running the plant. If the plant doesn't perform, customers can, in effect, fire you and take their business elsewhere. So you do, in essence, work for the customer.

Let's examine manufacturing strategy and operations now.

- Manufacturing is all about information and knowledge management. Manufacturers have to redefine themselves as managers of information — information about customers, products, and processes — not merely as "makers of things and stuff." Taking this view would really reinforce the importance of IT in the long term for global manufacturers.

I often refer to a *Business Week* article from 1999 in which Federal Express stated that it is "an information management company, not a transportation company." By viewing themselves this way, FedEx has expressed what it believes to be a critical core competency — information management — in support of its transportation infrastructure. If I use my evolutionary analogy here, FedEx's transportation infrastructure is its physical adaptive mechanism, and its IT capabilities are its cultural adaptive mechanism. Its systems capabilities will determine how well it can survive and maximize its physical structure in the age of E-business.

- Increasingly, access to all of this information and how it is used will make manufacturers winners or losers. For example, products will not be accepted without accompanying information about product and process quality.
- Manufacturers will not be selected as CMs without proof of their actual on-time delivery, proof of product and process quality, all in real-time. This implies a real-time window into the plant-level activities of your manufacturing partners to monitor their operations, their processes, and their performance.
- In the new economy, manufacturing will have to be as responsive as marketing, customer service, and other facets of your business are. This will be a change for many firms.

Let's next look at the Internet influence on new product development: new product development cycles will be shortened dramatically by Internet-based tools such as collaborative design with customers and key suppliers. These collaborative activities will begin during the buying and selling process and rapidly ripple through a virtual supply chain of core suppliers to prove out the concepts and bring them to market faster than ever before. (The Internet is the ultimate groupware, isn't it?) Speed to market will be shortened, prototyping and manufacturing launches will be facilitated by online simulations, and real-time sharing of product and process information will ensure manufacturability and product quality. Supply chains will be dynamically modeled and assembled based on the needs of the marketplace and the product to ensure customization appropriate to the geography, culture, and preferences of the buyers. See, we're finally getting to the mass customization model we've been talking about for so long. Contract manufacturing will be added and subtracted for increasingly shortened product life cycles, which will bring the focus on a new set of skills — how to assemble and disassemble supply chains dynamically according to the life cycle of your products.

Charles Fine addresses this topic quite nicely in his book, *Clockspeed: Winning Industry Control in the Age of Temporary Advantage*. He makes quite a compelling case, using evolutionary concepts I might add, for managing supply chains as a key adaptive core competency. He likens the horizontal and vertical fluctuation of supply chains to the double-helix structure of DNA. A company's ability to position itself properly within the structure of its particular industry during transitions from horizontal, disintermediated structures to vertical, integrated structures is the key to survival in this age of rapidly increasing clockspeeds.

Now, let's examine marketing and sales. A key difference for manufacturers today is that selling directly to individuals is quite different from selling to large distributors, large retailers, or other large corporations. There are differences in the way you treat customers, in the way that you ship product, in the way that you have to know your customers. For traditional manufacturers, taking credit card orders is often a big deal for firms that haven't done business this way before.

How about marketing and promotions and those types of skills? How does the Internet change them? For example, now people are rushing to set up corporate portals to attract customers to their Web sites. The business processes to maintain fresh content, to continually post interesting, personalized information, and even to attract eyeballs to a Web site are no mean feat. A recent client wanted to establish a portal strategy, but its divisional Web site was buried deep within its corporate Web site. I'd been with this client for months, and I still had difficulty finding its divisional Web site. These are simple things, but they are vital in the Internet age. Marketing and sales will be integrated with Internet strategies for handling orders, for attracting new customers, and for integrating sales and distribution channels into a cohesive corporate presence facing the customers. We haven't seen the end of the changes here, either. E-CRM, E-SFA, and other "E" words and "E" acronyms will continue to appear over the coming months and years.

Let's look at industrial automation. Yes, the Internet even reaches down into the equipment and devices on the plant floor. Three years ago or so, Group Scheider, or Modicon for you PLC romantics, developed a PLC architecture with an embedded Web server. This idea was a breakthrough! It demonstrated to the world of industrial automation that Internet technologies have compelling benefits in factory floor applications. E-business strategies and E-supply chain management efforts require E-factories to support them. Embedded Web servers in PLCs, drives and motors, valves, pressure transmitters, and other types of equipment will pave the way for dramatic improvements in factory floor operations, process and product quality, and remote equipment maintenance. They may even reorder themselves when they reach the end of their rated lives. Watch this space for new developments and rapid adoption of Internet tools and technologies.

Let's revisit on-line trading communities for a moment. They will not only allow manufacturers to shave costs from their operations and their products, but will provide new sources of revenue to global manufacturers — service revenues — that have previously been foreign concepts. GE made the move into services a few years ago and has shown admirable gains. But the Internet business model, the B2B business model of transaction fees and transaction cost reductions, will provide alternative sources of revenue to global manufacturers. Of course, when these trading exchanges go public, their IPOs will provide yet again more streams of alternative revenue.

Finally, let's discuss some E-business facts and fiction, as well as some other things to watch in the coming months and years.

- On-line marketplaces will continue to proliferate. Watch and see how these will evolve and respond to one another, how they will converge and morph as the technology changes, and as the winners and losers are selected by the marketplaces they are trying to serve.
- E-engineering around the Internet business model will be the theme for the foreseeable future. But let me assure you all about this "E-engineering" notion. From the projects I've been executing recently, the business process is still a critical success factor. You can have all the glitz and glamour you want, but if the processes don't support the business model, it will fail! Trust me on this! Never forget the process issues of E-business.
- Supply chain management will become a three-dimensional problem in cyberspace — trademarts, horizontal and vertical trade exchanges, these all add new dimensions to the puzzle of global manufacturing, global supply chain management, global customer relationship management, and global sales and marketing. E-business is global, and you have to think globally from the beginning to succeed.
- E-business will continue to be volatile, with new entrants every day, high rates of M&A activity, and accelerated rates of change. Hedging strategies will be used in selecting technology partners for business initiatives, at least until the breakaway firms are identified or selected, if you will, by the marketplace. But E-business cannot be conducted with a "wait-and-see" strategy. You have to dive in now and with full vigor and accept some degree of risk.
- What will happen with the traditional manufacturing software vendors? How will the old-line ERP companies adapt? Remember, these new ERP systems are already being viewed as legacy systems by E-business firms. How will software companies reposition themselves as E-business suppliers? And will they be credible in doing so?
- We use the term virtual corporation a lot these days. E-business doesn't have to be based on a virtual model. To be an E-business, it doesn't mean you have to outsource your manufacturing capacity and other physical assets. In fact, Amazon has recently built six DCs to be able to sustain its business model and service levels. In effect, Amazon has had to get real or get physical. So if you are a manufacturer and a consultant tells you that to be an Internet business you have to shed your physical assets, well I don't quite buy that.
- Having physical assets is not a weakness, nor does it prohibit E-business as a viable strategy. It means that your particular formula for success will have to be based on your company's culture, beliefs and

values, unique core competencies and skills, and physical assets such as R&D, manufacturing, and distribution. This is your adaptive framework from which your E-business capabilities must be derived. This is your corporate DNA, so to speak.

- Winners and losers will not necessarily be selected by a pretty Web site, although a slick Web site is nice. It is the combination of B2B and B2C capabilities as well as solid business strategy and marketing skills that will separate the winners and losers. All of this must be backed by outstanding manufacturing capabilities, world-class back-office processes, and customer-focused IT systems. I've been installing a private hosted trading exchange for a client — in fact, it goes live in two weeks — and trust me, there are a lot of issues beneath the covers of B2B E-commerce, as well as B2C E-commerce, that have to be addressed in order to ensure success. There is a big difference between announcing an Internet trading exchange and getting it online and running.

Finally, I'd like to share some key actions global manufacturers must take in order to help ensure their survival in this time of business upheaval — that is, to prevent themselves from being "information Darwined," so to speak.

FIRST, TREAT THE INTERNET AS AN OPPORTUNITY, NOT A THREAT

What a time we live in! This is an unprecedented period in history, and we're just beginning to see how things will change, given the reach and impact of the Internet. For example, I have mentioned online trade exchanges several times because it is a timely topic. Analysts expect B2B E-commerce companies to command an aggregate market value of $1.5 trillion by 2003, while taking transaction fee-based revenues of $55 billion this year and growing to $1.4 trillion by 2004. Those are astounding numbers. The Internet provided the opportunity, and many companies have seized it.

SECOND, INVEST IN IT

IT will be a key adaptive mechanism in every foreseeable future scenario. Global manufacturers must increase IT spending, in appropriate ways, by at least 50 to 100 percent in order to be positioned for survival. They must be willing to experiment with IT in ways similar to R&D. Put pools of funding aside for research. Give IT a role in generating top-line gains as well as driving bottom-line savings. In other words, engage these IT gurus in your core business operations. Believe me, they really know more about manufacturing than we sometimes give them credit for.

THIRD, PROMOTE YOUR IT STAFF TO OPERATIONS ROLES

As a result of Y2K efforts, your IT leaders have proven that they do indeed understand your business and how they impact its success. IT leaders suddenly were cast into the limelight with the whole Y2K phenomenon. They had a chance to rub elbows with senior leaders of major corporations as well as demonstrate their ability to meet a major challenge. I believe that the next five to ten years will be marked by IT management getting promoted to key leadership roles because their skills are absolutely necessary for the survival of firms in the modern age.

And remember, Internet technologies permeate every facet of your organization, so be sure to represent all functional disciplines in crafting your IT adaptive framework for the future. This means automation and controls engineers, manufacturing systems personnel, as well as the traditional IT disciplines, all have key roles to play in your future.

FOURTH, ENSURE ENTERPRISE AND ARCHITECTURAL AGILITY

This means that any investments must be made with a wary eye. Maintaining as many strategic degrees of freedom with respect to the marketplace, the competition, and the unknown is critical. This is especially the case in the Internet E-business arena where there are so many new entrants in all facets of this domain. The established software firms are scrambling to protect their flanks from these new competitors. But you have to invest in these new software tools to keep abreast of the environment. But invest and deploy using a hedging strategy versus a bet-the-farm strategy. The winners and losers of this battle have yet to be determined, but you don't have to be a loser just because one of your software partners has been deselected by the Darwinian forces of this Internet age.

Consider Intel's latest moves. Intel, we know, makes microprocessors like nobody else. However, under CEO Craig Barret, Intel is undergoing a major change — diversifying itself into multiple businesses that you wouldn't have expected. These include Internet services such as Web site and application hosting as well as selling branded Internet appliances. Intel couldn't even contemplate these changes without the architectural and business agility to execute them. This is adaptation at its finest — adding diversity in the face of uncertainty, which is the ultimate evolutionary advantage. Diversity wins the adaptation and natural selection game.

FINALLY, MAKE SURE YOU HAVE THE ADAPTIVE CAPABILITIES TO SURVIVE IN THIS WAVE OF RAPID CHANGE USING THE PUNCTUATED EQUILIBRIUM ANALOGY

I think you all understand now what I mean by that. Don't let your firms or yourselves become victims of Information Darwinism. We are in the age of information. Information is a key adaptive capability for survival for the foreseeable future. Don't be deselected by ignoring the growing information imperative of the Internet age. And remember, the rules of survival have been known for a long, long time: Adapt or die. That is the law of the jungle today. I think Charles Darwin said it best: "It is not the strongest of the species that survives, nor the most intelligent; it is the one that is most adaptable to change."

Chapter 7
Understanding E-Commerce Strategically: The Dawn of IT Fighting

Bernard H. Boar

In an industry well known for exaggeration and hype, the phenomenal ascent of electronic commerce (E-commerce) to the forefront of industry attention has set a new standard for user interest and business opportunities. Driven by the ubiquity of the World Web Wide, the global Internet, and the availability of universal browser interfaces, the growth and importance of E-commerce to the digital business of the new millennium cannot be over-hyped or exaggerated. Consider the following E-commerce forecasts:

- The size of the U.S. on-line population is expected to grow to over 100 million in 2001 from under 20 million in 1996.
- U.S. on-line retail sales are expected to grow to $17 billion by 2001 from less than $1 billion in 1996.
- It is anticipated that by 2003, close to 10 percent of all business-to-business commerce will be conducted through E-commerce.
- It is forecasted that U.S. business-to-business E-commerce revenue will grow by a factor of 10, to over $300 billion by 2002.

It is no wonder that every business will need to become a high-performance E-business in the coming years or become no business at all.

What is E-commerce? As the word gets widely used, its definition continually morphs. Consider the following recent definitions from industry publications:

- E-commerce encompasses all business operations and transactions based upon communication via electronic media.

- E-commerce is the buying and selling of goods and services on the Internet, especially the World Wide Web.
- E-commerce is the conduct of business on the Internet, not only buying and selling but also servicing customers and collaborating with business partners.
- E-commerce is Internet-based facilitation of trade between companies.
- E-commerce means conducting these business activities on-line and worldwide:
  - Company promotion
  - Product marketing
  - Negotiating and taking orders through virtual storefronts
  - Receiving payment
  - Interacting with customers for pre- and post-sales support

This author suggests that E-commerce is a very rich concept that needs to embrace all of these ideas and offers the following comprehensive definition:

> E-commerce is the use of Internet centric technologies to engage in business transactions with customers, suppliers, within the business itself, and/or any other business partners. E-commerce embraces:
>
> - E-tailing (electronic retailing) or virtual storefronts on the World Wide Web (WWW)
> - The gathering and use of customer demographic data through WWW contact
> - Customer pre- and post-sales care, service, and inquiry
> - Electronic data interchange, the business-to-business exchange of business transaction data
> - The creation of the electronic or digital enterprise wherein internal business transactions, embracing the entire value chain, are intermediated through Internet centered technologies

With the advent of E-commerce, competition and business opportunities migrate from physical marketplaces to the *marketspace* — a marketplace created, defined, nurtured, and exploited through information technology. A virtual realm where products and services exist in digital form, are delivered through information-based distribution channels, and that rewards speed, innovativeness, interactivity, and personalization.

Within the IT community, most of the E-commerce discussion naturally focuses on the *nets* of E-commerce, the Internet, intranets, and extranets (see Exhibit 1) and the enabling technologies such as HTML, XML, Java, software agents, and TCP/IP. While mastering these technologies is operationally important, it is beneficial to step back from a technology perspective of E-commerce and look at the underlying strategic logic that should guide our daily tactical work. What can one learn about E-commerce when one looks at it through a strategy lens?

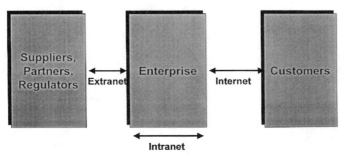

Exhibit 1. The "Nets" of E-Commerce

STRATEGY, ADVANTAGE, AND E-COMMERCE

The academic purpose of strategy is to provide direction, concentration of effort, sustainability of purpose, and flexibility as a business constantly moves to improve its positions in strategic domains. At a very pragmatic level, the purpose of strategy is to find a way — short (the shorter the better) of brute force — to accomplish one's ends. To a businessperson facing the chaotic new millennium, the purpose of strategy is very simple. The eternal struggle of business is the struggle for advantage. The one with more advantages wins, the one with fewer advantages loses. The purpose of strategy is the building and sustaining of advantage. The goals of strategy are to build new advantages, elongate existing advantages or reduce disadvantages. Thus, strategy is all about creating distinct attractions to customers while creating distance from competitors.

While there are endless ways to build advantage, all advantages can be classified into five generic categories:

1. Cost advantage: the advantage results in being able to provide products/services more cheaply.
2. Differentiation advantage: the advantage creates a product/service that offers some highly desirable and distinct feature/functionality.
3. Focus advantage: the advantage more tightly meets the explicit needs of a particular customer.
4. Execution advantage: the advantage permits operational processes to execute in a superior manner.
5. Maneuverability advantage: the advantage lets one to adapt to changing requirements more quickly than others. Being maneuverable allows one to constantly refresh the other types of advantage. It is the only advantage that one's competitors can never take away.

So, one wins by being cheaper, more unique, more focused, faster, or more adaptable than one's competitors in serving customers. At a minimum, the advantages must satisfy customers and, at best, delight or excite

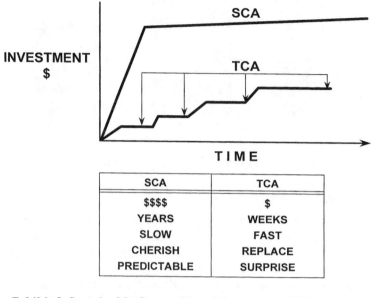

SCA	TCA
$$$$	$
YEARS	WEEKS
SLOW	FAST
CHERISH	REPLACE
PREDICTABLE	SURPRISE

Exhibit 2. Sustainable Competitive Advantage and Temporary Competitive Advantage

them. If an action does not lead to the development of an advantage, it is of no strategic interest. The struggle always has been, and remains, the perpetual struggle for competitive advantage.

Advantage comes in two flavors: sustainable competitive advantage (SCA) and temporary competitive advantage (TCA). As illustrated in Exhibit 2, what distinguishes them from each other is durability. Having struggled to create a sustainable advantage, it will last a long time, be cherished by the organization, be predictable to competitors, and difficult for competitors to replicate. Temporary advantages, as the name implies, are short-lived attractions. They create an advantage for a short period of time and can be rapidly duplicated or surpassed by competitors. At any time then, a company's success is a function of its portfolio of sustainable and temporary competitive advantages.

As illustrated in Exhibit 3, E-commerce is so strategically exciting because it is one of those rare entities that transcends all of one's choices in building advantage. E-commerce is such a rich concept that it can be used to create any of the classes of advantage (cost, focus, execution, differentiation, or maneuverability) in either of the time dimensions (sustainable or temporary). This is a rare occurrence. Most advantage opportunities are self-limiting to a few of the cells in Exhibit 3. The robustness of the impact of E-commerce on a business is such that how one builds advantage

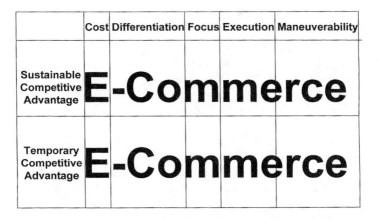

	Cost	Differentiation	Focus	Execution	Maneuverability
Sustainable Competitive Advantage	E-Commerce				
Temporary Competitive Advantage	E-Commerce				

Exhibit 3. Classes of Advantage and Time Dimensions for E-Commerce

with it is only constrained by the imagination. So, the first way to think about E-commerce strategically is to think of it as a rich and robust platform for the building of a dynamic portfolio of sustainable and temporary advantages. E-commerce should be appreciated as a platform that can mix all the different types of advantage to create limitless attraction to customers and ever-increasing distance from competitors.

PROCESS AND E-COMMERCE

One of the primary ways to build advantage is through execution excellence or process superiority. As shown in Exhibit 4, process embodies the entire product/service customer experience. Some strategists, therefore, argue that the primary focus of strategy should be the nurturing of the business processes that deliver value and satisfaction to customers. The logic of competition should concentrate on how to compete (e.g., the continual improvement of process).

Exhibit 5 illustrates the complicated relationship of process to customers. A customer will have many needs that must be satisfied, and a need can be shared by many customers. A need can be satisfied by multiple products/services, and a product or service can satisfy many needs. Finally, a product or service is delivered through multiple processes, and a process can support multiple products or services. Because of its complexity and importance, process provides a rich opportunity to distinguish oneself with one's customers.

Processes have many important attributes that can be attacked to satisfy customers and distant oneself from competitors. Processes can be judged by:

- Speed
- Consistency
- Exception processing
- Agility
- Innovativeness
- Accuracy
- Simplicity

- Quality
- Learning
- Costs
- Measurable
- Leverage
- Productivity
- Functionality

- Personalization
- Acuity
- Customer satisfaction
- Scalable
- Frictionless
- Collaborativeness
- Start/end with customer

What is strategically important about E-commerce is that it can be used to address all these dimensions. In particular, E-commerce is uniquely capable of addressing the attributes of speed, innovativeness, simplicity, frictionless, productivity, personalization, learning, and collaboration. So, the second strategic way to look at E-commerce is as a platform for creating attribute-rich processes that interact with customers, interact with business partners, and enable internal business activities.

HYPER-COMPETITION AND E-COMMERCE

More and more industires are entering into a state of competition called *hyper-competition*. Hyper-competition is a state of competition within an industry with some very alarming characteristics:

- Advantage: it is increasingly difficult, if not impossible, to create and maintain sustainable competitive advantages. The war of advantage migrates to creating an endless stream of overlapping and staggered temporary advantages from trying to defend a set of sustainable advantages.

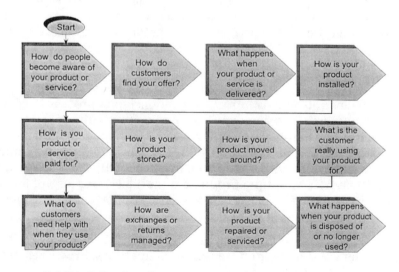

Exhibit 4. Product/Service Customer Experience Process

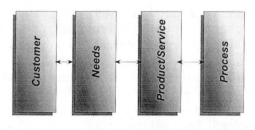

Exhibit 5. Relationship of Process to Customers

- Innovation: there is rapid and dislocating innovation in the industry. All forms of know-how are subject to rapid devaluation and must be continually refreshed.
- Competitive escalation: competitors continually raise the ante to play the game. A state of market equilibrium is neither achieved nor desired by winner-takes-all competitors.
- Customer power: customers become extraordinarily demanding and have ever-heightened expectations. These demands are made actionable by effortless substitution between supplier products and services.
- Value proposition: there is a continuing market redefinition of what is valued by consumers. Competitors constantly search for new combinations of basic products and add-on features that will entice customers. Nobody can either pause or rest based on past laurels. What is currently competitive gets old and dated quickly.
- End of chivalry: there is no respect for the status quo by competitors. Barriers to entry are viewed as challenges to circumvent. There is no tacit division of the marketplace pie with each supplier taking a share. Each competitor craves it all and acts relentlessly to satisfy that craving.
- End of customer loyalty: markets are characterized by excessive churn. Customer loyalty is fleeting and often needs to be bought. Dissatisfied, curious, and better-value-seeking customers vote quickly with their feet by taking their purchasing dollars elsewhere.
- Market disruption as the rule: competitors take actions to disrupt markets rather than protect markets. The objective of competitive strategy shifts from protecting what one has to taking what one does not have. Explicit actions are designed and executed to devalue the opponent's advantages and renew one's own advantages before a competitor decreases in value thos advantages.
- Hyper-competition is a state of intense and often lethal competition. Hyper-competition is driven by the concurrence of a number of market factors:
  - Shift of market power to customers: customers perceive a wide selection of choices and become accustomed to shopping across multiple alternatives.

- Rapid decline in barriers to market entry: ways are discovered to circumvent barriers to entry by creative and ambitious competitors. With ingenuity, it is often discovered that a seemingly inpenetrable barrier to entry is no barrier to entry at all.
- Accelerating technology/know-how change: the half-life of competencies is dramatically shortened by rapid innovation. The game of advantage through know-how is constantly being restarted with all the players having to start over again.
- Rise of multiple deep-pocket players: multiple companies enter an industry with the financial resources to fight it out. One big company can no longer bully all the others into submission and make them stay in their place.
- Deregulation: government and regulatory authorities disassemble legal barriers to entry. Often, the deregulation not only disbands legal barriers to entry, but also aggressively encourages intense competition.
- Inability to sustain advantage: the durability of advantages dramatically declines. Dramatic innovation, shifts in technological know-how, and creativity in redefining the product value proposition conspire together to reduce the resiliency of any advantage.
- Globalization: time and space barriers to market entry are overcome. Geographic strongholds become easily breached and foreign competitors can effectively invade markets — often with deep pockets, no respect for the status quo, and rich resources.

As illustrated in Exhibit 6, different models of advantage are associated with different market conditions. In hyper-competitive markets, what is

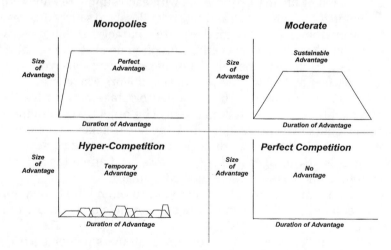

Exhibit 6. Four Models of Advantage Associated with Different Market Conditions

important is the ability to maneuver and continually refresh advantages. Hyper-maneuverability is the strategic coping response to hyper-competition and should convey the following imagery:

- The quality of a system that allows it to respond to change and variety
- The ability to deal with variance
- An action a_1 is more flexible than action b_1, if the set of possible actions following a_1 includes the set of possible actions following action b_1
- The capacity to take new/novel actions in response to new/changed circumstances
- The ability to respond to environmental disruption without disorganization or collapse
- The ability to reconfigure and remain in alignment with a changing environment
- The ability to add, modify, and delete without causing disruption
- The ability to adapt to fluctuations
- The only response that is viable to hyper-competition is to transform the business into a hyper-competitor. This means:
  - replacing moderate competitive behaviors with hyper-competitive behaviors
  - replacing one's devotion to sustainable advantages with an endless string of temporary advantages
  - making speed, agility, surprise, and the ability to maneuver and disrupt the cornerstones of one's strategy
  - being able to compete against time — time is of the essence

What it means most of all is that one must make a war of rapid and disruptive movements to replace the traditional strategy of defending one's strongholds. There is no safe harbor in retreat. Either one surrenders or one becomes a hyper-competitive predator. These are the only two choices. It is exaggerated, but only slightly so, that maneuverability is the primary type of advantage that a company must have to succeed in a hyper-competitive marketplace.

The problem of hyper-competitive business strategy reduces to being able to continuously turn the "front." Using a military analogy, armies line up against each other across a front (Exhibit 7). Then, as shown in Exhibit 8, the trick is to turn the front. The obvious reason is to permit the front-line forces to proceed unopposed; but the more compelling reason is that it disrupts the support infrastructure behind the front and displaces all the support systems from their positions. Turning the front ruins the plans of the opponent and causes tremendous friction for them as they try to reestablish order between the new front and their support infrastructure.

As shown in Exhibit 9, the same logic applies to business strategy. In a hyper-competitive business environment, it is necessary to be able to continually turn the front to create new value propositions for customers, or to

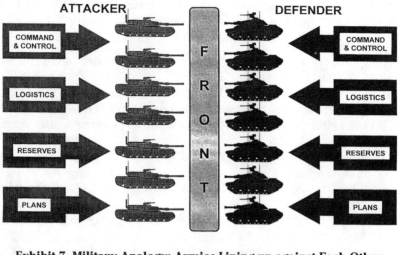

Exhibit 7. Military Analogy: Armies Lining up against Each Other across a Front

devalue the initiatives of one's opponents. In the information age, turning the front equates to being able to turn one's E-commerce systems. The competitor who has a deeper and more far-reaching strategy for commanding E-commerce will have a definitive advantage in an endless war of turning the fronts.

THE INFORMATION AGE, E-COMMERCE AND IT FIGHTING

One is now living through an era called the information age. It has the following distinguishing characteristics:

- The dominant technology of the era is the computer. Computing intelligence is dispersed into anything and everything that can be improved by being smart. The computerization of anything and everything is called mechatronics (mechanical electronics).
- The icon of the era is the microprocessor. Inexpensive and programmable chips permit products to be customized and made dynamically and personally responsive to each user.
- The output of the era is knowledge. Making products information-rich results in products and services with a high attraction to consumers.
- The basis of wealth of the era is information. Information drives the creation of knowledge that drives agile strategic actions that create temporary competitive advantage for the business.
- The defining work is the knowledge worker. Greater than half the workforce is involved with collecting, processing, and communicating information.

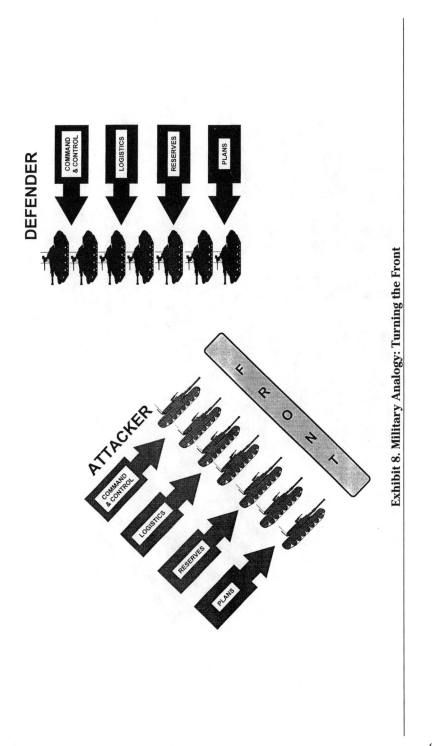

Exhibit 8. Military Analogy: Turning the Front

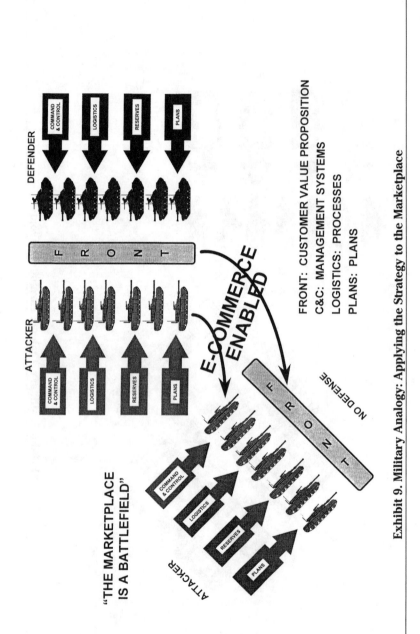

Exhibit 9. Military Analogy: Applying the Strategy to the Marketplace

- The means of moving things is communications networks. Logistics is concerned with moving bits (electronic products) rather than atoms (physical products).
- The marketplace, where people gather to buy and sell products and services shifts from the physical marketplace (a mall or shopping center) to the marketspace (an electronic marketplace in cyberspace).
- Information-based enhancements become the primary way to create new products and services and to embellish the value of existing products and services.
- People buy dynamic and variable nondiscrete combinations of information-based products. Value is created at the time of purchase through digitized customization.
- Customers are treated (marketed, sold, and serviced) as individuals — not as statistical averages. A broadly accessible information highway (currently personified as the Internet) permits global and interactive access to multimedia information.
- The convergence of information forms yields entirely new ways of working and living. Time and space constraints on markets collapse, permitting people to live where they please, work with remote employers, and purchase products from local or distant providers as the situation desired.

The information age means, more then anything else, radical shifts in the basis of wealth. In the industrial age, products were physical; in the information age, products become virtual. In the industrial age, the focus of effort was the automation of labor; in the information age, the focus of effort is the creation and exploitation of knowledge. In the industrial age, information flow was physical and paper based; in the information age, information flow is virtual and digitized. This results in the movement from manufacturing as the basis of societal wealth to knowledge as the linchpin of wealth. It results in the entire global economy becoming merged and information-centric.

In summary, the information age can be understood from five primary perspectives:

1. Technology. Continued innovation in information technologies results in information technology permeating all aspects of life. As the internal combustion engine permitted the automating of labor, the computer permits the informating of society.
2. Economics. The economy becomes information-centric. Wealth creation is closely tied to the ability to create new information based products and amend existing products with information. Information technology permits entirely new ways of collaboration to create products and services with closer ties to all value chain participants.

3. Employment. The density of employment shifts to knowledge workers. Most people make their living creating, moving, analyzing, interpreting, or disseminating information.
4. Spatial. The networking of computers throughout the world results in a collapse of the traditional market constraints of time and space. The world becomes one global marketspace.
5. Cultural. Society becomes media laden. Information is readily available in multimedia formats, customizable, and interactive. One expects information in forms that are readily accessible and convenient to one's needs. The social capabilities of computers and communications permit new social structures to emerge.

The information age is driven by three concomitant technological changes:

1. The digitalization of information, regardless of form. All forms of information — audio, data, image, and video become a series of bits. With the digitalization of all forms of information, all information shares the same bit-based DNA and becomes interoperable, transportable, and subject to interactive manipulation by the consumer. This has the net effect of radically changing business value chains, dramatically altering products and services, and completely revising consumer expectations as they are presented with interactive multimedia.
2. The rapidly declining cost of computing. The physics of computing has had only one impact on its price/performance for the past 30 years, and the exact same impact is anticipated for the foreseeable future — it will continue to dramatically decline. This cost efficiency is critical because it enables computing to become ubiquitous and available with sufficient power at an enabling and attractive price point.
3. The availability of broadband communications. The emergence of broadband communications is critical because multimedia is both storage intensive and time sensitive. The availability of gigabit communications will enable information-age companies to improve both the efficiency and effectiveness of work.

The key strategic implications of the information age are as follows:

- All information becomes digitized and is subject to interactive manipulation. The interface to the user becomes multimedia rich and is as much entertainment as it is instructive or transactional.
- The economy becomes digital. More and more, products and services take on electronic personas. Employment is dominated by knowledge work.
- Information becomes available to all — anywhere, anytime, and in any form.

- Information exchange occurs on a global basis. The location of information and the people with whom one interacts is virtual, and their location makes no difference. There is just one all-encompassing cyberspace.
- The economy becomes very knowledge-centric. Creating and applying knowledge rather than making things creates value.
- Business, shopping, leisure time, games, socialization, etc., all take on an electronic character. It is often easier, more efficient, and convenient to conduct daily affairs through electronic media than through physical presence.
- People become more self-sufficient in satisfying their needs through electronic distribution channels. This is the phenomenon of dis-inter-mediation.
- Products and services undergo mass customization. Information-age products undergo final assembly at the point of purchase in response to the exact desires of the consumer.
- Computing becomes ubiquitous. Everything that can benefit from being made smart is made smart. Once made smart, it is necessary that it be connected to be able to relate its knowledge to others. Like the availability of electricity today, the universal presence of computers will be taken for granted.
- Information becomes democratized. The first 30-year tyranny of text data comes to an end as image, video, audio, animation, etc., are all equally accessible and, often, much more valuable.
- Speed is of the essence. A digital society is a society where things happen quickly. A business must have the ability to respond ever more quickly to rapidly changing consumer tastes. In the industrial age, the large companies ate the small companies. In the information age, the fast and agile companies eat the slow and ponderous companies.
- Software agents that search, negotiate, and buy for you replace or complement human agents.
- Traditional barriers to market entry, as well as the historical market constraints of time and space, collapse. It becomes a war of all against all as customers become free to choose from a global marketplace. Market power shifts to consumers as information access creates a nearly friction-free marketplace where consumers have unlimited ability to comparison shop.
- Commerce becomes continuous. Business is conducted around the world around the clock without respite. Neither personal software agents nor the databases that they operate on ever need a vacation or time off.

As illustrated in Exhibit 10, companies engage in IT fighting and E-commerce becomes the weapon system to fight the market battle. Exhibit 10 should be understood as follows:

- The information age converts the marketplace to the marketspace.

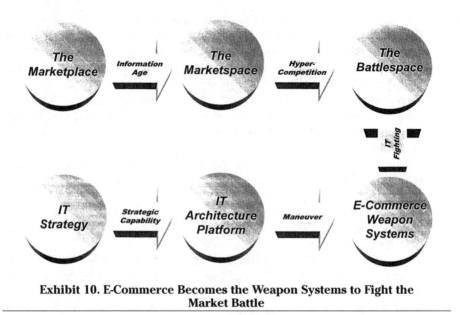

Exhibit 10. E-Commerce Becomes the Weapon Systems to Fight the Market Battle

- Hyper-competition converts the marketspace to the battlespace — a fiercely competitive virtual marketplace.
- To compete in the battlespace, the business will need highly maneuverable E-commerce weapons systems.
- With E-commerce weapons systems, the business can engage the batlespace by IT fighting — the use of IT systems to attract customers and deter competitors.

As shown in Exhibit 11, there is a dramatic change in the nature of advantage that is enabled by IT fighting, and E-commerce sits as the means to create those advantages.

Exhibit 11. IT Fighting: E-commerce Is the Means to Create IT Fighting Advantages

Industrial Age Advantage	Information Age IT Fighting Advantage
Mass production	Mass customization
Mass marketing	One-to-one marketing
Customer research	Customer participation
Optimization of physical value chains	Optimization of information chain
Physical collaboration with suppliers	Information collaboration with suppliers
Excellent customer service	Customer self-service
Physical location	Virtual globalization
Prompt delivery of physical products to door	Online delivery of virtual products
Knowledgeable sales help	Software agents

CONCLUSION

These are exciting times and at the heart of these times is the rise of the electronic enterprise. An electronic business (E-business) is an enterprise in which all the value chains are electronically inter-mediated — a business that is built upon and operated through E-commerce. How you strategically understand and implement E-commerce will make a dramatic difference to your success. Miyamoto Musashi in his great strategy classic, *The Five Rings,* wrote, "Essentially the weapon in and of itself is meaningless without the proper applications of its virtues by the Warrior." The weapon of E-commerce offers many virtues of advantage. It is a strategic challenge to build E-commerce weapons systems that permit a business to command the battlespace.

Chapter 8
Supply Chain Strategies

Jim Ayers

Supply chains are a hot management topic. Eyes are opening to a more global view of end-to-end material, information, and financial flows. As it is with most good ideas, commercial interest drives much of the hype. The management consulting industry contributes with new buzzwords to stimulate and sustain interest. So *supply chain synthesis* and *demand flow leadership* debut in press releases and seminars. Substantial contingents of software purveyors also vocalize the concept. Companies investing millions in new systems do not want yesterday's solutions.

"Supply chain thinking" is a better characterization. This term infers a more gradual infusion of new mindsets and methods into traditional tasks. Most managers have the same concerns today as managers had ten or 50 years ago. These concerns include products, markets, people and skills, operations, and finance. Supply chain thinking brings change to the tasks managers perform in dealing with these issues.

FIVE TASKS THAT WILL CHANGE

Exhibit 1 lists five tasks important to supply chain design and operation. Alongside each is a brief description of the impact of supply chain thinking.

Exhibit 2 shows the relationship of the tasks. Supply chain design begins with strategy, so it is at the center. The remaining tasks, including the development of information systems, need to align with these strategies. This article describes practical ways to bring supply chain thinking to the task of strategic planning. Too often strategic planning goes on in an operational vacuum. Gaining advantage from supply chains requires cross-functional thinking that is uncommon in most companies.

SUPPLY CHAINS AND STRATEGIC ADVANTAGE

The competitive field in most markets requires well-designed products. However, at the margin, other factors govern the buying decision. For

0-8493-1273-6/02/$0.00+$1.50
© 2002 by CRC Press LLC

Exhibit 1. Supply Chain Design and Operation

1. Designing supply chains for strategic advantage	Today's success stories show that innovation in supply chain design is vital to competitive advantage.
2. Implementing collaborative relationships	Functional command and control will give way to new structures.
3. Forging supply chain partnerships	Working together beats going it alone. The extended enterprise is for real.
4. Managing supply chain information	Opportunities to succeed wildly or fail miserably abound.
5. Making money from the supply chain	Pricing and cost always matter but ways of measuring and managing them will change.

example, most airlines offer clean, modern aircraft and maintain good safety records. This is the price of entry to the "club." If an airline did not qualify, we probably would not go near it. The way we view the airline likely depends on flight frequency, prices, frequent flier programs, or the coffee served on flights.

Every product occupies a different competitive position. Traditionally, features of the product itself have dominated in determining this position. Now products increasingly compete on the supply chains that deliver them. The variables in airlines are not in the planes they use or the routes they fly, but in supply chain design. Supply chain thinking has untapped

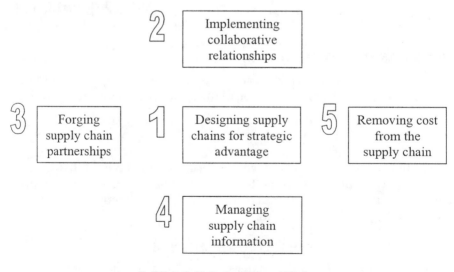

Exhibit 2. Relationship of Tasks

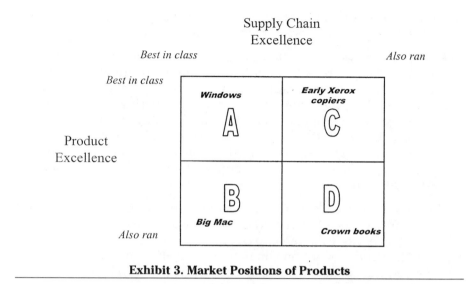

Exhibit 3. Market Positions of Products

potential for maintaining a competitive position or moving a company from an unfavorable to a more advantageous position.

For this discussion, we describe a *product* as its physical features or functionality. The *supply chain* includes all the processes that put the product in the hands of end users. This includes numerous transactions involving physical movement, exchange of information, and the flow of money.

PRODUCT POSITION GRID

Exhibit 3 illustrates how a product might be positioned in its market. It will probably excel or lag behind in product features or supply chain design, or both.

Companies with many products will have some in each category. As a matter of fact, most will prune underachieving products and businesses — characterized by "D's." The *Product Excellence* dimension rates the product against competitive products in its chosen market. The *best in class* will rank highest in terms of functionality, reliability, and value for price.

The *Supply Chain* dimension covers many activities. Examples include accompanying services, like technical support, financing, and distribution. The *best in class* often have great service reputations, if not exceptional products. The *also ran* companies are ones we avoid, if possible.

In the grid, "A" products have the best of all worlds. Products and supply chain processes are the best; makers of these products "own" their markets. Microsoft is a good example. Its Windows software is an automatic addition to a new PC, assuring widespread distribution. Also, no software developer would ignore it in developing a new application.

Most products we buy day to day lie in the "B" category. Competition is intense because there is little difference among products, so success requires supply chain innovation. "B" products may be former "A" products whose early success attracted competitive offerings. While their efficient supply chains remain intact, they are no longer the standard for product excellence. McDonald's has a widespread store network. It opens new outlets with precise, efficient procedures built on long experience. However, its product is, to many, dated and low quality — even for the price charged.

Wonderful products supported by sloppy operations populate the "C" category. Xerox, when it invented copier technology, was a "C" situation. Such companies are vulnerable to copycat competitors, just as Xerox was in time. "D" products are hanging on for dear life. Unless they move to another category, they will not survive. Crown Books, an early discounter, lost marketshare to Barnes & Noble and Borders who sell the same books, but with more amenities.

SUPPLY CHAIN THINKING ACROSS THE GRID

One's supply chain strategy will depend on grid placement. Exhibit 4 has examples of how supply chain thinking can apply to each box.

The remaining sections describe and apply this framework. A case study shows how a company with "D" products might move to friendlier environs.

Exhibit 4. Applying Supply Chain Thinking

Competitive Position	Supply Chain Thinking
A. Excellent product and supply chain	Continuously improve both product and supply chain to deter competitors. If there are any flanking, breakthrough innovations in product or supply chain design to be made, make them yourself. Do not let someone else.
B. Excellent supply chain, "commodity" product	Maintain parity in product design. Work hard to innovate the supply chain. Test new concepts for supply chain design.
C. Excellent product, unexceptional supply chain	Your technology lead will not last. Be prepared to move to the B quadrant. Work hard on supply chain innovations while you enjoy an advantage.
D. Poor product and supply chain	In the time you have (if any), innovate toward one of the other quadrants. If product innovations will take too long or are unavailable (a move to A or C quandrants), redesign your supply chain (a move to quandrant B).

ANALYTICAL FRAMEWORKS

Two notable articles by Marshall Fisher and Michael Porter prescribe ways to implement these strategies.[1,2] Fisher points out that supply chain design depends on the nature of the product. He divides products into *functional* and *innovative* categories. Functional products sell at low margins — equivalent to categories B and D on our grid. Supply chains for functional products should be efficient; customers are buying on price. Innovative products — equivalent to categories A and C — command higher margins. Delivery and availability, not efficiency, should drive supply chain design.

A supply chain contains multiple activities and processes. These processes include manufacturing, distribution, customer service, and selling functions. Porter maintains that linked activities and processes in the supply chain are especially resistant to competitive pressures. He emphasizes that, in any market, operations improvement can only go so far. The philosophy is consistent with the observation; "You cannot save your way to success." While product technology and supply chain imitators can duplicate an isolated activity, linked activities are difficult to duplicate. This uniqueness leads to invulnerability.

Both strategic frameworks are notable for their recognition that the supply chain should be a cornerstone for competitive success. Certainly products with superior features and design contribute greatly to company success. But innovation in the supply chain dimension is at least on a par with product design as a determinant of success.

CASE STUDY — APPLYING THE FRAMEWORKS

A case study for a fictitious company called Acme illustrates how to construct an activity system for innovative and functional products.

Acme had long manufactured a widely used line of aircraft fasteners, which Acme had originally designed. Fasteners hold aircraft together — they are essential components. Customers respected Acme for the quality of its product, but usually bought on price and availability. All suppliers were certified to quality standards.

Unlike other fastener companies, Acme maintained technical services to support its technologies. But quality and technical services — while desirable — seemed to carry little weight in most purchasing decisions.

Acme's profit had languished in a cyclical downturn in the commercial aircraft market. A recent boom in business brought profitless prosperity. Boeing, a price-driven buyer, dominated this market. Over the years, Acme had also aggressively licensed its technology. Many licensees had lower costs and greater marketshare, including sales to the dominant buyer, Boeing.

Many non-Boeing customers were turning to distributors for fasteners. This displaced manufacturers like Acme from dealing directly with customers. For these users, buying from distributors brought lower inventory, just-in-time delivery to assembly lines, and reduced purchasing overhead.

Despite these changes in industry supply chains, Acme maintained a one-size-fits-all production planning system. There were no supply chain accommodations for industry segments. Lack of innovative products and ignoring new supply chains caused most of Acme's products to fall into the D quadrant of the product grid. Particularly vexing to customers in a time of tight supply were long lead times for Acme's products.

The following sections illustrate how a supply chain redesign, using the conceptual frameworks of Porter and Fisher, might improve Acme's competitive position.

Select Strategic Themes to Underpin Your Strategy

Porter's framework begins with strategic *themes*. Strategic themes are the cornerstones of a supply chain strategy. The themes require clear choices regarding how to compete. This is a difficult but necessary step and not to be taken lightly. Too often companies try to be all things to all people. Failure to choose how one will compete means there is no strategy at all.

In Exhibit 5, the choices for Acme centered on the four themes listed in the left-hand column. The exhibit shows the "as-is" choice implicit in Acme's operation. These positions evolved historically and were not the result of conscious decisions along the way. The last two columns illustrate

Exhibit 5. Acme's Range of Choices

Theme	Acme "As-Is"	High End	Low End
Technical leadership	Provides a variety of resources — engineers, laboratories, etc.	Cutting edge.	Copy cat.
Service customization	No customization for segments. Services designed around direct sales to OEMs.	Tailored approaches to all segments.	Narrow choices directed at niches — at low prices.
Production flexibility	Inflexible scheduling. First in, first out.	Excess capacity, short lead times.	Take a number. Get it when it is ready.
Contribution margins	Not Managed, poorly measured.	Plush, service driven.	Narrow, price driven.

Exhibit 6. Acme's Possible Choices

Theme	Strategic Choice
Technical leadership	Maintain technical leadership position. Find. ways to more fully exploit the advantage from laboratories and engineering department.
Service customization	Develop different levels of service for different customer segments.
Production flexibility	Deploy production capability to match service levels.
Contribution margins	Price products and services to meet profitability goals.

the range of options from the high to the low end. Various competitors chose to compete along the spectrum from high to low. Most successful competitors had made conscience choices.

Acme had choices in each of these areas. A possible set of choices could include those shown in Exhibit 6.

Exhibit 7 shows how these choices of strategic themes might anchor a supply chain strategy.

Exhibit 7 displays an Acme decision to maintain its technical leadership position (1) while adding flexibility to its production and customer service systems (2 and 3). Profitable operations require new financial approaches (4). Therefore, pursuit of measures to assure that prices and costs align became a choice to be made.

Deceptively simple in concept, the four boxes represent real choices for Acme. As an example, Acme could choose to forego technical leadership.

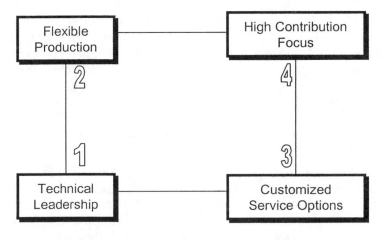

Exhibit 7. Anchoring a Supply Chain Strategy

That would produce a dramatically different company and supply chain. Gone would be laboratories, the engineering department, and the technical sales force. It would treat all its products as "functional," choosing to compete on price alone. It would operate as a "no frills" company (quadrant B in the product position grid), delivering little more than plain vanilla product. And several competitors did just that.

The flexible production and customer service themes (2 and 3) require major changes in the way Acme manages its capital resources and schedules its operations. These changes reflect focused strategies aimed at newly defined market segments. For Acme, this could mean three strategies:

1. A Boeing-specific strategy
2. A strategy for other aircraft makers
3. A distributor strategy

Each segment has different needs. For example, distributors want fast delivery of a variety of products. Price is secondary. Boeing wants long production runs and low cost.

With the complexity introduced by this strategy comes the need for better accounting. Therefore, pursuit of *contribution* is a theme. Note this is not *contribution margin*. The goal of increased contribution allows for both high and low margin business. To qualify, a low margin business with high volume would be desirable.

Define Unique Activities to Support These Streams

With strategic themes in place, Acme must develop supporting activities that uniquely implement those themes. Exhibit 8 shows some of the activities Acme might pursue to implement the strategic themes.

A renewed investment in product research and development (R&D) supports the theme of technical leadership. Also, Product R&D and Consulting support the technical leadership theme. Acme assumed its technical position was unique in the industry. That capability would have value to customers needing new solutions and advice on the use of the product, although it should "pay its way" instead of being given away for free. Acme faced the choice of many software firms. This choice was to support the paying customers through the product "break in" period and then charge for services thereafter.

Because demand had increased dramatically, Acme needed to use the plant and equipment capacity available. The Utilization Maximization activity supports this goal. It includes a number of measures like improved maintenance, reduced set-up, and cellular manufacturing to get more from scarce machine and personnel capacities. This activity was also important to enable Acme to get ahead of its backlog.

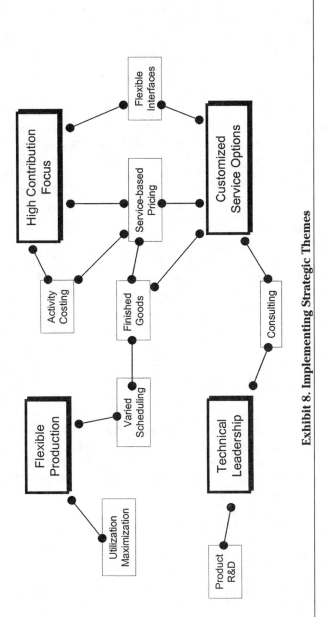

Exhibit 8. Implementing Strategic Themes

Varied Scheduling and Finished Goods support the Flexible Production and Customized Service Options themes. Acme had a policy not to carry finished goods inventory. This caused long lead times for all products. By selecting products for inventory, Acme can quickly satisfy at least a portion of its customers' requirements. Introducing Varied Scheduling would add predictability to production schedules and enable better management of production priorities.

In an environment of scarcity, offering different levels of availability is a strategic application of supply chain thinking. It recognizes that immediate availability has a value over delivery in six months. A supply chain providing product today at a higher price would solve some customers' needs. Other customers could choose to wait for their turns in the queue. Of course, the premium for short-term response will vary with the ebb and flow of market demand. At peaks in demand, the availability brings a premium price. At troughs, it is an edge in a more competitive marketplace.

Flexible Interfaces between Acme and its customers broadened the range of contracting and transaction options available to customer segments. Online ordering and production tracking are examples. The existing Acme customer interface system formed over time when end users placed direct orders. These options would especially accommodate the needs of the growing distributor base. Each distributor had a unique customer base with varying needs. Acme could "tune" its production system with more options.

Activity Costing would help Acme understand what business is profitable. Acme served many customers with a wide product range. But Acme had little left in the way of profit, despite a resurgent demand. Activity Costs would point the way to the profitable and unprofitable businesses. Activity Costs also supported Service-based Pricing. Service-based Pricing meant more services should cost more. It maintained that nonproduct supply chain services had value. A customer with customized interfaces drawing heavily on readily available finished goods inventory and technical support, for example, would pay more.

Make Sure the Activities Fit Together

According to Porter, sustainable advantage comes from "fit" between these activities. Fit has three flavors:

1. First order: fit between the activity and strategic theme. In the activity map, activity costing fits the notion of measuring contribution on different pieces of the business. Its application is as an internal control to evaluate product and customer profitability. Product R&D is another example of first order fit. That activity supports the Technical Leadership theme alone.

2. Second order: reinforcing activities. This type of fit is between activities where one activity supports another. For example, Activity Costing also reinforces another activity, Service-based Pricing. Activity costs provide the data needed to set pricing. Changing the way scheduling is done (Varied Scheduling activity) will enable maintenance of finished goods inventory (Finished Goods activity).

3. Third order: optimization of effort across the activities and with suppliers and distribution channels. Third order fit is supply chain integration. Flexible Production and Finished Goods provide options for distributor customers competing with just-in-time contracts. Flexible Interfaces increases the ability to link up with the supply chains of Acme's customers — notably distributors.

It is fit that provides sustainable competitive advantage. Competitors can usually imitate individual activities of successful companies. But they ignore the impact of second and third order fit — the greatest contributors to competitive position. To dislodge their successful adversary they must copy not just one, but multiple, activities and link them effectively. This is many times more difficult than imitating a single activity.

CONCLUSION

Thinking in terms of supply chains instead of individual operations or departments leads to more competitive strategies. These strategies, in turn, have fallout throughout the operation. In the case of Acme, the addition of new linked activities will bring the new need for new thinking, a shifting of organization roles, and new information systems.

The strategy is a vital first step to improvement. The implementation phase shifts from a "right brain" to a "left brain" exercise. There is an unprecedented need for cross-functional cooperation. Implementing Acme's new activity system will draw on skills from marketing, engineering, production, and finance. The devil lies in the details. Competent execution of the remaining four management tasks is mandatory.

Notes

1. Fisher, Marshall L., "What is the Right Supply Chain for Your Product?" *Harvard Business Review*, March–April, 1997.
2. Porter, Michael E., "What is Strategy," *Harvard Business Review*, November–December, 1996.

Chapter 9

Building a Leadership Organization

Brian Jeffrey

XYZ Company is a growing midsize retailer. The company has more than doubled its revenues during the last 5 years. Despite a weak economy, severe price cutting, and increased competition, gross margins have improved more than 30 percent over this period.

John is an XYZ customer. On XYZ's mainframe is a file on John, as well as files on more than 5 million other XYZ customers. This file contains details on all John's purchases from the company over the last 5 years. It also contains data on his income, his profession, details about his family, the car he drives, credit cards he uses, and more than 40 other categories of information.

XYZ has targeted John. The company has calculated exactly how much he spent in its stores last year. XYZ will try to persuade him to increase his purchases by 12 percent this year. If he buys less, XYZ will be concerned. He will receive personalized mailings, additional incentive coupons, and calls from a telemarketer. But it is not likely that he will buy less. John is an XYZ preferred customer. As such, he qualifies for discounts, special offers, and promotional rewards not only from XYZ, but also from more than 100 other businesses. This is why he buys from XYZ.

Preferred customers are only 15 percent of XYZ's customer base but account for more than 30 percent of sales and more than 40 percent of profits. XYZ's customer loyalty program is designed to keep preferred customers and get more. Today, John is going to a sale at XYZ. He received a personalized letter about it last week. XYZ has already calculated that there is a 36 percent probability that he will go to the sale, a 25 percent probability that he will buy something, and he will spend an average of $63.56. The cost of the letter, the sales it will generate, and the net profit contribution of John's projected purchase were all determined ahead of time.

John makes a purchase. An hour later, that purchase, along with hundreds of thousands of others, is being studied by XYZ's top management. They have gathered, as they do every afternoon — or during peak sales periods, every hour — to view information displayed on a large-screen computer terminal. This shows precise sales patterns for every product line and department of each of the company's stores. If necessary, management can examine sales of any of the 12,000 inventory items the company carries, for each single checkout nationwide. It shows not only the sale value, but also the profit contribution of each store, item, and customer.

Data is streamed upward from the point of sale systems in XYZ stores to a common customer data base. It is then analyzed automatically every hour for management by a highly sophisticated, custom-built command and control system. Illustrated in Exhibit 1, a common customer data base

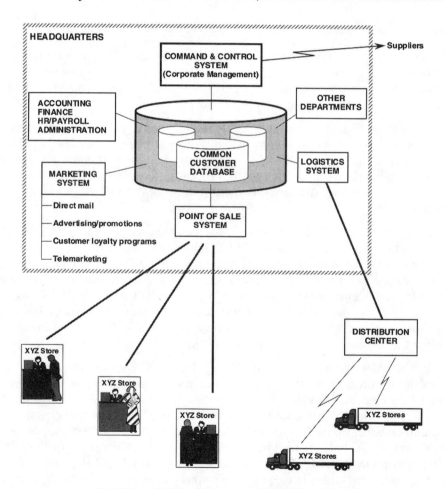

Exhibit 1. IS Infrastructure of XYZ Company

is the focal point of XYZ's entire IS infrastructure. Using analysis provided by the command and control system, decisions are made about whether to change product mixes, cancel or redirect orders, or place new ones. Orders are placed electronically, reaching suppliers immediately. The company's distribution center is also notified online. If necessary, deliveries for the next day can be scheduled immediately. For the distribution center manager, this is an automated task. A logistics system provides information about the precise location of all inventory items, as well as delivery trucks at any time during the day or night. The system calculates the most efficient way to schedule deliveries and automatically notifies all distribution center delivery personnel, regardless of their location.

Once a week — or once a day during peak sales periods — XYZ's marketing strategy is reviewed. Managers are alerted if sales of a hot item have dropped at several stores during the last week. If the trend continues, the item will become a loss maker by the end of the month. Personnel will analyze the problem, project alternative ways of dealing with it, and assess the profit implications. The results of this analysis will be available before the meeting ends.

At the conclusion of the meeting, the chief executive will address another problem area. Because a rival retailer opened a new store in a nearby city last month, the local XYZ outlet has lost 28 percent of its business from regular customers and, more disturbingly, 16 percent of its business from preferred customers. If the trend continues, it could cut XYZ's net profit margin this year by as much as 4 percent. A large-scale campaign is needed. It will include price discounts, direct mailings, special offers, along with new advertising and promotions. The company needs to analyze competitive product mixes and pricing, review marketing options, identify target customers, project costs against increased sales, calculate bottom-line profit gains from recapturing lost business, and start the campaign rolling. This is a major undertaking. It may take all day.

LEADERSHIP PROFILE

A projection of the future? Hardly. These systems and practices exist today. The XYZ Company profile is a composite of three top-growing retailers operating on three different continents. Similar examples can be found in a wide range of industries worldwide.

Leadership companies have a number of characteristics in common. First, they are highly focused in the way IS is used. In a large, diversified company, it may make sense to decentralize IS resources within the organization and subdivide responsibilities among business units and divisions. For fast-growing companies, the profile is different. Growing companies generally target well-defined customer bases, are more focused in the products and services they supply, and usually operate within specific geographic markets. Management chains of command are relatively short, organizations are compact, and reporting structures are uncomplicated.

In this type of organization, there are major benefits in concentrating IS resources. This does not preclude the use of PCs, workstations, or distributed servers. However, a leadership company is not one that just runs a few applications well, has placed a few new systems on minicomputers or servers, or has the latest word-processing package installed in all of its departments. It is a company in which all IS resources work together with maximum effectiveness, for maximum business yield.

A second common leadership characteristic is the ability to look beyond the ways in which IS has been used in the past. There is an important nuance here. Many companies that believe they are making advances in IS technology are simply reengineering, replacing existing applications, or changing the platforms on which these run. In contrast, a leadership company is more likely to deploy new, qualitatively different types of applications that its competitors do not have. And it is more likely to customize IS solutions to exploit its particular business profile, organizational strengths, and management skills.

The third and most important characteristic that distinguishes a leadership company from others is the way in which management views IS. In many companies, IS is seen as a means of automating rerouting operational tasks, handling accounting functions, and so on. It is considered an essentially static resource, part of the administrative machinery and is treated as a simple administrative overhead. In a leadership company, IS is seen as one of the most powerful business resources available to management. In many cases, it is viewed as the single most powerful resource — and is used accordingly.

FOCUSING IS ON COMPETITIVE PERFORMANCE

What, then, does a leadership IS strategy look like? There are many variations, because companies operate in different industries have different business profiles, and operate in different market conditions or competitive environments. The ability to design an IS strategy around such granularities is one of the hallmarks of a leadership company. There are also important commonalities. IS strategies, and the deployment of all IS resources, are driven by the goal of improving competitive performance. Specifically, IS resources are focused on three key variables: information, speed, and cost.

INFORMATION

Increasingly, the key to competitiveness is not just how well a business uses information technology, but also how effectively a business uses the information itself. Leadership companies employ IS to know more about their customers. Specifically, IS is used to know precisely who their customers are and how they behave, when and why their buying patterns change, and when and why they buy from competitors. This knowledge is used to acquire more customers, sell them more products and services, and retain their loyalty over time.

With a few modifications, the IS infrastructure also becomes the vehicle through which companies obtain even more valuable information about all the individuals, households, or businesses that should be their customers but are not — yet. And it is also about market trends, the actions of competitors, and all the other factors that affect what management will be telling their shareholders. However, this information not only drives the interface with customers and markets, but also generates information continuously about the company's internal operations. That information is used aggressively to maximize the efficiency with which all financial, material, and human resources within the business are used.

In a leadership IS strategy, the primary structure is the company's cored databases. These are the repository of its information resources. Applications generate and interpret information. Networks distribute it. PCs, workstations, and mobile computers provide access to it.

SPEED

In competitive markets, leadership companies are able to respond quickly and intelligently, supported by IS infrastructures designed to allow key business decisions and operations to occur in real time. The speed at which every activity is done, from strategic decision-making in the executive suite, to the tasks performed by front line employees, provides a critical competitive edge.

Some companies never understand this. There is not much point to having vast amounts of information if it takes too long to assimilate and act upon it. In too many businesses, information is turned into paper. Printouts are generated. Reports are compiled and read — or, more often, not read. presentations are laboriously compiled and given. Meetings are held to discuss the implications. More detail is needed. Analysts are sent off to massage the data some more, and another meeting is scheduled. In all companies, there is a path between the determination of a market requirement or the placing of a customer order, and the final delivery of the product and service. That path should be as short and direct as possible. However, all too often, that path goes through a succession of miniature bureaucracies. Clipboards, memos, forms, printouts, and slips abound, and one department after another checks, reviews, approves, signs off, and forwards the paper to another department, where the process begins all over again.

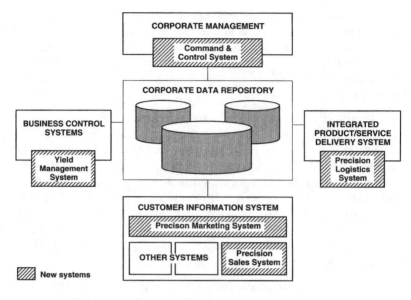

Exhibit 2. Blueprint for a Leadership IS Strategy

The way in which IS is set up has a major impact on the business process. Applications and databases are fragmented as departments and work groups work with separate, often incompatible computers. Data must be transferred between activities, function, or operations through less-than-high-technology information-handling techniques. All of this slows the business. This can be a problem, particularly if the competition is able to respond and deliver more efficiently.

A leadership IS strategy tackles these problems. First, it uses a new generation of precision information systems. These are powerful, fast systems that interpret large volumes of data and present information in a clear, easy-to-understand form that can be acted on, not only by management but also by front-line employees, sales personnel, and administrative staff. Exhibit 2 provides a blueprint for this type of system, which is a quantum leap beyond 1980s-style query and decision support tools running on PCs or departmental servers. As large-scale systems that operate company-wide, the impact on bottom-line business performance is radically greater.

Second, integrated product/service delivery systems are developed with new, flexible, highly functional software technologies. These eliminate administrative inefficiencies; consolidate fragmented applications and databases into single, streamlined systems; and replace paper-based procedures with electronic information handling. Such systems cut across traditional functional boundaries. Delivery of all products and services is accelerated, allowing the company to respond effectively and rapidly to changing market and competitive conditions.

Finally, there is the command and control system, one of the most valuable IS solutions available. Such a system will assist the company's management team in determining market strategies, monitoring business performance, and initiating change. It is highly customized, using advanced technology to adapt to the planning needs, thinking processes, and work patterns of management.

COST

Analyzing cost structures and projecting costs more effectively will increase the company's control of its financial resources, whereas improvements in throughput, resulting from streamlined delivery processes, mean that staff can be reduced and overhead costs cut. Cost reduction is not a by-product of a leadership IS strategy. It is one of its core mandates. This is critical. In many businesses, IS strategy has focused on revenue generation or marketshare growth, while neglecting the costs of achieving such goals. In others, it has been driven by intangibles such as empowerment or flexibility. These may be useful indicators of a company's vitality, but they are not business goals in themselves.

Growing companies are usually characterized by a strong, pragmatic emphasis on the bottom line. A leadership IS strategy reflects that. All applications and implementations are designed to achieve maximum efficiency in business operations. A new type of IS tool, a yield management system, ensures that this occurs.

CONCLUSION

Whereas information, speed, and cost are important, there is another, perhaps even more important variable. A leadership IS strategy requires one more ingredient: leadership. This means that IS strategy must be driven by top management. It is not necessary for management to understand IS technology. But it is necessary for management to understand its potential. IS strategies should be viewed from a business perspective, not a technology perspective. Customer information, product and service delivery, and strategic information are three key areas that can be addressed through a new type of IS strategy to deliver hard, bottom-line gains for any company.

Details of technical implementation, and the obvious questions that go with it (i.e., how to do it, what it will take, and what it will cost) should be dealt with based on specific business goals. In a leadership company, business goals are IS goals. Technology has no purpose other than to provide the necessary tools for realizing these goals.

Chapter 10
Stages in Information Systems Management
Djoen S. Tan

Rapid economic, social, and technological developments require ever-increasing flexibility and alertness of companies. New organizational forms, such as internal and external network organizations are required. Furthermore, companies need to apply information technology (IT) proactively instead of reactively. This means that existing organizational characteristics, such as business strategy, organization structure and business processes are not taken as given facts, but are changed to profit fully from the possibilities of IT. This can be business process redesign or reengineering or even business scope redefinition or business redesign. Applying IT in organizations and the way of IS management is a learning process. The more creatively IT is applied, the higher the costs and risks of IT investments, but the higher IT's potential to add value to the business and to succesfully support business redirection.

A CONSISTENCY MODEL OF IS MANAGEMENT

A consistency model of an organization views the organization as an open system with a limited number of basic subsystems (in systems thinking, often defined as aspect systems) or "forces," in which relevant variables can be arranged. To achieve internal and external stability, these subsystems strive towards mutual harmony and consistency through mutual adaptation and adjustment. Changes in one of the subsystems directly result in changes in the other subsystems until equilibrium is restored. Well-known consistency models are the McKinsey 7-S framework and the MIT90s framework. The MIT90s framework used in "The management in the 1990s" research program of the MIT Sloan School of Management, recognizes five "forces" (subsystems) that must be in dynamic equilibrium with each other: strategy, structure (functions and processes), technology, people (individuals and roles), and management (management processes). The external environment consists of a socio-economic environment and a technological environment.

0-8493-1273-6/02/$0.00+$1.50
© 2002 by CRC Press LLC

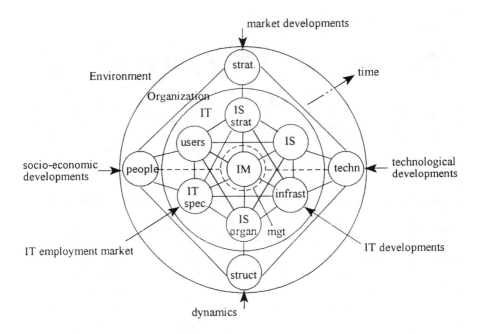

Exhibit 1. Consistency Model of IS Management

The MIT90s framework can be expanded to a more complete consistency model of IS management, which is shown in Exhibit 1. This model has three domains:

1. The environment domain
2. The organization domain
3. The IT domain (the IT facilities in the organization)

In accordance with the MIT90s framework, the five subsystems in the organization domain are:

1. Strategy: the organization's goals and how the organization tries to realize these goals; the selection of markets and products; and the marketing mix (the business plan)
2. Structure: the organization structure and process structure
3. Technology: the technology used for the business processes
4. People: the knowledge, skills, ambitions, attitudes, and social ties of people in the organization (the human resources)
5. Management: general management (senior and line management) responsible for the selection and realization of the business strategy and aligning the subsystems in the organization to each other

All the subsystems influence each other through mutual interaction. The first four subsystems are also influenced respectively by changes in the marketplace, the dynamics (rate of change), the technological developments, and the socio-economic changes in the environment.

The IT domain is a subdomain of the organization domain. In the IT domain, the subsystems of the organization should be focussed on problems concerning the application of IT:

- Strategy → IS strategy
- Structure → IS organization
- Technology → Information systems → Data and technical infrastucture
- People → IT specialists → Users
- Management → IS management

In the IT domain, Technology comprises all the IT resources. These resources are divided into Information Systems (applications) and the Data and Technical Infrastructure, because the data and technical infrastructure have greater long-term and common characteristics than do the applications. The subsystem People is divided into IT specialists and Users, because these groups usually have a different view of information systems and their managers often have different priorities.

The five subsystems of the organization domain interact with the following seven subsystems of the IT domain, that also are mutually influential:

1. IS strategy: the goals, preconditions, guidelines, selected standards, and plans of IT application
2. Information systems: the applications, including manual procedures
3. Users: the knowledge, skills, ambitions and attitudes of the information systems' users
4. Data and technical infrastructure (information infrastructure): the common data and knowledge bases and technical infrastructure (the hardware and systems software of computers and communication networks)
5. IS organization: the IS organization structure and process structure
6. IT specialists: the knowledge, skills, ambitions, and attitudes of the IT specialists
7. IS management: the management of the IS function by senior, line, and IS managers, who are responsible for adequate information facilities by aligning the above-mentioned subsystems

The first three subsystems express the demand for information facilities: the organization's need for information systems and the users' knowledge and skills to work with these systems. Subsystems 4 through 6 pertain to the available IS organization, the abilities of IT staff and the data and technical infrastructure: the supply of information facilities. The last subsystem, IS management, should balance supply and demand at an acceptable cost level.

There are also environmental forces that directly influence the subsystems of the IT domain in an organization. For example, the impact of IT developments on the technical infrastructure and the impact of the IT employment market on the IT specialists. Finally, Exhibit 1 shows time as a third dimension. This will be discussed in the next section.

IS MANAGEMENT PLATEAUS IN ORGANIZATIONS

In a constantly changing environment, an organization must continuously search for new situations where the subsystems are in equilibrium with each other. Time is a critical factor. To include the factor time and the changes in the environment and the organization in time, the consistency model of IS management should be combined with a stages model. Stages or development models help to understand the present and future positions of an organization. A stages model also illustrates the learning processes in an organization. A stage or phase cannot be skipped, but may be passed through faster. A well-known stage model of the application of IT in organizations is Nolan's Stages Theory. Nolan described six stages: initiation, contagion, control, integration, architecture, and demassing. Although this model was later updated, Nolan did not take proactive application of IT into account.

In this chapter, an *IS management plateau (ISM plateau)* is defined as a period of time during which the subsystems of an organization and its IT domain are in equilibrium. The ISM plateau is regarded as a development stage of IS management or IT application in an organization. On the basis of Venkatraman's levels of IT-enabled business reconfiguration, the following five ISM plateaus can be identified (Exhibit 2):

1. Functional integration
2. Cross-functional integration
3. Process integration
4. Business process redesign (BPR)
5. Business scope redefinition or business redesign (BR)

On each successive IS management plateau the organization is further tailored to the IT possibilities. Therefore, on each successive plateau, IT has more potential added value for the business; however, this also requires more complex information systems, more knowledge to build these systems, and more extensive organizational change to implement these systems and, therefore, higher costs and risks. On each ISM plateau, there must be a dynamic equilibrium between all the subsystems of the consistency model. Only then can the next plateau can be reached by means of an harmonic development of the seven subsystems. Thus, peri-

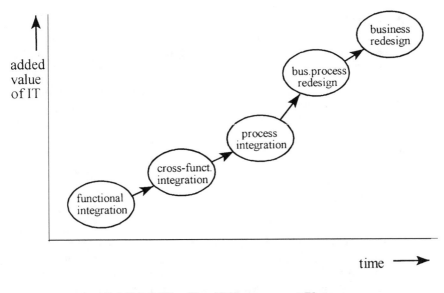

Exhibit 2. The Five IS Management Plateaus

ods of relative stability alternate with periods of change. A harmonic development is one that preserves unity through simultaneous and equivalent growth of the subsystems, which is only possible through mutual interaction and adjustment. The subsystems are mutually adjusted or aligned by means of communication and coordination within and between the organization domain and the IT domain. Each successive ISM plateau requires a higher degree (quality) of communication and coordination, because of the necessity of a progressively better alignment of the subsystems. A higher IS management plateau cannot be reached by, for example, merely changing the organization structure and building new information systems. If the IS strategy remains unchanged, the data and technical infrastructure unadapted and management, users and IT specialists improperly trained, the operation is bound to fail. The seven subsystems of the IT domain on each IS management plateau are briefly described as follows.

1. Functional Integration

On this first ISM plateau, the information systems support the existing workflow in the business functions (functional departments), such as manufacturing, sales, and finance separately. Aside from some procedural adjustments, no organizational changes are needed. The different business functions often exploit different technical platforms. The objective of the application of IT is operational efficiency. The IS plan is based on an inventory of users' demands. The IS organization basically mirrors the business organization. Depending on situational factors, this can vary from a completely centralized IS organization for a functional organization to a completely decentralized IS organization for a divisional organization. The information systems are developed and built by the IT specialists according to the users' functional specifications. Within the IT budget, IT decisions are made by the IS manager(s).

Until the early 1980s, most organizations were on this IS management plateau. Data processing in the sixties and seventies can also be characterized as functional integration, although the IS organization was completely centralized, with only one single technical platform because of the technological limitations (a mainframe's economies of scale) and the users' contribution were very limited because of their almost complete lack of IT know-how.

2. Cross-functional Integration

The information systems integrate the workflow across several related business functions, such as purchasing, inventory control, and accounting. The development and implementation of these systems are more complex than those on the first plateau. Minor organizational adjustments may be required, but the functional structure and the working methods remain largely unchanged. Naturally, the technical infrastructures of the functional departments concerned must work together. There should be at least some common standards. The objective of the application of IT is to improve the effectiveness of the business. The IS plan is derived from the business plan. The IS organization cannot be completely decentralized, because some form of central coordination is required. Depending on situational factors, the IS organization may vary from complete centralization to a federation in which agreements are made about, for example, common standards and joint projects. Here too, the information systems are developed and built by the IT specialists in accordance with the users' functional specifications. Many IT decisions are made by a steering committee of line and IS managers. Of course, if a management team with roughly the same composition already exists, it is better that this team functions as the steering committee.

Today, most organizations for which IT has a support or operational function are situated on this second ISM plateau. This is especially true for organizations in, for example, government and healthcare.

3. Process Integration

In this stage, information systems enable the work of integral business processes to be carried out across several organizational units. On this plateau management starts to adopt a process view instead of a functional view on the organization. The implementation of these information systems necessitates extensive organizational changes and an integrated data and technical infrastructure. The objective of the application of IT is to achieve (durable) competitive advantage in existing product-market combinations (PMCs). The IS plan and the business plan should be linked. The IS organization on this ISM plateau cannot be completely decentralized; on the other hand, a centralized organization is not in accordance with the line managers' responsibility for their information systems. Therefore, the IS function must be selectively decentralized (a combination of centralization and decentralization), so that the responsibility for IS is spread over different parts of the organization. For example, decentralized systems development and centralized management of the data and technical infrastructure. IT specialists and users together identify and analyze the most important business processes using, for example, Michael Porter's value chain method. A project manager (process owner) should be appointed for each main business process. Information systems are built by the IT specialists under the supervision of line management and IT decisions are made by a steering committee of line and IS managers and chaired by a member of senior management.

Most organizations where IT is of strategic importance, such as banks, insurance companies, publishing/printing companies, and transportation companies, are now on this ISM plateau.

4. Business Process Redesign

As with the former plateau, the information systems on this ISM plateau also enable the work of the most important business processes to be carried out as single entities. However, existing business processes are not taken as given, but are redesigned or reengineered to make use of IT in new ways (proactive IT application). Thus, business processes are performed in ways that were previously impractical or impossible. A customer order fulfillment process, for instance, can be eliminated by arranging for customers to place their orders electronically. Drastic organizational changes are usually necessary to implement these information systems. This is, of course, only possible with an integrated data and technical infrastructure. This infrastructure should also include development (CASE) tools and standard application modules to speed up systems development. The success of a process redesign project is often dependent on the speed of implementation. The objective of using IT is to realize competitive advantage in existing and new product-market combinations. The IS plan and the business plan are designed as one integrated strategic plan. The IT organization must be selectively decentralized with sufficient involvement by senior management, because IT has consequences for the entire company. Management consultants and user departments select and redesign the business processes together with IT specialists. The information systems are developed by the IT specialists and users together, under the supervision of line management. IT decisions are made by senior management following consultation with a steering committee, with the same composition as on the former plateau.

Nowadays, business process redesign or reengineering (BPR) is applied by most organizations where IT is of strategic importance. However, business process redesign is not a simple matter. Some large management consultancy companies have developed their own BPR methodology and some have also developed tools for specific parts. At this moment, a proven methodology is not available, which is why many reengineering projects fail. According to a study by the Arthur D. Little consultancy, involving 350 managers of Fortune 1000-listed companies, 85 percent of the respondents were not satisfied with the results of their reengineering projects. For organizations where IT is of strategic importance, reaching this ISM plateau was the main challenge for the nineties and beyond. Well-known examples of such organizations are IBM Credit Corporation and Ford Motor Company.

> IBM Credit finances IBM's products and services. Formerly, the entire finance process, from request to tender, was handled by four functional groups (with each group having their own information system) for, successively, checking the potential borrower's credit rating, modifying the standard loan covenant to the customer's requests, determining the appropriate interest rate and writing a quote. The four functional groups were replaced by a single group of generalists supported by a small pool of specialists for the difficult cases, all using one integrated information system. This reduced the throughput time from an average of seven days to four hours. The productivity increased no less than a hundredfold.

> At Ford the parts procurement process occurred as follows. The purchasing department sent a purchase order to a supplier, with a copy going to the accounts payable department. When the goods arrived, a clerk at the receiving dock sent a receipt form to accounts payable. Accounts payable payed the invoice after checking the purchase order and the receival document. A lot of time was lost when these three documents did not match. The procurement process was reengineered, so that now the data is entered into an on-line database when a purchase order is issued. When the goods arrive at the receiving dock, a clerk checks at the computer terminal to see whether the received shipment corresponds to an outstanding purchase order in the database. If so, the clerk accepts the goods with the press of a button; the computer then automatically makes out a check to the supplier. In this way, the accounts payable staff could be reduced by no less than 95 percent.

These drastic productivity improvements, caused by radical process changes, are typical for this ISM plateau. It is sometimes claimed that reengineering projects resulting in less than 50 percent improvement are not worth the name BPR. Productivity improvements on the first and second ISM plateau are usually no more than 10 to 20 percent. Therefore, a larger increase in IT's added value is shown between the third and the fourth plateau in Exhibit 2.

5. Business Redesign

Here too, information systems enable the most important business processes to be carried out using an integrated data and technical infrastructure. However, to make optimum use of IT, not only are business processes redesigned, even the business scope is enlarged or shifted if necessary. This requires not only redesigning the business processes, but the entire business. A new definition of the business objectives generally results in new business processes and the redesign of existing processes, which goes hand in hand with radical organizational changes. The objective of the application of IT on this plateau is to realize innovative product-market combinations. The business plan and the IS plan form one integrated strategic plan. A highly selective decentralization of the IS organization is required. The information processes are carried out by small process teams. Users and IT specialists together develop the new business processes and the corresponding information systems under the supervision of line management. An "enriched" information infrastructure is necessary to realize new applications quickly and to absorb new information technologies. IT decisions are made by senior management, because of the consequences for the business purpose. The intensive involvement of senior management and the close cooperation between users and IT specialists require the organization to be a so-called network organization (see section on network organizations).

It is expected that most companies will have reached this ISM plateau after the year 2000. The fact that this is the highest plateau does not mean that there will be no further developments after this level. By that time, however, the application of IT will have become as normal as using pencil and paper and information processes will have become ordinary business processes.

Exhibit 3 summarizes the seven subsystems of the IT domain for each IS management plateau. The ISM plateaus illustrate the "natural" development of the application of IT in organizations, as a result of learning processes of line managers, users, IS managers and IT specialists. Two breakthroughs can be distinguished:

1. A transition from looking at functions to looking at business processes in organizations due to experiences with quality management programs between the second and the third plateau
2. A transition from reactive to proactive application of IT due to the rising popularity of business process reengineering between the third and the fourth plateau

Exhibit 3. The Subsystems of the IT Domain on Each ISM Plateau in Organizations

Subsystem	Reactive IT application			Proactive IT application	
	Functional integration	Cross-functional integration	Process integration	Business process redesign	Business redesign
IS strategy	Improve efficiency. IS plan is inventory of users' demands	Improve effectivity. IS plan derived from business plan.	Competitive advantage in existing PMCs. IS and business plan linked.	Competitive advantage in existing and new PMCs. Integrated strategic plan.	Innovative PMCs. Integrated strategic plan.
Information systems	Support existing workflow in business functions.	Integrate workflow across business functions	Enable existing (complete) business processes.	Enable existing and redesigned business processes.	Enable redesigned and new business processes.
Information infrastructure	Platform for each function.	Common standards.	Integrated data and technical infrastructure.	Somewhat "enriched" information infrastructure.	"Enriched" information infrastructure.
IS organization	From completely centralized to completely decentralized.	From completely centralized to federated.	Selectively decentralized.	Selectively decentralized. Small teams.	Highly selectively decentralized. Empowered teams.
Users	Functional specifications	Functional specifications	Accountable for realizing IS	Redesign of business processes and realize IS	Design new business processes and realize IS.
IT specialists	Realize IS	Realize IS	Design and build IS		
IS management	IS managers decide within budget.	Steering committee of line and IS managers.	Steering committee chaired by senior management.	Senior management decides after consulting with steering committee.	Senior management decides.

134

Exhibit 3 can be used as a diagnostic tool to assess the functioning of an IS organization. For a proper functioning, the characteristics of the subsystems should be located in the same column (plateau). Subsystems situated on different plateaus is an indication of problems in an organization.

Different sections of an organization can be situated on different ISM plateaus. A faster transition to a higher plateau can be achieved by adequate planning and control of the necessary activities. The higher plateau is then regarded as the goal of the IS strategy. Intermediate plateaus can be defined, if necessary, to realize the transformation in smaller steps, thus increasing the manageability of the migration. A proper alignment between the subsystems through adequate communication and coordination must be attained as soon as possible after reaching a higher ISM plateau, to prevent falling back to the lower plateau.

The following conditions for a successful transition to a higher ISM plateau are suggested:

- All subsystems of the organization domain and the IT domain on the present ISM plateau are consistent with each other.
- Senior management believes that IT can be used as a lever for greater competitive advantage.
- A clearly defined IS strategy exists, supported by senior, line, and IS management.
- A climate of change is created in the entire organization (unfreezing).
- The IS strategy is defined as concrete action plans or projects for each subsystem.
- There is adequate control of the development of these projects.
- There is sufficient commitment and support from senior management.

It is, however, not always necessary to reach the highest ISM plateau as soon as possible. This is only the case if IT has strategic importance for the organization's survival, for example in the case of financial institutions, retailers and transportation companies.

IS MANAGEMENT PLATEAUS IN COALITIONS OF ORGANIZATIONS

Michael Porter has shown that companies, together with their main suppliers, distribution channels, and customers, form a value system through the vertical links between the value chains of each company. By working together, the value chain of each of the participating companies can be improved. Additionally, the exploitation of vertical links is difficult for competitors to copy. In this way, a market or even an entire branch of industry can be dramatically changed in favor of a group of cooperating organizations or coalition of organizations.

Coalitions or alliances are defined as long-term strategic cooperation between companies, encompassing more than the normal business transactions, but less than a merger or an acquisition. The following types of strategic cooperation are possible between businesses:

- An alliance, based on a long term cooperative agreement or contract
- A participation: acquiring a minority of the shares; this can also be a mutual interest, for example by exchanging shares
- A joint venture: jointly setting up a new business

Interorganizational information systems are the shared information systems of a coalition of organizations. These systems support business processes that extend to all the participating companies, enabling them to expand their scope and capabilities outwards to customers and suppliers. These systems support or trigger the redesign of business processes across the boundaries of multiple organizations. For example, with just-in-time delivery the outbound logistics of a number of suppliers are linked to or integrated with the inbound logistics of a company, resulting in considerable cost reduction for all the participating companies. The most simple form is linking by electronic data interchange (EDI) or Internet. In this way, the advantages of the familiar forms of horizontal and vertical integration of businesses can be obtained without actual acquisitions. Interorganizational information systems integrate businesses electronically without affecting the economic and legal independence of the separate businesses.

The consistency model of IS management (Exhibit 1) can also be applied to a coalition of organizations. In this case, a coalition rather than a single organization is seen as a collection of entities. The same subsystems can be identified in a coalition of organizations as in a single organization. After all, it is improbable that there are fundamental differences between a coalition of companies and, for example, a divisional organization with different business units. All the participating organizations make up the organization domain; the IT domain refers to the joint application of IT and the common IT facilities. The subsystems of both the organization domain and the IT domain apply to the entire group of cooperating organizations. Essentially, the five IS management plateaus in Exhibit 2, representing the development stages of joint application of IT or common IS management, also apply to a network of cooperating organizations. The following paragraphs offer brief descriptions for each ISM plateau, of the subsystems IS strategy, Information systems, Information infrastructure, IS organization, and IS management of the IT domain. The subsystems IT specialists and users also apply to all the participating organizations. The interorganizational information systems are generally developed by joint project teams, consisting of IT specialists and users from the participating organizations. User involvement increases at each successive plateau. Although the characteristics are similar to those of a single organization presented in the former section, there are higher barriers to close cooperation between IT specialists and users from different organizations, partly because of differences in company culture.

1. Functional Integration (Transaction Automation)

In a coalition of organizations, functional integration implies transaction automation. High-volume, repetitive paper transactions between the participating organizations are replaced by electronic messages (electronic mail or basic EDI transactions). The objective of the common application of IT is to increase the speed and reliability of the transactions between the organizations. Generally, the messages cannot link directly into the participants' main applications. Examples are sending and confirming orders, receipt notices, and invoicing. Only minor, peripheral alterations to the organizations' working procedures are necessary. The IS strategy, the data and technical infrastructure, the information systems, and the IS organization of the business participants can essentially remain the same and common IS management is fragmented. The situation is similar to a completely decentralized IS organization in a single company.

2. Cross-Functional Integration (Procedure Automation)

On this second ISM plateau, the interorganizational systems enable all transactions of a procedure to be carried out in the form of electronic messages. A procedure consists of a number of related transactions often performed by different functional departments of the participating companies, such as an invoice-to-payment procedure. Procedure automation requires a direct link into participants' application systems, because transactions must also trigger responses (e.g., an invoice initiates a payment). The objective of the common application of IT is cost reduction. Work methods within the participating organizations are affected by the procedural adjustments, but no significant changes to the internal organization structure and process structure of the participating companies are necessary. However, the IS strategies and technical infrastructures of the participating organizations should allow the realization of these systems. This implies at least an agreement on common IT standards. A steering committee of the involved line and IS managers must be set up to define these standards and to supervise the creation of these interorganizational systems. The situation is comparable to a completely decentralized IS organization with interdepartmental cooperation on a few applications in a single company.

Most EDI or Internet applications today are situated on the first or the second ISM plateau. These applications are used particularly by manufacturing companies, transportation companies, retailers, financial institutions, and government organizations.

3. Process Integration

In this stage, interorganizational systems enable the execution of some main business processes between the participants in a value chain, such as keeping shelves stocked. Of course, this is only possible if process integration has already been implemented in the individual organizations and if a common data and technical infrastructure is available. Process integration usually requires adjustments to the internal organization, process structure, and work methods of the participating organizations. The objective of the common application of IT is (durable) competitive advantage in existing product-market combinations. There must be a joint IS plan that is consistent with the individual business plans and individual IS plans. This joint IS plan must also address the development and maintenance of the common information infrastructure. The definition and implementation of the joint IS plan is controlled by a steering committee that includes members of senior management from the participating businesses. The IS organization has the federation form and is guided by the steering committee. Examples are companies with just-in-time supplying, such as Benetton, a worldwide supplier of knitwear based in Italy, and Wal-Mart, the largest retailer in the United States.

> Benetton agents, in different countries, relay orders for shops in their territories to Benetton's headquarters in Italy through a data network. An interorganizational order management system collects information from the agents' computers, updates the agents' product and price files, confirms orders, and routes them to the appropriate production plants in the various countries.

> Wal-Mart uses an interorganizational information system to replenish all their stores. The product inventory is minimized by letting day-to-day sales data automatically trigger orders to the suppliers and delivery to the stores. All Wal-Mart suppliers are linked up to point-of-sale computers and have on-line access to the database of product-purchase information fed by these systems.

4. Business Process Redesign

As on the former plateau, interorganizational systems enable all transactions pertaining to a shared main business process, on the basis of a common information infrastructure. The systems are fully integrated with the corresponding process-supporting applications in the participating organizations. However, business processes will be changed if this is necessary to optimize the IT potential. This often results in radical changes in the participants' internal organization and process structures. Sometimes, even the boundaries between the organizations must be reset. The objective of the common application of IT is competitive advantage in existing and new product-market combinations. Realization of these interorganizational systems and common information infrastructure requires a joint strategic

plan, integrating a business and an IS plan. The IS organization on this plateau is also federal. The decisions are made by a steering committee, that
includes senior management representatives from each of the participating organizations, because of possibly severe organizational consequences. In spite of the rising popularity of BPR, only a few pioneers, such
as the Blockbuster Entertainment stores in the United States, have reached
this fourth ISM plateau.

> Blockbuster Entertainment and IBM have developed a system that
> enables record shops to download CDs and videotapes on the spot
> using a central database filled by recording companies, movie studios,
> and game makers. Customers are thus presented with an almost unlim-
> ited availability and diversity of products, while shopkeepers can dras-
> tically reduce or eliminate the costs of shipping and inventory. Addi-
> tionally, unsold inventory and lost sales or rental revenues when
> popular copies are out of stock become things of the past.

5. Business Redesign

Business redesign (BR) or business scope redefinition is also possible in
a coalition of organizations. It is a logical step following the redesigning of
business processes across organizational boundaries. This implies boundary corrections and drastic organizational changes in the participating
organizations. The objective of the common application of IT is to realize
innovative product-market combinations, that may create completely new
business and market opportunities. This requires a common integrated
strategic plan and a common "enriched" information infrastructure. The IT
activities are functionally coordinated by senior management. Because of
the strong interdependence of the participating companies, the steering
committee on this highest ISM plateau takes the form of a board of directors of a holdings company. In effect, the coalition becomes a single (network) organization.

It is expected that coalitions of organizations will reach this highest plateau in the 2000s. The pioneers are today's core enterprises, described in
the section on network organizations.

Exhibit 4 summarizes the seven subsystems of the IT domain on each
ISM plateau for a coalition of organizations. Also in a coalition of organizations, all subsystems on each plateau must be in equilibrium before transition to a higher plateau can take place. On each successive ISM plateau, the
impact of IT on the individual organizations and on the relationships
between the organizations increases, the costs and risks rise, but so does
the potential competitive advantage generated by IT. Furthermore, more
and more knowledge and skills of the managers, users, and IT specialists are
necessary to realize the necessary interorganizational information systems.
On the highest two ISM plateaus, a common "enriched" information infrastructure is respectively desirable and required. IT is applied reactively on

Exhibit 4. The Subsystems of the IT Domain on Each ISM Plateau in Coalitions of Organizations

Subsystem	Reactive IT application			Proactive IT application	
	Functional integration	Cross-functional integration	Process integration	Business process redesign	Business redesign
IS strategy	Increase speed and reliability of transactions. IS plan based on users demands.	Improve efficiency. IS plan derived from individual business and IS plans.	Competitive advantage in existing PMCs IS plan adjusted to individual business and IS plans.	Competitive advantage in existing and new PMCs. Joint integrated strategic plan.	Innovative PMCs. Joint integrated strategic plan.
Information systems	Transaction automation with EDI or Internet.	Procedure automation with EDI or Internet	Enable existing joint business processes.	Enable existing and new joint business processes.	Enable innovative joint business processes.
Information infrastructure	Different information infrastructures	Common standards.	Common data and technical infrastructure.	Common data and technical infrastructure.	Common "enriched" information infrastructure.
IS organization	Project organization	Project organization	Federal	Federal	Functional coordination
Users	Functional specifications	Functional specifications	Accountable for realizing IS	Redesign joint business processes and realize IS.	Design new joint business processes and realize IS.
IT specialists	Realize IS	Realize IS	Design and build IS.		
IS management	IS managers decide within budget.	Steering committee of line and IS managers.	Steering committee chaired by senior management.	Steering committee of senior managers.	Steering committee of senior managers as a board of directors

first three ISM plateaus and proactively on the two highest plateaus. The interdependence of the participating companies increases on each successive ISM plateau. Thus, stronger forms of cooperation arise on the higher plateaus, such as joint ventures and mutual participation. Similar to a single organization, a coalition of organizations is transformed to one single network organization on the highest ISM plateau. Adequate planning and control of the required activities is necessary for a directed migration to a higher plateau. An essential condition for a successful migration is mutual trust within the coalition. Additionally, the conditions mentioned in the previous section also apply to coalitions of organizations.

Because a single (network) organization is formed on the highest ISM plateau, the five ISM plateaus can also be used as stepping stones to integrate a group of businesses into a single enterprise following mergers or acquisitions. It can start with EDI and Internet applications of the first and second ISM plateau, which will not affect the independence of the individual companies. The highest ISM plateau, where the business objectives of the individual companies are redefined and a single network organization is formed, is then chosen as the business strategy objective. The intermediate ISM plateaus can be used as intermediate steps for planning and control in order to increase the manageability of the transformation process. The companies' interdependence increases on successive plateaus because of the interorganizational information systems. In this way, IT can be used to lever the integration of acquired businesses into one enterprise. This will work especially for companies whose primary business process is a data processing process, such as banks and insurance companies.

NETWORK ORGANIZATIONS

New organizational forms are required to obtain a sufficient degree of flexibility and alertness of companies to survive in a complex and dynamic environment. Many different descriptions can be found in textbooks of these new (future) organization structures. Peter Drucker, for example, predicted the coming of the *information-based organization*. The intensive exchange of information makes whole layers of middle management and staff redundant. The operational work is executed by different specialists with a high degree of autonomy, such as in an orchestra. This does not take place sequentially, but is a synchronized team effort. James Quinn described the *intelligent enterprise*, concentrated around a few core competencies in which it is world leader and which provide a unique added value. Only those primary and support activities, in which the organization is the absolute best, are selected from the value chain. Any activity that can be performed better or more cheaply, elsewhere in the world, is outsourced. Modern management techniques and IT enable an effective control of contracted work.

This results into *boundaryless organizations*. The views of those authors named can be summarized in the following description of advanced organizations, referred to as *network organizations*. The three basic principles of a network organization are:

1. Integration of management and execution (task integration)
2. Concentration on core competencies
3. Coordination by means of IT rather than a hierarchy

These principles can be applied on a single organization or a coalition of organizations working together, here indicated as internal and external network organization respectively.

Internal Network Organizations

The most important characteristics of such an organization are:

- Minimal hierarchy because of the integration of management and execution and the use of IT for coordination
- The organization's center of mass is formed by managers and specialists (knowledge workers), that work together in changing multi-disciplinary self managed teams (strong selective decentralization)
- Self-organizing and self-learning features because of the integration of management and execution (a network organization is a learning organization)
- A large amount of work is outsourced to concentrate on core competencies
- A diamond-shaped, rather than a pyramid-shaped, organization due to the outsourcing of low-skilled work
- IT is used intensively at all levels: a network organization without IT is an impossibility because coordination and communication is mainly performed by IT (groupware)

Network organizations have no departments or sections. The organizational unit in a network organization is the (multi-disciplinary) self-managed team. The self-managed teams may have to deal with strongly differing assignments. Every team should have a goal, preferably quantified, that is clear to every team member. One-time activities can be assigned to a team as well-defined projects. As for the ongoing activities, each integral business process is assigned to a process team, consisting of a process owner or manager and a number of specialists from different disciplines. If parts of the business processes (subprocesses) are outsourced, the processes extend beyond the organization's boundaries and reach into the partner organizations. A team's composition and required information systems should be changed frequently, because business processes must continue to meet the customer's needs. Changing information systems rapidly is only possible with an "enriched" information infrastructure as described further on.

A critical factor in a network organization is the availability of people with the required knowledge, skills, and attitudes, because of the integration of management and execution (empowerment). Different expertises can fade away quickly in multi-disciplinary teams. A network organization therefore needs human resource managers or expertise coaches to develop and maintain specific expertise and to regularly rotate team members to ensure the necessary exchange of know-how between process teams. These managers are accountable for the knowledge management and supervise the necessary learning processes in the organization. Every team member has his or her own process manager and expertise coach, who are directly accountable to senior management. The process managers, the expertise coaches, and senior management together form the senior management team. Larger organizations can be subdivided in a larger number of business processes, that are then grouped into clusters of strongly interdependent processes, so that the exchange of information between the clusters is minimal. In this case, process managers and expertise coaches do not report directly to senior management, but to cluster managers, who are part of the senior management team. People in a network organization have no functions specifying their tasks, but roles indicating their goals and responsibilities. There are only five roles in a network organization: senior manager or director, cluster manager, process manager, expertise coach, and team member.

In a network organization, an important part of the management is carried out by the people themselves (self-organization through integration of management and execution). They have access to all the required information to make decisions independently. Both a clearly defined mission statement and goals are necessary to keep people directed towards the same objectives, and these should be easily translatable to individual actions. A network organization can only perform well in a customer-oriented company culture, because customer care is not concentrated into a separate unit. The company's results are expressed not only in sales and profit figures, but also in customer satisfaction. A customer-oriented company culture is encouraged if staff members have regular contact with clients and if clients are included in the process teams. Also, staff should have a high degree of self-motivation and strive for personal development through performing challenging assignments and having interesting experiences. Managers in a network organization convince rather than direct and are especially concerned with motivating their staff and stimulating them to high performances: in other words, they are good *coaches*. As "assisting foremen," process managers also execute tasks. The reward system is not only based on individual performance, but also on the team's results and the develop-

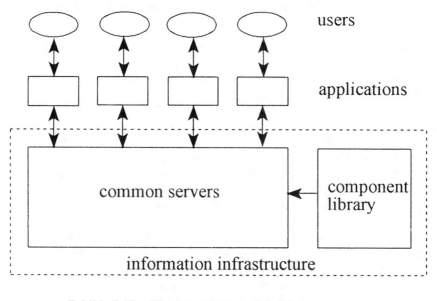

Exhibit 5. The "Enriched" Information Infrastructure

ment of required knowledge and skills. Recognition is mostly expressed through horizontal, rather than vertical, promotions, giving an employee the chance to pick up new skills and know-how and work on more interesting projects.

The "Enriched" Information Infrastructure

The current developments on open systems, three-tier client/server architecture, and object orientation make an "enriched" information infrastructure possible. Shared servers and object-oriented software components or building blocks (business objects) harbor the largest part of the functionality of all possible applications (Exhibit 5). The number of available servers is increasing rapidly. There are now special servers for storing text, images, and sound; servers for processing transactions; document imaging; workflow management and groupware; and servers for data mining (searching for characteristics and trends in databases). Reusable software components, which are partly self-made and partly purchased (class libraries), are stored in a component library that is part of the information infrastructure. Object orientation enables a distinction between objects that represent an organization's more fundamental properties and objects that represent the current (temporary) work methods. The result is a layered information infrastructure, with the more permanent elements in the lower layers and the temporary elements in the upper layers.

With an "enriched" information infrastructure, new applications can be realized quickly and existing applications can be adapted readily while maintaining a durable infrastructure. In other words, flexibility is combined with stability. There is also no need to make a distinction between central and local information systems, because the infrastructure is available both locally and centrally.

Organizations can also absorb new technologies rapidly by adopting new IT products and services, in the form of servers and object-oriented software components, in their "enriched" information infrastructure. Fast absorption of new technologies is a source of competitive advantage and therefore part of an organization's core competence. Because massive application systems have become obsolete, adopting new technologies no longer requires extensive conversions.

External Network Organizations

One of the characteristics of a network organization is a large amount of outsourcing. A network organization therefore needs a network of other organizations in order to function effectively. Today, an organization's success is largely determined by its strategic alliances with the world's best suppliers, designers, distribution channels, and other external services. In fact, expectations are that networks of companies will rule the global market in the coming years. Three constructions can be distinguished:

- Core enterprises or strategic centers
- Coalitions or federations of companies
- Virtual organizations

Core enterprises. Core enterprises create a network of small partner companies in which competition and cooperation are balanced by:

- Outsourcing as many activities as possible, that are not part of a core competence, in the form of strategic alliances with carefully selected companies that can make a valuable contribution to the whole. For example, this might be knowledge of local circumstances or capability of fast and cheap production.
- Developing partners' competencies and encouraging innovation through an intensive exchange of information and introducing a "knowledge competition," in which existing and new partners participate. Partners who can't keep up are shaken off.

Through standardization and task distribution among the various partners, core enterprises can realize economies of scale without losing flexibility or responsiveness, because this is innate to the small, autonomous partner companies. Core enterprises can also grow and adapt rapidly by attracting and rejecting partner companies. Examples of core enterprises

145

are the U.S. computer manufacturer, Sun Systems, and the Italian clothing business, Benetton.

Coalitions of companies. Companies can also enter networks of strategic collaboration with companies of about the same size. This results in a coalition or federation of independent companies. The value chains of the participating organizations can be strengthened by entering into alliances with suppliers, distribution channels, and customers using interorganizational information systems. On the higher ISM plateaus, a shared information infrastructure is required. This federation form combines autonomy with cooperation and the economies of scale of large companies with the flexibility and effectivity of small companies (see previous section).

Virtual organizations. Core enterprises and coalitions of companies are long-term alliances or stable networks. Alliances between companies may also be formed temporarily, for a specific task or project. When the task or project is completed, the coalition breaks up and the participating organizations are free to enter into new coalitions. This is referred to as virtual organizations or dynamic networks. A form of virtual organization is the so-called *broker organization*, a small core that manages independent specialty firms in different countries performing all the required business functions to realize certain products and services. Lewis Galoob Toys is an example of such an organization.

A NEW ROLE FOR IS MANAGEMENT

The proactive application of IT requires more from IS management than simply knowing what the company needs at a given moment. IS management's new role is to anticipate future demands, to stimulate innovation and organizational change by "enriching" the information infrastucture as soon as possible. In other words, the IS strategy is not a derivative of the business strategy, nor is the IS organization derived from the business organization. An integrated strategic plan is worked out and an integrated IS and business organization is set up. Exhibit 6 summarizes the changing role of IS management.

A successful launching of this new IS management role requires a new methodology to support this role. The Information Infrastructure Management (IIM) methodology is developed for this purpose. IIM is a methodology to integrally manage, develop, maintain, and use information infrastructures consisting of applications, databases, and technical infrastructure components (hardware and systems software of computer systems and communication networks). IIM has solved the difficulty of fitting an information infrastructure adequately to an organization, by making the *architecture* the focal point and defining architecture as the whole of business and information functions, business and information processes,

Exhibit 6. The Changing Role of IS Management

	Prevalent IS management	New IS management
Role	Supplier of IT products and services	Leader in organizational change
Purpose	Ensuring optimum IT facilities	Optimum contribution to achieving business goals
Products	IT products and services	Knowledge and information
Primary knowledge	Applying IT	Market, business strategy, and business processes
Method of IT application	Reactive	Proactive
Primary focus	Applications	Information infrastructure
IS strategy	Derived from business strategy	Integrated with business strategy
IS organization	Derived from business organization	Integrated with business organization

and information infrastructure. This results in a flexible IS organization that changes with the business organization. IIM offers a continuous improvement of the performance of business processes and can accommodate existing methods and techniques.

CONCLUSION

Consistency models describe the subsystems of an organization, while stages models describe its development phases. Combining the two types of models results in a complete picture of an organization, in both stable and dynamic environments. IS management plateaus can be defined by combining a consistency model of IS management with a stages model of the application of IT. There are five stages of IS management: functional integration, cross-functional integration, process integration, business process redesign (BPR), and business scope redefinition or business redesign (BR). For a successful application of IT, all subsystems of the organization domain and the IT domain should be in equilibrium. This requires good communication between users and IT specialists and adequate coordination by senior, line, and IS management. At each successive ISM plateau, IT yields more added value, but it requires greater organizational change, relatively higher IT expenditures, more IT knowledge on behalf of users and line management, more insight into business processes on behalf of IT specialists and IS management, and greater involvement from senior management. Each successive ISM plateau demands a higher degree (quality) of communication and coordination for an adequate alignment of the seven subsystems.

On the first three ISM plateaus, the application of IT is based on the current business strategy, organization, and culture. On these lower plateaus the subsystems of the IT domain are adapted to the subsystems of the organization domain. This reactive IT application results in productivity improvements of 10 to 20 percent. At the two highest ISM plateaus, the current organizational features are modified, if required, to enable an optimum utilization of the possibilities of IT. This means that, if necessary, the subsystems of the organization domain will be adapted to those of the IT domain. With this proactive IT application, productivity gains of more than 50 percent are possible. The third ISM plateau is a transition stage between reactive and proactive application of IT, where management starts to adopt a process view instead of a functional view of their organization. The transition to a higher ISM plateau requires adequate planning and control of the development of each subsystem, based on a clear business outlook and strategy. Progressing to higher ISM plateaus reduces the possible forms of IS organization. From the third ISM plateau on, only a selective decentralization of the IS function is appropriate.

The consistency model of IS management and the ISM plateaus can also be applied to a network of cooperating organizations or coalition of organizations. The further the interorganizational information systems intervene in the business processes of the participating companies, the greater the possible competitive advantages, but also the greater the costs, risks, and interdependence. Entering higher ISM plateaus means that the joint IS organization evolves from a completely decentralized form (with a project organization for the development and maintenance of the interorganizational information systems) to a federal form.

On the highest ISM plateau, both a single organization and a coalition of organizations transform into a network organization. The basic principles of a network organization are integration of management and execution, concentration on core competencies and coordination by means of IT rather than a hierarchy. A network organization also needs a network of other organizations in order to function adequately. This can have the form of a core enterprise with a network of small partner companies, a coalition of independent companies of roughly the same size or a temporary alliance (virtual organization).

Because a single network organization is formed on the highest plateau, the ISM plateaus could be use as stepping stones to integrate a group of businesses into a single enterprise following mergers or acquisitions. This applies especially to organizations whose primary business process is data manipulation, such as financial institutions. IT is then used as a lever in the integration of businesses.

A network organization requires an "enriched" information infrastructure, in which the greatest part of the functionality of all possible applications is in the form of shared servers and reusable object-oriented software components or building blocks. With an "enriched" information infrastructure, new applications can be realized rapidly and existing applications can be adapted readily while maintaining a durable infrastructure. Organizations can then also absorb new technologies quickly. The "enriched" information infrastructure illustrates the increasing importance of information infrastructures. The focal point of the IT facilities in an organization is shifting from information systems (applications) to the information infrastructure. IS management is becoming II management.

On the fourth and fifth ISM plateau, where IT is proactively applied, a new role of IS management is required. This new IS management is supported by a new methodology called Information Infrastructure Management (IIM).

Note

Tan, D. S., *From Information Systems Management to Information Infrastructure Management*, Lansa Publishing, Leiderdorp, 1996.

Section 2
Task 1: Designing Supply Chains for Competitive Advantage

This is a central management task often reserved for top management. It is the most important of the five supply chain tasks because it is here that an organization decides "what" to do. In our title, this task specifies the "design" of our supply chain.

The review of articles for this book revealed a great deal of agreement on the importance of this subject among Auerbach authors. Several of the selections stress that "optimization" is no longer sufficient. This means information systems that only reduce the cost of operations will not cut it in the competitive world. Systems and IS professionals must "add value" to the customer.

Software, one chapter on the "new value chain" observes, is not just for processes. It is also embedded in more and more products. Supply chain concepts also apply to the development of product-based systems. Another important theme, described in the chapter on "results-based IT" is that one system or one way of implementing a system does not necessarily transfer from one company environment to another's. Another chapter on ERP implementation has value for those who have not yet upgraded their backbone systems for managing suppliers and materials.

Chapter 11
The New Value Chain

Doug Aldrich

Recently I met with the CEO of a leading maker of heavy-duty consumer equipment. His company is thriving: revenues are up, profits are rising, and the current economic boom is favoring his industry in unprecedented ways. Despite the rosy picture, this CEO is quite concerned about two technology trends that together pose a significant threat to his company's business model.

First, he explained, his company's products are increasingly based on digital technology, rather than mechanical and analog technologies. Today, each of the machines it sells contains more computer technology than did a typical 1980s mainframe.

Second, there's the growing popularity of the Internet and other Web-based services among consumers, who are using these resources instead of relying on his company's traditional customers — the retailers — and consequently are buying the company's products at lower prices.

Although the CEO acknowledges that today's ideas of efficiency and cost reduction dictate eliminating the middleman — in this case, the retailers — he believes that this move is too simplistic. In fact, he champions the contrary view — that he will need more, not less, help from outside businesses to keep his customers happy. Why? True, it looks as though much of the traditional "value" provided by his retailers — disseminating product information, helping consumers make purchasing decisions, ordering highly customized parts and models, and providing follow-up support — is being eliminated by the Web's more efficient information-sharing and transactional capabilities.

But not all aspects of selling his company's high-ticket products can be accomplished "virtually." Someone has to physically hand over the product to the consumer. Someone else needs to provide very physical after-sales services for routine maintenance and in emergencies. In addition, the increasing complexity of these digital products — and the degree of technical integration they now involve — means that he is forging pioneering partnerships with an ever-widening array of disparate suppliers and integrators. This in turn complicates after-sales servicing of customers' needs, which is a critical determination of success in his industry.

In fact, in the digital age, a whole range of services is needed to support the new distribution channels. These services, necessary to ensure the end consumer's satisfaction, will no longer be determined by geographical or physical constraints. The CEO is smart enough to understand this reality. He is also smart enough to realize that traditional notions of efficiency don't work best in the digital age.

Considering all these changes and new realities, here's what we advise clients: instead of thinking of distribution chains, think of a value network. More specifically, put yourself in your customer's place and think about value from his or her point of view. Obviously, it makes sense to deliver your product or service at the lowest cost, but it's more important to figure out what the customer "values" about what you sell. Once you've found this out from your customer, what can you do to enhance that value? It may involve a strategic alliance with a surprising sort of business partner and involve more, not fewer, middlemen.

Chances are good that the digital age will drive these changes. For starters, technology welcomes entry into many markets. Whereas it used to take months or years to set up distribution channels, it now takes days — or even hours — using the Internet-enabled infrastructure. The Web has also cut down the need for retail storefronts and warehouses and the related capital required to build them. Most important, with breathtaking efficiency, technology provides direct access to consumers and information about their tastes.

In short, the digital economy is revolutionizing how we think about the traditional corporate value chain and redefining relationships between manufacturers, suppliers, distributors, and consumers. The value "chain" is in fact a value network, or "web," in which companies engage in multiple two-way relationships to bring increasingly complex products and services to market.

Of course, there are real competitive advantages to the cost-cutting tactics used by some mass-merchandise retailers. Their strategy is to go directly to the source of their basic products or raw materials, then to negotiate prices that cut out intermediary distributors and wholesalers and put other, less fortunate competitors out of business. And finally they tighten that supply-and-distribution chain until it is as taut as a drum.

But cost containment, or operational efficiency, is not the only answer. And CEOs are beginning to understand that concept. In A.T. Kearney's 1998 survey of CEO attitudes about information technology, only 10 percent said cost cutting was a key issue, down from 27 percent in 1996.

Rather, when you think of what electronically adds value to your product or service, compelling new opportunities emerge. The best way that technology can add value is by offering more time — the most precious commodity to businesses and individuals alike.

For example, automation has certainly armed manufacturers with rich databases filled with customers' likes, dislikes, and precise demographics that help manufacturers reduce inventories, the number and length of manufacturing cycles, and assembly costs. Again, the main — and largely unexploited — way that technology can help such businesses is to give consumers more time. For example, once your favorite clothing-brand supplier has your precise measurements, ordering a new suit requires a five-minute phone call, not six hours at the mall.

My prediction is that as the digital economy develops, entire industries will be created to fill gaps in the various electronic value webs that emerge.

Here's another example: To buy a Jaguar sports car, you go to a dealer. But now an enterprising businessman in Britain sells these luxury cars over the Internet. He will deliver to your door whatever model you choose electronically, with all the legal paperwork in order — for a whopping 35 percent discount. When your Jag needs a tune-up, another business on the Web puts you in touch with a dealer or repair shop. The second business adds further value to this particular electronic value web by using consumer-purchasing databases, global positioning technologies, and sophisticated telephony-call-center software. It allows you to summon people to your house when your car needs servicing. Then they deliver the car to the appropriate shop, verify that the work has been done properly, clean and wash it, and park it in your driveway. All for a hefty fee that people are willing to pay.

In the first instance, technology is used to swap one middleman (the local Jaguar dealer) for another one (the virtual Jaguar dealer) for the most traditional reason of all: to save the consumer money. In the second instance, technology is used to expand the value web, and the overall service costs more. But because value is offered, the business model works.

A NEW WAY OF THINKING

We encourage clients to think differently when developing strategies in the digital economy. It involves a concept called container versus content. Traditionally, products have been either predominantly containers (physical objects such as automobiles), or content (a service such as a book or magazine). But successful products in the digital economy will combine both content and container attributes in stunningly creative ways.

This concept often means bringing together previously unrelated technologies, products, services, and information — often from widely disparate sources. In short, it means building a value web.

We see how this happened in the home-banking software market. Products such as *Quicken* and *Managing Your Money* have been available for more than a decade, but they failed to attract a large following, primarily because consumers were unwilling to manually enter checking transaction data into the computer.

But when these software products were combined with another technology product — debit cards — home-banking software suddenly became attractive. Using a debit card, your bank allows you to post any debit-card activities — a grocery bill, an ATM withdrawal, a telephone payment — directly to your home-banking software, via the Internet. And it automatically records the transactions in your checking account. Consumers are willing for pay for this real value. These two formerly separate businesses formed a value web, one that innovatively combined container and content.

In the 1980s, the conventional wisdom was that businesses should focus on their "core competencies." In effect, they were to figure out what they did best and then to do it as well — and as efficiently — as possible. This was a good notion then, but it is outdated in the digital economy.

It's not enough to be the best at something unless that something offers real value in the marketplace. For instance, why did the Sony *Bookman* fail? It was a flashy "container" that was colorful, portable, cool even. But it didn't offer more than a book does. Yet another lower technology product is doing exceedingly well: books on tape or, increasingly, CDs, because it adds real value. People can drive their cars and absorb a book's information simultaneously.

So what can we learn from this? First, understand where your product or service fits into the existing value chain — and ruthlessly evaluate the value you give to the end customer.

Second, study your opportunities. Do you now offer container or content? What can you do? What sorts of value webs can you join or create to offer customers a truly valuable new combination of container and content? Finally, consider whether your restructured product or service saves your customers time. Can you help them get their goods to market faster or more easily? If you can work out solutions for your customers in those areas, you're on your way to succeeding in the new digital economy.

Chapter 12

Results-Based IT in an ERA of Process

L.R. DeJarnett

The development and automation of new processes seem to hold dominant focus. Some suggest following the mantra of first designing the new processes, then automating them. Others suggest automating first with ERP templates, and then reengineering further after the new system is installed. There are more than enough true believers, bigots, and demigods for any and all alternatives. The key point this writer has been trying to raise is that processes — in whatever sequences — are secondary. It is the results that count. Focus first and foremost on the overall business result that is needed. Insist that all actions contribute directly to achieving the significant economic outcome — the result! Then, following process best practices will get you where you need to be.

The theory and philosophy can be debated endlessly. This chapter highlights three example companies that adopted and followed a results-based IT strategy. The readers should judge the examples' successes and the merits of such a focus for their own IT initiatives.

THE RESULTS HIERARCHY AT WORK

Successful results-based management is a cascade of outcomes, but in our experience, each project cascade is different. This occurs despite the fact that the same processes may be pursued or that common technologies are being used, e.g., Microsoft Windows NT, the Internet, or SAP. In fact, how the technology is packaged — the deliverable results for supply chain, value chain, or whatever — is almost always unique to each company. Such differences add complexity and increase risk of failure, making results-based management even more critical. It is in these differences, however, where the magic happens:

- In the ability to do something your competitors cannot, or
- In the ability to optimize process for your particular market.

0-8493-1273-6/02/$0.00+$1.50
© 2002 by CRC Press LLC

TASK 1: DESIGNING SUPPLY CHAINS FOR COMPETITIVE ADVANTAGE

One size or one process definitely does not fit all. To illustrate this further, consider three companies that recently finished enterprise process improvements: a steel mill, a consumer products company, and a computer products distributor. All shared the same goal (i.e., a common top-level outcome). Each wanted to put the customer in charge of the supply chain. They also shared other qualities. Each company's process transformation turned out to be extremely successful. Each used a similar results-based management approach, and each success is attributed to knowing in advance what was wanted from the changes they were trying to administer.

Although all three wanted to get closer to the customer, the route and measurable intermediate results had to deal with the specific and particular challenges and opportunities of their respective businesses.

EXAMPLE 1: A STEEL COMPANY

A steel company wanted to replace a long-cycle manufacturing process with shortened, customer-driven production. Everything would be tied together, from sales order entry to production planning and control, to customer service. Processes would overlap and occur in parallel: materials ordered, hot steel molded and poured, orders taken, products shipped, and customers billed. Previously, steel had to be set, picked, slotted, and waiting in the yard for future orders — at which point it would be cut and rolled for the customer. Today, the company can make a decision while the steel is still hot: how it will be rolled and cut — including width, thickness, and so forth. The new process has allowed inventories to be cut to the bone, manufacturing costs to be cut by more than 20 percent, and cycle times to be reduced from 10 days to 90 minutes. Customers receive faster turnaround, greater product choice, and the ability to order the products they need later in their own production cycle.

A good deal of the change, of course, was in a newly constructed steel production facility. The new mill would be useless, though, without the software that could exploit the just-in-time nature of the new business model. Because the company no longer could depend on a safety net of stock, it had to be known precisely what was coming off the line, when, and for whom. In turn, integration with suppliers had to be tighter to make sure the right amounts of material were on hand the day it was needed. In other words, customers were essentially driving activity at the steel mill and at the mill's suppliers on a day-to-day basis. Electronically speaking, from the point of view of the customer (a car maker for instance), the steel producer and its suppliers were as much a part of the car building process as the assembly line. This would become a strategic advantage when competing for the car maker's business.

EXAMPLE 2: A CONSUMER PRODUCTS COMPANY

A consumer products company wanted to sell directly to customers (retail stores), bypassing distributors. The goal was to go from a supply-side push model, where product was produced (essentially) for warehouses, to a demand-pull model, where product was produced to satisfy specific customer needs. There were many similarities to the steel manufacturer, including reduction of inventories and a tighter integration with customers and suppliers. The key difference: the steel maker was reinventing its manufacturing; the consumer products company was reinventing its distribution.

This difference required the consumer products company to have a much sharper focus on forecasting, distribution, logistics, and inventory management functions. The consumer products company also had to push technology down into the hands of retailers and sales people, as opposed to the steel company, many of whose customers wanted to push technology up to suppliers.

The distribution transformation was no less massive. The number of consumer products company buyers increased to 150,000 from 15,000, whereas the number of orders processed increased to 300,000 a month from 3,000. One need only think about issues such as loading (consolidating daily shipments going to the same region or city) the order processing/billing process, to see what impact changes like this would have.

It is worth noting how hoped-for process results drove technology choices (i.e., hoped-for implementation results). Both the steel company and the consumer products company implemented SAP. The consumer products company also implemented a best of breed distribution and logistics solution — Manugistics — based on its need for different results at the to-be level (i.e., a distribution advantage). This, in turn, required changes in the SAP implementation, including custom interfaces between the two software packages. These differences impacted many lower levels in the project chain, affecting dozens of project teams and hundreds of developers, engineers, and process specialists. Managing all this activity at once was only possible when the results hierarchy was made crystal clear, deliverables were rigorously defined, and accountability for those deliverables assigned and tracked.

EXAMPLE 3: A COMPUTER DISTRIBUTOR

The desire to cut distributors out of the supply chain is not unique. Many companies and customers are using new computer technologies to bypass distributors and even retailers for improved value. Nowhere is this trend more striking than in the computer industry, Where consumers are ready to pull out their credit cards and order products over the Web. One company claims it generates a million dollars a day on its Web site. What is unique is the story behind this third example of results-based process improvement — a computer distributor that reversed its declining revenues, using the Internet, a unique inventory management approach, and innovative sales order-processing technology. The economic outcome was significant: revenue and net incomes in 1997 were at an all-time high, in contrast to 1995 when revenue plummeted and layoffs were the order of the day.

Again, the magic was not in the technology itself, but in the ability to differentiate the company, based on results achieved in both the supply chain and its technology project deliverables hierarchy. The company's objective was to streamline how it put knowledge into the hands of customers. The company concluded that it knew more than anyone else about the desktop computer market, including technology, current features, compatibility, and availability. The key would be to allow customers to take advantage of that knowledge before they went looking elsewhere. This was a daunting task, considering that the distributor carries more than 20,000 products that can be put together in countless varieties.

The computer distributor did what most companies could not do — it insulated and extended its legacy systems. It did not rip them out and replace them with package software. Among other things, that decision required the company to deal with the myriad of version control and compatibility issues that such do-it-yourself projects invariably entail. The company's objective was to clearly differentiate itself from other distributors. At the time, however, the real competition was not other distributors, but vendors and customers who might want to do business without this distributor in the middle. The company responded by creating a system so customers could access the distributor on the Internet, determine pricing and availability, and even configure hardware and software components online. The real difference, however, was that the company not only showed its pricing and availability, but also that of competitors. A customer could log on, find out who had the best deal, and then pick up the phone and do business with a competitor. Our case distributor's advantage was that they were easier to do business with, could monitor what customers wanted to know (compared with what was selling and compared with competitive offerings), and could change its own offerings instantly, in response.

The Gartner Group reports that 90 percent of its clients who try to reinvent their supply chain fail. Yet the three prior examples show companies that did not fail. They used results to master process, rather than being obsessed by process or technology. All three companies wanted essentially the same thing — closer integration with customers. Each approached the situation in a creative, different way, based on its own situation. To-be models were different, technology choices were different, and implementations were different, but the results, which drove those varying choices, were spectacularly good!

Enterprise package solutions may tempt management to adopt a slamit-in, one-size-fits-all strategy. But such strategy is unlikely to create high value through a commodity-type approach. Companies must learn how to differentiate throughout their value chains, without becoming lost in a process maze. The key is to visualize the hierarchy of results and the dependencies that exist among them. In an age of process mania, it is easy to lose sight of the fact that value comes from results, not activity.

Chapter 13
The Enterprise Resource Planning System as a Strategic Solution

Richard L. Jenson
I. Richard Johnson

Many large organizations are integrating core business processes throughout the supply chain by implementing enterprise resource planning systems such as Baan IV, SAP R/3, and Oracle Financials. System users have achieved savings by eliminating many different and often incompatible legacy systems as well as streamlining business processes. Although difficulties have sometimes been encountered during the rigorous enterprise resource planning (ERP) implementation process, most problems seem to result from users trying to map a previously ill-behaved system to work within the structure of the ERP system.

A reader of the business press or an observer of organizations will notice three recurring themes being played out in highly competitive companies. These companies are

- Focusing on core business processes that lead to customer satisfaction
- Tearing down functional boundaries that inhibit cooperation, fragment processes, and discourage communications
- Linking, integrating, and controlling processes with the use of powerful information technology, known as ERP systems

Proponents of various business process engineering approaches assert that the ineffectiveness of most organizational processes stems from a "division of labor" mentality held over from the industrial era where processes remain fragmented through overspecialization and spread across departmental boundaries. As a result, operations require more effort to coordinate, and it is often difficult to determine who is responsible for the entire process. Management interventions such as reengineering seek to eliminate process fragmentation, organize work around key business processes, and exploit the enabling technologies of modern information technology (IT) to link the core processes of the enterprise.

The emergence of IT as a process enabler and integrator also deserves emphasis. Traditionally, the role of IT has been viewed as merely *supporting* the enterprise. However, in observing the most successful companies in today's competitive corporate environment, it is clear that the role of IT has become much more dominant from both strategic and operational perspectives. Most modern organizations would have difficulty maintaining an identity apart from the IT infrastructure that controls their processes and facilitates communications and transactions with their trading partners. ERP systems have received considerable attention in the IT press and various practitioner journals over the last several years. Larger organizations are implementing information systems that link the supply chain of the organization using a shared database and tightly integrated business processes. The dominant enterprise systems integrator is SAP AG (Waldorf, Germany) with approximately 30 percent of the ERP market. Oracle, PeopleSoft, Baan, and J. D. Edwards round out the major players in this market.

The potential benefits of ERP solutions include greatly improved integration across functional departments, emphasis on core business processes, proven and reliable software and support, and overall enhanced competitiveness. In implementing a configurable off-the-shelf ERP solution, an organization can quickly upgrade its business processes to industry standards, taking advantage of the many years of business systems reengineering and integration experience of the major ERP vendors.

WHY ORGANIZATIONS ARE TURNING TO ERP

ERP system adoptions have recently accelerated. This can be attributed to several factors that are discussed in the following paragraphs:

- *Reengineering for Best Practice.* Because of emerging competitive pressures in their respective industries, companies are scrambling to make changes in their core processes that will both meet customer demand and slash logistics costs associated with meeting such demand. For example, SAP touts its R/3 enterprise software as having over 1,000 catalogued "best" business practices compiled within its reference model. According to SAP advocates, these practices have been refined over 25 years of experience over thousands of implementations. Rather than "reinventing the wheel," adopting organizations generally compare their existing practices to the R/3 reference model and then make the necessary changes to the old processes to accommodate the R/3 process implementation. Baan (Baan Company, N. V., Netherlands) delivers a somewhat smaller predefined process set, but provides tools (such as the Dynamic Enterprise Modeler) that enable customers to match their specific business processes and their organization model with the integrated Baan IV application suite.

- *Globalization and Multicurrency Issues.* The global economy has fostered a business environment in which multinational operations are the rule rather than the exception. Obviously, many companies locate facilities abroad to exploit lower labor rates. Moreover, localization requirements often make it necessary for companies to maintain a manufacturing presence in countries they sell in. Clearly, globalization presents almost overwhelming challenges, ranging from cultural differences to multicurrency and value-added tax issues. ERP software has been designed with global organizations in mind and provides an integrated, centralized database that can accommodate distributed transaction processing across multiple currencies.
- *Existing Systems in Disarray.* The authors assert that the wave of ERP implementations is at least partly due to a pent-up demand for an off-the-shelf solution to the general disarray across very large systems. The move to distributed processing appeased some end users as personal work stations and local area networks allowed users to participate in low-end processing. Generally, mission-critical applications remained on the legacy systems while the perceived gaps were filled through end-user computing. The resulting complexity and loss of centralized control are now almost universally recognized, and the push for server-side processing and "thin clients" is evidence of the backlash. Many organizations see enterprise systems as a return to centralized control over business processes.
- *Year 2000 Problems.* Clearly, a significant factor driving many ERP implementations was the much-hyped Year 2000 problem. This computer-programming artifact, often blamed on legacy-era software, could cause many date-sensitive programs to crash at the turn of the century. Companies spent millions of dollars to fix and test the millions of lines of existing computer code. Rather than spend this money on obsolete systems, the option of implementing a state-of-the-art ERP solution such as R/3 was especially attractive.
- *Integration and Discipline.* As Michael Hammer and James Champy emphasized in their bestseller *Reengineering the Corporation*[1] a major cause of broken systems is process fragmentation. That is, organizational processes tend to be spread across functional boundaries. As a result, many individuals and multiple departments must interact to complete a transaction. Coordination becomes complex with no individual or department assuming responsibility for the whole process. Often, no one knows the status of a transaction, or worse, the transaction "falls through the cracks." In addition, data entry and databases

are often duplicated as individuals and departments attempt to impose control on their portion of the transaction where none exists for the process as a whole. With ERP, organizations see opportunities to enforce a higher level of discipline as they link their processes and share their database.

THE BENEFITS OF ENTERPRISE SYSTEMS

Conventional wisdom says that no single system software company can be all things to all companies. This basic attitude set the stage for a blitz-krieg assault of North American companies by the German company SAP AG. The viability of enterprisewide software capable of managing information needs for the entire company was ludicrous. Only a few short years ago the concept was virtually unknown by the majority of corporate America. Times have changed. The list of companies that have either adopted or are in the process of adopting enterprise software is impressive and growing at an accelerating pace. A brief look at several companies that have made the switch and some of their experiences follow.

Data reported by SAP AG concerning the new Fujitsu SAP system reveal the following. Fujitsu was facing increasingly complex business processes with a series of aging mainframes and software that could no longer be upgraded. After a successful 10-month installation of SAP they enjoyed the following benefits:

- 90 percent reduction of cycle time for quotation from 20 days to 2 days
- 60 to 85 percent improved on-time delivery
- 50 percent reduction for financial closing times from 10 to 5 days[2]

"Manufacturers' Services Ltd. in Concord, MA is a $900 million company that has grown dramatically through acquisitions in Europe, Asia, and the United States. It is using The Baan Company software as the glue that keeps it all together. 'Traditionally, people have looked to ERP to run their basic operations,' says John Walshe, vice president of information systems. 'We want ERP to be an integrator for the company.'"[3]

General Motors selected SAP to enable common financial information and processes throughout the global corporation. The company expects the software to reduce greatly the cost and number of the many different financial systems currently employed throughout the world. Implementation of the new system is expected to be completed by the year 2002.

An interview with Boeing officials produced the following comment: "Baan forced us to look for ways to simplify our processes, and because the software is integrated, end users must now work together to solve problems within the internal supply chain."[4]

The incentive for adopting enterprise software varies greatly from company to company. One common thread, however, is the anticipated business improvement that will follow adoption. Roy Clothier, president of Pacific Coast Feather Company, explained the experience of his company as follows: "R/3 has all the tools we need to run our business," Clothier says. "We're already getting very satisfactory results — like reducing our inventory at the same time that we are improving our ability to service our customers — and we feel we're only scratching the surface of the benefits that are out there. Every day we find new ways to gain more value from R/3."[5]

The IBM Storage Products Company experienced the following success with its ERP system: 110 days after the system went into production, SPC recognized the following improvements: the time for checking customer credit upon receiving an order reduced from 15 to 20 minutes to instantaneously; responses to customer billing inquiries occurred in real time, versus 15 to 20 minutes; entering pricing data into the system took five minutes where it could take 80 days before; and shipping repair and replacement parts was done in three days, compared to as many as 44.[6]

Most companies adopting ERP software appear to be well satisfied. Not all companies, however, have enjoyed this same degree of satisfaction. One noted exception is FoxMeyer Health Corp. FoxMeyer expected the technology to cut cost, speed up inventory turnover, and increase the availability of useful information. Company spokesman Wade Hyde, however, sums up what FoxMeyer found, in the following comment: "The computer-integration problems we had were a significant factor leading to the bankruptcy filing."[7]

THE IMPLEMENTATION PROCESS

The IT press has focused significant attention on the trauma that often accompanies the implementation of ERP systems. Clearly, the introduction of an enterprise system is a nontrivial event in any organization. Given the scope of organizational change triggered by the typical implementation, it should not come as a surprise. Successful enterprise systems require a high degree of discipline from the organization. Consequently, organizations not accustomed to this level of discipline will struggle with such a comprehensive intervention. For example, an R/3 implementation forces the organization to examine all of its existing processes and compare them with the "best practices" incorporated within the package. In reconciling the differences (or "gaps"), the organization must generally reengineer its processes to fit R/3. Although it is theoretically possible to modify R/3 (make changes to the source code) to fit the existing organizational process, few experts would advise this approach. Current implementation wisdom emphasizes the need to leave the software in its "vanilla" state. The price to be paid for adding "chocolate chips" is higher implementation cost and increased difficulty of incorporating future software upgrades.

As is typical with any large-scale systems implementation, organizations adopting ERP use highly structured, phased methodologies. These projects are complex undertakings that must address issues such as process and task redesign, hardware, software, database administration, and software configuration. While such methodologies are beyond the scope of this article, a few of the major milestones are described as follows:

- *Form the Implementation Team.* While almost all organizations find it necessary to bring in outside ERP consulting expertise, the process requires a dedicated team of managers and other key employees that may convene for a period of months, perhaps years, to establish the plans, develop the objectives of the project, and manage the implementation process.
- *Blueprint the Current State.* The process typically begins with an assessment of the "current state" of organizational processes. The implementation teams will usually use process modeling techniques and software to document business events, the tasks that must be performed, the individuals and departments who perform them, the flow of information, and the linkages to other processes within the organization. From the current state, the team should identify existing weaknesses and opportunities to reengineer for best practice.
- *Gap Analysis.* With the enhanced understanding and documentation of the current state, the implementation team can then compare the current state with the business processes and solutions the system provides. As a practical matter, the organization will almost always adopt the ERP process version. Therefore, the gap analysis reveals the major process discrepancies that will require significant changes to existing processes. Occasionally, the ERP product may not offer a corresponding process. In such cases, the organization may require a work-around solution.
- *Design, Scripting, and Configuration.* The design of the new processes will generally evolve in an iterative fashion as the implementation team, assisted by key users, designs and documents the reengineered processes. The team prepares scripts of each of the redesigned processes to assist the user in navigating the system. The scripts will identify the steps within each process, the menu path the user must take, the system screens that will be accessed, explanations of the data fields that require input, and key decision points the user must address. The process designs will also drive the configuration of database tables that allow configuration of business objects such as data entry screens and reports.

- *Simulation, Testing, and Training.* As with any systems implementation, extensive simulation and testing is required with the newly configured system prior to going "live." Testing takes place on a test "instance," a logically distinct version of the database. Experienced ERP integrators recommend that simulations be conducted by nondevelopment team members. Similarly, users new to the environment are trained using a "sandbox" instance prior to introducing them to the live production system.
- *Going Live.* The intense implementation process culminates in the live activation of the actual production system. At this stage, master and transaction database files have been populated with genuine records. Basis administration has been established and technical support mechanisms are in place. Graphical user interfaces have been installed on the applicable work stations and users trained in their use. Assessment mechanisms must be implemented to assure the ongoing business integrity and to monitor basis systems performance.

THE CHALLENGES OF ERP IMPLEMENTATION

Obviously, many implementation problems relate to situations or processes that are unique to a particular company. The most frequent problem cited in the FoxMeyer experience described earlier was the inability of its enterprise software to handle the sheer volume of transactions required. In the Monsanto case, training its staff of some 18,000 employees to use the software after installation has turned out to be a significant problem. The lack of employees trained in the installation and use of ERP software is currently a global problem. With so much interest and movement toward such solutions in the past couple of years, there is a shortage of knowledgeable, experienced people to assist with the adoptions. Many, if not most, World Wide Web sites of ERP partners have a section dealing with systems-related employment opportunities.

CONCLUSION

Even though there appears to be a near stampede to adopt ERP systems worldwide, many significant questions linger. Not only are there the basic questions unique to potential adopters such as: Does the new system really fit the organizational needs? Does the organization have strategic business reasons for adopting the software? Do the cost of software implementation and the resulting disruptions of the business process outweigh the potential benefits that may be gained? Other broader questions can also be raised.

ERP solutions have been touted as "best practice" software. This claim is based on the long development period of a dynamic program. Given so many recent changes in the way the world does business, is it possible that this software incorporates all of these recent improvements? Does a company currently employing state-of-the-art business practices lose its competitive advantage by adopting standard practices used by all companies currently using ERP software?

These questions, along with many other questions, may be difficult to answer. Perhaps only time will provide clues into the wisdom of the global movement toward enterprise software. This much currently is known; many of the largest companies in the world are adopting the software and singing its praises. Improvements will undoubtedly be made as ERP vendors respond to the needs of the corporate world. The companies watching the show from the sidelines may be well advised to become part of the cast.

Notes

1. Hammer, Michael and Champy, James, *Reengineering the Corporation*. (New York: Harper-Business, 1993).
2. SAP America, 1998. SAP Consumer Products [online]. From Customer Successes, Fujitsu. Available from: http://www.sap.com/ [Accessed April 28, 1998].
3. Melymuka, Kathleen, "An Expanding Universe," *Computerworld*, September 14, 1998, p. 56.
4. Baan Company, 1988. From Customers, The Boeing Company. Available from: http://www.baan.com/ [Accessed September 22, 1998].
5. SAP America, 1998. SAP Consumer Products [online]. From Customer Successes, Pacific Coast Feather Company. Available from: http://www.sap.com/ [Accessed April 28, 1998].
6. SAP America, 1998. SAP Consumer Products [online]. From Customer Successes, IBM Storage Products Company. Available from: http://www.sap.com/ [Accessed April 28, 1998].
7. Hyde, Wade, "Technology (A Special Report): Working Together — When Things Go Wrong: FoxMeyer Drug Took a Huge High-Tech Gamble; It Didn't Work," *Wall Street Journal*, Eastern edition, November 18, 1996.

Chapter 14
Strategic Implications of Electronic Linkages

Dale Young
Houston H. Carr
R. Kelly Rainer, Jr.

Much has been written in the past decade regarding the competitive uses of information technology (IT) in industry. Organizations are encouraged to move into the supply chain, the system of interdependent activities used to produce a product or service, and to establish direct, electronic links with their suppliers and customers. Recent applications of IT, such as Web-based commerce, have targeted customers and distribution channels. These electronic links, or interorganizational systems (IOS), are a powerful competitive weapon for facilitating cost leadership and differentiating products and services.

A mature technology such as Electronic Data Interchange (EDI) allows users to examine the strategic relationships that develop over time between firms that share data electronically. EDI is a critical technology for establishing direct, electronic links between trading partners. Much of the past EDI research has described EDI technology and the activities necessary to implement EDI successfully. The strategic implications of EDI have not been studied as closely as its tactical concerns. This article addresses the need for a better understanding of the competitive effects of electronic linkages by examining the strategic issues associated with EDI usage. Users need to better understand the strategic implications of electronic linkages between firms as the amount of business-to-business commerce across the Web grows monthly.

It is often easy to overlook important strategic issues when a technology such as EDI becomes widely accepted as a way of doing business. Questions such as "Who benefits from these electronic linkages?" and "What are

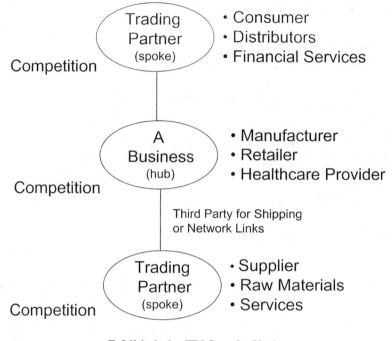

Exhibit 1. An EDI Supply Chain

the concerns of firms that are forced to use a technology?" should be explored. Unfortunately, the focus of many practitioners and researchers is solely on identifying and realizing the immediate benefits of EDI. This chapter attempts to bridge the gap between the tactical and strategic issues by examining the competitive implications of electronic linkages between trading partners, as exemplified by EDI.

STRATEGIC EDI ISSUES

EDI enables the direct, computer-to-computer exchange of standard paperwork, such as orders and invoices, between participating firms. EDI usage affects much more than the way of handling business between two firms. Multiple constituencies are involved in EDI activity, including

- The hub or EDI adopting firm
- The trading partners (spokes: customers or suppliers) of the hub firm
- Third-party firms that provide support services to EDI trading partners

These three parties are shown on the supply chain in Exhibit 1. Some of these hub firms have been very aggressive in implementing EDI. Others, especially spoke firms, have adopted EDI in reaction to threats of lost business.

Organizations occasionally adopt technologies like EDI simply to keep up with the strategic IS investments of other firms in the same industry. EDI becomes a necessary way of doing business rather than a competitive tool. Firms that make IS investments in response to pressure from customers or initiatives of competitors may gain strategic advantage over competitors that neglect to develop similar systems. However, the IS investment was a reactive move and not a carefully designed component of an IS strategic plan.

The strategic issues surrounding EDI implementation seem to be much more difficult to manage than the technical issues. Technologies such as the ANSI standards and communications software are maturing. But business issues (e.g., relations with trading partners) are evolving and affect organizations other than the firms that are exchanging documents directly. The authors' research into competitive IS applications and EDI implementation points to three key strategic EDI issues:

1. Business relationships between trading partners
2. Balance of power between buyers and sellers
3. Impact of EDI adoption on third parties

Business Relationships between Trading Partners

EDI implementation affects the amounts of data transferred between firms, influences the types and timing of information releases, raises concerns for security, and creates a need for changes in the business processes used by participants. Successful implementation of EDI dictates higher levels of cooperation, evidenced by the increased amounts of data that are exchanged between trading partners. Cooperation is mutually beneficial because it contributes to long-term relationships between buyers and sellers. High volume and simple products, which fit well into EDI-based systems, also are associated with long-term, stable, buyer–seller relationships. Fruit of the Loom has been successful in interacting with its distributors across the Web because of this high volume, simple product model. Conversely, complex products that require large amounts of information exchange during routine transactions may not adapt easily to electronic systems in which multiple buyers and sellers are exchanging data.

IOSs like EDI force changes in business processes. Firms that adopt EDI out of competitive necessity must realize cost savings to recover their EDI investment; this cost recovery comes about as basic business processes are redesigned or even eliminated. EDI usage affects the types and timing of information releases, forces changes in production methods used by supplier firms, and raises concerns for security and legal issues.

Changes in the relationships between trading partners are evident in both the types and timing of information releases. Some retailers are sending sales figures directly (i.e., via EDI linkages) to manufacturers, or alternatively giving online access to sales information in the retailer's database, to speed the reordering process. Manufacturers, in turn, must implement more efficient production methods and are informing their suppliers of manufacturing resource planning forecasts to ensure a steady flow of raw materials to feed just-in-time production processes.

Releasing internal data to a trading partner by way of a direct computer link requires a rethinking of the responsibilities or roles of each partner. Firms now are exchanging proprietary information. Allowing an outside firm to view transaction-level data places a premium on trust between trading partners because of the competitive risks associated with this type of access. Security concerns for on-site and communicated data can be addressed by internal accounting controls, passwords, callback routines, and encryption. Even the legal barriers to electronic contracting may not be as formidable as once thought. Trading partners should agree on terms and conditions up front and understand that electronic transactions are as enforceable as those that are paper-based.

Closely related to security and legal concerns are issues regarding the regulation of data flows between trading partners when the partners are located in different countries. Transborder data flows are subject to a variety of restrictions. Firms may be required to process data in the country in which the data originated, and organizations can be limited in the way communications facilities are used. Managers should be aware of the existence of constraints on international data movement because of the potential for reducing the benefits received from EDI or other forms of electronic commerce.

Cooperating with trading partners within a supply chain may encourage a firm to look at other electronic relationships. Competitors are jointly developing IT infrastructures to provide data to cooperative and EDI systems. The difficulties of sustaining a competitive advantage with IT, the risks involved in new, large-scale ISs, and the costs of such projects make joint ventures attractive. These jointly developed systems benefit buyers and sellers by lowering search costs and increasing the efficiency of interorganizational transactions. These systems make available competitive information in a single information system. EDI is a valuable extension to these joint systems because participants can perform price and product comparisons and electronically place orders.

Buyer/Seller Balance of Power

Systems that cut across company boundaries shift the balance of power in an industry. When a single, large firm mandates EDI usage by its suppliers, the balance of power between buyer and seller is changed. Large manufacturers, such as Ford and General Motors, and retailers, such as Wal-

Mart and Sears, are examples of companies that have made EDI usage mandatory. The organizations that operate these IOSs enjoy substantial economies of scale and benefit from the closer integration of steps in the supply chain, made possible by the systems.

The EDI-mandating firm — the hub — begins to dictate when business will take place, how that business will be transacted, and when shipment of product is expected. Some hub firms even dictate the EDI software and network that must be used. Suppliers that are slow to modify their business processes to fit the hub firm's demands may be endangering a much needed business relationship.

Responses by trading partners — the spoke firms — not only vary but actually may result in a loss of some of the expected benefits of EDI adoption when viewed from the perspective of the overall distribution system. For example, some firms use personal computers to receive and then print hard copies of EDI documents. These documents then are reentered manually into the receiving firm's computerized information system (IS). This manual process can result in errors, time delays, and other problems associated with data entry.

Other spoke firms, instead of developing fast production capabilities, build up inventories and thus their own costs to rapidly respond to orders. One survey of auto industry supplier firms revealed that the average lot size delivered by the suppliers was much smaller than the average lot size the supplier produced.[1] This production example shows how inventory holding costs can be shifted to other firms in the supply chain.

Although hub firms receive substantial benefit from using EDI, it is not at all clear that these benefits extend to each of the hub's trading partners in an equitable fashion. In fact, EDI usage may be disadvantageous to some members of a given supply chain. Another survey of firms that supply large automotive manufacturers found that most of the supplier firms were unable to identify any advantage to using EDI.[2] The suppliers had adopted EDI simply to avoid losing business with the mandating hub firm.

Some supplier firms cannot afford, or are not technically advanced enough, to move to EDI without assistance. The hub firm can assist in EDI adoption by providing software and training or by offering faster payment for EDI-based transactions.

All trading partners in a given industry share the direct costs of EDI programs. Industry experience suggests that these programs make participants more efficient, and thus reduce their operating costs. The savings should filter down to the ultimate consumer of the good or service in the form of lower prices, higher levels of service, or both. Unfortunately, it is hard to isolate the effects of EDI efforts from other competitive initiatives of user organizations.

There are cases in which electronic order entry systems that are controlled by a single firm have led to industry consolidations. The Economost system from McKesson Drug is an example of a system that caused smaller competitors, who were unable to develop their own EDI systems, to get out of the business or be taken over.

Third-Party Impacts

Improving the information flow between trading partners affects other organizations in the supply chain. These third-party firms often provide support services to the principle trading partners. Mandates for EDI usage can include demands by the hub firm that there be no middlemen (e.g., factory representatives) involved in the transaction. The result is that organizations that historically have brought together buyers and sellers now are excluded from participating.

Transportation firms are affected by EDI efforts in a significantly different manner. Retailers are advancing the concept of "Quick Response" or "Efficient Consumer Response" to provide just-in-time inventory to the store floor. Trucking firms have installed expensive ISs, such as satellite links in each truck, to improve the tracking of shipments while in transit. An electronic link between trading partners therefore can affect the supply chain component that provides the physical link between those firms.

A second way transportation firms are affected is when Quick Response retailers place small orders each day instead of larger orders monthly. Larger orders can be delivered to the retailer's distribution centers by trucking firms specializing in large containers. Next-day carriers such as UPS and Federal Express often deliver the small orders. Here a change in order size, as a result of a just-in-time program and electronic order exchange, leads to a change in both lot size and freight carrier.

Relationships among trading partners are affected by the decision to exchange data electronically. These relationships are experiencing substantial change due to forces both external (e.g., customer demand for higher levels of service) and internal (e.g., hub firm actions) to EDI-using industries. Exhibit 2 diagrams these competitive issues across a supply chain.

Summary of EDI Competitive Issues

EDI usage is having far-reaching impacts on competition and business practices in several industries, including

- Improvement in external links leading to better customer service, lower transaction costs, and more efficient intercompany information exchanges
- The shift of market power toward hub firms and away from spoke firms

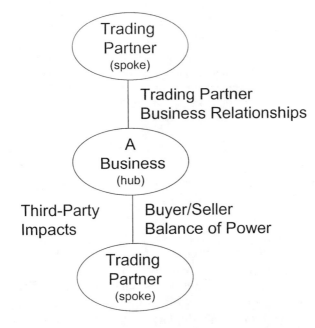

Exhibit 2. Competitive Issues Across a Supply Chain

- A willingness to share the risks and costs of large-scale EDI projects among groups of competing firms
- The lack of concern by some members of the supply chain for the needs of third parties that facilitate business transactions

Once all major competitors in an industry have adopted a technology, no single competitor gains any significant competitive advantage. The systems turn into a cost of doing business as adoption is a competitive necessity. An exception may be organizations that are "first movers" and so maintain a competitive advantage by developing strong ties with trading partners that are not quickly broken by competitors who adopt similar technologies. After all competitors have made a sizable investment in an IT infrastructure to support the electronic transfers of data, they actually may suffer lower profits as a result. IS applications that are strategic necessities are therefore candidates for cooperative development. Industry-specific EDI standards are an example of such cooperative efforts. Another example of cooperation is the use of VANs as a method of supplying a shared infrastructure for EDI.

There seem to be few penalties for using EDI, given the stable nature of the technology involved. However, in some industries (e.g., retailing and automotive), EDI is becoming a required component of doing business.

Exhibit 3. Description of the Respondents

Job Title	Description of the Firm	Annual Revenue
Vice President	Healthcare, insurance	$5.8 billion
Senior Vice President	Manufacturer, electronics	$5.8 billion
Senior Vice President	Manufacturer, forest products	$13 billion
Vice President, IS	Manufacturer, office products	$1.2B division of $3.8B firm
Project Officer	Gas and oil utility	$490 million division
Project Manager	Retailer	$3.5 billion

Firms that do not use the technology will be unable to keep pace with competition.

FINDINGS

To confirm the validity of these competitive relationships the authors asked several senior executives, who are familiar with day-to-day EDI operations, for feedback based on their personal experiences. Their comments provide a clearer understanding of the importance of trading partner relationships when firms exchange data electronically.

The Respondents

Exhibit 3 lists the job titles of the respondents, a description of each firm, and the firm's annual revenues. These multibillion dollar firms are typical in size of other EDI hub firms. The senior executive rank of these managers provides the strategic viewpoint necessary to comment on competitive issues and trading partner relationships.

One firm is a public utility; the others represent a mix of manufacturing and service industries. The three manufacturers compete in low-margin, high-volume lines of business against multiple competitors; thus, cost control and efficiency are critical. The retailer is an active participant in the current consolidation going on in that industry. The public utility services both residential and commercial accounts. The healthcare firm is under pressure to deliver higher levels of services while controlling the costs of interactions with doctors, hospitals, third-party providers, and insurance companies. Although the sample of firms is selective, it is an excellent cross-section of the types of firms and industries that are candidates for the efficiencies offered by EDI.

Data Collection

The authors contacted executives who have experience with EDI. The participating executives were mailed a brief questionnaire and a copy of a diagram that listed the strategic issues discussed here. They also met with several firms as part of this study. Respondents were asked to comment on the correctness of the EDI issues identified by discussing how well the items listed match their personal experience. Participants discussed their firms' EDI involvement with both customers and suppliers. Finally, the authors asked them about the competitive issues their firm considered when deciding to use EDI.

Direction of EDI Usage in the Supply Chain

The retailer uses EDI back down the supply chain with its suppliers. The healthcare firm also uses EDI in one direction — with other insurers, doctors, and hospitals. The other four firms use EDI in both directions — down the supply chain to suppliers and up the supply chain with customers. The gas company uses EDI with large suppliers and large commercial accounts. The three manufacturers use EDI with both customers and suppliers. The three manufacturers and the healthcare firm mentioned that they are initiators of the EDI relationships between themselves and their trading partners. Their role as initiator supports the idea that these are hub firms in the EDI relationship.

Competitive Issues

Respondents commented on two competitive issues: relationships with trading partners and the balance of power between themselves and their trading partners. The vice president from the electronics manufacturer noted that "… EDI causes change in every relationship, but the change is necessary for each industry to survive. I strongly believe everyone gains as opposed to your (the researcher's) comment that trading partners may not gain anything." This executive pointed to the mutually beneficial nature of the relationship change. Data exchanges between trading partners are an important part of the relationship: "Since we are the vital product link, meaning the ultimate producer of a major part of the customer's revenues, communications and information flow is absolutely vital."

The gas company viewed itself as small relative to the size of its suppliers and customers. They experience "substantial competition in large volume markets" and must be an efficient producer and distributor. EDI represents less than five percent of transactions with suppliers and commercial customers, and the gas company does EDI here due to competitive pressure. This firm views the balance of power issue as a real threat. The office products' vice president, however, stated that the buyer/seller balance of power is "rarely affected in the real world" by use of electronic interactions.

The retail respondent noted that larger retailers, "Federated, Bells, Sears, K-Mart, JCPenny," are "pushing" EDI, where previously the big vendors pushed the technology on retailers. The retailer sees a current change in the balance of power, swinging in favor of the retailer. The authors met with four textile and apparel industry firms that have implemented Quick Response (QR). They found the pressure for the use of bar coding, EDI, and automatic replenishment was primarily from the retail partner. Retailers wanted the suppliers to institute QR because inventory was pushed backward in the channel, away from the retail floor and the retailer's distribution center. Retailers pushed to have all deliveries from the supplier made directly to the store floor, ready to sell. Although the inventory ownership responsibility and even additional duties, such as tagging the goods, were pushed to the apparel manufacturer, it was not obvious that the retail partner passed funds to the supplier to cover these added costs. QR does allow the retailer to improve customer service by having goods in stock that are currently in demand by consumers.

The presence of well-defined EDI standards makes it easier for hub firms to switch between suppliers and can be an additional factor that increases the bargaining power of these large buyers. Our research uncovered charges that some retailers initiate business with a small-to-medium sized firm and gradually increase the amount bought, which means that the buyer is taking an increasing percentage of the seller's total volume. When the buyer gets to a significant percentage of the seller's business the retailer pressures the manufacturer to agree to new terms; otherwise the buyer will halt all business. The resulting loss of sales to the seller is, in some cases, over 75 percent of their production. With such a threat, the seller has little choice but to agree to the retailer's terms. EDI gives the buyer a greater chance to apply this pressure because the cost to switch between suppliers has been lowered.

When discussing competitive issues, one respondent mentioned the importance of changes to internal processes and procedures if the benefits of electronic transactions are to be realized fully. "I must emphasize that the use of EDI is only a minor part of the equation. What is done with the order, shipment, invoice, etc. internal to the company is much more important." To achieve the benefits of electronic trading partner links, a firm must change how it operates. These internal changes are a hidden cost of EDI.

An interesting comment by the retailer was that "few" are using electronic funds transfer with EDI because they want the float, or time lag. Here business strategy is the overriding factor, not technology. The authors found that one retailer paid its suppliers manually, managing the float, because the firm was cash-rich and other apparel industry members were not able to pay their bills.

WHAT WAS LEARNED

Firms in very diverse industries are having similar experiences with EDI. The balance of power between trading partners is a legitimate concern in some industries. The stresses introduced because of relative power ineq-uities must be balanced against the benefit of cooperation from electronic exchanges of data between these trading partners. Firms that initiate elec-tronic data exchanges are driven by competition and by a need to intro-duce efficiencies into day-to-day operations. Two study participants, the retailer and the healthcare firm, are under extreme pressures to control their cost of operations — the retailer from discounters and the healthcare firm from regulators. Both industries are experiencing consolidation as one way of accomplishing cost savings by gaining economies of scale.

These firms are looking beyond internal efficiencies — they are looking in all directions in their supply chains to leverage the benefits of informa-tion technology. What starts out as the simple automation of a manual pro-cess — the exchange of paperwork — becomes an issue with important strategic implications for each firm that participates in the supply chain.

Comments from these executives express that these strategic issues are important to how they manage their firms. These large firms are concerned about developing beneficial and efficient relationships with their trading partners. However, these same firms are interested in leveraging their size to influence the supply chain — to their benefit.

CONCLUSIONS

EDI is an important application of IT in a number of industries. Large EDI hub firms in these industries are forcing adoption by smaller companies. The largest share of the benefits seems to be accruing to the hubs.

EDI seems destined to be a technology that is adopted individually by all the major players in a given industry and so provides no enduring advan-tage to any one firm. Although joint efforts are underway to develop stan-dards, there is currently no evidence that competing firms are engaged in efforts to share EDI software or infrastructure costs.

The willingness of organizations to share internal, operational data is leading to other types of information exchanges and closer working rela-tionships between trading partners. Efforts at more efficient communica-tions between firms now extend to opening up internal electronic mail net-works to suppliers and customers and opening internal, Web-based ISs to trading partners.

There is still an enormous potential in industries where firms just now are beginning to consider seriously electronic exchanges of data. Lower-cost hardware, increased availability of EDI translation software, the move-ment of EDI transactions to the Internet, and the quality and variety of VANs are factors contributing to EDI acceptance. On the other hand, con-cerns arise today due to the fact that benefits from usage are spread unevenly, and implementation costs are not being shared by competitors.

TASK 1: DESIGNING SUPPLY CHAINS FOR COMPETITIVE ADVANTAGE

Although this study did not deal directly with electronic commerce over the Web, some speculation is not out of line. The authors believe that the strategic relationships that have evolved through EDI linkages may set a pattern for Web-based commerce that is now emerging. In both cases, organizations are accomplishing business-to-business linkages with technology, they dramatically are affecting the way information transfers take place with trading partners, and they are changing internal business processes as they exchange data with these trading partners. Finally, the authors suspect the strategic aspects of Web-based transactions will pass rapidly the tactical and technical issues, such as bandwidth needs and Web page content, as the most critical issues in electronic commerce.

Notes

1. Helper, S., How much has really changed between U.S. automakers and their suppliers? *Sloan Management Review,* 31, 7, 1990.
2. Bohl, D., Ed., *EDI at Work,* American Management Association, New York, 1989.

Recommended Reading

1. Benjamin, R., de Long, D., and Scott Morton, M., Electronic data interchange: How much competitive advantage? *Long Range Planning,* 23, 29, 1990.
2. Cecil, J. and Goldstein, M., Sustaining competitive advantage from IT, *The McKinsey Quarterly,* 4, 74, 1990.
3. Clemons, E., Corporate strategies for information technology: A resource-based approach, *Computer,* November, 23, 1991.
4. Kalakota, R., Whinston, A., *Frontiers of Electronic Commerce,* Addison-Wesley, Reading, MA, 1996.
5. O'Leary, M., Store-crossed lovers, *CIO,* 5, 40, 1991.
6. Waterhouse, P., Technology forecast: 1997, Price Waterhouse World Technology Centre, Menlo Park, California, 1997.
7. Radosavich, L., The once and future EDI, *CIO,* January 1, 1997.
8. Stalk, G., Evans, P., and Shulman, L., Competing on capabilities: The new rules of corporate strategy, *Harvard Business Review,* 70, 1992.

Chapter 15

The Evolution of EDI for Competitive Advantage: The FedEx Case

Margaret L. Williams
Mark N. Frolick

The purpose of this chapter IS to provide an understanding of Electronic Data Interchange (EDI), detail its advantages and disadvantages, and show how FedEx uses EDI to develop innovative solutions to resolve its complex business issues.

INTRODUCTION

EDI was the first method of E-commerce. Traditional EDI works in a method similar to using a telephone (before three-way calling). The computer systems are set up so that communication can occur only between two trading partners. EDI requires programming on the part of both trading partners to develop communication standards. In order to transmit data between the two companies, each is required to utilize a value-added network (VAN), which charges a fee for each bit of information that is sent over their networks. As a company adds other trading partners, programmers must develop additional transmission specifications based on the requirements of the new companies. This makes the prospect of using traditional EDI cost prohibitive for all except the largest, most profitable companies.

As technology has evolved, many of the problems originally associated with EDI have been mitigated. Instead of EDI being "hard coded" between companies and individual members of their supply chain, the new EDI is more accessible. Internet lines are used instead of expensive value-added networks. Software packages are now designed with electronic commerce modules. This means that there is less need for expensive consulting firms

0-8493-1273-6/02/$0.00+$1.50
© 2002 by CRC Press LLC

or large contingents of IT professionals to develop and design specialized communication. It helps both large and small companies lower their costs of business.

However, large companies that have heavily invested in EDI technology are not scrapping their networks. They are combining old and new technologies to create a more flexible system. FedEx, being both a technology leader and a customer-driven company, has found advantages to using EDI regardless of its form. It continues to use traditional EDI and has developed Internet solutions to assist its customers, vendors, and others in the supply chain to better communicate with the company. In addition, it has dedicated resources to assist trading partners.

OVERVIEW OF EDI

EDI is an automated method of transmitting information from computer to computer. EDI predates the Internet, chronologically and technologically, and it gained a level of acceptance before the Internet was even taken seriously.[2] Before the advent of the Internet, EDI was the only means of linking computers for the purpose of engaging in E-commerce.

In order to transmit EDI documents between computers, a VAN is normally used. A VAN is a company that offers fast, secure, access-restricted transportation of EDI documents between businesses. VANs also have additional functions such as message transport and tracking. The networks function by providing grouping and distribution of batches of electronic data to company servers via secure communications links. Translation programs interpret data from the EDI format to the internal systems of the individual companies.[3] Trading partners that rely on VANs pay for each transmitted character and often for multiple data pass-throughs. In addition to transmitting documents, the networks simplify communication because companies are dealing with one intermediary instead of a mass of customers and suppliers. VANs also streamline the business partnership by helping companies that use noncompliant or variant message formats operate smoothly in the business chain.[4]

EDI uses a standardized format created by a suborganization of the American National Standards Institute (ANSI) called x12. The x12 organization has assigned numbers to each type of business document. For example, invoices are the number 810; remittance advice is 820; the documents used for meter reads are 867; and purchase orders are 850.

X12 has tried to provide enough variation within each document type to allow it to be used by any industry. There are few mandatory fields, which support versatility while allowing for different interpretations by any company that uses the standard. Codes define the meaning of each data field. For example, a date field would contain a code to indicate the type of date that is stored in the field. The date could be an invoice date, a date of service, a birth date, or some other date.[6] Although EDI is considered to be old and outdated, there are still many advantages to using this technology.

ADVANTAGES OF EDI

The major benefit of EDI is that there is no human intervention once the programming has been completed. Transfers of data are set up to occur at intervals determined by both the sender and receiver. Because of this lack of intervention, faster, more accurate information can be produced in greater detail. With the normal information flow automated, users can focus on managing exceptions. Because the document flow is automated, the use of EDI can reduce the volume of paper required in order management and billing, help track shipments, provide status on in-transit purchases and proof of delivery, and give employees the opportunity to focus on more value-added job responsibilities.

Using EDI gives a company the ability to develop solutions to manage its inventory problems. This includes using a just-in-time (JIT) inventory management style. Companies utilizing JIT can also use EDI to prevent ordering too much or too little inventory. This in turn lowers the carrying cost of the inventory and increases the cash flow of the company. The business cycle becomes compressed, resulting in lower account balances for inventory, receivables, and payables.[7] Although EDI presents companies with distinct advantages, there is also a downside to choosing this technology.

DISADVANTAGES OF EDI

Because EDI links an individual supplier with an individual customer, the cost of implementing EDI can be prohibitive. Programmers must spend time to appropriately develop requirements. Many companies do not have this expertise in-house and must outsource in order to develop EDI. EDI may have standard formats, but each company is unique in the way it utilizes the standards. This means that each time a new customer or supplier is selected, programmers must build new requirements. This makes EDI less efficient than other methods of electronic commerce.

EDI also makes no allowances for data synchronization. EDI only provides for transmission of data over a VAN or over the Internet. This requires that each supply chain partner keep a copy of the product database on its own system. When changes are made to one business partner's copy of the file, EDI can automatically notify the other partner. However, there is no provision to ensure the originator that the alteration has been mirrored in the trading partner's copy of the database. To mitigate this issue, EDI provides for a UPC catalog. The UPC catalog reflects all the changes made by the vendor; however, there are no indicators that show which data elements have been changed. To see the changes, the partner must scroll through the database. In the meantime, transactions may be made with inaccurate information, which may cause discrepancies to arise between the supposedly identical databases.[8]

Another issue related to EDI is the unwillingness or inability of some trading partners to upgrade to the latest version of ANSI x12 standards. New EDI standards are released every few years. Not everybody upgrades at the same time, and many never upgrade. Some companies may be uncomfortable with change, find the process too labor-intensive, or have limitations in their own information systems. There are many versions of EDI being used today, and not every version is compatible.

Although using EDI is less expensive than paper for both the sender and receiver, it is still an expensive method of transmitting data. This is because EDI is conducted over expensive proprietary value-added networks. This makes it difficult for small- and medium-sized businesses to take advantage of the technology to improve their processes. This is evident by the amount of money large companies such as UPS spend on technology. For the past 11 years, UPS has spent more than $1 billion annually on technology, which is more than it has ever spent on trucks in a single year.[9] Smaller companies do not have and cannot afford to spend this large amount of money to secure the same technical advantages. Given the popularity of the World Wide Web, many companies are considering combining the benefits of EDI with the low cost of the Internet to create a more flexible method of data exchange.

INTERNET-BASED EDI

EDI continues to work well for those businesses that have committed the money and resources necessary to maintain costly networks. Increasingly, the global economy is forcing the use of less expensive methods of conducting business. Traditional EDI does not work well for global networking, and to compensate, many companies phone, fax, or e-mail information. However, these methods are prone to errors, and errors introduced at the beginning of the process can grow exponentially. The Internet is seen as an alternative, and it is forcing changes for traditional EDI as it evolves into a more complex yet more usable tool. Cost and ease of use drives many companies toward the Internet; however, most companies have combined the two technologies. Companies with traditional EDI systems in place are not ready to discontinue its use. They still use VANs when and where it is appropriate, but they also want to increase their flexibility. By combining the Internet with EDI, there is now the opportunity to reduce costs, introduce new capabilities, and expedite solutions to problems. This collaboration gives companies a more cost-effective and powerful form of EDI, and it has given smaller companies the ability to compete at the same level as their larger competitors.[10]

However, the Internet also has its problems. It is not as reliable as the value-added networks, and there are also problems with transmitting critical data. Security and privacy issues continue to deter some companies from pursuing EDI over the Internet, and there are computer server malfunctions, slow response time, and extensive training.[11]

FedEx is an example of a company that successfully combined EDI and the Internet and yet continues to use traditional EDI. The two technologies gave the company more flexibility for its customers and suppliers, reduced costs, and helped maintain the dominance of FedEx in the express transportation industry.

EDI AT FEDEX

FedEx Corporation is a leader in technology; however, it realizes that more can be done to increase efficiency, improve customer service, and lower costs. The company has been extremely innovative when computers and automation assist with the generation of sales. This is evident in its development of Internet tracking and Powership, an E-commerce tool that allows customers to key shipments, track packages, and print invoices and reports. The company is now looking for methods to automate internal processes in order to reduce inventory levels, decrease costs of purchasing products, and increase the efficiency of bill paying and accounting.

FedEx has been using traditional EDI for quite some time. In fact the company has a separate department that is dedicated to connecting with its many trading partners, developing translation maps, and making EDI transmissions ready for downloading into the many different mainframe and PC-based applications. There are also other departments that have technical resources that are responsible for determining the abilities of the trading partners and coordinating the transition to EDI. As competition has increased in the express transportation business, the need to decrease costs has become paramount. However, this decrease in costs could not come at the expense of the customer or of good business practices and procedures. FedEx has tailored its solutions to fit the business needs of the company. These solutions have taken the form of continuing EDI in its most traditional form and making some changes to the current business routines.

Traditional EDI at FedEx

FedEx has invested heavily in traditional EDI, and the decision has been made to continue to use this technology. Both the accounts receivable and accounts payable functions are using and will continue to use traditional EDI for billing and invoicing purposes. This is due to many of the company's customers and suppliers, who continue to embrace EDI as well. The use of EDI has enabled FedEx to lower costs associated with specialized printing, paper, personnel, mailing, or postage. In addition, EDI has allowed high-speed matching of purchase orders, receipts, and invoices.

Other departments also use traditional EDI as a method of communications. The company's largest contract trucking vendors send their invoices directly to FedEx via traditional EDI. The invoices are then downloaded and matched with the route details and pricing within the computer system. All matched invoices are interfaced with the accounts payable system and paid while others are held in the department until they are researched and adjusted.

Although some departments are content to continue to use EDI in the current manner, others are investigating different ways to utilize traditional EDI. Currently, FedEx is not fully utilizing electronic funds transfer (EFT) for payment of invoices, and very few customers are using EFT for the payments to FedEx. The costs to the company can be expressed in terms of loss of cash flow and costs for printing and mailing paper checks. In addition, lost payment checks must be canceled and reissued, while checks received from customers must be applied to their accounts. The process can be made more difficult if remittance advices do not contain enough data to properly adjust accounts receivable. An electronic process to send payments as well as apply accounts receivable appears to be an advantage to the company. FedEx is capable of sending an EDI remittance advice, but has found that many of its suppliers are not able to receive the electronic detail. The company has resolved the issues surrounding sending remittance advices and has given its suppliers several options that can be tailored to fit a company's specific need. Now, there is a search underway for trading partners who have the ability to receive remittance advices along with EFT.

While there are many examples of FedEx's use of traditional EDI, the company is also moving beyond the confines of this technology. It has found that combining EDI with the Internet has created a more flexible and user-friendly tool.

Traditional EDI Combined with Internet Applications

Because FedEx has committed to EDI, it will continue to utilize this technology whenever it is convenient to do so. However, as the Internet becomes the preferred method of transacting business, the company is finding ways to incorporate the Internet into its current business practices and is looking for more applications for Internet technology. Currently, the company uses EDI for transmission of data and the Internet to provide catalogs and other information to company employees.

To assist in decreasing the costs associated with purchasing products and to reduce inventory levels, FedEx has purchased a product from a company called Ariba. Ariba is a requisitioning system that is housed on the FedEx intranet. The system is set up so suppliers can maintain a database of catalogs that can be accessed by anyone in the company. Employees who need additional information about what product can be purchased can connect directly to the supplier's Web site. Once the employee has made a requisition, it is routed to the manager for approval through the intranet. After the approval has been given, the orders are sent to suppliers either via traditional EDI or over the Internet and invoices are sent to FedEx via EDI. To increase the number of suppliers and decrease the total costs of doing business, FedEx actively looks for vendors who are both capable and willing to use electronic means (either EDI or the Internet) for both purchasing and invoicing.

The Ariba system has achieved several benefits for the company. Because it allows individual, authorized employees to make purchases on behalf of the company, the need for additional procurement staff is eliminated. The system also has a module for desktop receiving. Once an item has been physically received, a manager can key the receipt into Ariba. By doing so, the need for additional people designated for that particular function is removed. Ariba also interfaces with the FedEx inventory systems. This means that inventory levels can be automatically updated for purchases of inventory items and that there can be a more accurate inventory replenishment process.

Other departments have also found uses for combined Internet and EDI applications. One area, with the assistance of its supplier, has developed an intranet site that will be used to order employee safety awards. The site is slightly different from what is offered by Ariba. Because there is no requisitioning module, ordering is restricted to management. However, every employee has the ability to review the catalog that is provided. The orders will be sent to the supplier via traditional EDI. The supplier will also send EDI invoices, and FedEx will pay invoices via electronic funds transfer (EFT).

Most large customers have embraced EDI in all its forms. However, not every customer has the capability of receiving EDI invoices. For those customers, FedEx provides invoices in the manner easiest for the customer. This flexibility has paid off for the company. Approximately 30 percent of FedEx invoices are sent electronically to its customers. To convert the remainder, the company is embracing Internet technology. The company has developed FedEx Invoice Online, an Internet tool, whereby customers can view their invoices and select the ones for payment. They can then choose a method of paying the invoices, which can be either payment over the Internet or electronic funds transfer (EFT).

Accounts payable is also taking advantage of both the Internet and EDI. While electronic invoicing methods have given the department the ability to move toward automation, 80 percent of the vendors sent ten or fewer invoices in a one year time span. Because of the costs involved in setting up EDI, this method is not suitable for the majority of the company's small suppliers. The newest project underway is for an extranet-based solution. FedEx is developing a means to have these vendors key their invoices on a secured Internet site. The invoices will then be interfaced with the company mainframe.

As hard as it may be to believe, there are trading partners that are not suitable for either an EDI or Internet solution. FedEx has developed a "proprietary method" to handle these unique types of situations.

The Proprietary Method

The proprietary method of transmitting data is simply a data file that can be downloaded directly into the FedEx mainframe. Normally, the file is sent via e-mail over the Internet. While it is not EDI in the pure sense of the word, the ability to receive data in an electronic format has been helpful. The biggest issue with using a data file is the potential for errors. Many times the file is not a download of information in the computer systems of suppliers or vendors; it is data that is entered by clerks into a specific format. The fact that there is human intervention in the process creates the potential for errors such as keying mistakes.

The proprietary method of invoicing has proven successful in areas where traditional EDI is too cumbersome. This includes departments where there must be an ability to approve, reject, or partially pay invoices. With EDI, the entire invoice must be paid; there is no opportunity to dispute or pay parts of a bill. The proprietary method gives them the flexibility to do this.

The proprietary method has also been used successfully in automating the automotive aftermarket vendors. Because of the large fleet of trucks owned by FedEx, these suppliers generate the majority of small-dollar invoices (individual invoices of less than $5000 in total). However, the vendors have computer systems that are owned by the parent company. These systems do not allow for computer-to-computer invoicing. Using the proprietary method of invoicing, the supplier is more efficient at processing these invoices, and FedEx also gains the ability to pay each vendor in a more timely manner. This has been a "win" for both the vendors and FedEx.

The New Frontier of EDI at FedEx

The key to being able to pursue trading partners effectively is flexibility. Each trading partner must be able to communicate in the most convenient manner, while at the same time, FedEx must have the ability to be able to accept and send communications that match those of their trading partner. This is challenging to a company the size of FedEx, especially when part of the overall goal is to develop electronic communications to the fullest extent possible. Although the use of Internet and the proprietary method have substantially reduced the costs of EDI at FedEx, the cost of using the value-added network continues to rise as the company becomes more automated.

To achieve the combined goals of lower costs and flexibility, FedEx has created its own secured method of sending and receiving electronic documents called FedExNet. In order to connect to FedExNet, trading partners are provided with software. The software uses several different platforms including URL (for Internet access) FTP, dial-up access through an Internet Service Provider, or direct access (computer to computer). FedExNet has two major advantages. First, trading partners no longer have to use a value-added network in order to transmit documents via EDI. This makes becoming a business partner a more attractive proposition and saves them money. Secondly, FedEx has been able to utilize FedExNet to send and receive transmissions. Every time FedExNet is used, the company's cost of transacting business decreases.

Of course, there are some trading partners that still prefer to use the VANs. The networks provide documentation of the information that was transmitted. This is particularly useful should there be disputes about transmission times or data or if the trading partner does not receive transmissions. Trading partners who choose to use VANs cannot connect directly to the FedExNet. As a result, FedEx cannot take full advantage of the benefits of electronic data transfer via FedExNet. Because many of the largest suppliers and customers use traditional EDI, new solutions must be instituted. As an enhancement, interconnectivity between FedExNet and the various value-added networks will be established. This means that even if the trading partner continues to use its VAN for its personal reasons, FedEx can use the FedExNet and benefit from the flexibility and lower cost that this technology provides.

CONCLUSION

EDI may be older technology, but it has been proven to be a valuable tool to business. The use of EDI has helped FedEx lower inventory levels, pay bills faster, account for purchases and payments of product, provide for better relations with its customers, and decrease the amount of labor required to perform these functions. In addition, FedEx has tailored its EDI presence to support customers that have no EDI ability, no access to EDI through traditional methods, or no Internet-based EDI.

Clearly, trading partners are moving toward Internet-based methods of communication. To support these customers and suppliers and to continue to develop new market opportunities, FedEx has also created innovative solutions that use the Internet. This includes using the Internet for tracking packages and as a means for transmitting orders, receiving invoices and providing secure communications.

FedEx has developed Internet-based solutions that provide small and medium-sized businesses the same advantages that are enjoyed by the large companies. This was accomplished by harnessing the power of the Internet while continuing to embrace the current methods already in use by FedEx and other large companies. This includes using the Internet so those vendors can track the progress of their payments and billings in a method that is similar to tracking customer packages. These new methods should prove cost-effective for both FedEx and its suppliers and customers.

Most important, FedEx is willing to develop services that will benefit the customer as well as decrease the costs for the company. Although FedEx will be focusing efforts on Internet solutions, it does not plan to move away from Electronic Data Interchange (EDI) unless the market does so. "We want to do business however our customers want to do business."[12]

References

1. Carbone, James, "Supply Chain Management Gets Outsourced," *Purchasing Magazine,* February 11, 1999, p 69.
2. "Operations Benchmark'99," *Catalog Age,* January 1999.
3. "Raising the Bar," *Purchasing Magazine,* January 14, 1999, p. 44.

Notes

1. Avery, Susan, "Internet Report; E-commerce; MRO Supplies Online Ordering Lets Buyers Focus on Strategy," *Purchasing Magazine,* April 22, 1999, p. s17.
2. Virgoroso, Mark, "On the Internet, E-commerce Tackles Direct Production," *Purchasing Magazine,* July 15, 1999, p. 182.
3. Werner, Tom, "EDI Meets the Internet," *Transportation & Distribution,* June 1999, pp. 36–44.
4. Werner, 1999.
5. Hawker, Louise and Schwab, Tom, "Re-Engineering for Multi-Entity Communications — EDI Requirements for the New Marketplace," *Utility Automation,* September 1999, pp. 32–36.
6. Hawker and Schwab, 1999.
7. Helms, Glenn L. and Mancino, Jane , "Auditing/Technology: The Electronic Auditor," *Journal of Accountancy,* April 1998, p. 45.
8. Scheraga, Dan, "Technology: The New EDI," *Chain Store Age,* October 1, 1999, p. 110.
9. Isadore, Chris, "Air Carriers Enhance Sites," *Journal of Commerce,* January 12, 1999, p. 10A.
10. Kernahorn, Carole, "Achieving Competitive Advantage," *Chain Store Age,* October 1, 1999, p. 114.
11. Virgoroso, 1999.
12. Hickey, Kathleen, "Ex Focus on E-commerce," *Traffic World,* December 21, 1998, p. 50.

Chapter 16
Portfolio Techniques Eliminate Lingering IT Management Problems

Mark Bills

Although many companies make investment decisions based on cost/benefit analyses, the techniques they use limit their effectiveness. Often, costs not directly associated with the acquisition and deployment of the technology are underestimated or missed completely, tangible benefits are overstated, and intangible benefits, when considered, are not valued appropriately.

Even with well-coordinated business and technology strategies, many project-level investment decisions are disconnected from those strategies because of a lack of formal methods for gauging alignment. Management dictates such as, "We will only fund strategic systems" are inadequate because they fall victim to funding gamesmanship, wherein all projects are reclassified to support the dictum.

Finally, many organizations pursue inappropriate technologies because they mistakenly believe that state-of-the-art is a proxy for quality of support. While new technologies may be very promising, often more traditional alternatives may be adequate, or nontechnical solutions may be more effective.

The way to improve returns, improve alignment with business strategy, and ensure that technology initiatives are appropriate for the organization is to manage all technology expenditures as a portfolio of investments, with the goal of maximizing the performance of the entire portfolio. As with financial investments, maximizing performance will require "portfolio managers" to focus on investments that support the goal of the portfolio (in this case, support for business strategies), then select a set of investments that provide the best return for the desired level of risk.

A portfolio approach will improve returns on technology investments by highlighting those that provide the greatest value over their lifetime, without favoring short-term investments. It will enable managers to balance the risk in their portfolio to improve the probability that the benefits are realized, and it will highlight poor and redundant investments quickly, so cost savings can be achieved early in the investment management process.

A portfolio approach improves alignment because it makes alignment a key performance parameter. In order to provide investment opportunities that support this goal, each investment must be analyzed to determine how well it supports a company's strategic direction, or how it helps create or enhance key organizational capabilities. Such an approach highlights the relative performance of each investment regarding alignment, so a portfolio manager can select investments that provide the best combination of return and alignment for any level of risk.

The consideration of economic value, strategic alignment, and investment risk greatly reduces investments in inappropriate technologies because such investments will be seen as low value (high costs for new technologies without adequate financial benefits), low alignment (technology for technology's sake, rather than business benefit), or high risk (technology is promising, but difficult for the company to realize its benefits).

Managing technology investments as a portfolio can eliminate the lingering problems associated with technology management. The approach outlined below will improve the financial performance of technology investments, improve the alignment of business strategies and technology initiatives, and deliver solutions built on appropriate levels of technology.

STEP 1: INVENTORY ALL POTENTIAL IT INVESTMENTS

Examine all company budgets and collect basic information on each IT investment. Any significant request for capital that involves the purchase or development of technology (e.g., development of a new claims-processing system, rewriting legacy systems using object-oriented technology, purchase of a new database technology, or technology required to switch from a mainframe to a client/server architecture) should be considered an IT investment.

Every request for capital should be classified, including ongoing initiatives. It is important to examine ongoing initiatives because the value to be derived from an investment, or its strategic relevance, can change during the time it takes to complete the project. This ensures that large-scale efforts requiring more than one year to complete do not take on a life of their own.

STEP 2: ALLOCATE ALL INVESTMENTS TO A PORTFOLIO

Allocate each investment to a portfolio that represents a meaningful business concept. Portfolios might be created for functions, such as marketing and distribution, or for processes, such as warranty support and order fulfillment. In a multibusiness company, an investment may be allocated first to a business unit and then to a specific portfolio.

When companies allocate budgets to organizational subunits, total IT investment often is not coordinated across the business. By allocating each investment to a portfolio, managers can get a quick indication of how much support each area of the business is receiving. This also provides an easy way to highlight redundant investments, which occur when several managers pursue equivalent initiatives unbeknownst to one another.

For example, a telecommunications company comprised of six business groups, each of which controlled its own technology development budget, created portfolios for "Switching Technology Development" and "Administrative Systems." After allocating all of its investments, it immediately realized two things: there were five separate projects focused on the development of asynchronous transfer mode (ATM) technology, and over $8 million was budgeted for new administrative systems. Three of the five ATM projects were canceled and a cap of $2 million was set for administrative systems. The company saved over $10 million simply by reaggregating and examining the nature of its technology investments.

After allocating all investment opportunities, each portfolio should contain at least four or five potential investments. If a portfolio has more than 15 investments, a business is investing heavily in one area or it is using investment categories that are too broad.

STEP 3: ASSIGN PORTFOLIO MANAGEMENT RESPONSIBILITIES (SEE EXHIBIT 1)

Assign a team of portfolio analysts to each portfolio (or set of small portfolios). This team should be comprised of one or more individuals from both the technology and finance organizations. It is their responsibility to work with business representatives to analyze each investment opportunity and estimate its value, alignment, and risk.

A portfolio manager, who oversees the team of analysts, should be assigned to one portfolio (or a set of small, related portfolios). This individual should be a middle-level manager (or above) who has an understanding of the area of the business represented by the portfolio and experience in managing technology initiatives. The portfolio manager is responsible for selecting the subset of investments that will maximize the performance of the portfolio and for managing the performance of the final set of investments within the portfolio.

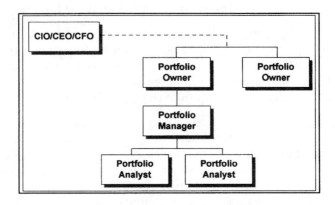

Exhibit 1. Portfolio Team Structure

A portfolio owner, who is advised by the portfolio manager, should be assigned to one portfolio (or a set of related portfolios). The portfolio owner is responsible for obtaining investment capital for the portfolio, working with other portfolio owners to ensure that total expenditures do not exceed investment limits, and establishing and enforcing general investment guidelines. The portfolio owner should be a senior executive whose area of responsibility is represented by the portfolio.

The CIO is responsible for setting and enforcing limits on total investment, setting spending limits for specific portfolios, and communicating general investment guidelines. (This assumes that the CIO has this authority. It may be the CFO or CEO.)

STEP 4: ESTIMATE THE VALUE CREATED BY EACH INVESTMENT OPPORTUNITY

Working with members of the business, the analysts estimate the economic value that will be created by each investment. A rough estimate can be used to highlight high-value investments quickly. A more rigorous analysis can then be used on this subset of investments.

Economic value provides a more comprehensive measure of value creation than other analytic techniques (NPV, IRR, etc.) because of its treatment of, among other things, taxes, depreciation, and working capital. Economic Value Analysis (EVA) also links operating performance improvements to financial performance, to ensure that both tangible and intangible benefits are properly valued.

For example, at a computer products manufacturer, a $600 thousand investment in a new customer service system was being considered, but it seemed only to have the "intangible" benefit of improving the productivity of the customer service representatives. Using EVA, a value tree was constructed that showed how reducing the average time per call for each representative would create $1 million of economic value for the company (with a return on invested capital of 179 percent). This previously labeled "intangible" benefit created tremendous value because customer service costs were shared across five different product divisions, so a small cost reduction had large-scale effects.

When performing this step, analysts should consider an investment's impact on the entire value chain, to ensure that implementation costs are not understated and financial benefits not overstated. An information services provider approved a data warehousing initiative because it would reduce annual data management costs by $6 million, but canceled it when further analysis revealed a downstream charge of $40 million for data conversion related to the production of client data bases.

STEP 5: DETERMINE HOW WELL EACH OPPORTUNITY SUPPORTS THE COMPANY'S STRATEGIC DIRECTION

Working with members of the business, the analysts assess how well each investment supports stated business strategies, supports key business processes, and creates or enhances key organizational capabilities.

The assessment requires investment proponents to explain to business and technology representatives how the initiative will support a company's strategic direction. The analysts conducting the assessment should offer alternative ways to achieve this support to ensure that apples-to-apples comparisons are considered.

A financial services company had several low-value investments in its Operations Support portfolio related to the development of an object-based applications platform. The investments provided little economic value because of the high costs associated with the development (development tools, training, etc.). But each investment was approved because it supported the development of a new organizational capability that the Executive Committee believed was essential to the company's continued success.

STEP 6: ESTIMATE THE RISK ASSOCIATED WITH EACH INVESTMENT

The CIO specifies which types of risk will be considered (operational, technical, etc.), and then the analysts estimate the risk associated with each investment. The assessment should tie risk to future cash flows for the investment being considered.

A business information services company was investing to convert one of its key mainframe systems to client/server. It considered the investment to be a "medium" risk (familiar business process, minimum operational change, high technology change). But when it tied risk to future cash flows, it realized that the technology risk might increase development costs significantly and delay release; and delayed release would jeopardize revenues in another part of the business. A complete analysis revealed that this "medium-risk" investment had only a 62 percent chance of creating any value at all, and a 4 percent chance of destroying significant value.

Formal assessment of risk forces investment proponents to consider how difficult it will be to adopt a specific technology and how difficult it will be for the organization to realize the financial and operating benefits calculated in previous steps. During this step, portfolio managers should work with business representatives to develop risk management strategies to reduce overall risk and improve the probability that the investment will deliver the stated benefits.

The level of formality used to estimate and manage risk can be tailored to the organization's comfort in dealing with risk. Early on, these are often high-level analyses that are refined as analysts and portfolio managers gain experience with the process.

STEP 7: ARTICULATE INVESTMENT MANAGEMENT GUIDELINES

Portfolio owners or other senior executives can influence the development of investment portfolios by articulating general guidelines that support business goals and investment priorities. For example, guidelines such as "no high-risk investments" or "favor value creation over strategic support" can guide portfolio managers as they select investments for their portfolios.

Investment guidelines should not be applied too rigorously early in the process because promising projects could be eliminated before construction of the final portfolio. The rigor with which the guidelines are applied should increase with each iteration of portfolio optimization.

STEP 8: OPTIMIZE THE INDIVIDUAL PORTFOLIOS

Each portfolio manager should work with the portfolio owner to analyze the relative performance of each investment and make initial investment decisions. The Opportunity Matrix (see sidebar) should be used for this analysis.

The initial decisions should be fairly straightforward, and the first pass should highlight fairly easy improvements (see sidebar). It is when the quality of investments is very good across the portfolio that the decisions get difficult.

If, after the first few passes, total spending limits require that more cuts be made, the total portfolio should be used to make investment decisions.

This ensures an optimal total return. (It should be noted that all investments in a portfolio may be eliminated if the portfolio contains low-grade or low-priority opportunities.)

STEP 9: COMBINE ALL PORTFOLIOS AND OPTIMIZE THE FINAL PORTFOLIO

When the portfolio managers and owners have optimized each portfolio, the portfolio owners and the CIO should analyze all of the investment opportunities and construct an optimal global portfolio.

This final step highlights redundancies, allows global management of risk, and allows the senior management team to enforce investment priorities. When cuts must be made on high-quality portfolios, the CIO should avoid the notion of sharing the pain by asking each portfolio owner to cut 10 percent more. Accept responsibility for establishing investment priorities and make cuts against specific portfolios.

STEP 10: INVEST IN AND MANAGE THE PROJECTS IN THE FINAL PORTFOLIO

Once a final portfolio of investments has been selected, each of the projects in the portfolio should receive funding. The individual portfolio managers have responsibility for overseeing the projects in their portfolio to ensure that they provide the anticipated returns.

During this process, the total number of investments is reduced significantly, allowing the portfolio managers to concentrate on the subset of projects that make important contributions to the long-term success of the business.

Investing in technology does not have to be fraught with error, uncertainty, and dismal returns. A process that highlights high-value investments that support the strategic direction of the business can eliminate lingering IT management problems and provide a framework for reasoned discussion among the many stakeholders and clients of the IT organization.

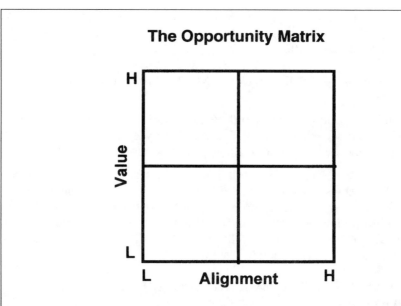

The Opportunity Matrix views technology initiatives as a portfolio of investment opportunities. It provides a framework that enables managers to:

- Determine the relative merits of each investment alternative
- Support the investment priorities of the business
- Ensure that the total portfolio provides unique benefits at an acceptable level of risk

Each investment is plotted on the matrix in a position that shows its potential for economic value creation and its support for the strategic direction of the business relative to other investment opportunities. The color or shading of the plot reflects the riskiness of the investment.

An investment opportunity may end up in any of the four quadrants, as follows:

High Value, High Alignment. These investments will create significant value for the company and enhance the company's strategic capabilities. For example, a financial services company may have the opportunity to invest in a new technology that would both reduce the costs associated with new service development and reduce its time to market for new services.

High Value, Low Alignment. These investments create significant value, but they do not support or enhance any strategic capabilities. For example, a manufacturing company that derives its competitive advantage by rapidly developing new products may find an investment in a new accounts payable system here. The investment would create significant value by reducing the costs associated with each payables transaction, but improving this area of the business would not enhance any strategic capability.

Low Value, High Alignment. These investments will not create significant value, but they will support or enhance one or more of a company's strategic capabilities. For example, a consumer packaged-goods company that derives its competitive advantage by being the first to market with new, high-end food products would find a system that improves their monitoring of consumer behavior here. The system may not deliver significant value directly, but it supports activities that do deliver value.

Many investments that have "soft" benefits or are related to the development of organizational infrastructure fall into this quadrant.

Low Value, Low Alignment. These investments will not create significant value, nor will they support or enhance any of the company's strategic capabilities.

Investment opportunities that fall into this quadrant should not be supported. If an investment in this area is necessary (e.g., a new payroll system), alternatives such as outsourcing and off-the-shelf purchases should be considered to ensure a minimum level of investment.

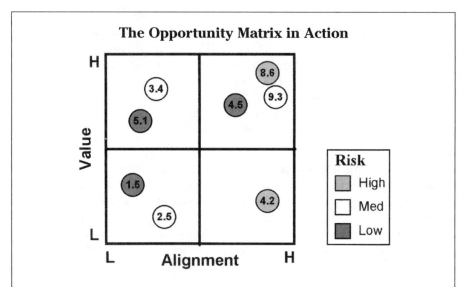

The Opportunity Matrix in Action

Functional managers at ABC Corp. submitted their budgets for the new fiscal year. The combined expenditures for information technology (IT) totaled $39.1 million. The CFO returned the proposed budgets and told them to work among themselves to ensure that IT expenditures did not exceed $20 million.

After the screams of agony and doubt subsided, the managers decided to use a portfolio approach to make their funding decisions. Their portfolio of opportunities is shown above. The numbers in the circles represent the amount of funding requested, in millions of dollars (project names and other details are omitted).

The group was pleased to see that over 57 percent of their planned expenditures fell into the High Value, High Alignment quadrant. Unfortunately, they realized that even if they funded only these projects, they would still exceed the $20 million limit ($22.4 million). They decided to examine each quadrant on its own, then see where they stood.

In the High Value/High Alignment quadrant, they decided not to support the $8.6 million request, since it was a large, high-risk investment. They kept the other two.

In the High Value, Low Alignment quadrant, they supported the $3.4 million request. They accepted its higher level of risk because it had a better return and required a smaller investment.

In the Low Value, Low Alignment quadrant, they eliminated the $2.5 million project and tried to eliminate the other, but found they needed to provide support for some in-house work that could not be outsourced. After further analysis, they found an alternative that required an investment of $800,000.

They decided not to fund the project in the Low Value, High Alignment quadrant because it required too large an investment for so little return and such high risk. They were comfortable with the decision since they felt the two projects in the High, High quadrant would provide adequate support for strategic capabilities.

When they added up the results, they were very pleased. Planned expenditures were reduced 54 percent to $18 million, with 77 percent of the total for High Value, High Alignment investments. The CFO was pleased too, and the company vowed to use this approach to manage all future IT investments.

Chapter 17
Developing a Global Information Vision

Tim Christmann

Information technology (IT) business executives are experiencing increasing professional pressures as their organizations strive to become truly global. In an effort to leverage their resources around the world and serve global customers, companies are turning to information technology as a means of achieving these objectives. IT capabilities have evolved to the point where some would argue that IT can, for the first time, be a strategic enabler in helping a company become truly global. For IT to be a strategic enabler for a company on a global basis, all major IT investments must be aligned with the business goals and strategies of the organization. One step toward aligning IT investments with business objectives and strategies is to bring key business and IT leaders to a common understanding or vision of how information will enable the company's strategy and future competitive position in the marketplace.

WHAT DOES IT MEAN TO BE GLOBAL?

In the age of economic globalization, it is not uncommon for companies to expand beyond domestic boundaries into foreign markets in search of new growth opportunities. If a company has operations around the world, does this make the company a global business? In short, the answer to this question is no. Being truly global involves mobilizing company resources around the world and presenting a common face for the company's key stakeholders — customers, suppliers, shareholders, and employees.

WHAT IS A GLOBAL INFORMATION VISION?

Start with what an information vision is not. It is not a statement conceived in the office of the CIO and posted above the door in the IT department. It is not about having the IT function achieve functional excellency through the use of leading edge technologies.

An information vision is a clear statement of how an enhanced information base will help the business achieve its strategic objectives. It is stated

0-8493-1273-6/02/$0.00+$1.50

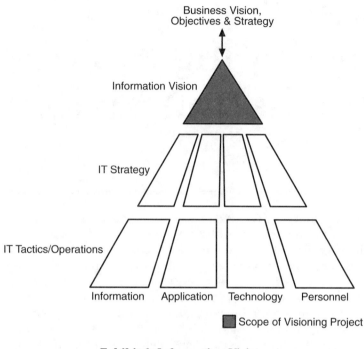

Exhibit 1. Information Vision

in business terms and contains a clear link to the competitive positioning of the business. A vision also indicates business outcomes that are recognizable by business and IT leaders alike.

As shown in Exhibit 1, within the IT decision-making hierarchy, the information vision provides a link between the business strategy and objectives and the IT strategy. Bringing the key business stakeholders to agreement on the information vision provides direction throughout the company on where IT investments should be focused to bring the most value to the company.

OBJECTIVES — PAY-OFF IDEA

Why is an Information Vision Needed in a Company?

There are a number of objectives that one should achieve while facilitating the development of a company's information vision:

1. Raise the understanding at all levels in the company of how information and information technology can and will add value for the company.
   - Often executives see the enormous operational and capital expenditures for IT and wonder what value they are getting for their

money. They fear that deployment of technology solutions may be based on an underlying desire to have the latest technological innovation rather than the pure business value of the investment. Demonstrating the value of IT investments does not stop once an information vision has been established. However, developing an information vision does put into clear business terms how information does and will add value to the business.

- Do business decision-makers think about information or IT when they are devising their business strategies? Business decision-makers often do not understand fully the capabilities of IT or do not think about how an enhanced information base can enable their business strategies. Engaging key business leaders in the exercise of developing a vision for information in the company will raise their level of awareness.

2. Promote better alignment of IT projects and the business objectives.
   - How often is it heard about companies that have sizable investments in state-of-the-art systems to improve an area or function that is not core to the business? Afterwards they often question how such an enormous investment of capital and human resources actually has changed the company's competitive position? By engaging key business and IT leaders in developing an information vision linked to clear business outcomes, a common understanding is reached with respect to where the value-adding opportunities exist for IT projects. Any project or opportunity not in line with the vision comes immediately under question.

3. Keep IT personnel focused on achieving an enhanced information base for the company rather than implementing new technologies for technology-sake.
   - The visioning exercise creates a better focus on the I rather than the T in information technology. Focusing on information forces people to question technology investments that do not result in a sufficient improvement to the base of information that will enhance the company's competitive position.

4. Develop an understanding of how a common information vision can benefit the global units and the company as a whole — not just another head-office exercise.
   - Often the words of a vision or mission mean little to those not directly involved in composing the statements. Especially if a company operates businesses around the world that have a certain amount of local autonomy, these units may offer some resistance if their interests have not been represented properly in developing the vision or if they fail to realize how the vision improves the position of their business. For this reason, it can be beneficial to indicate how enhanced use of information will benefit the local units as well.

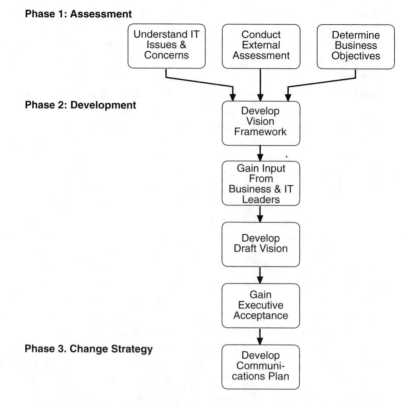

Phase 1: Assessment

Phase 2: Development

Phase 3. Change Strategy

Exhibit 2. The Process for Developing an Information Vision

The Process

To develop an information vision effectively, it is important to understand that perhaps the greatest value is in the process of developing the vision rather than in the words of the vision itself. To gain the full value of this exercise, the right level of people in the organization, from both the business and IT community, must be involved in developing the vision. Having the right people involved, especially from the business community, helps to ensure relevant content, organizational buy-in, and business ownership. To ensure relevancy and ownership, the vision must be articulated using words that the business community understands; therefore, the words themselves must come from key business leaders. Exhibit 2 outlines the process for developing a global information vision. Exhibit 3 provides the critical success factors for making this a reality.

Phase 1: Assessment

If one already has a clear understanding of the current situation of information and information technology in the company then this phase can be

Exhibit 3. Critical Success Factors

The following points represent critical success factors in ensuring successful development of an information vision.

- **The right level of sponsorship**

  It is important that this initiative be championed at the highest level in the organization to have the desired impact. An information vision should be viewed as an extention of the business strategy by stating how information will help the company achieve its business objectives. Therefore, a successful information visioning initiative will have a sponsor positioned at the same level in the company as the sponsor of a business strategy initiative. These initiatives might even be sponsored by the same individual.

- **Involvement from key business leaders**

  The objectives of the visioning process are aggressive given that they often require the thinking and decision making of management and staff throughout the company to be changed. One of the best ways to achieve buy-in from these people is to involve them as much as possible in the development process. Executive involvement is key. These people need to be involved to ensure that the vision is aligned clearly with the direction of the business. Also, their involvement lends credibility and importance to the initiative. Senior executives are often somewhat removed from decisions made at lower levels in the company, especially in a global company where decision making often is decentralized. Therefore, it can be beneficial to have management involvement in the development process from various business areas and geographic regions. Choose representatives from the business areas or regions that are seen as critical to the business and individuals who are viewed as leaders in their respective areas.

- **The right language**

  It is critical for the vision to be perceived as business-owned and business-led if the stated objectives are to be achieved. Therefore, the vision must be stated in business terms.

- **Linked to business outcomes**

  Linking the vision to specific business outcomes helps people to understand exactly how improving the information base in the company results in business value, especially if they are not involved in developing the vision. It also may help to reveal in which areas IT projects may provide the greatest opportunity in terms of positioning information as a strategic enabler for the business.

---

condensed. However, it is important to note that there are distinct benefits in conducting a formal assessment to ensure that the understanding is complete.

As part of the assessment, there are three main questions that need to be answered:

1. *What is the current state of the IT?*
The assessment phase provides an opportunity to gain a clear understanding of the current situation and bring to the surface any issues or concerns about the current state of information or information technology in the company. These issues or concerns not only represent areas of improvement, they also may represent significant barriers to changing the way

people think about the ability of the information and information technology to add value to the business. The business community needs to know that their concerns are being heard. Soliciting input from key business leaders also provides a prime opportunity to begin developing buy-in and ownership for the vision itself. It is also important to acknowledge past successes or progress that the company has made in IT projects. These successes are often not well-known throughout the company and serve to boost the company's collective confidence in its ability to deliver business value through IT.

2. What are the major external forces or pressures facing IT?
If possible it is beneficial to understand how competitors in the same industry or companies with similar operations are using IT. Presenting this information may serve two purposes. First, if it is determined that competitors are further advanced in the way they are employing IT, it may serve as a strong imperative for change. Exploring how similar companies use IT to gain competitive advantage also can raise the level of education within the company, heightening awareness of what is possible. In addition, it may be beneficial to articluate what the current possibilities are in IT today. People may ask, why does the company need a global vision about information? It is important for them to understand that for the first time, global communications and realtime information sharing are possible and can deliver significant business value.

3. What are the business vision, objectives, and strategy?
This third question is perhaps the most important for a number of reasons. First of all, the information vision must be aligned with the vision of the company as a whole. Often the company vision is not stated explicitly or understood well. Therefore, it is important to conduct interviews with key business leaders to gain a clear understanding of where the business leadership intends to take the company in the future and what the critical success factors are for the company as a whole and its core business areas. Secondly, conducting interviews with key business leaders helps build ownership for the vision within the business community. People are more likely to champion the vision when they are part of its development. Finally, it is critical for the vision itself be be stated in business terms. Exhibit 4 provides an example of typical findings that may result from the assessment phase.

The Change Imperative. One of the most important outcomes of the assessment phase is to build a clear understanding of the need for the company to change. The change imperative must be articulated clearly in terms of issues and challenges facing IT, changing business objectives and strategies, and the new IT capabilities that are available. It is important that the executive group understands the outcomes of the assessment phase and agrees on the need for change.

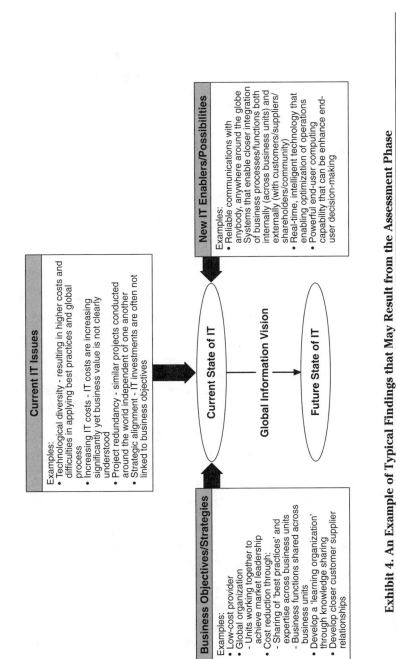

Current IT Issues

Examples:
- Technological diversity - resulting in higher costs and difficulties in applying best practices and global process
- Increasing IT costs - IT costs are increasing significantly yet business value is not clearly understood
- Project redundancy - similar projects conducted around the world independent of one another
- Strategic alignment - IT investments are often not linked to business objectives

New IT Enablers/Possibilities

Examples:
- Reliable communications with anybody, anywhere around the globe Systems that enable closer integration of business processes/functions both internally (across business units) and externally (with customers/suppliers/shareholders/community)
- Real-time, intelligent technology that enabling optimization of operations
- Powerful end-user computing capability that can be enhance end-user decision-making

Business Objectives/Strategies

Examples:
- Low-cost provider
- Global organization
  - Units working together to achieve market leadership
- Cost reduction through:
  - Sharing of 'best practices' and expertise across business units
  - Business functions shared across business units
- Develop a 'learning organization' through knowledge sharing
- Develop closer customer supplier relationships

Current State of IT

Global Information Vision

Future State of IT

Exhibit 4. An Example of Typical Findings that May Result from the Assessment Phase

213

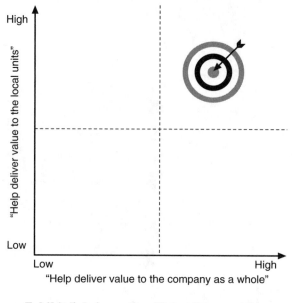

Exhibit 5. Information Vision Framework

Phase 2: Development

Different approaches may be used to develop the vision. Perhaps the most effective approach is to facilitate a group of key business leaders, including senior executives and key management personnel through each of the following steps. Although effective, this approach is often very difficult to execute especially if the key business leaders are situated around the world. It is important to keep in mind that having active involvement from as many key business leaders as possible is critical to the success of the initiative. Therefore, if it is not possible to conduct steps one through four as one group, it may be necessary to break the group of targeted participants into smaller focus groups.

Step 1: Develop Vision Framework. Establishing a framework may not be essential but can be beneficial both in developing the vision and communicating it. A framework can provide an effective structure in which to organize ideas regarding how an enhanced information base can enable the business to achieve its business objectives. The framework also can prove very useful in communicating how the vision can be linked to specific business outcomes. Exhibit 5 provides an example of a framework that could be used for a global company that is looking for ways to articulate how a common vision for an enhanced information base not only will improve the performance of the company as a whole, but also will improve the performance of the individual business units around the world.

214

Step 2: Gain Input from Key Stakeholders. Depending on the audience, different techniques can be used to gain input from key stakeholders. Often it is difficult to obtain extensive time with top executives. Therefore, it may be beneficial to include specific questions during the executive interviews in the assessment phase that will provide insight into how enhanced information may better enable the business to achieve its objectives.

The following are examples of specific questions that could be used to facilitate input from the key business leaders:

- How can information help the company attain its vision?
- What information would make a difference in the various business units? For customers? For managers?
- What impediments exist today to using information to add value to the organization and to make a difference to the bottom line?

Using the sample framework presented in Step One, Exhibit 6 provides some examples of possible ways to add value or enable business strategies. These examples, when linked to the vision, provide clear business outcomes that may result from developing an enhanced information base.

Step 3: Develop Draft Information Vision. This step involves developing a simple statement that combines the strategic objectives and critical success factors of the business with the feedback that has been given regarding how the business could change as a result of having an enhanced information base. An example of this is shown in Exhibit 7.

How the draft information vision itself is assembled depends largely on the development approach that has been chosen. If all key business leaders are in one room, then the words can be drafted by the group as a whole. If this approach is not possible or if there is already general concensus among the participants on the business outcomes that can be achieved through an enhanced information base, the vision can be assembled and presented to the key business leaders for review and approval.

Step 4: Gain Executive Acceptance. It is important that acceptance be given for the vision by the various business leaders involved in developing it. Once again, the vision must be business-owned and business-led. Acceptance will help to ensure that each of the leaders involved will serve as a champion for building an enhanced information base in his or her respective business area or region.

Phase 3: Change Strategy

A successfully executed information vision development process will generate a significant amount of awareness among key business leaders of how information can be a strategic enabler for the company. However, it is

Exhibit 6. Examples of Business Outcomes from Developing an Enhanced Information Base

An enhanced information base will deliver value to the company as a whole by	An enhanced information base will help to deliver value to the local units by
• enabling optimization of operations between business units • enabling a learning organization through experience sharing • capturing knowledge about customer needs so that, whenever pertinent, it flows through the company's value chain • allowing the internal organization to be transparent to the customer around the world • enabling people to be more a part of the company as well as their local groups; people then will act in the common interest of global company rather than only in the interest of their own group at the expense of the others • decreasing complexity, thereby decreasing costs and improving customer service • facilitating organizational change; reducing organizational boundaries; enabling the creation of virtual teams • increasing decision-making and implementation speed	• enabling optimization of operations within each business unit • capturing and exploiting innovative ideas and opportunities more quickly, more easily • tapping into global expertise for problem solving • tapping into global supplier options to reduce costs • improving operational stability, consistency, and reliability • enabling production capacity optimization • increasing decision-making and implementation speed

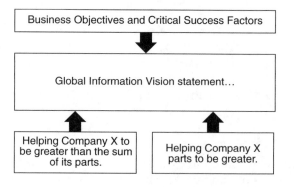

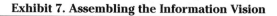

Exhibit 7. Assembling the Information Vision

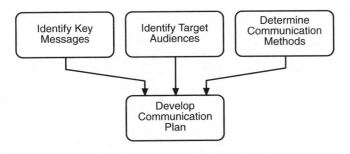

Exhibit 8. Approach to Developing Communication Plan

important to build on the momentum that has been achieved and have a plan for making all company management aware of the vision for how information will be leveraged to create business value. Do not make the mistake of relying on passive or informal communication methods. Instead, a detailed communication plan should be developed to ensure that all key stakeholder groups are aware of the vision. Exhibit 8 highlights a simple approach for developing a communication plan.

KEY MESSAGES

First, the key messages that the target audience should hear and understand must be identified. Given the visioning process that has just been completed, typical messages would include

- Business Vision and Strategy — Pick key phrases that link directly to the information vision.
- Information Vision — Emphasize that the statement has been developed and approved by key business leaders.
- Business Outcomes — The business outcomes that can result from developing an enhanced information base are key to making people understand how the vision will change the business.

AUDIENCES

Generally, all decision-makers in the company should be made aware of the key messages coming out of the visioning exercise. For the purposes of the communication plan, it is important to identify specifically those audiences that will require targeted communications. Once these audiences have been identified, it is a worthwhile exercise to determine the roles of each group with regard to their use of information and IT and to gain an understanding of their specific communication requirements. For example, some groups simply may need to be made aware of the key messages although others may need to incorporate this thinking into their decision-making. The level of communication required for a specific audience will dictate the method used.

COMMUNICATION METHODS

Typically, there are a variety of communication methods available within a company ranging from media tools, such as e-mail or company newsletters, to face-to-face communications, such as executive presentations. It may be necessary to create some specific communication opportunities to match the objectives of the visioning initiative. Compiling a list of the various methods available will help in developing the communication plan.

DEVELOPING THE COMMUNICATION PLAN

Assembling the communication plan involves determining which methods will be used to communicate the key messages to the target audiences.

CONCLUSION AND NEXT STEPS

Once the information vision has been developed and the communication plan has been launched, one may ask oneself, where to from here? Once again, given the momentum established during the visioning exercise, it is important to build on this momentum. The following are typical initiatives or deliverables that may provide further value to a company.

INFORMATION STRATEGY

Building on the stated business outcomes from the visioning exercise, an information strategy would provide further detail regarding what the specific information requirements are to achieve these outcomes. The strategy would answer questions such as: What knowledge is critical to the success of the company? How can this knowledge be leveraged further? What are the key strategic and operational decisions in the company? What information would enable these decisions to be made more effectively? An information strategy also provides detail regarding where IT investments should be targeted to deliver the greatest value to the company.

Information Management Plan

Once people acknowledge that information is a valuable resource for the company, they will begin to realize the importance of managing this resource effectively. An information management plan identifies how key information will be defined, managed, delivered, and protected. The plan also identifies who will be responsible for defining, managing, delivering, and protecting key information.

Chapter 18

Aligning Strategies, Processes, and Information Technology: A Case Study

Rainer Feurer
Kazem Chaharbaghi
Michael Weber
John Wargin

Process innovations and process redesigns must frequently employ technology to achieve major improvements in performance. Information technology has become an enabler for newly designed processes by eliminating limitations of time, location, or organizational structure or by providing a new basis for differentiation. This can only be achieved, however, when processes and information technology are carefully aligned with the overall organization's objectives and interfunctional teamwork.

While there is a general consensus among practitioners that business/IT alignment is necessary, the way to achieve it is often unclear. This is because business strategies are usually defined first, and the operations and supporting strategies, including technologies, are subsequently aligned. Such a sequential approach defines strategies, processes, and actions in light of the technologies available, as opposed to identifying technologies that drive the critical success factors.

A better approach is one in which strategies, processes, technologies, and actions are defined and aligned concurrently. The aim of this chapter is to present a business alignment approach, one used and developed by

0-8493-1273-6/02/$0.00+$1.50
© 2002 by CRC Press LLC

Hewlett-Packard Company for designing and implementing new business processes that are enabled and supported by new generations of information systems.

This approach has been practiced over several years, both internally and externally, generating a portfolio of best practices. The well-defined activities are closely linked and are applied by multifunctional teams for the purpose of business reengineering as well as redesigning core business processes. The whole approach is complemented by a strong focus on teamwork, specialized and objective-driven business units, and a commitment to quality and customer satisfaction.

FRAMEWORK FOR BUSINESS ALIGNMENT

Strategies are only effective when they are readily translated into actions. This implies that supporting information technologies need to be highly responsive. Business processes should be continuously optimized through the application of relevant technologies and carried out by high-performance teams. Strategies must therefore be:

- Formulated by closely examining the role of technology as an enabling source
- Translated into actions through highly interactive processes that consider all current and future business factors

In the past, the design of business processes and information technology applications focused on achieving incremental benefits. Flexibility and ability to react to major changes were largely neglected. The business alignment framework in Exhibit 1 links any given strategy and its corresponding actions.

Linking Strategy and Actions

Strategies determine the critical success factors that in turn define the necessary business processes and their information needs. The availability, cost, and flexibility of different technologies may limit their selection; therefore, business processes must be translated into feasible application models while information requirements are translated into workable data models. In this way, the gap between the ideal and workable solutions can be minimized, while ensuring a logical linkage between strategy and optimized actions.

The aim of such a framework is twofold:

1. To make process changes without being restricted by or limited to existing technology, applications, and suboptimal data structures
2. To make visible the impact of new technologies on processes, and vice versa

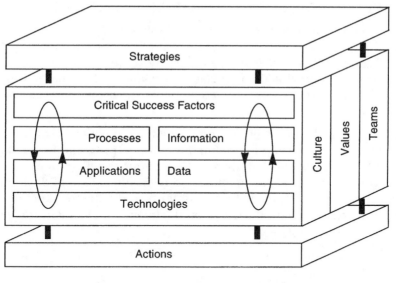

Exhibit 1. Business Alignment Framework

The business alignment framework takes into account the necessary process changes resulting from changes in the environment as well as potential advancements in technology. Because any change in strategy and technology potentially results in a change in the value system, culture, and team structures of the organization, it is vital to include these additional factors within the overall framework.

By employing this framework, Hewlett-Packard (HP) has experienced a number of benefits, including:

- The optimization of all the business processes with the support of integrated technology, as opposed to the suboptimization of individual processes and organization units with the support of fragmented technology
- A consistent focus on processes that maximize stakeholder values
- A common understanding of issues and future targets throughout the organization
- A high level of transparency and flexibility to act and react to changes stemming from the competitive environment as well as improvements in technology
- A high level of commitment from people throughout the organization

In this framework, target processes, technologies, and standards drive the selection of potential solutions. User participation forms an integral part of the framework and helps to ensure fast and effective implementation.

IMPLEMENTING THE BUSINESS ALIGNMENT FRAMEWORK

The business alignment framework is implemented by cross-functional teams that include members from different organizational and functional units. Team members are given a charter by senior-level management to initiate and implement major changes. To prevent tunnel vision, teams are sometimes supported by external consultants and a key role is assigned to management.

According to the structure of the framework, business processes and information requirements are defined in parallel to technology enablers and models, which are then linked throughout the alignment process. Objectives and measures are defined and reviewed in light of the intended overall strategy, which leads to adjustments and refinements of existing results. The approach used to develop the business alignment framework includes the following modules:

1. Breakthrough objectives and process links
2. Business models
3. Technology enablers and models
4. Solution mapping and selection
5. Functional mapping

Breakthrough Objectives and Processes

The alignment process commences with the existing business strategy or strategic direction of the organization or organizational unit. Based on a strategy review, potential breakthrough objectives are defined. Breakthrough objectives create a distinct competitive differentiation in the eyes of the customer when implemented. This can be achieved through significant improvements in performance in the area of cost, introduction or distribution of new products, outsourcing of noncore activities, consolidation scenarios, or modification of supplier relationships.

After a comprehensive list of potential breakthrough objectives is defined, the most critical (usually two to five) objectives are selected. These objectives form the basis of critical success factors, which in this sense are all those factors that have to go right to achieve a breakthrough. In parallel, potential obstacles that prevent the achievement of the breakthroughs are identified. These may fall in different categories including management practices, technology support, training, and goal conflicts between different stakeholders.

Innovative, Core, and Supportive Processes

The next step is formulating the key processes that have a major effect on achieving the breakthrough objectives. These processes basically support the critical success factors. Processes that support several critical

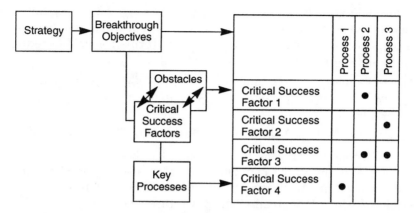

Exhibit 2. Breakthrough Objectives, Critical Success Factors, and Key Processes

success factors are classed as innovative processes. These usually involve multi-functional activities that directly create stakeholder value. They become the focus of business, process, and information models. Other process categories include supportive and core processes that, although important, do not result in a differentiation in the eyes of the stakeholders. This is because these processes usually correlate with only one or two critical success factors. Exhibit 2 shows diagrammatically the way in which breakthrough objectives and innovative processes are identified. Exhibit 3 demonstrates the classification process used to determine innovative, core, and supportive processes based on their potential impact on cost, quality, speed, and flexibility.

Business Models

Business models are developed for describing innovative processes and their role within the overall organization. HP designs business models not

Exhibit 3. Process Classification and Potential Impact

Major Processes	Process Classification	Process Impact			
		Cost	Quality	Speed	Flexibility
Manage product and parts information	Core	x		x	x
Control production	Innovative		x	x	x
Plan and procure material	Innovative	x	x	x	x
Manage material flow	Core/Innovative	x		x	x
Manufacturer products	Core	x	x	x	x
Distribution	Core		x	x	x
Financial	Supportive				x

only for facilitating communications and achieving consensus, but also as a basis for identifying enabling technologies that will allow the organization to achieve major improvements in performance or differentiation. This requires three equally important views:

1. The description of business activities or processes (process model)
2. The definition of business information requirements (information model)
3. The interaction between the business activities and information

Business models can yield highly adapted and flexible IT infrastructures that are geared not only to specific needs but also provide benefit to the entire organization. At HP, the creation of business models is performed by several cross-functional teams. The advantages include:

- Users can be closely involved in the modeling process and committed to the definition of their processes from a very early stage.
- Well-defined models can be reused and adapted to other business areas and subsidiaries.
- The work of parallel teams is more efficient if supported by a common structure and hierarchical decomposition.

The business models developed take a tree-shaped form in which each global process can be described as a collection of activities and subprocesses. While global processes are modeled by top-level management or core teams, the more detailed representations are produced by specialist subteams. In developing and linking the models, inconsistencies, omissions, and misunderstandings are observed and corrected. In parallel to developing the process hierarchy, information models are developed.

Information Models

Information models aim to identify and describe business data objects (e.g., assets, orders, locations), together with their interrelationships. For example, an order combined with a location creates the data object called Shipment. Information modeling is therefore concerned with two major questions: (1) What information does the business need? and (2) What interrelationship exists with other information?

To support this goal, data objects must be driven by business needs and defined in isolation from existing information systems and applications. This is in contrast to the approach used in the past, in which data was designed and created for a specific application system that supported a single function from a limited perspective. This method leads to a high level of data redundancy and inconsistency. Information models, however, regard information as detached from existing or potential applications with the aim of improving the timeliness, completeness, and accuracy of shared information while decreasing redundancy.

There are two levels of information models. At the highest level of abstraction, the global information model identifies the ten or twenty data objects or clusters that are critical for the implementation of breakthrough objectives. This model is primarily used for communication with senior-level management and setting a framework for detailed modeling performed by dedicated subteams.

The second type of model contains a more detailed explosion with approximately 100 to 200 data objects. This model is also used to validate the appropriate process models in the process hierarchy.

Although the process and information models are developed independent of any application systems , they help to determine where technology can play an enabling role, as discussed next.

Technology Enablers and Models

The impact of information technology has several characteristics, the most important ones being:

- *Integrative.* IT supports the coordination and integration between different activities and processes.
- *Direct.* IT is used to improve the sequence of activities and processes so that they can be carried out faster and in parallel. Furthermore, unnecessary intermediaries can be eliminated.
- *Information.* IT is used to capture process information for knowledge generation, process analysis, and decision making.

Standards

Technology can be a cost-effective enabler only if certain standards are defined and adhered to. It is therefore necessary to examine and define which technology elements based on today's technology and standards as well as likely future trends can be applied in the implementation of the business processes.

The selected standards should not be seen as a limiting factor but rather as a mechanism that improves exchangeability of technology, flexibility, and cost-effectiveness and efficiency. The definition of standards, for example, in the area of IT might include such considerations as the design of the physical and logical network concepts, including internal and external communications needs; operating systems; databases; as well as the definition of potential hardware requirements and implementation scenarios, including outsourcing and multi-vendor scenarios.

Solution Mapping and Selection

Once the business models and the technology standards are defined, the next step is to select solutions that best support and enable the defined

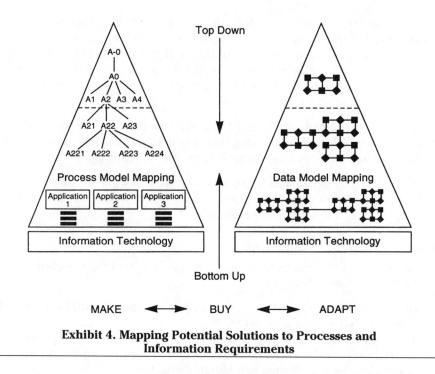

Exhibit 4. Mapping Potential Solutions to Processes and Information Requirements

business processes. This can be achieved by matching the defined process and information models to the process and data models of existing and potential newly developed solutions. This forms a top-down, bottom-up approach as shown in Exhibit 4.

Using this approach, processes that can be enabled or supported by information technology are combined into clusters of potential applications. These could include financial systems, manufacturing resource planning, production control, sales tracking, and customer databases. This clustering is performed at a very high level and as such does not yet include detailed functional requirements. In a parallel activity, key objectives for the selection of application solutions, together with importance ratings, are defined.

Based on the solution clusters and the selected objectives and weightings, a market analysis of existing application solutions is performed in which the top two to four candidates within each area are shortlisted and then checked as to their fit with the process and information models and their adherence to agreed-on standards and core concepts. In addition, business fit is evaluated according to criteria such as the vendor's size, availability of localized application versions, and references.

The selection process is continued by translating the process models into detailed functionality requirements; it may also include prototyping of

226

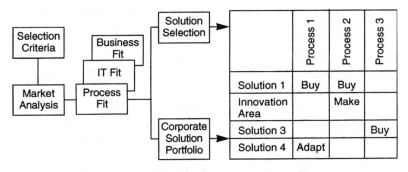

	Process 1	Process 2	Process 3
Solution 1	Buy	Buy	
Innovation Area		Make	
Solution 3			Buy
Solution 4	Adapt		

Exhibit 5. Solution Mapping and Selection

selected processes or parts of the process. This analysis is used to determine whether:

- The newly defined business processes can be supported or enabled using standard applications
- It is possible to modify and adapt existing application solutions
- It is necessary to develop custom application solutions

Developing a Corporate Solutions Portfolio

During this step, it is also possible to develop a corporate solutions portfolio of applications that can be shared across different organizational units or used for similar processes. Exhibit 5 illustrates the solution mapping and selection process.

Functional Mapping

Solutions and applications are selected on the basis of process and information models defined by teams of planners and users. Once a specific application is selected, it is possible to go back and really start the process of matching the key functions to the actual selected applications to determine the extent of application adaptation or process change required. This process is termed "functional mapping."

Functional mapping (Exhibit 6) is the beginning of the implementation process. However, it must still be regarded as part of the overall business alignment framework because modifications and changes in business processes and solution adaptation are still possible.

The defined business processes are checked with users in terms of the detailed fit with specific business or process events and compared to the functionality of the selected solutions. In cases where a gap exists, two alternatives are examined:

1. Modify the business process.

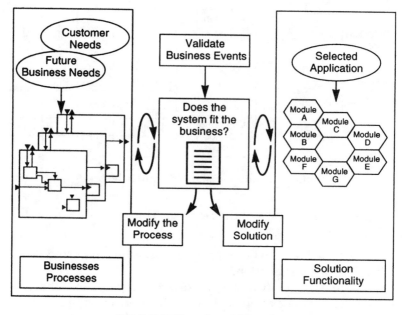

Exhibit 6. Functional Mapping

2. Modify the application solution, which may involve minor changes such as report generation or major changes such as recoding of specific software modules.

In cases where the implementation of a breakthrough objective depends on the existence of a specific process, the decision will always be the modification of the application, rather than sacrificing the process in the defined form. The process of functional mapping operates best if users can test to what extent the selected solution supports the newly defined processes; for this purpose, HP uses piloting centers and laboratories.

INDUSTRIAL APPLICATIONS

Two industrial applications demonstrate the potential of the business alignment framework. The first application reflects work carried out by HP for another organization in support of the construction of a transplant operation. This application illustrates the way in which the framework can be applied to a newly designed business and drive the selection of open systems based applications to significantly reduce IT costs. The second application is internal and demonstrates the way in which the framework can be applied to redefine existing operations. It incorporates additional considerations, such as finding a compromise between conflicting goals and objectives of different groups involved in the process of change.

Application to a Greenfield Operation

Hewlett-Packard was selected to help a large multi-national car manufacturer develop a new transplant operation in the United States. This transplant was considered to be the first step in the redesign of the organization toward a worldwide network of factories and represented a "greenfield" operation, and as such was not subjected to existing technologies, processes, work methods, and support systems. The only constraints were the short implementation time frame (18 months), certain environmental conditions, and the network of suppliers, customers, and the parent company.

The first step involved the creation of teams, together with the identification and definition of the key project requirements based on strategic considerations of the overall organization as well as internal and external benchmarks. The most important requirement was defined as achieving a premium on flexibility and adaptability in terms of new products or models, quantity, expandability, and "change of charter" (e.g., serving worldwide versus selected markets).

A balanced approach between using people and technology would allow the organization to more rapidly adapt the transplant strategy or processes to market requirements while at the same time being more motivational to the transplant personnel. The aim was to commit flexible resources at the latest possible moment in the production process, thus saving additional amounts of money. Another requirement was that the factory and infrastructures should be driven by innovative processes, thus allowing the acquisition and transfer of new knowledge and best practices. Finally, the project aimed to establish new levels and types of partnerships, thus recognizing the role of the transplant as part of a larger network. After having identified these and other key requirements, their significance and the competitive deficit of the organization were determined in form of a gap analysis. The resulting focus pattern (Exhibit 7) drove the execution of the business alignment and was regularly used for control purposes.

The breakthroughs in the area of process innovation and technology enablers were defined using cross-functional teams from both organizations. The breakthroughs, together with some of the critical success factors for the project, are shown in Exhibit 8. The next step was to identify key processes that would have a major impact on achieving the objectives. High-level business models of the transplant and its environment were developed and subsequently translated into key processes. These key processes were segmented into innovative, core, and supportive processes to identify those that would have the strongest impact on overall transplant performance. These subprocesses were subsequently modeled by cross-functional teams in a hierarchical way, as previously described. Exhibit 9 is a simplified representation of the highest level (A0) process model that contains the four subprocesses.

TASK 1: DESIGNING SUPPLY CHAINS FOR COMPETITIVE ADVANTAGE

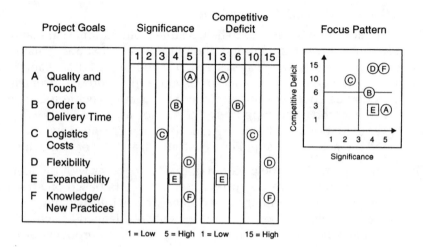

Exhibit 7. Project Goals, Significance, and Competitive Deficit

Critical Success Factors / Information Technology Breakthroughs	Open systems	Global vendors and suppliers	High level of transparency on process structure and interrelationships with other processes	Multifunctional teamwork	Multiple vendors	Scalability of systems	Standard solutions wherever possible	Incorporation of members of existing plants
Integrated and standardized applications (cost efficiency, flexibility, no vendor dependency)	•	•			•	•	•	
Process, team driven design and execution of approach			•	•				•
IT cost/product at 50% of cost level in existing plants	•	•	•		•	•	•	
Modularity of systems (for flexibility)			•		•	•	•	
Ability to transfer experience to other plants		•		•		•	•	•

Exhibit 8. Breakthroughs and Critical Success Factors in the Area of Technology Enablers

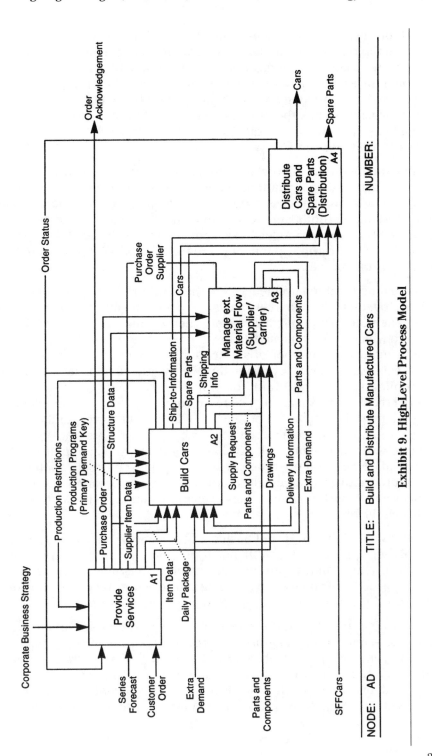

NODE: AD   TITLE: Build and Distribute Manufactured Cars   NUMBER:

Exhibit 9. High-Level Process Model

Each of the subprocesses was modeled and documented accordingly. While the top levels were modeled by a core team of planners, the subprocesses were modeled by dedicated and specialist subteams that included possible future users as well as experienced users of existing processes. This consistent modeling approach, supported by a computerized tool, made it possible to link the process models, rapidly and completely identify conflicts, and meet the required timeframe. In parallel to the process models, information models were generated.

Using the hierarchical process models, structure and resource requirements for material, information, financial flows, and personnel could be defined. In addition, process report requirements, including manual and computerized methods and access to central systems, could be easily identified. The process models were applied in the specification of potential solutions by drawing up functional requirements lists for the activities within a certain process.

These functional requirements were then clustered into potential applications, together with a market analysis of commercially available applications. The potential applications were then evaluated to determine the extent to which they would satisfy the functional requirements. It was possible to reduce the number of applications to five potential final candidates. This was achieved by evaluating the functional fit of several potential applications for different solution clusters (e.g., bill-of-material, material requirements planning, material flow), together with their level of integration. In the evaluation of functional fit, a level corresponding to 60 percent or above was considered acceptable. The analysis also served as a cross-check that commercially available solutions could be applied in the running of a transplant operation in general. If only one application would have scored above 50 percent, it would have been necessary to reconsider the decision to aim for commercially available solutions in the first place or to change the processes.

Besides functional fit, IT and business fit were also evaluated. The overall fit of each application was obtained by mapping all the applications with the help of a three-dimensional matrix. Exhibit 10 diagrammatically summarizes the process of application mapping and selection, together with some example criteria used for the evaluation in each of the three dimensions.

The project resulted in the selection of several standard applications that would support highly optimized processes, ensure effectiveness and efficiency, and maintain a high level of flexibility. The structured approach with which the project was performed, together with the standard solutions used, made it possible to achieve the intended implementation time frame without compromising the quality of the project outcomes.

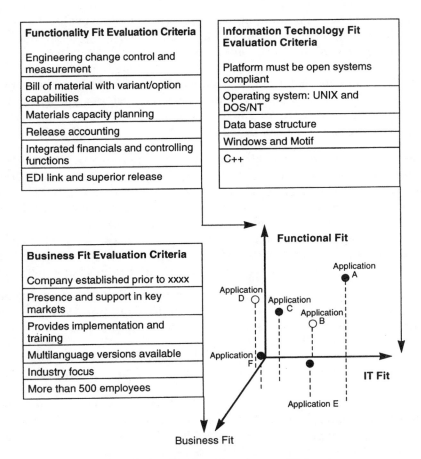

Functionality Fit Evaluation Criteria
Engineering change control and measurement
Bill of material with variant/option capabilities
Materials capacity planning
Release accounting
Integrated financials and controlling functions
EDI link and superior release

Information Technology Fit Evaluation Criteria
Platform must be open systems compliant
Operating system: UNIX and DOS/NT
Data base structure
Windows and Motif
C++

Business Fit Evaluation Criteria
Company established prior to xxxx
Presence and support in key markets
Provides implementation and training
Multilanguage versions available
Industry focus
More than 500 employees

Functional Fit

Application A
Application D
Application C
Application B
Application F
Application E

IT Fit

Business Fit

Exhibit 10. Application Mapping and Selection

Application to an Existing Business

HP has used the business alignment framework to redesign its order fulfillment process. Although the application of the overall framework remained the same as in the previous example, two additional dimensions had to be addressed:

- Because the business process already existed, it was necessary to evaluate the impact of potential changes.
- Because the process spanned several business units and product groups (some of which had conflicting goals), it was necessary to decide where and how compromises could be achieved.

In this case, the greatest benefits could be achieved when concentrating on improving on-time delivery, speed of new product introduction, and price performance in a common way. Other, group-specific factors were then dealt with independently by the different business units. This analysis also formed the basis for the definition of breakthrough objectives, such as 100 percent delivery on customer date and 30 to 40 percent cost reduction for each group and business unit, that would clearly improve the performance of the overall organization for the selected business goals. Based on these and other breakthroughs, a new order fulfillment process was designed using an end-to-end perspective.

Strategy Impact. Because different groups had differing requirements, it was necessary to incorporate a vector called strategy impact. Determining strategy impact was used to fine-tune the overall process to the requirements of individual groups. It also made it possible to incorporate the changes arising from the competitive environment or product-specific marketing programs and adjustments of inventory levels due to specific component shortages or trends. Exhibit 11 is a high-level view of the redesigned order fulfillment process, together with the strategy impact vectors.

To ensure high levels of flexibility, the process models attempt to balance the use of human support and technology support. Wherever no major improvements could be achieved, human support was favored.

Cost Justification. Because order fulfillment processes were already in place that had evolved through numerous continuous improvement efforts, it was necessary to justify the implementation costs of the newly defined processes, including the cost of the new information technology systems and applications. The cost of nonalignment that represents the cost of tolerating non-value-adding activities had to be determined for comparison purposes. Here, different techniques were employed, including:

- Actually tracking a customer order from the moment of quotation to final delivery
- Measuring the time involved in handling exceptions
- Benchmarking with related and nonrelated industries
- Reexamining core competencies that, for example, resulted in subcontracting all post-manufacturing delivery activities
- Establishing common performance measures

When it was determined that the cost of nonalignment outweighed the cost of new process development and implementation, the core processes and relevant subprocesses were modeled and translated into functional requirements so that potential solutions could be selected or developed.

Because the requirements for each business unit were different, it was impossible to select one uniform application. A portfolio analysis determined the best compromise for limiting the number of application solutions for implementation. Exhibit 12 shows the outcome of the portfolio

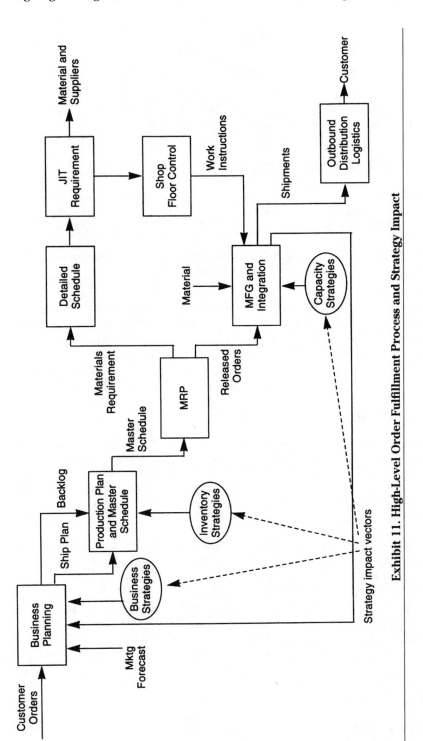

Exhibit 11. High-Level Order Fulfillment Process and Strategy Impact

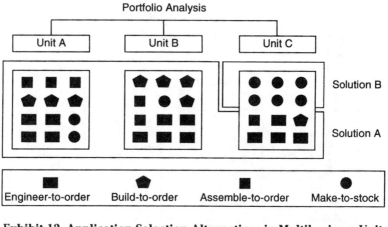

Exhibit 12. Application Selection Alternatives in Multibusiness-Unit Environments

analysis. For example, business units A and B have similar product portfolios for which application solutions can easily be applied. For business unit C, solution A lends itself to a limited number of products. Therefore, a second application solution was necessary. These solution clusters allowed HP to implement the new processes using a few standard applications while redefining a speedy implementation and minimizing the overall cost.

RECOMMENDED COURSE OF ACTION

IS managers recognize the need for aligning strategies, people, processes, and technologies in dynamic business environments in which speed of implementation is critical. The two examples illustrate step-by-step how the framework can be applied to define new business models and modify existing ones. This structured framework for alignment allows the user organization to:

- Develop processes that focus on breakthroughs that make a clear difference in the eyes of customers
- Identify and use appropriate enabling technologies
- Achieve a high level of transparency and reduce redundancies
- Use standard applications based on open systems wherever possible to reduce cost and implementation time while ensuring integration
- Allow for flexibility that changes arising from the competitive environment as well as advancements in technology can be rapidly implemented

Section 3
Task 2: Implementing Collaborative Relationships

Collaborative relationships, as we define them, are those inside the organization. Many, if not most, organizations are comprised of departments. In most, it is these departments where budget accountability occurs, where sponsorship for new systems comes from, and where process ownership resides.

The situation encountered by many in the IS organization is that processes cross multiple department boundaries. However, systems are optimized for each department's piece of the process. This occurs ar the expense of the overall process, and the organization as a whole. One has to wonder if an organzation cannot produce an effective internal process, how can it make its supply chain processes effective?

This section looks at the impact of supply chain management on internal organizations and the IS function. It also contains selections describing the leadershi role IS has in introducing the right kind of technology to the supply chain.

Chapter 19
Supply Chain Information Systems: Putting the Process First

James B. Ayers

Companies around the world spend billions on "solutions" to improve their supply chains. These billions include expenditures for capital equipment; launching new systems; and opening or closing plants, warehouses, or sales offices. With such large investments at stake, managers want the changes to "stick" (i.e., not wither away soon after the project is over). To the chagrin of many, organizations are like rubber bands — they quickly return to their original state once the pressure is off. Once the wave passes, business as usual returns.

Making change stick is particularly vexing when it comes to systems projects. That costly new integrated, enterprisewide system may hold a mountain of data but the data is often not in a form useful for supply chain decision-makers. Promises from software purveyors to "mine" these databases for information nuggets are unconvincing without an understanding of the needs throughout the chain. What decisions must be supported? Who will make those decisions? What information do they require to make the decisions? The answers to these questions require an understanding of supply chain processes, the organization, its people, their roles, and measures of their performance. A company is not ready to "mine" data until these issues have been resolved.

STRATEGY AND SUPPLY CHAIN DESIGN

Supply chains have a profound affect on the way companies are organized. The traditional organization structure, the one that continues in most companies today, divides people according to their functions. Sepa-

0-8493-1273-6/02/$0.00+$1.50
© 2002 by CRC Press LLC

rate departments perform each function. The supply chain in a manufacturing company, for example, has the procurement department, the manufacturing department, and the distribution department. Decision-making becomes a functional mission, with too little overview of the total supply chain process.

In some situations, this arrangement makes sense, but these situations are becoming fewer and fewer. The obsolescence of the functional organization is driven by increased customer segmentation, resulting in tailored processes to meet the needs of those customers. The "one-size-fits-all" supply chain organization is probably doomed in most markets. So too is the one-size-fits-all enterprise system incorporating so-called best practices.

Segmenting markets is something of an art form. This chapter describes that concept briefly, along with other marketing concepts. It is important to understand that segmenting and attacking markets with improved products and supply chain processes happens all around us in competitive markets. For any company, segmentation and focused supply chain design constitute a two-edged sword — both a threat and an opportunity. The threat is that a focused competitor can tailor a supply chain to the needs of a particular segment served by an entrenched company. If the competitor's supply chain does a better job of meeting customer needs, market share will be lost. The opportunity, on the other hand, is that a focused company not now serving a market can use the same methods to bypass an entrenched competitor.

Supply chain process redesign including customer segmenting and decision support requirements should precede planning new systems What follows are several concepts useful for designing the organization and its requirements for information support.

Should There Be a Supply Chain Organization?

With regard to organization, a company has two basic options. The first is to pursue or maintain a functional structure, as has been described. The second is to adopt a supply chain structure, in which multiple focused supply chain-oriented structures exist side by side. Before proceeding with systems tasks like enterprise systems, decision support, and mining data, however, the question of should there be a supply chain organization must be answered.

Answering this question requires an understanding of the position of products relative to competitors and where they are in the product life cycle. The "product grid," as shown in Exhibit 1 displays that company products occupy different quadrants on the grid and require strategies suited to the quadrant.

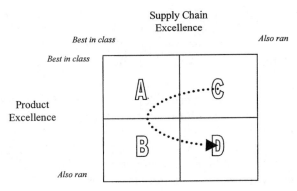

Exhibit 1. Supply Chain Excellence

Companies in the A quadrant have the best of all worlds — an exceptional product delivered by an exceptional supply chain. Microsoft's Windows and Office products are examples. They face little competition.

Quadrant B products are the ones consumers buy every day. Product features vary little from competitor to competitor. In the computer world, this "commoditization" has taken place over time. The competitive field is more likely to be determined by supply chain innovation than by innovation in the product itself. Accordingly, Dell could charge, at least for a time, a premium price in return for over-the-phone convenience and high-end customer service. Some observers refer to these amenities as the "extended" product. For Starbucks Coffee, it is less a matter of what is in the cup but more the surroundings in which it is served.

Customers eagerly seek quadrant C products. But, for whatever reason, the supply chain is not as developed as the product itself. However, the company can "do no wrong," and efficiencies in the supply chain are a secondary concern. Xerox was such an organization in the early days of its copier technology. A breakthrough drug under patent may present a similar opportunity to a pharmaceutical company. Boeing reflected C quadrant status when it tried to increase production rates. Its supply chain could not respond. The company, in spite of having great products and a dominant market share, lost money and marketshare when it failed to make its committed deliveries.

A product in the D quadrant is in deep trouble. It cannot survive for long without moving to another quadrant.

The quadrants also track movement of products through what is called "the product life cycle." Readers may know this as the "S" curve taught in marketing courses. The life cycle holds that products pass through four phases: an introduction phase, a growth phase, a mature phase, and a decline phase. Recognizing the life cycle is an important underpinning of product strategies and of supply chain organizations. For high-technology products, this life cycle is shortening dramatically. The dotted arrow in Exhibit 1 traces the life cycle phases on the product grid.

The products of a start-up business unit might be in the C quadrant. The company's products may be in great demand and hold promise in a growing market. Product developers and marketing types probably rule the roost. Supply chain issues take a back seat to product development and marketing. The chief supply chain challenge is dealing with product changes and meeting demand. In some technology products, a particular challenge is finding suppliers with the capacity and technical capabilities needed.

As the product moves to quadrant A, the organization becomes of such a size that formal procedures are necessary. At this point, the functional structure starts to take shape in a new company. In a mature company, the new product may "transition" from the new product development team to the functional organization. Profits are still plush in the growth market, driven by the novelty of the product and growth in demand. The principal supply chain mission is to ensure that the demand is met. A danger is that needs of particular customer segments are neglected while growth is strong, and the company becomes vulnerable to losses in market share.

In quadrant B, competition stiffens and growth slows. Pricing is a dominant consideration. Competitive initiatives center on cost reduction across the supply chain. Innovation in the supply chain may lead to competitive advantage. Focused competitors, no longer able to ride growth in the overall market, look for ways to take business away from their competitors.

The product that has moved to quadrant D is in decline. The life cycle can possibly be extended by supply chain innovation (moving it back to quadrant B) or a new platform product (moving to quadrant C). Most quadrant D products are, however, discontinued or sold off to better positioned companies.

The organization that has been in business for a while may manage products in all the quadrants. It is likely to do this through a supporting functional supply chain structure. In effect, it has one "compromise" supply chain. This supply chain is not particularly suited to producing or delivering products and services in any of the quadrants. The organization is vulnerable to competitors with distinctly focused supply chains or is likely to break up into focused divisions or "spin-offs."

Choices for Supply Chain Design

Better management of supply chain evolution and associated decision-making processes can sustain a product's profitability and shorten reac-

Exhibit 2. Alternatives to Supply Chain Organization for Acme Corp.

Acme Corporation Product Lines	Product Grid Quadrant	Segment 1	Segment 2	Segment 3
Product line Alpha	B	$$$	$$	
Product line Beta	D			$
Product line Charlie	A		$$$$	
Product line Delta	C	$$		

tion time to competitive moves. Exhibit 2 illustrates the alternatives to supply chain organization in the Acme Corporation.

Acme has three customer segments and four product lines. The number of "$" symbols represents the profit earned in each segment by product line. For example, the exhibit shows that Alpha's product line Charlie has the most profitable product/customer combination in segment 2. Beta products produce the lowest profits. Segment 3, the market for Beta, is the least profitable.

Each product is in a different quadrant of the product grid. Charlie, the most profitable, is in the A quadrant. Things are going well. But Acme must be wary that the "golden goose" is not stolen, particularly if market maturity is near at hand. Alpha products serve two mature market segments. One of the segments is shared with product Charlie. Delta is an innovative new product sold to customers in segment 1. Product Delta is the "dog" in the portfolio. It generates neither profit nor business for other products with its customer base in segment 3.

Acme has a functional organization. Its procedures dictate that each product line be sourced, produced, and distributed the same way. Traditional functional departments, such as procurement, operations, and distribution, make this happen. They use a common system for each customer/product combination. Inventory policies are the same. Lead times are the same. Acme is a company with a one-size-fits-all supply chain.

Unfortunately, Acme is very, very typical. Like many others, it plans a new enterprise resource planning (ERP) system. While implementing its ERP system, it will tailor, at considerable expense, the information generated to the perceived needs of the "as-is" structure.

If Acme were to shift to a supply chain structure, it has two basic alternatives to the functional supply chain. It can

1. Form tailored supply chains according to products. This might result in one or more product lines sharing a distinct supply chain. The chains are "product-centric."

Exhibit 3. Acme Corp.'s Market Factors

Type of organization	Preferred in cases of:	Not preferred in cases where:
Functional	Narrow product line Small organization Mature business	Diverse product/customer base Speed is important in adjusting to changing conditions
Product-centric supply chain	Multiple products with differing production technologies Cost driven business (B on the product grid) Homogeneous customer base Capital intensive production technology	Varied customer base with differing requirements Relative low cost production technology Cost secondary to service in production decision
Customer-centric supply chain	When strategy calls for targeting attractive segments Style driven business requiring fast response (A and C on the product grid) Heterogeneous customer customer base/many segments	Too many segments to serve practically Lack of scale could cause loss of control or focus Price sensitive market

2. Form tailored supply chains according to market segments. There could be one or more supply chains organized around segments. The chains are "customer-centric."

If Acme follows the first alternative, it might discontinue Beta and form one product-centric supply chain for Alpha, its mature business, and another for its growth businesses serving products Charlie and Delta. If Acme dropped Beta and selected a customer-centric approach, it would likely have supply chains for segments 1 and 2. The roles and information needs of decisionmakers would certainly be different under the two scenarios.

In choosing an alternative, Acme should consider several market factors. Exhibit 3 describes them. Acme's selection will depend on a reading of these factors. It is not uncommon to mix these basic models. For example, incoming generic commodity items are increasingly sourced centrally and bought locally. This makes sense for copier toner, paper, forms, and so forth. These items have little effect on competitive position, and purchasing them in greater quantities may yield savings.

In determining decision support needs for Acme, the choice of supply chain designs will be vital. Overlaying new technology on the existing function organization may result in incremental improvement, but large increases in sales and profits call for a different approach.

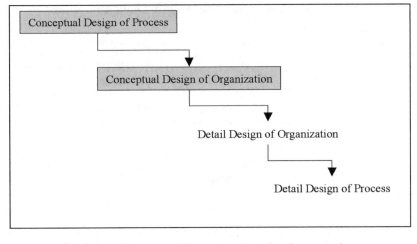

Exhibit 4. A Successful Approach to Implementation

Timing the Implementation of Organizational Change

An aggressive supply chain transformation will rattle an organization. How should the design and implementation phases be sequenced for the greatest effectiveness? The question often arises regarding shifting from one supply chain focus to another, whether it is functional to a product-centric or customer-centric focus. The sequence shown in Exhibit 4 is a successful approach that has been used in several situations.

The shaded activities produce the supply chain design — which includes processes and organization — at a conceptual level. These are all the activities needed to compete effectively. They are functional, product-centric, or customer-centric depending on business needs. The organization design includes roles, responsibilities, and measures for decisionmakers in the organization. These, in turn, define high-level decision support needs.

Once the conceptual design is complete, the actual organization that will execute processes should pursue detail. This should start with the organization and proceed to detailed process design. Out of the detailed process design will come the information requirements for decision support. The capability of new systems enables information to be provided "proactively."[2] Such systems "push" needed information to decision-makers in a timely way.

STAYING ON TRACK: PERFORMANCE MEASURES

Unless supply chain designs include the appropriate measures, changes will not last. In the mature organization, new measures may challenge decades of precedent. Also, if the financial management decisions

Exhibit 5. Common Examples of Supply Chain Innovations

Balanced Scorecard Measures	Supply Chain Examples
Financial perspective	Supply chain changes should improve balance sheets and cash flow. Sales and profits should increase from providing targeted premium services.
Customer perspective	Shifts to customer-centric supply chains will better take into account customer requirements.
Internal business perspective	Restructuring to supply chain organizations produces fundamentally different ways of doing business. Processes are linked to competitive realities.
Innovation and learning perspective	Redefined roles in product or organization-centric supply chains will call on a broader range of skills than a functionally organized enterprise.

are not consistent with the new direction, needed changes will lag for want of funding.

Kaplan and Norton have introduced a tool for measurement that applies well to supply chain management.[3] The authors call their tool the "balanced scorecard." The balanced scorecard has value in locking in supply chain changes. The scorecards also evaluate whether changes are having the desired affect.

The approach takes broad corporatewide goals and cascades them down into meaningful measures for departments, groups, or individuals. The "balanced" aspect of the technique comes from the breadth of the measures. Rather than limiting measurement to financial information, the approach is fourfold:

1. Financial perspective — the traditional viewpoint including owner value
2. Customer perspective — how the organization measures up to customer requirements and expectations
3. Internal business perspective — what the organization must excel at to be successful
4. Innovation and learning perspective — how the organization can improve and create value

All four areas are susceptible to enhancement through supply chain innovations. Some common examples are shown in Exhibit 5.

The authors recommend developing lower-level measures to match strategies. For example, if lead-time reduction is a supply chain initiative, specific goals for each element of lead time should be assigned to the appropriate group or department that has the job of making the goal a reality.

Exhibit 6 shows how a supply chain goal like "reduced lead time" can "peel" down into lower-level objectives. In the case of Acme discussed subsequently, a corporate goal is translated into balanced goals for the manufacturing department.

The exhibit shows that Acme wants to reduce lead times for one or all of its products. This is one of many goals as indicated by the band of "Corporate Level Goals." The manufacturing department has four goals, accompanied by measures to support lead-time reduction. A strength of the balanced scorecard is that measures in all four areas support the goal. Current practice in most companies for a goal like lead-time reduction does not include the measures for each perspective.

Acme recognizes that set-up times are a principal contributor to longer lead times. It wants to shorten these to make smaller runs more feasible from an operating point of view. So management sets a goal of training workers on upstream and downstream jobs, which will add flexibility in the light of fluctuating demand.

Acme assesses that an understanding of where products are used by customers will increase awareness of the importance of response time. So management plans visits by front-line workers to customer operating sites. Because the measures should decrease costs, it also sets the goal of removing hours from budgeted labor levels.

CONCLUSION

Innovation in supply chain management principles and techniques puts new demands on information system implementers. Companies implementing major systems such as ERP have or soon will have an important enabler that can lead to improved competitiveness. But many will apply their new capability to outmoded supply chain processes. Putting technology ahead of competitive position and operational requirements is a frequent shortcoming of many management teams.

New process design based on the competitive and life cycle positions of products should drive supply chain design. A candid self-assessment, a conscientious redesign, and careful implementation will reap competitive benefits.

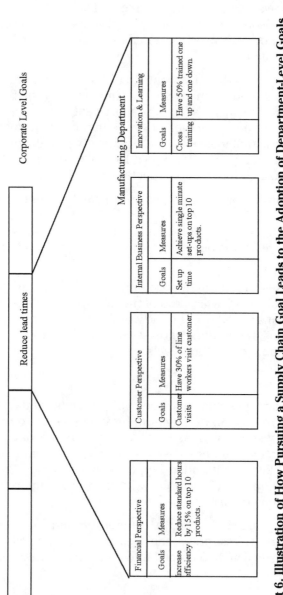

Exhibit 6. Illustration of How Pursuing a Supply Chain Goal Leads to the Adoption of Department-Level Goals

Notes

1. Ayers, James B., "Supply Chain Strategies," *Information Strategy: The Executives Journal,* (Winter 1999), pp. 2–10.
2. Lewin, Marsha; Kennedy, Keith; and Ayers, Jim; "Transformation Through Proactive Systems: A Case Study," *Information Strategy: The Executive's Journal,* (Spring 1996), pp. 29–35.
3. Kaplan, Robert S. and Norton, David P., "The Balanced Scorecard — Measures that Drive Performance," *Harvard Business Review* (Jan.–Feb. 1992), pp. 71–79.

Chapter 20
The New Enabling Role of the IT Infrastructure

Jeanne W. Ross
John F. Rockart

Recently, some large companies have made some very large investments in their information technology (IT) infrastructures. For example:

- Citicorp invested over $750 million for a new global database system.
- Dow Corning and most other Fortune 500 companies invested tens of millions of dollars or more to purchase and install enterprisewide resource planning systems.
- Johnson & Johnson broke with tradition by committing corporate funds to help its individual operating companies acquire standard desktop equipment.
- Statoil presented all 15,000 of its employees with a high-end computer for home or office use.

At firms all over the world senior executives in a broad cross-section of industries are investing their time and money to shore up corporate infrastructures. In the past, many of these same executives had, in effect, given their IT units a generous allowance and admonished them to spend it wisely. Now, in contrast, they are engaging in intense negotiations over network capabilities, data standards, IT architectures, and IT funding limits. The difficulty of assessing the value of an IT infrastructure, coupled with technical jargon and business uncertainties, has made these conversations uncomfortable for most executives, to say the least. But the recognition that global markets are creating enormous demands for increased information sharing within and across firms has led to the realization that a powerful, flexible IT infrastructure has become a prerequisite for doing business.

The capabilities built into an infrastructure can either limit or enhance a firm's ability to respond to market conditions (Davenport and Linder, 1993). To target a firm's strategic priorities, senior executives must shepherd the development of the infrastructure (Broadbent and Weill, 1997). Sadly, most senior executives do not feel qualified to do so. As one CEO described it: "I've been reading on IT, but I'm terrified. It's the one area where I don't feel competent."

New infrastructure technologies are enabling new organizational forms and, in the process, creating a competitive environment that increasingly demands both standardization for cost-effectiveness and customization for responsiveness. Most firms' infrastructures are not capable of addressing these requirements. Accordingly, firms are ripping out their old infrastructures in an attempt to provide features such as fast networks, easily accessible data, integrated supply chain applications, and reliable desktop support. At the firms that appear to be weathering this transition most successfully, senior management is leading the charge.

Over the past three years, we have done in-depth studies of the development of the IT infrastructure at 15 major firms. We have examined their changing market conditions and business imperatives, and we have observed how they have recreated their IT infrastructures to meet these demands. This chapter reports on our observations and develops a framework for thinking about IT infrastructure development. It first defines IT infrastructure and its role in organizations. It then describes how some major corporations are planning, building, and leveraging new infrastructures. Finally, it describes the roles of senior, IT, and line managers in ensuring the development of a value-adding IT infrastructure.

WHAT IS AN IT INFRASTRUCTURE?

Traditionally, the IT infrastructure consisted primarily of an organization's data center, which supported mainframe transaction processing. (See Exhibit 1.) Effectiveness was assessed in terms of reliability and efficiency in processing transactions and storing vast amounts of data. Running a data center was not very mysterious, and most large organizations became good at it. Consequently, although the data center was mission critical at most large organizations, it was not strategic.

Some companies, such as Frito-Lay (Mead and Linder, 1987) and Otis Elevator (McFarlan and Stoddard, 1986), benefited from a particularly clear vision of the value of this infrastructure and converted transaction processing data into decision-making information. But even these exemplary infrastructures supported traditional organizational structures, consolidating data for hierarchical decision-making purposes. IT infrastructures in the data center era tended to reinforce existing organizational forms rather than enable entirely new ones.

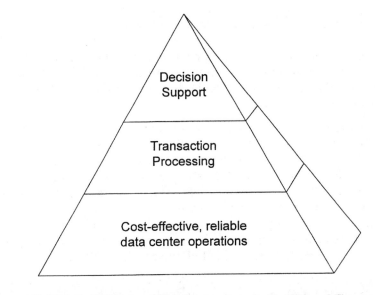

Exhibit 1. The Role of IT Infrastructure in Traditional Firms

In the current distributed processing era, the IT infrastructure has become the set of IT services shared across business units (Broadbent and Weill, 1997). Typically, these services include mainframe processing, network management, messaging services, data management, and systems security. While still expected to deliver reliable, efficient transaction processing, the IT infrastructure must also deliver capabilities, such as facilitating intraorganizational communications, providing ready access to data, integrating business processes, and establishing customer linkages.

Delivering capabilities through IT infrastructure is much more difficult than managing a data center. Part of the challenge is technological because many of the individual components are immature, making them both unreliable and difficult to integrate. The bigger challenge, however, is organizational, because process integration requires that individuals change how they do their jobs and, in most cases, how they think about them.

CHANGING ORGANIZATIONAL FORMS AND THE ROLE OF INFRASTRUCTURE

Historically, most organizations could be characterized as either centralized or decentralized in their organizational structures. While centralization and decentralization were viewed as essentially opposite organizational structures, they were, in fact, different manifestations of hierarchical structures in which decisions made at the top of the organization were carried out at lower levels (See Exhibit 2). Decentralized organizations dif-

Decentralized   Centralized

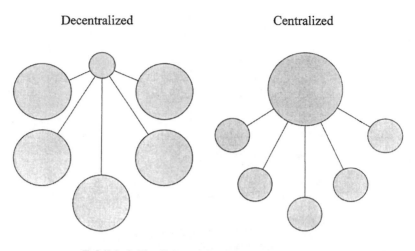

Exhibit 2. Traditional Organizational Models

fered from centralized in that more decision-making was pushed down the hierarchy but communication patterns were still vertical and decisions involving two business units were usually made at a higher level, so that business units rarely recognized any interdependencies. Centralization and decentralization posed significant trade-offs in terms of their costs and benefits. Simply stated, centralization offered economies of scale while decentralization allowed firms to be more responsive to individual customers. Thus, the degree to which any firm was centralized or decentralized depended on which of these benefits offered the most value. As global markets have forced firms to speed up decision making and to simultaneously recognize both the global scope of their customers and their unique demands, firms have found it increasingly important to garner the benefits of both centralization and decentralization simultaneously. Johnson & Johnson and Schneider National demonstrate how firms are addressing this challenge.

Johnson & Johnson

For almost 100 years, Johnson & Johnson (J&J), a global consumer and healthcare company, achieved success as a decentralized firm (Ross, 1995a). Both J&J management and external analysts credited the autonomy of the firm's approximately 160 operating companies with stimulating innovation and growth. In the late 1980s, however, top management observed that a new breed of customer was emerging, and those customers had no patience for the multiple salespersons, invoices, and shipments characteristic of doing business with multiple J&J companies. For example, executives at Wal-Mart, the most powerful of the U.S. retailers, noted that J&J companies were sending as many as 17 different account representatives in a single month. In the future, Wal-Mart mandated, J&J should send just one.

In response, J&J created customer teams to service each of its largest multi-business accounts. The teams consolidated data on sales, distribution, accounts receivable, and customer service from the operating companies and presented a single face to the customer. Initially, much of the reconciliation among the businesses required manipulating spreadsheets populated with manually entered data. Ultimately, it meant that J&J would introduce complex structural changes that would link its independent operating companies through franchise management, regional organizations, and market-focused umbrella companies.

Schneider National

In contrast, Schneider National, following deregulation of the U.S. trucking industry in 1980, relied on a highly centralized organizational structure to become one of the country's most successful trucking companies. Schneider leveraged its efficient mainframe environment, innovative operations models, centralized databases, and, later, satellite tracking capabilities to provide its customers with on-time service at competitive prices. By the early 1990s, however, truckload delivery had become a commodity. Intense price competition convinced Schneider management that it would be increasingly difficult to grow sales and profits.

Schneider responded by moving aggressively into third-party logistics, taking on the transportation management function of large manufacturing companies (Ross, 1995b). To succeed in this market, management recognized the need to organize around customer-focused teams where operating decisions were made at the customer interface. To make this work, Schneider installed some of its systems and people at customer sites, provided customer interface teams with powerful desktop machines to localize customer support, and increasingly bought services from competitors to meet the demands of its customers.

Pressures toward Federalist Forms

These two firms are rather dramatic examples of a phenomenon that most large firms are encountering. New customer demands and global competition require that business firms combine the cost efficiency and tight integration afforded by centralized structures with the creativity and customer intimacy afforded by decentralized structures. Consequently, many firms are adopting "federalist" structures (Handy, 1992) in which they push out much decision making to local sites. In federalist firms, individuals at the customer interface become accountable for meeting customer needs, while the corporate unit evolves to become the "core" rather than headquarters (See Exhibit 3). The role of the core unit in these firms

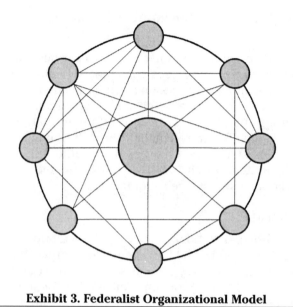

Exhibit 3. Federalist Organizational Model

is to specify and develop the core competencies that enable the firm to foster a unique identity and generate economies of scale (Hamel and Prahalad, 1990; Stalk, Evans, and Shulman, 1992).

Federalist firms require much more horizontal decision-making to apply shared expertise to complex problems and to permit shared resources among interdependent business units (Quinn, 1992). Rather than relying on hierarchical processes to coordinate the interdependencies of teams, these firms utilize shared goals, dual reporting relationships, incentive systems that recognize competing objectives, and common processes (Handy, 1992). Management techniques such as these require greatly increased information sharing in organizations, and it is the IT infrastructure that is expected to enable the necessary information sharing. However, an edict to increase information sharing does not, in itself, enable effective horizontal processes. To ensure that investments in information technology generate the anticipated benefits, IT infrastructure must become a top management issue.

ELEMENTS OF INFRASTRUCTURE MANAGEMENT

At the firms in our study we observed four key elements in the design and implementation of the IT infrastructure: organizational systems and processes, infrastructure services, the IT architecture, and corporate strategy. These build on one another (as shown in Exhibit 4) such that corporate strategy provides the basis for establishment of the architecture

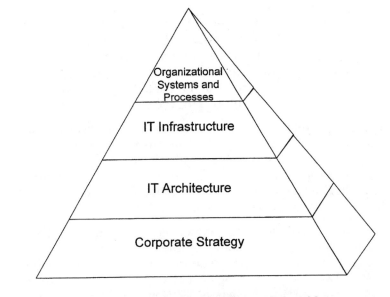

Exhibit 4. The IT Infrastructure Pyramid

while the architecture guides decisions on the infrastructure, which provides the foundation for the organizational systems and processes.

Corporate Strategy

The starting point for designing and implementing an effective infrastructure is the corporate strategy. The strategy defines the firm's key competencies and how the firm will deliver them to customers. Many large decentralized firms such as J&J have traditionally had general corporate strategies that defined a firmwide mission and financial performance goals, but they allowed individual business units to define their own strategies for meeting customer needs. In the global economy these firms are focusing on developing firmwide strategies for addressing global customer demands and responding to global competition.

For purposes of developing the IT infrastructure, senior management must have an absolutely clear vision of how the organization will deliver on its core competencies. General statements of financial and marketing goals do not provide the necessary precision to develop a blueprint for the foundation that will enable new organizational processes. The necessary vision is a process vision in which senior management actually "roughs out" the steps involved in key decision-making and operational processes.

Based on a clear vision of how it would service customers, Federal Express developed its Powership product, which allows any customer —

be it an individual or a major corporation — to electronically place and track an order. Similarly, JC Penney's internal management support system evolved from a clear vision of the process by which store managers would make decisions about inventory and sales strategies. This process included an understanding of how individual store managers could learn from one another's experiences. Such a clear vision of how the firm will function provides clear prescriptions for the IT infrastructure.

A corporate strategy that articulates key processes is absolutely essential for designing an IT infrastructure because otherwise neither IT nor business management can define priorities. The vision peels back corporate complexities so that the infrastructure is built around simple, core processes. This peeling provides a solid foundation that can adapt to the dynamics of the business environment.

Some firms have attempted to compensate for a lack of clarity in corporate goals by spending more money on their infrastructures. Rather than determining what kinds of communications they most need to enable, they invest in state-of-the-art technologies that should allow them to communicate with "anyone, anytime, anywhere." Rather than determining what data standards are most crucial for meeting immediate customer needs, they attempt to design all-encompassing data models. This approach to infrastructure building is expensive and generally not fruitful. Money is not a good substitute for direction.

IT Architecture

The development of an IT architecture involves converting the corporate strategy into a technology plan. It defines both the key capabilities required from the technology infrastructure and the places where the technologies, the management responsibility, and the support will be located. Drawing on the vision of the core operating and decision-making processes, the IT architecture identifies what data must be standardized corporatewide and what will be standardized at a regional level. It then specifies where data will be located and how they will be accessed. Similarly, the architecture differentiates between processes that must be standardized across locations and processes that must be integrated.

The architecture debate is a critical one for most companies because the natural tendency, where needed capabilities are unclear, is to assume that extensive technology and data standards and firmwide implementation of common systems will prepare the firm for any eventuality. In other words, standard setting serves as a substitute for architecture. Standards and common systems support many kinds of cross-business integration and provide economies of scale by permitting central support of technologies. However, unnecessary standards and common systems limit business unit flexibility, create resistance and possibly ill will during implementation, prove difficult to sustain, and are expensive to implement.

The elaboration of the architecture should help firms distinguish between capabilities that are competitive necessities and those that offer strategic advantage. It guides decisions on trade-offs between reliability and state-of-the art, between function and cost, and between buying and building. Capabilities recognized as strategic are those for which a firm can justify using state-of-the-art technologies, de-emphasizing standards in favor of function, and building rather than buying.

IT Infrastructure

Although firms' architectures are orderly plans of the capabilities that their infrastructures should provide, infrastructures themselves tend to be in a constant state of upheaval. At many firms key elements of the IT infrastructure have been in place for 20 to 30 years. Part of the infrastructure rebuilding process is recognizing that the fast pace of business change means that such enduring infrastructure components will be less common.

Architectures evolve slowly in response to major changes in business needs and technological capabilities, but infrastructures are implemented in pieces with each change introducing the opportunity for more change. Moreover, because infrastructures are the base on which many individual systems are built, changes to the infrastructure often disrupt an uneasy equilibrium. For example, as firms implement enterprisewide systems, they often temporarily replace automated processes with manual processes (Ross, 1997a). They may need to construct temporary bridges between systems as they deliver individual pieces of large, integrated systems or foundation databases. Some organizations have tried to avoid the chaos created by temporary fixes by totally replacing big pieces of infrastructure at one time. But infrastructure implementations require time for organizational learning as the firm adapts to new capabilities. "Big bang" approaches to infrastructure implementations are extremely risky. Successful companies often rely on incremental changes to move them toward their defined architectures, minimizing the number of major changes that they must absorb.

For example, Travelers Property & Casualty grasped the value of incremental implementations while developing its object-oriented infrastructure. In attempting to reuse some early objects, developers sometimes had to reengineer existing objects because new applications clarified their conceptualizations. But developers at Travelers note that had they waited to develop objects until they had perfected the model, they never would have implemented anything (Ross, 1997c). Stopping, starting, and even backing up are part of the learning process inherent in building an infrastructure.

Organizational Systems and Processes

Traditionally, organizations viewed their key systems and processes from a functional perspective. Managers developed efficiencies and sought continuous improvement within the sales and marketing, manufacturing, and finance functions, and slack resources filled the gaps between the functions. New technological capabilities and global markets have emphasized three very different processes: (1) supply chain integration, (2) customer and supplier linkages, and (3) leveraging of organizational learning and experience.

For many manufacturing firms, supply chain integration is the initial concern. To be competitive they must remove the excess cost and time between the placement of an order and the delivery of the product and receipt of payment. The widespread purchase of all-encompassing enterprisewide resource planning (ERP) systems is testament to both the perceived importance of supply chain integration to these firms and the conviction that their existing infrastructures are inadequate. Supply chain integration requires a tight marriage between organizational processes and information systems. An ERP provides the scaffolding for global integration, but a system cannot be implemented until management can describe the process apart from the technology.

At the same time, firms are recognizing the emergence of new channels for doing business with both customers and suppliers. Where technology allows faster or better customer service, firms are innovating rapidly. Thus being competitive means gaining enough organizational experience to be able to leverage such technologies as electronic data interchange and the World Wide Web and sometimes even installing and supporting homegrown systems at customers' sites.

Finally, many firms are looking for ways to capture and leverage organizational learning. As distributed employees attempt to customize a firm's core competencies for individual customers, they can increase their effectiveness if they can learn from the firm's accumulated experiences. The technologies for storing and retrieving these experiences are at hand, but the processes for making that happen are still elusive.

Firms that adapt and improve on these three processes can be expected to outperform their competitors. It is clear that to do so will require a unique combination of a visionary senior management team, a proactive IT unit, and a resourceful work force. Together they can iteratively build, evaluate, redesign, and enhance their processes and supporting systems.

IMPLEMENTING AND SUSTAINING THE INFRASTRUCTURE

It is clear that the top and bottom layers of the IT pyramid are primarily the responsibility of business managers, whereas the middle layers are the

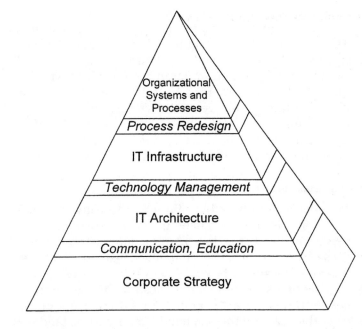

Exhibit 5. Partnership Processes in Infrastructure Development

responsibility of IT managers. Three partnership processes provide the glue between the layers as shown in Exhibit 5.

Communication and Education

The process of moving from a strategy to an IT architecture involves mutual education of senior business and IT managers. Traditional approaches to education, such as lectures, courses, conferences, and readings, are all useful. Most important, however, is that management schedules IT-business contact time in which the focus of the discussion is business strategy and IT capability. For example, at Schneider Logistics, senior business managers meet formally with IT managers for two hours each week. This allows IT management to identify opportunities while senior management specifies priorities and targets IT resources accordingly.

Thus, the IT architecture debate is a discussion among senior managers with insights and advice from the IT unit. Senior management articulates evolving strategies for organizational processes, whereas IT clarifies capabilities of the technologies. A key role of IT becomes one of explaining the potential costs of new capabilities. Typical return-on-investment computations are often not meaningful in discussions of infrastructure development, but senior managers need to know the size of an investment and the accompanying annual support costs for new capabilities before they commit to large infrastructure investments.

To avoid getting bogged down in arguments over who would pay for new capabilities, some firms have made "speed bump" investments. Texas Instruments (TI), for example, traditionally funded infrastructure by attaching the cost of incremental infrastructure requirements to the application development project that initiated the need. But when the corporate network proved inadequate for a host of capabilities, senior management separately funded the investment (Ross, 1997b). In this way TI avoided the inherent delays that result from investing in infrastructure only when the business units can see specific benefits that warrant their individual votes in favor of additional corporate taxes.

Technology Management

Moving from the architecture to the infrastructure involves making technology choices. Senior managers need not be involved in discussions of the technologies themselves as long as they understand the approximate costs and risks of introducing new capabilities. Instead, core IT works with local IT or business liaisons who can discuss the implications of technology choices. Selecting specific technologies for the corporate infrastructure involves setting standards. Local IT staff must understand those choices so that they can, on the one hand, comply with standards and, on the other hand, communicate any negative impacts of those choices.

Standards will necessarily limit the range of technologies that corporate IT will support. This enables the IT unit to develop expertise in key technologies and limits the costs of supporting the IT infrastructure. However, some business units have unique needs that corporate standards do not address. Negotiation between corporate and local IT managers should allow them to recognize when deviations from standards can enhance business unit operations without compromising corporatewide goals. IT units that clearly understand their costs have an edge in managing technologies because they are able to discuss with business managers the value of adherence to standards and the trade-offs inherent in noncompliance (Ross, Vitale, and Beath, 1997).

Process Redesign

Although the infrastructure can enable new organizational forms and processes, the implementation of those new processes is dependent on the joint efforts of business unit and IT management. Successful process redesign demands that IT and business unit management share responsibility and accountability for such processes as implementing common systems, establishing appropriate customer linkages, defining requirements for knowledge management, and even supporting desktop technologies. The joint accountability is critical to successful implementation because the IT unit can only provide the tools. Business unit management needs to provide the vision and leadership for implementing the redesigned processes (Davenport, 1992).

Many process changes are wrenching. In one firm we studied autonomous general managers lost responsibility for manufacturing in order to enable global rationalization of production. Initially, these managers felt they had been demoted to sales managers. A fast-food firm closed the regional offices from which the firm had audited and supported local restaurants. Regional managers reorganized into cross-functional teams and, armed with portable computers, took to the road to spend their time visiting local sites. In these and other firms changes rarely unfolded as expected. In most cases, major process changes take longer to implement, demand more resources, and encounter more resistance than management expects.

IMPLICATIONS OF INFRASTRUCTURE REBUILDING

We observed significant obstacles to organizations' attempts to build IT infrastructures to enable new federalist structures. Most of the changes these firms were implementing involved some power shifts, which led to political resistance. Even more difficult to overcome, however, was the challenge of clarifying the firm's strategic vision and defining IT priorities. This process proved to be highly iterative. Senior management would articulate a vision and then IT management would work through the apparent technological priorities that the strategy implied. IT could then estimate time, cost, and both capabilities and limitations. This would normally lead to an awareness that the strategy was not clear enough to formulate an IT architecture. When the organization had the necessary fortitude, management would continue to iterate the strategy and architecture, but most abandoned the task midstream and the IT unit was left trying to establish priorities and implement an architecture that lacked clear management support. This would lead either to expensive efforts to install an infrastructure that met all possible needs or to limited investment in infrastructure that was not strategically aligned with the business (Henderson and Venkatraman, 1993).

Although it is difficult to hammer out a clear architecture based on corporate strategy and then incrementally install an IT infrastructure that supports redesigned organizational processes, the benefits appear to be worth the effort. At Travelers, the early adoption of an object environment has helped it retain a high-quality IT staff and allowed it to anticipate and respond to changing market opportunities. Johnson & Johnson's development of a corporatewide infrastructure has allowed it to address global cost pressures and to respond to the demands of global customers. Senior management sponsorship of global systems implementations at Dow Corning has enabled the firm to meet due dates for implementation and anticipate potential process redesign.

TASK 2: IMPLEMENTING COLLABORATIVE RELATIONSHIPS

As firms look for opportunities to develop competitive advantage, they find it is rarely possible to do so through technological innovations (Clark, 1989). However, the firms in this study were attempting to develop infrastructures that positioned them to implement new processes faster and more cost effectively than their competitors. This kind of capability is valuable, rare, and difficult for competitors to imitate. Thus, it offers the potential for long-term competitive advantage (Collis and Montgomery, 1995). Rebuilding an infrastructure is a slow process. Firms that wait to see how others fare in their efforts may reduce their chances for having the opportunity to do so.

Notes

Broadbent, M., and Weill, P. 1997. Management by maxim: How business and IT managers can create IT infrastructures. *Sloan Management Review* 38(3): 77–92.

Clark, K.B. 1989. What strategy can do for technology. *Harvard Business Review* (November–December): 94–98.

Collis, D.J., and Montgomery, C.A. 1995. Competing on resources: Strategy in the 1990s. *Harvard Business Review* 73 (July-August): 118–129.

Davenport, T.H. 1992. *Process innovation: Reengineering work through information technology.* Boston: Harvard Business School Press.

Davenport, T.H., and Linder, J. 1993. Information management infrastructure: The new competitive weapon? Ernst & Young Center for Business Innovation Working Paper CITA33.

Hamel, G., and Prahalad, C.K. 1990. The Core Competence of the Corporation, *Harvard Business Review* 68 (May-June).

Handy, C. 1992. Balancing corporate power: A new federalist paper. *Harvard Business Review* 70 (November-December): 59–72.

Henderson, J.C., and Venkatraman, N. 1993. Strategic alignment: Leveraging information technology for transforming organizations. *IBM Systems Journal* 32(1): 4–16.

McFarlan, F.W., and Stoddard, D.B. 1986. Otisline. Harvard Business School Case No. 9-186-304.

Mead, M., and Linder, J. 1987. Frito-Lay, Inc.: A strategic transition. Harvard Business School Case No. 9-187-065.

Quinn, J.B. 1992. *Intelligent enterprise: A knowledge and service paradigm for industry.* New York: Free Press.

Ross, J.W. 1995a. Johnson & Johnson: Building an infrastructure to support global operations. CISR Working Paper No. 283.

Ross, J. W. 1995b. Schneider National, Inc.: Building networks to add customer value. CISR Working Paper No. 285.

Ross, J.W. 1997a. Dow Corning: Business processes and information technology. CISR Working Paper No. 298.

Ross, J.W. 1997b. Texas Instruments: Service levels agreements and cultural change. CISR Working Paper No. 299.

Ross, J.W. 1997c. The Travelers: Building an object environment. CISR Working Paper No. 301.

Ross, J.W., Vitale, M.R., and Beath, C.M. 1997. The untapped potential of IT chargeback. CISR Working Paper No. 300.

Stalk, G., Evans, P., and Schulman, L.E. 1992. Competing on Capabilities: The new rules of corporate strategy. *Harvard Business Review* 70 (March-April): 57–69.

Chapter 21
Are Human Resource Departments Ready for E-HR?

Marie Karakanian

Watching the sweeping changes that the E-wave is throwing at the shores of all business disciplines one cannot help but wonder if HR is ready for E-business? The question for HR is whether to embrace and formally describe the meaning of E-HR, or remain a spectator for competitor actions and miss the boat dashing across the E-waves. Of course, these questions raise a slew of others, like whether HR has finally managed the time to reach the comfort zone in their HRMS systems or if HR is ready to declare the addition of its client/server applications to the ranks of legacy systems.

Is this technology wave truly important for HR, considering that despite all the hoopla surrounding the digital revolution shaping the new economy, HR continues the struggle to align to the ever-dynamic business strategies, to hunt rare talents, and to develop compensation strategies for high-tech and high-touch people? How will this E-wave impact the HR agenda? Will it facilitate HR's attainment of its objectives, or will it eradicate HR? Should HR jump on the E-procurement and supply chain bandwagon, clarify the enterprise integration points, and wave the business case flag once again and convince everyone of how the HR activity chain can add value and strengthen the E-business promise?

All valid questions that have no definite, clear-cut answers. However, as the promise of global network technology shapes the lives of all sizes of businesses today and questions the very existence of so many of those businesses, HR has no option but to go back to the drawing board and pull together the blueprint of their E-existence.

WHAT DOES E-BUSINESS MEAN?

E-business is the overall business strategy that redefines the old business models and uses digital media and network technology to optimize customer value delivery. It relies on Internet-based computing, which is the platform that supports the open flow of information between systems. It capitalizes on an existing technology backbone consisting of front-end and back-end enterprise business systems; and it makes effective use of component technology and interacts with customers via business portals established over the Internet. Technology is used in this case both as the actual cause and also driver of business strategy. It is used not only to develop the product or the service, but also to provide better choices to customers and enhanced delivery options.

E-business requires a complete replacement of the old business designs — new outsourcing and partnership alliances that not only reduce costs and speed solutions but also improve customer options. In one word, it is the re-invention of the old ways of doing business and aligning business strategies, partnerships, processes, applications, and people — truly fast and right.

HOW TO DESCRIBE E-HR

When mapping the above description of E-business to the world of human resources, one can say that E-HR is the overall HR strategy that lifts HR, shifts it from the HR department and isolated HR activities, and redistributes it to the organization and its trusted business partners old and new. E-HR ties and integrates HR activities to other corporate processes such as finance, supply chain, and customer service. Its premise is that HR is the owner of the strategy and, when required, it is the service broker as opposed to the provider.

What this philosophy demands is dedicated HR homework; executive participation; excellent appreciation of technology and utilization of technology, including a well-developed and integrated HRMS system; and wise use of network technologies and various communication channels such as Web, wireless, and perhaps kiosks. The HRMS system acts as the HR data and business rules backbone; it interfaces to the enterprise intranet and it connects to HR service suppliers and business partners via an extranet and links to the internet via HR portals.

Thus, a potential critical dimension of the HR role becomes that of a services broker as opposed to a deliverer. Considering the proliferation of the variety of HR-related services within the marketplace — including business process, application services, candidate search, survey data, and a variety of function-specific expert service providers — the concept of HR service broker will probably soon turn into a larger reality than it is today.

WHY WOULD INTERNET-ENABLED HR TECHNOLOGY BE IMPORTANT FOR HR?

Here are some of the reasons why Internet-based technology is important for HR business:

- Provides cost-effective universal access to HR data to all authorized parties, including employees, managers, executives, HR service providers, relevant communities, corporate customers, and also the public-at-large
- Offers more cost-effective options for HR information systems management, especially for small and mid-size organizations via application service providers (ASPs)
- Allows the capture of significant amounts of data truly at source, thus almost eliminating data collection turnaround time and enhancing data accuracy
- Reduces the uncomfortable distance between the HR department and its internal customers by optimum integration between the corporate processes, potentially covering purchasing to payables, new employee request to candidate identification, and compensation surveys to performance increases
- Enables the globalization of corporate HR information and its accessibility at significantly reduced costs

The next section focuses on some business scenarios to illustrate the potentials currently available for E-HR.

Scenario A

A typical HR business scenario can explain the usage of all the above links. Say the Canadian headquarters of a multinational pharmaceutical company called B-Tec is looking for biotechnologists and has outsourced this process to a specialized global service provider, BPO.Com. BPO.Com posts the vacancies on the Internet. Applicants e-mail their resumes to this service provider, which shortlists three candidates for interviews and e-mails their resumes to B-Tec. B-Tec stores these resumes on its HRMS system, and selects and authorizes two candidates to create their profiles using the HR portal on the company's Web site. BPO.Com arranges electronic tickets to the candidates from two different countries using its own travel business partner. At the completion of the interviews, B-Tec authorizes the selected candidate to access and accept a job offer waiting for her on its Web site. The candidate accepts the job and advises B-Tec of the candidate's preferred arrival date subject to an employment visa. BPO.Com processes the employment visa for the selected candidate and assists with accommodation arrangements.

B-Tec creates a temporary employee ID upon candidate's acceptance of the offer and grants her access to the self-service portion of its Web site. The potential employee listens to a welcome Webcast by the president of the company, chats with her new manager, and familiarizes herself with the company's organizational chart. The candidate also selects her benefit preferences and registers for a company orientation session based on her arrival date. A B-Tec-assigned coach and the candidate chat on the Internet regardering her questions. E-mail from BPO.Com notifies her of her employment visa at the Canadian consulate.

Upon arrival to her country of employment, she presents herself to an HR consultant, who transfers her temporary employee record from the company's Web site to its employee database to complete the hiring process. The built-in business rules and edits ensure that the record has complete data.

A computer is allocated to the new employee right away. B-Tec's e-mail system advises the new employee of her temporary password to the Web site that has a to-do checklist waiting for her. One of the to-do items is her expense claim from BPO.Com. BPO.Com deposits owed monies to the employee's bank account.

Sound like a fairy tale? Examine the next scenario.

Scenario B

A small U.S. branch (1000 employees) of a Japanese giant automaker, H-Flyer, finally decides to replace its existing Y2K-patched HRMS system. One of the requirements is delivery to Japan, on a bi-weekly basis, of a variety of HR information, including employee core data, head count, training information and budgets, compensation changes, and employee turnover and reasons. After a long analysis, including multi-layer security administration requirements, the U.S. branch decides to use the services of an ASP, as this turns out to be more cost-effective, less disruptive, and more quickly implemented. This approach allows all employees of the branch to update their personal and benefit information via self-serve; it allows the HR department to access/maintain HR data in traditional ways; and it also allows managers access to a variety of authorized employee data. All data maintenance and access is enabled over the Internet, considering that H-Flyer's HRMS database resides on the ASP's servers. The ASP provides the application implementation, data conversion, and maintenance and post-implementation support services, some of which it subcontracts to expert partners such as Speedo Consulting Services and the E-Infrastructure Gurus.

In addition to a variety of information outputs from the database, the ASP provides three files in the format required by the Japanese parent and posts it on a dedicated Web site accessible by the Japanese headquarters and the Canadian HR branch. These files are in a predefined format required by the Japanese headquarters, who in turn download them via its translation engine into Japanese and update its global HR data repository, which is maintained in Japanese.

The organizations in both scenarios A and B can be described as E-HR-enabled, wherein all employees and managers can interact directly with the supporting technologies, HR professionals can communicate directly with HR service suppliers and vendors, and the public-at-large can access company information to the extent the companies allow them. HR assumes accountability for the coordination and delivery of the right service at the right cost to the right party at the right time.

THE TRENDS SHAPING E-HR

Similar to E-business, there are certain market and business trends that are shaping the world of E-Human Resources. These trends are driven by users/clients, processes/services, organizational entities, and, of course, technology. Exhibit 1 describes these trends and provides contextual examples. However, risk and security management is perhaps more crucial to HR-related information than any other because it involves private and highly sensitive individual data. The disclosure and cross-border movement of HR data is a critical issue that needs to be managed very carefully based on country, organization-specific, as well as individual authorizations. Thus, data and multi-platform security aspects are perhaps the most serious factors that need to be taken into consideration during the formulation of an organization's E-HR strategy.

The value of the HR chain of events is derived from the unique combination of business strategy, people and knowledge assets, technology resources, and business processes within a given environment. This value should be recognizable not only by the employees of an organization, but also by its customers in the form of affordability, quality accessibility, and usability of its products and services.

CONCLUSION

One can safely say that Web technology is here to stay and its muscle is strengthening day-by-day and impacting business strategy in a way not experienced before. Therefore, as HR becomes more of a refined business discipline, with processes more sophisticated than those of the traditional back office, it should optimize the use of all available technology to support and help accomplish the business goals. The HR department, however, needs to recognize some of the current limitations related to Web technology and its integration into the HRMS backbone. These challenges include multi-platform security, the inability to perform extensive transaction processing, and concurrent Web site and database updates. There is no question about the complexity of a technology environment that operates on the principle of ubiquitous availability, yet needs multi-layered technologies to help slice-and-dice the unrestricted cyberspace. Similar to most E-business ventures, the security of private HR information is a top priority. Organizations looking seriously into Internet enabling of their HR business should evaluate the authentication, secu-

Exhibit 1. Trends and Realities Impacting HR Business

Driver	Trend	Impacts	Examples/Application Related to HR
Users/clients	Service delivery speed	Employees Managers Executives Job candidates	• Reimbursements • Recruitment processes • New system implementations • Change of personal information
	Self-service and self sufficiency	Employees Managers Executives Business partners	• Performance management and feedback • Career planning and training • Pay information • Performance-based increases and bonuses, including Web-enabled employee communication
	Integrated solutions	Employees Managers Executives	• Web-enabled CBTs with updated competency profiles • Operational budgeting and monitoring • Strategic information management, trend analysis, performance score cards
Process	Integration Partnership/alliances Adaptation Consistency Convenience Enterprise extension	Employees Managers Public-at-large Business partners Service providers Competitors	• E-recruiting, hiring, and orientating new employees using multimedia • Sharing costs and benefits of same sources, such as job candidate databases and technology infrastructures • Dedicated portals over company intranet targeted to various employee groups such as sales staff, executives, high-tech staff, etc. • Use of repeatable, consistent, well-organized multi-channel communication based on specific questions related to benefits, pensions, policies, and procedures • Accessing of multi-channel information for 24 hours from anywhere • Company property management and tracking

New business models	Outsourcing: BPO, ASP Innovation	Employees (jobs) Business partners Technology vendors	• Reviewing shortlist of candidates from an executive search partner's online system and scheduling interviews • Accessing and maintaining own HR information over the Internet
Technology	HR systems bridging Enterprise application integration Multi-channel integration Internet business portals	Employees Managers Customers Public-at-large Technology vendors	• Feeding overtime information from work management systems to the payroll system • Linking HRMS to customer relationship management systems to improve customer service • Linking HRMS to company supply chain system to integrate internal and external processes, such as supply of training material, receivables, and payables • Accessing expert systems provided by external suppliers, such as compensation surveys and benchmark jobs
Globalization	Profitability Growth Sharing knowledge assets	Shareholders Governments Employees	• Using the Internet to link to shared HR data across all operational countries where a company operates • Using a combination of the intranet, network, and other technologies to extend operations across different countries • Using existing technologies to develop consistent company image, culture, and processes across geographies where possible. • Accessibility to internal knowledge resources across the globe through networking and groupware technologies

rity, access rules, and audit trails related to service providers' networks, servers, and applications.

Web technology is currently not capable of capturing employee time, checking pay rates, and running transactions such as payroll processing all at the same time. However, it allows the capture of employee time data via self-serve that can be transported to a backbone HRMS system, and get validated and calculated into employee pay dollars, thanks to payroll engines — some of which still use good old COBOL programs. Data captured on a corporate intranet — such as benefit changes, overtime data, or organizational change — that is using Web technology needs to be fed somehow to the backbone HRMS database or the payroll system. HRMS vendors have started exploring the potential for concurrent updates of the Web sites as well as the HRMS database, regardless of which end is accessed for updates.

Chapter 22
The CIO Role in the Era of Dislocation

James E. Showalter

Peter Drucker has suggested that the role of the CIO has become obsolete. His argument suggests that information technology has become so mission critical for reaching the company's strategic goals that its responsibility will be ultimately subsumed by the CEO or the CFO. After years of viewing information technology as an excessive but "necessary cost," executive management has now awakened to the recognition that failing to embrace and manage "dislocating" information technologies can mean extinction.

A dislocating technology is defined as a technological event that enables development of products and services whose impact creates completely different lifestyles and commerce. The Internet has been such a dislocating force, and others are on the horizon. Navigating these dislocations requires leadership and vision that must span the total executive staff, not just the CIO. This, I believe, is Drucker's point: The management of dislocating technologies transcends any individual or organization and must become integral to the corporate fabric. However, I also believe there is still an important role, albeit a different role, for the CIO in the 21st-century enterprise.

In his book, *The Innovator's Dilemma — When New Technologies Cause Great Firms to Fail*, Clayton Christensen provides a superb argument for corporate leadership that takes the company to new enhanced states enabled by technological dislocations. The Silicon Valley success stories have been *entrepreneurs* who recognize the market potential of dislocations created by technology. I believe the 21st-century CIO's most important role is to provide *entrepreneurial leadership* during these periods of dislocation for the company.

FROM PUNCTUATED EQUILIBRIUM TO PUNCTUATED CHAOS?

Evolutionary biologist Stephen Jay Gould theorizes that the continuum of time is periodically "punctuated" with massive events or discoveries that create dislocations of the existing state of equilibrium to a new level of

0-8493-1273-6/02/$0.00+$1.50

prolonged continuous improvement (i.e., *punctuated equilibrium*). The dinosaurs became painfully aware of this concept following the impact of the meteorite into the Yucatan peninsula. In an evolutionary sense, the environment has been formed and shaped between cataclysmic dislocations — meteorites, earthquakes, droughts, plagues, volcanoes, and so on. Although exact scenarios are debatable, the concept is plausible even from events occurring in our lifetime.

There are many examples of analogous technological discoveries and innovations (the internal combustion engine, antibodies, telephone service, interstate highway system, etc.), which promoted whole new arrays of products and possibilities that forever changed commerce and lifestyles. In each of these examples our quality of life improved through the conveniences these technologies enabled. The periods between dislocations are getting shorter. For example, the periods between the horse, the internal combustion engine, and the fuel cell took a century whereas the transformations between centralized computing, distributed computing, desktop computing, network computing, and ubiquitous computing have occurred in about 40 years.

In the next century, technological dislocations in communications, genetics, biotechnology, energy, transportation, and other areas will occur in even shorter intervals. In fact, change is expected so frequently that Bill Gates has suggested that our environment is actually in constant change or upheaval marked by brief respites — *punctuated chaos* rather than punctuated equilibrium. We are currently in the vortex of a dislocation or transition period that many companies will not have survived into the 21st century. With certainty, many new companies, yet unidentified, will surface and replace many of the companies currently familiar to us. No company is exempt from this threat, even the largest and most profitable today. The successes will be those that best leverage the dislocating technologies. To protect their companies from extinction, CIOs must understand the economic potentials and consequences of dislocating technologies.

THE ERA OF NETWORK COMPUTING

We are currently experiencing a new technological dislocation that embodies the equivalent or possibly greater potential of any previous innovation. This new dislocation is *network computing,* or perhaps a better nomenclature, *ubiquitous communications*. Network computing involves the collaborative exchange of information between objects, both human and inanimate, through the use of electronic media and technologies. Although network computing could arguably be attributed to early telecommunications applications in which unsophisticated display terminals were attached to mainframe computers through a highly proprietary communications network, the more realistic definition begins with the Internet.

Moreover, thinking must now focus on anything-to-anything interchange and not be limited only to human interaction. Navigating this transition will challenge every company — a mission for the CIO.

From today's vantage, networking computing includes (1) the Internet and Internet technologies and (2) pervasive computing and agent technologies.

The Internet and Internet Technologies

The compelling and seductive power of the Internet has motivated all major worldwide enterprises to adopt and apply Internet technologies within their internal networks under local auspices. These private networks, called intranets, are rapidly becoming the standard communications infrastructure spanning the total enterprise. Intranets are indigenous and restricted to the business units that comprise the enterprise. They are designed to be used exclusively by employees and authorized agents of the enterprise in such a way that the confidentiality of the enterprise's data and operating procedures are protected. Ingress and egress to and from intranets are controlled and protected by special gateway computers called firewalls. Soon additional gateway services, called portal services, will enable the enterprise to create a single portal to its network of internal Web sites representing specific points of interest that the company allows for limited or public access.

In general, the development and stewardship of intranets are under the auspices of the CIO. Whereas the Internet conceptually initiated the possibilities afforded by network computing to an enterprise, it is the intranets that have enabled the restructuring or reengineering of the enterprise.

Essentially all major enterprises have launched intranet initiatives. Due largely to ease of implementation and low investment requirements, enterprises are chartering their CIOs to implement intranets posthaste and without time-consuming cost justifications. In most cases, enterprises are initially implementing intranets to provide a plethora of "self-service" capabilities available to all or most employees. In addition to the classic collaboration services (e-mail, project management, document management, and calendaring), administrative services such as human resource management and financial services are being added which enable employees to manage their respective portfolios without the intervention of service staffs. This notion enables former administrative staffs to be transformed into internal consultants, process specialists, and other more useful positions for assisting in the successful implementation of major restructuring issues, staff retraining, and, most important, the development of a new corporate culture. Over time, all applications, including mission-critical applications, will become part of the intranet. Increasingly, these duties are being outsourced to trusted professional intranet specialists. Clearly, CIOs must provide the leadership in the creation and implementation of the company's intranet.

Companies in the 21st century will be a network of trusted partners. Each partner will offer specific expertise and capabilities unavailable and impractical to maintain within the host or nameplate company. Firms producing multiple products will become a federation of subsidiaries each specific to the product or services within its market segment. Each company will likely require different network relationships with different expert providers. This fluidity is impossible within the classical organizational forms of the past.

To meet these growing requirements and to remain profitable, companies are forced to reduce operating costs and develop innovative supply chain approaches and innovative sales channels. Further, in both the business-to-business (buy side) and the business-to-customer (sell side) supply chains, new "trusted" relationships are being formed to leverage supplier expertise such that finished products can be expedited to the customer. Initially, this requirement has motivated enterprises to "open" their intranets to trusted suppliers (buy side) and to dealers, brokers, and customers (sell side) to reduce cycle times and cost. These extended networks are called extranets. However, the cost of maintaining extranets is extreme and generally limited to large host companies. In addition, lower-tier suppliers and partners understandably resist being "hard wired," maintaining multiple proprietary relationships with multiple host companies. This form of extranet is unlikely to persist and will be replaced by a more open approach.

Industry associations such as SITA (Societé Internationale de Telecommunications Aeronautiques) for the aerospace industry and the Automotive Network Exchange (ANX) for the automotive industry have recognized the need for a shared environment in which companies within a specific industry could safely and efficiently conduct commerce. Specifically, an environment is needed in which multiple trusted "virtual networks" can simultaneously coexist. In addition, common services indigenous to the industry, such as baggage handling for airlines, could be offered as a saving to each subscribing member. These industry-specific services — "community-of-interest-networks" (COINS) — are evolving in every major industry. COINS are analogous to the concept of an exchange. For example, the New York Stock Exchange is an environment in which participating companies subscribe to a set of services that enable their securities to be traded safely and efficiently.

For all the same reasons that intranets were created (manageability, availability, performance, and security), exchanges will evolve across entire industries and reshape the mode and means of interenterprise commerce. Supply and sales chain participants within the same industry are agreeing on infrastructure and, in some noncompetitive areas, on data and transaction standards. In theory, duplicate infrastructure investments are eliminated and competitiveness becomes based on product/customer relationships. The automotive industry, for example, has cooperatively developed and implemented the ANX for all major original equipment manufacturers and (eventually) all suppliers. In addition, ANX will potentially include other automotive-related market segments, such as financial institutions, worldwide dealers, product development and research centers, and similar participants. Industries such as aerospace, pharmaceuticals, retail merchandising, textiles, consumer electronics, and so on will also embrace industry-specific exchanges.

Unlike the public-accessible Internet, which is essentially free to users, exchanges are not free to participants. By agreement, subscription fees are required to support the infrastructure capable of providing service levels required for safe, effective, and efficient commerce. The new "global internet" or "information highway" (or whatever name is ultimately attached) will become an archipelago of networks, one of which is free and open (Internet) while the others are private industry and enterprise subscription networks. The resulting architecture is analogous to today's television paradigm — free channels (public Internet), cable channels (industry-specific exchange), and pay-for-view channels (one-off service, such as a video teleconference).

Regardless of how this eventually occurs, intranets are predicted to forever change the internal operations of enterprises, and exchanges are predicted to change commerce among participants within an industry. Again, the CIO must provide the leadership for his or her firm to participate in this evolving environment.

Pervasive Computing and Agent Technology

The second dislocation is ubiquitous or pervasive computing. Currently there are an estimated 200 million computers in the world. By 2002, Andy Grove of Intel estimates there will be 500 million. In most cases, today's computers are physically located in fixed locations, in controlled environments, on desktops, and under airline seats. They are hardly "personal" in that they are usually away from where we are, similar to our automobiles. But this will change dramatically.

Although there are "only" 200 million computers today, there are already 6 billion pulsating noncomputer chips embedded in other objects, such as our cars, thermostats, and hotel door locks throughout the world. Called "jelly beans" by Kevin Kelly, in his book *Out of Control and New Rules for the New Economy*, these will explode to over 10 billion by 2005. Also known as "bots," these simple chips will become so inexpensive that they can affordably be attached to everything we use and even discarded along with the item when we are finished using it, such as clothing and perishables. Once the items we use in daily life become "smart" and are capable of "participating" in our daily lives, the age of personal computing will have arrived.

Programmable objects or agents are the next technological dislocation. Although admittedly sounding futuristic and even a bit alarming, there is little doubt that technology will enable the interaction of "real objects" containing embedded processors in the very near future. Java, Jini, Java chip, next-generation (real-time) operating systems are enabling information collection and processing to be embedded within the "real-life" objects. For example, a contemporary automobile contains between 40 and 70 microprocessors performing a vast array of monitoring, control, guidance, and driver information services. Coupled with initiatives for intelligent highway systems (ITS), the next-generation vehicles will become substantially safer, more convenient, more efficient, and more environmentally friendly than our current vehicles. This same scenario is also true of our homes, transportation systems, communications systems (cellular phones), and even our children and persons

Every physical object we encounter and employ within our lifestyles can be represented by a software entity embedded within the object or representing the object as its "agent." Behavioral response to recognizable stimuli can be "programmed" into these embedded processors to serve as our "agents" (e.g., light switches that sense the absence of people in the room and turn off to save energy and automobiles that sense other automobiles or objects in our path and warn or even take evasive actions). Many other types of agents perform a plethora of other routine tasks that are not specific to particular objects, such as searching databases for information of interest to the reader. The miniaturization of processors (jelly beans), network programming languages (Java), network connectivity (Jini), and appliance manufacturers' commitment will propel this new era to heights yet unknown. Fixed process systems will be replaced by self-aligning systems enabled by agent technology. These phenomena will not occur naturally but, rather, must be directed as carefully as all other corporate resources. In my judgment, this is the role of the 21st-century CIO.

SUMMARY

In summary, the Internet has helped launch the information age and has become the harbinger for the concepts and structure that will enable international communication, collaboration, and knowledge access for commerce and personal growth. Although the Internet is not a universal solution to all commerce needs, it has, in an exemplary manner, established the direction for the global information utility. It will remain an ever-expanding and vibrant source for information, personal communication, and individual consumer retailing. Intranets, developed by enterprises, are reshaping the manner in which all companies will structure themselves for the challenging and perilous journey into the 21st century. Complete industries will share a common exchange infrastructure for exchanging information among their supply, demand, product, and management support chains.

Pervasive computing will emerge with thunder and lightning over the next few years and offer a dazzling array of products that will profoundly enrich our standard of living. Agent technology coupled with embedded intelligence in 10 billion processors will enable self-aligning processes that adapt to existing environmental conditions.

CIOs who focus on the business opportunities afforded by dislocating information technologies will be the ones who succeed. Even if the CIO title changes in the future, an officer of the company must provide leadership in navigating the company through technological transitions or dislocations. As we enter the new millennium, however, there is a lot of work to be done to create the environment discussed in this chapter. As Kevin Kelly observes:

> …wealth in this new regime flows directly from innovation, not optimization: that is, wealth is not gained by perfecting the known, but by imperfectly seizing the unknown.

Successful CIOs will adopt this advice as their credo.

Notes

Christensen, C. 1997. *The Innovator's Dilemma: When New Technologies Cause Great Firms to Fail.* Boston: Harvard Business School Press.

Drucker, P. 1994. Introduction. In *Techno Vision,* edited by C. Wang. New York: McGraw-Hill.

Gates, B. 1999. *Business @ The Speed of Thought,* New York: Warner Books.

Kelly, K. 1997. The new rules for the new economy — twelve dependable principles for thriving in a turbulent world. *Wired,* September, 140.

Schlender, B. 1999. E-business according to Gates. *Fortune,* 12 April.

Chapter 23
Enterprise Transformation and Data Management

Richard Lee

Globalization and rapid technological change has forever changed the competitive landscape. There has been a great advance in information technology, and telecommunications that accelerate productivity and supply chain integration. This rising sophistication, and expectations of customers around the world, has given rise to implications in the way companies manage processes and data.

Whether it is through the Internet, information kiosks, or some other means, there now exists the "virtual customer" who decides what, when, where, and how they will purchase goods and services. Customers have virtual access through cyberspace to products and services to which they previously could not gain access. Not only do customers now have access, they will demand products and services "on-line" and almost in "zero-time." Consequently, this will have dramatic effects on the way companies manage, process, and organize data. Organizations that traditionally retrieve and use "old data" to plan, forecast, and execute, will have a difficult time in meeting customers' needs in the future.

Leading organizations have shifted their focus from cost to growth strategies. These companies are building flexibility and rapid-response capabilities in their products and services. They are redesigning business processes, and leveraging technology to develop innovative, integrated solutions. Studies (conducted by Deloitte Consulting) conclude that the speed of adaptability to customers — not incumbency, size, or technological elegance — has become the chief determinant of success in the industry. In all regions and sizes of organizations, the ability to innovate and respond quickly to changing market conditions was cited as the most critical advantage. The most profitable companies recognize the power of

0-8493-1273-6/02/$0.00+$1.50
© 2002 by CRC Press LLC

21st-century customers and are adapting to a new customer value paradigm and proactively changing the basis of competition.

Organizations that collect, leverage, and utilize data effectively will have a distinct advantage over their competitors. Organizations that excel at data management will be more efficient at rolling out their key capabilities into new markets. Success depends on linking the organization's strategic objectives with data management. There must be clear strategic decision making for data sharing, and the appropriate infrastructure — both technical and nontechnical. As well, organizations must address a number of issues including the mind-set to share data, the resources to capture and analyze the data, and the ability to find the right people and data.

IMPROVEMENT ON PROCESSES

Almost all enterprise transformations have involved some degree of reengineering, whether it has been minor incremental improvements to major dramatic change. Regardless of the degree of change, any transformation of an enterprise necessitates a reevaluation of the management of data.

Many enterprise transformations have improved processes through information technology integration and centralized data management. The advantage of integration allows a worldwide organization to run as a small business. Standardizing business processes all over the world with one system allows an organization to manage data in multiple languages and multiple currencies more effectively. Most IT managers cite that standardizing business processes is the primary advantage for integrating computer systems. Organizations also benefit by generation of better data through more effective utilization of resources. As well, the data that can be monitored through integrated systems allows an organization to know how it is actually producing, instead of knowing the forecasted or theoretical capacity of an operation. Once an integrated system is in place, it can also be less expensive to operate.

Finding Profits in Data

Companies must recognize the potential for utilizing data for profit. Improved processes and integrated systems do not necessarily make enterprises more successful. To sustain growth and take advantage of the enterprise transformation improvements, companies are consolidating internal databases, purchasing market research data, and retaining data longer in efforts to better focus their marketing efforts. To better serve their customers, organizations are analyzing behavioral characteristics of customers. If organizations can start tracking a customer's purchasing behavior, the kinds of things he or she likes and doesn't like, the organization can use the organization's data mining tools and data warehouses developed to target market the customer. There would be a lot less junk mail and better deals that the customer really cares about.

However, building and managing data through centralized or decentralized databases is not an easy task. Many organizations have had difficulty in finding adequate tools to manage such an ordeal. Many IT departments have found that the tools required to manage these databases are inadequate, immature, and possibly nonexistent.

The business process should dictate the tools and data required for users to perform the responsibilities that enhance the enterprise. Business processes should be developed to maximize the value of the enterprise to customers, employees and shareholders. Identifying the correct tools and data translate into specific business goals that match the organization's unique objectives.

Critical Success Factors

Enterprise transformation not only impacts technical, and organization structures, but data structures as well. Companies must recognize the importance of managing information as an asset. Successful companies recognize the need to carefully manage their data as well as they manage other valued assets. Critical success factors include managing data from an enterprisewide basis, managing data quality, assigning data ownership and empowerment, and developing long-term data strategies to support the enterprise.

Managing Data from an Enterprisewide Basis. An effective approach to managing data on an enterprise scale is to transform data from a "functional-silo" view to a business-unitwide and enterprisewide view. The data should address not only functional areas, such as sales, financial, and products, but also how their relationships with enterprise processes, such as marketing, finance, distribution, are mapped.

The culture of an organization usually dictates how data is distributed across its business units. A large multinational organization that has business units operating autonomously may have disparate technology architectures and distributed local databases. This environment provides more of a challenge than companies that have a strategy of centralizing data for current and detailed historical data, while allowing each business unit to retain corresponding summary data.

The purpose of an enterprise view of data is to:

- Share data between multiple organizations or among business units that are critical to the enterprise.
- Identify and control data that have dependencies with other systems or subsystems.

285

- Improve the quality of data resources.
- Establish effective data change management processes that maximize the value of information while ensuring data quality.
- Minimize data duplication due to collecting, and processing information.
- Facilitate external partner data access and sharing.

Many companies can benefit from managing data on an enterprisewide basis. Data just sitting in a local database is just data. However, when data is shared on an enterprisewide scale, then other business units may be able to take advantage of that data. From a customer relationship perspective, when demographics and psychographics are added to customer data, the company can gain extensive knowledge about that customer. Business intelligence is gained when the results of a competitive analysis are added to base customer data. When this intelligence is utilized within the enterprise's planning process, it will result in value-added ways to manage and expand the customer base.

Managing Data Quality. One of the many benefits for improved data management through enterprise transformation is improved data quality through elimination of data duplication. Most companies have many individuals throughout different parts of the organization that enter data relating to a certain process or business function. Consequently, it is very difficult to identify the integrity of the various types of data that is entered.

Data error can be attributed to a number of factors including:

- Multiple data entries from multiple users
- Lack of corporate standards
- Data distributed across disparate sources and legacy systems
- Data redundancy between different applications
- Data entry errors

An example of this was cited in an article in *Automotive Manufacturing & Production*. A first-tier automotive supplier, having seven divisions that shared some of the same vendors, did not utilize the same vendor codes. Each division not only assigned a unique identification number to each of those vendors, but each division also had its own descriptions for the components supplied by those vendors. Also, the seven divisions had a mix of legacy hardware platforms, software applications, and financial systems. To say the least, monthly roll-ups for divisional product sales, as well as component and supplier costs, were difficult for the parent company to obtain.

In order to improve quality of data, there have been a number of approaches utilized throughout industry. Companies have achieved improved labor time and cost by achieving gains in speed and accuracy of data entry. Directly related to this, is the higher degree of work satisfaction from staff, since the users will not have to re-key the information. As a result, companies that invest an amount up front in improving labor and data entry processes will save an organization a substantial amount of effort and cost providing batch work solutions later.

Assigning Data Ownership and Empowerment. Enterprise transformation typically leads to a change of responsibility for users. As a result, it is very important for organizations to manage data effectively. A number of roles involved in creating and distributing data are important for effective data management. Roles have been identified in the *Enterprise Data Management* article as:

- *Business Process Owners:* The business process owner defines and maintains the processes and subprocesses across multiple business functions. Operational business processes may include market products/services, perform order management, procure materials/services, manage logistics and distribution, and provide customer support. Infrastructure business processes may include the following: perform financial management, manage human resources, manage information systems, and provide support services. Business process owners have the responsibility of evaluating and managing the proposed changes to data has on the impact of their business process.
- *Data Owner:* The data owner is usually a business-function manager that is responsible for the data resource. For example, a person in the finance department should own the tax-rate data. A data owner should be able to assess the validity of the data from a business point of view, and not necessarily a computer programmer. The data owners should drive and review proposed changes to the data and assess the impact on their own data.
- *Data User:* The data user is anyone who completes a simple, fill-in-the-field change to a data item. A data user tends to be a task-based role rather than a position, and can be anyone from a customer-support representative to a head of a plant temporarily changing the inventory capacity for a given item. Data entry should be performed under careful access, security, and data-validation controls.
- *Data Custodian:* The data custodian is a person who often resides in an information technology department or MIS, providing services to several data owners. The data custodian is a person who actually manipulates the data structure for the data owner. Data custodians manage data dictionaries under change-control processes, implement proposed functional changes at the data level, and assess the broader impacts of proposed data changes. This role typically involves a combination of a database administrator, a data analyst, and an application-knowledgeable analyst.

TASK 2: IMPLEMENTING COLLABORATIVE RELATIONSHIPS

Transforming enterprises usually occur through technology-enabled business processes. This transformation must include an in-depth knowledge of the enterprise's application, data, and technical infrastructure. Just as important as the technical infrastructure is the organizational infrastructure that must be in place. This includes a strong management committee that is involved in program management, selection committees, implementation teams, and ongoing support teams.

In order to achieve a successful enterprise transformation, extensive training, education and overall project leadership are required. Resources must be both technically and business knowledgeable. Achieving an effective data management process during enterprise transformation is not easy, but it is essential to achieve the business improvements required in today's competitive economy.

Developing Long-Term Data Strategies to Support the Enterprise. Enterprises that undergo transformation look to improved data planning, and access through the use of appropriate methods, tools, and technologies. Companies must learn to promote internally and externally the importance of data as a valuable resource and properly manage its creation, use, storage documentation, and disposition.

In a survey conducted by *LAN Times* in *BusinessWeek*, 500 organizations found that a vast majority of the businesses have already implemented technology to provide intranet or browser-based access to corporate data. The major driving forces toward this Internet- or intranet-based technology is the demand for mobile knowledge workers and the opportunities for revenue and efficiency by E-commerce. As a result, enterprises are now reformulating their data strategy to take advantage of the benefits of the Internet. Most companies have a long way to go, but are now looking at the most efficient ways to build database infrastructures and user-friendly, standardized access paths. The benefits are tremendous for enterprises looking to get useful information directly to the people, inside or outside the company, who need it most.

The Internet

The Internet provides companies with the ability to distribute data to end users. Through consolidation and simplifying data on one universal client, companies can contact their customers and work with their business partners much more easily. The Internet makes it easier for companies to manage geographically distributed databases and organizations. Companies are now identifying ways to consolidate data onto a central server to allow access from users anywhere, with the proper data security, and integrity features in place.

Allowing customers to gain access to a company's database via the Internet provides many benefits to organizations. Customers can obtain information regarding billing, invoices, and their accounts via the Internet. Cost savings is just one of the reasons for companies managing their distributed databases via the Internet. According to the *LAN Times*, "A lot of organizations are interested in decentralizing the IT management operations because database administrators are so expensive. Rather than have a database administrator for each regional office, you can have one DBA team in the central office that can manage all the regional databases. The Internet will move that paradigm along because in the world of the Internet, physical location is more or less irrelevant."

The leading application for companies tends to be customer support followed by decision support, financial transactions, E-commerce, and EDI. Other internal uses are support for mobile employees, interactive intranet-based databases, and salesforce automation.

CONCLUSION

Enterprise transformation requires a robust strategy for enterprisewide data management. Managing data on an enterprisewide basis is increasingly crucial to running almost every aspect of today's business. Effective data management requires a combination of efficient processes, robust and flexible technology infrastructures, and skilled people. There is a growing need for enterprises to manage data on an enterprisewide base, through data ownership and empowerment, while maintaining data quality. Companies are also developing long-term data structures to meet the business needs. The Internet is just one of the tools which enterprises are utilizing to manage their data.

References

Anonymous, "Data cleanliness is next to enterprise efficiency," *Automotive Manufacturing & Production*, Vol. 10, Issue 6, June 1998, p. 66.

Bartlett, Jeffrey, "Business needs driving data dependency," *LAN Times*, May 11, 1998, Vol. 15, No. 10, p. 15(1).

Caron, Jeremiah, "Access methods change it all," *LAN Times*, May 11, 1998, Vol. 15, No. 10, p7(1).

Deloitte Consulting, Deloitte & Touche, "1998 Vision in Manufacturing" study, 1998.

Gibbs, Jeff, "The power of enterprise computing," *Internal Auditor*, February 1997.

Greenfeld, Norton, "Enterprise data management," *Unix Review*, February 1998.

Miller, Ed, "A solution approach to PDM," *Computer-Aided Engineering*, April 1998.

Moriarty, Terry and Swenson, Jim, "The data requirements framework," *Database Programming & Design*, April 1998 Vol. 11, No. 4, p. 13(3).

Mullin, Rick, "IT integration programmed for global operation," *Chemical Week*, Vol. 159, Issue 6, Feb. 12, 1997, p. 21–27.

TASK 2: IMPLEMENTING COLLABORATIVE RELATIONSHIPS

Perez, Ernest, "Savings from data entry engineering," *Database*, Vol. 21, Issue 3, June/July 1998, p. 76–78.

Schwartz, Karen, D., "Distributed databases, distributed headaches," *Datamation*, June 1998.

Singh, Colin and Hart, Max, "Changing business culture: Information is the key," *Australian CPA*, Vol. 68, Issue 8, September 1998, p. 50–52.

Trussler, Simon, "The rules of the game," *Journal of Business Strategy*, Vol. 19, Issue 1, January/February 1998, p. 16–19.

Chapter 24
Transformation through Proactive Systems: A Case Study

Marsha Lewin
Keith Kennedy
James B. Ayers

In recent years, many companies have engaged in extensive (and expensive) reengineering projects that relied on technological tools. Their results have often been disappointing. Studies suggest that those projects that failed lacked technological tools for rapidly delivering accurate and meaningful information that could be used to identify and exploit opportunities in a controlled manner. Because decision-makers need different kinds of information, such tools must work with both commonly used data and specialized data that meet unique user needs. This is a significant challenge. Running a business today is fraught with problems: insecurities caused by changing marketplaces and legislation, new technologies that render recent acquisitions obsolete, and tax laws that alter the profitability of long-term strategies. Managers must respond quickly with effective decisions; and to make those decisions, managers depend on the rapid delivery of accurate information. Many businesses have installed advanced systems infrastructures, common databases, and workgroup software to provide this information. Technology has thus infiltrated not only the products and services that businesses deliver, but also the means by which they deliver them. If the use of technology is ubiquitous, however, how can a company use it to gain a competitive edge? The answer is by incorporating technology both into the company's products and into the management of the company itself (this is the subject of this chapter). How a company wields technology determines the degree of control it exercises over

0-8493-1273-6/02/$0.00+$1.50
© 2002 by CRC Press LLC

its business environment, that is, its ability to monitor changes in this environment and to respond to these changes with the best decisions it can make in the quickest timeframe.

WHAT IS BETTER INFORMATION?

Better information is not necessarily more information — as any manager knows who must sift through pounds of paper or spend hours at a computer to extract the few pieces of information needed to make a decision. Better information is more accurate, timely, and especially more usable information than that which was previously available.

Because each decision-maker has his or her own data needs, data must serve many different purposes. The more the same sets of data are used by multiple groups or individuals for different purposes, the more trusted they become. The more people trust the integrity of the data, the more they trust the groups that produced the data and the easier team development becomes.

If It Ain't Broke ...

Coordination among business components — as in a construction project or joint venture — is costly and extremely difficult. Achieving the necessary balance among department, division, or company needs takes great amounts of time, discussion, and trust. More often than not, the participating groups give up and return to their previous ways of doing things (e.g., creating marketing plans, sales materials, or job cost information). When one group needs information from another, it is then grudgingly asked for or "guesstimated."

In many large construction projects, weekly or more frequent meetings bring together the firms involved in the projects. These can be rancorous events in which each company tries to establish the correctness of its position — as reflected in the lists of data it carries in, the number of outstanding items, and the additional costs required to accomplish agreed-on activities. Naturally, each firm uses different systems and procedures to collect and report information.

Reconciling conflicting data is expensive and time-consuming. Often, participants spend so much time deciding what the situation really is that unnecessary emergencies develop, resulting in cost and schedule crises. Money is wasted and sales are lost. In construction, these disputes often move into the courts.

A Case Study

The proactive approach to information gathering can improve the administration of a large construction project. A pioneering proactive system is being sponsored by San Bernardino County in southern California to help manage the construction of a $600 million medical center. Project participants must cooperate closely to complete the center on schedule and within budget.

The business environment for the construction project is similar to that faced by many other enterprises. Several partners, including the owner, construction manager, architect, general contractor, and many subcontractors, must coordinate their efforts. All must work together to build the project on time. However, contracts include specific accountabilities for timely processing of information, and a failure of any partner to perform can lead to expensive claims.

Documents are the backbone of formal communications for such a project, and their management is challenging. Similar projects can involve more than a million documents transmitted among decision makers in partner firms.

Project managers for these partners must contain costs, meet deadlines, and avoid costly problems after completion of the project. In working with other organizations on the project, they must take into account their partners' different motivations, cultures, procedures, and ways of handling information. To avoid litigation and cost overruns, the project managers chose the proactive systems approach to address these barriers and clarify the tasks of managing the project.

What Is a Proactive System?

Proactive systems have evolved with advances in technology. Early systems were procedure-based; they next became data-based, usually operating at the department level. For example, accounting systems dealt with accounting functions, and sales order systems addressed the needs of the sales and marketing functions. In this environment, the departments (e.g., sales order processing or inventory management) had custody of their own pieces of the system. The processes that the systems supported therefore tended to be sequential in nature. That is, information moved from department to department for action by specialists. Accountability was fuzzy because multiple departments were involved.

This model worked as long as decisions made by management did not cross functional lines. However, data generated by one function was often needed by another; therefore, systems were improved to provide access to data across departments. Information needed to be entered only once — perhaps into the sales system — but could be read by the inventory system. This was important progress, but the systems were still passive. Through experience or personal rules of thumb, decision-makers had to know instinctively when conditions demanded decisions.

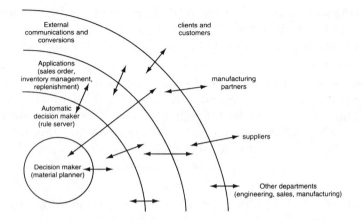

External communications and conversions

Applications (sales order, inventory management, replenishment)

Automatic decision maker (rule server)

Decision maker (material planner)

clients and customers

manufacturing partners

suppliers

Other departments (engineering, sales, manufacturing)

Exhibit 1. Structure of a Proactive System

Current competition demands a broader operational view than these methods of data access can provide. A proactive system that integrates its inventory system with its sales system can suggest when to initiate a sales campaign based on excess inventory. This is the benefit of a contemporary proactive system: when it detects certain situations, the system can route information to decision-makers according to predetermined rules. The rules are customized to each organization to reflect its unique lines of authority, and they can be altered quickly to accommodate changes in the business environment.

For example, the proactive system facilitates the approval of change orders by sending messages immediately and simultaneously to each person who must approve a given action. The system also measures the time that elapses before each action is taken and reminds late responders of what they need to do.

Exhibit 1 illustrates the structure of a proactive system in a manufacturing company. What makes the structure of this system proactive is the rule server that processes some of the inputs to the company decision-maker — in the case of Exhibit 1, a material planner. For example, a system's rule server can be designed to notify a company's planner if the sales department places an order that exceeds the company's stock. This person is then presumed to know what to do.

More aggressively designed rules can interpret the sales order, deciding to order that more product be manufactured. The rules server could then print purchase orders and direct them electronically to suppliers for raw material. Then, the server could notify sales forecasters to review their planning assumptions. Finally, the rules server might recast income statements and balance sheets to reflect the order, notify the bank of a need for more credit, and print supplier checks.

In this arrangement, preset rules matching the needs of the decision-maker reflect the authority vested in that individual. They grow out of a management philosophy of empowerment and continuous improvement. Management values and decisions, not technology, dictate these rules. For this reason, proactive systems further many of the goals supported by reengineering.

Proactive systems automate the processing of information, replacing production meetings or messengers carrying paper. Just as automation in the factory has streamlined metal cutting through numerical control and has sped material handling through robotics, proactive systems now speed information flow.

Developing a proactive system offers many opportunities for short-term improvement. In many cases, the critical examination of required decisions reveals alternative solutions that produce improved decisions. For example, a company creating a proactive system could replace an individual material planner's rules with uniform best practices.

Software and Hardware in Proactive Systems

The San Bernardino proactive system uses 40 commercially available database and applications software packages, including workflow, e-mail, imaging, document management, networking, and communications systems. Developing such a system involves constructing the interfaces between these systems and the network and then developing the rules that make the system proactive.

However, previously acquired hardware and software meet past requirements. Existing systems may or may not be suitable as the applications layer in a proactive system. A team developing a proactive system should critically evaluate these existing systems before incorporating them.

Issues Faced

The distinctive advantage of proactive systems is that they return control of business processes to management. Business rules built into these systems ensure that each member of a staff works efficiently and that the workload in and across departments is balanced.

In many circumstances, the net financial benefits of implementing a proactive system can be spectacular. Exhibit 2 shows how much time managers at the San Bernardino construction site spent performing their various duties before and after a proactive system was implemented. They estimate that the time they could spend managing increased four-

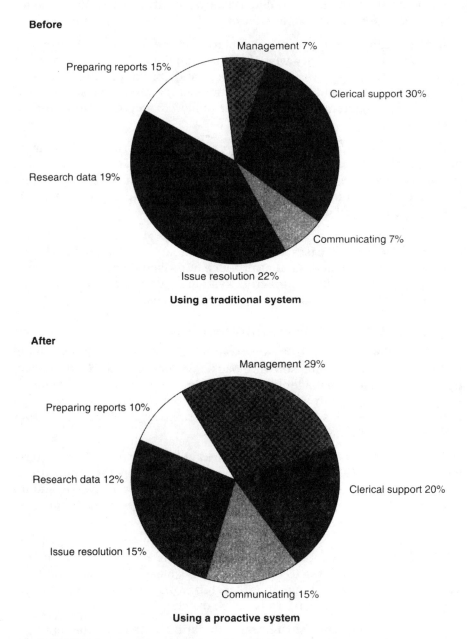

Exhibit 2. Comparison of Using a Traditional and a Proactive System at the San Bernardino Construction Site

fold with the proactive system. When documents are stored and transmitted electronically, information is more readily available, and managers spend less time on administration, issue resolution, and researching information. They can spend more time on communicating, and human relations are therefore better.

Paper slows down business processes, but proactive event-driven systems improve customer service, increase office productivity, and free time for managers to manage and motivate. The San Bernardino system created similar savings in work and process costs. For example, one construction procedure (processing requests for information) was reduced from 64 to 17 steps.

Roadblocks

The implementation of a proactive system is not without impediments. At San Bernardino, the participating partners had little choice in adopting the new system and its constraints on their customary flexibility. San Bernardino County made them accept it. Other organizations, however, have a choice — at least in the short term. The following paragraphs outline some objections commonly made to implementing a proactive system.

Reluctance to Change. Learning to use a new system is frustrating and tedious, but it is definitely worth the effort. Organizations implementing a proactive system should budget time and money to train users on it. Those firms that commit to training their people and to using proactive systems experience higher productivity than those that do not.

Need for Familiar Data. People often learn by rote how to work with reports and do not understand the underlying relationships and meaning of the data the reports contain. During reengineering, new formats, and even data definitions, are routinely introduced, disturbing users' comfortable familiarity. Users can become confused even when a horizontal representation is made vertical. Mapping old reports to new ones is a sound practice but is often not possible. User-by-user training speeds acceptance.

Internecine Rivalries. Competitive and adversarial positions are institutionalized in construction projects, not to mention within departments of a firm. For each construction change order awarded to a contractor, for example, the owner may pay additional money. The owner wants to keep costs low, and the contractor wants a profitable project. If both parties are working off the same data throughout the life of the project, the opportunities for differing opinions on what is really happening are reduced.

Home Office Requirements. Because the San Bernardino project involves many firms, differing company requirements were an issue in developing a proactive system. The parent companies of the project partners all had different policies and procedures that were reflected in different data formats and governing procedures they used at job sites. Sometimes, these formats and procedures conflicted with the project team's needs and, if followed, could have reduced the effectiveness of the system by limiting its scope. For example, the system requires that all file names end with a common suffix. Home offices did not follow this convention; but after they were informed of this requirement and the reason for it, they supported the change.

Heavy Training Requirements. A proactive system eliminates many of an organization's administrative tasks. Those that remain, it redefines and reorganizes. Users must be trained in these new procedures as well as the new system. An organization that fails to allocate sufficient time for this training can expect its new system to be improperly used, duplicative (i.e., it will not replace the organization's old ways of exchanging information but merely exist beside them), and intimidating to users who lack confidence in their ability to properly navigate it.

The Desire for Invisibility. Although the basis of a proactive system is sharing the same information among all parties, keeping information close to the chest is a hard habit to overcome. By making data invisible or inaccessible, people often feel they cannot be questioned too deeply about it. An atmosphere of openness can be sustained only if all parties feel that sharing information benefits them — usually financially.

Less Paper, Not Paperless Systems. Although the ultimate goal of the San Bernardino system was to produce a paperless system, some paper still flows in the project. Large drawings are available both electronically and in hardcopy so they can be easily read and carried onto the site. Tremendous reductions occurred in internal administrative documents: where dozens of copies had been needed, none are now. As confidence in the new approach soared, hardcopies were no longer requested as security blankets.

Who Should Develop Proactive Systems?

Proactive systems are not for everyone or every situation. They require a great deal of teamwork to develop and are expensive to implement. An organization should consider implementing a proactive system when it needs any of the following:

- *Consistency.* Because of process reengineering, government regulations, or company policy, many organizations need to treat the delivery of goods or services according to a consistent set of policies (or rules). A proactive system institutionalizes these requirements.
- *Need for leverage.* When a company is growing quickly or cannot get enough qualified decision-makers, or when its managers' areas of control are too wide for traditional methods of information transfer to

work, a proactive system relieves over stretched managers of many of their administrative tasks, giving them additional time to manage.

- *Reduced administration and coordination costs.* A company implementing a proactive system realizes its greatest cost reductions by automating the tasks required to move paper: the generation, filing, tracking, and retrieval of documents.

A Word of Advice

An organization implementing a proactive system cannot train its users too much. The San Bernardino users needed to learn new ways of thinking about information and data. A phased data representation process would have helped those users who were frightened when data did not appear in the formats they had traditionally seen it in. In the first phase, users would have seen data in the old formats; in the second phase, it would have appeared in new formats. As users grew to trust the accuracy of their data, they could then move to the new representations more comfortably.

The San Bernardino system was the first of its kind for the construction industry; its users were learning the system as it was being developed. This fact compounded the difficulty of the educational process. When already developed proactive systems are introduced, users can be trained on the actual screens and processes they will later use. This facilitates the learning process.

Chapter 25
EUC Professionals as Change Agents

Stewart L. Stokes, Jr.

As business computing becomes more user-centered, EUC professionals must learn to present themselves as a value-adding resource whose services benefit the organization and its customers. EUC professionals must also learn to champion technological and other workplace changes.

BECOMING A CHANGE AGENT

The word *vortex* is defined by the *American Heritage Dictionary* as "a situation that draws into its center all surrounding it." End-user computing (EUC) is firmly ensconced in the vortex of the changes surrounding information systems and information technology. As information processing becomes increasingly user-centered, EUC professionals face change on two fronts: with their colleagues in the business units and with their associates in the IS organizations.

EUC professionals are at the critical intersection where escalating business demands collide with rapidly evolving technologies. Continuous learning and "just-in-time training" are now the norm. End-user computing requires that those who live at the center of business and technological change become highly competent change agents. EUC professionals can learn to confidently master change by:

- Understanding the factors that are driving change in end-user computing
- Focusing on the value they and their services add to customers and the enterprise
- Avoiding the unintended consequences of change
- Taking a series of action steps to better manage change in their organizations

PERCEPTIONS OF IS PERFORMANCE

The results of a survey of IS managers, IS staff members, and business unit managers emphasize the need for EUC professionals to understand their roles as change agents.

0-8493-1273-6/02/$0.00+$1.50
© 2002 by CRC Press LLC

TASK 2: IMPLEMENTING COLLABORATIVE RELATIONSHIPS

The survey, conducted and reported by *Computerworld* in January 1996, examined perceptions of overall IS performance, IS/end-user relations, and the value of information services. The survey was administered to representatives from IS and users from the business units.

All three groups agreed more than they disagreed on the critical issues surveyed. Representatives of both IS and the business units agreed that end users should be the driving force in determining the direction of IS. In agreement with this statement were 71 percent of end-user business managers, 62 percent of IS managers, and 65 percent of the IS staff.

Two other areas of IS/end-user agreement relate to the value of information services to the business units. First, fewer than one-third of those surveyed agreed with the statement, "IS technologies should not be the driving force in designing the business processes."

Second, over two-thirds of the respondents agreed with the statement, "Information systems do not benefit the business unless accompanied by business practice changes." Among business unit managers, 71 percent agreed; followed by 60 percent of IS managers and 60 percent of IS staff.

Even though modest differences remain, IS managers and staff agree with their business unit associates on the principle that IS should not be the dominant driver in business process reengineering. It is also apparent that if enterprisewide computing is to reach its potential, EUC professionals need to play key roles in communicating business knowledge as they interface with both those who represent the business units and those who represent IS.

SHIFTING PRESSURES AFFECTING END-USER COMPUTING

Because of the advent of packaged software and the personal computer, EUC has emerged as a key player within enterprisewide computing. In the old information processing paradigm, IS was a monopoly — focusing only on controlling the supply side of the IS supply/demand equation and producing systems on time and within budget.

Today, IS faces competition from the enterprise's business units. Department walls continue to fall and enterprises of all sizes continue to restructure themselves into flatter organizations with more cross-functional teams involved in the applications development and construction process.

These structural changes are major challenges for business professionals as well as for their IS counterparts. As organizational boundaries blur, both groups must reinvent themselves as value-adding business professionals.

Adding Value to an Organization

The process of value adding is the responsibility of every department. Every employee is expected to add value to the organization's products, services, and customers.

EUC professionals are well equipped to position themselves as value-adding resources, but to be successful they must first understand and appreciate how value is defined and perceived by their customers. According to internal customers, value-adding contributions of EUC professionals include:

- Accelerating the cycle time of applications development, thus enabling business units to reduce their time-to-market of products and services
- Working closely with the IS staff to eliminate technical roadblocks and improve internal/external customer responsiveness
- Collaborating with business unit managers and staff to assist in the integration of IT across work group, organizational, and geographic boundaries
- Controlling work group, departmental, and enterprisewide expenditures
- Serving as communication links between technical and business-unit resources

Understanding EUC's Role in the Internal Value Chain

EUC professionals can enhance their ability to add value to their internal customers by closely examining the different environments within their organizations.

EUC should consider its roles and responsibilities in the context of the larger organization. Such evaluation includes understanding external customers, market segments, industry trends, and the economy and overall business environment. To understand their role better, EUC professionals might ask themselves:

- How are the needs of the external customers changing and how can they be met?
- What added value should be contributed to the external customers? How can that be done?
- What added value should be contributed to the internal customers and members of IS?
- What is the best way for EUC support to become a visible and viable part of the internal value chain?
- What added values are currently being contributed to the company and the customers?

The Unintended Consequences of Change

EUC professionals may discover that well-intentioned changes some-times lead to unintended negative consequences. For example, it is not unusual to find that changes in computer technologies that promise to deliver major improvements in employee productivity result instead in ill will among the users. Upon investigating, business unit managers find that the real problems lie not with the technology but with new working rela-tionships and expectations affecting those performing the work. The new working relationships may have been formed because of new technologies or process improvement changes. Either way, change that was intended to be positive resulted in unforeseen negative consequences.

Unforeseen negative consequences are often a result of political forces that were either unrecognized or ignored during the change management process. EUC professionals should remember that the most important question people ask themselves when faced with change is "What's in it for me?" EUC professionals will also benefit from knowing something about the recognition and reward systems in their business units. Knowing how people are recognized and rewarded reveals a great deal about how new technologies will be received and used.

Avoiding the Unintended Consequences of Change

No change takes place in isolation, but IS often introduces and manages as if it did. Changes in one area frequently cause a ripple effect of changes in others. Such unforeseen and unintended results may adversely impact how work is performed by other departments or locations. For example, changes in procedures made possible by new technologies in one work area may result in the need for unplanned changes in both procedures and technologies by those in other locations. Although the overall impact of the changes may be positive, time and energy that could have been saved with better planning may have to be expended. Such unplanned change may also needlessly increases already high stress levels.

In one example, changes were implemented but the company paid a high price in unintended negative consequences. There was widespread resentment that the company was interfering in the private lives of its employees by mandating home workspace without first consulting with those affected. Compensation for the workspace was never offered or dis-cussed. Morale plummeted. The changes could have been implemented more smoothly and effectively if two principles of change management had been observed:

- *Those affected by the change should be involved in its planning.* In this case, prior consultations could have been held with the em-ployees being affected by the change. People respond to change

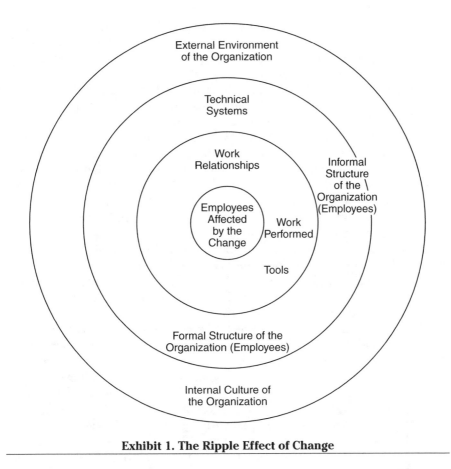

Exhibit 1. The Ripple Effect of Change

better when they are at least presented with an opportunity to voice their concerns.

- *Possible ripple effects of the change should be considered in the planning stage.* In this case, changes in working arrangements had a ripple effect that created many other unintended, negative changes. Exhibit 1 illustrates how changes affecting employees create additional changes that affect other aspects of the organization.

HOW TO CHAMPION CHANGE: 10 ACTION STEPS

Following are 10 action steps that EUC professionals can take to better position themselves as knowledgeable change agents within their business units and the enterprise. In the face of change, EUC professionals should:

1. Understand the external and internal pressures causing the change. Change management begins with an understanding of the reasons for change. External pressures for change come from customers,

competition, new technologies, financial conditions, laws and governmental regulations, and public opinion. Internal pressures to change come from management, new strategies, restructuring, and adaptations to new technologies.

2. Create a vision of what conditions will be like after the change. Both those initiating the change and those individuals and groups affected by it need a point on the horizon toward which to steer.

3. Understand the benefits that will result from the change and communicate them often to those individuals and groups affected. During times of change there can never be too much communication.

4. Know as much as possible about the history of change in the workgroups and departments. The more change has been experienced successfully, the more comfortable people will be and the easier change management will become. The reverse is also true. If there is a history of difficult change, people may be uncomfortable and require more training and time to adjust.

5. Pay attention to why change has been either successful or difficult. What factors have accounted for successful or failed results? Try and replicate the success factors.

6. Know the training, education, and coaching resources that are available and plan ahead for their use. Training is a critical success factors for effective change management.

7. Know the stress levels already present in the workgroup. Most change results in stress, even if the change is welcome and beneficial. Attempts should be made to curtail the stresses of change in departments already saddled with a great deal of stress.

8. Understand that all change brings with it some degree of resistance. Listen to those affected by the change and attempt to understand their concerns.

9. Avoid secrecy and dispel rumors.

10. Recognize, reward, and celebrate progress toward the goals of change. As new systems are designed, created, implemented, tested, and used, celebrate progress and results.

Chapter 26

An Information Architecture for the Global Manufacturing Enterprise

Robert L. Sloan
Hal H. Green

Global manufacturers must leverage their IS capability and information assets in ways that can create cost or competitive advantage and distinctive services across the supply chain, up to and including the customer. IS needs to create the necessary computing infrastructure and adopt an organizational model that reflects its new primary product: information delivery. This chapter addresses some of the fundamental data integration and architectural issues related to global manufacturing and information delivery.

PROBLEMS ADDRESSED

The two most important responsibilities of leadership are to establish a vision or strategy for the organization and to put in place the systems, processes, and structures that enable the organization to progressively achieve that vision. One of the structures used by manufacturers to create competitive advantage is integrated information systems. Competitive advantage, including cost and differentiation, can be won or lost by marginal differences in the speed, accuracy, and comprehensive nature of information being delivered to decision-makers.

An organization's competence in timely decision support capabilities has been given impetus by the total quality movement; the Malcolm Baldrige criteria state that "the ability to access and act on timely, reliable busi-

0-8493-1273-6/02/$0.00+$1.50
© 2002 by CRC Press LLC

ness data is requisite to the achievement of quantitative continual improvement in the delivery of products and services."[1]

Michael Porter has described the importance of horizontal strategy as the interrelationship between business units. Integrated information and control systems support horizontal strategy, enabling independent business units to share key product and process information along the whole supply chain.

HORIZONTAL BUSINESS INTEGRATION STRATEGY

Manufacturers are providing increased service levels in response to competitive pressure and to create differentiation in product offerings. One trend is toward smaller, custom lot sizes on the part of the process manufacturer and custom product configurations on the part of the discrete component manufacturer.

As manufacturing assumes these higher levels of service, the strategic model of the manufacturing organization is moving toward a professional context, in which the operating work of an organization is dominated by skilled workers who use procedures that though difficult to learn are well defined.[2] In this model, empowered workers are given greater decision latitude. In other words, with increased automation of the manufacturing processes, the nature of the work in the plant or factory shifts from manually effecting the independent processes to using information systems in support of customer-driven operating objectives related to production. The empowered worker equipped with business operating objectives makes decisions using information that previously was the purview of manufacturing management. Information systems, integrated with factory automation systems, therefore enable both differentiation and flatter organizational structures.

Compared with the conventional machine concept of the manufacturing organization, empowered or high-performance work teams typify a more people-centered, organic culture. This new manufacturing organization depends on high-speed access to high-quality information. For example, Total Quality Management prescribes the use of statistical quality control (SQC) techniques. Manufacturers use Statistical Quality Control techniques software to help workers process the sheer quantity of data required by the application of SQC principles in manufacturing, further illustrating the affinity between strategy, organization, and information technology.

The IS organization within the global manufacturing enterprise must understand the impact organizational strategy has on the information technology (IT) infrastructure. Furthermore, it must determine and create the optimum IT architecture to best support a horizontal business integration strategy.

DIFFERENTIATING INFORMATION SYSTEM PRODUCTS AND SERVICES

Historically, IS has delivered custom computer applications to business functions to improve effectiveness and reduce cost. System projects were justified on their stand-alone return on investment. The IS management structure reflected project team independence and aligned applications development teams with their respective customers (i.e., manufacturing, finance, or distribution). This approach to systems development avoided the long-term need to integrate data between applications. Viewed separately, each system met its functional objective. Viewed collectively, they presented a set of conflicting interfaces and incompatible information, thereby constraining a horizontal business integration strategy.

As businesses flatten their organizations, their dependence on integrated information flow across worldwide boundaries increases. The IS organization must find ways to remove the functional and technical incompatibilities of existing computer systems that are barriers to business-centric information access.

Trends in Manufacturing

More business managers recognize that information-related service extensions to their product/service mix can effect their companies' ability to compete favorably in international markets. They are also beginning to recognize that existing computer systems were designed in a way that is inconsistent with the view of information as an asset to be managed by the corporation, which has led to concerns about the return on investment for older systems.

Plant-level information systems, once the domain of process control engineers and production personnel, are being drawn into the scope of the IS function from the standpoint of integrating the operational data in these systems with horizontal supply-chain business strategy. The span of the IS organization's responsibility may expand to include multiple operational (e.g., manufacturing) systems from which enterprise information is collected and delivered. The charter of IS becomes focused on assimilating and combining manufacturing-process data with other forms of business data to enhance the quality of customer service, to support integrated operations objectives, and to provide value-added decision support across the corporation.

QUANTITY OF MANUFACTURING DATA

Information systems are pervasive across the manufacturing supply chain. The entire manufacturing supply chain uses information, but the epicenter of information technology in a modern industrial manufacturing company usually exists at the manufacturing plant site. Here, a variety of systems, using data at different levels of abstraction, are employed to control manufacturing processes, provide decision support to operations, and perform planning functions such as those offered by MRPII (material requirements planning) systems.

The problem of functionally integrating manufacturing software applications is exacerbated by the total volume of data employed in manufacturing. In the case of the process/batch manufacturer who employs process control systems, extensive quantities of process data may exist within the process control applications. Most of that data is needed by other parts of the manufacturing organization. It is common, for example, for a process manufacturing plant to generate 8 to 10 million pieces of information every 24 hours.

A central concern when manufacturing-process data is integrated into enterprisewide information systems is the requisite changes necessary to derive information from elemental process data. For example, a Fortune 100 diversified chemical company needs to maintain a complete history for each lot or batch of material made, including details of the processes used to make any given batch. A maker of an automobile safety device needs similar detailed information for each discrete component and assembly produced. In addition, the customer, the automotive industry, and proper business practice all specify that the detailed information be maintained indefinitely and be available on demand during the anticipated 20-year life of the product.

NATURE OF MANUFACTURING DATA

The problems outlined in each of these situations can be understood when the nature of manufacturing data itself is examined. Exhibit 1 identifies four categories of data that exist in manufacturing:

1. Derived data needed for longer-term business decision support
2. Transaction-driven, product-oriented data
3. Event-driven, operations-oriented data
4. Real-time, process-oriented data

The columns of Exhibit 1 contrast the key attributes of these different data types. Nonsite-specific positioning of derived data is critical to successful horizontal business integration for the multisite manufacturing enterprise.

Process data possesses the lowest level of integration in manufacturing, whereas decision support data has usually been integrated or summarized to afford the user a basis for broad business and planning decisions. These two extremes can be illustrated by considering the questions the business user of manufacturing data might ask as compared with those asked by a

Exhibit 1. Manufacturing Data Framework

Categories of Data	Example Data	Key Attributes of Data			
		Typical Orientation	Typical Use	Integration Scope	Typical Volume
Multi-site Decision Support	Lot/Batch Quality Summary	Subject/Table	Multi-site Read Only	Business	Low
Cross-Area Integrated Operations	Lot/Batch Quality Detail	Transaction Subject/Table	Driven	Site	Medium
In-Area Operations	In-Area Quality	File/Field	Event Driven	Area	Medium
Process/Machine Control	Process/Quality Parameter	Tag or I/O	Real Time	Machine/Process	High

process engineer concerned about the problem of manufacturing process optimization.

Business users of manufacturing data might want to know about the yield for a given product manufactured at all sites during the previous month. A typical process engineer might inquire about the historical trend of temperature for one or more tag (i.e., input/output) values, related to a particular piece of equipment or process. Both questions have equal relevance and potential merit, but they are fundamentally different, being based on the type of data needed to render a valid response.

The process-related question requires access to manufacturing (i.e., process control) data at its lowest atomic level. The product yield question requires access to data stored at a higher level of abstraction. Process data such as lot/batch yield must be collected and derived uniformly into a value for product yield at each site. This type of query represents a significant change in the level of abstraction and integration of the data across multiple plant sites.

The operations data presented at the middle levels of Exhibit 1 reflects the transformation of data from process (tag) to subject (table). An operations database often provides a repository for manufacturing data that is clearly outside the process domain but is still necessary for manufacturing. Operating conditions, procedures, recipes, and specifications, organized by product, equipment/cell/area, or manufacturing team, are often candidates for operations data. If material requirements planning is employed, the operations information data base is also often used to provide the MRP system order-operations as they are completed by product, line, or plant.

DATA-DRIVEN MANUFACTURING APPLICATION FRAMEWORK

Past efforts to computerize manufacturing focused on the automation of isolated process steps or organizational functions. The success of the global manufacturing enterprise depends on new application architectures, predicated on data integration, and the availability of derived production data for use in multi-site business decision support. Using the categories of manufacturing data from Exhibit 1, a data-driven application framework can be constructed for a typical manufacturing site (see Exhibit 2). This framework takes advantage of the existing differences in data, provides for the horizontal separation of multiple manufacturing process steps, and recognizes the need for operational integration. The upper level in this manufacturing site application framework supports the business need for horizontally integrated, multi-site production information access.

Adoption of a consistent manufacturing site application framework both enables multi-site integration and presents a major cost-reduction oppor-

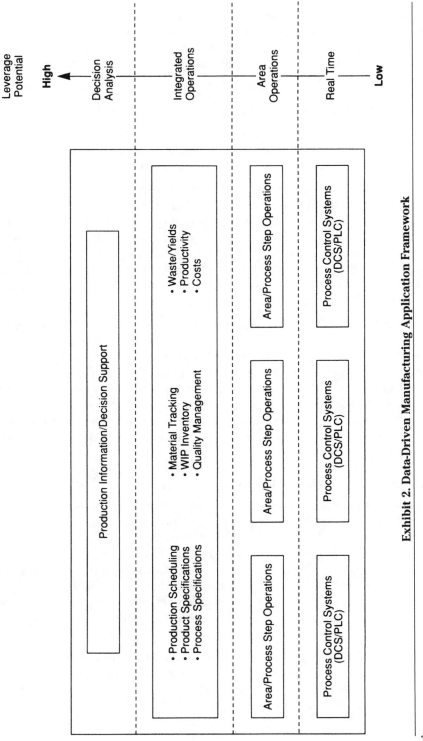

Exhibit 2. Data-Driven Manufacturing Application Framework

tunity. The lack of a consistent framework for site applications all too often results in unique site applications requiring expensive life cycle support. Use of a consistent framework enhances the prospects of multi-site applications development (or commercial purchase), which significantly lowers life cycle support cost.

EFFECTIVE INFORMATION DELIVERY

In view of the strategic use of IT and the vast quantity of manufacturing data now available, what should be the product of the IS organization? What should be the role of IS in the world-class manufacturing organization?

The manufacturing IS organization is required to reduce total cost of ownership of software systems, reduce lead times, increase flexibility of developed applications, deliver integrated (i.e., customer, supplier, and internal manufacturing) information to a wide variety of users across the enterprise, and develop and acquire applications suitable for multiple sites. The manner in which these conventional business objectives and their implied information needs are provided must improve for the manufacturer seeking integrated information and control systems.

Information collection and delivery is replacing applications development as the IS organization's prime responsibility. The advent of consistent manufacturing site application frameworks and the growing availability of commercial applications to satisfy operational needs can reduce, over time, the IS role in the development and support of operational applications. As a result, IS can focus on the development and support of a new infrastructural layer of decision data services and networks built above the existing base of manufacturing site and centralized order entry/product distribution systems.

Infrastructure for Worldwide Decision Support

This infrastructural layer is designed to collect and position the requisite information for horizontal supply chain integration and worldwide decision support. William Inmon's unified data architecture with data warehouses holding decision support information separate from operational systems is gaining acceptance in manufacturing and nonmanufacturing industries alike.[3] The IS organization's prime responsibility is to implement and maintain this secure worldwide decision support infrastructure (see Exhibits 3 and 4)and to provide business with effective information access and delivery mechanisms.

The IS organizational model has evolved so far to optimize its traditional primary product: custom applications development. To accomplish worldwide information delivery, IS must adopt an organizational model that reflects its new primary product.

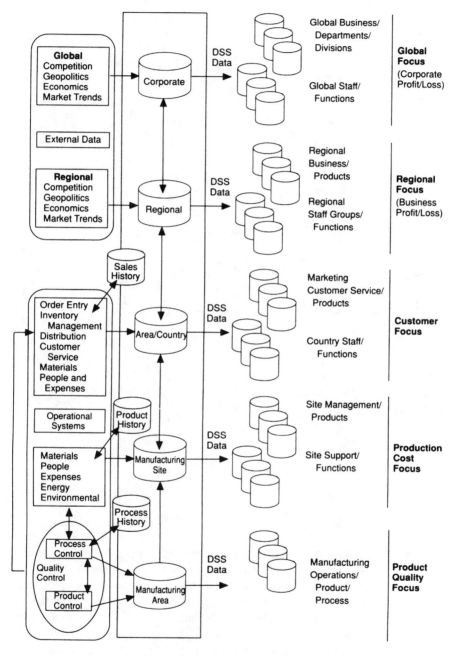

Exhibit 3. Data Delivery Architecture

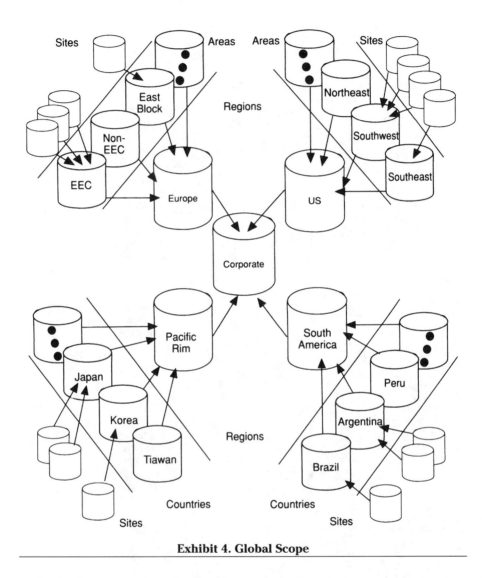

Exhibit 4. Global Scope

As the IS organization changes from a custom manufacturer to a product distributor, with enterprise information as its essential product, the central focus of IS becomes information supply, inventory, regional warehouses, and business delivery mechanisms. The responsibility for this nonoperational data storage, structure, and content must be separated from applications development and controlled centrally or regionally, driven by the need for data integration, end-user data access, and enterprisewide data integrity (see Exhibit 5). Distributed information storage and access mechanisms, predicated on the use of client/server technologies, can be implemented to insulate both the business users and Decision

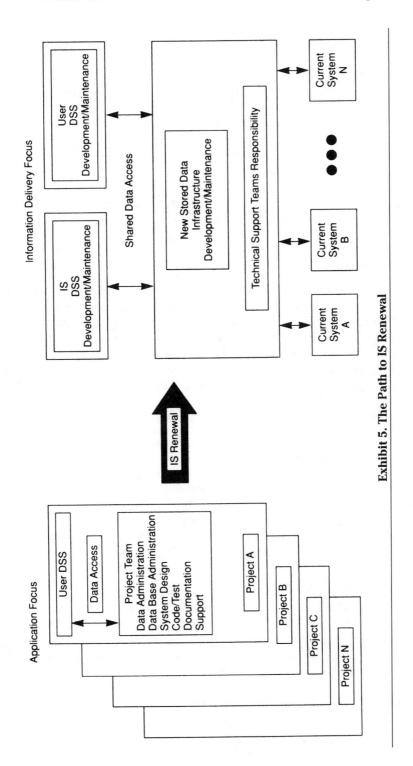

Exhibit 5. The Path to IS Renewal

Support System developers from the incompatibilities of existing operational applications.

New or reengineered operational systems are required to pass selected data from manufacturing sites and centralized order entry/product distribution operational systems to the infrastructure layer, thereby taking advantage of the infrastructure's ability to provide data to decision support applications. New operational systems can be downsized and optimized to best meet the immediate operational tasks. History, nonoperational analysis, and reporting could be accomplished as extensions of the infrastructure layer using commercially available analysis tools. Such a strategy allows users to select analysis tools according to their own business needs, with IS ensuring the integrity of the data managed within the infrastructure layer.

DELIVERY TEAMS

A consistent set of development policies, principles, methods, and tools is needed to govern the secure development and delivery of information products and services. On-line metrics relating to the performance of the infrastructure layer need to be made available to determine who is using information, as well as when, why, and where information is being used. A single (i.e., logical) decision support environment can provide insulation from underlying hardware and operating system incompatibilities. Decision support applications can be accomplished as a unified effort by IS or others, independent of the facilities or physical location of the developer.

A new IS business-focused organizational model emerges in which internal technical support teams assume the responsibility to design, build, and support the infrastructure layer. Radiating from the core are information delivery teams working directly with the businesses to identify information needs and ensure information delivery. Exhibit 6 details the relationships among the different members of the business-focused information delivery team. Exhibit 7 shows the overall organizational model for optimizing information delivery.

RECOMMENDED COURSE OF ACTION

The actual steps required to move an IS organization toward the described information delivery paradigm depend on current IS business practice and how quickly the IS and business cultures can accept change. Although the individual paths forward will differ, the overall goal is to establish sustainable change in both the IS technology and the people processes.

Organize Around Information Delivery

If the IS function is to be a provider of information as opposed to a provider of automation, then change is a prerequisite. The IS culture can begin

318

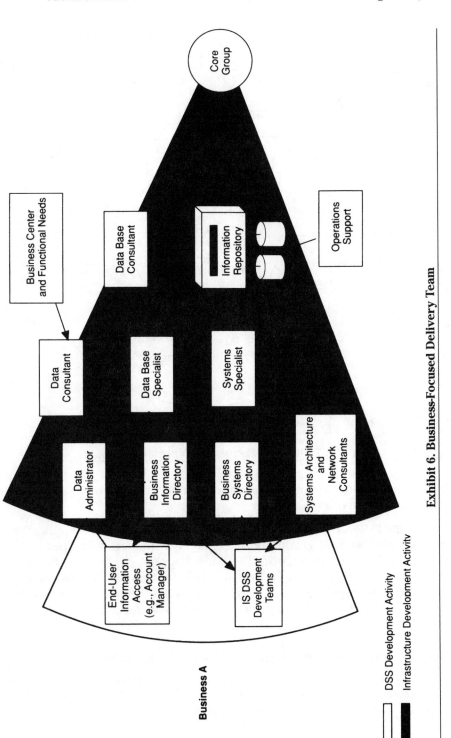

Exhibit 6. Business-Focused Delivery Team

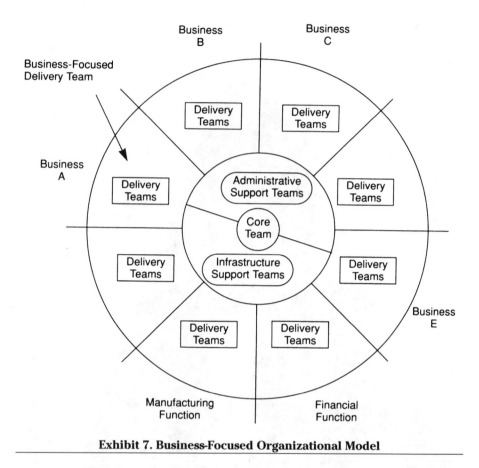

Exhibit 7. Business-Focused Organizational Model

by defining its purpose as that of empowering its user community through access to information.

Existing IS organizational structures that optimize custom applications development should gradually be replaced with structures promoting cross-application integration. Decision support capability should be removed as a task of individual applications development teams and organized as an enterprisewide infrastructural activity. Employee recognition and reward mechanisms must be redesigned to reinforce and sustain these new IS directions.

Develop and Implement an Enterprisewide Architecture

The plant sites of the global manufacturer are often littered with locally optimized IT solutions that defy integration into a multi-site supply chain strategy. The stand-alone nature of these solutions reflects the fact that no shared business rules or IT framework exists to provide the technical integration ground rules.

An essential IS path forward is the establishment of the architectural framework that provides a consistent technical context for horizontal business integration strategy. This framework should provide specific guidance for both existing and proposed applications, technology, and data. Data is not only a valid architectural consideration, it is fundamental to establishing integrated information delivery mechanisms. The data models resulting from data architecture development become the product catalogs for the IS function's information delivery business.

Information strategic planning (ISP) offers a valid approach to designing the overall enterprise architecture. The deficiency in information engineering has been a lack of recognition of the fundamental differences and uses in manufacturing data at different levels in the architecture. Exhibits 1 and 2 reflect these differences and their implications for manufacturing systems. Exhibits 3 and 4 reflect the logical placement of the data warehouses in the global manufacturing architecture. The use of encyclopedia-based Computer-Aided Software Engineering technology is strongly recommended in the development of the enterprisewide architecture. The distributed nature of this technology allows IS to both automate and share reusable software assets while teaming across geographical boundaries.

Notes

1. Malcolm Baldrige National Quality Award, U.S. Department of Commerce and the National Institute of Standards and Technology, Gaithersburg, MD.
2. H. Mintzberg and J.B. Quinn, *The Strategy Process* (Englewood Cliffs, NJ: Prentice Hall, 1991).
3. W.H. Inmon, *Building the Data Warehouse* (Wellesley, MA: QED Information Sciences, 1992).

Chapter 27

Organizational Pitfalls of Reengineering

D.P. Cardarelli
Ritu Agarwal
Mohan Tanniru

For the leaders of many companies considering or engaged in reengineering efforts of any magnitude, a stream of advice and influence from diverse sources sets the tone and tenets of successful reengineering. Relying on the veracity of this advice, corporate leadership embraced certain organizational initiatives and behaviors. Unfortunately, these behaviors sometimes detracted from successful implementation and at times accounted for failure of the effort altogether.

Only recently has the academic and practitioner literature[1] examined or addressed the reasons for reengineering effort failures. Failure is attributed to several organizational considerations, including an unwieldy project scope, the inability to demonstrate benefits quickly, a lack of top management commitment, a nonsupportive social culture to make the needed radical change, and inadequate resources.[2] Success factors, on the other hand, include top management commitment, an incremental implementation of radical plans, a reduction in the gap between espoused and practiced strategies, commitment from all members of the business process reengineering (BPR) team, and resource adequacy.

Ironically, some of the reasons for failure of reengineering efforts involve initiatives that arose out of the very tenets of success espoused over the past several years. This chapter explores why common wisdom can turn into a trap and what IS leaders can do to more proactively avoid and mitigate the adverse consequences of such traps. In addition, this chapter seeks to further illuminate understanding of a critical organizational challenge: How can the likelihood of success for process reengineering projects

0-8493-1273-6/02/$0.00+$1.50
© 2002 by CRC Press LLC

be improved? This understanding is based on a leader's perspective, his experiences with extensive reengineering projects, and interaction with other organizational leaders. A leader's insights suggest that there are some common organizational pitfalls that, if not anticipated and managed appropriately, can doom a reengineering project to failure.

WHAT ARE ORGANIZATIONAL PITFALLS?

A pitfall is defined here as a barrier to the successful execution of a given step. Frequently, pitfalls are either not easily observable or often not recognized by the project team members as hurdles they need to clear to complete a given step. Indeed, more prevalently and more disturbingly, the pitfalls are viewed as enablers or requirements for successful implementation. Experience suggests that there are three primary pitfalls:

1. BPR is a strategy.
2. A BPR effort needs a leader.
3. A BPR effort is big and new.

PITFALL 1: BPR IS A STRATEGY

Organizations that exhibit declining financial performance, an erosion of marketshare, or declining quality advantage to their competitors tend to view the radical change attributed to BPR as their savior. By emphasizing dramatic cost reductions or performance improvements that firms have achieved, published success stories of BPR only underscore this view.[3] Often, the search for such radical performance improvements provides the impetus for executives to engage in a major BPR effort with the expectation that such an engagement will address their financial woes.

BPR Is Not a Strategy

Organizations need to evolve strategies to address weakness in financial performance or competitiveness by first identifying what contributed to these weaknesses (a diagnosis) and then addressing these weaknesses (with a set of solutions). The solutions may necessitate improvements in quality, an expansion to new markets, a reduction of costs, or the creation of a market niche. A BPR effort may then be linked to one of these strategies.

For example, a firm might consider a reengineering of its processes along the customer order processing value chain to improve service quality if it is determined that a "quality improvement" strategy addresses the firm's need for better financial performance. The key point is to recognize BPR for what it is — a process to bring about change. The desired change and the strategic reasoning behind the change must be clearly identified before the process of BPR can even be assessed as appropriate. Perhaps one of the reasons why so many BPR projects fail is precisely this: Management did not focus attention on what the underlying business rationale and strategic intent was; rather, it viewed BPR as a strategy unto itself.

BPR Should Not Disguise Cost-Cutting Strategies

Several early BPR efforts such as those at Ford and IBM demonstrated how the consolidation of processes and elimination of workflows can reduce the number of people needed to provide quality service. Clearly, any reduction of labor directly contributes to cost reductions, and process reengineering appears attractive to firms looking for a quick way to improve financial performance or appear fiscally sound for potential investors. However, reducing labor without clearly linking a reduction to explicit corporate strategy can have severe ramifications, including loss of employee morale and expertise and loss of productivity as a result of job-related uncertainties. In some cases, cost reduction may not even be feasible if the BPR effort is intended to improve decision quality and market responsiveness.

Cost reduction can be a strategy and a BPR effort can, in fact, support such a strategy by reducing employment levels. For example, improved inventory management at the retail store may eliminate the need for warehouse operations, and electronic invoicing and order processing may reduce the number of employees involved in such operations. However, it is critical that a firm clearly articulate such a corporate strategy and explain the anticipated impact on employment levels.

A philosophy of deferring implementation of needed cost reductions until the initiation of a BPR effort, rather than acting on them immediately, can only result in adverse consequences. There is nothing more distressing to employee morale than finding out about job loss through rumor mills or newspaper reports — or finding out that job loss was an intended outcome of the BPR effort from the beginning. It is important that leaders implement cost reductions first under the existing framework for action to the extent possible, then seek to reengineer the framework as appropriate. It reduces anxiety in the long run and truly creates the right mental model for BPR efforts in the minds of the workforce: as a means of making fundamental changes in the way business is done rather than associating it with a work force reduction.

Technology Is Not a Solution

Early successes in process reengineering have been achieved, in part, by a firm's effective use of information technologies, such as electronic data interchange (EDI) technology to link suppliers and firms, knowledge-based technology to centralize processing knowledge so customer service can be improved, and workflow and document management technology to cen-

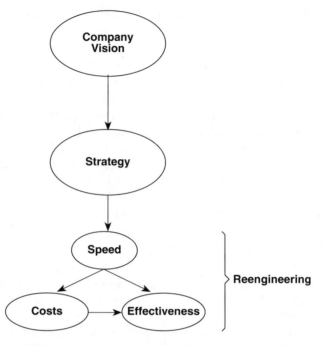

Exhibit 1. Overview of an Effective Approach to BPR

tralize document processing so responsiveness to customer requests may be improved. Hence, the tendency is to look toward technology to address a BPR problem. In some earlier reports, a BPR effort, as opposed to total quality management, was often actively linked to the use of IT. Although IT can be used to reduce costs and improve responsiveness, its utilization should be derived to support a process redesign effort that is identified as necessary to address an explicitly stated strategy. In other words, the technology cart should follow the strategy horse, with the process redesign decision linking the two.

In summary, to avoid pitfall 1, managers should perform the following activities:

- Focus on speed of reaction to market demands, cost of producing a product or providing service, and effectiveness in delivering quality product or service to meet customer satisfaction as strategies to address corporate vision.
- Redesign processes to address these strategies.
- Seek out technologies to support these redesigned processes.

Exhibit 1 provides a schematic overview of this approach.

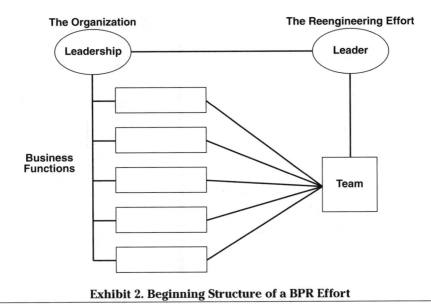

The Organization

The Reengineering Effort

Leadership

Leader

Business
Functions

Team

Exhibit 2. Beginning Structure of a BPR Effort

PITFALL 2: A BPR EFFORT NEEDS A LEADER

Conventional wisdom for implementing BPR suggests the following:

- Name a reengineering leader.
- Establish cross-functional teams to define the project.
- Select the best people for the job.
- Give these people the needed resources.
- Give them top management support and priority.

In many cases, the reengineering effort starts as shown in Exhibit 2 and ends up as shown in Exhibit 3. As the initial excitement wanes, the organization loses the BPR focus and the BPR team evolves into an independent entity. Eventually, barriers develop between two key entities — the BPR team and the management team — and communication breakdowns occur. Commitment becomes less forthcoming and direction for the BPR effort becomes less focused, as the changes called for in the BPR effort appear to come from or dictated by the BPR team as opposed to the management team. The following sections describe some ways to avoid this trap.

Avoid Naming a Leader

The owner of the company or the manager of the operations immediately affected by the BPR effort owns the reengineering effort. The project belongs to the owner/manager and its success is the responsibility of these individuals. He or she then, *ipso facto,* is the leader of the BPR project.

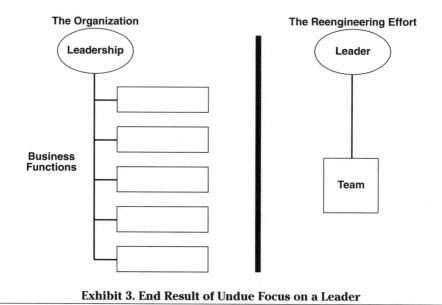

Exhibit 3. End Result of Undue Focus on a Leader

Management Should Not Define the Effort

Management is responsible for defining, in as much detail as possible, what needs to get done and how these steps eventually lead to fulfilling the espoused strategy through the BPR effort. The degree of specificity of these steps may vary depending on the level at which management is involved in the effort, and each of these steps must relate to the corporate strategy. Cross-functional teams are formed to get the work done and not to define the effort. If they start defining the effort, they have to start selling the effort to management, which becomes complex and time-consuming over time. The teams need to focus on executing tasks defined in the BPR effort and not spend too much time communicating the effort to management.

Recruit New Skills to Move the Effort to Completion

The best people within a firm are often the best at current practices (i.e., what they are doing now). This is somewhat inconsistent with the objective of a BPR effort, which is frequently intended to change the current practices. Because these so-called best people may not necessarily be the most suited for implementing the BPR effort, it is critical to define what needs to get done, to identify the skills needed to effectively complete these tasks, and to aggressively recruit those (from within or outside) that have these skills. Whereas bringing people from outside can infuse new knowledge or skills into a firm, the objective of recruitment again should be related to the effort and the skills needed to complete the effort.

Resources, Support, and Priority Are Not Important

Give people the goals, direction, and feedback. Let the BPR teams move the effort toward its intended conclusion and let management focus on directing this effort and providing appropriate feedback so the team stays on course. The resources needed to complete the task will be addressed by management as they move the effort toward its intended conclusion. The support and priority are implicit and will be forthcoming when the effort is led by managers.

In summary, management's role in a BPR effort includes the following responsibilities:

- Define the steps needed to complete the BPR effort.
- Identify and recruit the appropriate talent to complete this effort.
- Use cross-functional teams to implement the effort.
- Provide direction and feedback to keep the effort on track.

PITFALL 3: A BPR EFFORT IS BIG AND NEW

BPR efforts are promoted as a major undertaking, requiring massive organizational resources and commitment. Such a characterization creates an atmosphere of crisis and forces management to pump in resources with the expectation that such a commitment is needed to ensure success. Although a BPR effort could necessitate a large investment in resources depending on its scope, one should not let the scope cloud management's judgment of fiscal, organizational, or social responsibility. Organizations have probably handled crises before and will do so in the future, BPR or no BPR. Thus, it is critical to place the whole BPR effort in context and plan for its implementation using the same type of sound business judgment that is afforded to any other major investment The following sections address ways to avoid this trap.

Avoid Scope Creep

Many projects start small with a narrow scope but mushroom in size over time. BPR efforts start big and continue to grow even bigger, as size becomes secondary with all the high visibility and initial excitement. The size of the effort should be determined by the espoused strategy. At times, when reengineering gets too big, it can stop or distract the people from productive work needed to keep the business running. Thus, like all efforts in which a firm engages, both big and small, a BPR effort has to be planned so it remains consistent with the strategy and shows incremental progress. In this way, each of these incrementally progressive steps builds competence, confidence, and momentum toward eventually achieving a big goal.

Ensure Accountability

Management should measure everything and make appropriate individuals accountable for each and every step. Management should not leave anything to chance or make assumptions about who does what. Personal accountability is the best motivator to get things done. Again, this accountability is needed for any effort: big or small, BPR or no BPR.

Focus on the Process, Not the Event

A reengineering effort will merely be one event in the firm's history. The process that is redesigned will have a longer lasting impact on the firm than the effort itself. So, management must focus on the process and make sure that the redesigned process affects the strategy positively now and into the future. In other words, management must make sure that the redesign effort continues to deliver the intended benefits or support the strategies over time, as BPR efforts may be transitory but processes and the organization itself hopefully have greater longevity.

Perpetuate the New Way of Bringing Change

Even after the reengineering effort is completed, processes have to be continuously changed or redesigned as market demands change and new strategies evolve. It becomes critical then to alter the change management culture so the firm perpetuates a new way of bringing about change. In other words, it is imperative that changing a process becomes a natural part of completing the process, especially when it appears that the process is not meeting organizational needs. Note that making a change to a process is not the same as patching a process to handle a new situation; the latter is a quick-fix solution that is likely to produce only short-term benefits, whereas the former focuses on evaluating the current process and changing (or redesigning) it to ensure its ongoing relevance and salience.

In summary, the pitfall of thinking of BPR as a new and big effort can be avoided by handling it just like any large organizational effort. The following activities are crucial to achieving success in this endeavor:

- Ensure incremental progress to sustain confidence, competence, and momentum.
- Make people accountable by measuring progress and effort.
- Focus the effort on the processes that are being changed to meet the strategies.
- Ensure that process change becomes a part of process completion.

Notes

1. Bashein, B.J., Markus, M.L., and Riley, P. (1994). "Preconditions for BPR Success and How to Prevent Failures," *Information Systems Management* 11 (2), pp. 7–13; Clemons, E., Thatcher, M.E., and Row, M.C. (1995). "Identifying Sources of Reengineering Failures: A Study of the Behavioral Factors Contributing to Reengineering Risks," *Journal of Management Information Systems,* 12 (1), pp. 9–36.
2. Stoddard, D. and Jarvenpaa, S.L. (1995). "Business Process Redesign: Tactics for Managing Radical Change, *Journal of Management Information Systems,* 12 (1), pp. 81–107.
3. Hammer, M. and Champy, J. *Reengineering the Corporation: A Manifesto for Business Revolution* (New York: Harper Business, 1993).

Chapter 28
Quality and Change Management

Yannis A. Pollalis

Business process reengineering (BPR) has become one of the most cited management issues in the managerial, academic, and trade press. It has also been listed as a top priority by most surveys of corporate executives, business planners, and management consultants. The BPR concept was introduced during the late 1980s primarily by a few influential consultants and academics. BPR uses information technology (IT) to radically change (or redesign) the business processes within organizations to dramatically increase their efficiency and effectiveness. Although some of the concepts and methods of previous management practices are similar to those of BPR (e.g., total quality management and activity value analysis), BPR is still perceived by some advocates as a different way of management thinking. Thus, many of the mistakes committed with BPR's predecessor concepts and methods have been repeated.

Furthermore, evidence indicates that a great percentage of BPR efforts have failed. Research on these failures produced a list of critical failure factors that include lack of management commitment and leadership, resistance to change, unclear specifications, inadequate resources, technocentricism, a lack of user/customer involvement, and failure to address the human aspect of planned change.

Although BPR reflects a relatively new way of thinking about process change, similar efforts have already taken place in the areas of information systems planning (ISP) and total quality management (TQM). Thus, integrating BPR, ISP, and TQM into a holistic model capitalizes on the lessons learned from ISP and TQM efforts and avoids repetition of past mistakes.

ISP AS PLATFORM FOR INTEGRATING BPR AND TQM

TQM's main goal is to improve the processes within an organization and the organization's ability to meet the needs of the customer by emphasizing continuous quality improvement and responsiveness to customer

0-8493-1273-6/02/$0.00+$1.50

demands. Overall, TQM activities involve improving business processes and implementing incremental change by:

- Focusing on satisfying customer needs
- Analyzing business processes continuously to increase efficiency and customer service
- Emphasizing teamwork and employee empowerment across and within the firm to ensure the previous two activities

ISP activities include:

- Identifying information resources that support or redefine the goals of the firm and the IS organization
- Identifying opportunities to use IT and improve the firm's competitive advantage
- Implementing process change through IT
- Meeting the systems requirements of internal and external users

More specifically, ISP aims to reduce the uncertainty associated with the internal and external business environments. Uncertainty in the internal environment is generated by process changes in an organization. Its successful resolution depends on the ability of IS management to understand the interrelationships among the various organizational functions and processes and minimize redundancy and inefficiencies. This type of uncertainty requires that ISP consider process quality improvements along with user satisfaction goals.

Uncertainty in the external environment results from IT developments and competitive market pressures. ISP's role in this arena is to identify opportunities and threats in the environment and successfully integrate them with the IS organization's goals.

Thus, ISP can be defined as a proactive process that emphasizes IT-based process change to improve an organization's ability to:

- Respond successfully to external threats and opportunities
- Strategically apply its own capabilities and competencies through information resources

Based on this definition, ISP focuses on three areas common to both BPR and TQM:

1. *Technological improvement — which* reflects the IT focus of BPR's process redesign and innovation efforts
2. *Process improvement — which* emphasizes both the redesign of existing organizational processes and the employee empowerment concepts used in TQM's cross-functional and coordination activities
3. *Strategic improvement — which* concentrates on BPR's and TQM's alignment with corporate objectives

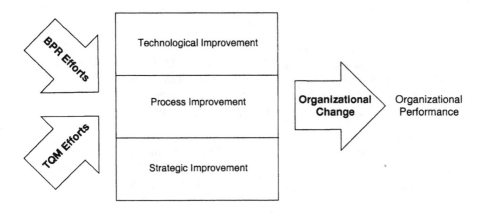

Exhibit 1. Planning as a Platform for Integrating BPR and TQM Efforts

Thus, as illustrated in Exhibit 1, IS planning can act as a platform that integrates an organization's BPR and TQM process change efforts.

COMMON DIMENSIONS OF ISP, BPR, AND TQM

IS planning has four major components that overlap with the objectives of BPR and TQM.

1. Alignment of Corporate and IS Goals

In IS planning, information resources are used to support business goals (usually efficiency, effectiveness, and competitive uniqueness), as well as to lead corporate strategic efforts to capitalize on external opportunities and internal competencies derived from IT. For example, Wal-Mart's integrated distribution network and United Services Automobile Association's (USAA) state-of-the-art document-handling system represent two such IT-based distinctive competencies. These competencies were aligned with corporate strategies and brought competitive advantage to the two companies.

2. Customer Focus

The ultimate goal of ISP should not be to use IT to implement organizational change for the sake of technology's potential capabilities. Rather, ISP should address various concerns of quality and customer needs, and improve and sustain linkages between the organization and its internal and external customers. In general, IT systems that help the customer to order, choose among alternatives, and purchase products and services contribute to both BPR's radical change and TQM's continuous improvement efforts. Thus, IS planning becomes the hub for a value-added network that includes linkages to both external customers (e.g., suppliers, buyers, and competitors) and internal customers (e.g., functional departments and divisions).

For example, the legendary systems of American Airlines' SABRE, American Hospital Supply's ASAP, and McKesson's ECONOMOST have helped to build strong ties with external customers (i.e., travel agents, hospitals, and drugstores, respectively) owing to their user friendliness, convenience, and value-added services offered with the total package.

Similarly, ISP can facilitate relations and linkages among an organization's internal customers (e.g., accounting, purchasing, production, and marketing) by improving the quality and efficiency of IS services. Examples of such cases include Charles Schwab's integrated account environment (called cashiering), which allows faster and more reliable retrieval of customer/investor account information by the various Schwab brokers; and Citicorp's workgroup computing environment, which integrates the business divisions of leasing, retail banking, institutional banking, capital markets, and real estate loans to promote reliable information and overall organizational effectiveness.

3. IT-Based Process Change

By changing, updating, or replacing existing information systems and processes within a firm, ISP facilitates restructuring of a firm's business processes. Prerequisites of such planned IT-based change include management support, strong IT leadership, and involvement of IS executives in corporate planning and systems thinking. The efforts of Pacific Bell, Xerox, and Texas Instruments in this area are discussed in the section on successful integrations.

4. Organizational Learning

By forcing its participants to understand a firm's various processes, their critical success factors, and the way IT can improve them, the ISP function becomes a facilitator for learning about organizational processes. Various techniques, such as scenario-based planning and simulations of internal or external crises, promote such learning and prevent unexpected disasters. Among the classic examples of such efforts toward organizational learning through strategic planning is Shell's crisis management simulations, in which what-if exercises resulted in major redesign and process changes that helped the company anticipate and prevent market- and technology-based disasters.

Exhibit 2 depicts the integration of an organization's BPR and TQM process change efforts with IS planning.

Exhibit 2. Integrating BPR and TQM with IS planning.

Major Components of IS Planning	Interrelated BPR Efforts	Interrelated TQM Efforts
Strategic Alignment: Dynamic relationship between corporate and IS goals; focus on capitalizing on external opportunities and internal capabilities and cornpetencies derived from IT.	Reengineering efforts begin with the corporate objectives and aim to realign operational capabilities with corporate strategic goals.	TQM's efforts include alignment with the IS organization's goals to improve IS operations (e.g., introduce new software tools and promote acceptance by organizational users).
Customer Focus: Introduction or adoption of IT to increase customer satisfaction and create value-added services.	Reengineering is driven by customer demands and is taking advantage of the market opportunities derived from customer needs.	TQM is focusing on both internal customers (e.g., business divisions) and external customers (e.g., buyers, suppliers, competitors, support institutions).
Process Change: Changing, updating, or replacing existing IT-based processes to improve organizational effectiveness and efficiency (i.e., change management and systems planning).	BPR asks whether organizational processes can be redesigned to increase their effectiveness and looks at the interrelationships among the organizational processes affected by IT.	TQM emphasizes coordination among IS professionals and the rest of the organizational functions and continuous improvement of the processes across the organization's value chain.
Organizational Learning: Understanding the firm's critical success factors, the relationships among its cross-functional processes, and its capacity to prevent crises and disasters (i.e., scenario-based planning).	Reengineering examines the possibility of changing organizational members' business mental models by challenging management's existing assumptions and learning both from past failures and successes and from new IT developments.	TQM focuses on incremental changes similar to prototyping systems development methodology and learning by completing small steps in implementing change, using workgroups, and sharing information across functional areas.

INTEGRATED PROCESS CHANGE MANAGEMENT

Recent research and case studies confirm the similarities between ISP, BPR, and TQM. Organizations that engage in uncoordinated and sometimes concurrent efforts for ISP, BPR, and TQM engender the following problems and concerns:

- Different organizational members advocate and participate in often similar ISP, BPR, and TQM change initiatives, which results in redundancy, inefficiency, and inconsistency in organizational projects and goals.
- Some organizational members participate in more than one of the three initiatives, resulting in confusion and inability to define clear and consistent goals across the organization. In addition, because participants in ISP and TQM activities often fear that the reengineers will eliminate or ignore their efforts in the eagerness to start with a clean slate, they are reluctant to commit needed resources to ISP and TQM activities.
- Because of the confusion and lack of trust among the participants in the preceding two scenarios, very few ISP, BPR, and TQM projects can be successfully implemented.
- There are no clear and compatible measures or criteria of success for ISP, BPR, and TQM projects, resulting in inadequate evaluation of efforts to implement organizational change. Furthermore, although BPR advocates might view organizational change as strategic, TQM and ISP advocates might regard it as simply operational, thus making it almost impossible to set priorities for projects and coordinate change efforts across a firm.

Success Stories

Companies such as Pacific Bell, Xerox, and Texas Instruments (TI) are among the few firms that, under the concept of process management, have integrated traditional TQM procedures with IS process-modeling and BPR techniques. In these organizations, in contrast to what Michael Hammer and James Champy preached in *Reengineering the Corporation* (New York: Harper Business, 1993), BPR and TQM are viewed as two sides of the same coin and IS planning is integrated with their efforts toward process change management. For example, Pacific Bell and TI created central-process-management teams responsible for providing tools and methods to concurrent BPR efforts and for ensuring that IS, TQM, and BPR teams are coordinated and learn from each other's successes and failures.

More specifically, at Pacific Bell, process management efforts include IS projects responsible for aligning systems development strategies and tools with the current needs of BPR projects. At Texas Instruments, various process-capture tools allow continuous improvement methods to be integrated with BPR and IS development processes; similarly, Xerox has created the concept of process owners who decide what kind of change needs to be performed in a broad business process (e.g., tweaking versus a major overhaul) and how IS, TQM, and BPR groups can work together to provide the necessary tools and methodologies.

In contrast to these integrated environments, some companies continue to view BPR as a radically different type of activity for IT planning and TQM. Such companies take a more top-down approach that allows BPR consultants to identify specific projects and procedures and ignore any organizational learning accrued before their involvement. The problem with uncoordinated approaches, however, can be traced back to TQM efforts that attempted to deliver competitive advantage without considering key external and organizational factors (i.e., technology developments, market conditions, and corporate strategy) and focusing instead on internal improvements and process changes.

BPR is not an entirely new activity, different from ISP and TQM. As Exhibit 3 illustrates, all three are complementary elements of efforts

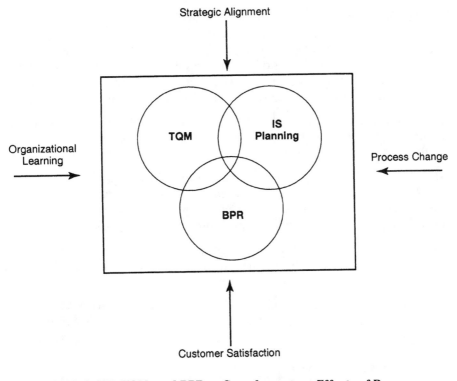

Exhibit 3. ISP, TQM, and BPR as Complementary Efforts of Process Change Management

toward process change management. Although ISP, BPR, and TQM should be coordinated within an organization, certain activities are unique to each of them. These activities are shown as the nonoverlapping areas in Exhibit 3 and include the following:

- TQM usually involves bottom-up, incremental design changes focusing on specific processes.
- BPR usually involves a top-down orientation, focusing on innovation and radical change.
- ISP can be both top-down (i.e., strategic) and bottom-up (tactical) to identify corporate strategies as well as IS implementation problems. Successful ISP practice involves both top-down and bottom-up orientations to anticipate short-term organizational changes and long-term technology developments and market forces that could affect corporate goals.

STEPS FOR INTEGRATING ISP, BPR, AND TQM

The following steps form the basis for process change management and will help IS professionals integrate ISP, BPR, and TQM.

Determining priorities and organizational goals for each initiative. For example, does process change mean the same for ISP, BPR, and TQM groups? Organizational priorities can be established through the techniques of critical success factors (CSFs) and benchmarking, or be based on the organization's distinctive competencies (IT-based or otherwise). ISP, BPR, and TQM task forces should collaborate with top management in this stage.

Bringing participants from each initiative together to discuss their projects and identify similarities and differences among them. The shared dimensions of the three initiatives as delineated in Exhibit 1 should be used in this step.

Establishing collaborative meetings or groups to discuss organizational learning issues over the course of ISP, BPR, and TQM efforts. Such groups discuss what the organization has learned from each initiative so far to make use of successful processes and avoid repetition of past mistakes.

Avoiding redundant activities. Scheduling regular informative meetings at which teams disclose their findings helps ensure that activities are complementary rather than redundant.

Setting synchronous and clear goals. This step is accomplished by having teams agree on measurement criteria or participate in one another's evaluation procedures.

ROLE OF IS MANAGEMENT

The importance of IT resources in any BPR and TQM effort gives IS management a central and sensitive role in the integration process. By conveying the following key concepts to the BPR and TQM groups, IS managers clarify the necessity of integration as well as the IS function's supportive role in the effort toward organizational change.

Shared Resources and Expertise. The whole organization benefits when teams share resources and expertise while working toward process innovation (BPR), continuous process improvement (TQM), and IT-based strategic advantage (ISP). Stressing the common goals among the three initiatives (e.g., alignment, customer satisfaction, process improvement, and organizational learning) helps clarify this concept. IS managers can also play the role of the outside IT consultant for both BPR and TQM initiatives.

Alignment of Technology with Corporate and Customer Needs. Teamwork and inclusion of IS managers in BPR and TQM decision processes and projects increases the likelihood that the systems delivered by IS will be aligned with corporate goals, as well as with customer (internal and external) specifications. Furthermore, senior executives are more likely to accept and support recommendations for organizational change when participants from all three initiatives are involved in and accountable for final process change results.

Commitment and Accountability. Integrating ISP, BPR, and TQM efforts is not about giving more control to the IS organization and management. It is about commitment and accountability — both at the individual and group levels — to build a platform for shared expertise and organizational goals.

Strategic Advantage. The ISP–BPR–TQM think tank promotes competency-based strategies and creates processes and systems that optimize the organization's unique capabilities and resources.

Prototyping for Success. Prototyping procedures in which pilot systems and processes are tested before full-scale implementation and full commitment of resources increase the success rate for the perspective change and enhance the learning capacity of the ISP, BPR, and TQM groups.

Common Measurement Criteria. Consistent measurement criteria across all three initiatives eases the transition from independence and redundancy to integration and sharing. Common criteria among BPR, ISP, and TQM include process quality, product quality, system quality, customer satisfaction, cost reduction, faster delivery, and value-added service to customers.

Measurement should not be based on a bottom-line approach that continuously monitors costs and benefits. Such an approach eventually results in micro savings and demoralization of the ISP–BPR–TQM alliance. Measurement should be flexible, because there is no guaranteed way to include or predict all benefits and costs from a system or process, and allow for innovation and guided risk-taking. This approach gives partici-pants a certain degree of responsibility for decision-making and brings bet-ter results in the long run. In summary, measurement should be able to see both the forest and the trees in regard to the short- and long-range goals of a BPR, ISP, and TQM alliance.

CONCLUSION

Organizations that quickly jump from one management trend to another without first learning from past experience have high failure rates in their efforts toward process change management. In contrast, organizations that have a universal management philosophy embedded in all activities related to improvement and change compete successfully. In an age when global competition and continuous technology developments are the norm, the ISP–BPR–TQM holistic model capitalizes on and integrates the learning that occurs in IS planning, business process reengineering, and total quality management.

Chapter 29
Developing Reward and Compensation Systems to Motivate Self-Managed Teams

Madeline Weiss

Leading-edge IS departments are using empowered, customer-focused teams — self-managed teams — to provide innovative uses of information technology to the organizations they serve. Teams require sustenance if continuous improvement is to be achieved. This chapter describes how information systems (IS) management can motivate teams and individual team members by rethinking traditional methods for reward and compensation.

PROBLEMS ADDRESSED

Moving up within the organization has long been seen by IS professionals as a reward worth working hard to attain. However, such traditional expectations of career growth are beginning to shatter as hierarchies in IS departments flatten. Long-term security has also been a traditional expectation of IS professionals, who have always been in demand. However, major corporations are laying off people as part of downsizing, rightsizing, and outsourcing strategies to become competitive.

This chapter discusses methods to motivate IS employees to perform at ever-higher levels of quality, productivity, and customer service as IS departments change their unwritten contracts with employees. The recommended actions center around rethinking traditional methods for rewards and compensation.

0-8493-1273-6/02/$0.00+$1.50
© 2002 by CRC Press LLC

DETERMINING WHAT MOTIVATES INFORMATION SYSTEMS MANAGERS AND PROFESSIONALS

Rewards serve to address individual needs or motives in order to motivate individuals to meet the organization's needs. The first step is to consider the needs or motives of IS managers and professionals. Studies and experience consistently point to the following motivators:

1. They want praise, recognition, and respect.
2. They want to control their own destiny by making decisions related to work and having control over their careers.
3. They want to know how they are doing.
4. They want to feel they are contributing to something worthwhile.
5. They want to be challenged and to grow professionally.
6. They want the chance to play another game of "pinball." The pinball analogy is that if you win the game, you get to play another round. Tracy Kidder, author of *The Soul of a New Machine,* noted the high level of motivation of a Data General Corp. team charged with building a new computer. In this example, the team members were compelled to succeed on the project so they would get the chance to build another computer.
7. They want to be financially compensated for their performance and participate in the organization's success.
8. Some professionals want social relationships. (Research shows, however, that many other IS professionals have low social needs and do not want as much social interaction as other professionals.)
9. They want to be secure.
10. Some professionals want more flexibility in hours and location.

Managerial Implications

Of course, motivations vary among individual IS managers and professionals. Individuals are motivated to perform at a high level if the reward for doing so is attractive (i.e., meets their needs), if they believe they can achieve the specified goals, and if they believe that performance will lead to the desired rewards. This has several managerial implications. First, motivation varies by individual; not everyone values the same rewards. Second, goals must be clear and perceived to be attainable. Finally, people have to believe that rewards are linked to performance. Therefore, the organization must make visible the link between performance and rewards.

MOTIVATIONAL REWARD STRATEGIES FOR THE NEW IS ENVIRONMENT

The following reward strategies are proving to be effective in this new environment. Compensation is considered last because studies of IS and other high-technology professional workers indicate that the most important rewards are the professional, rather than financial, ones.

Providing a Vision People Want to Achieve

IS professionals are motivated to contribute to something worthwhile. Successful leaders can inspire others with the power and excitement of their vision and give people a sense of purpose and pride in their work. An example is an experiment in which two groups are given an unassembled puzzle. One group is given the pieces in a plastic bag and the other, in a box with a picture of the completed puzzle. There is little doubt that the second group would complete its puzzle first. The leader's job is to paint the big picture and to give people a clear sense of what the puzzle will look like when all have put their pieces in place.

Giving People the Opportunity to Learn and Grow

The chance to learn new skills or apply them in new arenas is an important motivator in a turbulent environment because it is oriented toward securing the future. It also meets the need for growth and recognition. Access to education, training, mentors, and challenging projects can be very motivating.

Tomorrow's careers will be more professional, in which opportunity involves the chance to take on more challenging assignments. New careers will also be more entrepreneurial (i.e., success is starting a new venture either within the organization or outside it) and less bureaucratic (i.e., success is measured by advancing up the hierarchy). The overall effect of these changes in careers, as well as of downsizing and outsourcing, is a loosening of employment bonds between organizations and people. Job insecurity is a consequence.

Employability. If employment at a particular organization cannot be guaranteed, then organizations must help satisfy the need for security through employability. Employability security comes from the knowledge that today's work enhances the person's value in terms of future opportunities. It comes from the chance to accumulate human capital — skills and reputation — that can be invested in new opportunities as they arise. IS departments must invest in people's learning and growth, give them opportunities to apply their skills in new arenas, encourage innovative contributions, and reward their performance. The IS department benefits because people are willing and eager to take on challenging assignments.

Methods for enhancing employability include work-related seminars; tuition reimbursement; funds for travel to professional meetings; funds for professional association memberships, journal subscriptions, and books;

cross-functional job rotation; challenging assignments; and an environment in which failure is used as a learning opportunity.

Sharing Power and Information: Empowerment

IS professionals want to be informed and have control over their work environment. Without gasoline (power), the capabilities of the most finely tuned, high-performance automobile would be useless. This is true of people as well. Without power, people cannot perform at their best level.

The more people feel a sense of power and influence, the greater their ownership and investment in the organization's success, the better their ability to perform their jobs, and the greater their sense of personal well-being. Empowerment leads to better performance than if employees feel like bureaucrats who have to ask permission at every step.

Empowerment benefits leaders as well. When people are empowered and can accomplish more on their own, the leader's own sphere of influence is enhanced because people feel grateful. Leaders build credits they can draw on when extraordinary efforts are needed.

Ways to share power and information include giving people discretion and autonomy over tasks and resources, asking people what they need to do their jobs most effectively and getting it for them, giving problem-solving teams a budget to implement ideas, keeping people informed, giving people greater visibility and recognition, building relationships for others, and encouraging employees to evaluate their managers and each other.

Establishing Teamwork as a Way of Doing Business

Teams — corrective action, quality improvement, or self-managed — are proliferating in IS departments driven by Total Quality Management (TQM) initiatives, flattening hierarchies, and the need to produce higher-quality products faster and cheaper. Teams address individuals' motives for social relationships, their need to be more in control of their destiny, as well as challenge and professional growth. In organizations with true rather than nominal team cultures, teams transform relationships and work processes — they challenge virtually everything about how business is conducted.

Conceptually, teams are based on the incorporation of several core job dimensions that research has shown lead to high motivation and satisfaction, as well as performance. These dimensions are skill variety, task identity (the team owns a complete task or process), task significance, autonomy, and feedback (see the Job Characteristics Model in Exhibit 1). The model can be used to design teams and identify elements to build into jobs to make teams successful. The model is especially suited to people with high growth needs, which studies show to be a key characteristic of IS professionals.

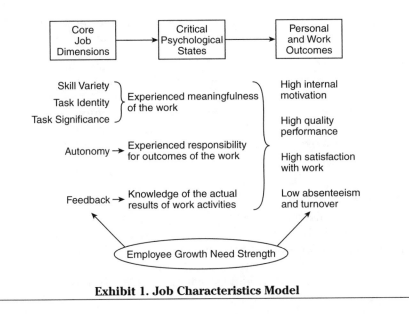

Exhibit 1. Job Characteristics Model

Showing an Interest in Employees' Performance and Careers

Coaching and expressing confidence in employees are ways of taking an active interest in them. These actions address employees' needs for praise and growth. Coaches of IS professionals should give feedback regularly, not simply at the end of the performance evaluation season. Managers should also provide material support whenever possible and moral support at all times.

Enhancing Reputation

Reputation is a key resource in professional careers and the chance to enhance it can be an outstanding motivator. Enhancing reputation is a way to meet needs for recognition, for individuals to see themselves as winners, and for security (i.e., employability). Managers can enhance reputation — and enhance motivation — by providing public recognition and visible awards, crediting the authors of innovation, publicizing people outside their own departments, and linking people into organizational and professional networks.

Acknowledging Accomplishments

Organizations traditionally focus on financial ways of recognizing accomplishments. Nonfinancial awards can also be motivating, especially for IS professionals. Awards satisfy needs for recognition.

Too many organizations shroud awards (financial and other types) in secrecy, worrying that those who do not receive them will be jealous and demotivated. If the message the organization wants to send is that it values performance and rewards it, awards should not be kept a secret.

Methods of recognizing and celebrating accomplishments include holding recognition events and special lunches to acknowledge extraordinary efforts, praising people in memos to senior management or in organizational newsletters, and sending letters directly to employees. With long, multi-year IS projects, milestones can instead be recognized. People who feel like winners like to up the ante and raise their work standards.

Creating Dual Career Ladders

Most IS departments can cite examples of excellent IS professionals who became less-than-excellent IS managers. Unfortunately, many outstanding IS professionals have found the only avenue for increasing financial rewards to be promotion into management. However, many talented technical people experience frustration and failure as managers. In the future, those who might be successful as managers may not have the chance as hierarchies flatten.

Some IS departments have instituted dual career ladders as a way to address these issues and keep senior professionals in positions where they can succeed and continue to make significant contributions. In some cases, technical tracks do not go as high as senior IS management positions, but they do overlap at least with the lower- to middle-management positions.

Promotion up the technical ladder should be based on carefully defined criteria representing excellence in the discipline. As with research and development professionals, where dual career ladders are now common, selection and evaluation can be conducted through a committee of professionals and, in some cases, managers who hold higher ranks. At the highest levels, committee members may even be drawn from a distinguished list of professionals who do not necessarily belong to the organization. Although movement up the managerial ladder is usually associated with increasing power and decision-making authority, movement up the professional ladder is usually indicated by greater autonomy in the practice of the individual's craft.

Providing Midcareer Breaks

Managers can send high performers, who either are or will be in management positions, to management development programs at business schools. These programs help prepare someone with a specialized background for general management responsibilities. This is a reward because it meets people's needs to grow and be recognized. The organization is rewarded in turn because it welcomes back a more skilled employee.

Free Time and Flexible Work Hours and Location

These rewards reflect respect and trust, and give people greater control over their destiny. They are effective vehicles for rewarding and retaining performers who need flexible work structures, such as those with day-care or elder-care responsibilities.

Giving People a Share of the Value They Create

Most IS managers would say their compensation systems are based on paying for performance, rather than for time in the job. However, the reality in many cases is that differentials in salary increases are small, performance appraisal is not done well, and performance measures are inadequate. Because subjective performance measures are not trusted, people do not believe that pay based on such measures is really a result of performance.

In practice, the so-called merit raise is based less on merit and more on cost-of-living adjustments that often do not satisfy even those who receive the raises. The tiny range of difference among employees is usually just enough to create conflict. Past merit payments become part of the individual's base salary, thereby creating an annuity, and people continue to get paid for past performance. To be motivating, however, changes in pay should be 10 to 15 percent, rather than the often-seen 2 to 6 percent.

Too many managers are unwilling to recommend large and small pay actions, even when they are warranted. Consequently, people get raises even if they do not actually meet their objectives. One reason is the unpleasant task of explaining to subordinates why they are getting a low raise. If managers make excuses, such as their hands were tied by the budget or by the personnel department's policies, it clearly communicates to the employee that pay increases are beyond the manager's control and thus not based on performance.

The practice of allocating a budget amount to a manager to divide among employees on the basis of merit can be disruptive to teamwork. It clearly puts team members in a competitive situation in which team performance does not matter, but individual performance does. In many cases, managers are asked to distribute their ratings using a forced-distribution format because a normal distribution is usually assumed, although the people being rated are not a random sample of the population. These IS professionals have been carefully selected and trained. In addition, the number of individuals being rated is far too small to render a normal distribution.

Organizations are moving to new strategies in compensation. According to the American Quality and Productivity Center, 75 percent of organizations use at least one nontraditional pay plan. Most of these programs share two characteristics: they put more of each employee's pay at risk and they link that pay more closely to performance. Incentive pay systems not only induce individuals and teams to produce more, but they also hold down wages and wage-related benefits and let compensation costs rise and fall with the organization's fortunes.

FINANCIAL COMPENSATION SYSTEMS BASED ON PERFORMANCE

Four nontraditional pay plans that should be considered are profit sharing, gain sharing, performance bonuses, and share of venture returns.

1. Profit Sharing

Profit sharing returns a share of business profits to employees at the corporate or business-unit level. Most plans set a profit goal and pay back a share of all profits achieved above that goal. According to compensation experts, profit sharing is not a very effective motivator, primarily because most employees perceive they have little influence on overall profits.

2. Gain Sharing

Gain sharing operates somewhat like a corporate profit-sharing plan, but is based solely on business-unit results. Because of the narrow scope, gain-sharing plans are more motivating than profit sharing. When participants meet or exceed group performance goals, they receive bonuses. Early gain-sharing plans focused narrowly on such productivity measures as cutting labor costs and were used mainly with operational staff at the plant level.

Service providers are experimenting with gain-sharing programs. At one credit services department in a manufacturing company, staff members receive quarterly bonuses that are based on how much they collect in accounts receivable. In one example, the manager invested $22,000 and got back more than $100,000 in collections. Staff members, informed of quarterly objectives and monthly collection amounts, recognize the direct impact of their performance on income.

IS departments are also exploring gain-sharing programs, especially among self-managing teams. At Corning, Inc., an applications development team is part of a gain-sharing pilot in the corporate Administrative Services Center. The plan includes incentives for spending within budget, customer satisfaction, process improvement, and cost reduction.

3. Performance Bonuses

Performance bonuses are cash incentives paid to individual employees or teams for exceptional performance. Bonuses do not roll into base pay. In some IS departments, managers decide who should receive bonuses. In others, anyone in the organization can nominate recipients and a panel of peers makes the decisions.

Sometimes, bonuses are paid out in cash equivalents. An IS department might award "American Express Be My Guest" chits; another might award gift certificates and tickets. Still another might award gifts to families of IS staff members who work overtime. One high-technology company in the Boston area offers a competitive bonus of 25 percent of an engineer's salary based on the performance of the team. Each team can submit a proposal to management explaining why it deserves a bonus based on costs saved or value added to the organization. In another IS department, an applications development team proposed taking over a critical project that had been outsourced and was foundering. The team stipulated that if it came in under budget, ahead of schedule, and met specific quality requirements, it should receive a bonus. The team met its criteria and got the bonus. Still another IS department awards $500 to each member of teams that complete projects with no more than 5 percent variance.

In the IS department at Medtronic, Inc., a medical device manufacturer headquartered in Minneapolis, bonuses are granted in lieu of salary increases. Salaries are adjusted based on the market, but not performance. Bonuses are granted annually on the basis of performance and awarded as a lump sum. Exceptional performers can earn annual bonuses of 24 percent, while those whose performance is rated in the expected category receive no bonus (thereby freeing up more funds for exceptional performer rewards). Employees must earn their bonuses each year. Managers at Medtronic believe that their new compensation system has actually helped recruit and retain star performers.

4. Share of Venture Returns

This compensation method focuses on long-term company success. Company stock is distributed to employees as part of a bonus payment or through company-sponsored stock option or stock purchase programs. A stock plan addresses individual needs for security and participation in the organization's financial success. Its intent is to make employees at all levels think and act as if they were owners.

Research indicates that employee owners tend to be more committed to their organizations. It gives them a financial incentive to figure out ways of working smarter. Organizations that combine ownership and employee involvement have consistently been shown to improve performance.

KEY SUCCESS FACTORS IN IMPLEMENTING REWARD SYSTEMS

Several factors should be kept in mind when implementing new reward systems for the IS department.

Develop a Vision of Organization Strategy and Culture. Those organizations with a clear vision of the strategy and culture to be served by the reward system usually install more successful nontraditional reward programs. They focus on the links between business priorities and reward design issues, taking time to prepare the organization for implementation and develop accurate measures.

Make Sure Employees Understand Performance Priorities. Employees must also know what they should do to support these priorities and that this support leads to rewards. Effective two-way communication is key to ensuring that employees understand the link between goals and rewards. Providing rewards that are attractive ensures that employees will be motivated to meet goals.

Track Programs for Success. Any program must be audited and controlled to ensure that it stays on course. A one- or two-degree correction one month out is much easier to accomplish than a 40-degree correction 12 months out. View incentive programs as ongoing, constantly monitored management programs.

Let People Make a Difference. Successful programs focus on work designed with wide margins for employees to exercise discretion. People can make a difference on their jobs, and management values the additional contribution sufficiently to pay additional rewards when peak performance is achieved.

Separate the Incentive from the Base Pay. The reward of traditional merit adjustments is lost when folded into base pay. Moreover, adjustments to salaries contribute to high fixed costs and pay compression, especially among long-term employees.

Stay Flexible. Adapt programs as business conditions and plans change.

Reflect Upside and Downside Risk. Programs that reflect risk reinforce a sense of partnership among stakeholders.

Make Information about the Pay System Public. Disclosure enhances the credibility of the link between pay and performance. Secrecy leads to consistent distortions of people's perceptions of how pay is administered. It leads to overestimates of the pay of others so that in comparison, individuals feel more poorly paid than in fact they are.

Establish a Performance Evaluation System Consonant with Reward Systems. An effective performance evaluation system should include:

- Clear, measurable objectives created with the active participation of those being evaluated and perceived as tough but achievable
- Understanding on the part of those being evaluated of the impact of accomplishing the objectives on financial compensation

- A mechanism for soliciting input on performance from as many relevant sources as possible, both inside and ouside the IS department
- Open communication on performance so that those being evaluated feel they had meaningful input; in addition, the organization's culture must value effective performance evaluation

Foster a Climate of Continual Learning. All IS members need a dose of humility sprinkled on their basic self-confidence. Humility acknowledges that there are always new things to learn to improve the future.

RECOMMENDED COURSE OF ACTION

The dream of having organizations appreciate that effective information services contribute to their ability to compete globally is coming true. For IS departments not yet positioned to meet the challenge, the dream begins to take on the quality of a nightmare of ever-greater demands for the latest and greatest technology solutions and services. To adapt, IS departments need highly motivated and skilled IS professionals who are prepared to meet and exceed the company's sometimes daunting requirements — even as pressures to reduce costs constrict their ability to do so.

Overall strategies to help the IS department meet these challenges successfully include flattening the management hierarchy, adopting Total Quality Management, and establishing self-managed teams that are empowered and customer focused. Another strategy detailed in this chapter is to create reward and compensation systems that motivate. New reward systems are different from those of traditional bureaucrats. They are based less on status and more on contribution; and they consist not of regular promotion and automatic pay raises, but of excitement about a vision, challenging assignments, and a share of the glory and gains of success. For IS professionals, the new security is not employment security, but employability security.

Leading-edge IS organizations are demonstrating that, taken together and implemented in an integrated fashion, these strategies unleash creativity, commitment, and ownership in IS. As a result, the minds, hearts, and spirits of IS professionals are enlisted in delivering world-class services and systems that their organizations truly value.

Bibliography

1. Kanter, R.M., *When Giants Learn to Dance,* Simon & Schuster, New York, 1989.
2. Lawler, E.E., *Strategic Pay: Aligning Organizational Strategies and Pay Systems,* Jossey-Bass Publishers, San Francisco, 1990.
3. Robbins, S.P., *Essentials of Organizational Behavior,* Prentice-Hall, Englewood Cliffs, NJ, 1988.

Section 4
Task 3: Forging Supply Chain Partnerships

This section addresses partnerships outside the immediate organization. This is the area where SCM often has the most visible impact on an organization. What have traditionally been arm's-length transactions, often driven by price, are giving away to cooperative relationships among suppliers and customers. A major hurdle to the performance of this task is the traditional role the procurement function plays and the mindset of people in that function.

There seems to be no limit to the creativity applied in the shaping of supply chain partnerships. Falling into this category are solutions such as exchanges, electronic data interchange (EDI), extranets, Web sites, applications service providers, and outsourcing. All these change the relationships with existing partners or establish new relationships, falling into our definition of Task 3.

Not to be ignored are the nontechnical alternatives for linking with customers or suppliers. Several of these are explored as well. The IS professional as well as the general manager, should be aware of the alternatives to what can be very expensive IT solutions.

Chapter 30
Reengineering the Supply Chain: The Next Hurdle

Scott Stephens
Craig Gustin
James B. Ayers

American business is rapidly adapting to the supply chain paradigm. This paradigm moves beyond department or company efforts, to supplier and customer collaboration in supply redesign. Confining improvement efforts, the paradigm goes, to single departments or even single companies, will not cut it in today's competitive economy.

Changes brought by supply chain reengineering are in the news almost daily:

- The Big Three automakers strive to turn their suppliers into systems suppliers — not component makers. The outsourcing of key components reduces costs, but leads to strikes and plant shutdowns.
- Proctor and Gamble reports saving $1.6 billion over five years and expects to save even more in the future through more efficient supply chain management.
- A grocery chain called David's sues its distributor, Fleming, for overcharging on its business. The suit forces an "unbundling" of distributor charges.
- A major natural gas producer and pipeline operator, Enron, buys an electric utility to integrate its supply chain and compete with deregulating electric utilities for end-user customers.
- A top producer of entertainment content, Disney, buys a television network, ABC, to ensure distribution channels for its product.
- Over 70 of the nation's largest manufacturers and shippers form a Supply Chain Council to standardize supply chain nomenclature and pro-

cess descriptions. The Council is one of several organizations developing tools for more efficient supply chain management.

- After a review of internal processes, the Department of Defense moves to adopt commercial supply chain processes and accelerate initiatives to electronically link its systems with commercial suppliers and carriers.
- Microsoft teams with Net Logistics to launch a zero-cost Web site for conducting shipping transactions in a standard format.
- A coffee chain consolidates non-coffee product (muffins and other extras) delivery to reduce frenetic early-morning, shelf-stocking by multiple vendors.

These examples illustrate the breadth and depth of supply chain reengineering. Their scope illustrates the major difference between supply chain and traditional reengineering efforts. Because these efforts are intercompany, the difficulties in their undertaking are orders of magnitude larger than traditional efforts. By the same token, the impact of such initiatives can transform an industry.

The purpose of this chapter is to explain the challenges in supply chain reengineering and offer insight into the shape of future large-scale reengineering projects. Admittedly, no one has all the answers, but those who get supply chain reengineering right will be winners in their markets.

The Supply Chain

The supply chain includes the organizations and processes for the acquisition, storage, and sale of raw materials, intermediate products, and finished products. Supply chain product flow is linked by physical, monetary, and information flows.

Supply chain management is a term that can mean different things to different people. In the broadest sense, it encompasses all logistics activities, customer-supplier partnerships, new product development and introduction, inventory management, and facilities. The concept, as shown in some of the examples, applies equally to service businesses.

Many professionals define supply chain management more narrowly. They often confine the definition to activities internal to any one company, minimizing the scope of improvement efforts outside the walls of their own enterprise. This perspective is often justified by the daunting task of implementing internal change. After all, smaller reengineering efforts at the local level often fall far short of either promises or expectations. And the risks of missteps and wasted time and money increase as project scope increases.

Craig Gustin, in cooperation with the University of Georgia and the consulting firm of Ernst & Young, conducted a study of logistics systems reengineering efforts directed at supply chain integration. Results of the 1995 study showed that reengineering efforts, most of which were one-company affairs, are still in the beginning stages. Only 9 percent of the respondents deemed they had been successful. Another 42 percent were in progress at various stages, and 20 percent were ignoring the effort entirely.

Supply chain thinking is fundamentally different in the mindset and management approach needed to be successful. The need for a new mindset is a by-product of growing interdependence among organizations. As the name implies, it requires a top-down perspective, often of an entire industry, beyond the boundaries of any one enterprise.

Exhibit 1 illustrates the point. Inputs (raw material, information, intellectual capital) to Enterprise A are processed in Departments 1, 2, and 3. The output of Enterprise A moves on to Enterprise B. Enterprise B, in turn, adds its value through four departments. Enterprise B's output proceeds down the chain toward the end user. Thus, the supply chain covers many different departments and contributing enterprises, each with its own values, information systems, structures, and economics.

This exhibit simplifies the situation. However, the problem of adopting one common view in undertaking a reengineering program remains. Depending on whom one talks to, at least four views are prevalent:

1. *The strategic view.* The supply chain design offers a different way to compete. It is a chain of resources used to support a product's market positioning in terms of the target customer, pricing, and promotion mix. The end result is improving margins on product sales.
2. *The functional view.* The supply chain consists of the individual organizations needed to procure material, convert it, and sell it. It is supported by material, transportation, and other groups. The end result is lower costs in the dominant functions.
3. *The logistics–transportation view.* The supply chain is the physical path of a product through a set of facilities linked by a transportation network. Those facilities include factories, warehouses, sales offices, trucks and ships, and distribution centers. The objective is lower logistics costs.
4. *The information management view.* The supply chain is integrated by the movement of information among the many participants. An integrated supply chain has a common information base as well as the mechanics in place to share this information among participants. The objective is low information-processing cost.

The authors have seen only one or two of these views incorporated in their observations of reengineering efforts. While none of these views are wrong, any one of them alone will produce an incomplete solution. Without

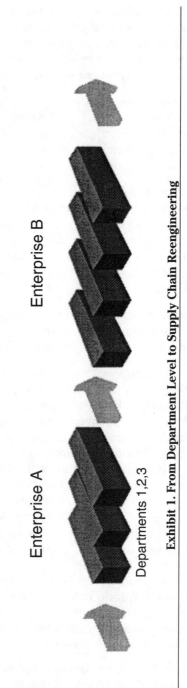

Exhibit 1. From Department Level to Supply Chain Reengineering

taking all views into account, supply chain reengineering efforts are doomed. A key challenge is to somehow incorporate all these views into a single reengineering effort.

Reengineering

Like supply chain management, business process reengineering (BPR) has many interpretations. Hammer and Champy, the authors who popularized the term, distinguished BPR from other process changes by its radical and dramatic nature. Others[1] classify a broad range of initiatives under the term "reengineering." Many, if not most, seek less than dramatic results or even goals. The authors believe that the focus of reengineering, or whatever term succeeds it, will continue to evolve. Stephens, Gustin, and Ayers believe the evolution has had three stages.

At Stage 1, the efforts are department focused. Process improvement is conceived, developed, and managed at that level. These efforts often create department "silos." The result is optimization at the department level, while perhaps doing damage in other departments or even in other enterprises beyond the walls.

In Stage 2, enterprisewide solutions emerge. Reengineering begins to affect the entire company with top-management sponsorship. Efforts such as cellular workgroups and focused factories, organized around segmented customer requirements, are examples of enterprisewide solutions.

Stage 3 is supply chain focused, going beyond the organization to multi-enterprise processes. There are many reasons to pursue a supply chain strategy. The best is improvement in strategic positioning. Michael E. Porter, a prolific writer on strategy, believes that strategic positions are built on hard-to-copy activity systems. Sustainable competitive advantage derives not from cost-cutting, but from excellence in executing activities that reinforce value to customers.[2] For manufacturers, the supply chain is integral to these sustainable strategies.

At Stage 3, a supply chain reengineering effort will have four characteristics; it

1. Has the potential to shift the basis for competition
2. Involves multiple enterprises in the supply chain
3. Has an aggressive, not incremental, quantified improvement objective
4. Will incorporate a balanced approach encompassing the four views described above

According to these measures, the efforts of most organizations are Stage 1. A few have ventured into Stage 2. Stage 3 examples are still emerging. There is growing recognition that each business is mutually dependent on its customers for sure, and its suppliers in all probability. Chief executives realize they need proactive — rather than reactive — strategies to capitalize on the supply chain threats and opportunities.

Report Cards on Reengineering

Much anecdotal evidence, as well as published research, supports some general conclusions about the success of reengineering. A study by consultants of McKinsey & Company suggests five keys for success.[3] Their advice includes the following points:

- Set an aggressive reengineering performance target.
- Commit 20 to 50 percent of the chief executive's time to the project.
- Conduct a comprehensive review of customer needs, economic leverage points, and market trends.
- Assign an additional senior executive to be responsible for implementation.
- Conduct a comprehensive pilot of the new design.

These conclusions came after an in-depth study of 20 reengineering projects. In 11 cases, the business unit results gained less than 5 percent. This occurred despite the fact that process results were often much greater. The few surveyed organizations that had favorable results performed projects with broad scopes.

Another contributor to success was the depth of solutions. The successful efforts went beyond just one dimension, like information systems. They included structure, skills, measures, and values, as well as technology and systems.

Another review of reengineering success factors looked at project management issues applied to the effort itself.[1] The factors contributing to success and failure are shown in Exhibit 2 in decreasing order of their contribution to success. Note that technology is ranked at the bottom of the heap

Exhibit 2. Issues Related to Reengineering Success

- *Human resources:* training and organization value development
- *Project management:* communication and lack of management tools; failure to assess project performance
- *Management support:* goal-setting, sponsorship, continuity of involvement
- *Change management:* addressing organizational resistance
- *Tactical planning:* resource commitment and financial justification
- *Process delineation:* measurable goals, scoping of process, scoping of effort, and incrementalism
- *Strategic planning:* alignment with strategy and business vision for the project
- *Timeframe:* timeliness of implementation, ability to ensure schedule performance
- *Technological competence:* capabilities in technical areas of the project

as a contributor to success. Both retrospectives concluded that "soft" issues played the leading role in ensuring the success of reengineering.

That view was reinforced by Dr. Michael Hammer, creator of "reengineering." When queried about reengineering success, he admitted, "I wasn't smart enough about that (getting more out of people to support revenue growth). I was reflecting my engineering background and was insufficiently appreciative of the human dimension. I've learned that's critical."[4]

How Stage 3 Reengineering Management Will Work

Although traditional Stage 1 and 2 reengineering efforts have yielded mixed results, the success factors found in these two stages can be used to draw conclusions for Stage 3. The following list of features will help to characterize successful Stage 3 supply chain reengineering initiatives.

- A focused goal for the effort with objectives including strategic positioning, increased revenue, and profit improvement
- Multi-company groups partnering and funding the effort
- Third-party "honest broker" to facilitate the effort and provide an outsider's perspective
- CEO steering committee with representatives from each partner firm
- Multi-year projects with self-funding, short-term wins; this allows the program to be sustained by its own cash-flow benefits
- Contracting that distributes costs and rewards based on achieving measures of performance
- Balanced deployment of technology with integration of legacy systems where the likelihood of disparate systems will hinder progress toward improvement

At the operational level, a supply chain reengineering program could evolve as described in the following paragraphs.

First, a sponsor firm must determine that there is a compelling requirement to reengineer some or all of its supply chain activities. This firm will invite key suppliers and customers to participate. The invitees add significant value to the chain or have a high level of interdependence with the sponsor.

Next, the participants will form a supply chain working group (SCWG). This group will choose the processes and build a business case for the effort. At this point, the honest broker will begin to guide the evolving project. The SCWG produces a master plan for the project. The plan will cover participation, reward, and cost distribution, and issues in areas such as information technology, facilities, and product development.

Finally, implementation should occur locally but be monitored globally. The SCWG should retain responsibility for ongoing progress toward the stated objectives. In concert with the planning, the team members can pursue specific implementation projects based on criteria such as impact on baseline measures, time to completion, and contribution to competitive positioning.

Information technology issues become important for firms with existing investments in technology and processes. The financial commitment and risk associated with replacing existing information technology with state-of-the-art systems are often prohibitive. These firms require an open architecture framework approach that incorporates existing systems and permits inserting technology when appropriate.

CONCLUSION

Supply chain reengineering is the next hurdle in improving competitive position. Like many of today's technologies, the half-life of a reengineered process is short. This means that supply chain reengineering will become an ongoing process requiring a continuous effort by all partners in the supply chain.

Notes

1. Grover, V., Jeong, S.R., Kettinger, W.J., and Teng, J.T.C. "The Implementation of Business Process Reengineering," *Journal of Management Information Systems*, 12(1), 109–144, Summer 1995.
2. Porter, Michael E., "What Is Strategy?," *Harvard Business Review*, 74(6), 61–78, Nov./Dec. 1996.
3. "How to Make Reengineering Really Work," *Harvard Business Review*, 71(6), 119–131, Nov/Dec. 1993.
4. White, Joseph B., "Reengineering Gurus Take Steps to Remodel Their Stalling Vehicles," *The Wall Street Journal*, November 30, 1996, p. 1.

Chapter 31

Interorganization Systems and Supply Chain Management: An Information Processing Perspective

G. Prem Premkumar

In recent years, supply chain management has been touted as one of the major strategies to improve organizational performance and generate competitive advantage (Ellram, 1990; Fisher, 1997). A variety of changes in the business environment including time-based competition, fast product cycle, just-in-time production, cost leadership, use of interorganizational systems, and global competition have fueled interest in supply chain management (SCM). The growth in business-to-business (B2B) commerce has highlighted the role of supply chain management in the modern digital economy.

Supply chain management encompasses many activities, but for the purposes of this chapter, it is defined as follows:

> Supply chain management is the integration of all activities associated with the flow and transformation of goods from new materials, through to the end user, as well as associated information flows, through improved supply-chain relationships to achieve a sustainable competitive advantage (Handfeld and Nichols, 1998).

This definition clearly identifies the two major flow components of the supply chain: materials and information. The growth in interorganizational systems (IOS) has made it possible to have electronic flow of information across the supply chain. Another definition of supply chain management from a business-process perspective that highlights the role of interorganizational systems is "Integration of business processes from end user through original suppliers that provides products, services, and information that add value to customers." Supply chain management reengineers the chain and adds value by exploiting the information in the value chain.

Traditional research on supply chain has focused on the flow of material and information independently. The operations and logistics researchers focused on movement of materials (Cooper et al., 1997) and the IT researchers focused on electronic flow of information (Premkumar et al., 1994). In this chapter, an attempt is made to integrate the findings from these two research streams and identify critical management issues related to implementation of an electronic supply chain that integrates the traditional supply chain with interorganizational systems.

SUPPLY CHAIN MANAGEMENT

A supply chain is a series of linked suppliers and customers that takes a basic raw material at one end and delivers a finished product to the ultimate end user at the other end. Exhibit 1 shows the various players in a supply chain.

The supply chain can be decomposed into many levels. There could be a single-level supply chain that includes only the focal firm's immediate set of suppliers and customers, or one could go down n levels to include the raw material supplier on one end and the disposal of used finished product at the other end. A supply chain becomes sufficiently complex beyond two levels. The complexity stems from the fact that it is not a simple linear chain as shown in Exhibit 1, but a complex web of chains as shown in Exhibit 2. Each customer and supplier in the chain has many supply chains with its own suppliers and customers. A small change in any of the partners' supply chain, or a weak or broken link in the web, can create a major reaction in the entire chain. Because most organizations have neither the

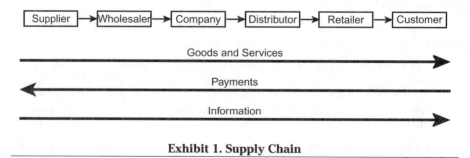

Exhibit 1. Supply Chain

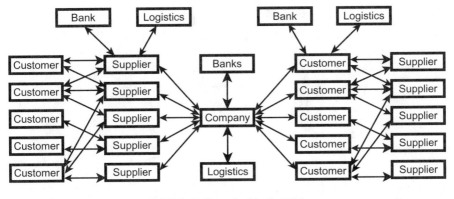

Exhibit 2. Supply Chain Web

control nor the resources to monitor the entire web, they normally restrict their focus to one or two levels.

There are three components flowing through the supply chain: goods and services in one direction, payments in the other direction, and information in both directions. Sometimes payments are shown as an information flow and not as a separate flow, although the characteristics are different and require different set of entities. To facilitate the movement of these three components, the service of other entities is required. While transportation carriers and logistics firms are used for movement of goods, banks and financial institutions are used for movement of payments. Information flow can occur between the entities directly or through an outsourcer or third party. In recent years, direct links between firms are becoming more popular than third-party links. However, there are large third-party, industrywide, interorganizational systems that create the infrastructure to facilitate the movement of information. An example of such an agency is the airline reservation system (e.g., Sabre) that facilitates movement of information among various entities in the transportation industry (airlines, travel agents, customers, rental car agencies, hotels).

Exhibit 3 shows the various players for the first level of the supply chain in an organization. Some of the major objectives of the supply chain management are

- Customer service
- Cycle time reduction
- Inventory turnover
- Flexibility and adaptability in the system
- Effectiveness of business processes

Supply chain management covers a broad area of partnership between two trading partners, including operations and logistics coordination,

TASK 3: FORGING SUPPLY CHAIN PARTNERSHIPS

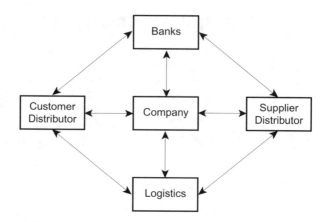

Exhibit 3. Business-to-Business Interorganizational System

partnerships in market research and product development, and coordination of customer service. Some of the implementation issues in supply chain management are

- Alignment of business interests of partners
- Long-term relationship management
- Reluctance to share information
- Complexity of large-scale supply chain management
- Competence of personnel supporting supply chain management
- Performance measurement and incentive systems to support supply chain management

INTERORGANIZATIONAL SYSTEMS

Information flow between organizations has existed ever since human beings traded their goods and services. What is unique about the current environment is the availability of a communications infrastructure to electronically transfer information, with minimal effort and time lag, resulting in the easy availability of information. Interorganizational systems, also called extranets, are application systems that link various partners in the supply chain using a public or private telecommunications infrastructure. These systems provide the ability for computer-to-computer communication of business transactions and documents. Interorganizational systems became popular with the introduction of electronic data interchange (EDI). Although EDI has been in existence for more than 20 years, it is only during the past five to ten years that it has been widely used. There are basically two types of interorganizational systems: electronic dyad (i.e., a system that exists between two firms) and electronic networks or multilateral information systems.

There are three levels of sophistication in interorganizational systems: communication, coordination, and cooperation. These are discussed in the following paragraphs.

At the simplest level, interorganizational systems can be used for electronic *communication* of messages between trading partners. This provides the basic infrastructure for electronic transmission of information. These messages may or may not be integrated with the rest of the information systems in the organization. Essentially, at this level, firms are substituting paper, phone, or fax modes of communication for computer-to-computer communication. Very often this happens in the initial stages of EDI, when a novice partner uses the computer to collect the EDI messages and later print them or rekey them for internal consumption.

The second level of sophistication is *coordination*, in which the computer-to-computer communication is integrated with the internal information system. An order from a customer is automatically entered, after routine validation, into the order processing and production planning system of the organization. There is active coordination in terms of production planning, delivery schedule, and logistics coordination between the partners. The level of coordination or coupling can be tight or loose depending on the level of information sharing and slack existing in the coupling. For example, Dell coordinates with its logistics firm and the computer monitor supplier (Sony) to directly deliver the computer monitor to the customer's premises along with the computer from Dell's warehouse, instead of receiving the monitor at Dell's warehouse, packaging with the computer and reshipping it to the customer. This saves Dell considerable time and cost. It does, however, require Dell to share order and customer information with the vendor and the logistics provider.

The final level of sophistication is *cooperation*, where two business partners share common goals and use similar performance measures to evaluate the performance of their interorganizational activities. Cooperation can occur over a wide range of levels, spanning many functional areas within the organization. For example, the firm can provide initial product design information to the suppliers and get their input in the design of the product; or the distributor can share customer information with its partners to support cross-selling of some products or develop joint promotional campaigns. Information technology plays a critical role in many of these cooperative ventures. This level of sophistication forms the advanced level of supply chain management at which firms graduate from traditional logistics to the entire gamut of business processes linking the two partners (Cooper et al., 1997). Automobile firms are experimenting with such partnerships with a few selective vendors.

TASK 3: FORGING SUPPLY CHAIN PARTNERSHIPS

Transaction-Cost Economics Framework

The field of transaction-cost economics provides a theoretical framework for discussion of market structures (Williamson, 1975). Two questions asked by firms are

1. Which activities should a firm keep within its boundaries and which activities should it outsource from outside?
2. How should it manage its relationship with its customers, suppliers, and other business partners?

A firm could have all the activities within its boundary and operate as a hierarchy, or it could outsource most of the activities, except for its core competencies, and operate as a virtual corporation, depending on the market for most of its inputs (Applegate and Gogan, 1996). Exhibit 4 shows these two possibilities. There are hybrid structures in which a firm may outsource only a few activities. Firms make decisions on organizational design based on various factors, including what investments have to be made specific to the relationship (asset specificity), what activity is critical for effective business performance of the firm, uncertainty in the relationship with partners, and product complexity. Investments specific to the relationship lock in the supplier and increase the costs of switching to

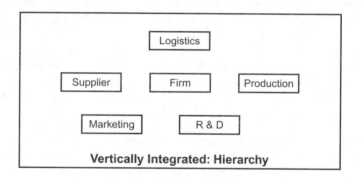

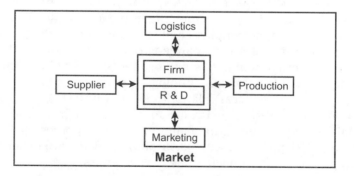

Exhibit 4. Markets and Hierarchies

another customer. Demand uncertainty may force a firm to develop a closer relationship with its supplier to better meet market requirements, or alternatively to develop standardized products and have extra inventory to counter the uncertainty.

The design of the organization and the structuring of the industry are to some extent dependent on the two cost components: production and transaction cost. Production cost is the direct cost to produce the product. Transaction cost includes coordination cost, operations risk, and opportunism risk (Clemons and Row, 1993). Coordination cost includes search cost, negotiation cost, financing cost, and distribution cost. Search cost involves the cost of exchanging information on product details and buyers' needs along with the cost for finding the right product or service that meets the needs. Negotiation and financing cost involve the cost of determining the appropriate price and payment terms and identifying suitable financing to pay for the product or service. Distribution cost is the cost of the physical transfer of goods to the buyer's location. Operations risk is the risk that other partner may misrepresent or withhold information or underperform on the contract. It stems from differences in the objectives of the partners and information asymmetry. This could also be considered as a cost if a buyer factors in the cost for policing the contract, obtaining additional information, enforcement, and dispute resolution. Opportunism risk is the risk due to the lack or loss of bargaining power because of a relationships specific investment. While in markets the production cost is low as a result of economies of scale and specialization, the transaction costs are higher. In hierarchies, the production costs are higher because of the lack of economies of scale, and the transaction costs are lower because of limited coordination and less risk.

Interorganizational systems reduce coordination cost by reducing the cost of exchanging and processing information. Interorganizational systems also increase information availability and processing capacity, enabling better monitoring, and thereby reducing operations risk. The use of open standards in interorganizational systems reduces relationship specificity for IT connectivity, enabling connection with more suppliers and customers, thereby reducing opportunism risk.

Electronic Integration Issues

Electronic integration along with free flow of information among the supply chain partners opens up a wide range of business opportunities (Clark and Lee, 1997). However, implementation is not always easy; there may be resistance, because integration may not provide the same level of benefits to all partners. Typically, EDI has been implemented in a hub-and-spoke arrangement, where the initiator (hub) takes proactive steps to get the smaller firms (spokes), mostly suppliers, to adopt interorganizational systems. They may even coerce the spoke firms into adopting EDI by using veiled threat of loss of business. Studies have found that the initiator tends to gain more at first but, in the long run, all parties benefit from the implementation. A similar situation is found in the implementation of a supply chain, where a firm normally takes a proactive lead to integrate the chain (Handfeld and Nichols, 1998).

Most of the discussion of supply chain and interorganizational systems is based on the premise that information will be freely shared among the partners. However, a critical issue is how much information can be shared between partners. Even though technology provides the ability to share information easily, firms may not share information for various business reasons. Businesses thrive and make money on information asymmetry. Therefore, there are strong disincentives to share information. Unless there is positive proof that sharing information is equally beneficial to all members of the supply chain, it will be difficult to convince all members to share information. The withholding of information by even one member in the chain can lead to loss of trust and dysfunctional behavior among all members, despite the best technology to facilitate information flow. For example, Wal-Mart began to suspect Rubbermaid's promise of lowest pricing for its supply chain management initiative, when Wal-Mart came to know through their buyer, who was recruited from another discount retailer, that Rubbermaid quoted lower prices for that retailer (Mariotti, 1999). It took many years for Rubbermaid to regain the trust of Wal-Mart.

UNCERTAINTY, INFORMATION ASYMMETRY, AND THE ROLE OF INTERORGANIZATIONAL SYSTEMS

Organizations often have twin objectives in managing uncertainty: (1) reduce their environmental uncertainty by obtaining as much information as possible, and (2) to increase information asymmetry to gain maximum benefits from interaction with their partners. The following section discusses the role of interorganizational systems in influencing uncertainty and information asymmetry.

Most organizations attempt to reduce uncertainty in their operations by improving the availability of appropriate information for decision-making. Information asymmetry among the participating units leads to uncertainty, which in turns leads to inefficiency of the total chain. While all organizations in the supply chain want to reduce their uncertainty, it may be at the expense of others in the supply chain (Sheombar, 1997). For example, the buyers may be waiting for a sale to buy in bulk rather than provide advance information of their requirements. Some businesses are built on brokering the information among the participating units. Therefore, reducing information asymmetry in the supply chain, while ideally optimal, may be threatening the business of these brokers (Lee and Clark, 1996). The designers of interorganizational systems need to be cognizant of practical realities.

Uncertainty can be broadly defined as "the difference in the amount of information required to perform the task and the information already possessed by the organization," (Galbraith, 1977). Daft and Lengel (1986) identified two forms of uncertainty: (1) uncertainty due to lack of knowledge regarding occurrence of events, and (2) uncertainty due to not knowing how to respond to an event when it occurs (also known as equivocality). In an open supply system, it is difficult to completely eliminate uncertainty because the organization deal with customer orders, which are randomly generated. Similarly, there is uncertainty related to supplies from the firm's vendors. The uncertainty could be due to variations in lead time or the quality of the products. Hence, a firm has both demand and supply uncertainty that is normally beyond its control. A firm absorbs the external uncertainty by designing suitable internal systems. It tries to design forecasting systems to better predict the external events. It adds some slack in internal design such as excess inventory (safety stock) or excess processing capacity or longer lead time to deal with external environmental uncertainty. The lower the external uncertainty the less slack the firm has to build in its internal design and thereby lower the operation costs. Hence, there is significant incentive to reduce uncertainty.

Organizations also experience uncertainty in their internal subunits. Whenever there is transfer of goods or information between subunits that requires coordination, uncertainty is created. For example, variation in production (due to quality or production problems) can create uncertainty in downstream subunits. Internal uncertainty among the subunits is influenced by two factors: (1) how the external uncertainty is distributed among the internal subunits, and (2) uncertainty created by its internal operations and information flow. The level of information sharing among the subunits influences the uncertainty experienced by the subunits. The internal units can be isolated from external uncertainty by building inventory on the inbound or the outbound side, or the units can be totally exposed to external uncertainty where everything is made to order. If the information flow between the sales department receiving the orders and the production department producing the products is constrained either by the time it takes to reach the other end or by the accuracy of the information, then it is going to add uncertainty in the production department. For example, if the order lead time is one week and it takes three days for the information to reach the production department, then they have less time to react to the orders. Similarly, if the information in its entirety is not completely transmitted (e.g., some product options are not known), then it creates uncertainty. The flow of information need not be one way. For example, the salesperson should have information on production lead time and inventory for them to promise appropriate delivery schedule.

TASK 3: FORGING SUPPLY CHAIN PARTNERSHIPS

The internal design of the organization is influenced by the performance parameters set by the firm in terms of lead time, cost, reliability, and the like. These parameters are to some extent determined by the external environment — the industry, customers, competitors, and suppliers. The lead time for order completion can determine the decoupling point between the external and internal environment. A short lead time may require a closer decoupling point to absorb the uncertainties in the demand. Reliability could determine the level of inventory and the level of capacity to meet demand. Cost has the opposite effect, but is equally important in determining the level of capacity and the decoupling point. Organizational design is modified to ensure that information processing capacity matches task uncertainty. Mismatch causes reduced performance through budget/time overruns. The performance parameters determine which variables of external events need to be predicted and the levels of slack in internal design. Firms need to match uncertainty with the level of coordination and information sharing with external environment, acceptable level of variation or deviation from required performance, and the cost of emergency measures to meet certain critical performance measures.

In summary, the design of interorganizational systems should ensure free flow of information across the supply chain. This leads to an interesting question. Is it feasible to design an information system that increases free flow of information across all partners in the supply chain? The answer is theoretically, yes; practically, maybe.

INTEGRATED SYSTEM: A UTOPIA OR A MYOPIA

The concept of an integrated system linking information from order processing, inventory control, production planning, warehousing, and accounting has been a dream for IS professionals for more than three decades. In the days of centralized mainframe systems, IS designers envisioned systems that integrated various functional areas. However, they never considered the organizational reality. Organizations, or even subunits within an organization, have two types of information — public and private information. The proportion of the two information types is dependent on the culture of the organization. If information is power, and information asymmetry between subunits provides better opportunities and negotiation capabilities, then there will be reluctance to share information. Although information asymmetry may cause greater uncertainty among the partners, it also provides the ability for one to exploit that uncertainty. Hence, even if it is technically feasible to integrate systems and share information, organizationally it may not be feasible because it may cause major upheavals in the power structure.

Dearden (1972), in a classic article in *Harvard Business Review,* claimed that it would be foolish to wish away the organizational realities and attempt to develop these integrated systems because they are bound to be implementation failures. Despite these predictions, IS designers in modern organizations have been slowly increasing the level of public information in an organization for the improved performance of the whole organization. A wave of new technologies in the last decade, including large database systems, strategic IS planning, IT infrastructure design, and client/server development have tried to achieve this objective with varying success rates. The recent introduction of enterprise resource planning (ERP) systems integrating internal information systems is also a step in that direction. The problems and challenges in implementing ERP highlight some of the organizational constraints. Even though information flow in current organizations is much better compared to organizations ten years ago, basic information is still not totally transparent within the organization.

If the process of opening up the information flow within the organization was a difficult task, it will be even more difficult across organizations that have widely different business objectives, different stakeholders, and servicing of multiple business partners. It will require a very high level of trust among trading partners. For example, a sales department would be unwilling to reveal its promotional campaign because it hopes to get as much sales without the promotion before using the promotion to attract new buyers. The development of interorganizational systems and integration with the supply chain has many management issues to be dealt with. A few of them are highlighted in the following sections.

MANAGEMENT ISSUES

In focus, both supply chain management and interorganizational systems are external to the organization and therefore they involve many unique management issues that are outside the control of senior management. Many of them involve developing better relationships and partnerships with the trading partners (Crum et al., 1996; Lambert et al., 1996). The successful implementation of interorganizational systems requires the cooperation of a large number of external trading partners. It is also a complex technical endeavor, as it is necessary to link widely diverse and technically incompatible systems. Management of interorganizational systems projects brings in additional challenges to IS managers trained on traditional IS projects, because they have to interact with partners whom they do not control and require of more senior management's guidance and approval in dealing with external partners. The major technical and management issues are discussed next.

Commonality of Objectives

Interorganizational systems are built on the premise that all organizations in the supply chain gain from sharing information. However, the benefits from sharing information for some may be more than for others. The free flow of information may even be a threat to the business of some of the intermediaries as their existence may be based on being only an information agent or a buffering agent to overcome uncertainty (Lee and Clark, 1996). For example, if flow of information from the retailer to the manufacturer is instantaneous, the existence of a distributor may be in jeopardy, as its primary role is to act as an information broker between the two or as a warehouser, stocking inventory to buffer for uncertainty and variation in demand. Direct marketers such as Dell Computers have leveraged the Internet to directly provide information to the end-consumer, thereby bypassing part of the chain (Stein and Sweat, 1998). In the airline industry, the ability to directly sell to consumers has put the information broker's (travel agent) business in jeopardy. The middlemen have some clout in the chain and can exert significant influence on the development and adoption of these systems. Airlines are reconsidering their strategies for rolling out interorganizational systems that will not alienate one of the major partners in the supply chain. Compaq, a major PC manufacturer, had to reformulate its Internet marketing plan because it alienated its retail dealer network with its Web-based online shopping foray, resulting in a reduction in retail and total sales. Therefore, although extranets are technically feasible, the lack of commonality of objectives may create major roadblocks to implementation. Goal congruence between two business partners, intent on maximizing their business goals, is a difficult issue, especially considering the fact that the organization participates in multiple dyads both at the upstream and downstream end.

Data Security

Extranets provide access to information in databases to their trading partners. While various security measures can be implemented to ensure security, it still exposes the firm and its trading partners to some data risk. The firm would be concerned about intruders hacking into the database and getting confidential information about its operations. The partners would be concerned about whether its competitors would get information about its business dealings with the firm. For example, when there are multiple competing suppliers to a retailer, it would be very useful for each of the competing suppliers to obtain information about marketshare, price, commission, and the like of its competitors to enable it to formulate its marketing strategy. The problem becomes more serious if there is a possibility of vertical integration. Trading partners would be concerned about safeguards to protect their information in their partners' databases.

Alignment with Business Strategies

It is not only feasible to design and build a technically sophisticated interorganizational systems, but also to formulate business and marketing strategies that complement and support these systems. If a firm's IS strategic objectives are not in alignment with its business strategies, then these interorganizational systems are bound to fail. For example, if a firm wants to design an interorganizational system that establishes a long-term relationship with its supplier, it needs to provide the supplier information on its requirements and perhaps even let the supplier monitor its inventory and replenish it periodically. A key component for the success of this system is the mutual agreement and trust that the supplier will supply at a certain price and the firm's buyer will not resort to buying it in bulk during sales promotions in alternative channels. Hence, there needs to be an alignment of business strategies and commitment among the organizations for long-term business cooperation if the system is to succeed.

Internal Systems and Performance Measures

It is not only important to align the external partners' business strategies but also to look inward and redesign internal control systems and performance measures to ensure the success of these systems. For example, if the buyer's performance is evaluated based on the level of savings achieved through innovative buying practices (e.g., sales promotions), then the buyer will continue to engage in buying practices that is advantageous to him or her, but is dysfunctional from an organizational perspective and detrimental to the success of the system. The organizational structure and the internal systems have to be modified to reflect the new buying arrangements. The automation of some of the buying activities may entail relocation of the buying personnel or redesign of their jobs. Resistance to such changes is inevitable in implementing these systems.

An equally important aspect, particularly in the context of supply chain management, is the performance measurement for the entire supply chain. Suitable benchmark measures must be developed that all members of the chain can use to evaluate. It is very unlikely that the benefits will be equally distributed or have a single measure as a reflection of performance. An important consideration is how does the chain perform against competing chains, and can it sustain its competitive advantage.

Internal control systems and audit measures for interorganizational systems are not very well developed. While some of the contractual and legal aspects are considered during the initial phase of setting up the interorganizational systems, not all the issues are considered. The controls system should evaluate various aspects of security, information exposure risk, and possibilities for fraud.

Technical Compatibility Issues

If an organization is planning for tight integration of various systems with its many trading partners, it needs to resolve various technical compatibility issues. While it may be relatively easy to establish a simple system to exchange messages (using EDI or other messaging technologies), the order of complexity increases many fold if information flow is tightly integrated across multiple systems spanning multiple partners. The use of vendor-specific hardware and software considerably increases the compatibility problems. The only solution would be the use of open systems that can exchange information regardless of the hardware and software, or use such intermediaries as value-added networks (VAN) that provide translation services. The development of XML (extensible markup language) and its integration with EDI provides opportunities to create open systems. Another major technical issue is the transformation from a message-passing interorganizational system to an event-driven system in which events trigger messages, which in turn trigger various actions. There are significant technical challenges in integrating multiple ERP systems across organizations.

GUIDELINES FOR INTERORGANIZATIONAL SYSTEMS IMPLEMENTATION

The implementation of interorganizational systems must be well planned and carefully implemented. Here are some guidelines for successful implementation.

Assess the Business Strategy and Internal Climate of the Organization

Before embarking on any major interorganizational systems it is important to assess the business strategy of the organization and senior management's views on interorganizational systems. If the firm is committed to supply chain management as a business strategy, then it makes sense to launch an interorganizational systems initiative. However, if the organization has not considered or is not in favor of supply chain management, then it is an uphill battle to sell the idea. Sometimes it may be necessary to be proactive, because some organizations may not have visualized an opportunity or formulated a formal business strategy relating to these ideas. It is important to realize that interorganizational systems implementation may not be the best strategy for all organizations. Interorganizational systems can create major changes in the industry structure and eliminate a few intermediaries in the supply chain. Hence, an organization has to carefully examine the long-term implications of introducing an interorganizational systems in the industry and to determine the threats and opportunities coming from the new environment.

Once the organization decides to evaluate the technology, the sponsoring department, normally the IS function, can take the lead in championing the adoption by creating an awareness of the technology, its potential, and its impact on the organization. It is important to find support from the functional areas that would benefit from interorganizational systems implementation. Explore the potential for interorganizational systems in the inbound (purchase) or outbound (sales) side and identify a strong champion for the technology. If they have already started an initiative in supply chain management or a related concept, interorganizational systems can be piggybacked on that initiative. Another strategy that is used in some firms is the "fear" factor. In some organizations, interorganizational systems implementation is initiated in response to external pressure from powerful customers or suppliers. The external environment can be examined to identify a potential customer or supplier who may be able to exert pressure to implement interorganizational systems. In summary, before launching the interorganizational systems project assess the internal environment for synergy with the business strategy, evaluate the long-term implications of introducing interorganizational systems in the industry, determine the level of support from functional areas, and identify champions in the functional area to sell the idea to senior management.

Assess the External Environment for Interorganizational Systems Partners

Once it has been determined that there is adequate internal support, it is necessary to identify one to three potential trading partners for the pilot phase of interorganizational systems implementation. Criteria that could be used for the selection of the partner include:

- Implementation focus, inbound or outbound side
- Desirability of establishing a long-term relationship from a business perspective
- Partner's willingness to participate
- Technical compatibility
- Technical expertise of the partner

Senior management must decide from a business strategy perspective whether the supply chain and interorganizational systems must be implemented on the inbound or the outbound side. While traditional supply chain efforts start on the purchase side, some organizations have proactively implemented it on the sales side. The decision is based on the level of support in the functional areas, external pressure, and maximization of benefits. The firm has to identify a few partners with whom it desires to have long-term business partnership, because the systems may evolve to very sophisticated levels of integration and cooperation between the firms. It is necessary to explore with the partners and determine the level of cooperation possible in these activities. Also, the availability of technical expertise at the partners' end and the technical compatibility of their systems must be assessed to determine the level of complexity and effort required for interorganizational systems' implementation.

Plan the Technology Infrastructure

The development of a strong information technology infrastructure is critical, because the scope of interorganizational systems in terms of the variety of applications and the number of partners can grow rapidly. The applications and communications architecture, the two pillars of IT infrastructure, must be planned to provide a strong foundation for growth of interorganizational systems. The firm has to first determine the level of sophistication (communication, coordination, and cooperation) required in the system. Although these systems evolve through these three levels over a period of time, it is important to decide on the level of integration for the next three years so that the infrastructure to support that can be built.

The applications architecture provides a blueprint of the various applications in interorganizational systems that users interact with as well as the supporting infrastructure. Some of the major issues that need to be addressed in developing the architecture are

- What will be the primary technology?
- What will be the client/server architecture?
- What will be the nature of linkage?

Technology Choice. The technology choices available are EDI, proprietary application software, simple Web-based system, XML, or a combination of these. Some of the factors to be considered in the selection of a technology are the level of sophistication required, technology trends and commercial availability of the technology, technical expertise of the firm and its partners, partners' preferred technology, type of linkage (one to one, one to many), and resource availability. EDI is a natural choice for a firm wanting to establish a one-on-one connection with its partner to transact at the lowest level of sophistication. Newer technologies such as XML/EDI integrate the Web to EDI and provide more opportunities. A Web-based interface is popular for one-to-many interactions with many customers using a "virtual storefront" metaphor. Firms such as GE are attempting it on the purchase side by allowing suppliers to bid on GE's requirements posted on the Web. An organization may use all of these technologies, choosing the technology that best fits each application. While EDI may be appropriate for large-volume event-triggered transaction applications, a Web-based user interface may be better for online interaction for information retrieval and decision making.

Client/Server Architecture. The client/server architecture provides the blueprint for applications development. While the Web or EDI determines the user interface to communicate with the partners, a firm has to decide on the back-end system that either provides or uses the data, and how the front-end and back-end systems will be integrated. Typically, middleware exists between the two, creating a three-tier architecture. Middleware is responsible for a variety of services, including mapping data from the front-end system to the specifications of the back-end system, facilitating communication between the two through translation and protocol services, providing a common applications programming interface (API) to a widely divergent set of front-end and back-end system and network protocols, and incorporating some validation and business logic for transaction processing. For example, the middleware may receive the EDI message (eg., sales order), map the contents to data fields, validate the data, convert it to a SQL statement, update the back-end database system, and, if necessary, trigger some downstream action. Organizations could use one or more tiers in the middleware depending on the complexity of the system, hardware and software and networks used, vendors' preferences, and performance issues.

Linkage. The nature of system linkage between the partners can be defined in terms of three dimensions: access mode, access type, and update mode. *Access mode* could be message-based or interactive. EDI systems are message-based systems in which there is computer-to-computer communications but normally minimal direct user interface for the external users. Alternatively, interorganizational systems could have a direct user interface to enable the user to directly interact with the partner's system. The user interface could be proprietary, Web-based, or a combination of both. For example, Federal Express provides a proprietary interface for large corporate clients to access their tracking system but also provides a Web-based interface to the general public. Similarly, the airline reservation systems have a proprietary interface for travel agents but also provide a Web-based interface for the general public. Currently, the proprietary systems have more functionality and better performance compared with Web-based systems.

Access type describes the operations the users are allowed on the system — only query or query and update of information. A firm may provide product information to customers but may not allow placing orders online. The access type is to some extent dependent on the firm's level of trust with its partners. Organizations have to assess the level of risk exposure from providing external access. The risks could arise from damage or corruption of data, data security issues, and information privacy issues in terms of access to others' confidential information in the database, along with other legal issues.

Update mode specifies the frequency of update of the back-end system with the transaction data from interorganizational systems, whether in batch mode or in real-time mode. In most EDI installations, where tight coupling between the two systems does not exist, the data is updated at periodic intervals in a batch mode. The other option is a real-time update of the database. This could create a significant load for the back-end system if the number of external users and their transactions increase significantly, leading to system performance problems for internal operations. The nature of linkage in terms of access mode, access type, and update mode is determined to some extent by the level of interorganizational systems sophistication.

Communications Architecture. The communications architecture is designed to support the applications architecture. It is dependent on a variety of other factors, including the partners' preferred mode of communication, cost, level of security and reliability, traffic volume, number of partners, and level of communications expertise. The options available are

- Direct connection using a modem
- Value-added network (VAN)
- Public Internet infrastructure
- Virtual private network (VPN)

If the company has only a few partners and infrequent communications, a direct connection using a modem may be the least-cost alternative. If the organization has large-volume communication with only a few partners, a leased line between the partners that provides continuous communication may be justified. If the firm or its partners do not have the necessary communications expertise, then a value-added network that provides various EDI-related services (e.g., translation, store-and-forward mail boxes, conversion, and integrated on-site services including front-end and back-end systems) would be a good choice to facilitate the adoption of interorganizational systems. The growth of the Internet has created a public packet-switching data communications infrastructure that is almost ubiquitous and provides a public highway for communication. However, the Internet suffers from perceptions of insecurity and unreliability. If adequate security precautions, such as encryption and digital authentication are used, it provides a cost-effective infrastructure for communication, especially for one-to-many communications where there is not a fixed set of trading partners. For firms that require a higher level of security and reliability in their communications infrastructure, virtual private network (VPN) provides all these services in a packaged form. VPN piggybacks on the public Internet protocol and infrastructure but uses additional security measures and better quality transmission.

Design and Implement the System

The firm, depending on its expertise and resources, can choose one of the following options:

- In-house development
- Packaged solution from a vendor

- Third-party development of software solution that specifically meets its needs
- Combination of the foregoing options

Unlike traditional information systems, interorganizational systems are implemented across organizational boundaries. The success in implementation is not only dependent on the firm's level of preparedness but on all their partners' readiness. Hence, implementation of interorganizational systems is a more complex issue that needs advanced planning. A firm's partner can have a wide range of IS expertise, ranging from novice to expert, a wide range of hardware and software platforms, and numerous other interorganizational systems with other trading partners. This web of connections brings in significant technical complexities to overcome, especially if a proprietary system is being used. Apart from the technical complexities, some of the partners may not have adequate technical expertise and may require handholding and training to enable them to implement the interorganizational systems. Because success of interorganizational systems is dependent on usage of systems across multiple partners, the firm has to manage the implementation process not only locally but also across all partners. A firm could use supportive or coercive strategies, or both, to ensure success in implementation. Firms that have economic power over their partners have been successful in using coercive strategies such as demanding interorganizational systems for doing business with them. They have found a supportive strategy, such as offering training and technical support, to be more beneficial for diffusion of interorganizational systems.

Plan for Next Level of Integration

As organizations realize the enormous potential from electronic integration between firms, interorganizational systems evolve into more sophisticated levels of integration. As described earlier, firms go through three broad phases of evolution: communication, coordination, and cooperation. Depending on the level at which a firm started, it has to develop a timeline for evolution. If a firm started with a simple EDI system for one to two transactions with one partner, it could plan to expand its scope. Strategies for expansion include:

- Increase the variety of transactions, thereby improving the coordination of various activities between the two firms.
- Expand the scope of coverage from one firm to multiple firms, both on the inbound and outbound side, thereby increasing the proportion of transactions communicated using the interorganizational systems.
- Automate many of the routine transactions (e.g., order processing, delivery scheduling) to an event-based trigger system that directly com-

municates to the partners' computers without any human intervention.

- Evolve from a message-based system to an interactive system providing the partners direct access to information.
- Expand information sharing beyond business transactions to other areas of cooperation.

The first strategy is attractive for firms that want to develop close working relationships with a few partners so that they could graduate to tight integration of their operations in a short time. The second strategy increases the breadth of coverage of partners. This is helpful if a firm decides to completely automate at least one of its interorganizational systems activities so that it does not have to maintain two systems, manual and interorganizational, for an extended period of time. Event-based triggering is a good strategy if a firm has excellent information systems with suitable controls and can provide clear guidelines to trigger business transactions using interorganizational systems. On-line access to information is a natural evolution for partners reaching their limit in message-based communication. Finally, as more information become available, organizations have to leverage the information availability for more extensive cooperative ventures such as collaborating on product design, joint promotional campaigns, and improving logistics.

SUMMARY

Supply chain management has become an excellent strategy to effectively link all the trading partners and ensure cost-effective and timely movement of materials from the raw material supplier to the final end-consumer of the finished product. Interorganizational systems or extranets provide the technology infrastructure to facilitate the flow of information along the chain, thereby ensuring the smooth flow of goods. The basic premise in both these initiatives is that organizations are willing to share information with their business partners on their internal operations including orders, inventory, and shipments. However, the reality may be the opposite. Firms are interested in protecting information, and this may become the primary inhibitor to successful implementation of these two initiatives. A climate of trust and true partnership must be created among the partners for these initiatives to be successful.

References

1. Clark, T.H. and Lee, H., 1997. "EDI Enabled Channel Transformation: Extending Business Process Redesign Beyond the Firm," *International Journal of Electronic Commerce*, 2(1), 7–22.
2. Cooper, M.C., Lambert, D.M., and Pagh, J.D., 1997. "Supply Chain Management: More Than a Name for Logistics," *International Journal of Logistics Management*, 8(1), 1–13.

3. Crum, M., Premkumar, G., and Ramamurthy, K., 1996. "An Assessment of Motor Carrier Adoption, Use and Satisfaction with EDI," *Transportation Journal*, 35(4), 44–57.
4. Daft, R.L. and Lengel, R.H., 1986. "Organizational Information Requirements, Media Richness and Structural Design," *Management Science*, 32(5), 554–571.
5. Dearden, J., 1972. "MIS is a Mirage," *Harvard Business Review*, 50(1), 90–99.
6. Ellram, L.M., 1990. " Supply Chain Management — The Industrial Organization Perspective," *International Journal of Physical Distribution and Logistics Management*, 21(1), 13–22.
7. Fisher, M.L., 1997. "What Is the Right Supply Chain for Your Product?" *Harvard Business Review*, March–April, 105–116.
8. Galbraith, J., 1977. *Organization Design*. Addison Wesley, Reading, MA.
9. Handfield, R.B. and Nichols, E.L., 1999. *Introduction to Supply Chain Management*. Prentice Hall, Englewood Cliffs, NJ.
10. Kalakota, R. and Whinston, A.B., 1996. *Frontiers of Electronic Commerce*. Addison Wesley, Reading, MA.
11. Lambert, D.M., Emmelhainz, M.A., and Gardner, J.T., 1996. "Developing and Implementing Supply Chain Partnerships," *International Journal of Logistics Management*, 7(2), 1–17.
12. Lee, H. and Clark, T.H., 1996. "Impacts of the Electronic Marketplace on Transaction Cost and Market Structure," *International Journal of Electronic Commerce*, 1(1), 127–149.
13. Malone, T.W., Yates J., and Benjamin, R., 1987. "Electronic Markets and Electronic Hierarchies," *Communications of the ACM*, 30 (6), 484–497.
14. Mariottie, J.L., 1999. "The Trust Factor in Supply Chain Management," *Supply Chain Management Review*, Spring 1999, 70–78.
15. Premkumar, G., Ramamurthy, K., and Nilakanta, S., 1994. "Implementation of Electronic Data Interchange," *Journal of Management Information Systems*, 11 (2), 157–186.
16. Premkumar, G. and Ramamurthy, K., 1995. "The Role of Interorganizational and Organizational Factors on the Decision Mode for Adoption of Interorganizational Systems," *Decision Sciences*, 26(3), 303-336.
17. Sheombar, H.S., 1997. "Logistics Coordination in Dyads: Some Theoretical Foundations for EDI-Induced Redesign," *Journal of Organizational Computing and Electronic Commerce*, 7(2&3), 153–184.
18. Stein, T. and Sweat, J., 1998. "Killer Supply Chains," *Information Week*, November, 36-42.

Chapter 32

Are You in Control of Your E-Commerce Strategy?

Andrew J. Czuchry
Mahmoud M. Yasin
Paul Bayes

Day by day, CEOs and owners are pressured to enter the E-commerce arena because their competitors are jumping on the bandwagon. However, many abandon their traditional disciplined approach and unknowingly expose their companies to significant financial and legal risks.

In a recent informal survey of CEOs and business owners conducted by one of the authors during regional roundtable business meetings, over 70 percent were unaware that failure to include formal disclaimers on their Web sites could expose their companies to significant liabilities. An equal number tended to abandon their sound contractual principles when conducting business-to-business transactions over the Web. An interesting observation is that these risks can be avoided with relatively little effort and without seriously altering the speed at which business transactions are conducted in this exciting arena.

Electronic commerce is having a dramatic impact on the way business is being conducted and is causing many of the rules of competition to be rewritten. During a recent television interview, representatives of the national Baldrige Award-winning Eastman Chemical Company estimated that the E-commerce window of opportunity was limited to three years for the chemical industry. By this they meant that Eastman must aggressively move into the E-commerce arena within the next three years, or face the consequences of losing marketshare to their competitors who are using the Web to conduct business-to-business transactions. Those in the chemical industry have only three years to respond to competitors' E-commerce

0-8493-1273-6/02/$0.00+$1.50
© 2002 by CRC Press LLC

initiatives. If they delay beyond this time window, it will be too late! Large companies, such as Eastman, have the financial, information technology, legal, and marketing resources to capitalize on the E-commerce opportunity within this relatively short timeframe. But what about the small- to medium-sized business?

If a small- to medium-sized business fails to implement an effective E-commerce strategy, it may easily find itself out of business. On the other hand, if such organizations were to implement an E-commerce initiative without mitigating the often hidden legal, operational, customer, technical, managerial, and organizational cultural risks, their resulting liabilities and shortfalls may still force them out of business. Are these small- to medium-sized businesses doomed when they approach the E-commerce arena? Fortunately, there is a way out of this dilemma.

The objective of this chapter is to present a practical, systematic, strategic approach in order to ensure the effectiveness of the E-commerce effort. First, the relevant literature is highlighted. Next, a conceptual framework is presented for mitigating risks associated with an E-commerce business strategy. Finally, a simple checklist of managerial do's and don'ts is offered as a guide to managers as they attempt to deal with the tactical and strategic facets of E-commerce.

THE RISKS

While most previous innovations have taken years to have a major societal impact, this cannot be said of E-commerce. The use of E-commerce is increasing exponentially, leading to additional business opportunities and risks. It took radio 38 years to be used by 58 million people; it took only five years after the birth of the World Wide Web to be used by twice as many people. The American Institute of Certified Public Accountants defines E-commerce as follows:

> E-commerce involves individuals as well as organizations engaging in a variety of electronic transactions, without paper documents, using computer and telecommunication networks. These networks can be public, private, or a combination of the two. Traditionally, the definition of E-commerce has focused on Electronic Data Interchange (EDI) as the primary means of conducting business electronically between two entities having a pre-established contractual relationship. More recently, however, the definition of E-commerce has broadened to encompass business conducted over the Internet (specifically the Web) and includes entities not previously known to each other.

E-commerce can also be defined as a broad array of strategic opportunities.[3] These electronic commerce opportunities can be evaluated by means of a series of questions to determine the potential (cost versus benefit) associated with E-commerce. Such questions include: Can we extend our geographic reach? Can we bypass the traditional channels of doing business? Can we add value to our traditional markets? Can we boost service? Can we improve our message delivery to customers? Positively answering these questions is the first step toward establishing an E-commerce presence. However, focusing only on the opportunities may result in overlooking potential risks. Therefore, risk assessment should be an integral part of a sound E-commerce strategy.

The risk assessment process must evaluate and react to several kinds of risks. A recent Lloyd's of London survey found that 62 percent of more than 200 Atlanta-based insurance executives considered E-commerce risks in terms of loss of reputation or brand as two of the most significant business risks.[1] It is estimated that most companies can expect to lose $1 per $1000 of Internet-based transactions due to fraud.[2] E-commerce-related risks are multifaceted. Even worse, additional risk types may emerge, because the E-commerce business is relatively new. The known categories of risk associated with E-commerce are addressed next.

The first risk to be considered is what impact will this failure have on the company's customers and business partners if it chooses not to participate in the new wave of E-commerce? If the company does not develop an E-commerce strategy, will its competitors? Do customers or suppliers expect the company to develop new ways of doing business?

The second risk is that of developing an E-commerce strategy but failing to consider the problems of future development and maintenance of E-commerce strategies. Many firms develop an E-commerce strategy, but the process either becomes stagnant, with no changes in the process, or fails to consider what others are doing. With the speed of technological change, there needs to be constant monitoring of new enhancements for the company's E-commerce strategy. For example, have the needs of customers or suppliers changed? Has E-commerce enhanced the company's operations by increasing revenue, reducing costs, or improving employee morale? Each of these questions must be considered before either venturing into E-commerce or maintaining a presence in this new realm of business activity.

Third are the legal risks, as defined by past and future court cases, as E-commerce technology evolves and changes. For a sample of recent court cases involving copyright infringement issues visit Webreview.com.[4] These cases involve such companies as Ticketmaster, The Church of Scientology, *Playboy*, and Sega. The legal risks consist of copyright infringement and violation of local, state, national, and international standards, policies, and laws. Additional issues involve jurisdictional taxation, where and if sales taxes are to be collected, privacy issues, and medical problems (e.g., carpal tunnel syndrome).

Fourth are the operational risks. These risks consist of additional employee training and screening, increased hardware and software expenditures, and increasing visibility (site registration). Site registration and exposure can be expensive in that addresses need to be placed on all company literature, and customers as well as suppliers need to be notified of this site address. Other risks include product defect policies, including return and multi-functional currency. How does the company handle the returns from a customer that can be thousands of miles from its physical location? How does it handle transactions from others with different currencies? Included in this issue is the monitoring of exchange-rate fluctuations.

The fifth category of risks is related to the external parties involved in E-commerce. The external risks are associated with relationships developed with partners in the E-commerce process such as customers, suppliers, and creditors; investors; and potential investors. Reliance on suppliers also increases vulnerability if one partner fails to meet its obligation in a contract. Investors and potential investors may require immediate access to company information, reducing reaction and response time for business changes. This also puts more pressure on companies to make sure information is up-to-date and accurate.

Sixth are the technical risks of an E-commerce network, including hardware and software issues. These risks are related either to lost cash flow or to the possibility of future cash outflows due to legal actions resulting from technical problems. In this context, the types of hardware, software, firewalls, and passwords and the delay of a system administrator must be considered carefully. Issues such as network configuration, off-site backups, and the integration of Web page and order processing are also items that need analysis before establishing an E-commerce network. Failure to carefully construct a secure E-commerce network can lead to systems downtime, which stops the cash or transactions flow for an organization. Failure to control for externally induced problems (i.e., viruses,) can result in damage to data centers and transmission networks. Failure to maintain the integrity of transactions can lead to lost documents and duplications. Changed and incorrectly processed orders can lead to lawsuits. In addition, the failure to develop an E-commerce network that responds quickly to users results in loss of trading partners and damage to reputations.

Management, while accountable for all previous risk categories, does incur specific risks of its own. For example, failure by management to adopt a systematic E-commerce-based strategy may provide competitors with a competitive advantage in cost reductions, data collections, or improved customer/supplier relations. On the other hand, if management chooses to adopt an E-commerce strategic orientation, it must be able to integrate business and marketing plans. Failure to do so increases the risk of deterioration in customer relations, supplier relations, and service quality and can lead to dysfunctional policies. Finally, careful analysis of dot.com partners is needed. By the end of 2000, several firms, as a result of financial difficulties or mergers, were not providing services. Many firms have suffered losses for a period of time, and investors are more wary of providing continuing support.

To offset these aforementioned risks, the E-commerce strategic and tactical efforts should address employee training along with technical considerations such as encryption, private networks, Internet security systems, and insurance. Employee training, including hiring quality employees, is important, because it is estimated that more than one-half of the frauds involving technology come from within an organization.

A ROADMAP TO E-COMMERCE EFFECTIVENESS

The approach presented in this section attempts to answer the questions of what to do and how to do it involved in an effective E-commerce strategy. What is needed is a systematic approach for formulating and implementing an effective E-commerce strategy. Exhibit 1 outlines the components of such a systematic orderly approach. Starting on the left-hand side of Exhibit 1, we recognize that market realities demand an effective E-commerce business strategy as a response to customer expectations and competitive pressures.

The alternative E-commerce types are intra-business, business-to-business, business-to-consumer, and value/supply chain management. We suggest that each alternative be evaluated from an open system perspective that brings the customer and the external legal and regulatory environment into consideration. In this context, managerial influence is utilized internally to modify business processes, information infrastructure, and organizational culture and externally to influence the legal system. However, to effectively determine the appropriate strategic E-commerce course of action, management must have means for assessing the potential risks and for quantifying the potential effectiveness of alternative strategies.

The framework shown in Exhibit 1 suggests that risk assessment be conducted along legal, operational, customer, technical, managerial, and organizational culture dimensions. Exhibit 2 provides a checklist to facilitate this process. For each risk type, the subjective probability of occurrence and resulting impacts are assessed. Risks having a high likelihood of occurrence and high impact on operational efficiency or strategic effectiveness mandate that detailed risk mitigation plans be developed and implemented.

Finally, completing the system diagram shown in Exhibit 1, the effectiveness of E-commerce business strategies is evaluated in terms of the effectiveness of the measures provided. These outcome measures include financial benchmarks, customer-related benchmarks, operational benchmarks,

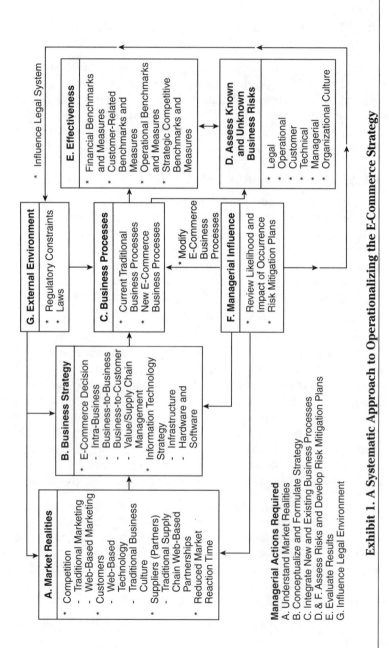

Exhibit 1. A Systematic Approach to Operationalizing the E-Commerce Strategy

Exhibit 2. Risk Mitigation Checklist for E-Commerce Business Strategies

E-Commerce Types	TYPES OF RISKS TO BE CONSIDERED				
	Legal	Operational	Customer	Technical	Managerial
1. Intra-Business 2. Business-to-Business 3. Business-to-Consumer 4. Value/Supply Chain Management	• Copyright infringement (intellectual property) and patent protection (2,3,4) • Advertising of products and services must conform to standards, laws, and policies (2,3,4) • Using an unauthorized link — intellectual property • Copyrights, trademarks, and advertising practices • Lack of written contract (2,3,4) • Different buyer/seller jurisdiction (2,3,4) • Taxed by which jurisdiction (2,3,4) • Cost of defending lawsuits in jurisdictions (2,3,4) • Violation of privacy • Risk of carpal tunnel syndrome • Regulatory compliance in multiple states such as credit cards • Website design, development, and hosting: Who owns your site?	• Employee training and screening • Off-site backups • Alternative host sites • Finding qualified employees • Making sure of visibility of site (registration) • Cost to put address on company literature • Multifunctional currency (2,3,4) • How to handle product defects (2,3,4)	• Understand the market and competition • Conceptualize and formulate stage • Integrate into existing business processes • Improved customer services and recognition of buying patterns • Recognition of customer changes	• Loss-prevention techniques such as losing credit card numbers, customer database information, etc. (2,3,4) • Security (software cost, firewalls, passwords, administrator for system) • Problem of Web page integration and order processing • Making it possible to view account information • Stakeholders can view interactive financial statements • Client/server relationship • Electronic documentation of all business transactions • Continuous system testing • Damage to data centers, transmission networks, viruses	• Need integration of business and marketing plans • Identify core business • Affiliate relations impact integration • Drill-down capabilities by outside parties (2,3,4) • Increase efficiency, cut delivery costs, collect data on customers • Provide better customer service • Benchmarking • Acquisition of new, technology-based skill sets • Improved distribution of digitized data sets • Developing and managing supplier relations • Evaluate stability of dot com partners

Note: Numbers indicate dominant risks relevant to E-commerce types. Where no numbers are given, the risks are applicable to all. See also Managerial Do's and Don'ts.

and strategic competitive benchmarks. Throughout this process, the importance of a detailed assessment of high-risk areas that emerge is underscored. Exhibit 3 is helpful in identifying these potential risks.

CONCLUSION

Businesses have a window of opportunity to capitalize on the potential of E-commerce. Some, such as the chemical industry, have estimated that this window is no more than three years wide. Although large firms may have the resources to capture this opportunity, they may lack the business agility to respond.

Small- to medium-sized businesses, on the other hand, may have the agility but lack the resources to respond. Driven by market and competitive pressures, these managerial decision-makers may overlook potentially catastrophic risks associated with the different types of E-commerce.

This chapter suggests a practical, systematic approach for identifying and mitigating the sometimes forgotten E-commerce business risks. The approach advocated here attempts to overcome the difficulties associated with a piecemeal and me-too E-commerce approach. In this context, it is intended to guide decision-makers as they attempt to chart E-commerce strategies in order to survive in today's information technology-driven, globally competitive environment.

Notes

1. Robert E. Umbaugh, Ed., *Handbook of IS Management,* Auerbach Publications, 1997.
2. PRNewswire, "Atlanta Executives Cite E-Commerce Risks and Loss of Reputation or Brand as Most Significant Threats to Corporation," January 21, 2000, p. 7247.
3. Smith, Michael 1999. "Comment: E-Commerce Risks Overstated but Real (Statistical Data Included)," *American Banker,* October 1, Vol. 164, I 198, p. 6.
4. Webreview.com, "Court Cases Regarding ISP Liability."

Exhibit 3. Managerial Dos and Don'ts

A. Understand Market Realities

— Do know how existing and potential customers are using Web-based technology.

— Don't look at the market from a traditional sense only.

— Do consider the blurring between products and services.

— Do consider the new Web-based marketing approaches such as permission and viral marketing.

— Don't overlook market trends.

— Do cater to customers in target markets.

— Do evaluate stability of dot com partners.

B. Conceptualization and Formulation Strategy

— Don't let the current strategy limit future strategic options.

— Do know where the company wants to be and capitalize on information technology to get there.

— Do not hesitate to be strategically innovative.

C. Integrate New and Existing Business Processes

— Do consider reengineering existing processes.

— Do realize that a new strategy may require updated or modified processes.

— Don't hesitate to introduce orderly change.

— Do build synergy between existing and new processes.

— Do make sure that the Web site is easy to navigate.

— Do create an organizational culture that views change positively.

— Don't have complex, time-consuming downloads.

D. and F. Assess Risk and Develop Risk Mitigation Plans

— Do realize that it is better to plan for it now than to pay for it later.

— Do realize that testing a plan is the best way to determine its effectiveness.

— Do realize that the cost of risk may be more than just dollars and cents.

— Don't rely only on the firm's expertise in the risk assessment area.

— Don't think that if the likelihood of a given risk is low that the risk is insignificant.

E. Evaluate Results

— Don't be hesitant to use qualitative as well as quantitative measures of performance.

— Do establish target benchmarks, but always try to improve them.

— Do be willing to take the experience of other organizations into account.

— Don't forget that the marketplace is the ultimate judge of performance.

— Don't forget that "good performance" is relative.

G. Influence Legal Environment

— Do establish the firm's policies and procedures, so the government does not have to do that instead.

— Do know that any firm, along with and others in the same industry, can influence laws and regulations.

— Do know the difference between what is legal and what is ethical.

— Don't forget that laws and regulations tend to lag behind technological advances.

— Do realize that if it concerns your business, it is not just a legal issue; rather it is a strategic issue.

— Do realize that it may be a job for lawyers, but management is ultimately responsible for the outcome.

Chapter 33
Business-to-Business Exchanges

Marie Tumolo

Business-to-Business (B2B) exchanges are central, electronic marketplaces in which multiple buyers and multiple suppliers come together to exchange goods and services. Exchanges are a significant component of the business-to-business electronic commerce market, estimated to reach $600 billion to $3 trillion in U.S. revenues by 2003.

Exhibit 1 outlines the three major aspects of exchanges. Exchanges are used to match buyers and suppliers and facilitate transactions between the two. They also maintain a technical, institutional, and compliance infrastructure that supports their offerings. Exchanges are typically run by independent, third party intermediaries rather than by individual buyers (e.g., General Motors Corp. or General Electric Co.) or suppliers. In the single-firm case, a buyer opens an electronic market on its own server and invites suppliers to bid on specified parts or services needed, or a supplier sells its products or services only to approved customers. Third-party exchanges, on the other hand, do not take title or physical possession of goods but facilitate the matching of buyers and suppliers. The terms "exchange" and "marketplace" are used interchangeably in discussions of electronic commerce. Exchanges serve a variety of industries including aerospace, agriculture, automobive, banking, chemicals, education, employment, energy, food, hospitality, insurance, paper, and steel.

Exchanges are a form of outsourcing, enabling a company to shift much of the work performed by the purchasing function to a third party. The exchange searches for suppliers matching the buyer's request, compares prices and product features, and provides recommendations. All of these services replace ones now usually performed by employees in the purchasing department. For suppliers, exchanges provide another channel of distribution, one that does not require support by sales personnel. Exhibits 2 and 3 illustrate the differences between using an exchange for transactions and using it for conventional means.

Exhibit 1. How Exchanges Work

Matching Buyers and Suppliers
- Establishing product offerings
- Aggregating and posting different products for sale
- Providing price and product information, including recommendations
- Organizing bids and bartering
- Matching supplier offerings with buyer preferences
- Enabling price and product comparisons
- Supporting negotiation and agreement between buyers and suppliers

Facilitating Transactions
- Logistics: delivery of information, goods or services to buyers, identification of company administrator to:
  - Provide billing and payment information including addresses
  - Define terms and other transaction values
  - Input searchable information
  - Grant exchange access to users and identify company users eligible to use exchange
- Settlement of transaction payments to suppliers, collecting transaction fees
- Establishing credibility: registering and qualifying buyers and suppliers, communicating exchange transaction and other fees, maintaining appropriate security over information and transactions

Maintaining Institutional Infrastructure
- Ascertaining compliance with commercial code, contract law, export and import laws, intellectual property law, rules and regulations of appropriate agencies
- Maintaining technological infrastructure to support volume and complexity of transactions
- Providing interface capability to standard systems of buyers and suppliers
- Obtaining appropriate site advertisers and collecting advertising and other fees

Exchanges operate throughout the supply chain, facilitating everything from the acquisition of raw materials to the sale of finished goods. When exchanges are integrated with automated procurement processes and customer requirements management systems, the supply chain is streamlined within and across organizations and industries. A typical supply chain includes the components shown in Exhibit 4.

Estimates of the number of exchanges in existence vary from 600 to 1000. Announcements of the formation of new exchanges continue to appear in the press, despite the announcements of exchanges closing down or scaling back. Many of the exchanges are unlikely to last beyond the initial press release or survive beyond the first year. AMR Research predicts that only 50 to 100 of the current exchanges will survive through 2001.

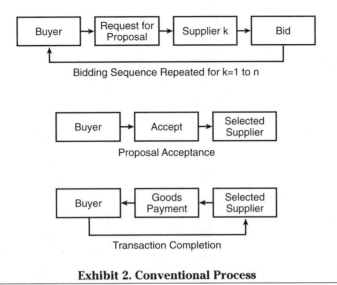

Bidding Sequence Repeated for k=1 to n

Proposal Acceptance

Transaction Completion

Exhibit 2. Conventional Process

a. RFPs Submitted and Bids Made

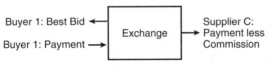

b. Best Bid Accepted

Exhibit 3. Exchange Process

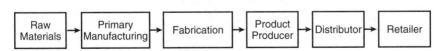

Source: J. R. Galbraith, "Strategy and Organization Planning," in *The Strategy Process: Concepts, Contexts, Cases, 2nd ed.,* edited by H. Mintzberg and J. B. Quinn (Englewood Cliffs, NJ: Prentice Hall, 1991), P. 316.

Exhibit 4. Typical Supply Chain

401

TASK 3: FORGING SUPPLY CHAIN PARTNERSHIPS

How Exchanges Evolved

Since the 1980s, IT experts have predicted that information technology would reduce many of the coordination costs incurred by businesses, such as the costs of gathering information, negotiating contracts, or protecting against opportunistic behavior. Coordination costs, along with other factors such as the degree of complexity of a particular product and the level of specificity of assets used in a particular business, influence the decision whether to use markets for economic activity or to directly control more aspects of business through ownership and hierarchical management. The reduction of coordination costs along with lower asset specificity leads to higher use of market mechanisms. Exchanges are market mechanisms that use information technology and the Internet to reduce the cost of gathering information and negotiating contracts for products that are fairly standard either across or within industries.

B2B E-commerce has its roots in electronic data interchange (EDI) networks established between large buyers and suppliers within a specific industry. The automobive, aerospace, and chemical industries used EDI extensively to reduce costs and improve operational efficiency. EDI consists of private networks between companies that facilitate communication of orders, status, invoicing, and payment. Expensive to build and maintain, EDI networks were often limited to the largest companies within that industry. Many of the buyer- and supplier-oriented marketplaces evolved from EDI, facilitated by the on-line automation of the procurement process made possible by the Internet.

Exchanges came about when several companies (predominantly Ariba, Inc., Commerce One, Inc, and W. W. Grainger, Inc.) took their E-procurement software and used it to establish open markets on their own servers. Many of the initial exchanges were on-line catalogs. However, continued technological development is increasing the scope of services provided by the exchanges. A number of exchanges are beginning to provide additional functions. For example, Messmer11 points to such functions as:

- Sharing of synchronized, real-time updates on prices and shipment information
- Pushing and pulling data directly from corporate back-end enterprise resource planning and database systems
- Flagging errors before problems multiply on the production and shipping end

In addition, Trombly describes the following functionality:[15]

- Generating Extensible Markup Language (XML) forms, which can be viewed with a Web browser
- Evaluating product availability, by linking into a supplier's inventory application

- Pacing orders from a buyer's procurement application, then following through with a supplier's order-fulfillment package
- Supporting different contract terms or purchasing agreements for different buyers
- Fulfilling orders electronically, which requires real-time order validation and downloads for applications such as software or content sales
- Electronic invoicing and payments including automated clearinghouse payments
- Credit checks and financing
- Security and authentication

Types of Exchanges

Most exchanges can be categorized as either horizontal or vertical. Horizontal exchanges provide many commodity products that can be used across most industries. Typical horizontal exchanges involve the purchase and sale of

- Office supplies
- Uniforms
- Furniture and equipment
- Maintenance services
- Electronic components
- Repair and operating supplies

The primary benefits of horizontal exchanges are the variety of products offered and lower prices.

Vertical exchanges focus on a specific industry, providing participants with

- Specialized products
- In-depth industry knowledge
- Greater opportunities for collaboration

There are also meta-exchanges that combine aspects of both vertical and horizontal markets and support a full range of market-connecting mechanisms, including bid/ask exchanges, auctions, and reverse auctions.

Horizontal and vertical exchanges can take various forms. Specifically, the major forms of exchanges are

- Aggregate catalogs (Chemdex)
- Trading (TradeOut)
- On-line exchange of goods (FreeMarkets)
- Labor exchange (Guru.com)
- On-line auctions and reverse auctions (PlasticsNet)
- Fully automated with order matching such as stock exchanges (Altra Energy Technologies).

Exhibit 5. Major Forms of Exchanges

Exchange Name	Type	Form	Functions
Chemdex	Vertical	Catalog	Academics, scientists, pharmaceutical firms buy and sell science research products
OrderZone	Horizontal	Catalog	Merged with Works.com. Sells uniforms, office supplies, maintenance, repair, laboratory and safety equipment, and electronic components
TradeOut	Horizontal	Trading	Virtual storefront posting surplus assets representing over 100 product categories
FreeMarkets	Horizontal	Online	Purchase and sale of industrial parts, raw materials, and commodities and services
Guru.com	Horizontal	Labor	Posting of projects requiring contract workers
PlasticsNet	Vertical	Online Auction	Auctions and reverse auctions for used and excess products in the plastics industry; materials and news for buyers and suppliers
Altra Energy Technologies	Vertical	Fully Automated	Trades natural gas and other energy. Traded $4 billion in 1999
e-STEEL	Vertical	Automated	Entire steel industry. Supports prime and non-prime steel products
PaperExchange	Vertical	Automated	Buys and sells all grades of paper
Covisint	Vertical	Catalog, auction, and automated	Formed by auto industry manufacturers

Examples of these forms are shown in Exhibit 5.

Exchange Technology

Exchanges are basically Web sites that use a standard language, XML, to facilitate application-to-application data exchange, similar to EDI. XML allows information regarding orders, purchases, payments, and products to be easily understood by other computers. XML, in effect, makes the benefits of EDI accessible to organizations of all sizes.

Three software companies, Ariba, Commerce One, and Oracle, dominate the exchange software market by providing packages, installation help, and consulting. These software packages evolved from buy-side software developed to help purchasing departments.

Although XML is a standard language, different versions exist, hampering the ability for exchanges to communicate with one another. In response, a number of software companies such as i2 Technologies, Extricity, Mercator, and IBM are developing software to help buyers and suppliers use multiple exchanges to transcend the barriers erected by using different versions of XML.

Full automation of the supply chain is one of the primary benefits often claimed for B2B E-commerce. That is, the software covers all functions from salesforce and materials buying to billing. However, only 10 of 600 exchanges tracked by AMR Research as of April 2000 actually provide integration from the exchange to a supplier's or buyer's back end systems.

Sell-side electronic commerce systems enable the exchange to tap into the suppliers' systems to determine available quantities and price for quotations. Software companies dominating the supply side include Calico, Ironside, and SAP. On the buy side, E-procurement systems, such as those developed by Oracle, Ariba, and Commerce One, allow buyers to streamline the processes of requisitioning parts and services, retrieving necessary documentation, obtaining and evaluating bids, and receiving the items.

BENEFITS OF EXCHANGES

Exchanges promise significant benefits including

- Cost savings
- Increased operational efficiency
- Improved information.

Most of these benefits have yet to be realized, although some participants predict annual cost savings of anywhere from 7 to 30 percent. Benefits vary among buyers and suppliers, but both parties achieve the benefit of better information. Exchanges are information tools, providing buyers and suppliers with the ability to screen and compare products, prices, sources, terms, availability, and potential substitute products. In addition, some exchanges provide product recommendations, often one of the most valued features for participants. In addition, both buyers and suppliers have the added benefit of reduced negotiation costs because the exchange enables both parties to a transaction to meet electronically and come to agreement rapidly.

Buyer Benefits

Because exchanges bring together multiple buyers and suppliers, buyers can expect to pay lower prices when purchasing through an exchange. Smaller orders can be aggregated by the exchange so that each individual buyer receives the high-volume discount. Buyers have more suppliers to choose among and gain greater price transparency. It is much easier in an exchange to see how prices for the same product may vary based on geographic region, size of the order, or customer relationship. In addition, customers may compare the price they typically pay with the current exchange price and ask why any difference exists. Using an exchange also enables buyers to obtain information about product availability and potential substitute products more quickly than before and at a lower search cost.

Even more significant are the cost savings that can be achieved by automation of the procurement process and integration of a company's systems with those of the exchange. Lower administrative costs result from reductions in the number of employees required to support the purchasing function, streamlining the approval process for purchases and enabling managers to make purchasing decisions directly by using the exchanges. Integration of a company's back-office systems with those of the exchanges also facilitates improved inventory management.

Supplier Benefits

Suppliers that participate in exchanges are able to expand their markets, acquire new customers at a very low cost, aggregate smaller orders into larger bundles, and service customers at a lower cost. Suppliers reduce their dependence on their salesforces and eliminate the expensive costs of continually producing expensive catalogs. In addition, suppliers can often eliminate traditional market intermediaries because the exchange acts as an automated intermediary. It may be possible for suppliers to appropriate and retain a portion of the discount previously given to the middleman. Integration of exchange information with customer relationship management information already under development by the major software companies will allow suppliers to obtain customer information such as purchasing history and to automate sales and services.

COSTS

Fees vary by exchange: some exchanges charge a fee per transaction; others charge a percentage of the revenue on the transaction or a percent of the cost savings achieved. Some exchanges also charge membership fees, but competition for participants is reducing the number of exchanges charging such fees. Recent trends indicate that exchanges are increasingly favoring open (non-fee) membership to qualified participants. Downward pressure continues to be exerted on all types of fees. Additional information on the example exchanges and their fees is shown in Exhibit 6.

Suppliers often are required to pay a fee to post items for sale or for sales transactions that occur. Suppliers, however, are critical to the success of exchanges. For an exchange to be successful, it must provide buyers with a large number of suppliers from which to choose products and

Exhibit 6. Additional Information on Example Exchanges, Including Fees

Exchange	Date Opened	Ownership	Membership	Available Fee Data	Supply Chain Integration
Horizontal:					
TradeOut	1998	Independent	Open	Supplier: 5% of — $10 listing fee — $1000 annual membership fee	No
Works.com (OrderZone)	1999	Consortium	Open	Service fee: $1 per order	Pending
FreeMarkets	1995	Independent	Open	Seller: 5% of winning bid	No
Guru.com	1999	Independent	Open	$200 per project or $1000/qtr	No
Vertical:					
Altra Energy	1996	Independent	Qualified		Yes
eSTEEL	1999	Independent	Qualified	Supplier: .875% of transaction value	Pending
PaperExchange	1998	Commercial investors	Qualified	Supplier: 3% of total purchase price	No
PlasticsNet	1997	Independent	Qualified	Yes	Yes
Covisint	Pending regularoty approval	Consortium	Qualified	To be determined	Future enhancement
Chemdex		Independent	Qualified		Yes

services. To attract suppliers, exchanges must keep fees charged to suppliers reasonable. With so many exchanges being developed and as yet few clear dominant players, most exchanges are more concerned with attracting suppliers than making money from high fees.

Buyers' costs can include membership fees as well as transaction fees, depending on the exchange. The actual cost of the goods to the buyer includes the amount paid to the supplier, the commission paid to the exchange (if any), and the freight costs. In particular, if a buyer selects a supplier located further away, the savings from lower costs of goods may be eaten up by the additional freight charges.

DISADVANTAGES OF EXCHANGES

To achieve the benefits of the exchange in terms of a more efficient process, buyers must make a large number of transactions over this channel. In effect, the exchange becomes the buyer's single (or major) source for supplies or vital inputs. Although cost savings are associated with using the exchange, the buyer assumes the risk of exchange failure or deterioration. Buyers also still run the risk that changing suppliers when buying through the exchange may result in poor product performance, particularly when buying critical parts and components. Exchange recommendations and comparisons may provide insufficient information regarding input specifications unique to an individual buying company.

From a supplier's standpoint, the primary disadvantage is that exchanges may dominate over all other selling channels, leaving those companies that do not join the right exchange out of the bulk of the business. Mediocre suppliers (in terms of quality and price) face particular disadvantages because the widespread use of exchanges will most likely force out of business those suppliers that cannot meet the exchange's standards.

CRITICAL SUCCESS AND FAILURE FACTORS FOR EXCHANGES AND PARTICIPANTS

Critical Success Factors

- *Mass.* Exchanges require sufficient mass, that is enough buyers and suppliers to make participation worth it for both. Mass also increases liquidity of the exchange and enables the exchange to improve services offered. Because exchanges are so new, it is difficult to determine what sufficient mass is for each market. Dollar volume of transactions and the stability of transaction fees are considered to be important criteria of exchange liquidity.
- *Seamless integration.* Increasingly, exchange members want to integrate their company's back-office systems seamlessly with the exchange as well as clearing the financial transactions with each party's

bank. As a result of this integration, exchanges can be expected to evolve from marketplaces to full supply chain automation. Exchange members also want to use information generated by the exchange to forecast demand for their products better as well as to compare prices, product characteristics, availability, terms, and sources.

- *Income.* The problem for exchanges is how to balance the need for revenues to keep going against the need for participants to realize the cost-saving benefits of participation. Having a sufficient number of suppliers is critical to the survival of an exchange because it increases the willingness of buyers to participate. Yet many suppliers are increasingly concerned about participating in exchanges that are too focused on price as the only determinant of the purchasing decision. Suppliers have little incentive to encourage deterioration of their own profits.

Critical Failure Factors

Many of the exchanges that closed recently — for example, Industrial-Vortex, a marketplace for industrial automation products; M-xchange, a horizontal exchange for minority-owned suppliers; and Fleetscape.com, a marketplace for commercial truck aftermarket parts and service — were unable to obtain additional funding. Venture capitalists are becoming more reluctant to invest in exchanges with heavy reliance on transaction fees. So many exchanges have been formed that one analyst at Keenan Vision estimates that some 4,200 exchanges will exist by 2003. The numbers are driving down transaction fee revenues in many markets. Originally, exchanges anticipated charging 1 to 3 percent of each transaction amount. Downward pressure led many exchanges to reduce their fees to 1/4 percent to retain sufficient membership and liquidity. For this reason, exchanges that are backed by significant players in an industry are considered most likely to survive.

IMPLICATIONS OF B2B EXCHANGES

Business Issues

Exchanges need to ensure that suppliers listed on the exchange are able to supply the quality and quantity of goods demanded by buyers and have the integrity to be participants to a contract. Buyers will quickly stop using an exchange if the products and services offered by the supplier do not meet expected standards. Exchanges that will survive are those that exert an effort to prequalify both buyers and suppliers in terms of conventional business factors such as reputation, creditworthiness, size, and experience.

Distribution logistics are also an important consideration when using an exchange. Although exchanges bring together multiple buyers and suppliers, enabling each to expand their scope of operations, basic logistics require the ability to actually deliver products, limiting the transactions to those companies best able to deliver where and when the buyer needs it.

As with any intermediary function, exchanges are subject to concerns by participants that the exchange is reputable, complies with all relevant laws and regulations governing transactions, and has adequate procedures in place to qualify participants, secure private information and safeguard financial assets.

Antitrust Considerations

Both the FTC and the European Commission are examining exchanges and their potential impact on the competitiveness of various industries. The exchanges attracting the most regulatory attention are those that strive for full supply chain automation within a specific industry and that evolved from industry consortiums. For this reason, the FTC continues to look closely at Covisint, the automakers' exchange, after granting it guarded approval on September 11, 2000. The European Commission is looking at MyAircraft.com, a joint venture for the sale of aircraft spare parts and engines set up by Honeywell International, Inc.; United Technologies Corp., and i2 Technologies, Inc. One potential violation of competition rules concerning the EU is the ability of the exchange to compare price and other sensitive information — in effect, forming a cartel. Both regulatory agencies are concerned with the ability of exchange members to share information about prices and the potential for that to lead to price fixing. They are also concerned that exchanges may so dominate an industry that nonmember firms are forced out of business and that price sharing may lead to downward price pressure, squeezing out smaller players and creating oligopolistic situations.

Exchanges are carefully constructing firewalls and other security measures designed to alleviate potential antitrust concerns. Many exchanges, such as eSTEEL, do not allow individuals from other companies to see final agreed-on prices between buyers and suppliers. Automated exchanges are concentrating on commodities and using existing commodity exchange markets as guides.

Relationship Management

One of the potentially most interesting effects of exchanges is their impact on supplier relations, customer loyalty, and customer retention. During the past ten years, academics and the popular business press advocated the formation of deep relationships between buyers and suppliers, partially facilitated by EDI and customer relationship software. Strengthening relationships with key suppliers enabled companies to reduce costs and defects of parts and raw materials. Customer intimacy enabled companies to respond to the evolving needs of their targeted customers with tailored products and services. Flexible customer response often depended on speed to market, increasing the importance of strong supplier relationships.

The exchanges have the potential to fundamentally change the nature of those relationships as buyers become aware of new suppliers and increase their ability to compare prices and service across a broader range of businesses. Yet at the same time, customer/supplier intimacy is increasingly critical to a company's ability to differentiate itself from the competition.

The depth and criticality of customer/supplier relationships will drive the type of exchange used by a company. For noncritical supplies and equipment, a third-party horizontal exchange is appropriate. Companies would use vertical exchanges to purchase industry-specific and commodity items and to monitor changes and evolutions in the industry that may affect future customer/supplier relationships.

LESSONS FOR MANAGERS

- *Determine what role exchanges should play in your business.* Although exchanges are considered most effective for commodity products and services, the development of industry-specific exchanges with full supply chain integration may lead to the use of exchanges for acquisitions of strategic materials and services as well. Many exchanges are working diligently to improve security around requisitions, bids, negotiations, and transactions. Strategic functions, products, and services need to be carefully identified, and the process of developing and acquiring strategic components needs to be carefully examined to determine how best to take advantage of developing opportunities. Fragmented industries are particularly able to benefit from the use of exchanges.
- *Identify all potential exchanges. Look at exchanges being used by other companies in the same industry.* Determine whether companies of similar size with similar business models are using certain exchanges more than others. Closely examine geographic dispersion of suppliers and buyers in a particular exchange in light of the unique logistic issues specific to the company's product or service.
- *Evaluate the exchanges based on how the company will use them.* Look for focus and participants that are appropriate for the company's buying or selling needs. Review content carefully to determine whether products offered are of acceptable quality and quantity, include name brands, and are priced competitively. Examine exchange investors and partners. Most of the exchanges that have closed are independent third-party exchanges with no equity participation by any significant players in the industry. Look at the history of the exchange and fee structure to determine how sustainable the exchange is.

411

- *Select the right exchanges to join.* Realistically, companies will probably need to join more than one exchange. The most successful exchanges to date focus on a particular industry or type of product but have sufficient breadth to attract many buyers and suppliers. Liquidity is key as well as integration and the ability of the exchange to facilitate linkage to other exchanges, enabling a buyer or supplier to participate seamlessly in the most appropriate exchanges. Although many experts define liquidity as sufficient buyers and suppliers, it also is important to look at the nature of transactions — whether buyers and suppliers will find sufficient products and services to keep using the exchange over the long term.
- *Extract value from the exchanges.* Closely monitor cost savings achieved compared with those anticipated. Use the exchanges' information-gathering and reporting capabilities to improve planning and forecasting of product demand. Monitor enhancements offered by the exchanges and carefully consider how they may help you improve your business.
- *Evaluate results.* Calculate your return on investment, cycle time improvements, and impact on the business. Look at cost savings over time. Periodically review trends over time in prices. Keep a close eye out for process savings. Determine what information gained from participating in the exchange means in terms of improving business performance or avoiding costly mistakes.

CONCLUSIONS

Peter F. Drucker tells us that the best way to determine what will happen in the future is to look at what has already happened. For example, a number of independent exchanges closed down or merged into other exchanges because they had liquidity problems. Consortium-led exchanges, such as Covisint and MyAircraft.com are experiencing regulatory scrutiny as well as delays due to the need for consensus among industry members. These instances do not mean that exchanges will disappear, rather that only the best will survive, resulting in easier decisions for managers trying to determine which to join. The number of enhancements being developed to improve exchange functionality and service is another indication of which exchanges may ultimately deliver the greatest value to participants.

References

1. eMarketer (2000). *Changing B2B Exchanges* [Business 2.0 Web site]. August 14.
2. Backes, A. and Butler, S. (2000). "New eCommerce: B2B Report Examines Wide Range of Projections for B2B Growth." *eMarketer*, August 8.
3. Bakos, Y. (1998). "The Emerging Role of Electronic Marketplaces on the Internet." *Communications of the ACM* (August), 35.

4. Copeland, L. (2000). "Trade Exchange Closes Virtual Doors." *Computerworld* (July 24).
5. Drucker, P. F. (1997). "The Future That Has Already Happened." *Harvard Business Review,* 75 (5, Sept.–Oct.), 20–24.
6. Greenemeier, L. (2000). "Buying Power." *Information Week,* 780 (Apr. 3), 67–68.
7. Gubman, Edward I. (1995). "Aligning People Strategies with Customer Value." *Compensation and Review* (Jan.–Feb.), 15–22
8. Kaplan, S. and Sawhney, M. (2000). "E-Hubs: The New B2B Marketplace." *Harvard Business Review,* 78 (3, May-June), 97–103.
9. Lundegaard, K. (2000). "FTC Clears Covisint, Big Three's Auto-Parts Site." *Wall Street Journal.*
10. Malone, T. W., Yates, J., and Benjamin, R. I. (1987). "Electronic Markets and Electronic Hierarchies." *Communications of the ACM,* 30(6), 484–497.
11. Messmer, E. (2000). "Online Supply Chains Creating Buzz, Concerns." *Network World,* 17 (Apr. 24), 12.
12. Nash, K. S. (2000). "Reality Check for E-Markets." *Computerworld* (June 5), 58–59.
13. Segal, R. L. (2000). "Online Marketplaces: A New Strategic Option." *Journal of Business Strategy,* 21 (2, Mar./Apr.), 26–29.
14. Sweat, J. (2000). "E-market Connections." *Information Week,* 780 (Apr. 3), 22–24.
15. Trombly, M. (2000). "Top U.S. Bank to Open B-to-B Marketplace." *Computerworld*, 34 (15, Apr. 10), 6.
16. Vizard, M. (2000). "Business-to-Business-to-Consumer Signals the Next Generation of e-Business." *InfoWorld*, 22 (14, Apr. 3), 111.
17. Walker, L. (2000, April 5). "B2B: Almost as Old as the Internet." *The Washington Post*, pp. G03.
18. Wilson, T., and Mullen, T. (2000). "E-Business Exchanges Fight For Survival." *InternetWeek* (August).

Chapter 34
Partnering on Extranets for Strategic Advantage

Steven Chan
Tim R. V. Davis

Recently, the managers of a failing steel supplier gambled on an investment in Internet technology. The company created an extranet so that major customers could view available steel inventory and submit bids over a secured Internet environment. By giving customers direct access to the firm's inventory data, bids were more rapidly evaluated and time spent by salesclerks in faxing out information and answering customers' questions was greatly reduced. The company then extended the system to include order entry and order tracking. This application allowed customers to track the progress of their own orders in the plant or yard and in transit. Customers liked the new system better than talking to salesclerks over the phone; it was more convenient and quicker. The steel company, which had been in danger of being shut down, was able to increase sales while cutting sales and service people. The system was inexpensive to introduce and provided a rapid payback. What seemed like a gamble ended up saving the company.

Internet technology is building electronic commerce into a major economic force. But three problems currently beset commerce on the Internet: security, privacy, and speed. Most companies want to control access to their computer systems and ensure privacy. They also need to be certain that trading partners can log on to the system without any delays. Doubts and concerns these issues are prompting firms to install intranet and extranet systems. Intranets are closed networks based on Internet technology that are used for intracompany communications. Extranets extend intranets and enable companies to communicate with other parties outside the firm. Both intranets and extranets create high-quality interaction while ensuring security, confidentiality, and speed. Extranets are more private than the Internet but more permeable than an intranet. They are likely to become the most popular intercompany communication tool in the new millennium. This chapter explains how extranets are being used and describes how leading companies are gaining strategic advantages from this technology.

EDI AND EXTRANETS

During the 1970s and 1980s, businesses extended their computing power beyond the company's walls by sending and receiving purchase orders and invoicing and transmitting shipping notifications electronically via EDI (electronic data interchange). This enabled companies to form much closer ties with suppliers and customers. EDI is the computer-to-computer exchange of business data in standards formats. With EDI, information is organized according to a specified format set by the parties involved. EDI computer transactions are usually transmitted over private communication networks called value-added networks (VANs) that require no human intervention or rekeying. The information contained in an EDI transaction set is, for the most part, the same as that on a conventionally printed document. There are several hundred standards currently being used to conduct these business-to-business transactions.

While companies can gain tangible benefits from using EDI, the cost of specialized hardware, software, and the installation and maintenance of VANs has put electronic communication out of the reach of many small- and medium-sized companies. These businesses still rely on the fax and telephone for most of their communications. Even larger companies that use EDI do not realize the full savings because many of their business partners cannot afford to install it. Realizing the shortcomings of EDI, big corporate users are now supporting EDI messaging formats on the Internet. They are using open standards to broaden the reach of the technology to smaller partners that could not afford the costly software and VANs required for traditional EDI.

Compared to the audience of 100 million that already exists for Internet communication, the use of EDI is much more restricted and delivers far less value. For companies that have already made the investment in EDI, it will continue to be a valuable method of intercompany communication. However, it does not provide the flexibility of extranets, which can assist companies in doing other forms of communication — e-mail, multimodal marketing, product and company profiles, to name just a few. Forty percent of business-to-business electronic commerce applications are expected to be replaced by extranets in the next three years.

Developing applications based on Internet technology means that the company need not supply its partners with a lot of special hardware or develop custom front-ends. By choosing Internet-based applications that are supported by technology already in use by the partner, companies avoid most of the obstacles that EDI users experience. These obstacles include maintaining and supporting client hardware, dealing with compatibility issues, and providing frequent upgrades. With the help of the open Internet, companies can now communicate much more effectively and efficiently. By using a modem, a browser, an account with an Internet service provider (ISP), and a personal computer, the limitations of EDI can be minimized and the number of partners increased dramatically.

EXTRANET SOFTWARE

Major software companies are embracing the development of corporate extranets and teaming up to ensure their success. For example, Netscape, Oracle, and Sun Microsystems have alliances to ensure that their extranet products work together. Their efforts have been aided by the general acceptance of standardized system architecture such as Common Object Request Broker Architecture (CORBA). CORBA is an important step on the road to object-oriented standardization and interoperability.

CORBA, users gain access to information transparently, without having to know what software or hardware platform the information resides on or where it is located on an enterprise's network. Among the other standard development languages is Java, which was developed by Sun Microsystems (Sun) in the early 1990s. Sun made Java available free to the public in 1995. Because Java delivers a "write once, run anywhere" capability, over 100,000 developers rapidly adopted the language. The rollout of JavaScript in December, 1995 by Netscape Communications Corp. also serves as a general purpose Internet/intranet/extranet application development language.

EXTRANET APPLICATIONS

Early applications of extranets demonstrate the technology's versatility and wide-ranging potential. The possible uses of extranets should stimulate management to rethink business strategies, how services are delivered, and how the company is connected with customers, suppliers, contractors, and consultants. Some companies are using extranets as the main vehicle to deliver their products. Others provide services to a group of other companies, such as on-line banking applications managed by one company on behalf of affiliated banks.

One of the earliest and best known examples of an extranet is the one built by Federal Express. FedEx has expanded its range of services from the mere pickup and delivery of packages to the full logistics of order processing and associated services. Part of FedEx's stated strategy is to serve companies that need assistance in conducting business on the Web. FedEx has used the extranet to offer a fuller range of customer services. The company opened its shipment-tracking system to the public so that FedEx's customers can go to the company's Web site and schedule shipments, fill out forms online, and even track their own shipments. FedEx's shipment tracking system evolved into a business-to-business service that displays Web catalogs, takes orders, and delivers merchandise. This system has saved over $10 million in customer service costs alone. Seeing the success of FedEx's system, other companies have followed its example and designed extranets to fulfill a variety of different functions.

For example, McDonnell Douglas's commercial aircraft division, Douglas Aircraft, designed an extranet to improve document distribution to customers. The company used to send four to five 25-page bulletins each year to its customers around the world. This accounted for over 4 million pages of documentation. By most of the information electronically, Douglas Aircraft has reduced paper expense and cut customer service support costs. The new system is more flexible than a paper-based system, and it helps Douglas Aircraft save more than half of its previous mailing cost. Updates and revisions are delivered faster and no longer get mislaid or lost in the mail.

The Goodyear Tire & Rubber Co. has made dealer support a major priority for its extranet. The company spent a year developing its extranet system, which is called Xplor. Before the birth of Xplor, Goodyear's marketing department was spending a significant portion of its budget and manpower on composing, printing, and mailing out its monthly promotions to independent dealers in the United States. A similar effort went into making sure dealers had up-to-date technical and marketing information on their tire sales. Since the company introduced the Xplor system, the costs of customer service and printed material have been greatly reduced.

With most of the technical information on-line and just a mouse click away, Goodyear has shrunk its Customer Sales and Service Center and redeployed these resources to other areas of the company. Dealers no longer call the Customer Sales and Service Center to request brochures or product information. Anytime dealers need promotion material, they log onto the extranet and print it themselves. Xplor gives dealers direct access to the corporate ordering system. Dealers can check tire availability, order tires on-line, and check the status on orders 24 hours a day, 7 days a week. Goodyear's dealers now possess the power to do business anytime and anywhere they want. Geographic and time differences are becoming increasingly irrelevant. This is a major improvement over the old order-entry system, which involved faxes, phone calls, and manual tracking.

Hyundai Motors launched its Hyundai Enterprise Internet Commerce System to make it easier for dealers and small garages to do business with Hyundai. The system is used by Hyundai dealers, distributors, and consumers, but the main strategic objective of the system was to expand the volume of business with independent auto repair shops. Previously, independent garages and body shops had to wade Hyundai's paper catalogs and microfiche system, which was slow and tedious. With Hyundai's new extranet system, once the order is placed, the system routes the order to the nearest dealer, processes the transaction, and fulfills the order. The new system is fast and much more convenient. It allows Hyundai's business partners to locate and order parts, orders, and even access specific repair instructions.

The Toro Co., maker of lawnmowers and snowblowers, developed its Web site as a two-part system: one unsecured, the other secured. The unsecured side lets consumers access information about the company's lawnmower and snowblower products and services. The secured extranet lets suppliers and distributors exchange information, make purchases, design promotions, and plan forecasts. Through the sites' forums, dealers and distributors can help customers solve specific problems as well as place and track orders.

Many firms are using extranets to form closer ties with vendors and to reduce purchasing costs. For example, Liberty Mutual has been trying to reduce expenses in the highly competitive insurance industry. In a few months, the company built an application to improve the purchasing of office supplies. Liberty places more than 17,000 purchase orders annually. The company's old centralized system involved quarterly purchases of key supplies which were stored in the office stockroom. Now the company's 2,200 administrators order supplies on-line whenever and where they need them. The company negotiated a 48-hour delivery arrangement with its office-supply vendor, Staples, which has reduced the need to stock items. The system limits the items available in the on-line Staples catalog to just the ones preselected by Liberty Mutual's purchasing department. The system automatically calculates the sales price, tax, and total and then electronically transmits the order to Staples. Invoicing is aggregated monthly and is paid by one check. Departments are then assigned monthly charges. With this system, Liberty Mutual has reduced the number of purchase orders to less than 8,000 annually, saving millions of dollars in purchasing and accounts payable processes. The company is now expanding its extranet application to cover the purchase of computers, furniture, and fleet cars. Others companies (e.g., Ford) also see the benefit and are aggressively pursuing these applications with vendor partners.

Marshall Industries, a large U.S. electronics distributor, has made its extranet the centerpiece of its business strategy. In most sectors of the electronics industry, time is being compressed. Product design cycles are falling from several years to several months. "Speed to market" is assuming greater importance. Marshall's extranet helps facilitate the flow of information from the company to hundreds of its customers, suppliers, and systems integrators. Marshall supplies global support to its 65,000 customers and 100 suppliers worldwide through strategic alliances with SEI in Europe and Serial System in Asia. These allies offer coverage in 36 countries from 164 locations. The extranet system connects suppliers and customers to products, services, and information from anywhere in the world. Marshall was named the number-one business-to-business Web site in the world for two consecutive years in the NetMarketing 200, an independent company that analyzes and business-to-business Web sites. Its customers can check out any promotions, locate product availability, scan technical data sheets, perform real-time ordering of products, and take interactive training sessions and product seminars through video, audio, and interactive chat technologies.

Marshall has formed partnerships at both ends of the supply chain. Customers can see the status of their orders immediately and interact with different parts of the company. They can log-on to the extranet anytime to check product pricing, availability, and order status. When customers place orders, Marshall uses United Parcel Service (UPS) to deliver products. Marshall's extranet provides a direct link with the UPS extranet so that package tracking can be easily accomplished. The company's Help@Once section inside its extranet site is a chat service offering its business partners online support, 24 hours a day. After customers enter the chat room, a Marshall Technical Support Engineer is available to answer questions and provide technical assistance. This has helped many customers resolve technical problems promptly as well as settle ordering, shipping, and payment issues. Suppliers get point-of-sale reports at any time, day or night. Suppliers can log-on to the company's extranet using unique account numbers and passwords and check on sales volume and pending sales opportunities. They can also respond to requests for quotations from Marshall's purchasing department.

Marshall Industries' extranet has helped increase productivity. Even though company sales and profit have doubled in recent years, sales staff has been trimmed from 1,600 to 1,450 employees.

There are many other creative uses of an extranet. CyberSource's extranet is used to manage the intellectual property rights of CyberSource's customers, including publishers, distributors, and resellers and merchants. Extranets extend the corporate information system to channel partners outside the corporation. They can help expand their businesses internationally while maintaining increased control over channel partners and end-customers. A lot of companies venture to new markets or geographic locations by using regional distribution centers and signing on local distributors and resellers in order to leverage contacts that can gain market access quickly. A disadvantage of dealing with independent distributors is that control over the customers or end users is often lost. Extranets allow corporations not only to connect, but also to totally integrate their sales, marketing, and customer support systems, not just with channel partners, but directly with the end-customer.

EMBEDDED EXTRANETS

Some companies are extending the functionality of their systems with embedded extranets. An embedded extranet is a corporate Web site that queries a second company's database and transmits information transparently. Cisco Connection Online, the networking giant's extranet site, is one of the first such applications. Instead of manually checking Federal Express Corp.'s Web site to find out when their network equipment orders will arrive, Cisco customers can query the FedEx database from within Cisco's extranet site under a partnership between the two companies. FedEx lets its largest customers have access to its intranet, allowing them to build Web applications that query its databases. Customers enjoy the convenience. Cisco has realized considerable costs savings in order entry. A major advantage of embedded extranets is that they keep users in the company's own site. Other companies' Web sites do not have to be contacted, which eliminates a step for the user. Embedded extranets will become increasingly more popular as companies collaborate on each other's Web sites.

Another example of an embedded extranet is the one developed by Dell Computer, the world's leading computer systems supplier. Dell opened an extranet Web storefront and started on-line, direct selling in 1996. Dell's extranet is presently used mainly for order entry, customer support, and relationship management. Like Cisco, Dell connects customers with its shipping partners. Customers can check the delivery status of a particular item in real time without having to leave Dell's Web site. In March, 1997, Dell launched Premier Pages[SM] as a free service to high-volume small-business customers. The Premier Pages[SM] service is a tailored, business-to-business commerce tool. It offers customized Web site access for order entry, order status tracking, service and support, and account team contact 24 hours a day. Dell developed more than 19,000 Premier Page extranet sites worldwide since the service was introduced. Dell helps customers personalize these pages so that they can be rapidly connected with relevant company information. Workflow capabilities in the Premier Pages[SM] enable customers to pick suitable computer configurations from Dell's catalog and forward chosen setups to their purchasing departments. Authorized buyers can then review each outstanding internal order, give approval, and submit orders to Dell. This on-line process helps streamline the workflow for customers's purchasing agents. The service tracks of customers' purchases and purchasing history put customers in instant contact with their service teams, and keeps customers up-to-date on all of the latest product announcements and price changes. Dell's customers can obtain assistance as needed from a Help Desk. They have multiple levels of access, which they control themselves. Dell has also incorporated dynamic service upgrades that are tailored to each customer, easier navigability with drop-down menus, and a wide range of available service options for buyers. Sales through Dell's extranet surpassed $18 million per day by the first quarter of 1999. This accounted for 30 percent of the company's overall revenue.

The most important benefit of an extranet is this ability to build closer relationships with customers, business partners, and sometimes the general public. These diverse applications demonstrate its versatility.

CHOOSING WHOM TO PARTNER WITH ON EXTRANETS

Companies need to identify potential partners before building an extranet. The system should accommodate and benefit as many partners as possible. A logical way of evaluating partners is to stratify them by importance to the company. This allows management to evaluate the benefits and security risks of creating extranet applications for specific partners or entire groups of suppliers and customer segments. Managers can classify partners as follows:

- *Strategic partners.* Strategic partners are organizations that are crucial to the company's success (e.g., customers that contribute more than 10 percent of the company's revenue or profit). Customers that contribute less may also qualify if they have significant growth and profit potential. Exclusive suppliers that contribute a high proportion of material cost and pose risks of manufacturing downtime may also be classified as strategic partners.
- *Major partners.* Major partners have an important but less critical influence on the company's success. These may be medium-sized customers and suppliers. They may also include professional partners such as corporate attorneys, management consultants, or contract employees.
- *Minor partners.* Minor partners are all other customers and suppliers who do not individually carry a lot of weight. They might be small commodity suppliers, small customers, occasional customers, and less important service providers, such as insurance brokers.

This type of partnering status can be used as an incentive to the company's bigger customers. The management of Bell Fasteners of Pawtucket, Rhode Island limits access on the company's extranet to large customers. Major industrial customers can now search Bell Fasteners' inventory of over 35,000 nuts, bolts, and screws and execute orders through Bell's Web page. For the rest of the customer base, Bell Fasteners will continue to send out the inventory data on diskettes. The system may be viewed as an incentive to do more business with Bell and become a strategic partner.

CONCERNS IN IMPLEMENTING EXTRANETS

Even though the extranet can provide significant benefits to companies, managers need to be aware of some of the potential pitfalls. Managers should not implement new systems just because competitors are doing it. Most of the extranet implementation difficulties are due to product or service mismatches. Applications should not begin with questions like "which browser should we select" or "which operating system should we use?" They should begin by asking "what are the strategic applications of the technology?" "How can a competitive advantage be achieved by installing an extranet?" Managers who have successfully implemented extranets evaluated the company's situation and decided which areas of the business would benefit from the new technology.

If a company does not already have a sound information infrastructure, these problems will be magnified on the firm's extranet. Granting external access to ineffective internal information systems is likely to create chaos. Sufficient testing of the extranet must be performed before putting the system on-line. Companies must clean up their data and improve their core processes. A study by consumer goods manufacturer, Procter & Gamble found that more than 30 percent of all its electronic orders contained manual mistakes due to keying errors by order-entry clerks and customers.[1] Companies need to reengineer processes for error-free ease of use before automating them. Dell's easy-to-use and navigate Web site is a model for other firms to follow. A viable information infrastructure must be built before proceeding with building a highly visible extranet system. This will increase the start-up costs of an extranet.

An IS department must also have fallback plans and failsafe procedures to cope with system failure. Charles Schwab & Co., the largest on-line brokerage company in the world, has a robust and fault-tolerant extranet trading system with more than two million user accounts. The company recently increased its capacity from 100,000 to 250,000 "concurrent logons" by adding a new mainframe to the existing system. A configuration error with this new system brought the company's entire on-line trading system down on several occasions in early 1999. Investors trying to make trades during the crash could execute transactions by phone or go directly to a Schwab branch office. Those investors who had to hold on the phone for more than five minutes were offered $500 off commissions on future trades. The high cost of system outages on E-commerce sites of all sizes demonstrates the need for management to rigorously test new systems and components, institute strong failover and backup procedures, and be ready at all times to implement these procedures quickly when things go wrong.

Extranet applications need to be prioritized. Applications should start small and build on successful projects. By implementing high-priority projects that produce impressive results, managers can gradually extend the use of the extranet to other areas of the business.

A major concern in implementing an extranet is the security of corporate data. Joint efforts are needed by information system managers, business managers, vice presidents of operations, IT directors, and corporate counsels. Protecting information requires firewalls, proxy servers, passwords, encryption, digital certificates, public key infrastructure, and the like. Corporate counsels can draw up warnings to deter casual intruders as well as agreements to protect the company in the event of misuse of data.

Most of the costs of installing an extranet are "people costs" for training. This includes training for content creation on the Web site as well as system management. Hardware upgrade costs may also be incurred in modifying the information system. Some of the artwork that was previously done by an advertising agency's graphic designers will be taken over by office employees who are trained in the use of computer graphics. While off-the-shelf software can help content creators maintain the site, employees must have sufficient training so they can use these tools effectively. Employees will spend considerable time organizing and posting information to the net.

Allowances must also be made for extranet partners. Extranet partners may not be technically sophisticated, fluent in the corporate language, or deeply committed to the extranet. Applications must be developed with "ease of use" in mind. These applications should have intuitive interfaces that "push" information to users.

JUSTIFYING AN EXTRANET

Developers can use various approaches to justify the implementation of an extranet system. It should be seen, initially, as a necessary cost of doing business, like the expense of office administration. Some companies may be able to justify an extranet on the basis of short-term revenue enhancements and cost savings. With Goodyear's Xplor system, operating costs for distributing technical documents and marketing information to national dealers grew to millions of dollars per year. In this case, it was relatively easy to cost-justify implementing the extranet on the basis of the immediate cost savings that were realized. In other companies, benefits may be less apparent or immediate. However, certain departments are likely to be the most active users of an extranet and may stand to benefit more directly. Cost information should be gathered from these departments on how much they are currently on communication and information sharing. These costs can be compared with the expense of installing equivalent functions on an extranet. Another consideration, when examining alternative systems, is that extranet applications are far less expensive to implement than EDI systems and can provide considerably more functionality.

The cost of establishing supply chain links using EDI are as high as $50,000 per partner, compared with $1,000 per partner or less for forming extranet links. Nevertheless, managers should not just look at the immediate application in justifying the cost but should consider all the alternative uses to which the system may be put later.

CONCLUSION

According to *Business India* (October 16, 1998), which used data from International Data Corp., E-commerce is expected to grow from $12.4 billion in 1997 to a whopping $425.7 billion by 2002. The U.S. share is projected to be $268.8 billion; the European Union, $55.5 billion; Japan, $21.4; and Asia, $15.6 billion. More than 100 million users are connected worldwide currently, and the number is expected to top 320 million by 2002. Extranets allow firms to extend their intranet applications and give them the reach and function of the Internet. The whole system is built on open standards. This eliminates many compatibility problems. The cost of implementing an extranet is substantially lower than EDI. Extranets can directly affect the way a company conducts business and can significantly impact the company's competitive position.

The Internet makes electronic commerce affordable to the smallest home office. Companies of all sizes can now communicate with each other electronically, through the public Internet, through intranets for company use only, and through extranets that link a company and its business partners. Internet commerce through the implementation of extranets is now expanding rapidly. It may be used to coordinate the purchasing operations of a company and its suppliers; the logistics planners in a company and the transportation companies that warehouse and move its products; the sales organizations and the wholesalers or retailers that sell its products; and the service and maintenance operations that link the company to customers or end users. Forward-thinking managers are creating an expanding array of extranet applications that are transforming the way companies compete.

Note

Karpinski, R., "Real world issues, real challenges," *Internet Week,* March 1, 1999, p. 15.

Recommended Reading

1. Baker, R.H., *Extranets: The Complete Sourcebook,* New York: McGraw-Hill (1997).
2. Bayles, D., *Extranets: Building the Business to Business Web,* Englewood Cliffs, NJ: Prentice Hall (1998).
3. Bort, J. and Bradley, F., *Building an Extranet: Connect Your Intranet with Vendors and Customers,* New York: Wiley Computer Publishing (1997).
4. Cronin, M.J., "Intranets reach the factory floor," *Fortune*, August 18, p. 208 (1997).

5. Johnson, M.E., "Give 'em what they want: broken links in supply chain management can prevent your product from getting to customers when they need it," *Management Review,* November 1998, pp. 62–67.
6. Koehler, J.W., Dupper, T., Scaff, M.D., Reitberger, F., and Paxon, P., *The Human Side of Intranets: Content, Style and Politics,* Delray Beach, FL: St. Lucie Press (1998).
7. Maitra, A.K., *Building a Corporate Internet Strategy: The IT Manager's Guide,* New York: Van Nostrand Reinhold (1996).
8. Urbaczewski, A., Jessup, L.M., and Wheeler, B.C., "A manager's primer in electronic commerce," *Business Horizons,* Sept.-Oct., 1998, pp. 5–16.

Chapter 35
An Implementor's Guide to E-Commerce

John Care

The paradigm of Internet Time is now starting to stretch Internet projects after several years of compression. Internet systems are becoming increasingly complex as tools and languages gain in complexity. In 1996, all an IT organization, or even a power user in sales and marketing, needed to cope with was setting up a Web server and a relatively small subset of HTML commands.

Since that time, a complete Internet architecture (see Exhibit 1) has evolved, and it is a rare project that now gets built in weeks instead of months. Increasingly, "Net" projects need to look outwards, capitalizing on tried and trusted user requirements' documents, QA procedures, while simultaneously capturing the technological zest and frenzy of the Web.

Meanwhile, business-to-consumer Internet commerce will grow to $93 billion in 2002 from $13 billion in 1998. More impressively, business-to-business Internet commerce will reach $1.3 trillion in 2003 from a mere $43 billion in 1998.[1] In late 1999, the value of goods and services traded over the Internet was doubling every three to four months. *The Industry Standard* reports that from 1998 to 1999, the number of Web users increased by 55 percent worldwide, the number of hosts grew by 46 percent, the number of Web servers by 128 percent and the number of new Web addresses by 137 percent.[2] And, the Federal Reserve Board's chairman, Alan Greenspan, made this observation about the development of E-commerce:

> The newest innovations, which we label information technologies, have begun to alter the manner in which we do business and create value, often in ways not readily foreseeable even five years ago.

Against this backdrop, a corporation's senior officials have determined that an electronic commerce site is now critical to profitability and revenue growth. The information technology (IT) group is mandated to make it happen. Implementation of anything but the simplest site requires the input

0-8493-1273-6/02/$0.00+$1.50
© 2002 by CRC Press LLC

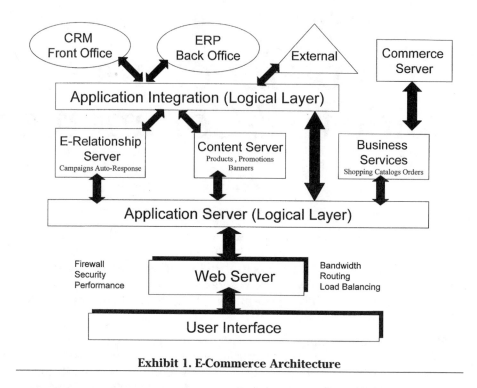

Exhibit 1. E-Commerce Architecture

and work of multiple departments and project stakeholders and can now rival the complexity of an ERP installation. So where to start?

A BROAD DEFINITION OF E-BUSINESS

The Center for Electronic Commerce broadly categorizes E-business into five distinct types:[3]

1. *Self-services* provide 24x7 access to important business and personnel data. The most common examples in this category include online employee benefit enrollment, updates of personnel or 401(k) records, access to shipping status of customer orders, and some forms of on-line banking.
2. *Information access* provides search and retrieval capabilities for both public and proprietary domain data archives. Examples would be credit agencies such as Equifax and financial sites such as Edgar Online and Hoovers.
3. *Shopping services* allow customers to seek and purchase goods and services though electronic networks. Although retail sales sites such as Lands End and The Gap are usually associated with this category, the classification can be extended to business-to-business (B2B) sites for purchasing used industrial equipment and commod-

ities. On-line auction sites such as eBay are also a variation within the category.

4. *Interpersonal communication services* provide a mechanism for individuals, groups, or corporations with mutual interests to exchange information and ideas in a cooperative environment. Examples include on-line interactive help desks, updated files sent to a printer by a publisher, joint supplier/customer groups building product specifications, and even e-mail communications between suppliers and purchasing agents.

5. *Virtual enterprises* are business arrangements such that trading partners are able to join in complex business activities, although separated by geography, as if they were a single enterprise. This includes true supply chain integration, transmitting forecast and planning data throughout a multi-tier chain. Another more common example is a grouping of allied suppliers allowing a common customer to do business with them ("one-stop shopping") via a single transaction.

The purpose of such broad classifications is actually one of focus. The fewer categories covered by an initial E-commerce project, the higher likelihood of both a business and technological success. This is in reality nothing more than the time-honored "contain the scope" mantra preached by project managers for generations.

More Than Taking Orders

Designing customer-facing applications instead of inward (internal) applications is still new to most organizations. Not only does the interface need to be functional, it also needs to be visually appealing. The E-customer, whether in business-to-business (B2B) or business-to-consumer (B2C) will only repeatedly visit a Web site for a limited number of reasons:

* The E-customer saves time
* The E-customer saves money
* Products and services are only available via the Web site
* Comparison shopping

A recent *USA Today* report showed that 60 percent of purchase transactions are abandoned prior to pressing the "Buy" button. Major reasons cited included incorrect pricing, special offers, customer service questions, and general uncertainty. This is hardly the standard fare of software bugs and slow performance technologists are typically concerned with.

WEBSITE DESIGN

Aside from some basic infrastructure decisions, Web site design represents the most contentious area between the technologists and the business people. The fundamental issue is that of who owns the site and the content. The usual King Solomon style answer is to have the technology group be responsible for the day-to-day operation of the site and to keep it running, but to charge either sales, marketing, or, in more forward-looking organizations, the on-line content group with the appearance and structure of the site. The Web site represents the "brand" of the corporation and as such needs to be designed by marketing — or with heavy input from them, as opposed to several HTML/Java programmers building the outward face of the company. Web developers know the difference between Java and JavaScript, and they like downloading plug-ins. Visitors to the site say, "So, how can I buy this?"

The four most common Web site operational requirements cited by users in numerous surveys are:

1. *Content.* The content of a site needs to be fresh and interesting. Matching this requirement is frequently the prime operational cost once a site goes live.
2. *Ease-of-use.* An intuitive interface that guides a user from screen to screen, with complete on-line help. Additionally, provide an option to remain on the Web page and contact customer support to resolve any questions.
3. *Fast downloads.* Filling a page with large .gif or .jpeg graphics, animations, or Java applets dramatically slows download times. The longer a page takes to load, the higher the chance a transaction will be abandoned. As a datapoint, Zona Research estimated that slow download times cost U.S.-based sites $4.6 billion in 1999.
4. *A search engine.* Many sites operate with search engines that are not up to the task. Either they cannot handle long queries like "Black Tommy Hilfiger Sweater" or they produce multiple pages of useless information based on a single keyword ("Tylenol").

Above all, it is key to be consistent. Once a corporate style has been decided upon, all pages within the system need to follow the style and the interface.

It is also worthwhile to note several things *not* to do.[4] Do not:

1. Use frames. Although a marvelous piece of programming technology, frames tend to be confusing and can radically cut down on the amount of free space available on a page for display. In particular, double-frames (top and bottom or top and side) receive extremely poor ratings.
2. Require scrolling. If a user needs to scroll left and right, or up and down to get to vital information, the page immediately loses its impact. The keep-it-simple philosophy is an excellent guideline.
3. Forget to confirm. A user needs to know that a requested action has actually taken place. These range from something as simplistic as an order acknowledgment to more complex error trapping.

4. Ignore the 12-second rule. If an action has not occurred in 12 seconds, a user has a higher probability of canceling or refreshing a screen. (*Note:* Various Web pundits place different values on the wait factor, but the principle is that a measurable limit needs to be set.)
5. Design for T-1 speeds if dealing with B2C systems, international systems, or remote dial-in. 56k access is a good guideline.
6. Provide an English-only system if dealing with international trade. Although used by 57 percent of the world's surfers, English is only spoken by 8 percent of the population.[5]

PRIVACY

On March 7, 1999, *The New York Times* revealed that the world's most powerful software company was collecting data about its customers with an apparent total disregard for privacy. This incident, although quickly corrected by Microsoft, thrust the concept of privacy squarely under the nose of the American public.

A privacy violation occurs when an organization uses information collected from its customers, or prospects, in ways the end user did not explicitly agree to when providing the data. This information can be anything from on-line behavior patterns to phone and fax numbers to demographic data. Although the buying and selling of consumer information has long been a staple of marketers worldwide, the speed of collection, collation, and dissemination via the Internet is an order of magnitude faster.

The establishment and publishing of a privacy policy is essential for any commercial Web site dealing in B2B or B2C transactions. On-line privacy statement generators are available via the Direct Marketing Association.[6] Several third-party organizations such as TrustE and BBB Online (a unit of the Better Business Bureau) also provide audits and seals of approvals. For a high-volume, major site, the American Institute of Certified Public Accountants CPAWebTrust program supplies the most vigorous trustmark.

For an IT project manager, this is a task to pass off to the legal department in terms of the wording and certification. However, ensuring that no illicit data collection is actually performed behind the scenes and that no consumer's data is visible to anyone else is the responsibility of the project team. The most common avenues for "accidental" collection are typically remnants of debug code or stub CGI scripts left by the programming team.

The counterpoint of privacy is that the more a vendor can learn about a customer, the more value the vendor can provide by customizing for that customer. This is the basic tenet of one-to-one marketing. Eventually, as the relationship evolves, it becomes a matter of trust — more data can be voluntarily collected and put to good use.

Exhibit 2. Basic Definitions of Web-Centric Marketing Terms

Term	Definition
Click-through rate	Percentage of viewers who click on a banner ad
Conversion rate	Percentage of visitors who purchase
Abandon rate	Percentage of visitors who abandon a transaction before purchase
Up-sell rate	Percentage of transactions where a higher cost item was sold measured against the original intended purchase
Eyeballs	A net-centric term indicating the number of unique views each item or site obtains
Impression	Number of views (per link or page) by product or feature category during entire visit
Cross-sell rate	Percentage of completed transactions which included an additional product outside of the original intended purchase

ADVERTISING AND MARKETING

At first glance, this is hardly the realm of information technology, but through the extended project team it is a critical function of any E-commerce site. This reaches further than simple Web site design, which is covered elsewhere. First, the prime consideration is if advertising (banner) space will be featured on the site. If so, then both inbound and outbound traffic need to be monitored.

Web traffic analysis by slicing Web server log usage data is a common adjunct to any commercial site and many tools exist[8] to extract and examine such data. Standard analysis details the total hits, ranks popular pages, and shows the entry and exit points of the site by user, and where that user came from. The breakdown from the E-commerce viewpoint is that such tools do not provide linkage to the end result (i.e., a sale or order).

The marketing department will be interested in various Internet metrics (see Exhibit 2).

A newer form of analysis, microconversion, with more of a focus on ROI has been proposed by IBM researchers[7] and is gaining credence in the marketplace. While the conversion rate of an on-line store is the percentage of visitors who purchase from a store, it does not indicate the possible factors affecting sales performance. The notion of microconversion extends the traditional measures by considering the four general shopping steps in an on-line store, product impression, click-through, basket insertion, and purchase. Microconversion rates are computed for each adjacent pair of measures resulting in three additional functional rates.

1. Look-to-Click rate: product impressions converted to click-throughs
2. Click-to-Basket rate: click-throughs converted to basket placement
3. Basket-to-Buy rate: basket placements converted to purchases

The end result for IT is that measurement, both inbound to one's site and outbound (potentially to partners paying royalties), needs to be included in the initial project scope in order to generate any form of meaningful ROI for the site and its marketing programs.

SALES CHANNEL CONFLICT

Opening up the corporate sales process to one's customers will undoubtedly save the company money and streamline delivery for customers. However, depending on the sales model used, there may be considerable conflict between the different sales channels within an organization. (An example of channel conflict might be a full-service brokerage offering $20 trades to its clientele and not compensating its field brokerage force.)

Although not an issue for IT to directly resolve, requirements from the sales and partner organizations are likely to revolve around lead management, compensation, and quota recognition — all of which add to the complexity of the operation and will involve batching data to payroll or external systems.

INTEGRATING EXISTING AND NEW SYSTEMS

Barring the most recent "dot.com" companies, every corporation has a collection of legacy systems that contains useful information for the enterprise. In addition, there are invariably operational systems running on a current technology set which also require linkages to the E-commerce site. In numerous implementations witnessed by this author, the critical path to bringing a site live actually relies on the speed of integration as opposed to the base commerce technology itself.

Although not an exhaustive list, the types of systems shown in Exhibit 3 need to be examined for integration to the site.

Exhibit 3. Potential Integration Points

IVR/VRU	Interactive voice recognition for customer service
Inventory	Is the product or service actually in stock?
Pricing tables	Current pricelists (commercial, retail, government, etc.)
Shipping/Fulfillment	To provide status updates for orders
External shipping	Realtime linkage to UPS, FedEx, or chosen vendor
Financials	Credit check, E-cash
Billing and invoicing	To ensure payment is made for the transaction
Credit card	Credit card authorization
External	Trading partners supply chain systems
Marketing	Lead and campaign management, personalization
eCRM	Electronic customer relationship management

Taking Care of the E-Customer

A much quoted Jupiter research report[9] showed that over 40 percent of the top 120 Internet commerce stores either did not respond to customer e-mail or took longer than five days to do so. A number of these sites did not even provide an 800-number or an e-mail address for queries. There are also many individual stories, including several experienced by this author, about the lack of integration between sales, service, and Web site. Unless a corporation provides a truly unique and monopolistic service, the maxim "the competition is only a click away" is one to live by.

Based on a corporation's desire to have customer service as a differentiator, linkage to a CRM (customer relationship management) system becomes an added requirement. Despite the proliferation of Web self-service sites, at some point customers and prospects may need to speak to a live customer service person. Even Amazon.com, which bombards the consumer with status and update messages, still has live bodies on the end of the phone. The benefits of a CRM package are manyfold, including the ability to:

- Attract, acquire, and then retain customers
- Determine who are the most profitable customers
- Allow anyone in the corporation access to appropriate customer data
- Provide base data for marketing campaigns
- Obtain eventual linkage to field sales force automation system

How Much Does It Cost?

Exhibit 4 sets out an approximate cost schedule to build an industrial-strength E-commerce site, based on estimates from various suppliers.[10]

These are undoubtedly daunting figures, with a wide degree of variance, but nevertheless bolster the assumption that building an E-commerce site is neither a trivial nor cheap project for any reasonably sized corporation. Naturally, a significant part of the implementation costs can be absorbed internally if both the manpower and budget dictate.

SUMMARY

Internet application development and deployment has gained the reputation of being fast and not tied to prior systems and methodologies. Unfortunately, as the tools and requirements imposed on such E-systems have become more complex, the project scope, reach, and budget have risen dramatically. The needs of an E-commerce site cross multiple departmental boundaries — from sales and marketing to legal to shipping to product management and finance — and all of these groups need to be stakeholders in the E-commerce project and be part of the E-team constructing the site.

**Exhibit 4. Approximate Cost Estimates for "Industrial Strength"
E-commerce Site**

Cost of Technology	Low	High
E-commerce applications	$ 1,000,000	$ 2,000,000
Integration to existing systems	$ 50,000	$ 500,000
eCRM software	$ 500,000	$ 1,000,000
Chat, discussion, bulletin boards	$ 200,000	$ 200,000
Operations	$ 1,000,000	$10,000,000
Site Hosting and network infrastructure	$ 250,000	$ 2,000,000
Total technology cost	$ 3,000,000	$ 15,700,000
Cost of Implementation		
E-commerce applications	$ 2,000,000	$ 8,000,000
Integration to existing systems	$ 300,000	$ 1,000,000
eCRM software	$ 1,000,000	$ 2,000,000
Chat, discussion, bulletin boards	$ 50,000	$ 50,000
Operations	$ 1,000,000	$ 10,000,000
Site hosting and network infrastructure	$ 250,000	$ 2,000,000
Total implementation cost	$ 4,600,000	$ 23,050,000
Overal Project Cost	**$ 7,600,000**	**$ 38,750,000**

A simple four-step process, remarkably similar to methodologies around since the COBOL era, forms the basis for development.

1. Perform a needs analysis to determine how to leverage existing legacy and operational systems. Obtain input from all departments that will integrate their business to the site. Nominate at least one member from each department to the E-team.
2. Choose an open-standards-based platform solution. Search for the optimum combination of the scalability and reliability for the company's requirements.
3. Connect the E-commerce application to the corporate ERP (enterprise resource planning), CRM (customer relationship management), and legacy systems.
4. Test and test again.

Notes

1. Forrester Research Papers, 1999, www.forrester.com.
2. My How We've Grown, Maryann Jones Thompson, *The Industry Standard,* April 26th, 1999, www.thestandard.com.
3. The Environmental Research Institute of Michigan, www.erim.com.
4. A detailed study of aesthetic Web design is located at www.creativegood.com.
5. Reference www.emarketer.com.
6. Found at www.the-dma.org.
7. E-Commerce Intelligence: Measuring, Analyzing, and reporting on Merchandising Effectiveness of Online Stores, Gomory, Hoch et al., IBM Research Center, Yorktown Heights, NY.
8. Doubleclick www.doubleclick.com, Media Matrix www.mediamatrix.com, Marketwave www.marketwave.com.

TASK 3: FORGING SUPPLY CHAIN PARTNERSHIPS

9. Jupiter Research (www.jup.com).
10. Estimates provided by USWeb/CKS (www.usWeb.com), Interactive Week (www.zdnet.com/intweek), Clarify Inc. (www.clarify.com), and Eloyalty (www.eloyalty.com).

Chapter 36
Root Cause: Weak Links

James B. Ayers

Linkages are the ways partners in the supply chain coordinate their joint enterprise. They include any of the supply chain components — physical, information, financial, or knowledge flow. Strong links lead to a well-coordinated effort; weak ones to an uncoordinated effort.

Supply chain partners are like warships at sea, where their combined strength is presumably greater than that of any one member. When under way, the movements of the fleet must be coordinated. For example, to maintain their formation, all must turn at the same time when the course they are steering is changed. Moving independently creates chaos, and leaves the fleet vulnerable to attack. Ships at sea have many ways to communicate their course changes. These include radio transmissions of voice messages; semaphore (signaling flags); encrypted radio signals; blinking lights; and, particularly if submarines are part of the formation, underwater telephones. The supply chain has similar needs for linkages. As one might expect, there are many variations as well.

Some have also likened the supply chain to a symphony. At the symphony, the conductor leads musicians. The sheet music defines the production and timing of contributions from each orchestra member. In supply chain management (SCM), linkages play the roles of conductor and sheet music.

Supply chain linkages are a special category. Supply chain linkages can range from "tight" to downright "unwieldy." So supply chain partners must be careful in their design. In general, "less is more" and "elegant simplicity" will win out over complex, expensive linkages. This chapter points to some of the efforts under way to establish strong links across supply chains.

THEORY OF CONSTRAINTS

In formulating the theory of constraints, Eli Goldratt and Robert Fox observe that a production system can produce no more than its "capacity

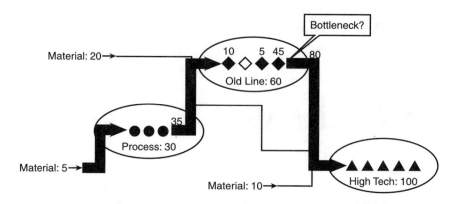

Exhibit 1. Identifying the CCR in a Supply Chain

constraint resource," or CCR. They use this principle as a foundation for what they call the "drum–buffer–rope way." While the authors focus on individual factories, the lessons apply equally to the supply chain.

To illustrate its application, we use a supply chain case study. From Exhibit 1, we see that the longest lead-time operation in the supply chain is 45 days at a company we call *Old Line*. This is likely to indicate the presence of a CCR at that operation. Managing the CCR is the core of the drum–buffer–rope, or DBR approach. The *drum* sets the beat determined by the capacity of the CCR. This is equivalent to takt time, or the interval at which products are produced. A supply chain that operates 5000 minutes a week and is designed to produce 1000 units per week will have a takt time of five minutes (5000 minutes/1000 units) with level loading of work centers in the supply chain. This drumbeat paces the entire supply chain's production. Because it is the constraining resource, there is no point in letting other operations march faster than the "drum" will allow.

The *buffer* is a device to protect capacity at the CCR. This protection is in the form of inventory that assures a supply of work for the CCR in case of upstream disruption in supply. The size of the inventory is equivalent to the number of days needed to recover from any anticipated disruption upstream interruptions. If a disruption at *Process* stops the flow of material to Old Line, a buffer will keep the CCR at Old Line going until the disruption is fixed.

The DBR system's final component is the *rope*. The rope is symbolic of the link between the CCR and the front end of the production process, or gating operation. Its purpose is to prevent production in excess of capacity at the CCR. This avoids the common problem of launching more production into the supply chain than it is capable of handling.

Like the ships at sea, the linkage that communicates along the supply chain should fit the situation. Alternatives range from digital signals from linked information systems to physical forms like the Kanbans. For an automated linkage, a proactive system approach could establish the routing of the signal and the appropriate responses.

The DBR system assures maximum output from the CCR, hence the entire supply chain system. For example, assume the supply chain partners determine that Old Line's operation is the system's CCR. As such, it will set the pace for the entire supply chain. Linkages will pace operations at both Process and High Tech. The form is less important than the realization that it is needed. Options include periodic (hourly, weekly, or even monthly) status or automated linkages for continuous monitoring.

REPLENISHMENT RULES

Another component of supply chain linkage is the quantity–timing decision for production. This decision includes the rules by which partners will order and replenish stock along the supply chain. Monden also describes the alternatives used to set up Kanbans in the Toyota Production System.[2] The first option is *constant quantity*. With the constant quantity decision, the same quantity is produced when a production need is triggered. This is particularly appropriate for operations with high setup costs. The selected quantity should be sufficient to assure an economic transfer. The second decision option is *constant cycle*. With this rule, stock is replenished on a fixed cycle. The quantity is determined by the actual amount used.

Both methods pull material through the supply chain. According to Monden, the constant cycle method is favored for subcontractors in the Toyota Production System. These may take the form of "milk runs" to the supplier several times a day, a constant cycle method, to pick up material for assembly lines. The constant quantity method is favored for internal suppliers. The difference is the distance factor. Constant cycle delivery leaves less to chance from transportation disruptions over longer distances.

The supply chain requires linkages to trigger movements of material. In general, they will follow either the constant quantity or constant cycle rule. But one or the other should govern the movement of each item in the supply chain. Exhibit 2 displays the advantages and disadvantages of each.

Working out which method to use is subject to objectives for the supply chain, contractual discussions, experimentation, and logistics between partners in the supply chain. But agreement to linkages and replenishment rules will be vital to orderly and low cost movement of work through the supply chain.

Exhibit 2. Constant Quantity or Constant Cycle?

Option	Advantages	Disadvantages
Constant quantity	• Better for close operations with minimal transportation requirements. • Can take advantage of EOQ economies for operations involving high set up costs. • Fast, does not require counting or tracking of inventory. • Simplicity. Compatible with visible signaling. Examples are the two-bin system and Kanban approaches. • Easier to predict time requirements once orders are placed.	• Can cause excess inventory in the system. Better for low cost, "C" items. Some companies expense items in this category.
Constant cycle	• Establishes a regular rhythm in the supply chain. Decreases variability from uncertainty about schedules. • Can take advantage of setup economies when setup times depend on sequence. An example is paint lines where different color sequences require different setup efforts.	• Variation in quantities can cause production to run behind. • Have to track production through the chain. Need to know usage at various points to signal correct quantity. • Fits higher value "A" items.

THE 3C ALTERNATIVE

Three managers from Lucent Technologies operations in Spain have devised and road-tested a simplified tool for optimizing supply chain performance.3 They call their methodology "3C," which stands for *Capacity, Commonality,* and *Consumption.* The method is an alternative to what they view as flawed MRP approaches. In particular, they object to the reliance on forecasts inherent in the MRP methodology.

In the 3C method, supply chain *capacity,* the first C, is the governing parameter over the amount of inventory in the system. Under 3C control, the chain should have a sufficient number of any one part on hand to produce to the capacity of the chain for usage of that part. To the extent parts are *common,* then the overall inventory is less, because a single part will support several products.

Exhibit 3 provides an example to explain the concept. The simple system we describe has four parts and three products. The capacity of the

Exhibit 3. The 3C Alternative Method

	Product 1	Product 2	Product 3	Target
Part A	1	1	1	20
Part B	2		1	20
Part C	1		3	30
Part D		1		20
Capacity	10	20	10	

supply chain is the number of units of each product that can be produced in a given period. This assumes that the system is producing nothing but that single product. The "target" inventory is determined by the maximum potential demand for the part during the period. For example, Part A's target inventory should be 20, because the Product 2 capacity is 20. Part C's target is 30 due to potential demand from Product 3. A level of 20 for Part A and 30 for Part C will cover the needs of any potential demand scenario.

As parts are *consumed*, then they are replaced in sufficient amounts to maintain the target inventory. This concept is applied to all "points of consumption" through the supply chain. Thus, actual demand provides the signal for replenishment in the chain. No stock is reserved for any single forecasted need. So a company using the 3C method would do away with forecasts for each of their products — eliminating a source of confusion and inventory overbuilding. With 3C, only capacity, not lack of parts, restricts what can be delivered to the customer. Frequent updating is abolished. Changes in the targets occur only at times when product or market changes make it necessary.

The authors have performed simulations demonstrating that 3C bests the MRP method in many cases. 3C is a valuable addition to thinking about both supply chain systems and "rules of the road" among partners. We believe that supply chain management will call for simpler rule-making with respect to inventory maintenance and restocking rules. 3C fulfills the criterion for simpler methods.

COLLABORATION

Many tools and techniques have been developed to help create effective supply chains. One initiative addresses both the cultural and technical barriers to collaboration among supply chain partners. It is Collaborative Planning Forecasting and Replenishment, CPFR for short. CPFR requires a business relationship between partners and has taken root in the retail industry. Collaboration strives to better match demand and supply, improve inventory management practices, and capitalize on new systems through sharing. CPFR is primarily a link between retailers and their manufacturer suppliers. It is expected that the concepts will expand to other industries.

CPFR is moving forward with standards for communications, innovations in placing and filling orders, and roadmaps for business arrangements. The obstacles are not technical, however, but cultural. Top management commitment is necessary to forge partnerships. A key to successful implementation of CPFR will be removing these barriers. A primary barrier is the evolution of the "flow model." Often the planning cycles of manufacturers and their retail customers are unsynchronized. CPFR attempts to implement a common forecast that represents a compromise between the needs of both parties.

Notes

1. Goldratt, Eliyahu M. and Fox, Robert E., *The Race,* Croton-on-the-Hudson, NY: North River Press, 1986.
2. Monden, Yasuhiro, *Toyota Production System,* Institute of Industrial Engineers, 1983.
3. Fernández-Rañada, Miguel, Gurrola-Gal, F. Xavier, and López-Tello, Enrique, *3C: A Proven Alternative to MRPII for Optimizing Supply Chain Performance,* Boca Raton, FL: St. Lucie Press, 2000.

Chapter 37
Outsourcing and Long-Term Strategy

William R. King

Outsourcing is often viewed in dollars-and-cents terms, and traditional make-or-buy thinking can prevail in making the decision to outsource operations. However, this approach ignores the long-run and possible strategic implications. When this thinking is applied to IS, or any other major function of an organization, it can be dangerous or even fatal.

INTRODUCTION

A senior business executive justified a $1 billion, decade-long IS outsourcing contract on two grounds."First," the executive said, "the vendor buys our IS assets and pays us money up front; the annual contracted expense is less than we incur now; the vendor hires all of our people and guarantees them jobs for at least a year; and there's no learning curve, because the people who used to do the work will still be doing it; they'll just be working for the vendor." "Second," the executive continued, "we decided that IS is not a core competency, so we could afford to make this judgment strictly on economic grounds. In fact, it was a no-brainer."

The executive might have added that outsourcing is currently a major trend in U.S. business: 85 percent of banks have outsourced their IS function, and up to 50 percent of the firms in other major industries have done so as well.

If he were not avoiding insulting his IS people, the executive might well have said that IS is notorious for the enormous demands it places on scarce capital investment budgets, for its cost and schedule overruns, for its inability to clearly demonstrate its direct impact on the bottom line, and for its arcane content and language. If a business manager can outsource the function, reduce costs, improve the balance sheet, and avoid or reduce the need to deal with millions of instructions per second, computer-aided software engineering, and UNIX, and the like, why not?

0-8493-1273-6/02/$0.00+$1.50
© 2002 by CRC Press LLC

There was a time when business managers wanted to tightly control everything. They vertically integrated and created many small, inefficient functions. Now they are doing an about-face. They are not even pretending to be able to do everything well in-house; thus, outsourcing is popular.

But, of course, in an era in which quality and customer service are paramount, there is grave danger of outsourcing functions that can directly affect either quality or service. Who wants to depend on outsiders in dealing with customers or in retrieving data that is crucial to servicing customers?

OUTSOURCING IS A STRATEGIC ISSUE

Decisions regarding outsourcing significant functions are among the most strategic that can be made by an organization, because they address the basic organizational choice of the functions for which internal expertise is developed and nurtured and those for which such expertise is purchased. These are basic decisions regarding organizational design. Therefore, decisions concerning outsourcing should not be made because a vendor makes an offer that is too good to refuse or because the current fad is to outsource a particular function or service.

Major outsourcing decisions are strategic and should be made after other key choices pertaining to a vision, a mission, core competencies, and key success factors. Although this may seem like a textbook approach, the fact is that outsourcing a function that might potentially be a core competency or a key success factor, merely because it may be economically desirable to do so in the short run, may result in the unplanned "hollowing" of the organization, thus jeopardizing its *raison d'etre*. (This notion was first discussed in "The Hollow Corporation," a 1986 *Business Week* report that focused on companies that had outsourced production to the degree that they had little or no production base to support the products that they marketed.)

Factors in Deciding to Outsource

A wise decision about outsourcing IS depends on having a solid understanding of some fundamental factors, including:

- The overall consequences of any make-or-buy decision
- An explicit multiple-criteria understanding of what constitutes a core competency
- An assessment of whether IS might be a future key success factor, although it has not been one in the past
- The new skills and attitudes that are required for effective outsourcing
- Alternatives to outsourcing

CONSEQUENCES OF A MAKE-OR-BUY DECISION

One simple view of outsourcing is to characterize it as a simple make-or-buy choice. However, the textbook version of the make-or-buy decision is inadequate because it usually views the choice as an isolated one that has no long-term implications. Even in the simple case of the decision to make or buy a part or component, it should never really be a do-whatever-is-cheapest decision because, when an organization chooses to buy, it is to some degree foreclosing on the possibility of having both options in the future.

The reason, of course, is that with every "buy" choice, the capability of "making" in the future is, to some degree, lost. Eventually, in a series of make-or-buy choices, this loss of expertise comes to dominate the decision, and it is always less expensive to buy than to suffer the fixed costs of rebuilding the degraded expertise. Eventually, such rebuilding is not even feasible to do, and the expertise has been forever lost.

Former Secretary of Labor Robert B. Reich has described a situation in which a company's engineers complained that "[the company] thinks it's cheaper to buy rather than build, and it is today. But if we don't make it in-house, we don't gain the experience and knowledge that goes with making it. And then we can't develop a whole range of technologies that are likely to evolve from that component."[1]

WHAT IS A CORE COMPETENCY?

The notion of core competencies is clearly important to outsourcing decisions. The idea that companies should follow a contrived "hollowing" strategy, in which only core competencies are retained and other capabilities are purchased, is very much in vogue. The identification of IS as a function that is not a core competency is often made casually and in retrospect, when in fact the parameters of what constitutes a core competency should be carefully spelled out and assessed before such a decision is made.

Criteria for Core Competencies

Just because a business is good at something does not necessarily mean that it is a core competency, although it may have been the basis for considerable competitive advantage in the past. Conversely, just because something has not been of critical importance in the past does not mean that it is not, or might not be, a core competency.

A core competency is a capability that:[2]

1. Evolved slowly through collective learning and information sharing
2. Cannot be quickly enhanced through additional large investments
3. Is synergistic with other capabilities

4. Cannot be easily imitated or transferred to others
5. Confers competitive advantage in the perception of customers
6. Can be a key success factor for the industry (one that historians will use to explain who won and who lost in the marketplace)
7. Cannot readily be "cashed out" (i.e., one in which investment is irreversible)

A careful look at many organizations that do not typically think of IS as a core competency reveals that IS can be seen to have (or be very close to having) many of these traits. For example, IS often meets the first three criteria, and significant elements of IS usually meet the fourth criterion. IS often has the potential to meet the fifth and sixth criteria as well. Such an assessment should give pause to anyone who wishes to dismiss IS as a bothersome service function for which an outsourcing choice is a no-brainer.

A FUTURE KEY SUCCESS FACTOR

Although IS may not meet the key success factor criteria from a historical perspective, the critical question is: Does it have the potential to be of critical importance?

In an information age, a wise business manager will not be too quick to dismiss the possibility of developing strategic systems those that can create competitive advantage or systems that are competitive necessities those that can match the competition and keep the business in the ball game. Similarly, the potential for using IS to make products or processes more information intensive should be carefully thought through. Information-based innovations in products and processes are some of the most common that are currently being implemented, so it seems unwise to forfeit this opportunity.

Of course, defenders of IS outsourcing will argue that most large organizations do not outsource critical elements of IS, such as the development of new applications; so many of these things can still be done even after some IS operations are outsourced. However, this may be too clever a distinction. When it comes to IS expertise — the kind that can confer competitive advantage or add value to products or processes using IT — there is no way of ensuring that the "right" capabilities are kept and people and the wrong ones are outsourced.

Thus, outsourcing IS may lead to the loss of a capability that could potentially be a key success factor. This has been demonstrated in many industries that are not information intensive, as well as in those that depend on IS.[3]

New Skills and Attitudes Required for Effective Outsourcing

Outsourcing is often viewed as a way of reducing the total administrative and coordination costs within an organization and of avoiding the management headaches associated with IS. However, this may be a simplistic and unrealistic view because outsourcing requires the organization to develop a new set of skills and new ways of managing, which increases other costs and creates new headaches.

Difficulty in Managing Outsourcing Contracts

Executives who believe that they simply sign a contract and walk away from their problems need only look at the U.S. government, which outsources the procurement of everything from soap to complex weapons systems. The federal government's contract management system, which is necessitated by this outsourcing, is a professional discipline in itself, one whose best-known manifestations are the purchase of $300 hammers and $800 toilet seats.

Many organizations have several IS outsourcing vendors: one for data center operations, one for network administration, one for disaster recovery, for example. Managing a single large, complex outside vendor relationship is difficult; managing several of them amplifies the difficulties.

Lack of Options. Contract changes are a major issue in managing outsourcing. Many government contractors are alleged to buy into contracts with unrealistically low prices, and then make a profit on the changes that are invariably required in long-term contracts involving complex systems. So, the government's purchase of overpriced toilet seats and hammers stems partly from the lack of alternative sources that are available to the purchaser after it becomes subject to a long-term contract and from the need to provide fair compensation when changes are made or new requirements are placed on the vendor. The hammer may be something that seemingly should cost only a few dollars because it is similar to one available in any hardware store. However, when a hammer is added to a large weapons systems contract, it often has a special purpose; thus (to use an IS analogy), it must be tested so that it does not introduce bugs into the system, and the vendor must be compensated for the extra costs (including overhead), involved in providing it in small quantity.

The Fine Print. In outsourcing contracts, the devil is truly in the details, and careful, detailed management is therefore required. Changes are inevitable in a long-run contract and many cannot be foreseen. However, when many changes that could be foreseen are added to those that could not, contract management can become a nightmare. It is not uncommon for an IS executive to be surprised when the IS vendor bills for software license transfer fees, or when the IS executive finds that no provision has been made for obtaining the cost data needed for negotiating contract extensions or enhancements.

Who Is a Partner? Of course, vendors attempt to sell outsourcing contracts as "partnerships." In general, they are no such thing! Partnerships require a significant degree of commonality of objectives; outsourcing vendors are primarily motivated by their own profit.

In one highly publicized case, Massachusetts Blue Cross and Blue Shield's (BC/BS) large outsourcing contract was hailed as a model in 1992, in part because of its applications development partnership provisions.[4] However, in January 1994, Blue Cross and Blue Shield was ordered to pay $7 million to employees who had been transferred to the vendor on short notice (some of whom were subsequently terminated). A representative of the vendor is quoted by *InformationWeek* as reacting that the court judgments "… were against Blue Cross [not against us] and from [our] … perspective were probably justified."[5] Therein lies a lesson — both in partnerships and in details.

Once IS is outsourced, top management no longer has direct command authority over it. Every special or emergency request becomes the subject of a contract change proposal that must be formalized and negotiated. So, an entirely new set of attitudes and way of managing are required when IS is outsourced.

Alternatives to Outsourcing

Suppose that a manager is considering outsourcing the IS function and that it has already been determined that it is not now, or ever likely to become, a core competence. Then, is not it best to farm out this nettlesome function?

Well, perhaps it is, but IS should be viewed as a window on the world of information and communications technology, which clearly is going to become even more important to everyone. Is it really sensible to not pay attention to this significant function and its associated technologies? Is it reasonable to expect that an organization will adequately keep aware of the latest technological opportunities when it does not have specialists with intimate knowledge of the technologies, or if it has far fewer of them? Hardware and software vendors quickly learn that there is no payoff in calling on those who have outsourced IS. IS executives who once viewed these salespeople as irritants can quickly come to feel that they are out of the loop when it comes to new developments.

The alternatives to outsourcing are not just the status quo, which may well be unsatisfactory. The first to be considered is the partial outsourcing that is done by many large organizations. Many organizations retain applications development in-house, for example. In effect, by doing so, they are insourcing new, potentially important systems and outsourcing legacy systems that are necessary but not important to the future of the business.

Other alternatives should include consideration of the same strategies that are currently being employed in other core business activities redesign of the IS function and processes, new IS training programs, IS quality programs, and new incentives such as productivity gain sharing. There is evidence that such efforts can produce results that might represent a significant improvement to the IS status quo.

CONCLUSION

In an era in which most organizations have given up trying to perform all functions, it is reasonable to consider outsourcing rote utility-like systems while retaining the expertise to develop a strategic infrastructure, an information architecture, and a suite of strategic systems. However, this must be done very carefully after consideration has been given to the long-term loss of expertise, a sophisticated notion of core competency, a serious assessment of potential future key success factors, a realistic assessment of the new problems that outsourcing is likely to create, and the alternatives that are available.

Notes

1. R.B. Reich, Companies Are Cutting Their Hearts Out, *The New York Times Magazine*, December 19, 1993, pp. 54–55.
2. This list is based on several sources, including: P.J.H. Schoemaker, How to Link Strategic Vision to Core Capabilities, *Sloan Management Review,* Fall 1992, pp. 67–81; and I. Diericky and K. Coll, Asset Stock Accumulation and Sustainability of Competitive Advantage, *Management Science*, 35, 1504–1514, 1989.
3. W.R. King, V. Grover, and E. Hufnagle, Using Information and Information Technology for Sustainable Comparative Advantage, *Information and Management,* 1989, pp. 87–93.
4. N. Margolis, Massachusetts Blue Cross Tries EDS Rx, *Computerworld,* 26(4), 1, 131, Jan. 27, 1992.
5. J.P. McPartlin, Crossed Up: Ruling in Blue Cross Case Send Pointed Message to Outsourcers and Their Clients, *Information Week,* January 31, 1994, p. 12.

Chapter 38

Public Web Sites as a Component of Corporate Supplier Communication

Dale Young

Public and private Web sites are a cost-effective way to communicate up and down the supply chain to trading partners, both customers and suppliers. The Web has rapidly become a channel for conducting business-to-business (B2B) transactions. Firms are using the Web for such functions as taking orders, supporting business customers, and publishing information.

This chapter focuses on one aspect of these trading partner interactions, the use of public Web sites by large firms for communicating with existing and prospective suppliers. It describes the categories of supplier communication most often found on corporate public Web sites, notes business objectives for supplier communications, measures the extent or depth of those communications, differentiates between public and private Web site content, and offers suggestions for "best practices" based on an analysis of the public Web sites of the Fortune 100.

PREDOMINANT USES OF CORPORATE PUBLIC WEB SITES

Corporations use public Web sites to reach four key audiences: customers, suppliers, potential employees, and stakeholders such as investors. Investors are interested in financial reports. Job seekers look for discussions about the work environment, specific job openings, and ways to post résumés interactively. Customers want the convenience of placing orders over the Web and find the Web an easy way to get support, through site features such as "frequently asked questions" (FAQs). A public Web site is an efficient way to provide product or service information. Firms use the Web as an avenue for publicizing contributions and other civic activities. Sup-

0-8493-1273-6/02/$0.00+$1.50

pliers may come to a public Web site to learn how to do business with the host firm.

The content of a corporate public Web site should reflect both the business objectives for developing the site and the information needs of its various audiences. Many firms view the Web as an alternative sales channel. They develop transactional Web sites to meet the business objective of selling to as many customers as possible in ways that are convenient to those customers. Large retailers such as Wal-Mart and Sears offer products for sale through the Web. Newspapers such as *The Chicago Tribune* and *The New York Times* create electronic editions to provide customers one more outlet for receiving news. Customer service is a second content area on a public Web site. UPS and Federal Express allow customers to check the status of a package over the Web as an efficient alternative to a customer support call. Third, a public Web site is an effective way to distribute information and interact with various parties. The different audiences of the firm come to a single public Web site and, depending on their interests and needs, use the site to place orders, get customer support, interact with the firm via electronic mail, and gather financial or product information.

This chapter focuses on the supplier content of the Fortune 100 public Web sites. The Fortune 100 are appropriate for studying supplier interactions through the Web because of the size, resources for information technology investments, public exposure, and the mix of different industries within this group of firms. Corporate public Web sites can be used to recruit new suppliers by discussing "mutually advantageous" business opportunities, and can also provide information to existing suppliers. Obviously, many of these large firms are interacting with their suppliers through private network links such as electronic data interchange (EDI) and Web-based extranets. This chapter examines the content of the nonprivate portions of these firms' Web sites to better understand how corporations are using public Web pages as one component of supplier communication.

GROWTH AND BENEFITS OF ELECTRONIC SUPPLIER LINKAGES

Web-based B2B commerce is growing dramatically. The Boston Consulting Group expects U.S. B2B transactions over the Web to exceed EDI transaction volume, and on-line purchasing (e.g., ordering and replenishment) to represent 40 percent of total inter-company purchasing by 2004.[1] The Yankee Group is a bit more conservative, estimating that companies will purchase 30 percent of all goods and services electronically by 2004, while cross-industry MRO products reach the 40 percent figure.[2]

A recent survey by the National Association of Manufacturers (NAM) found that 68 percent of respondent companies were not currently using the Web for business transactions.[3] In that survey, 80 percent of the manufacturers had a Web site, but most were being used simply for informational purposes. The NAM survey found B2B utilization to be very low for buying raw materials (7 percent), buying intermediate materials (12 percent), and arranging logistics (10 percent).

Retailers have been equally slow in enabling transactional Web sites with their suppliers. CSC's annual retail survey found that only 7 percent of retailers with Web sites used them to collaborate with trading partners.[4] Many of the surveyed retailers plan to implement Web-based EDI to communicate with suppliers, and others are adding private extranets to link with suppliers.

There are a large number of significant benefits from these Web-based trading partner linkages, such as:

- Eliminating costs from the supply chain by improved procurement and resource planning
- Cutting out intermediaries, such as brokers and factory representatives, for on-line purchases
- Lower prices for direct and indirect (MRO) purchases
- Reducing delivery times from weeks to days and thereby improving cycle times
- Reducing the amount of on-hand inventory and the associated carrying costs
- Removing paperwork and people from the reordering process by use of electronic documents
- Reducing the need for human operators to take orders and answer questions
- Tailoring orders for individual stores based on an analysis of product movements
- Broadening the available selection of trading partners through elimination of prior-generation EDI, and dropping expensive value-added networks by moving to lower-cost data transfers over the Internet

A Cahners In-Stat Group survey found that 63 percent of its respondents will move from EDI to the Internet as the preferred way of conducting business with suppliers. Several studies also mentioned that these Web-based supplier systems are an important way to deepen relationships with suppliers.

Although the first generation of Web-based systems primarily faced customers, companies are now looking to gain benefits in the areas of procurement, distribution, inventory, and supplier relationships through B2B systems.[5] The Meta Group study found that firms in industries such as retailing, transportation, financial services, and manufacturing view supply-related Web systems as a means of process and cost improvement.

In short, recent studies point to a dramatic growth in B2B commerce over the Web. A sizable portion of that B2B commerce will focus on procurement. Firms enjoy substantial benefits from implementing B2B trading partner systems. Existing B2B systems are moving from EDI to the Web. However, to date some industries have been slow in Web-enabling their supplier interactions.

Several questions arise in the discussion of how firms make this move from private, value-added networks and proprietary EDI solutions to Web-based supplier interactions. First, given the critical importance of security in B2B transactions, do all supplier interactions occur over private (e.g., virtual private network or extranet) connections, or are some supplier transactions initiated after login from a public Web site? Second, what types of supplier communications are most common on a public Web site? Answering the second question aids in understanding the role of a public Web site for supplier communications. This study examined these two questions.

SUPPLIER CONTENT ON FORTUNE 100 PUBLIC WEB SITES

All of the Fortune 100 firms have a public Web site. The list of Fortune corporations and their Web addresses is available at the *Fortune Magazine* Web site (Fortune.com). During visits to each of these public Web sites, the entire site was reviewed to identify content of interest to suppliers. The site's search tool was used to complete a search on the word "supplier" if no site content relating to suppliers was immediately identified. The researcher developed a data collection form to facilitate the site visits and ensure that the reviews were consistent across sites. Although not representative of all public Web sites, the sites of the Fortune 100 show how some of the world's largest firms use their public Web sites for B2B interactions.

Just over one-third (34 firms, 34.3 percent) of the Fortune 100 have content for suppliers on their public Web sites. The 34 firms are in 18 different industries, including aerospace, computers, general merchandisers, telecommunications, petroleum refining, and chemicals.

There are four categories of supplier content on these 34 Web sites:

1. *Expectations* — about what the firm purchases (price, quality, what items the firm buys)
2. *Operations* — how business is to be conducted (electronic orders, product labeling, ethics)
3. *Application procedures* — how to become a supplier
4. *Diversity programs* — for small, minority, and women-owned businesses

Exhibit 1 lists items that make up these categories of supplier content on the 34 public Web sites. With the exception of "Supplier Development Programs," most of these content items are appropriate for prospective sup-

Exhibit 1. Supplier-Related Content on Fortune 100 Public Web Sites (n=34)

Content Categories and Items	#	%
Expectations About What the Firm Purchases		
What Items the Firm Buys	18	52.9
Product Pricing	15	44.1
Product Quality	15	44.1
Service (e.g., on-time delivery)	11	32.4
Supplier Development Programs (to improve quality, lower costs)	3	8.8
How Business Is to Be Conducted		
Electronic Order Linkages	11	32.4
Electronic Data Interchange (EDI) Required	11	32.4
Gift Policy, Ethics	7	20.6
UPC Labeling Required	5	14.7
Labor Law or OSHA Compliance	4	11.8
How to Become a Supplier		
Application Procedures (on-line form — 11; print form — 9; request proposal — 2)	22	64.7
Submit Financials/Annual Sales	14	41.2
DUNS # or SIC Codes	10	29.4
Provide Business References	6	17.6
Georgraphic Coverage (regional, national)	5	14.7
Diversity Programs for Small, Minority, and Women-Owned Businesses		
Web Site Mention of These Programs	27	79.4
Require Supplier to Be Certified	19	55.9
Letter from President/CEO Regarding Supplier Diversity	6	17.6
Provide External Links for Certification	5	14.7
Mention Diversity of Second-Tier Suppliers	3	8.8

pliers. Other supplier-related items that appear on a few sites include a key word search specific to the supplier area (3 sites), awards from minority councils (1), and success stories with small or minority suppliers (1).

When discussing expectations about what the firm purchases, the buying firms use their public Web sites to emphasize the importance of product or component quality (e.g., "zero defects," "our quality standards are extremely high") and continuous improvement ("continuous value improvement"). Price and quality are mentioned on nearly half (44.1 percent) of the sites, and they are often linked together ("high quality merchandise...at competitive prices"). The sites often describe the competitive bidding process and note that prices of goods and services must be competitive with what the firm currently purchases ("we work with vendors to drive costs out of the system," "cost effective...lowest total cost").

TASK 3: FORGING SUPPLY CHAIN PARTNERSHIPS

When discussing "service," the firms mention on-time deliveries, support for just-in-time programs, order lead times, the ability of the supplier to handle expected distribution volumes, the importance of a single point of contact, a national sales force, and cycle time improvement.

Over half (18 of 34, 52.9 percent) of these corporate public Web sites with supplier content have specific lists of products (e.g., raw materials, merchandise for resale, nonmerchandise items such as equipment and packaging) and services (e.g., technical and professional, advertising) that are currently purchased by the buying organization in order to assist suppliers in identifying business opportunities. Three firms mention supplier improvement programs ("we want to keep our suppliers competitive") to help suppliers with product quality improvements, price reductions, and data integrity. Kmart mentions a specific program for working with vendors in managing inventory.

Concerning how business is to be conducted, nearly one-third (11 of 34, 32.4 percent) of the firms use public Web pages to discuss the importance of electronic order linkages. Intel states that it "expects to do significant business on the Internet now and (it) will be the only way we do business in the future" and PG&E says it "communicates electronically where possible." AT&T asks if the prospective supplier will add electronic data interchange (EDI), while Bank of America asks about electronic billing. Others list EDI transaction requirements or EDI mappings or have an EDI handbook and note they "do not deviate" from requiring EDI (e.g., "all suppliers must be EDI capable"). Federated Department Stores set up a separate Web site to provide operational details to existing suppliers on issues such as EDI, labeling, and shipping. The retailers are very concerned about labeling of both individual items and the cartons they receive. However, only 20.6 percent of these firms are explicit on their public Web sites about offering "gifts" to their buyers.

Nearly 65 percent of the firms with supplier-related content on their public Web sites explain how to become a supplier and sell to that firm. In their application procedures, these firms ask for the expected data, such as company name, address, and names of key officers. The buying firms also ask a number of questions of prospective suppliers concerning the supplier's ability to provide coverage to all the buying firm's locations (i.e., extent of geographic coverage — national and regional), sales volume, and financial situation by requiring income statements. Boeing even uses the phrase "prove financial stability." A few ask the supplier to provide its number of employees and years in business. These large buyers are concerned about the stability and longevity of any prospective supplier. They ask for business references ("list your top customers") to get a sense of the supplier's ability to deliver. A surprising entry on one application was "Are you a customer of (company name)?" which may imply that current customers have a better chance of becoming suppliers. Some of the electronic application forms list issues such as insurance certification, OSHA or labor law compliance, human rights standards, and SIC codes. After an initial screening of the form or proposal, certified suppliers are added to a supplier database that is accessed by the buying offices of these firms. Instead of an on-line form, Sears and United Technologies discuss putting together a proposal letter or package so the prospective supplier can be evaluated.

The site segment with the highest number of participating firms — 79.4 percent of the public Web sites with supplier content — is diversity programs for small, minority, and women-owned businesses (some also include disabled veterans). Many of the public sites encourage these businesses to apply to become a supplier. An important part of the application process for these supplier diversity programs is certification of the supplier as a small, minority, or woman-owned firm. Generally, buying firms require supplier certification before establishing a business relationship. The sites list certifying agencies such as the Small Business Administration and the National Minority Suppliers Development Council. Some of the buyer sites provide external Web links to these and other agencies, such as the Department of Defense Office of Small and Disadvantaged Business. A few firms note the percentage of business they do with minority or small businesses; the range is from 5 to 25 percent. General Motors has a specific policy concerning second-tier suppliers; it requires its direct suppliers to source 5 percent of their business to GM with minority suppliers. Bank of America and Duke Energy use their public Web sites to encourage first-tier suppliers to expand minority and women business opportunities.

In some cases the supplier diversity sections are extensive, covering multiple Web site pages, while others are simply a paragraph in the "Selling to Us" section. Letters from the President/CEO imply strong support from the top of the organization for these programs. Several sites mention small business liaison officers (e.g., supplier diversity manager) or offices, or a minority business development director. In part, these sections reflect regulatory compliance, because firms that do business with the U.S. government are required to source from small, minority, or disadvantaged suppliers. However, many firms recognize the value of diversity in all its aspects and encouraging supplier diversity through a public Web site is simply one component of corporate diversity efforts.

Most of the Fortune 100 public Web sites with supplier content (23 of 34 firms, 68 percent) have an open access area for supplier information. The other 11 Web sites have both public access and private areas reserved for existing suppliers to login. For example, Wal-Mart has a "Retail Link" program that is accessible after a potential supplier has been certified and its products accepted for resale; Kmart has a secured section entitled "PIN — Partner Information Network;" and existing Federated suppliers can log into "FDS Net." Therefore, some supplier transactions are initiated after login from a public Web site.

Six of the 11 firms with private login areas for suppliers reveal features of the secured sections through their public Web pages. Existing suppliers can log into an extranet, have Web browser-based access to an internal or company private information system, and they can

- View daily store-level sales and review in-store inventory.
- Look up specific purchase orders and check the status of payments well as chargebacks.
- Submit new items for approval by buyers.
- See weekly demand forecasts or planned parts needs from the buying firm.
- Read an evaluation of the supplier's performance based on metrics from the buying firm.

From this list of extranet features, it is evident that private Web pages are becoming a substitute for in-store visits and some telephone calls to buyers or to accounts payable. These extranet features also suggest that there are different functions assigned to public and private Web sites. The extranet pages contain proprietary or company private information (e.g., inventory levels) that firms do not want to be shared with competitors, hence the login requirement. Exhibit 2 summarizes these primary content areas on both public and private corporate Web sites.

The names of the supplier areas on these public Web sites vary. Fortune 100 firms use supplier section names such as "vendor (or supplier) programs (or relations)," "working together with suppliers," "supplier resource center," "purchasing Web site," "supplier link," "supplier net," and "vendor

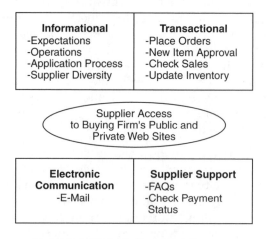

Informational	**Transactional**
-Expectations	-Place Orders
-Operations	-New Item Approval
-Application Process	-Check Sales
-Supplier Diversity	-Update Inventory

Supplier Access
to Buying Firm's Public and
Private Web Sites

Electronic Communication	**Supplier Support**
-E-Mail	-FAQs
	-Check Payment Status

Exhibit 2. Web Sit Supplier Content

communications." General Motors uses the name "Global Supplier Network." Other firms emphasize their diversity efforts through supplier section names such as "building supplier diversity," "supplier (or vendor) diversity program," "minority (or small) business development group (or program)," "minority and women business development (or enterprise)," "small business programs" and "U.S. supplier diversity policy." DuPont uses the acronym TEMPO — "To Encourage Minority Purchasing Opportunities."

SUPPLIER CONTENT AND PUBLIC WEB SITE OBJECTIVES

The four categories of supplier content (expectations, operations, application procedures, and diversity programs) reveal the types of supplier communication most commonly found on public Web sites. The categories also suggest that these large firms use the supplier sections of their public Web sites primarily for information publishing. Only 9 of 34 firms (26.5 percent) have a communication link in the supplier section, so e-mail interactions with prospective suppliers are not a priority on these public Web sites. The overwhelming goal for the supplier section(s) of these corporate public Web sites is publishing information, especially to prospective suppliers. This informational focus is appropriate, given the mixed audience for these public Web sites — both prospective and existing suppliers.

Few firms initiate supplier transactions from their public Web sites. Less than one-third (11 of 34, 32.4 percent) of these firms offer supplier login for transactions (e.g., submit items for approval) from their public Web sites. The login or extranet features suggest that private Web sites are used for most transactions. Only Compaq has both a supplier-area electronic mail link and login access to a secured section from the public Web site. Support is another objective for a Web site; the FAQ section of the General Motors site is an example of carrying out this objective. Other vendor support features of these sites may be hidden behind the login areas that are reserved for existing suppliers.

The emphasis on electronic order linkages by nearly one-third of these companies suggests that after vendor certification, business transactions are electronic — they encourage electronic interactions via electronic mail and EDI. The emphasis of these sites on EDI rather than Web-based linkages is at odds with the survey data presented earlier, and indicates that many B2B transactions are currently executed using prior-generation technology. The maturity of B2B transactions through EDI and the perceived lack of security on the Web both contribute to the informational focus of public Web pages that are dedicated to suppliers. This informational focus in the supplier sections of these corporate, public Web sites suggests that these firms have different objectives for their public Web sites than for existing, secured networks. Transactions are reserved for private, secured network links.

DEPTH OF WEB-BASED SUPPLIER INTERACTIONS

Web sites add value for visitors and so gain competitive advantage through several factors, including the "richness" of the site — the depth and detail of information the site gives out to visitors. There are noticeable differences between firms in the richness of supplier information provided on each public Web site. Some sites are very "shallow;" the Web site facilitates an initial screening, such as collecting the supplier's name and address. Other public Web site's supplier information is very "deep" (i.e., very rich); the site provides extensive information about doing business with the firm, provides an on-line application form, and lists contact names and electronic mail addresses.

Examples of shallow supplier content on a corporate public Web site include:

- A buying office name and address, but no e-mail link or individual names listed, or an "800" number and a message to "contact us for further information"
- Use of the Web site to pick up the names of prospective suppliers, but no other information or services to vendors are provided
- No specific supplier information section on the public Web site, simply a listing of press releases related to suppliers or to diversity programs

Corporations with shallow supplier content have chosen not to use their public Web sites as an outlet to support or publicize vendor diversity efforts, even though the firm may have extensive off-line diversity programs.

Conversely, corporate public Web sites with deep supplier content:

- Provide public and private (login required) access areas, e-mail links, and list buyer's names and addresses that can be searched on-line.
- Develop specialized applications (e.g., to assess inventory status and stock turns) within the secured area for vendors, or provide unique services (e.g., an annual supplier conference).
- Explain expectations for suppliers and discuss how to apply to become a supplier.
- Offer extensive operational support resources such as on-line manuals, handbooks. descriptions of training sessions, EDI technical specs, and express a willingness to develop electronic linkages with all suppliers.
- Indicate strong support for supplier programs through letters from top officers, or listing the steps the buying firm has taken to support supplier diversity; formalize supplier diversity efforts by naming a specific organizational unit for small, women-owned, and minority vendors (e.g., office of minority affairs), or listing the name of the firm's top diversity officer (e.g., a minority business development director or supplier diversity manager); personalize diversity efforts by displaying photographs of both buyer and diversity personnel, and in-

Exhibit 3. Web Site Items Contributing to Depth of Supplier Interactions (n=34)

Supplier-Related Items	#	%
Supplier Diversity Programs	27	79.4
Application (forms, proposal explanation) for Supplier Certification	22	64.7
Expectations (regarding price, quality, service)	18	52.9
Operating Procedures (electronic links, operating manuals)	14	41.2
Site Friendliness (contact names, not siply a department name)	13	38.2
Security (login to area reserved for suppliers)	11	32.4
Electronic Mail Link in the Supplier Segment of the Web Site	9	26.5
Unique Programs	7	20.6
Easy Access (supplier link on home page)	5	14.7

cluding case histories of successful small and women-owned suppliers; or encourage supplier diversity by creating external links to relevant certifying agencies.

Firms deepen the interactions they have with suppliers through public Web sites as they add elements from this list. By placing this information on their public Web sites, corporations suggest that they are open to solicitation from new vendors. The buying firms also increase internal efficiency by using the Web to provide information and support services interactively. These indicators of the depth of supplier interaction build on the supplier-related content categories identified previously and can be combined into nine items (see Exhibit 3).

For all 34 public Web sites with supplier content, the average number of supplier-related items is 3.7, meaning the average site has less than four of the nine items listed in Exhibit 3. The range was from zero to six. The relatively low average (3.7 items) for the number of supplier-related items suggests that the public Web sites of the Fortune 100 have business objectives other than creating links with suppliers. Very few (5 of 34, 14.7 percent) of these public Web sites have direct links to supplier information from the home page; site visitors must move to secondary pages for this material. Most of the firms (27 of 34, 79.4 percent) with supplier content use this segment of their public Web sites to publicize their diversity efforts, and the majority (22 of 34, 64.7 percent) automate some segment of the supplier application and certification process.

Corporations give trading partner interaction from public Web sites high priority by placing links to supplier information on the home page. Firms that provide a contact name and e-mail address present a friendlier "face" than those with only a department contact. Offering multiple content areas (e.g., expectations, diversity, operating procedures) does not simply tell more but enables prospective vendors to make a more professional approach to the buying firm.

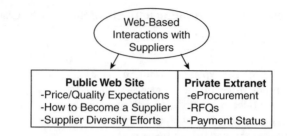

Exhibit 4. Role of a Public Web Site in Supplier Communication

Several corporate public Web sites mention unique programs to enhance supplier relationships. Wal-Mart has a program to evaluate products that have less than six months of sales history. Kmart runs a supply chain management and compliance seminar that discusses bar-coding quality and data integrity. Compaq and Lockheed-Martin host annual conferences to discuss supplier issues. Intel has an on-line course on how to deal with the company. Federated Stores and the Bank of America have set up separate Web sites devoted to supplier issues.

PUBLIC AND PRIVATE WEB SITE CONTENT

The benefits, such as lower costs and shorter cycle times, for transactional communications (e.g., RFQs, procurement) over private extranets and EDI systems have been widely reported. The large firms in this study clearly differentiate between public, informational content for suppliers (e.g., how to become a supplier), and private transactions such as placing a bid. There appears to be a clearly defined role for both types of content on corporate Web sites. This difference between public and private Web site content is summarized in Exhibit 4.

SOME BEST PRACTICES

The fact that 18 different industries are represented in this study shows that very diverse firms in widely different supply chains are able to utilize public Web sites for supplier interactions. Web links to suppliers are not just for manufacturers that order raw materials or retailers that order products for resale. Firms in industries whose primary output is a service, such as insurance and banking, use public Web sites to interact with vendors. The firms in this study that have supplier content are a "best practices" example for other corporations in utilizing a public Web site for interacting with suppliers.

What are these best practices for supplier segments on a corporate public Web site? Several firms in the study are doing an effective job of balancing the divergent uses of a public Web site regarding links with vendors.

These firms are using the Web to publish information — for example, price and quality expectations — and change processes, such as on-line forms to be completed by a prospective vendor. They also provide password-protected access to specialized or customized applications (e.g., weekly demand forecasts) for authorized supplier personnel. These sites enable electronic communication via e-mail and provide supplier support through FAQ sections. Relative to supplier interactions, these firms are accomplishing three fundamental objectives for public Web sites: transactions, trading partner support, and information sharing.

Supplier diversity is another example of a "best practice" for corporate public Web sites. Most (27 of 34, 79.4 percent) Fortune 100 public Web sites with supplier content use the site to discuss supplier diversity programs and to automate some aspect of the vendor application and certification process. However, only 27 of the Fortune 100 mention supplier diversity on their public Web site, and finding these pages on the site usually requires the visitor to move off the home page.

In addition, general content related to suppliers may be buried under the "About Us" section. In some cases, there is no identifiable supplier-related content on these public Web sites, and the site's search engine must be used to find the appropriate pages. If supplier diversity and trading partner linkages are a priority, corporations should consider listing these initiatives on the home page of their public Web sites.

OPPORTUNITIES FOR SUPPLIER COMMUNICATION ON PUBLIC WEB SITES

Public Web sites present a significant opportunity for corporations to enhance relationships with suppliers by clearly communicating expectations about pricing, quality, and service issues such as on-time delivery. A corporate public Web site is an efficient way to transmit "generic" information (e.g., the distribution of manuals and operating procedures) to current supplier's employees who have Web access. It is also well-suited for making contacts with potential suppliers and in handling the initial stages of the supplier certification process for those prospects. Public Web sites are insecure and thus poorly suited for giving access to accounting or ordering data. Having existing suppliers log into an extranet or use a secure server or virtual private network provides the necessary security. In general, a public Web site is an efficient way to carry out some supplier interactions, but as with other B2B links, data security and privacy control site content (see Exhibit 4).

The frequent mention of electronic order linkage suggests that these corporations have private network connections with suppliers, but only 34 of the Fortune 100 firms' public Web sites contain supplier content. Therefore, 66 percent of the Fortune 100 do not provide Web-based vendor content from their public Web sites. The low number of Fortune 100 firms with supplier content, combined with the lack of depth in supplier information for the public Web sites with supplier content, suggests that many of these large firms are not fully exploiting public Web pages to develop relationships with vendors.

The shallowness of supplier information on these corporate public Web sites indicates that this aspect of trading partner interaction is not mature or well developed. Firms in such industries as banking and retailing are rapidly developing transactional Web sites for linking with their customers. Conversely, their supplier interactions from public areas of their Web sites tend to be less well developed, are placed off the home page, and are primarily informational. The initial emphasis in the development of public Web sites, at least among the Fortune 100, has been on building new sales channels and less on inbound logistics for supplies and services. Shallow supplier interactions from a public Web site may send the unintended signal that vendor relations are not important. The dual business objectives of reducing inventories within supply channels and shortening replenishment times are examples of why supplier relationships are important.

Rather than bury their supplier efforts in news releases on the site, corporations with significant programs for suppliers should publicize these efforts in their public Web pages. Using a public Web site for supplier interaction can help create a more diverse set of suppliers and generate savings in the way firms distribute information to existing suppliers.

The ease with which a supplier can get on the Web argues for expanding supplier linkages through corporate public Web sites. The Web is almost universally available to supplier firms, at least in the United States. Software applications for accessing the Internet are not proprietary, and they are inexpensive. Granted, the development of a transactional Web site is costly, but the access features most needed by vendors are relatively inexpensive. The wide availability of Internet service providers contributes to ease of Web access for suppliers. These two critical issues of low costs and ease of implementation through nonproprietary software are important to many of the supplier firms that tend to be smaller than these large, Fortune 100 corporations that they sell to.

What are the potential benefits corporations can realize from effective use of supplier communications on a public Web site?

- First, frequently updated documents (e.g., brochures) can be published to the Web, saving the cost of printing and physical distribution. Similarly, press releases, announcements, and related items can be posted on the public Web site, replacing conventional mailings (or perhaps electronic mail) to all suppliers.

- Second, a public Web site provides an effective forum for explaining and "selling" corporate diversity programs and for recruiting diverse suppliers. Applications and certifications can be completed on-line, reducing paperwork.
- Finally, these sites can augment or replace procurement and buying office responsibilities related to handling questions from suppliers about issues such as technical standards for exchanging electronic documents. The public Web site becomes a place to publish frequently asked questions instead of fielding those questions through telephone support.

Therefore, relative to supplier communications, corporate public Web sites can improve internal efficiency by reducing or eliminating paperwork and telephone calls, reengineer processes by automating applications procedures for new or diverse suppliers, and raise the accuracy and timeliness of support provided to existing suppliers. These applications of a public Web site represent an important companion to the private extranet that is used for procurement transactions such as posting RFQs and handling replenishment orders.

CONCLUSION

This study of Fortune 100 public Web sites suggests that many corporations have not fully recognized the potential of their public Web sites for linking with suppliers. Even the most fundamental application of a Web site — information publishing — is underutilized today because so many large firms are not using their public Web site to distribute information to suppliers.

This underutilization of corporate public Web site capabilities relative to suppliers is a critical issue because vendors affect materials availability and the costs of products and services that are deliverd to customers. A public Web site provides an unusually efficient way to build relationships with this key constituency, and it can augment the transactions currently carried out over private, Web-based extranets and EDI systems. If public Web sites are not being used to their potential, as is the case for many corporations today, they are overlooking an important opportunity for cost savings. Building private, transactional Web sites for selling to customers and buying from suppliers is important, but corporations should be equally concerned about interactions with their suppliers over public Web sites so they can effectively manage all aspects of the supply chain. The current focus of the supplier sections on public Web sites is an important first step, but not an end point. Much more can be accomplished as corporations begin to take advantage of the informational and support capabilities of their public Web sites for communicating to and building relationships with potential and exsting suppliers.

ACKNOWLEDGMENTS

The author acknowledges the support of the R.T. Farmer School of business at Miami University, Oxford, Ohio, for completing this research.

References

1. Ashman, A. (2000) "Researcher Says B@B Market Will Reach $4.8 Trillion by 2004." *Internet World News,* (2, 172), September 6.
2. Yankee Group (2000). "How Will the $3 Trillion B2B eCommerce Opportunity Affect Your Industry, Your Company, and Your Internet Strategy?" Press Release, April 24.
3. eMarketer (2/23/00). "B2B: Not as Easy as It Looks."
   http://www.emarketer.com/estats/022300_nam.html.
4. CSC (2000). "The E-merging Future in Retail."
   http://www.csc.com/features/060100_feature.html.
5. Meta Group (2000). "Study Finds Most Major Firms are Missing the Mark on e-Business." Press Release, February 9.

Chapter 39
Application Service Providers

Dawna Travis Dewire

The latest trend in the use of technology has spawned a new breed of companies called application service providers. An application service provider (ASP) provides a contractual software-based service for hosting, managing, and providing access to an application from a centrally managed facility. Customer companies have remote Web access to applications that are live on the ASP-provided servers.

ASPs provide business solutions to small-, medium-, and large-sized companies on a rental basis. Customers of ASPs are seeing cost savings in total cost of ownership and improved time to deployment. ASPs, referred to as outsourcing companies by some, are often restructured software companies or strategic partnerships between consulting groups and infrastructure providers. ASPs provide organizations an alternative to the high fixed costs associated with software projects as well as the impact of these projects being over budget and past deadline.

Traditional applications such as enterprise resource planning (ERP), commerce, and call centers are natural markets for the ASP model. The trend is actually extending the model to include vertical as well as horizontal applications. ASPs are looking at applications within banking, retail, sales management, medical imaging, and groupware, as well as the oil and gas industries.

International Data Corp. (IDC) describes an ASP scenario as "an end user accesses an application resident on a server, just as he or she would on a LAN or in the enterprise data center. However, the server resides at the ASP's third-party data center and is reached via a dedicated line or the Internet (or extranet). The applications can range from low-end, productivity programs (e.g., word processing) to high-end ERP modules. The service is provided on a subscription basis and can bundle a full range of hosted application services."

Compare the process of leasing a car. Not much upfront money is required, consumers get something they might not be able to buy outright, they pay for it monthly, and at the end of the lease they decide what to do with the car. By just licensing a few seats from an ASP, organizations get a full-functioning application that might be something more powerful and sophisticated than they could buy outright. They have access to the application without having to pay for hardware, software, or installation. Organizations can realize financial cost savings, reduce capital investments, and lower IT management requirements. Such an option also allows organizations to focus on their core businesses and react quickly to changes in the marketplace — both opportunities and threats.

Packaged software developers can use the ASP model to convert the infrequent buyer into a steady revenue stream customer. Usually, a customer buys version 4.2 of a software product and then elects not to upgrade for two or three generations. Under the ASP model, an ASP customer is provided with the latest version of a software package and pays a monthly fee to use that software, thereby generating a steady stream of revenue for the software package developer.

The software vendor upgrades only the master copies on licensed ASP servers. The software vendor is not required to maintain old code or support multiple versions of a product. If customers do not like the upgrade, they cannot go back to a prior version.

Customers of ASPs usually pay a flat fee to sign up and from then on a monthly fee. For that monthly fee, the customer gets all upgrades automatically as soon as they are released — all the new drivers, the new features, everything. However, because the ASP is monitoring the customer's payments, if the customer stops paying, it no longer gets the use of the software. It is as simple as that.

IDC estimates that the ASP market will be $7.7 billion by 2004, and Forrester Research estimates $6.7 billion by 2002. The Information Technology Association of America (ITAA) did a survey of more than 1,500 IT executives. Nearly one-fifth were already using ASPs. Nearly 24 percent were planning to evaluate their use over the next year, and 19 percent expected that they would be using ASPs before the end of the year.

An ASP service is not the timesharing of the 1960s or the outsourcing of the 1980s. The ASP model is much more than the rental of a slice of time. The model allows an organization to decide the location of the computing capability based on economic and financial grounds. It provides an option for sharing information and conducting transactions. The ASP model uses client/server architecture and relies on secure, cost-effective data communications. The IT staff does not need to have expertise in the application or the infrastructure that is being handled by the ASP. ASPs can be used to fill gaps in an application portfolio. So, the focus is on saving time as well as cost, and time and cost are two major variables of any IT project.

In traditional outsourcing arrangements, the entire business process is handed off to the outsourcing company — operations, the legacy application itself, the infrastructure it was built on, and some of the internal IT staff to support it. Today, every level of the IT infrastructure (network, data, messaging, system management) can be selectively outsourced. With the ASP model, the software and its required infrastructure (including support) are provided by the application service provider, but the actual business process operations are still handled by the organization. If an insurance company outsources its claims processing, the outsourcer receives the claims and processes the claims on its hardware using its software and its staff. With the ASP model, the insurance company's staff receives the claims and processes the claims on the ASP's hardware using the ASP's software and infrastructure.

ASP BUSINESS MODEL

ASPs provide access to and management of an application. An ASP owns the software or has a contractual agreement with the software vendor to license it. Customers gain access to the environment without making investments in application license fees, hardware, and staff. The application is managed from a central location (the ASP site) rather than the customer's sites. Customers access the application via the Internet or leased lines. The ASP is responsible for delivering on the customer's contract regardless of its structure — sole provider or partnered. If a problem arises, the ASP is responsible for resolving the issue. Service guarantees usually address availability, security, networked storage, and management and are spelled out in service level agreements (SLAs). ASPs enforce these guarantees by closely monitoring the server environments and often add proprietary modifications to ensure performance uptime and security.

An ASP provides the application service as its primary business. The service may be delivered from beginning to end by a single vendor or via partnerships among several vendors. A single-source vendor controls everything from implementation to ongoing operations and maintenance of the application. The customer deals with only one vendor, and that vendor has complete control over the process. Oracle Corp. is offering ASP services using this model. Under this model, the vendor must have expertise in a variety of areas, maintain a data center infrastructure, and have high capital requirements.

In the best-of-breed model, the company partners with other organizations to leverage expertise. In effect, the ASP has its own supply chain. One partner might be providing data storage, another the Web hosting services, and another the application itself. Two successful ASPs use this model.

TASK 3: FORGING SUPPLY CHAIN PARTNERSHIPS

USinternetworking (USi), listed on the NASDAQ, has partnered with Cisco to supply networking infrastructure and operates its own data centers. USi currently has four data centers around the world. Corio has a partnership with Sun Microsystems to supply infrastructure and partnerships with Exodus Communications and Concentric for storage of data. With this model, a customer has many players to deal with but should, ideally by contract, have only one interface point — to the ASP itself.

DRIVING FORCES

The growth of the ASP market can be attributed to a variety of factors. On one hand, it reduces the risk associated with buying software — no huge consulting fees, no huge capital investment in hardware, no huge software cost (ERP package software alone can cost $100,000), just a monthly fee. It also reduces the technology complexities involved in installing such software — the hardware, the network, the support. It allows an organization to focus on selecting a business solution.

Growth of this market is also fueled by reduced network costs, the growing capabilities of communication bandwidth, and improved security on the network. As the cost of connectivity declines as predicted by Moore's law, its capabilities will increase. The ASP market is positioned to take advantage of this trend. Deloitte Research predicts a range of "xSP" companies. BSPs (backbone) will provide high-capacity, long-haul connectivity. ISPs (Internet) will provide access to the Internet gateways and the BSPs. SSPs (storage) will provide remote data storage locations. CSPs (commerce) will provide delivery, Web design, and ISP service. ASPs (application) will rent software via the Internet to any user with a Web browser.

The negative perceptions of outsourcing and off-the-shelf software are changing. Cost/benefit analysis is being used to determine the best alternative. Organizations are weighting the option of off-the-shelf software rather than custom-developed applications, of in-house production versus purchased services. The ASP model provides perpetual maintenance and the latest versions of software, unlike internal efforts; typically, when an application is finally tested and released, the organization has to immediately start planning for the next version, which is already on the horizon.

The business climate is changing quickly with mergers and acquisitions and the rapid growth of E-business. Organizations need to find flexible solutions while still focusing on their core competencies. IT departments are already busy maintaining existing applications and lack the resources to respond in a timely fashion. ASPs allow an organization to respond to changes and opportunities in a user-friendly Internet-based environment. An E-commerce site can be up and running within a short time.

IT talent is harder and harder to find and retain. Using an ASP frees IT from supporting commodity applications and allows companies to use their scarce IT resources for strategic projects. Using an ASP eliminates the need to hold up implementing critical software while trying to find IT talent such as experienced E-commerce people.

Mid-sized companies are turning to ASPs to implement high-end applications. Such companies typically do not have the IT talent or resources to deploy such software or the capital required to license the software and implement it; in some cases, implementation costs can run three to five times as much as the license fee. ASPs give these mid-sized organizations access to these high-end applications at a reasonable price, at lower risk, and more quickly.

CATEGORIES OF ASPs

Currently, application service providers fall into one of four categories based on the types of applications they offer.

1. Enterprise

These ASPs offer high-end applications that require customization. This category of ASP is offering ERP, customer relationship management (CRM), supply chain management (SCM), or workflow and imaging software services. The software vendors include SAP, Baan, PeopleSoft, Oracle, and Siebel. ASPs in this market segment also offer professional services for design, implementation, systems integration, and ongoing operations management.

2. General Business

These ASPs are targeting the small- to mid-sized companies that need general business applications that require little or no customization. These are relatively simple applications. Templates are used by the user to configure the application to its specifications.

3. Specialist

These ASPs are focused on a particular type of application such as human resources.

4. Vertical

These ASPs provide packaged or specialized applications for a vertical market segment such as medical practice management software for medical practices and claims processing for insurance companies.

ASPs may also offer various levels of service. Core services include the basic level of services: managing the application environment, monitoring the application, network support, and providing upgrades, as they are available. Managed services enhance the core services by offering additional services and guarantees related to security, application performance, and data redundancy. Finally, extended services further enhance the managed services by satisfying demands for strategic planning, application configuration, and training.

ARCHITECTURE

The keys to an ASP's successful delivery of an application are reliable, remote data access and network management. The technology requires four different architectures to work together efficiently and effectively as shown in Exhibit 1.

The applications being delivered use client/server architecture. Client/server architectures consume large amounts of bandwidth between PCs and servers. To provide a high level of quality network service, ASPs typically partner with telecommunications providers. The choice of the network platform ultimately determines the level of service that the ASP can actually deliver.

Hosted application environments require a different architecture from internally hosted environments, because the external environment cannot rely on the high bandwidth of the internal LAN. Internet connections can vary from dial-up to T1 lines. Internet connectivity directly affects the way an ASP can provide access to the hosted application.

The network platform drives the architecture choices for the computing architecture as well as the choices for hosting the application itself. The computing architecture must support the management of the software as if it resided locally. It must also support remote management of the application and desktops.

For organizations with high bandwidth, an ASP can use regular PC clients and traditional client/server software architecture to deliver the application over the high bandwidth, corporate connections. Users access the application via their browsers using a portal site. The ASP manages the browser application and the individual desktops.

Exhibit 1. ASP Architectures

Application Software Architecture

Hosting Platform   Computing Architecture
  Architecture

Network Infrastructure Architecture

If the network is a limiting factor, an ASP has to consider alternative computing architectures: Java applications or thin client architectures. With Java, an ASP can simplify the Web-based environment. The application is downloaded and run transparently on the user's machine. However, Java downloads work best with high bandwidth and may not perform as well as thin client/server architectures.

Thin client architectures can be used with low bandwidth, including dial-in. The application is run within the data center. Users run the application remotely with the network transporting only keystrokes and screen updates. The ASP administers and manages the desktops from the data center. Thin client architecture is also viewed as the best way to provide the level of reliability and security required by the ASPs.

SERVICE-LEVEL AGREEMENTS

As mentioned earlier, SLAs spell out the customer's expectations for service, which might range from expected response times to minimum bandwidth. Some ASPs include guarantees such as 99.9 percent uptime and disaster recovery. ASPs will add security to an already secure platform (e.g., Windows NT) to guarantee security levels.

An SLA details the day-to-day expected service. There should be means to award exceeded minimum requirements that can be offset against days that failed to meet expectations. The SLA might also include provisions for days when the ASP's servers are off-line for maintenance. An SLA should also include a clause that allows the customer to terminate the contract without penalty if it receives poor service. A customer should also make sure that it can get out of the deal with whatever it needs to bring a new ASP on board — data, customized software, and the like.

Customers, should keep the contract term as short as possible — no more than three years. It is difficult to know what hosting will look like in five years. Make sure that the performance penalties truly motivate the ASP to address the organization's issues (remember, the ASP has other customers) and that penalties escalate each time the problem occurs. Establish metrics that truly measure growth. Choose two simple ones, and agree on a firm price for the service as usage grows. Furthermore, customers should not try to trade reduced service for lower monthly fees. The only way for an ASP to lower the orginization's costs is to cut service levels. The quality of the service is key to the customer's successful use of, and therefore its derived benefit from, the ASP.

CHALLENGES AND RISKS

The ASP market is still in its infancy. In order to reach its projected revenue levels, the market has many challenges to overcome and risks to manage.

ASPs need to gain customer acceptance as well as IT acceptance. The selling focus is usually to business management — pitching a business solution or business service. The focus is on value added. The IT organization often comes into the discussions to address security and network issues. IT needs to view the ASP as an alternative, not an interloper. IT needs to become advisors, not turf protectors.

Potential customers must be convinced that their application and its data will be available to them 24x7 but yet secure from outsiders. As Internet traffic continues to grow, potential customers must also be convinced that their access will not slow down. As mobile use escalates, ASPs need to deal with the needs of employees out of the office and the security requirements mobile access demands.

How well the market grows will also depend on how well ASPs can deliver on promised service levels. Can they meet or exceed customer expectations? Since USinternetworking had its successful IPO, ASPs have been springing up seemingly overnight, fueled by venture capital money. Some will not make it. GartnerGroup estimates that of the 300 or so current ASPs, more than 80 percent will disappear because of poor service or market consolidation.

WHOSE CUSTOMER IS IT?

An interesting question that remains to be answered is Who owns the customer — the end user? Is it the software vendor of the application itself or the ASP or some combination? Software agreements might give the ASP a master license, which can be leveraged across multiple customers, or might give the ASP a discounted license fee and the ability to resell the application directly to the end customer. However, as software vendors are beginning to realize the potential of the ASP market, agreements are being restructured.

The initial agreement between Siebel and USi was as a reseller. The agreement has since been restructured so that Siebel's salesforce is the main distribution point for its ASP offering. Under the new agreement, USi fulfills the back-end hosting role. Oracle decided to maintain complete control over its ASP offerings from software sale to implementation and hosting. This way, Oracle maintains full control over the customer.

The ownership issue will be an interesting one to watch. It is expected that most software vendors will enter this market by partnering with an ASP that wishes to leverage its existing data center infrastructure. Consequently, the two organizations must work together to balance customer ownership. However, if the customer's point of interface is the ASP (predictably, because the ASP is implementing and hosting the application) and not the software vendor, the ASP will have ownership tipped in its favor.

NEW PLAYERS TO WATCH

As the ASP market matures and proves itself, more players will try to join in. There will continue to be ASPs that focus solely on the ASP market. Traditional systems integrators will begin to enter the ASP market using their integration expertise as their strength. IBM Global Services and EDS have already announced that they are adding application hosting to their service portfolios. EDS has a partnership with SAP. Qwest Communications and KPMG have a joint venture named Qwest Cyber Solutions. Qwest provides the data network infrastructure, and KPMG provides nearly 500 application developers and integrators.

However, systems integrators are not noted for their ability to change gears quickly. ASPs are smaller organizations and more agile. The systems integrators are also used to long projects, not the mindset of an ASP turnkey service. The entry of systems integrators into the ASP market could be viewed as validation of the concept rather than a threat.

Web hosting companies will need to improve their professional service capabilities before they become major players in the ASP market. Many will find their way into the market by partnering with other ASPs as back-end data center providers. The same holds true for telecommunications companies. The ASP market would help them leverage their large infrastructure investments. To enter the ASP market, they will have to improve both their value-added capabilities and their service capabilities. Telecomm companies will also most likely end up as partners in the ASP marketplace.

SUMMARY

An application service provider offers organizations business solutions. The ASP delivers the service, handling all aspects of the service: the hosting environment, the network infrastructure, the data center, and the application itself. Organizations typically pay a monthly fee to use the service. Using an ASP allows an organization to reduce capital costs and implement applications in a timely fashion.

As outlined in Exhibit 2, there are many reasons why an organization should consider an ASP for its commodity applications. The prevailing economy forces organizations to focus on what they do best and hire others to do the rest. That is exactly what the ASP model allows an organization to do.

Certainly the trick is picking the right application and the right supplier — in this case an ASP, but isn't it always? So if you saw your own organization as you read the statements in Figure 2, start researching which application service providers can supply your needs. Don't wait for the competition to pass you by.

Exhibit 2. When to Consider an ASP

- The organization is a start-up and doesn't have the capital resources to make significant IT investments
- The organization is undergoing rapid growth and needs to scale its IT infrastructure quickly
- The organization is undergoing mergers and acquisitions and needs a flexible IT infrastructure
- The organization can't afford a huge IT capital outlay at the time
- The organization needs to be able to switch environments in the future
- The organization needs to deploy applications rapidly
- The organization is finding it difficult to attract and retain IT staff
- IT isn't a core competency

References

1. Application Hosting Market, August 2, 1999, Legg Mason Equity Research — Technology Group.
2. "Application Service Providers," http://-www.star- dock.net/media/asp_primer.html.
3. "ASP & Ye Shall Receive," *CIO*, May 1, 2000
4. "ASP: Market Hype or a Real Option for Your Business?" an IDC White Paper, *Computerworld*.
5. Butler, Michelle, "Supply Chain Management: Eliminating the Weak Links," June 5, 2000, http://- www.aspstreet.com/archive/default.taf/what,show- /1,pv/sid,14/id969/cid,110.
6. Carter, Todd, "Beginner's Guide to ASP: SLA," May 23, 2000, http://www.aspstreet.com/resources/stores/- default.taf/what,show/id,865.
7. "How ASPs Deliver Value: Next Generation Portals for Business Applications," May 3, 1999, http://www.trg- international.com/HTML/giotto.htm.
8. McPherson, Amanda, "Application Service Providers — A New Software Distribution Model," May 13, 1999, http://www.greatconnect.com/transofmr/-projects_s99/amcpherson_project.html.
9. "Monster in a Box?" *CIO*, May 1, 2000.
10. Rutherford, Emelie, ASP Primer, *CIO*, http://www.- cio.com/forums/asp/edit/030600_primer_content.-html.
11. Seymour, Jim, "How Application Service Providers Will Change Your Life," The-Street.com, http://www.sac cess.com.com/-theStreet/comment/techsavvy- /7599565.html.
12. The Internet-Based ASP Marketplace, Deloitte Consulting and Deloitte & Touche.
13. Wainewright, Phil, "ASP Insider: An Application Service Primer," ASPnews.com, http://www.asp news.com/news/article/0,,4191_373981,00.html

Section 5
Task 4: Managing Supply Chain Information

All the selections in this book address aspects of information management. The chapters in this section describe trends related to the information itself and different ways to manage it. Organizations have a growing range of options for managing supply chain information. They include data warehousing, E-commerce alternatives, and applications service providers (ASPs). Effective management of information in a supply chain environment will increase the need for IS staff to work effectively with other supply chain partner organizations.

Chapter 40

Infocentric Automation: An IT View of Controls

Eric A. Marks

A clash of cultures, technologies, and business perspectives is inevitable given the trends in technology and business strategy. Even the Year 2000 issue has shown how these two disciplines have become similar over time. With the juxtaposition of these two disciplines — controls and IT — comes the potential clash over ownership of the architectural and technological decisions at the boundary between these two worlds. Although this boundary is blurring and becoming more of a cultural firewall than a technological barrier, the strategies, organizational issues, skills, and tools have not been defined to manage this rapidly changing space.

This chapter discusses some key trends in manufacturing that are bringing the IT and controls environments into closer collaboration. It will also identify the issues that must be resolved at the interface between the two environments, including architecture, technology, and networks. Finally, a framework for an Infocentric Automation Strategy™ will be presented that will allow controls and IT professionals to collaborate on the information needs of the factory of the new millennium. This framework will also suggest ways to develop the necessary skills for manufacturing in the next decade. Like it or not, the worlds of automation and IT must work conjointly in order to implement the key business strategies of world-class manufacturing today.

HISTORY OF MANUFACTURING IT AND CONTROLS

The development of IT systems separately from control systems created different organizational and computing paradigms within manufacturing organizations. Tom Gunn in his book *21st Century Manufacturing*[1] provides a concise history of manufacturing IT systems. The first manufacturing planning systems were developed in the late 1960s and were called material requirements planning (mrp or little MRP). These systems included two software modules run in batch mode: material requirements planning and capacity requirements planning. Over the next 20 years, mrp software underwent two to three generations of enhancements, which were concurrent with advancements in information technology, including relational databases, computing hardware, and operating systems. The new systems included order entry, forecasting, distribution requirements planning, resource requirements planning, master production scheduling, material requirements planning, capacity requirements planning, shop floor control, purchasing, and cost accounting. When accounting and financial applications were added in the early 1980s, the name changed to MRPII to reflect those enhanced capabilities. Today, these systems include ability to manage multi-plant and multi-country operations, have preventive maintenance modules, advanced scheduling and planning, utilize expert system-based scheduling and artificial intelligence, and include enterprise logistics planning. These systems are now called enterprise resources planning (ERP) systems. Today the ERP vendors include SAP, J. D. Edwards, Baan, Oracle, PeopleSoft, and others. The ERP market today is approximately a $30 to $50 billion industry if associated services, hardware, and other software products are included.

Control systems developed differently. Although computer automation has a rich history, the current programmable logic controller (PLC) paradigm is based on a New Year's Day 1968 specification for a programmable controller that would replace hard-wired relays in the electrical control system of a manufacturing facility. The creation of the incipient Modicon 084 controller (*MO*dular *DI*gital *CON*troller) is attributed to Dick Morley, the "Father of the PLC." However, it was the Modicon 184 PLC that blossomed into the industrial automation market of today. The notation for programming is relay ladder logic, which was similar to electrician's notation for wiring diagrams. The hardware platform was the PLC, a specialized computing device with very fast and deterministic logic-solving capabilities for controlling machinery and devices in a safe and reliable fashion. While PLCs became more powerful with more instructions, memory, and processing capabilities, the software to manage the devices, the communications between them, and the data to and from them was slower to be developed. Very little classical data management was applied to control systems because they derived their functions from a device control and safety perspective, not from a data management and information sharing perspective.

Control systems today include PLC-based systems, distributed control systems (DCS), supervisory control systems, and other real-time-oriented systems that control how process equipment, material handling equipment, heating, ventilation and air conditioning (HVAC), and facility management equipment operate in a manufacturing facility. Some emerging trends today include PC-based control, where Windows NT is used to run a deterministic "software PLC" program rather than classical PLCs, as well as Windows CE and Java as embedded real-time operating systems for device control.

The divergent development of the IT and controls disciplines resulted in different programming methods, different data management philosophies, and completely different architectures. Recently, many of the architectural and programming differences began disappearing due to several factors:

1. Adoption of general-purpose technology for plant floor control systems, e.g., Microsoft Windows operating systems, PCs for real-time control applications, general purpose programming tools, and relational database technology
2. Increased use of commercial, open networks such as Ethernet TCP/IP to connect PLCs to one another as well as to the MES and ERP systems of an enterprise; Ethernet TCP/IP is rapidly taking over the space occupied by proprietary Level 1 fieldbus networks
3. Development of standards for programming PLCs, e.g., IEC-1131-3, as well adoption of development tools such as Visual Basic, Java, C, and C++
4. Adoption of Internet technologies into industrial automation solutions and products, such as World Wide Web browsers, XML/HTML, Java, and ActiveX
5. Development of standards for data exchange, e.g., SQL, ODBC, and OLE DB, Microsoft's object linking and embedding (OLE), OLE for Process Control (OPC), CORBA, COM/DCOM, and ISA's SP95 standard

These technology trends are the forces driving the convergence of controls and IT in manufacturing organizations today. However, the business drivers of competition, market responsiveness, cost reductions, quality improvements, and others are forcing global manufacturers to rethink how information can be exploited as a lever for competitive advantage.

BUSINESS TRENDS IN MANUFACTURING

The convergence of IT and controls is being driven by both the inevitable onslaught of technology as well as the adoption of business strategies that require manufacturing capacity to be tightly linked to the business systems and customer management systems of global manufacturers.

From a business-strategy perspective, IT and controls are being pushed closer together in support of the supply chain management strategies being adopted by global manufacturing companies. Managing capacity closer to demand necessitates tighter links between manufacturing facilities and the business systems of manufacturers. Supply chain management results in removing inventory waste and slack from the inbound logistics and supplier processes, from manufacturing processes, and from out-bound logistics and distribution processes. However, removing these inventory buffers from the supply chain can cause manufacturing sched-ules to be more variable with "lumpy" demand profiles, as opposed to level and smooth schedules that help manufacturers optimize asset utilization and resource allocation while minimizing setups and changeovers at key manufacturing operations.

This mass customization scenario puts a heavy burden on product con-figurators, product data management (PDM) systems, and even computer-aided design (CAD) systems to accommodate the increased variety coming from the marketplace. When customers' orders become manufacturing work orders, bidirectional data traffic across the manufacturing enterprise sharply increases. Sources of data traffic include recipe management sys-tems, computer numerical control (CNC) repositories, uploading/down-loading of PLC programs, MES, data historians, and document manage-ment systems. The infrastructure supporting these systems has not been designed for this agile, mass customization environment.

In particular, MES strategies are increasingly becoming critical for achieving world-class manufacturing performance as well as for managing the information requirements of make-to-order manufacturing strategies driven by mass customization, electronic commerce, and supply chain management initiatives. The access to relevant customer, product and real-time information is essential to MESs to support the business objec-tives of global manufacturers. (See Fraser and Marks, 1998[2] and Marks, 1997[3] for discussions of MES in general and MES as an enabler for opera-tional excellence.)

Even E-commerce strategies are having an impact the relationship between manufacturing facilities and the business management systems. An E-commerce business is much more than a dressy Web site with ani-mated Java applets and a secure server for managing financial transac-tions. The act of customizing a product, whether it is a vehicle from Ford or a shirt from Land's End, means that customers directly interact with and affect manufacturing capacity, schedules, and asset utilization of manufacturers. Successful Web commerce for global manufacturers may require retooling the manufacturing systems behind the scene. Those systems include logistics, transportation and warehousing systems, sup-ply chain planning and finite scheduling systems, and ERP systems, among others. Data warehousing systems may be needed to drive a more thorough understanding of customer purchasing behavior through cor-porate Web sites. Decision-support systems will help make key informa-tion available to business management to support planning and decision-making activities.

CONTROLS VERSUS IT?

So given that technology and business strategies are forcing controls and IT personnel to work closer together, what issues will arise during this collaboration? To a large extent, we can anticipate differences of perspective and opinion simply based on the divergent heritage of these two disciplines.

Exhibit 1 contrasts controls and IT along several dimensions to show that the differences derive from the training of personnel, from the evolution of the technology foundation that underlies each discipline, and even from the culture of the plant floor relative to the front office.

The differences between the controls and IT disciplines come from their divergent heritage. Both organizations must accept is that their respective differences are valid, real, and legitimate. They must also understand that neither discipline has sole authority for the information architecture of the manufacturing enterprise of the new millennium. That responsibility must be shared, with controls and IT personnel integrated into the information delivery function of today's business.

Implementing business strategies such as the ones discussed above will require new organizational policies and information management approaches for manufacturers. The next section will develop an organizational philosophy that will help implement those concepts. This will be presented in two steps: First a set of guiding principles will establish the high-level goals and objectives of an infocentric automation framework. Second, ten specific steps are offered as a beginning for executives to adopt the framework and begin to implement it in their IT and controls organizations.

ADOPTING AN INFOCENTRIC AUTOMATION FRAMEWORK

Adopting an infocentric automation strategy revolves around the following guiding principles that will become crucial in the coming years. These are a set of foundational policies that will help drive toward an architecture and information management strategy that supports the business imperatives of global manufacturers.

Some guiding principles are:

- Information will become increasingly critical for managing the global manufacturing enterprise. Any information-creating assets in the company must be managed from an information perspective, including automation devices and systems.
- Access to information will not be inhibited by proprietary architectures, proprietary networks, or proprietary products. Where possible,

Exhibit 1. A Contrast between IT and Controls

	IT Systems	Controls
Staff training	Computer science	Electrical and Mechanical Engineering
Heritage	Mrp/MRPII	Electrical relays
Culture	Business	Plant floor
Processes	Business, financials, transactional	Machines, processes
Architecture	De Facto Standards/Open	Proprietary
Programming tools	C, C++, Java, Object Technology, Cobol, Fortran, Assembler, JCL	Relay ladder logic, Sequential function chart
Data management requirements	High	Low
Networks	Ethernet, TCP/IP, Open	Level 0 and 1 fieldbuses, proprietary
Technology rate of change	Rapid	Slow
Budgeting	Expensed	Capital equipment
Data handling	Transaction/batch	Real-time
System life	Short to medium term	Long term

proprietary technology will be replaced with open and standards-based products and technologies.

- Technical resources will become increasingly scarce. Leveraging shared expertise and knowledge will be the rule, not the exception. Where possible, technologies will be implemented that leverage the existing resource pool, e.g., TCP/IP, Internet technologies, database products, etc.
- Open standards will be the first selection criterion for all information and automation products. Proprietary products will be phased out of the architecture over time.
- Corporate standards will be defined for all architecture elements, including automation, network infrastructure, databases, development environments, and integration middleware.
- Where there is an issue impacting the production equipment, safety considerations will have top priority, followed by information considerations. Controls and IT personnel will jointly work through all issues pertaining to implementation of technology with original equipment manufacturers, systems integrators, and other product and service providers to the enterprise.
- Cross-training of IT personnel and controls personnel will be essential to developing "bilingual" technical resources capable of managing both aspects of manufacturing — the IT side and the automation side. In-house development will be the primary method of employee training.
- Technologies of IT and controls will continue to converge (e.g., TCP/IP, Ethernet). Therefore, supporting staff will help define the manufacturing architecture, technology selection processes, and all related investments in information assets and infrastructure.

With these principles in place, the following steps will guide IT and manufacturing management in the transition to an infocentric automation framework. These steps are a starting point in the journey to a world-class organizational structure poised to support and even drive the business and IT strategies of visionary manufacturing companies. The steps toward an infocentric automation framework are as follows:

- Communicate the need for action. Develop an awareness presentation and obtain buy-in from key stakeholders.
- Prepare a mission statement for the IT/controls joint efforts. Begin to consider the budgetary issues of controls compared to IT. Allocate shared budgets for integration and collaborative projects.
- Understand and document the interfaces between IT systems and automation systems, e.g., ERP, MES, HMI/SCADA, maintenance management systems, material control, etc.
- Document the current interface methods and the desired future state of IT/automation integration.

- Inventory your organization's current skills, including IT personnel, controls and plant electricians, and maintenance engineers.
- Determine the skills required of the future technology environment. Create a five-year vision of what technologies will become prevalent and what skills will be needed to manage that environment. This should be a joint IT/controls exercise.
- Prepare a technology policy for future automation and IT investments. This is also a joint IT and controls effort. This should map to the business plan, the IT strategy, and the manufacturing strategy.
- Develop a training plan for grooming the skills required of your current and future technology and business environment. Determine what skills can be developed in-house and through professional classes.
- Implement a cross-training strategy to rapidly increase the awareness of the needs and issues of IT and automation. Rotate key staffers through areas of each discipline to facilitate mutual understanding of the technology and support needs of each environment.
- Implement technology policy, training program, and joint IT/controls work teams on key projects. Document successes, failures, and benefits from leveraging skills, knowledge, and most important, the information created and needed by both organizations.

COMMON INTERESTS (OR BONES OF CONTENTION)

Key areas of the collaboration between controls and IT will be very important to both organizations and functions during the transition to an infocentric automation framework. The following issues will inevitably arise as the boundaries between the two worlds blur:

Architecture

The architectural decisions of controls and IT must now be considered with a larger purpose — enterprisewide information access — as opposed to legacy approaches that preclude information access. Keep in mind that these legacy approaches are not necessarily active attempts to block information access by IT. But they are prohibitive in that proprietary architectures typical of automation systems, as well as the cultural and organization boundaries between information professionals and controls engineers, prevent access to needed production data except as allowed by clumsy and cumbersome methods inherent in proprietary systems and architectures.

Architectural decisions should be made jointly *vis-à-vis* the interfaces between manufacturing automation systems and IT systems as well as the standards that will be supported in deploying these systems, e.g., operating systems, networks and protocols, database standards, hardware platforms, network infrastructure. Consideration should also be given to treating automation platforms as infrastructure.[4,5]

Infrastructure

Spending on computing infrastructure such as backbones, networks, media, hubs, routers, gateways, switches, and related technology can be standardized within an enterprise, thereby minimizing support issues and possibly leading to volume discounts from strategic vendors. For automation systems, this means eliminating proprietary networks where possible unless the engineered machine or process absolutely requires proprietary technology to carry out its function safely and reliably. It may also mean treating automation technology as infrastructure[6] based on the useful life of automation systems once implemented.

Programming paradigms

Given that C, C++, Visual Basic, and Java are becoming more prevalent in automation systems development, it makes sense to agree on documentation standards, naming standards for software and programs, and other related conventions for shared systems or interfaces between the two domains. In fact, based on trends toward a more graphical programming paradigm for both IT and controls, it is expected that the venerable relay ladder logic will gradually give way to simpler and more intuitive programming methods that will be common for both IT and controls. This will accelerate as the electricians and maintenance staffs in manufacturing facilities retire over time and are replaced with personnel with more current skills in traditional electrical engineering as well as exposure to Internet tools, general programming languages and methods, and object technology. In fact, object technology is expected to become the dominant paradigm in all software development activities for controls and IT.

Data management

Data management is emerging as an important activity in manufacturing automation systems and their interfaces into IT systems. Firms are realizing that the time invested up front in defining the data and information needs of systems from a combined controls/IT perspective will reduce the need for custom integration and reprogramming of automation and IT systems after the fact. Developing naming conventions for real-time database tags, database schema, PLC registers, and named variables all will result in open data access via data management standards for plants and all systems in the modern manufacturing enterprise. Data management techniques will dramatically eliminate system analysis, programming, and testing effort and increase access to and the value of real-time information in managing plants in the global manufacturing enterprise. This activity will be facilitated by systematic analysis of what information is needed by what application, what departments, what personnel, and how frequently. The information needs should also forward look with regard to emerging technologies and anticipated system investments that may require real-time information.

MES

Manufacturing execution systems (MESs) are more important than ever in the realization of supply chain management strategies being implemented by global manufacturers. MES will continue to play an increasingly vital role in delivering *actual* manufacturing performance information in real-time to support ERP and supply chain planning systems for all industries, including discrete, electronics, batch/process, pharmaceutical, automotive, and aerospace. Even continuous manufacturers have invested in MES solutions recently. Without MES, these systems do not have access to needed real-time production information. The nature of MESs — because they reside between the ERP systems of manufacturers and the automation and control systems — forces the need for integration planning and teamwork between different organizations in the manufacturing structure of the firm. Interfaces are often required for various PLCs (such as Modicon, Telemecanique, Allen-Bradley, and Siemens), software human machine interface (HMI) packages (Wonderware, Intellution, USData FactoryLink), maintenance management systems (Maximo, Datastream, Indus), and even middleware platforms (Cycle Software, EnvisionIT Software). Because MES tends to fall between many organizations in a plant or a manufacturing firm, collaboration is crucial not only for a successful integration of MES into the plant floor systems environment, but also for accessing needed data from controls and other systems. As the technology platforms of various manufacturing systems continue to converge, the integration burden will lessen over time, particularly as object technology matures. Nonetheless, the integration of MES to a wide variety of systems of differing architectures can be expected for the foreseeable future.

Integration strategies

An emerging need given the trends documented above is agreement on the integration strategies required to unite automation systems with the strategic business applications of the IT world. Decisions about integration middleware, database integration, object request brokers (ORBs), messaging middleware, distributed object architectures, and more all have implications for how integrating systems will be accomplished in support of the organization's information needs. With the rapid adoption of distributed object architectures for controls applications, this will be an exciting technology space to watch. This will become a very strategic architectural decision for both controls and IT over the next few years if it is not one already.

Vendor management

Vendor management will become very critical as controls and IT share more technologies and vendors. One area of concern is managing vendor risk. Managing vendor risk involves spreading technology and infrastructure spending across multiple vendors by having a primary supplier for the majority of spending and a secondary vendor as a backup. Some corporations purposely maintain fixed ratios of automation spending with multiple vendors for that reason, as well as to minimize the technology refresh spending from year to year. With emerging technologies such as those associated with Internet technologies, integration middleware and others, vendor risk must be mitigated and still support the ever-changing information needs of the organization.

This becomes a challenge as the industrial automation vendors adopt more general-purpose technologies from the IT world. This is because automation technologies have not been prone to the same pace of technology change that IT has, and IT staffs have traditionally had more experience managing faster technology change rates than the controls staffs in manufacturing plants. One point to be made here is that experience managing quickly changing technologies in the IT domain does not necessarily mean success.

Budgeting issues

Budgeting is another problem to be tackled as a collaborative approach between controls and IT is implemented. This stems from the different budgeting practices of the two organizations. Controls investments are traditionally associated with capital equipment purchases. These are big-ticket expenditures for entire new plants, manufacturing lines, or work cells. The opportunity to invest in new technology occurs infrequently and in the form of large capital projects with long lead times. IT spending is expensed for a large percentage of the spending, and it is somewhat easier for IT to periodically invest in new technology compared to controls. Keep in mind, though, that large-scale computing purchases, e.g., mainframe computers, data center projects and large infrastructure projects, may be amortized or treated as capital equipment depending on the project.

There are two implications of the different budgeting practices of controls and IT. First, the project schedules are rarely synchronized. So if there are overlapping architectural or technological issues, they are not treated jointly. Whoever has the budget at the time decides the issues. Second, because of the organizational gap between controls and IT, there is rarely, if ever, any budget allocated to integrating the two environments. This means that when a need arises to link an IT system to an automation system (because there was no joint information management planning in place), the integration methods and budgets are an afterthought, the optimal solution probably is not possible, and the near- and long-term costs of the project are higher as a result.

Another observation by Bruce Richardson[7] of AMR Research bears mentioning. Richardson noted at a AMR Executive Conference (September 1998) that there are no longer large computer integrated manufacturing (CIM) staffs in manufacturing organizations that can specify and approve large-scale plantwide system projects. For many large manufacturers, these groups have been dissolved and the resources and budgets have been moved into other organizations. This helps explain the lack of budgets and organizational responsibility for plant integration projects.

Lastly, the budget and cultural issues both become apparent when software companies attempt to sell products into the controls organizations. The automation industry is becoming more of a software business as the hardware products become commodities. But an interesting phenomenon noted by these software suppliers is that controls personnel are not used to paying for software despite it becoming more and more critical to the industry. They are used to getting the needed software for free when purchasing PLCs and related control and automation products. But this will change as software becomes the key differentiator for automation suppliers and as controls and IT integration become crucial to implementing supply chain management strategies in manufacturing firms.

Technology absorption

Finally, a key issue to be resolved is the rate of technology absorption in support of the joint controls/IT information delivery architecture. Differential rates of technology change and adoption characterize both domains, but as controls and IT merge to a nucleus of core technologies based on Internet standards, Microsoft Windows technologies, and CORBA/COM/DCOM distributed object architectures and others, these two groups must agree on the key technologies to implement into production systems. In controls, where safety considerations still dominate the decision calculus, the technology adoption rates tend toward more conservative choices. In IT, there is some degree of latitude with regard to new technology adoption, although vendor risk and technology risk are still important factors behind these decisions. The key point is that these two organizations will have different tendencies toward absorbing new technologies into their specific systems, depending on the function and the criticality of the system to the organization.

This list of issues is not exhaustive, but it foreshadows some of the major points to be resolved as the touchpoints between controls and IT become more prevalent and their functions become more interdependent.

SUMMARY

The industrial automation world and IT are headed toward an uneasy alliance in support of current business strategies of leading global manufacturers. The business trends and technology trends are bringing these domains ever closer together via the convergence of key shared technologies. The organizational and technical collaboration of controls and IT will become a differentiatal for visionary manufacturers that link their manufacturing systems more tightly to their business systems. This chapter has presented a view of the business and technology trends that are driving this convergence of controls and IT, as well as the critical issues to be mutually addressed by the two organizations. The Infocentric Automation Framework™ presented will provide a foundation for developing the organizational and technical competence to proactively manage these rapidly changing business and technology forces. Visionary manufacturers will take advantage of these forces to affect positive change in their controls and IT organizations to help drive the business and manufacturing strategies of the future.

Notes

1. Gunn, Thomas G., *21st Century Manufacturing,* (Essex Junction, VT, Oliver Wright Publications, 1992) p. 157–190.
2. Fraser, Julie and Marks, Eric, "MES: Foundation for Operational Excellence," *Future Focus Systems,* December 1998.
3. Marks, Eric, "MES as an Operational Excellence Enabler: The Groupware for Manufacturing," *Information Strategies: The Executive's Journal,* Spring 1997.
4. Marks, Eric, Industry Outlook, "Manufacturing's New Mandate," *Managing Automation,* June 1998.
5. Marks, Eric, Industry Outlook: "Rethinking Manufacturing IT Infrastructure," *Managing Automation,* July 1998.
6. Infrastructure spending has important implications for enterprise success, as documented by Weill and Broadbent in their book *Leveraging the New Infrastructure* (1998) and Marks (endnote 4). Therefore, automation purchases should perhaps be evaluated in light of the information infrastructure and requirements of manufacturing firms, not merely from the automation perspective.
7. Richardson, Bruce, Speech at Fall 1998 AMR Research Strategic Manufacturing and Automation Conference, Boston, MA.

Chapter 41

Web-Based Data Warehousing: Fundamentals, Challenges, and Solutions

Lei-da Chen
Mark N. Frolick

Billions of bytes of business-critical data are being created by organizations' computer systems daily, yet only a small portion of them will ever be used in business-related analysis. Most companies today are "data rich" and "information poor," as their ability to manipulate data and deliver information lags far behind the growth rate of the data. An organization's competitiveness lies in its ability to utilize information. Data warehousing and the Internet are the two key technologies that offer potential solutions for managing corporate data. Data warehousing liberates information, and the Internet makes it easy and less costly to access information from anywhere at anytime. The combination of the two technologies makes the processing and distributing of key information more efficient and economical. The marriage of these two technologies produces Web-based data warehousing. Web-based data warehousing involves accessing, analyzing and distributing the information extracted from a data warehouse through the Internet, intranet, or extranet using a Web browser as the user interface. As a result of the explosive development in the data warehousing and Web-related technology available today, Web-based data warehousing is starting to gain more and more popularity among organizations. It was estimated that by 2001, the Internet serves as the primary decision-support delivery platform for intra- and extra-enterprise applications (Ladley, 1998).

0-8493-1273-6/02/$0.00+$1.50
© 2002 by CRC Press LLC

TASK 4: MANAGING SUPPLY CHAIN INFORMATION

The purpose of this chapter is to provide an overview of Web-based data warehousing, beginning with the discussion of the limitations of data warehousing in its current form. It then introduces Web-based data warehousing and illustrates how it can be used by organizations to overcome the limitations of traditional data warehousing. A model is provided to further readers' understanding of the components of Web-based data warehousing. Even though a number of compelling advantages of Web-based data warehousing can be realized by organizations, several challenges exist in the implementation. These challenges and their potential solutions are discussed, as are the implications of this Web-based data warehousing phenomena for both researchers and practitioners.

THE LIMITATIONS OF DATA WAREHOUSING IN ITS CURRENT FORM

William Inmon defined the data warehouse as "a subject-oriented, integrated, nonvolatile, time-variant collection of data organized to support management needs." (Castelluccio, 1996) The purpose of a data warehouse, as stated in the definition, is to facilitate managerial decisionmaking. The market segment for this technology is estimated currently at over $15 billion (Reinaner, 1998). A data warehouse differs from operational databases, which mainly support the daily business transactions, and management information systems, which supply information to managers in the form of periodical reports. A data warehouse collects data from multiple sources and stores it in a fashion that allows end users to have faster, easier, and more flexible access to key information. In some organizations, a subset of the data warehouse is captured in a data mart. Data marts are functional or departmental data warehouses. Implementing data marts to interface with end users not only reduces the cost and time for development, but increases the performance and security of a data warehousing environment (Murtaza, 1998). Exhibit 1 depicts the data warehousing environment as seen in many organizations today.

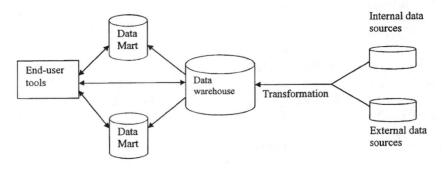

Exhibit 1. Data Warehousing Environment

A data warehouse is user driven. It provides greater flexibility in using data than traditional information systems. Orr (1996) identified eight interconnected parts of a data warehouse architecture (DWA). The eight parts represent the overall structure of data, communication, processing, and presentation in a data warehouse environment. Among them, the information access layer is the layer that end users deal with when using the data warehouse. It includes the hardware and software that constructs the user interface with the data warehouses. The major goal of the user interface is to make the raw data available easily and seamlessly to the end users. Currently, most organizations implement data warehousing in either a standalone or traditional client/server environment, and most data warehousing applications implement their information access layer using applications with graphic user interface (GUI) running on desktop computers.

Although this approach seems to be the most intuitive and appropriate for now, a number of drawbacks exist. First, the client/server infrastructure is expensive to establish and maintain. The high level of coordination among different systems on networks has proved to be both difficult and costly. Moreover, if the data access tools are client-centric, scalability becomes an issue when handling complex reporting requirements and a large number of users in a client/server environment (*IQ Software,* 1997). Second, using one user interface is no longer sufficient, because of the increasing number of mobile users. The Gartner Group estimates that by the year 2003, 137 million business users worldwide will regularly work outside the boundaries of the enterprise and without continuous LAN or high-speed WAN connections (Reinaner, 1998). Providing information and decision support to these users becomes an inevitable challenge to organizations today. Third, system compatibility is always a problem for the traditional client/server environment; deploying multiple computing platforms enormously increases the cost of administration and maintenance.

Besides the technological limitations, changes in the business horizon also require new solutions to data warehousing. Today, supply chain management (SCM) has becoming increasingly important. Successful SCM requires an organization to invest heavily in interenterprise coordination, distribution and channel partnerships, and customer responsiveness (Kalakota and Robinson, 1999). Information visibility among companies in the supply chain is crucial. Therefore, limiting the information access to a small number of highly trained specialists within an organization is no longer sufficient. Information access must be extended to include an organization's internal users, suppliers, partners, and customers.

To resolve these drawbacks, a new form of data warehousing, adopting a thin-client configuration, is gaining popularity. This new form of data warehousing is Web-based data warehousing. In addition to remedying the technical shortcomings of the current data warehousing solutions, the

TASK 4: MANAGING SUPPLY CHAIN INFORMATION

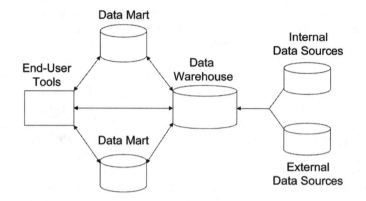

Exhibit 2. The Architecture of Web-Based Data Warehousing

most important contribution of Web-based data warehousing is assisting an organization to create innovative relationships with its suppliers, partners, and customers. It has tremendously enhanced the communication and decision-support capabilities both within and beyond an organization. These new capabilities allow all companies in the supply chain to operate efficiently and effectively as one company in better utilizing data resources and reacting rapidly to opportunities. The architecture of Web-based data warehousing and its advantages over a traditional data warehousing environment are discussed subsequently.

ARCHITECTURE OF WEB-BASED DATA WAREHOUSING

The Internet and data warehousing are highly complementary for developing systems to implement widespread data warehousing. Nevertheless, a wide range of technologies are crucial to the success of Web-based data warehousing, and understanding the fundamentals of developing a Web-based data warehouse begins with analyzing its architecture. Exhibit 2 depicts the architecture of Web-based data warehousing. The architecture is three-tiered and includes client, Web server, and application server. On the client side, all a user needs is an Internet connection and a Web browser (preferably Java-enabled). The client computer can be of any platform, including PCs, Macintoshes, UNIX machines, network computers (NC), and so on. The Internet/intranet/extranet is the communication medium between client and servers. On the server side, a Web server is used to manage the inflow and outflow of information between client and server. It is backed by both a data warehouse and an application server, which houses downloadable Java applications, Common Gateway Interfaces (CGI) programs, and other applications that are utilized to manipulate the data in the data warehouse. The query results are displayed on Web pages that are constructed on-the-fly or by Java-based data visualization tools. The success of a Web-based data warehousing system requires a three-tier architecture to work seamlessly.

ADVANTAGES OF A WEB-BASED DATA WAREHOUSING SYSTEM

The move to Web-based data warehousing offers many advantages. Web-based data warehousing allows end users to use Web browsers as a user interface in order to access and manipulate data. Such applications can be Internet, intranet, or extranet based. Web-based data warehousing offers several compelling advantages, including ease of access, platform independence, and lower cost.

Ease of Access

The increasing number of mobile users, such as telecommuters and field sales representatives, are increasing the demand for powerful analytical tool availability in corporate networks. The recent emphasis on SCM requires a high level of information visibility among all parties in the supply chain. Web-based data warehousing makes the corporate data warehouse and its application easily accessible from any computer with Internet connectivity. In order to justify an organization's data warehouse investment, the data warehouses must be fully utilized by its internal business, customers, suppliers, and partners in the value chain. The Web-based data warehouse provides a Web-centered approach to extensibility and ease of access. In recent years, end users have become more experienced in using the Internet for both business and leisure purposes; this phenomenon makes the Web browser an easy-to-use interface for users of all levels of computer skill.

Platform Independence

The Internet provides a way to distribute data to a large number of users in a low-cost and platform-independent environment. The Web is built on standards, including TCP/IP for communications, HTTP for application navigation, and HTML for display. These standards are supported by almost every major client/server computing environment (Howie, 1998). By using Web browsers as the information access layer of a data warehouse, the vital business information can be accessed by users adopting any computing platform without the need to customize. This makes Web browsers a perfect user interface for any client system.

To ensure complete platform independence, the Java programming language is being increasingly used for mission-critical data warehousing applications. Its promise of "write once, run anywhere" allows organizations to leverage and extend their data warehousing investments across the entire enterprise. The Java-based applications, which can be interpreted by most Web browsers, are designed to access, analyze, and publish corporate information over the Internet, intranet, or extranet. For example, Java-based data visualization tools allow users to convert multi-dimensional databases into interactive charts and graphs effortlessly.

Lower Establishment and Management Cost

Web-based data warehousing reduces the establishment and management cost by offering a thin-client solution (White, 1998). The thin-client solution moves most of the application processing to the server; therefore, there is a reduced need for hardware and software cost and support on the desktop. A thin client brings the power of many computers into one relatively simple desktop device connected to the network. The use of the thin-client solution allows organizations to adopt such new technologies as network computers (NC). Many system managers like the concept of a centrally managed network and its promise of cost advantages, easier administration, and greater security. In Web-based data warehousing, applications are stored on the application server. They are either downloaded to clients as required to manipulate data locally (i.e., Java applications) or executed on the server (i.e., CGI applications). Therefore, preinstallation of the software is not required, and future upgrading and maintenance are performed only on the server, which saves an enormous amount of resources.

The foregoing discussion demonstrates the advantages of using Web-based data warehousing. Web-based data warehousing provides a platform-independent solution to increase the availability of corporate decision support to internal and external users. At the same time, a remarkable cost saving in administration and maintenance can be achieved.

CHALLENGES AND SOLUTIONS IN IMPLEMENTING WEB-BASED DATA WAREHOUSING

Web-based data warehousing is most appropriate for distributing business-critical data and decision support tools to a large number of end users within or beyond an organization. Web-based data warehousing leverages and extends the organization's data warehousing investment and provides great flexibility for users in their ways of using the data resources. Nevertheless, a number of challenges still exist in implementing Web-based data warehousing due both to the immaturity of this technology and to some management concerns. These challenges and potential technical and managerial solutions are discussed in the following sections.

Challenge 1: Scalability

The Internet provides a way to distribute data to a large number of users at a relatively low cost. When the data warehouse is accessible through the Internet, intranet, or extranet, it is sometimes difficult to anticipate the number of users who will be accessing the data warehouse concurrently. In addition to the internal users, the data warehouse may be available to tele-commuters at home, sales representatives at sites, and business partners or customers who want to access technical support and product information. This has significant implications for the hardware and software resources used to deliver and process data. Too many concurrent "hits" to the data warehouse create an extra burden on the network, and the results of an overly congested network are slower transmission, lower performance, and increased server problems, all of which lead to lower user satisfaction. Therefore, a Web-based data warehouse system must be highly scalable to handle a large number of audiences concurrently (Howie, 1998). Server-based processing is the key to Web-based data warehousing, so server capability is crucial to the scalability of a Web-based data warehouse. The solutions to the scalability challenge today are to increase the server capability, ensure server reliability, and improve network bandwidth from the Intemet to Web servers.

To meet the scalability challenge in the future, IS managers must think ahead when developing a Web-based data warehouse. They need to realize that users' information needs, the number of users, and the volume of data will grow considerably in the next few years, hence the hardware and software resources for maintaining the data warehouse should be planned to have sufficient scale to meet the increasing demand. Before acquiring the hardware and software, IS managers must determine both the transaction speed and network performance requirements. A wide range of hardware tools is available today to meet the performance requirements of data warehouses of any scale. A small- to medium-sized departmental data mart may be able to serve a limited number of users sufficiently using high-pow-ered workstations or servers with symmetric multi-processor (SMP) plat-forms, whereas an enterprise data warehouse used by thousands of users will require multiple mainframes with massive parallel processors (MPP).

One key managerial consideration to solve the scalability issue is under-standing end users' information needs. The Web is characterized as an interactive, "pull" medium. Users have greater control over the selection of information content, the sequence of content, and the process of content exposure compared with other media. However, most users are interested only in data related to their specific functions (Gardner, 1998). Presenting users with information pertinent to almost all aspects of the organization and scores of analytical tools sometimes prevents users from focusing on the data resources that are really useful to them. Another recommended means of information dissemination is to use the "push" method. Using the "push" method, information that is considered most relevant to a user is pushed to the user. Therefore, the user is presented only with information that she is most likely to need. It is suggested that an organization imple-ment a combination of "pull" and "push" approaches when delivering information to users. With a combination of "pull" and "push" approaches, users are presented only with information directly related to their functions, while they still have the option to receive additional information on demand. By analyzing the information needs of users, an organization is able to effectively segment its data resources into functional data marts and identify the potential users for each data mart. A data mart is a scaled-down functional data warehouse used by a limited number of users; hence, it is more manageable than an enterprise data warehouse. Using a data mart architecture, the number of concurrent users, future growth in the number of users, and average amount of data feed becomes easier for IS managers to predict.

Challenge 2: Speed

Speed is a criterion often used to judge the performance of a Web-based system. An organization's ability to deliver information rapidly over the Web is dependent on many factors. In addition to the communication devices, other factors (e.g., network and switch traffic, noise, crosstalk, interference, the distance) contribute to the transfer speed on the Internet (Devoney, 1997). In a data warehouse environment, the complexity of user queries and the large amount of data involved add an extra burden to the processing. The slowed processing speed due to these factors reduces the overall speed of information delivery by a Web-based data warehouse as well. In an intranet environment, speed is often much less an issue. However, the internal network still can be overloaded and slowed down if large blocks of data are transmitted.

Many used to believe that a Web-based data warehouse should be limited to simple tasks requiring little data transmission and that it is not suitable for more complicated decision support. Today, however, technologies are available to deliver complex business information in the forms desired by users at high speed. Some of these technologies are: ISDN, cable modems, TI and T3 lines, satellite networks, and XDSL options. The company should connect itself to the Internet backbone with a high-speed communication line to ensure fast transfer speed.

While most organizations turn to their network bandwidth to look for ways to improve the speed of information processing and delivery, another viable solution to the problem is caching. This technique is used to reduce the time necessary to access data from disks. For example, every time a report is requested, the system checks the disk cache first. If the report has been accessed previously and is present in the disk cache, no re-accessing of the data warehouse is necessary (Gardner, 1997). When the caching technique is used properly, it effectively reduces the amount of data that must be manipulated and the number of tasks that must be performed.

Challenge 3: Security

According to Ernst & Young's 1997 Information Security Survey, nearly 80 percent of 1,300 U.S. organizations surveyed suffered at least one type of data loss during the past year, which was a 25 percent increase over the previous year (Schwartz, 1997). Network security issues generally fall into two categories: (1) unauthorized attempts to access private data via internal and external communications networks, and (2) computer viruses that can disrupt or corrupt data (Hansen, 1997). Security of Web-based data warehousing is a matter not only of managing the rights of different users on the systems but of preventing the theft of information during the transfer, as well as any other harmful action to corporate data resources. Information sent over the Internet travels through many unsecured computer systems, and it is at risk for interception and misuse. Therefore, the security concerns on the Internet should be extended to corporate databases, corporate Web servers, and data transferred through the networks. Application and user level security must be implemented to limit users' privileges of accessing and manipulating data, and extremely sensitive data should not be made available through the Internet. An organization can also implement a number of technologies — for example, encryption, secure protocol, and public/private key protocol — to ensure the security of corporate data (Calkins, 1998). Organizations can choose from various types of software- and hardware-based protective systems to provide the level of security they feel is adequate and cost-effective. Another solution is to focus on the intranet integration with the data warehouse rather than the Internet, because the intranet is usually more secure and manageable than the Internet.

The emphasis on information visibility among organizations in the supply chain to quickly identify business opportunities will certainly raise the question of security. Consequently, an organization must determine what information and analytical tools can be shared on the extranet. In order to accomplish this successfully, a deep analysis of the information needs of external users must be performed. Data and analytical tools that support the strategic missions of the organization are not suitable to be made available to external users. For example, an organization's manufacturer may be granted access to the past and current sales volume data to project the short-term production schedule, but it should not have access to the organization's long-term sales forecast and marketing strategies. The strategic decision-making data and tools should be made available only to the relevant internal users through a more secured channel (i.e., intranet). One tool that an organization can use to prioritize the security needs for different types of data is the data security priority grid presented in Exhibit 3. An organization can classify its data resources both in terms of security priority and internal or external use to help it decide the proper security measure for each type of data.

Exhibit 3. Data Security Priority Grid

	Low Security Priority	Medium Security Priority	High Security Priority
Internal	Operational level: operation data, inventory data	Tactical level: short-term sales forecast, short-term production planning, human resources	Strategic level: long-term production and marketing strategy, capital requirements for future growth
External	Operational level: technical support database, product catalog, product documentation	Tactical level: short-term sales forecast, inventory management	Strategic level: distribution planning, interorganizational alliances

CONCLUSION AND IMPLICATIONS

Building a Web-based data warehousing system to expand the use of the corporate data warehouse and extend corporate investment in it is a challenging yet rewarding process. This chapter provides an overall map of the Web-based data warehousing phenomenon. Its advantages, challenges in implementation, and proposed technical and managerial solutions are the focus of the chapter. The architecture and advantages of Web-based data warehousing presented herein offer readers a conceptual understanding of the system. For IS managers seeking a viable solution to extend their organizations' investment in data warehousing, the chapter can serve as a resourceful guide to the many aspects of a Web-based data warehousing system. Understanding the system will assist them in assessing the feasibility and value of such systems in their organizations. For researchers interested in the areas of electronic commerce and data warehousing, the chapter introduces them to a rich field for future research. A number of challenges of implementing Web-based data warehousing were discussed. Research in solving these problems will be highly useful in the future development of such systems.

References

1. Calkins, M., "Internet Security for Data Warehouses," *Journal of Data Warehousing* (3:1), 1998, pp. 12–17.
2. Castelluccio, M., "Data Warehouse, Marts, Metadata, OLAP/ROLAP, and Data Mining — A Glossary," *Management Accounting* (4:78), 1996, pp. 59–61.
3. Devoney, C. "In Search of 56K," *Computerworld* (39:31), 1997, pp. 77–80.
4. Gardner, D., "Cashing in with Data Warehouses and the Web," *Data Based Adviser,* February 1997, pp. 60–64.
5. Gardner, S.R., "Building the Data Warehouse," *Communications of ACM* (41:9), September 1998, pp. 52–58.
6. Hansen, M.D. "Scared Bitless: Internet Safety & Security," *Professional Safety* (8:42), 1997, p. 18.

7. Howie, G., "Warehouses: Innovate, Integrate and Liberate," *Computing Canada* (24:15), 1998, pp. 35–36.
8. IQ Software, "Automating Information Dissemination Across the Extended Enterprise on the World Wide Web," 1997, Available at www.iqsc.com/products/misc/web-paper.htm.
9. Kalakota, R. and Robinson, M., *e-Business: Roadmap for Success,* Addison-Wesley, Reading, MA, 1999.
10. Ladley, J., "Data Warehousing Trends," *Data Web Adviser,* January 1998, pp. 35–36.
11. Orr, K., Data Warehousing Technology, 1996-1997, Available at www.kenorrinst.com/dwyaper.httnl.
12. Reinaner, R., "Self Storage; Lower Data Warehouse Management Cost with Web Access; Industry Trend or Event," *Communications News* (35:8), August 1998, pp. 35–37.
13. Schwartz, S., "Internet Security: the Bane of Electronic Cornmerce?" *Insurance & Technology* (9:22), 1997, pp. 40–46.
14. White, C., "Building Web Information Systems," *Byte* (23:7), July 1998, pp. 80–83.

Chapter 42

A Guide to Web-Enabled Data Warehouses

Mary Ayala-Bush
Walter Kuketz

Delivering data warehouse access through Web browsers has a variety of benefits. Inside a corporate intranet, Web-enabled data warehouses can increase ease of use, decrease some aspects of training time, and cut costs by reducing the number of proprietary clients. Upgrades can also be accelerated given a standard client, and data warehouses can more easily integrate with other applications across a common platform. When extended to corporate trading partners through an extranet (a secure extension of an intranet outside a firewall), the information contained within a data warehouse may become a revenue source.

Although the internal and external benefits of Web-enabled data warehouses are appealing, they do not come without complicating issues. In traditional implementations, data warehouses have been used by a small population of either highly trained or high-ranking employees for decision support. With such a small number of users having the warehouse application on their desktop, access control was straightforward: either users could access a given table or they could not. Once the warehouse is to be entered by more people — possibly including some outside of the company — access may need to be restricted based on content. Security concerns also change as the user population increases, with encryption over the public Internet becoming one likely requirement.

Because Web-based access to a data warehouse means expanding the community of people who access the data, the types of queries are likely to be more varied. Better business intelligence may thereby be derived, but once again not without complications. In addition to security, performance (and therefore cost) issues become immediately relevant, dictating reconsideration of everything from replication patterns to login requirements.

TASK 4: MANAGING SUPPLY CHAIN INFORMATION

This chapter discusses how Web-enabled data warehouses change the strategy, architecture, infrastructure, and implementation of traditional versions of warehouse applications.

STRATEGY

Business Relationships

The strategy for a Web-based data warehouse should answer at least the following two questions:

1. Who is being granted access?
2. Why are they being granted access through the Web model?

Answering these two questions supplies important information for the cost justification of broader access. Possible justifications might include getting better service from vendors, facilitating better relationships with customers, shortening time of products in the supply chain, and receiving revenues from an internal application. The implications of broader access include having to design an architecture flexible enough to allow for new audiences with needs and requirements that may not be well identified. In addition, going into the information business can distract a company from its core focus by raising the following questions:

- How are pricing levels determined?
- How does revenue derived from a potentially unexpected external source change payback and ROI models?
- What are the service level agreements and how are they determined?
- Who becomes the customer service liaison, especially if the IS organization is already running at full capacity for internal constituencies?

Access Control and Security

Security is a primary consideration when Web access to sensitive corporate information is under consideration. Authentication can be required at three separate stages, allowing administrators to fine tune who sees what when, whereas encryption (typically through the use of the secure socket layer or SSL) protects both queries and responses from being compromised in transit. Initially, the Web server can require either name and password login or the presence of a certificate issued by the data warehouse administrator. This grants access to the site and triggers the SSL encryption if it is implemented.

Once inside the data warehouse, the user might also be required to authenticate himself at the query server, which allows access to the appropriate databases. This might be a dedicated data mart for a vendor, for example, that precludes vendor A from seeing anything pertaining to vendor B, whose information is held in a logically (and possibly physically) separate data mart. Finally, authentication may be required by the database to limit access within a given body of data: a clerk at vendor A can see only a selected portion of the A data mart, whereas A's president can see that company's entire data mart.

The logistics of security are extensive. Maintaining certificates requires dedicated resources, and planning for and executing multitiered logins is a nontrivial task. At the same time, limiting access could limit the value of the data warehouse. For this reason, security must be designed to be flexible and as friendly to legitimate users as possible.

New Components

Broader access to a data warehouse introduces several new elements into the traditional application model, such as what happens to the query engine vendor's pricing model as its proprietary desktop clients are no longer required? Where are the skill sets and hardware to implement Web servers and connect them to the query engine? How much will data be transformed (and by whom) if it is moved out of a central data warehouse into data marts for security, performance, or other reasons?

ARCHITECTURE

If strategy is concerned with goals and objectives, architecture is the unifying conceptual design or structure. It defines a system's component parts and relationships. Effective architectures ensure that the component hardware and software pieces fit together as an integrated whole.

A Web-enabled data warehouse introduces additional components within a system architecture, which must be expanded to include:

- The Web server component
- The components that connect the Web server to the query engine
- The component that formats the results such that they are viewable by a Web browser

The system architecture may also need a component for integrating data marts.

Even with these elements, the architecture must be flexible enough to change rapidly to match the pace of innovation in the Internet arena and the evolving place of data warehouses in contemporary business. The warehouse components may change as a result of the increasing numbers of people using the warehouse, changing aggregations based on security or performance requirements, new access paths required by technological or organizational evolution, and so forth.

New design considerations are introduced by each of the components listed. Web servers introduce new complications, particularly regarding scalability issues. Secure transactions over a dial-up connection can be painfully slow, but detuning the security at either the firewall or the Web server can expose the corporate network to risk. Middleware between the Web server and the query server can dramatically affect performance, particularly if common gateway interface (CGI) scripts are used in place of APIs. Database publishing to hypertext markup language (HTML) is reasonably well advanced, but even here some of the newest tools introduce Java programming into the mix, which may cause implementation problems unless the skills are readily available. Java also presents the architect with new ways to partition the presentation layer and the application logic, with implications (for the network and desktop machines in particular) that are only beginning to be experienced in enterprise computing.

The system architecture must support competing enterprises accessing the data sources. One challenge is to support competing vendors where access control is data dependent. Both vendors can query the same tables — for example, product, by region, by week. If a given retail outlet sells both vendors' products, and people from the sales outlet are allowed to query the data warehouse, they will need to access to both vendors' history.

An effective system architecture must include the facility for access control across the entire Web site, from Web server through to the database. If a mobile sales force is given access while on the road, the architecture must have a component to address the types of connections that will be used, whether they are an 800 dial-up service, local Internet service providers (ISPs), or national ISPs such as CompuServe or America Online.

INFRASTRUCTURE

The infrastructure required to support the Web-enabled data warehouse expands to include the Web site hardware and software, the hardware and software required to interface the Web server to the query server, and the software that allows the query server to supply results in HTML. The corporate network may have to be altered to accommodate the additional traffic of the new warehouse users. This expansion increases the potential complexity of the system, introduces new performance issues, and adds to the costs that must be justified.

The Web-enabled warehouse's supporting infrastructure also introduces new system administration skills. Because the warehouse's database administrator should not be responsible for the care and feeding of the Web site, a new role is required: the Web site administrator, often called the Web master. This term can mean different things to different people, so clarity is needed as the position is defined. Depending on the context, corporate Web masters may or may not be responsible for the following activities:

- Designing the site's content architecture

- Writing and editing the material
- Designing the site's look and feel
- Monitoring traffic
- Configuring and monitoring security
- Writing scripts from the Web server to back-end application or database servers
- Project management
- Extracting content from functional departments

The amount of work that may have to be done to prepare for Internet or intranet implementation varies greatly by company. For example, if the warehouse is going to be accessible from the public Internet, then a firewall must be put in place. Knowing the current state of Web-based applications development is essential: if organizational factors, skills, and infrastructure are not in place and aligned, the data warehouse team may either get pulled from its core technology base into competition for scarce resources or be forced to develop skills that greatly differ from those traditionally associated with database expertise.

Web Site

Web site components include the computer to run the Web server on and the Web server software, which may include not only the Web listener but also a document manager for the reports generated from the warehouse. The common gateway interface (CGI), one of the Web protocols, allows the Web browser to access objects and data that are not on the Web server; in this way the Web server accesses the data warehouse. The interface used does not access the warehouse directly but accesses the query engine to formulate the queries; the query engine still accesses the warehouse.

The CGI has been identified as a bottleneck in many Web site implementations. Because the CGI program must incur the overhead of starting up and stopping with every request to it, high-volume systems lead to a situation of pronounced overhead and noticeably slow response time. API access tends to be faster, but it depends on the availability of such interfaces from or in support of different vendors.

Application Query Engine

The infrastructure must support the application query engine, which may run on the same computer as the data warehouse or on a separate computer networked to the data warehouse computer. This component must be able to translate the query results into HTML for the server to supply to the browser. Some of the query engines present the results in graphic form as well as in tabular form. Where such quantitative information is rendered into image form, the images will change as Java redefines the relationships between clients, servers, and networks. Traditional warehouses have supported relatively small user communities, so existing query engines have to be monitored to see how their performance changes when the number of users doubles, triples, or increases by even larger multiples. In addition, the type and complexity of the queries also have performance implications that must be addressed based on experience.

Data Warehouse

The infrastructure for the data warehouse is not altered simply because Web browsers are being used; instead, the expanded number of users and new types of queries that may need to be executed forces changes to be made. When a data mart architecture is introduced for performance or security reasons, a change may be necessary as to where the mart is located: on the same machine as the warehouse, or on a separate machine. The infrastructure has to support both the method of replication originally specified and new patterns of replication based on DASD cost considerations, performance factors, or security precautions.

SECURITY

Security should be addressed in the following four categories:

1. Web server access
2. Communication transport security
3. Query server application
4. Database access

Web Server Access

Access to the Web server can be controlled through the following:

1. Requiring the user to log into the Web site by supplying a user name and password.
2. Installing client certificates into the browsers of the clients to whom access is granted.
3. Specifying only the IP (Internet Protocol) addresses allowed to access the Web site.

The client certificate requires less interaction on the users' part because they do not have to supply a user name and password to access the system. The client's certificate is sent to the Web server, which validates the certificate and grants the user access to the system. (Part of the process of enabling a secure Web site is to install a server certificate. This must be requested from a third party, called a certificate authority, that allows you to transmit certificates authenticating that you are who you say you are.) A less secure strategy is to configure the Web server to allow connection from a selected number of computers, with all others being categorically denied access. This scheme lets anyone from an authorized computer — as opposed to authorized persons — access the Web site. Because this method is based on an IP address, DHCP (dynamic host configuration protocol) systems can present difficulties in specifying particular machines as opposed to machines in a particular subnet.

Communication Transport Security

Both the query and especially the information that is sent back to the browser can be of a sensitive nature. To prevent others along the route back to the browser from viewing it, the data must be encrypted, particularly if it leaves the firewall. Encryption is turned on when the Web server is configured, typically through the secure socket layer (SSL) protocol.

Query Server Application

To access the query server, the user may be asked to supply a user name and password. The information supplied by the certificate could be carried forward but not without some custom code. Various approaches are used to develop the user names and passwords: one can create a unique user name for each of the third parties that will access the system (allowing the login to be performed on any machine) or for each person who will access the warehouse. Each approach has implications for systems administration.

Database Access

Database access is controlled by limiting the tables' users and user groups can access. A difficulty arises when there are two competing users who must access a subset of the data within the same table. This security difficulty is solved by introducing data marts for those users, each of which contains only the information a particular user is entitled to see. Data marts introduce an entirely new set of administrative and procedural issues, particularly concerning the replication scheme to move the data from the warehouse into the data mart. Is data scrubbed, summarized, or otherwise altered in this move, or is replication exact and straightforward? Each approach has advantages and drawbacks.

IMPLEMENTATION

The scope of implementing a Web-enabled data warehouse increases because of the additional users and the increased number of system components. The IS organization must be prepared to confront the implications, both of the additional hardware and software and of potentially new kinds of users, some of whom may not even work for the company that owns the data in the warehouse.

TASK 4: MANAGING SUPPLY CHAIN INFORMATION

Intranet

Training should cover the mechanics of how to use the query tool, provide the user with an awareness of the levels (and system implications) of different queries, and show how the results set expands or contracts based on what is being asked for. The user community for the intranet is some subset of the employees of the corporation. The logistics involved with training the users are largely under the company's control: even with broader access, data warehouses are typically decision-support systems and not within the operational purview of most employees.

Implementing security for the intranet site involves sensitizing users to the basics of information security, issuing and tracking authentication information (whether through certificates, passwords, or a combination of the two), and configuring servers and firewalls to balance performance and security. One part of the process for enabling a secure Web server is to request a server certificate from a certificate authority. Administratively, a corporation must understand the components — for instance, proof of the legal right to use the corporate name — required to satisfy the inquiries from the certificate authority and put in place the procedures for yearly certificate renewal.

Monitoring a Web-based data warehouse is a high priority because of the number of variables that need tuning. In addition, broader access changes both the volume and the character of the query base in unpredictable ways.

Intra/Extranet

In addition to the training required for internal users, training is extended to the third parties that will access the warehouse. Coordination of training among the third parties is usually more difficult: competing third parties do not want to be trained at the same time, and paying customers have different expectations compared to captive internal users. In addition, a public, purchased service may necessitate more thorough user interface testing of the look and feel within the application.

Security gets more complex in extranet implementations simply because of the public nature of the Internet. It is important to keep in mind the human and cultural factors that affect information security and not only focus on the technologies of firewalls, certificates, and the like. Different organizations embody different attitudes, and these differences can cause significant misunderstandings when sensitive information, and possibly significant expenditures, are involved.

Monitoring and tuning are largely the same as in an intranet implementation, depending on the profiles of remote users, trading partner access patterns, and the type and volume of queries. In addition, a serious extranet implementation may introduce the need for a help desk. It must be prepared to handle calls for support from the third parties and combine customer service readiness with strict screening to keep the focus on questions related to the data warehouse. It is not impossible to imagine a scenario in which third-party employees call for help on topics other than the warehouse.

CONCLUSION

Because Web browsers have the ability to save whatever appears in them, information that appears in the browser of a Web-enabled data warehouse application can be saved to the desktop. Protecting information from transmission into the wrong hands involves a balancing act between allowing for flexibility of queries and restricting the information that can potentially move outside corporate control. Legal agreements regarding the use of information may need to be implemented, for example, and these tend not to be a specialty of the IS organization. Pricing the information is another tricky area, along with managing expectations on the part of both internal and third-party users.

By their very nature, however, data warehouses have always been more subject to unintended consequences than their operational siblings. With changing ideas about the place and power of information, new organizational shapes and strategies, and tougher customers demanding more while paying less, the data warehouse's potential for business benefit is increased by extending its reach while making it easier to use. The consequences of more people using data warehouses for new kinds of queries, although sometimes taxing for IS professionals, may well be breakthroughs in business performance. As with any other emerging technology, the results bear watching.

Chapter 43
Data Warehousing Stages of Growth

Hugh Watson
Thilini Ariyachandra
Robert J. Matyska, Jr.

Ten years ago, data warehousing was largely unknown. Today, many companies are receiving considerable business value from their warehousing efforts, as seen in the following examples:

- First American Corporation (FAC), a regional bank located in the Southeast, lost $60 million in 1990 and was operating under letters of agreement with regulators. A new senior management team developed a customer intimacy strategy with a data warehouse at the heart of the strategy. Using warehouse data, FAC was able to determine the profitability of all of their clients and products; develop programs to attract, maintain, and enhance their customer base; create profitable new product and service offerings; and redesign their distribution channels to increase profitability and better meet customers' needs. Data warehousing helped FAC to become a profitable, innovative leader in the financial services industry.
- Owens & Minor is the leading distributor of branded medical and surgical supplies and serves thousands of hospitals, integrated healthcare networks, and group purchasing networks. The company purchases nearly 130,000 different products from some 1,400 suppliers and sells them to more than 4,000 hospitals and healthcare providers. In order to identify cost savings opportunities in their large and complex supply chain, a data warehouse was built to analyze sales, inventory, and accounts receivable data, resulting in millions of dollars of savings. The company then gave suppliers and customers access to the warehouse, providing them with up-to-the-minute reporting and analysis of customer sales and usage, product inventory, contracts, pricing, and orders. This information is so valuable that suppliers pay for it.

- Whirlpool is the world's largest manufacturer and marketer of home appliances. Whirlpool manufactures thousands of products, every one with hundreds or thousands of components, in 12 major factories, which are stored in 28 places. Over 16 million appliances a year are sold. A major use of Whirlpool's data warehouse is to track and analyze everything associated with the appliances that they manufacture, starting with the components purchased from suppliers and continuing through customers' life-long experiences with the products. Quality engineers can easily track the performance of component parts which allows them to detect problems with particular parts and identify the high and low quality suppliers. Purchasing agents have information from around the world so that they can find the lowest-cost, highest-quality part available on a global basis. Suppliers can access Whirlpool's data to assess the performance of the parts that they are supplying.

In these and other companies, the benefits from data warehousing did not occur all at once. Typically, there was a specific business problem that motivated the development of the warehouse, such as at Owens & Minor where comprehensive supply chain information was needed; or at First American Corporation where there was a need to integrate data about the bank's customers from a variety of disparate systems; or at Whirlpool where there was the desire to reduce costs, improve quality, and increase customer satisfaction.

Initial success typically leads to an expansion of the warehousing initiative, with more data, applications, and users. Experts say that data warehousing is "a journey, not a destination" in order to emphasize its constantly evolving nature. This ongoing evolution creates many additional organizational opportunities, but also generates issues that must be addressed if the warehouse is to live up to its potential.

Even when a data warehouse reaches maturity, it continues to change. It becomes the foundation for organizationwide reporting systems, predefined and *ad hoc* queries, decision-support systems, executive information systems, and data mining. It becomes critical to performance management (e.g., Balanced Scorecarding), E-commerce (e.g., storing and analyzing clickstream data), and customer relationship management.

In this chapter, we present a stages of growth model for data warehousing. How a warehouse goes through initiation, growth, and maturity stages and the variables (i.e., characteristics) that define each stage are described. The chapter also discusses where leading companies are going with their data warehousing efforts. This information should help organizations plan for the evolution of their warehouses. The model and future directions were developed based on interviews with eight leading authorities in the field. These interviews make it clear that while data warehousing has been successful, its greatest impacts are in the future as it becomes integrated with operational processes and E-commerce and is extended to all parties in the value chain. We begin, however, with background information on data warehousing, the stages of growth concept, and how the study was conducted.

BUSINESS DRIVERS AND TECHNOLOGY ENABLERS

During the mid-to-late 1990s, data warehousing became one of the most important developments in the information systems (IS) field. Virtually all of the Fortune 1000 companies now have a data warehouse, and many medium- and small-sized firms are developing them. The Palo Alto Management Group predicts that the data warehousing market will grow to a $113.5 billion market in 2002, including the sales of systems, software, services, and in-house expenditures.[1] As the new millenium emerged, Year 2000, data warehousing, and electronic commerce were at the top of CIOs' strategic initiatives.[2]

The rapid growth is due to the combination of business need and technological advances. Businesses are capturing much more data than ever before, especially about their customers, and want to turn this data into actionable information. In the case of FAC, they wanted to know their customers better than anyone else and to use this information to increase profits and value for their customers. This requires collecting, storing, and processing revenue and cost-related data, data about every client transaction, and demographic and psychographic (e.g., client preferences) data about its customers. When data on customer transactions is collected, data warehouses quickly go over a terabyte in size. Wal-Mart's data warehouse is over 125 terabytes in size. Warehouses this large could not exist without recent advances in computer hardware and software technology. Everything must be done in parallel, including the computing hardware and database software.[3]

DATA WAREHOUSING FUNDAMENTALS

A data warehouse (or smaller-scale data mart) is a specially prepared repository of data designed to support decision-making. The data comes from operational systems and external sources. To create the data warehouse, data is extracted from source systems, cleaned (e.g., to detect and correct errors), transformed (e.g., put into subject groups or summarized), and loaded into a data store (i.e., placed into a data warehouse). The data in a data warehouse has the following characteristics:[4]

- *Subject oriented* — The data is logically organized around major subjects of the organization, e.g., around customers, sales, or items produced.

- *Integrated* — All of the data about the subject is combined and can be analyzed together.
- *Time variant* — Historical data is maintained in detail form.
- *Nonvolatile* — The data is read only, not updated or changed by users.

A data warehouse draws data from operational systems, but is physically separate and serves a different purpose. Operational systems have their own databases and are used for transaction processing; a data warehouse has its own database and is used to support decision-making. Once the warehouse is created, users (e.g., analysts, managers) access the data in the warehouse using tools that generate SQL (i.e., structured query language) queries or through applications such as a decision-support system or an executive information system. "Data warehousing" is a broader term than "data warehouse" and is used to describe the creation, maintenance, use, and continuous refreshing of the data in the warehouse.

THE STAGES OF GROWTH CONCEPT

The stages of growth concept is widely used in organizational[5] and IS research.[6] The fundamental concept is that many things change over time, in sequential, predictable ways. It has been used to describe, explain, and predict organizational life cycles, product life cycles, and biological growth. In information systems, it has been used with overall computing activities in an organization,[7] in the evolution of information centers,[8] and in the integration of information and business systems planning.[9]

The stages of growth are commonly depicted graphically using an S-shaped curve, where the turnings of the curve mark important transitions. The number of stages varies with the phenomena under investigation, but most models have between three and six stages. Also, over time, additional stages can emerge that were not known or foreseen when the model was first developed. For example, Gibson and Nolan first described a four-stage model[7] and a couple of years later revised it to include two additional stages.[10] Each stage is uniquely identified by a set of benchmark variables. These variables change their values as the phenomena move through the stages of evolution.

Data warehouses also evolve over time. For example, the initial rollout of a warehouse is likely to contain data for only a few subject areas and is used by only a subset of the organization's personnel. If the warehouse is successful, additional subject areas and users are added. At the Maturity stage, the warehouse becomes enterprisewide in terms of the data it contains and the user base that it supports.

THE STUDY

To develop a stage model for data warehousing, leading experts in the field were contacted and asked to participate in telephone interviews in

Exhibit 1. Study Participants

Name	Position	Company
Karolyn Duncan	Consultant	Information Strategies
Jane Griffin	Consultant	Arthur Andersen
Bill Inmon	Consultant	Pine Cone Systems
Randeen Klarin	Data warehousing manager	NASD Regulations
Theresa Leahy	Data warehousing manager	First American Corporation
Don Stoeller	Data warehousing manager	Owens & Minor
Ron Swift	Strategist and consultant	NCR
Jim Thomann	Consultant	Web Data Access

order to identify the stages and the variables that identify the stages. Every expert who was contacted agreed to participate. The experts included (1) highly regarded and experienced consultants and (2) managers of highly successful data warehouses (see Exhibit 1). Karolyn Duncan has her own consulting firm and teaches courses for The Data Warehousing Institute (TDWI). Jane Griffin heads up Arthur Andersen's data warehousing practice in the Southeast. Bill Inmon is widely regarded as "the father of data warehousing." Theresa Leahy is the data warehousing manager at FAC, which won the 1999 Society for Information Management award for leading practice. Randeen Klarin is the data warehousing manager at NASD Regulations, which won the 1998 TDWI Leadership Award. Don Stoeller received the 1999 TDWI Leadership Award for the data warehouse at Owens & Minor. Ron Swift is a strategist and consultant for NCR CRM Solutions. Jim Thomann is a data warehousing consultant and teaches courses for The Data Warehousing Institute.

The telephone interviews were 20 to 45 minutes in length and focused on three topics:

1. The number of data warehousing stages
2. The variables that define the stages
3. Descriptions of the evolution of data warehouses

Based on the information collected, an initial stage model was developed. This model was then sent to the experts for their review and comment. The experts' reactions to the model varied from agreement, to recommendations for minor changes, to suggestions for a model with more stages.[11] The stage model was revised to reflect the experts' comments.

DATA WAREHOUSING STAGES

Three stages describe the current evolution of data warehouses (see Exhibit 2):

1. *Initiation* — the initial version of the warehouse

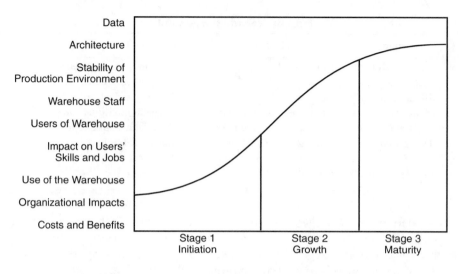

Exhibit 2. The Stages of Growth for Data Warehousing

2. *Growth* — the expansion of the warehouse
3. *Maturity* — the warehouse becomes fully integrated into the company's operations

There are indicators, however, that there will be additional stages in the future, based on what leading-edge companies are doing with their warehouses. Furthermore, there are iterations within the growth and maturity stages.

Nine variables describe the different stages:

1. *Data* — the number of subject areas, the data model(s) used, and the quantity of data stored
2. *Architecture* — the structure of marts and warehouses
3. *Stability of the production environment* — established processes for maintaining and expanding the warehouse
4. *Warehouse staff* — the experience, skills, and specialization of the warehouse staff
5. *Users* — the types, numbers, and locations of users of warehouse data
6. *Impact on users' skills and jobs* — how users' jobs and required skills change because of the warehouse
7. *Applications* — the kinds of applications that utilize warehouse data
8. *Costs and benefits* — the costs and benefits associated with the warehouse
9. *Organizational impact* — how much impact the warehouse has on organizational performance

Exhibit 3. Bill Inmon Talks about the Data Mart Approach

Even though most firms take the data mart approach, Bill Inmon feels strongly that this is the wrong way to go. According to Inmon, most firms develop four or five marts, only to discover after six to nine months that they need to start over again and develop an enterprisewide warehouse. The reason for this is that the architecture of marts and warehouses is "genetically" different and marts do not evolve into warehouses. He says, "You don't plant a seed, see it grow into a tumbleweed, and then become an elm." A data warehouse needs to be designed differently from a data mart because of:

- The volume of data
- The amount of historical data
- The need for greater data integration
- The need for greater flexibility in how the data can be used
- The need for easy expansion
- The need for greater data reconciliation

These requirements lead to hardware, software, data modeling, and business decisions that are different than those made with marts.

Even though we present a stage model for data warehousing, it is important to recognize that the model is a generalization that does not perfectly describe every company's experiences. Factors such as business need, executive support, and the availability of resources influence how a company's warehousing initiative unfolds. It is also important to recognize that two competing approaches to data warehousing exist. The first is the top-down, enterprisewide approach advocated by Bill Inmon.[4] The second is the bottom-up, data mart approach associated with Ralph Kimball.[12] The latter will be described because it is the more common approach, but the first approach has strong proponents.[13] Exhibit 3 lists some of the reservations that Bill Inmon has with the data mart strategy. Actions that can be taken to ameliorate the potential negative aspects of the data mart approach will be described. If followed, the actions provide a middle ground between the two competing approaches.

Initiation Stage

Warehousing initiatives usually start small.[14] A department, often sales, marketing, or finance, has a need for specific data, and the intended use of the data is clear. In order to meet this need, the building of a data mart is approved (as opposed to a larger data warehouse). When the cost of the mart is relatively modest and it has a strong business sponsor, funding for the project may come from the business unit. The data mart stores only a single or a few subject areas, and the amount of data stored is relatively small. The data are stored in a multidimensional format (e.g., a star schema), so that it matches the way that users think (e.g., customers, products). Given its newness and time pressures to roll out the data mart quickly, populating the mart (via data extraction, transformation, and loading processes) is *ad hoc* and evolving. To some extent, the data mart is a decision support experiment. The in-house IT personnel assigned to the project have experience with databases, but are typically new to data warehousing. As a result, it is common to bring in consultants to help with the work and provide knowledge transfer. The learning curve for in-house personnel is steep. The initial users of the data mart are analysts in the unit that requested the mart. They are typically more computer literate and savvy than most of the users who will follow. These analysts use a variety of data access tools (e.g., SQL and managed query environments) to access and analyze the data in the mart to address the issues for which the mart was built. The mart allows the analysts to perform their jobs more quickly and thoroughly. Some reporting systems may also be cleaned up and expanded because of the availability of more reliable, consistent, integrated, and timely data. Although the cost of a data mart is less than for a warehouse, it typically runs into at least six figures when hardware, software, and personnel costs are included. The primary benefits provided by the mart are time savings for analysts and IT personnel (e.g., fewer requests for data extracts and special reports), more thorough analyses, answers to specific questions that previously went unanswered, and better decisions. These benefits are realized within the unit that was responsible for building the mart; consequently, the organizational impact is local.

Growth Stage

If the data mart proves successful, it provides a "proof of concept" for data warehousing. This typically leads to additional initiatives, such as the expansion of the initial data mart and the demand for additional data marts. The building of more data marts marks the beginning of the growth stage. The company is at a dangerous point. It cannot allow data marts to be developed independently. To do so only perpetuates the "silos of information" problem that is so common in organizations today. There must be an overall plan and architecture for the larger data warehousing initiative. Some of the issues that must be addressed include what are the "official" data sources for the data marts, what data definitions apply across the data marts, and what common dimensions (e.g., product, location, time) are used with the various data marts. The production environment is still somewhat unstable in this stage. Considerable effort is going into expanding the number of data marts and serving a growing user base, so there is little time for formally documenting extraction, transformation, and loading procedures or putting data warehouse performance measurement systems in place. The company's internal data warehousing staff has moved up the learning curve and most of the consultants and vendors are no longer needed. Consultants may still be brought in, but they typically provide highly specialized services, such as database performance tuning. Members of the internal staff assume more specific, specialized roles, such as data modeling new subject areas. As new subject areas and data marts are added, new users come on board. They often are not as savvy as the initial set of users and know less about the data warehousing initiative. They also are more diverse in their information needs and how they want to gain access to the data in the data mart(s) (e.g., custom-built applications, predefined queries). This diversity creates challenges in areas such as end-user training and support and data access tool(s) selection. Some users may find that the requirements of their job (e.g., much more analytical) change so much that they are either unable or unwilling to adapt to the changes and move on to other positions. As people become aware of the potential of data warehousing, new applications emerge. Some of the applications are in the business units served by the new data marts, but there is often a change in the nature of the applications themselves. Whereas the initial applications are often backward facing (i.e., what was), some of the new applications allow users to perform "what-if" analysis about future scenarios. As the number of users and applications grows, so do the benefits, but the benefits still are largely in the form of time savings, new and better information, and improved decision making. At some point in the growth stage (e.g., often about 18 months after the initial rollout), the benefits begin to exceed the costs. Companies often do not know when this occurs because of the time and difficulty of quantifying the benefits. The organizational impact of data warehousing in this stage is still largely tactical rather than strategic. There are exceptions, of course, such as when the warehouse was created to support applications that are an integral part of corporate strategy.

Maturity Stage

In the maturity stage, the volume of the data maintained grows, it covers multiple subject areas, it is highly detailed, and it provides considerable historical detail. New subject areas are still added, often in three-month iterations. A warehouse is a "journey" not a "destination" in that there is never an end point. To store the data, a data warehouse has replaced most, if not all, of the data marts. There probably still are data marts, but the marts are different from those in previous stages. The earlier marts were "independent" in that they were fed by their own source systems. In the maturity stage, the marts are "dependent" because they are created and fed by an enterprise warehouse. This approach ensures that the organization has a "single version of the truth," because all of the data used for decision support comes from the same source. There are two reasons for creating dependent data marts — (1) improved response time for users and (2) providing users with a simpler view of the data (e.g., just sales data). The data in the warehouse is stored in a relational database (the same kind used with operational systems) in order to manage the vast amount of data efficiently. The multidimensional data model is still used for the data in the dependent data marts. By this time, the production environment is stable. Data extraction, cleansing, transformation, and loading processes are routinized and documented. Good metadata (i.e., data about the data, such as when data in the data warehouse is refreshed) exists. The data warehousing staff is experienced and there is little need for outside consultants. Members of the staff have well-defined roles and responsibilities, including operating and monitoring the warehouse, providing training and support for users, adding new data and applications, and ensuring that the warehouse is aligned with business objectives. The number and range of users continues to grow. Executives may be given an executive information system that draws heavily on warehouse data. Sales representatives in the field may be able to access warehouse data over the Web. The data warehousing staff needs to offer courses (e.g., a data warehousing university) and support (e.g., perhaps decentralized to the business units) that is appropriate for the different kinds of users. Almost everyone in the organization needs some minimal competency in accessing and using warehouse data. Many jobs and how they are performed are affected by the warehouse. Applications that use warehouse data can be found throughout the organization. They range from reporting, to predefined and *ad hoc* queries, to decision support systems, to executive information systems. Data mining applications surface as the organization searches for important relationships (e.g., the characteristics of people who are most likely to respond to a direct mailing) in the massive amount of data stored in the warehouse. Many warehouses become more strategic to the organization as they become important enablers for accomplishing corporate objectives. E-commerce, connecting suppliers and customers along the supply chain, and supporting customer intimacy initiatives are some of the more significant developments that are currently emerging. These applications commonly have warehouse data being used for operational purposes. These recent and important developments are discussed in the next section. The stages and the benchmark variables are summarized in Exhibit 4.

The Future

The evolution of data warehousing does not end with the three stages described here. Already, developments are occurring that point to additional stages. Some of the developments are seen in the vignettes that opened this chapter, while others were suggested by the data warehousing experts. Here are some of the developments that are taking place now or that can be expected in the near future.

Many of the future developments will involve the World Wide Web, and they will occur in a variety of ways. Companies that sell products over the Internet are increasingly collecting, maintaining, and analyzing "click-

Exhibit 4. The Stages of Growth and Benchmark Variables

Benchmark Variables	Initiation Stage	Growth Stage	Maturity Stage
Data	Limited amount for a single or a few subject areas	Data for multiple subject areas	Enterprisewide data, well integrated and for multiple time periods
Architecture	A single data mart	Multiple data marts	A warehouse, with dependent data marts
Stability of the production environment	Procedures are *ad hoc* and evolving	Procedures are not well established	Procedures are routinized and documented
Warehouse staff	In-house personnel inexperienced; consultants are frequently used	In-house personnel have gained experience and consultants are not heavily relied on	In-house personnel are experienced; the staff has well-defined roles and responsibilities
Users	Analysts in the business unit served by the data mart	Users from all of the business units served by the data marts; diverse in their information needs and computer skills	Users from the throughout the organization access the warehouse; suppliers and customers may have access to warehouse data
Impact on users' skills and jobs	Some users may not have the skills or inclination for the more analytical jobs	More users experience changes in the skills they need in order to perform their jobs	Users throughout the organization need improved computer skills in order to perform their jobs
Applications	Reports and predefined and *ad hoc* queries; backware looking to what has already occurred	Reports and predefined queries; more analysis of why things occurred and "what-if" analysis for future scenarios	Reports, predefined queries and ad hoc queries, DSS, and EIS; data mining provides predictive modeling capabilities; integration with operational systems
Costs and benefits	Costs are moderate; benefits include time savings, new and improved information, and improved decision-making	Benefits include time savings, new and better information, and improved decision-making; the benefits exceed the costs for the first time	Benefits include time saving, new and better information, improved decision-making, redesigned business processes, and support for corporate objectives; high ROI may be realized
Organization impact	Operational and tactical in a few business units	Operational and tactical in additional business units	Organizationwide and often strategic as well as operational and tactical

stream" data — the mouse clicks at a Web site. This data can be used in two major interrelated ways. The first is with applications that react immediately to the clicks and personalize the shopping experience. What the shopper is presented with is determined "on the fly" based on the shopper's clicks and the intelligence built into the application. The second use is to place clickstream data in a warehouse for analysis purposes. For example, the data might be analyzed to track how people proceed through a Web site, to determine what triggers purchases, to assess what types of information are selected by different categories of shoppers, and to discern what attracts people and keeps them coming back. Data warehousing products are appearing to support these applications.

We can expect data mining to become increasingly common. For years companies knew important relationships (e.g., what products sell together) were hidden in corporate databases, but did not know how to find them. Academicians had methods for discovering the relationships (e.g., neural networks), but there were no software products available to easily apply them. A data warehouse provides the clean, highly granular (i.e., very detailed) data that are required for data mining. Vendors are introducing software that offers "data mining in a box." With this software, the application, such as credit card fraud or market basket analysis, is predetermined. The software provides a set of tools to extract data (often from a data warehouse), analyze the data interactively using an appropriate data-mining algorithm, and present the findings in a way that can be understood. These packaged data mining "solutions" make "rocket science algorithms" usable by companies without "rocket scientists." Many of the data mining applications will be used with customer-centric data warehouses such as at First American Corporation.

To fully understand customers, it is necessary to integrate data from multiple systems and sources. Taking a banking example, data is potentially stored in separate, nonintegrated checking account, credit card, and mortgage loan systems. Additional demographic data about customers is available in external databases. Only by integrating all of this data in a data warehouse is it possible to have a comprehensive understanding of customers. Data warehousing is the critical enabler of one-to-one marketing and customer relationship marketing, and more companies will move their warehouses in this direction.

Another major development will be the closer integration of operational systems and data warehouses. The potential benefits of integration are great. Consider, for example, a call center where a customer representative has access to a profile of every previous interaction between the customer and the company which allows the representative to talk through issues, cross-sell, or give additional information. Currently, the information needed for this kind of information is seldom available through a single system.

CONCLUSION

We have described a stage model for data warehousing that identifies the stages that a data warehouse goes through and the variables that define each stage. We have also considered future directions for data warehousing, directions that suggest a vibrant, important future. By understanding the stage model, managers should be able to better plan their companies' data warehousing initiatives.

When moving through the stages, there are potential pitfalls that should be understood and avoided. In closing, the major ones are discussed.

- *Failure to have a scalable design.* The first data mart is relatively easy to build. It requires limited sponsorship, is relatively inexpensive, and has little impact beyond the business unit that creates it. However, there are technical and business issues that must be addressed early on if the data mart is to evolve to a successful enterprisewide data warehouse. The architecture and technologies used must be scalable to accommodate more subject areas, data, and users. Failure to do this can result in costly and time-consuming scrapping of previous work. On the business side, the data must be viewed as a company-wide resource, rather than the property of the unit that creates it, common data definitions must be established for warehouse data, and the warehouse should be viewed as an enabler of corporate strategy.
- *Failure to bring in external help.* Most internal IT staffs need help in getting their data warehousing initiatives started correctly and in planning for the rapid expansion of the warehouse. Building a data warehouse is much more difficult than building a large database. It involves complexities, technologies, and issues that are usually beyond the current staff's experiences. Supporting decision-making is very different from developing and maintaining transaction processing systems.
- *Failure to anticipate changes in job skills and personnel.* The warehouse changes how jobs are performed and the skills that are needed. Some people will not be able to make the required changes and new personnel will have to be brought in to fill the positions.
- *Failure to train and support users.* Data warehouses have a wide variety of users who perform different jobs, have varying information needs, and possess different computer skills. Training and support for all of these different kinds of users must be provided.
- *Failure to understand changes in sponsorship.* The first data mart can be built with business unit sponsorship and help from IT. Over time, however, the sponsorship needs to expand to include senior management, other business units, and IT. This is necessary because of the role that the warehouse plays in corporate strategy, its organizational impacts, its resource requirements, and its use throughout the organization.

- *Failure to create a stable production environment.* As the data warehouse becomes better integrated into how people perform their jobs and the running of the organization, it is important that it is always available, with the information that is needed. People and processes need to be put in place to ensure that this happens.
- *Failure to view the warehouse as a strategic resource.* The largest returns from data warehousing occur when senior management sees the warehouse as an enabler of corporate strategy. In the new economy, data warehousing will be critical to many strategic initiatives.

References

1. Eckerson, Wayne. W., "Post-Chasm Warehousing," *Journal of Data Warehousing,* 3(3): pp. 38–45, Fall 1998.
2. Eckerson, Wayne W. "Evolution of Data Warehousing: The Trend toward Analytical Applications," The Patricia Seybold Group, April 28, 1999, pp. 1–8.
3. Swift, Ron. *Accelerating Customer Relationships Using CRM and Relationship Technologies,* Upper Saddle River, NJ: Prentice-Hall, 2000.
4. Inmon, William H. *Building the Data Warehouse,* New York: John Wiley & Sons, 1992.
5. Greiner, L. E. "Evolution and Revolution as Organizations Grow," *Harvard Business Review,* 50(4), pp. 37–46, July/August, 1972.
6. Burn, J. M. "A Revolutionary Staged Growth Model of Information Systems Planning," *Proceedings of the Fifteenth International Conference on Information Systems,* Vancouver, British Columbia, Canada, pp. 395–406, December, 1994.
7. Gibson, Cyrus F. and Richard L. Nolan, "Managing the Four Stages of EDP Growth," *Harvard Business Review,* 52(1), pp. 28–40, January/February, 1974.
8. Magal, Simha R., Houston H. Carr, and Hugh J. Watson. "Critical Success Factors for Information Center Managers," *MIS Quarterly,* 12(4), pp. 413–425, September, 1988.
9. King, William R. and Thompson, S. H. Teo. "Integration Between Business Systems Planning: Validating a Stage Hypothesis," *Decision Sciences,* 28(2), pp. 279–308, Spring, 1979.
10. Nolan, Richard L., "Managing the Crises in Data Processing," *Harvard Business Review,* 57(2), pp. 115-126, March/April, 1979.
11. Swift, Ron. *Accelerating Customer Relationships Using CRM and Relationship Technologies,* (a six-stage model is presented).
12. Kimball, Ralph. *The Data Warehousing Toolkit,* New York: John Wiley & Sons, 1992.
13. Goff, Leslie. "Beware of Marts, Experts Agree," *Computerworld,* April 6, 1998, p. 65.
14. A notable exception is in the telecommunications industry, where the intended purpose of the warehouse (e.g., analyzing customer call data) is such that the warehouse is large even at the beginning.

Chapter 44
Leveraging Developed Software: An Economic Perspective

Hal H. Green
Ray Walker

Leveraging is the reusability or portability of application software across multiple business units. Leveragability is the extent that the application can remain unchanged as it is installed and made operational at each location. Because leveraging can reduce the cost of acquiring and maintaining application software, it should be part of the IS (information systems) strategy.

INTRODUCTION

The result of leveraging, successfully done, is a continual reduction of both the up-front costs associated with acquiring and installing software applications, as well as the long-term support costs. These cost reductions are achieved through economies of scale realized as (1) common elements of a software application are repetitively applied and (2) costs are prorated across a larger set of installations.

This chapter examines the issues of leveraging application software in a manufacturing context. Leveraging, or the reduction in application life-cycle costs (illustrated in Exhibit 1), can be discussed in either a context of spanning multiple manufacturing locations within a single business unit or spanning multiple businesses within a single product type.

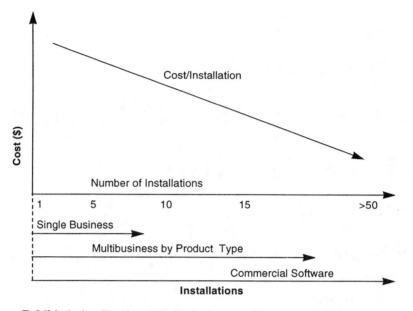

Exhibit 1. Application Life-Cycle Cost and Leverage Opportunity

MAINTENANCE AND SUPPORT COSTS IN MANUFACTURING ENVIRONMENTS

The process of acquiring automation, process control, and plant information systems has traditionally involved one-of-a-kind development projects. The needs of each site were individually assessed, software was selected and purchased, and local resources (often in the form of system integrators) were contracted to provide services. This business paradigm is easily executed, but it has resulted in a profusion of unique, site-specific systems. By multiplying atypical applications, manufacturers discovered that the costs of supporting these unique sets of applications increased because of the lack of commonality or no economy of scale. Compounding the problem is the plethora of applications serving different needs or functions of the manufacturing user communities.

Business structure and organization are also issues to consider. Manufacturing sites are usually autonomous, with at least cost-center responsibility if not profit-and-loss responsibility. A large manufacturing site may make multiple products or product grades. Production areas within a single site are usually product defined. A single product may be made at multiple sites for sourcing, distribution, and marketing reasons. Business units are formed around one or more product lines. A business unit may span multiple products on multiple sites. Hence, any given site may support many business units.

Information and control systems (e.g., process control, product control, and quality control) are usually required to be in-plant systems. Enterprise systems (e.g., Material Requirements Planning or material requirements planning, warehousing and distribution, and order management) are most often shared across multiple sites as supply chain functions.

Manufacturing applications that directly affect the manufacturing process have historically been contained on-site. This situation has resulted in a physical architecture different from a central mainframe with dumb terminals at remote sites. Whereas manufacturing applications are often computer-intensive, few simultaneous users are served.

Unique site manufacturing applications crowd the IS landscape, owing their existence to differences in product or area requirements. Factors that have contributed to this condition include:[1]

- The need to exchange process control data with other manufacturing systems
- The autonomy of manufacturing sites to make IT investment decisions
- The lack of a vision for future integration of direct manufacturing systems with other plant IS applications and systems

Historically, manufacturing applications were constructed in a purely vertical sense with automation — not integration — in mind. Shared applications, while functionally isolated, were often interfaced with other applications through a variety of means. The resulting set of disparate and unique legacy systems has driven support costs higher, even as support resources are shrinking.

One textile fibers manufacturing business estimates that for every dollar invested in development, $0.25 per year is incurred for maintenance and support, including both direct and indirect costs.[1] Taken over a ten-year anticipated life of an application, this amounts to a present value for support of about 2.5 times the total cost of the initial development.

ECONOMICS OF LEVERAGING

As leveraging is foremost a business objective, it is important to note the economic effects of leveraging as a capital decision process. As leveraging occurs, the costs of application software per site go down. Assuming that benefits from the software are constant, the Net Present Value of the per-site investment increases. Exhibit 2 shows a sample discounted cash flow curve from an initial investment in an application.

The costs associated with bringing a software capability on-line at a site include the following cost categories:

- Initial planning, analysis, consulting, and specification

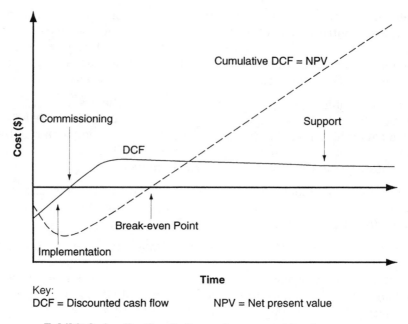

Exhibit 2. Application Software Investment Performance

- Construction/implementation, staging, integration, and factory acceptance
- Hardware, system software, and networking
- Installation, database population, commissioning, site acceptance testing, and training

Taken together, these cost categories can be counted as the investment toward an anticipated improvement in manufacturing operations. Most investments are driven by an anticipated series of positive future cash flows. This is, of course, standard financial analysis for capital decisions. The word "benefits" is frequently used to describe enhancements to the manufacturing operation that result from using an application. For an investment to yield a net present value (NPV), the sum of the present value of the future cash flows resulting from the initial investment must be greater than the present value of the costs associated with realizing the benefits.

The investor (plant site) expects benefits (future cash flows) from the investment (initial costs) at an appropriate discount rate. One method of organizing and analyzing benefits in manufacturing seeks to maximize net present value (NPV) of a set of information system projects identified through a strategic planning acitivity.[2] Exhibit 2 illustrates the shape of the curve of cash flows over time when costs are assigned as negative cash flows for an application project and benefits as positive cash flows. Development costs (cash outflow) initially cause the curve to go down. After commissioning and allowing some time for use of the application to reach maximum effectiveness, cash flows become positive as benefits (cash inflow) begin to be realized. Support costs (cash outflow) continue but should be small compared to the benefits accruing per period. Discounted cash flow (DCF) causes the net cash flow over time to steadily decline, assuming constant support cost for the application. A break-even point occurs when the cumulative data communications function is equal to zero; that is, the present value of application benefits is equal to the present value of costs.

The principal business drivers for leveraging are economic, not technical. A successfully applied program of leveraging an application or capability across multiple manufacturing sites reduces the installed costs per site while minimizing the ongoing support and maintenance costs of the delivered applications. Assuming manufacturing benefits result from the application, the result of leveraging is a maximum net present value (NPV) of the investment across one or more manufacturing sites.

Exhibit 3 illustrates the economy-of-scale effect as a measure of the resources required per installation. Leveraging has the effect of driving the total costs per site to some base level that is set by the costs of off-the-shelf system components plus resources required to install and make operational the system at each respective site.

Leveragability, then, can be economically measured by the extent of the costs associated with planning and implementing each site's respective requirements. Exhibit 4 illustrates the effect of leveraging as the number of sites to receive the application increases. Leveraging is therefore an economy-of-scale effect. The greater the number of sites in the leveraged effort, the greater the net present value (NPV) of the investment across the collection of target sites or installations.

CONSISTENT DATA

Because the business drivers for leveraging are clear, it is reasonable to ask why leveraging is not a pervasive business practice. Some of the barriers to achieving leveragable software include:

- Misperceptions of leveraging
- Absence of a long-term manufacturing applications migration plan
- Lack of a consistent architectural framework
- Corporate culture ("not invented here" thinking)
- *Ad hoc* approaches to applications development
- Conflict between corporate IS/engineering and the manufacturing sites' objectives

Whereas application leveraging does not have to mean "one size fits all," some consistent framework must exist so that applications can be

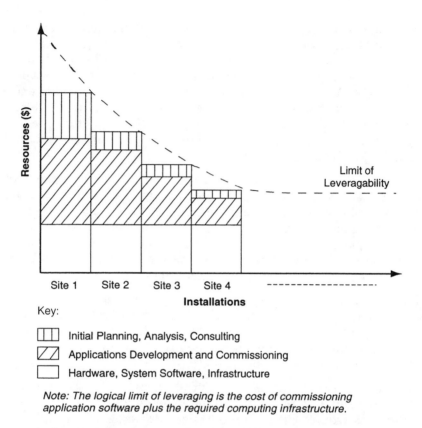

Exhibit 3. Leveragability as a Measure of Resources per Installation

designed to be consistent with this framework. Although the data content of applications varies between businesses or sites, applications should fit into a common architecture across the domain of sites or businesses over which the applications are implemented. Without such a common framework, leveraging does not occur.

The common architecture must not stop at the point of defining hardware, communication protocols, or even database types. A consistent way of understanding the types of data to be stored and the type of repository for those data should be planned. If a real-time database is to be employed for process control and monitoring, for example, what are the valid types of data to be managed by this portion of the plant manufacturing application architecture? What are the valid functions to be addressed by this part of the architecture?

Often, the answers to these questions are blurred by misconceptions. Sometimes, companies select a particular database vendor and perceive they have accomplished leveraging. On the contrary, the applications must

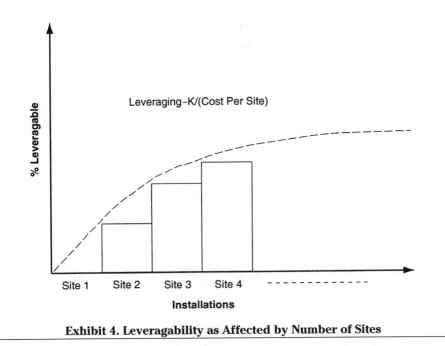

Exhibit 4. Leveragability as Affected by Number of Sites

be able to plug-and-play in the target database existing at the sites if they are to be leverable. This degree of leveraging implies standards for the development of applications that use the selected database, ideally determined before development and acquisition of applications.

Data Standards

Data standards go beyond a textual specification of functionality, however. Textual specifications usually emphasize desired functionality of the application and fall short of defining a model of the data to be employed. Information engineering, which is now rapidly becoming a standard for database design, is an improvement over narrative specifications. This methodology incorporates data modeling and functional modeling using the entity-relationship diagram (ERD) and activity hierarchy diagram (AHD), respectively.

To prepare for leveraging applications, IS management must answer several questions:

- What are the standards of technology to support applications?
- What are the standard tools for building and maintaining manufacturing applications?
- What are the standards for modeling and describing requirements?
- What types of data will be stored and operated on by these systems?
- What are the standards for screen design and user interaction?

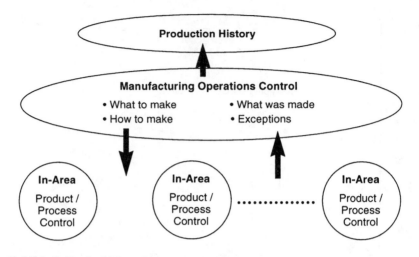

Exhibit 5. Typical Manufacturing Information Processing Requirements

TECHNICAL ARCHITECTURE ISSUES

It is often impractical to know every aspect of each plant's or site's technical IS architecture before commencing development. It is important, however, to have a common way of viewing existing and proposed systems in the context of the types of data they are to manage.

A data-centered architectural framework can be used for information and control systems in manufacturing.[3] Exhibits 5, 6, and 7 provide an overview of the framework. Data is viewed in three distinctive categories: "in-

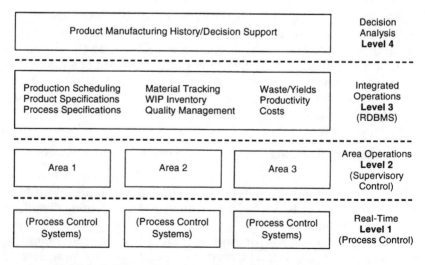

Exhibit 6. Direct Manufacturing Application Framework

Exhibit 7. Manufacturing Data Types and Usage

	Example Data	Typical Orientation	Typical Usage	Integration Scope	Typical Volume
Multi-site Decision Support	Lot/Batch Quality Summary	Subject/Table	Multi-site Read Only	Business	Low
Cross-Area Integrated Operations	Lot/Batch Quality Detail	Subject/Table	Transaction Driven	Site	Medium
In-Area Operations	In-Area Quality Results	File/Field	Event Driven	Area	Medium
Process/Machine Control	Process/Quality Parameter	Tag or I/O	Real-Time	Machine/Process Step	High

area" for process control," manufacturing operations and control" for plantwide product control, and "production history" for plantwide and businesswide decision support. This architecture places such functions as material requirements planning, order management, and inventory management as business-level or supply-chain functions. Exhibit 6 decomposes these three categories of data stores into further detail. Exhibit 7 maps a specific example set of data concerning the subject of quality to the architecture of Exhibit 6.

Exhibits 5, 6, and 7 portray a topological way of viewing manufacturing data. They also reveal a fundamental obstacle to leveraging. Without some type of agreed-on taxonomy of data, leveraging becomes difficult. An application framework should recognize and position the desired suite of application software during the planning or analysis phase of the project.

Many workable approaches can be applied to modeling manufacturing applications, but both data types and functions must be central to any discussion of modern plant IS architecture. In the end, it is the types of data to be managed that must be understood between applications if cost-effective integration is to be obtained.

Given optimum conditions of similar or like plant logical and physical architectures, the ability to leverage an application nevertheless remains influenced by a variety of factors. First, it is important to note that the closer the application is to the manufacturing process equipment, the less the application will lend itself to leveraging. Process control applications are inherently tied to the site process control systems, which often vary greatly. It is a rare process control application that is totally independent from the field/equipment instrumentation that is measuring and controlling the process.

A valid approach to designing leveragable applications is to place only real-time applications at the process control level of the architecture. These are applications that must, by the nature of the data they manage, be positioned such that they can access the real-time process control database.

In contrast, applications that can be logically positioned farther from the front-end process control database tend to offer greater leveragability. Such applications are usually database applications related to the product rather than the manufacturing process. The integrated operations or manufacturing execution level of type 3 applications in Exhibit 6 (previously referenced) lists some of these product or subject-based applications.

Leveragability, then, is limited to the extent that it is specific to the site's manufacturing processes. It is therefore incumbent on the applications designer or purchaser that applications be properly positioned within an

Category	Examples	Leveraging
Core Capability	User/Client Screens, Data Model, Data Base Implementation	High
Auxiliary Functions	Reports, Specialized Functions, Particular Screens	Medium-High
Site-Specific Functions	I/O Processing, Data Occurrences, Quantity of Users, Hardware, System	None-Low

Exhibit 8. Taxonomy of Leveraging

IS architecture and, further, be constructed to be as generic as practical with respect to the process control system.

MEASURING LEVERAGABILITY

The ultimate measure of leveraging is the resulting business benefit: the reduced cost of delivering a working capability from site-to-site across an enterprise. Can leveraging be quantitatively analyzed before commencing a rollout in order to forecast the required resources/costs per incremental site? The following paragraphs illustrate one approach.

It is helpful to map the various functional elements of the application against an expected quantity of its leveragability. A spreadsheet can be used to view the various components according to three categories:

- Core functionality
- Auxiliary functions
- Site-specific functions

The data types and functions comprising the application set can be decomposed into these three categories. Exhibit 8 depicts such a decomposition.

As the data model underpinning the application is foundational and can be understood independently of user screens and reports, it is likely the purest representation of core capability. Functions of one or more applications can be separated by some rationale into independent subfunctions. Subfunctions can be assigned to one of the three leveraging categories:

1. *Site-specific functions* are those that must be customized to a particular site and therefore offer the least leveragability.
2. Auxiliary functions may be items like reports, specialized functions, or perhaps particular user screens. Such functional items may be leveragable across a subset of sites but perhaps not the whole of the target domain.
3. Core functions are those that can be leveraged across every site in the target domain without modification.

541

Analysis of Target Domain

There are two possible sources for meaningful information on which to base estimates for assessing leveraging. The best information source results from an exhaustive analysis across the target domain. An analysis of the subject areas across multiple sites is able to calibrate the data/functional model according to the extent of changes likely as the application is moved from one site to the other.

Pilots and Prototypes

Another valid source of information is from completed projects, pilots, or prototypes. These assets are excellent because they provide a test bed for quantifying leveragability. In any case, usually more than two sites must be sampled to have a meaningful representation of the whole.

Weighting Factors

Assuming one of these two possible sources of information, it is possible to assign leveraging weighting factors to each function or process of the application. Weighting factors should reflect, more or less, the extent of variability in each subfunction or capability of the application with respect to target sites. Weighting factors can also be used to assess resource requirements as measured in development resources or costs. This discipline reinforces an effort to maintain as much of the application as practical within what may be called the core, thus driving greater leveragability.

Breakpoint values for leveragability can be defined, quantitatively, by what is in the core, auxiliary, or site-specific categories: 100 percent leveraging means that no modification is required in the application to make the application operational across all sites in the target domain, 0 percent leveragability implies unique tailoring of the applications to each site. The end state of the leveraging analysis should portray the incremental costs of moving the complete application across all sites in the target domain.

CONCLUSION

Leveraging is driven by management's recognition of the inherent costs of unique site-specific solutions. An effective business practice will explicitly declare leveraging to be part of the IS manufacturing strategy. The goal of leveraging is to maximize the net present value (NPV) of the IS investment.

As manufacturers continue to invest in information technology, significant assets are being created in plants. The management of these assets should be performed with the same decision process as applied to other important capital assets.

This chapter has presented a financial perspective on leveraged software. Chapter 45, entitled "Leveraging Developed Software: Organizational

Implications," describes an effective environment for leveraging software development and support.

Notes

1. R.L. Sloan, Executive Briefing, Maximizing Return on Plant IS Investment, November 17, 1993, Houston, TX.
2. L.B. Koppel, Information System Master Planning, *Hydrocarbon Processing,* May 1993.
3. R.L. Sloan and H.H. Green, An Information Architecture for the Global Manufacturing Enterprise, *Information Management: Strategies, Systems, and Technologies,* 5(5), October 1993.

Chapter 45

Leveraging Developed Software: Organizational Implications

Hal H. Green
Ray Walker

Leveraging application software is a business objective that seeks to provide common solutions across numerous sites. A businesswide effort to leverage application software has organizational implications. Roles and responsibilities of the analysis team and the user community are described within a manufacturing context. The technical aspects of leveraging are discussed in Chapter 44.

INTRODUCTION

Leveraging is the reusability or portability of application software across multiple business sites. The extent to which an application can remain unchanged as it is installed and made operational at each location is referred to as leveragability.

Leveraging can reduce the cost of acquiring and maintaining application software. However, the ultimate measure of leveraging is the resulting business benefit — the cost of delivering a working capability from site to site across an enterprise.

Whether a manufacturer chooses an off-the-shelf or custom software solution, achieving leveraging requires the cooperation of multiple sites, beginning with the initial phases of the process. In downsized companies and companies with greater decentralization of decision-making, this type of businesswide effort can become difficult. This is especially true when the application is not necessarily a supply chain level-application, but one affecting more directly the manufacturing process.

ASSESSING PREPAREDNESS FOR LEVERAGING

Where a leveraging opportunity exists, limiting the scope of the target sites to a common business, product type/configuration, or other shared interest may mitigate some of the management challenges to leveraging. This strategy contains the leveraging activity to sites that are apt to benefit most. These sites are likely to be willing to compromise on functional requirements to realize the reduced costs of acquiring and supporting the leveraged application.

Analysis Team Responsibilities

Leveragability of software is affected by the initial choice of platforms. Ideally, the application should result from a rigorous data and function modeling phase that clearly depicts the natural systems of the sites. All too often, hardware, operating systems, and database platforms are the decisions that precede, shape, and limit the follow-on choices. As is the case for all good design practice, business requirements should drive technical architecture, not the other way around.

If a solid data and function model exists for each site, the choice of acquiring or developing software becomes clearer. When an off-the-shelf application exists that is capable of serving most of the business needs, then the choice becomes a selection between vendors' offerings relative to the specification. When no commercial offering exists on the market that satisfies the site's information model, then new development or modification of some existing software are the obvious choices. In either case, the following questions are germane to understanding the number of sites that can apply the application to be acquired or developed:

1. Will changes in product or the manufacturing differences affect the applications?
2. How do manufacturing business practices change from site to site?
3. What type of process control or I/O systems exist at each site?
4. What hardware, system software, and networking protocols exist at each site?
5. Do the user communities differ at each site with respect to their information needs?
6. What user communities should be interviewed to assess requirements?
7. What type of training or follow-on consulting must be provided to make the application effective at each site?
8. Who will be responsible for first-line support at each site once the application is commissioned?

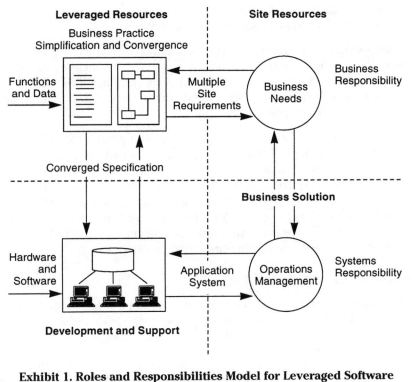

Exhibit 1. Roles and Responsibilities Model for Leveraged Software Development and Support

Answers to these and a host of other questions should be captured as part of the deliverables that result from the analysis process. Once the architecture *vis-à-vis* the applications are known, the quality and location of sites to be included in the analysis can be selected.

Exhibit 1 presents an overview of the process of requirements analysis or documenting the common specification across the target business. In Exhibit 1, leveraged resources represent the analysis team responsible for designing and delivering the application across multiple sites. Site resources consist of two groups:

- *The user community.* Users provide the business objectives and needs.
- *The IS community.* IS maps the effect of systems on manufacturing operations.

The analysis team captures information needs across multiple sites. In a manufacturing context, information needs may be similar to these examples:

- Amount of product waste on yield on each line by shift
- Statistics of key process/quality parameters

- Recipe or formulary for each product
- Trend of selected process values over time

A successful modeling effort results in a shared specification that enjoys system independence in that it describes what the business does, not simply "how" it does it. The use of a shared data and functional model is an effective means of creating a living specification that reflects the information needs of the business.

Data and functional models resulting from analysis can also be used to complete development. Whether the design team elects to purchase off-the-shelf application components or develop custom software, the model-based specification is useful. Whether full life-cycle CASE tools or 4GL tools are employed, the data and functional specifications are foundational to the applications. Fourth-generation client/server tools that allow decoupling of client processes from the database server can be used effectively to capture user screen requirements during prototyping.

ORGANIZING FOR LEVERAGING

Leveraging is a business objective, originating from a purposeful decision to provide common solutions across numerous manufacturing sites. Leveraging begins, therefore, with the affected organizations sharing this business objective.

Businesses that enjoy a culture in which ideas germinate at the lower levels of the organization can offer some of the greatest challenges to leveraging. These businesses often build strong IS capabilities at the plant and manufacturing sites to support and build new manufacturing software applications. For such organizations, their strength is also their weakness when it comes to leveraging applications software. Overcoming the cultural and organizational barriers at a site to a businesswide or corporate-wide convergence effort or solution can become a serious hurdle to the planner and analyst. One means of mitigating this problem is the use of a leveraged application workgroup that represents the various sites.

Leveraged Application Workgroups

The leveraged application workgroup is responsible for capturing the business benefits that accrue across multiple manufacturing sites during the definition, development, and deployment of an application. The workgroup is composed of representatives from each business or site that derives benefit from the application, as well as a project engineer or analyst and a sponsor from the corporate staff function that is held accountable for the program's success.

The workgroup is formed soon after an individual business unit or site requests development of a new manufacturing application. Additional sites and business units are solicited for membership in the workgroup by distributing a brief description of the application and anticipated benefits from deployment across multiple sites. A project engineer or analyst is assigned to draft a detailed specification that is then reviewed and upgraded by the workgroup. Upon reconciliation of all the requested modifications to the specification, the document is reviewed with the application supplier. The supplier provides a proposal for developing the application (functional design concepts, cost, and schedule).

Funding from each site and business unit for the development of the application is a key component in the success of leveraging software. Funding from multiple sources reduces the cost for each individual site.

Upon delivery of the application analysis and detailed design documents from the supplier, the application workgroup reviews the design and decides what modifications or scope changes are required. The workgroup is responsible for making certain that the final design will bring the maximum benefit across the different sites.

The application workgroup decides which site is appropriate for piloting the application. Selection of the first site is important because this site's learnings will be the basis for deployment at additional sites. After installation at several sites, the workgroup compiles all the installation learnings and benefits information. A best practices/implementation guide is compiled for rollout at multiple sites.

A communications bulletin is distributed to all the business units and sites for potential reuse of the application. This communication alerts sites considering development of a similar or redundant application.

DELIVERING LEVERAGED APPLICATIONS

If as a result of the analysis and design it is determined that an off-the-shelf package exists to provide the desired solution, the construction phase assumes the characteristics of a rollout. Key considerations revolve not around code development but around applying the packaged software in the target sites. Key concerns are:

- Integration with existing systems (if necessary)
- Database population plans
- Interfaces with I/O devices
- Any necessary modifications of the off-the-shelf software
- User training
- Ongoing support

The use of pilot or prototype systems is encouraged as a means of continuing to align user expectations for leveraging the application. Working pilots in plants are an excellent means of identifying potential benefits of

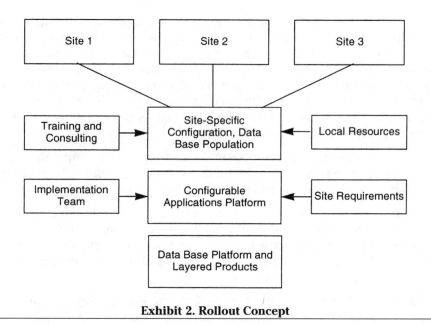

Exhibit 2. Rollout Concept

the application if a solid base case is first established for comparison. Pilots serve as a platform for technical and performance evaluations while at the same time providing a test bed for the user community before full implementation or rollout.

PLANNING THE APPLICATIONS PLATFORM

The analyst and designers must plan for leveraging from the initial phases of the project. Common database platforms, common user interfaces, and even common I/O drivers are not sufficient to realize the full benefits from leveraging. Exhibit 2 presents an overview of an applications platform and illustrates delivery of leveraged applications.

Beginning with the database, standards should be set around database configuration. If the database engine is relational, then the data model becomes the common basis of configuration. If the database is part of a real-time process control system, then standards could include tag naming conventions, data types, screens, process icons, trends, and SPC charts.

Layered over the database engine are the applications that will operate on data in the database. The applications should be sufficiently complete such that database population need only occur once the systems are delivered to the site. This means that metadata is known and fixed. Likewise, user screens are complete and ready to work out-of-the-box. Process control systems that use configurable graphical user interfaces are a convenience and a luxury if uniquely configured for each site.

Common graphical user interface screens with generic capabilities from site to site offer greater economy to create and less cost to support. Where graphical screens are being leveraged across multiple sites, there is usually sufficient economy created by the leveraging approach to produce higher-quality graphics. The quality of the delivered applications should increase with leveraging.

Ideally, applications can be made operational quickly once hardware and system-level software is operational. A factory acceptance test should be performed where the complete system is staged, integrated, and checked before rollout.

CONCLUSION

There are organizational implications in any effort to effectively leverage software. Leveraged software development and support requires the cooperation of multiple sites beginning with the initial phases of the process.

It is also appropriate to point out that the business model for leveraging software reviewed in this chapter implies fewer contributors to the effort. The need to have a different system integrator provide development or application programming per site is diminished, if not eliminated. The leveraged application workgroup is likely to find that the applications can be made operational with a small dedicated team systematically moving from site to site.

Chapter 46

Business-to-Business Integration using E-Commerce

Ido Gileadi

Now that many of the Fortune 1000 manufacturing companies have implemented ERP systems to streamline their planning and resource allocation, as well as integrate their business processes across the enterprise, there is still a need to be integrated with the supply chain.

To reduce inventory levels and lead-times, companies must optimize the process of procurement of raw materials and finished goods. Optimization of business processes across multiple organizations includes redefining the way business is conducted, as well as putting in place the systems that will support communication between multiple organizations each having their own separate systems infrastructure and requirements.

This type of business-to-business electronic integration has been around for some time, in the form of EDI (electronic document interchange). EDI allows organizations to exchange documents (e.g., purchase orders, sales orders, etc.) using standards such as X.12 or EDIFACT and VANs (value-added networks) for communication. The standards are used to achieve universal agreement on the content and format of documents/messages being exchanged. EDI standards allow software vendors to include functionality in their software that will support EDI and communicate with other applications. The VAN is used as a medium for transferring messages from one organization to the other. It is a global proprietary network that is designed to carry and monitor EDI messages.

The EDI solution has caught on in several market segments but has never presented a complete solution for the following reasons:

- High cost for setup and transactions: smaller organizations cannot afford the cost associated with setup and maintenance of an EDI solution using a VAN.

0-8493-1273-6/02/$0.00+$1.50

- EDI messages are a subset of all the types of data that organizations may want to exchange.
- EDI does not facilitate on-line access to information, which may be required for applications such as self-service.

With the advance of the Internet both in reliability and security and the proliferation of Internet based E-commerce applications, E-commerce has become an obvious place to look for solutions to a better and more flexible way of integrating business-to-business processes.

The remainder of this chapter discusses a real-life example of how internet and E-commerce technologies have been implemented to address the business-to-business integration challenge.

BUSINESS REQUIREMENTS

The business requirements presented to the E-commerce development team can be divided into three general functional area categories:

1. general requirements
2. communicating demand to the supply chain
3. providing self-service application to suppliers

General requirements included:

- 100 percent participation by suppliers: The current EDI system was adapted by only 10 percent of suppliers
- minimize cost of operation to suppliers and self
- maintain high level of security both for enterprise systems and for data communicated to external organizations
- utilize industry standards and off-the-shelf applications wherever possible; minimize custom development.
- supplier access to all systems through a browser interface

Demand requirements included:

- send EDI standard messages to suppliers
  - 830: Purchase Schedule
  - 850: Purchase Order
  - 860: Purchase Order Change
- provide advance notice of exceptions to demand through exception reports

Exhibit 1 describes the flow of demand messages (830, 850, 860, exceptions) between the manufacturer and supplier organization. The demand is generated from the manufacturer ERP system (Baan, SAP, etc.). It is then delivered to the supplier through one of several methods (discussed later). The supplier can load the demand directly into its system or use the supplied software to view and print the demand on a PC. The supplier can then

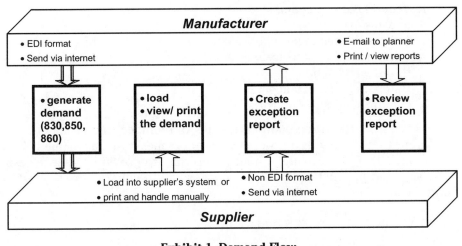

Exhibit 1. Demand Flow

produce an exception report, indicating any exception to the excepted delivery of goods. The exception report is sent back to the manufacturer and routed to the appropriate planner. The planner can view the report and make the necessary adjustments.

Self-service application requirements included:

- ability for suppliers to update product pricing electronically, thereby ensuring price consistency between manufacturer and supplier
- provide on-line access with drill-down capabilities for suppliers to view the following information:
  - payment details
  - registered invoices
  - receipt of goods details
  - product quality information

TECHNICAL REQUIREMENTS

The technical solution had to address the following:

- transport EDI messages to suppliers of various levels of computerization
- provide complete solution for suppliers that have no scheduling application
- support small and large supplier organizations seamlessly
- provide batch message processing and on-line access to data
- provide security for enterprise systems as well as data transmission
- utilize industry standards and off-the-shelf products

Once again, the technical requirements are divided into three categories:

TASK 4: MANAGING SUPPLY CHAIN INFORMATION

1. general requirements:
   a. low cost
   b. low maintenance
   c. high level of security
   d. industry standards
2. Batch message management
3. On-line access to enterprise information

In reviewing the three main categories of technical requirements it is apparent that one needs a product to support message management (EDI and non-EDI), and the same or another product to provide on-line access. The selected products will have to possess all the characteristics listed under general requirements.

E-COMMERCE PRODUCT SELECTION

Selection of E-commerce products to construct a complete solution should take the following into consideration:

- What type of functionality does the product cover (on-line, batch, etc.)?
- Is the product based on industry standards or is it proprietary?
- Does the product provide a stable and extensible platform to develop future applications?
- How does the product integrate with other product selections?
- What security is available as part of the product?
- What are the skills required to develop using the product, and are these skills readily available?
- Product cost (server, user licenses, maintenance)?
- Product innovation and further development?
- Product base of installation?
- Product architecture?

The E-commerce team selected the following products.

WebSuite and Gentran Server from Sterling Commerce. This product was selected for handling EDI messages and communication EDI and non-EDI messages through various communication mediums. This product provides the following features:

- secure and encrypted file transfer mechanism
- support for EDI through VANs, Internet, and FTP
- browser operation platform using ActiveX technology
- simple integration and extendibility through ActiveX forms integration
- simple and open architecture
- easy integration with other products
- EDI translation engine.

Baan Data Navigator Plus (BDNP) from TopTier. This product was selected for on-line access to the ERP and other enterprise applications. The product has the following main features:

- direct on-line access to the Baan ERP database through the application layer
- direct on-line access to other enterprise applications
- integration of data from various applications into one integrated view
- Hyper Relational data technology, allowing the user to drag and relate each item data onto a component thereby creating a new more detailed query providing drill-down capabilities
- access to application through a browser interface
- easy-to-use development environment

Both products had just been released when the project started using them (Summer of 1998). This is typically not a desirable situation because it can extend the project due to unexpected bugs and gaps in functionality. The products were chosen for their features, the reputation of the companies developing the products, and the level of integration the products provided with the ERP system already in place.

E-COMMERCE SOLUTION

Taking into account the business and technical requirements, a systems architecture that provided a business and technical solution was put together. On the left side of the diagram are the client PCs located in the supplier's environment. These are standard Win NT/95/98 running a browser capable of running ActiveX components. Both the applications (WebSuite and TopTier) are accessed through a browser using HTML and ActiveX technologies. As can be seen in Exhibit 2, some suppliers (typically the larger organizations) have integrated the messages sent by the application into their scheduling system. Their system loads the data and presents it within their integrated environment. Other suppliers (typically smaller organizations) are using the browser-based interface to view and print the data as well as manipulate and create exception reports to be sent back to the server.

Communication is achieved using the following protocols on the Internet:

- HTTP, HTTPS: for delivery of on-line data
- Sockets (SL), Secure Sockets (SSL): for message transfer

All traffic enters the enterprise systems through a firewall for security. Security is discussed in the following section.

On the enterprise side, the client applications first access a Web server. The Web Server handles the HTTP/HTTPS communication and invokes the server-side controls through an ASP page.

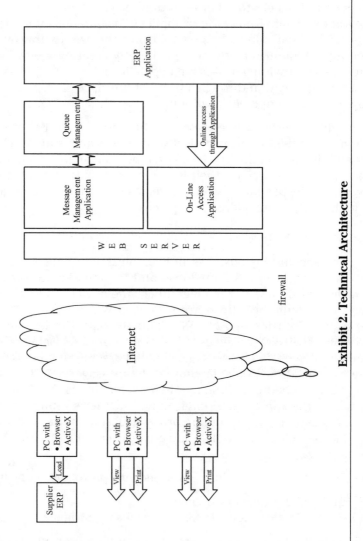

Exhibit 2. Technical Architecture

The on-line application (TopTier) intercepts the HTTP/HTTPS communication address to it and interprets the query. It then provides a result set and integrates the result set with an HTML template to be sent back to the client PC as an HTML page. The on-line access application communicates with the ERP application through the application API or through ODBC.

The message management application (WebSuite) communicates to the message queue using server-side ActiveX controls and FTP to send and receive files between systems. The message management application communicates with the ERP and other enterprise applications using a set of processes that can read and write messages to a shared mounted disk area.

The above system architecture supports a mechanism for transferring messages in a secure and reliable fashion as well as providing on-line access to data residing in the enterprise systems — all through a browser interface with minimal requirements from the supplier and minimal support requirements.

SECURITY

The are two categories of security that must be handled:

1. enterprise systems security from outside intrusion
2. data security for data communicated over the web

Security for the enterprise is intended to prevent unauthorized users from accessing data and potentially damaging enterprise systems and data. This is handled by various methods that are far too many to have a meaningful discussion in this chapter. One can review the steps taken to secure the system on this project; these are by no means the only or the complete set of measures to be taken. In addition each organization may have different security requirements. For this project the following steps were taken:

- Use a firewall that provided the following:
  - limitation on IP and PORT addresses
  - limitation on protocols allowed (HTTP, HTTPS, IP)
  - user Authentication at the firewall level
  - abstraction of Server IP address
- Authentication:
  - front-office application layer
  - back-office application layer
  - operating system layer
  - firewall layer
- Domain settings:
  - The Web server machine is not part of the enterprise domain
  - The Web server machine has IP access to other servers

TASK 4: MANAGING SUPPLY CHAIN INFORMATION

Data security is required to protect the information that is transferred between supplier and manufacturer over the public domain of the Internet. The intent is to secure the data from unauthorized eavesdropping. There are many methods to protect the data; these methods can be grouped into two main categories:

- Transferring data through a secure communication channel (SSL, HT-TPS). This method utilizes:
  - authentication
  - certificates
  - encryption
- Encryption of data. This method is typically used in conjunction with the previous method, but can be used on its own. There are various encryption algorithms available. The encryption strength (cipher strength), which can be defined as how difficult it would be to decrypt encrypted data without the keys, can vary and is designated in terms of number of bits (40 bit, 128 bit, etc.). This project employed Microsoft Crypto API, supported both by the Web server (IIS 4) and by the client browser (IE 4). The cipher strength selected was 40 bits to allow non-U.S. countries and Canada access to the application; 128-bit cipher strength is not available for browsers used outside of the United States and Canada.

CONCLUSION

Manufacturing organizations striving to reduce inventory levels and lead-times must integrate business processes and systems with their supply chain organization. E-commerce applications utilizing the Internet can be used to achieve integration across the supply chain with minimal cost and standard interfaces.

When implementing E-commerce applications, it is recommended to select application that can be used as an infrastructure to develop future business solutions to address new requirements. Selecting applications that provide technology solutions with a development platform, rather than applications that provide an integrated business solution, will provide a platform for development of future business applications as the use of E-commerce proliferates through the organization.

Chapter 47

The Future of Application Service Providers

Mahesh Raisinghani
Mike Kwiatkowski

Application service providers (ASPs) have received a large amount of attention in the information technology (IT) service industry and the financial capital markets. Numerous firms have made recent announcements concerning partnerships and service offerings aimed at corporate customers to outsource their business applications using the Internet as the medium to provide service.

Conceptually, ASPs have a great deal to offer customers (Exhibit 1). They can maintain applications such as e-mail, enterprise resource planning (ERP), and customer relationship management (CRM), while providing the business with higher levels of service by utilizing economies of scale in order to provide a quality software product at a lower cost to the organization. In particular, the ASP value proposition has particular value to small- and mid-sized enterprises (SMEs) that do not possess the IT infrastructure, staff, or capital to purchase high-end corporatewide applications such as SAP, PeopleSoft, or Siebel. The goal of ASPs is to enable customers to use mission-critical enterprise applications in a better, faster, and more cost-efficient manner.

A quote from Scott McNealy, CEO of Sun Microsystems, is typical of the enthusiasm industry leaders have for the ASP service model: "Five years from now, if you're a CIO with a head for business, you won't be buying computers anymore. You won't buy software either. You'll rent all your resources from a service provider."

FUTURE IMPLICATIONS

Role of ASPs in the 21st Century Organization

Many business scholars have attempted to define the shape and structure of effective organizations in the future. Overall, they unanimously predict technology will dramatically change the delivery methods of products and services. Organizational structures such as the "networked organizations" and "virtual organizations" will prosper.

Networked organizations will differ from traditional hierarchical organization in a few major ways. First, the structure will be more informal, flatter, and loosely structured. Second, employees will be more empowered, treated as an asset, and their contributions will be measured based on how they function as a team. Last, information will be shared and available both internally and externally to the organization.

The ASP industry model can facilitate each of the major areas in the networked organization. Structurally, ASPs are a perfect fit for organizations that desire to become flatter and loosely structured because all of the IT staff overhead and data center infrastructure required to support the business is outsourced to the ASP. The increased need for employee empowerment to make decisions requires additional knowledge. This knowledge must be provided to employees through advanced information systems such as intelligent systems and the Internet. ASPs have the potential to provide the expert and intelligent systems required for supporting "knowledge workers." Historically, these systems have been cost prohibitive to install and maintain. The ASP model lowers the cost by sharing the system with many users and capitalizing on economies of scale. Information sharing is more efficient via the ASP's delivery method than compared to traditional private networks or value-added networks. These networks required expensive lease lines and specialized telecommunications equipment for organizations to pass data and share information. In the ASP model, a business partner can access your systems via the Internet simply by pointing their browser to your ASP's host site.

The virtual corporation (VC) is an organizational structure that is gaining momentum in today's economy, especially in the "E-economy" or world of electronic commerce. It can be defined as an organization composed of several business partners sharing costs and resources for the purpose of producing a product or service. Each partner brings strength to the organization such as creativity, market expertise, logistical knowledge, or low cost. The ASP model has a strong value proposition for this type of organization because it can provide the application expertise, technology, and knowledge at a lower cost.

Exhibit 2 lists the major attributes of VCs and highlights how ASPs can fit the attribute and service the organization's needs. The continued evolu-

Exhibit 1. ASP Provider Summary

Company Name	Products and Services Offered			Service Delivery Method
Applicast, Inc.	Agile Microsoft SAP	Siebel Tumbleweed		GTE Data Services
Breakwaway Solutions, Inc.	Strategy Consulting Esolutions	Application hosting Systems Integration		Co-location at 11 data centers with Exodus and Level 3
Corio, Inc.	Broadvision Cognos and E.piphany Commerce One	PeopleSoft SAP Siebel		Co-location with Exodus and Coincentric for Web-hosting
EbaseOne Corporation	Great Plans Logility Sales Marimba	Microsoft Logix		Co-location with Level 3
EOnline, Inc.	SAP Financials HR CRM			Owns data center, partners with UUNET for connectivity
Futurelink Corporation	Corel Epicor Great Plains Microsoft	Onyx Pivotal SalesLogix		Owns 2 data centers
Interliant, Inc.	Consulting Web-hosting Application outsourcing (numerous) AppsOnline.com			Owns 3 data centers
Interpath Communications	SAP Financials HR R/3			Owns a data center and an 850-mile fiber optic network from Atlanta to Washington, D.C.

Exhibit 1. ASP Provider Summary (*Continued*)

Company Name	Products and Services Offered		Service Delivery Method
Push, Inc.	Alliance HRMS Great Plains Microsoft	QuickBooks SalesLogix Solomon	Building "community ASP" centers throughout California
Qwest Cyber.Solutions	Ariba Captura Oracle	PeopleSoft SAP Siebel	Global network with 4 data centers
Surebridge, Inc.	Baan Epicor Great Plains	Microsoft OneSoft Solomon	Not disclosed
TeleComputing, Inc.	Microsoft Office Microsoft Exchange	Back Office E*biz	Co-location with UUNET
USInternetworking., Inc.	Ariba Broadbase Broadvision Lawson Microsoft	Oracle PeopleSoft Sagen Niku Siebel	Global network with 4 data centers
Xuma	Pre-integrated E-business solutions		Owns one data center
AristaSoft Corporation	Agile Clarify	JD Edwards Webridge	Co-location arrangement with Exodus
The LearningStation.com	Learning software from numerous education publishers		Owns 1 data center
TriZetto Group, Inc.	Healthcare software designed for PPMs, payors, and administrative and financial systems		Developed 2 data centers
Agillon	Provides a comprehensive customer management solution		Partnered with Exodus for data center services
Capstan Systems, Inc.	Provides a proprietary designed Web-based supply chain management solution		Partnered with Exodus for data center services

Company	Service	Infrastructure
EALITY, Inc.	Provides proprietary applications for day-to-day business functions not provided for in ERP systems	Partnered with Pilot Network Services for data center services
Employease, Inc.	Provides Internet based human resources, employee benefits, and payroll administrative functions	Co-location arrangement with NextLink
UpShot.com	Developed a Web-based sales force automation solution	Partnered with Exodus for data center services
Critical Path, Inc.	Provides Web-based messaging and collaboration solutions	Hosting arrangements with Exodus, Level 3, and Qwest
Mail.com, Inc.	Provides advanced Internet messaging services	Co-location arrangement with Telehouse
NetEx	Provides secure e-mail delivery services	Owns 1 data center
WebEx	Developed a real-time, Internet-based collaboration service that enables participants to conduct meetings and presentations on-line	Co-locates servers with Frontier Global Services
AmQwest, Inc.	Enables and provides advanced hosting and monitoring services	Owns 1 of the largest data centers in the South
Centerbeam, Inc.	Provides a subscription computer service designed to meet the infrastructure needs of small businesses; offers five key components: office infrastructure, data center services, private Internet access, business services, and customer care	All infrastructure provided via a "plug and play" offering to businesses
Digex	Provides advanced Web and application hosting services	Operates 4 Internet SmartCenters located in Maryland and California
Jamcracker	Provides the service as an ASP aggregator through its portal	Co-location agreement with Exodus
NaviSite, Inc.	Provides Web-hosting, E-commerce, and hight availability solutions	Owns 4 data centers

tion of VCs presents ASPs with unique opportunities. The first is a greater need for messaging, collaboration software, and tools. Some ASPs are currently targeting the corporate e-mail application, with many firms outsourcing mail services for large ISPs at this time. A few firms such as Interliant and Accenture offer Lotus Notes via the Internet to fit the niche for collaboration and groupware applications. However, the majority of ASPs are attempting to host Microsoft Exchange as their performed collaboration platform. Hotoffice.com is an example of a firm that is offering a variety of document management, calendaring and e-mail, bulletin boards, and online conferences in the SME market via a subscription model that starts at $12.95 per month.

Because partners of virtual corporations can be located anywhere, but will not relocate to join a VC, the need for interorganizational information systems (IOS) will grow. WSVs will need to address this need by developing systems that can be effectively utilized between organizations because currently most systems are primarily designed for a single firm use. Ease of integration and the use of Internet standards such as TCP/IP and XML by software vendors will allow ASPs to offer system access to many organizations in a secure and integrated environment.

These changes in organization structure will impact the current information technology organization (ITO) in numerous ways. The Gartner Group predicts: "IT organizations will transform from a provider of technology services into an organization that is responsible for business processes since business processes drive the need for information technology."

POTENTIAL IT MANAGEMENT ISSUES

According to the Gartner Group, "The ASP model has emerged as one of the foremost global IT trends driving phenomenal growth in the delivery of applications services. Long term, this model will have a significant impact on IT service delivery and management." IT organizations will have to deal with a variety of changes in the culture of the organization, make infrastructure improvements, and manage the people, technology, and business processes.

Culture Changes

With the increased adaptation of the ASP delivery model, IT organizations will need to adapt culturally to being less responsible for proving technology internally and begin embracing the concept that other organizations can provide a higher degree of value. Most IT professionals take a negative view of outsourcing because successful adaptation of this principle means fewer projects to manage, fewer staff members to hire, and a perception of a diminishing role in the organization. Self-preservation instincts of most IT managers will view this trend with negativism and

Exhibit 2. Strengths of ASPs in the Virtual Corporation

Attribute of VC	Strengths of ASPs
Excellence — Each partner brings its core competence and an all-star winning team is created. No single company can match what the virtual corporation can achieve.	By providing in-depth application expertise, technology experience, and the ability to provide high levels of service, the ASP organization is suited to deliver the technology excellence sought by VCs.
Utilization — Resources of the business partner are frequently underutilized or utilized in a merely satisfactory manner. In the virtual corporation, resources can be put to use more profitability, thus providing a competitive advantage.	The economies of scale that allow ASPs to provide low-cost service, require a high degree of system utilization; therefore they are incented to partner with VCs to ensure their resources are efficiently utilized.
Opportunism — The partnership is opportunistic. A VC is organized to meet a market opportunity.	To capitalize on opportunities in the marketplace, VCs can utilize ASPs to implement required support systems quickly.
Lack of borders — It is difficult to identify the boundaries of a virtual corporation; it refines the traditional boundaries. For example, more cooperation among competitors, suppliers, and customers makes it difficult to determine where one company ends and another begins in the VC partnership.	The ASP business model is characterized by many business partnerships between software vendor, systems integrators, and infrastructure providers. VC partnerships can leverage a shared data center or shared data center or shared application. Because costs are determined by number of users, technology costs can be shared among partners and not owned by one firm in the VC.
Trust — Business partners in a VC must be far more reliant on each other and require more trust than ever before. They share a sense of destiny.	As organizations evolve into more trusting environments, this will lower some of the barriers to ASP adoption. ASPs must focus on maintaining good service levels to ensure VC customers continue to trust an ASP with valuable data and mission-critical systems.
Adaptability to change — The VC can adapt quickly to the environment changes in a given industry or market.	ASPs in today's marketplace are a constantly evolving duet to the uncertainty in the industry and the pace of technology changes. Successful ASP organizations will possess an innate ability to change and assist their customers in implementing technology rapidly.
Technology — Information technology makes the VC possible. A networked information system is a must.	Because technology is a critical component and VCs do not want to build their own IT infrastructure, the ASP service delivery model or outsourcing is the only alternative. Additionally, the ASP model is a networked delivery system and therefore a perfect match for the VC.

skepticism. Therefore, increased trust of service providers and software companies will be required to effectively manage the ASP relationships of the future.

In order for IT professionals to survive the future changes ASPs promise, they must evolve from programming and technical managers to vendor managers. Additionally, they should think strategically and help position their organization to embrace the competitive advantages an ASP can provide with packaged software and quick implementations.

IT leaders will need to gain a better understanding of the business they support rather than implementing the latest and greatest technologies. With an increased understanding of the business drivers and the need for improvements in efficiency and customers service, IT practitioners must focus increasingly on business processes and understanding how the technology provided by an ASP can increase the firm's competitive advantage. Reward and compensation programs should be modified whereby IT compensation plans are based on achieving business objectives rather than successful completion of programming efforts or systems integration projects. IT managers should work to improve communication skills because they are required to effectively interact within the VCs and the many partnerships they represent.

Infrastructure Changes

There are five major components of the information infrastructure. These components consist of computer hardware, general-purpose software, networks and communication facilities (including the Internet and intranets), databases, and information management personnel. Adaptation of the ASP delivery model will require changes in each of these areas.

Typically organizations deploy two types of computer hardware, desktop workstations and larger server devices, which run applications and support databases. The emerging ASP model will impact both types of hardware. First, desktop systems can become "thinner" because the processing and application logic is contained in the ASP's data center. The desktop will also become increasingly standardized with organizations taking more control of software loaded on the workstation to ensure interoperability with the applications provided via the Internet. Second, there will a decreasing need to purchase servers or mainframe computing environments, because the ASP will provide these services. Also, support staff and elaborate data center facilities will not be required in ASP adopters.

General-purpose software such as transaction processing systems, departmental systems, and office automation systems will reside at the ASP and be accessed via the network. End-user knowledge of the system's functionality will be required, however, and users will gain the knowledge through training provided by the ASP rather than the in-house application support staff. Programming modifications and changes will be reduced because the low customization approach of ASPs will force organizations to change business processes and map themselves to the application.

While the expenditures in hardware and software dwindle, infrastructure investment will be focused on better communication networks. The next generation networks will be required to support many types of business applications such as voice, data, and imaging, as well as the convergence of data and voice over a single network. The continued improvements in fiber optical technology and increased use of high-speed networking protocols such as ATM will over time provide an Information Superhighway.

Network infrastructures must be flexible to accommodate new standards such as TCP/IP version 6, which is the next generation of Internet telecommunications language that improves the speed and security of networked communications. People required to support these advanced networks will be in high demand and difficult to retain in-house. However, ASP providers are not likely to offer internal network support directly, but may partner with third-party firms to manage the internal networks of an organization. Today, traditional telephone and network equipment providers do offer turnkey solutions in an outsourced delivery model today.

Perhaps the most critical piece of an organization's infrastructure whose role is not fully defined in the ASP model is the role of data. The speed and direction of how this issue is addressed will be critical to the ASP industry's future growth. Typically data architecture was a centralized function along with communications and business architecture. The emergence of the improved Internet data standards such as XML (or extensible mark-up languages) will be a factor in the adaptation of ASPs due to the improvements XML promises in easing the integration of different systems. Most corporate data is not in XML format. This presents an integration issue for organizations to synthesize two different data architectures namely, Internet data in XML format and legacy data. However, given the advanced tools and systems employed to support data warehousing today, this issue can be resolved.

Another large concern for many corporations is the security of the data because many consider customer data one distinct competitive advantage they possess in their marketplace. Given the importance of knowledge workers in the 21st century economy, how well an organization manages to transform data into information and then information into knowledge may be the single most strategic advantage a firm may possess. Considering that this data might provide a strategic advantage and should be considered vital to the "core business," many firms will not want to outsource the care and management of the data to an outside firm.

CONCLUSION: THE FUTURE OF THE ASP INDUSTRY

To achieve the forecasted success, ASPs will need to gain acceptance in the larger more diversified organization by delivering on the promises made to existing customers. Of particular importance are the quality of service (QOS) issues ASPs will face as they add more clients. Most industry observers agree that the industry will undergo a consolidation period over the next few years because the larger software and system integration firms will purchase ASPs with market share and delivery knowledge, in an attempt to catch up in the market. Also, infrastructure companies will begin to acquire the successful start-ups to improve profit margins and expand their current business offerings.

The ASP industry future is heavily dependent on software vendors to:

- Provide Internet-architectured applications
- Develop formal ASP distribution channel programs
- Refrain from competing against these channels
- Implement new licensing programs for the ASP customer

The evolution of contracts from a cost per user to a cost per minute service agreement is also hypothesized; however, an ASP organization will require an exceptionally large customer base to offer this type of billing program. Additionally, software packages must be flexible to allow the mass customization required and provide all the functionality many different types of organizations require. A large opportunity exists in other specialized business applications not addressed by the ERP and CRM vendors. ASPs who can partner with "best of breed" solutions for an industry, possess the industry experience, and have an existing distribution channel will succeed. Therefore, the current FSP may evolve into more vertical solutions providers which segment their offerings along industry specific lines.

"Renting" applications to consumers is a topic not specifically addressed in this chapter, but it holds the potential to be a large market, serviced by existing ISPs such as AOL or vendors of popular consumer-oriented software such as games, personal finance, and specialty applications. Given the low licensing cost of these products and the continual price decreases in the hardware to store and run these applications on a home PC, there is currently not a large financial case for this delivery model. However, as the Information Superhighway grows, and bandwidth becomes cheaper than media storage devices, the economics of continually purchasing upgrades and upgrading hardware to execute the programs might foster an application-renting approach.

Lastly, the emerging trend of Internet appliances and the "smart home" could become the first large-scale application to be offered directly to consumers via a service model. With the increased complexity of integrating all the systems and devices in the home, there will be software vendors building applications to support the demand. The application will allow consumers to manage appliances, heating systems, cooling systems, security, lighting, telecommunications, and entertainment systems from a Internet-based application via a cell phone, PDA, or Internet appliance located in the home or office.

Notes

1. Caldwell, Bruce, Outsourcing deals with competition, *Information Week,* (735): 140, May 24, 1999.
2. Caldwell, Bruce, Revamped Outsourcing, *Information Week,* (731): 36, May 24, 1999.
3. Dean, Gary, *ASPs: The Net's Next Killer App,* J.C. Bradford & Company, March 2000.
4. Gerwig, Kate, Business: the 8th layer, Apps on Tap: Outsourcing hits the Web, *NSW,* September 1999.
5. Hurley, Margaret and Schaumann, Folker, KPMG Survey: The Outsourcing Decision, *Information Management and Computer Security,* May 4, 1997, pp. 126–132.
6. Internet Research Group, *Infrastructure Application Service Providers,* Los Altos, CA, 2000.
7. Johnson, G. and Scholes, K., *Exploring Corporate Strategy: Text and Cases,* Prentice-Hall, Hemel Hempstead, U.K.
8. Larson, Kent D., The Role of Service Level Agreements in IT Service Delivery, *Information Management and Computer Security,* June 3, 1998, pp. 128–132.
9. Leong, Norvin, *Applications Service Provider: A Market Overview,* Internet Research Group, Los Altos, CA. 2000.
10. Lonsdale, C. and Cox, A., Outsourcing: Risks and Rewards, *Supply Management,* July 3, 1997, pp. 32–34.
11. Makris, Joanna, Hosting Services: Now Accepting Applications, *Data Communications,* March 21, 1999.
12. Mateyaschuk, Jennifer, Leave the Apps to US, *Information Week,* October 11, 1999.
13. McIvor, Ronan, A Practical Framework for Understanding the Outsourcing Process, *Supply Chain Management: An International Journal,* 5 (1), 2000, pp. 22–36.
14. PA Consulting Group, *International Strategic Sourcing Survey 1996,* London.
15. Porter, M.E., *Competitive Advantage: Creating and Sustaining Superior Performance,* Free Press, New York, 1985.
16. Prahald, C.K. and Hamel, G., The Core Competence of the Corporation, *Harvard Business Review,* July–August, pp. 79–91.
17. Teridan, R., ASP Trends: The ASP Model Moves Closer to Prime Time, *Gartner Group* Research Note, January 11, 2000.
18. Turban, E., McLean, E., and Wetherbe, J., *Information Technology for Management: Making Connections for Strategic Advantage,* John Wiley & Sons, 1999.
19. Williamson, O.E., *Markets and Hierarchies,* Free Press, New York, 1975.
20. Williamson, O.E., *The Economic Institutions of Capitalism: Firms, Markets, and Relational Contracting,* Free Press, New York, 1985.
21. Yoon, K. P. and Naadimuthu, G., A make-or-buy decision analysis involving imprecise data, *International Journal of Operations and Production Management,* 14 (2), 1994, pp. 62–69.

Chapter 48

Refurbishing Legacy Systems: An Effective Approach to Maintenance

William F. Lenihan

If IS is to play an active role in the effort to better control cost, then system refurbishment should be included as part of an overall cost-reduction plan. This chapter specifically targets legacy systems by presenting an approach for maintaining and repositioning these aging systems to make them more cost-effective and competitive. IS can similarly use this approach to achieve substantial benefits from refurbishing newer systems that have been developed using loose standards or that have experienced several modifications.

INTRODUCTION

In its effort to support the business need for more information to be available in less time, the IS department has implemented a variety of proprietary technologies, developed new systems, and added capabilities to existing ones. The amount of systems integration, development, and maintenance activity required to satisfy these demands has left IS with little time to properly care for the base of old and rapidly aging systems. These legacy systems are often in a state of disrepair, suffering from the use of outmoded technologies and years of changes at the hands of different IS personnel who used different programming styles and formats. For many companies, these systems have been left to age with few (if any) improvements to the program structure, complexity, or hardware and software technologies.

Currently, however, the IS department's new directives are to reduce cost and improve financial performance. Departmental budgets are being cut, business processes and computer systems are being reengineered, application systems are moving away from a centralized data center and distributed to the operating divisions, and IS is being outsourced or downsized. When the cost associated with maintaining legacy systems is evaluated, it is increasingly apparent that, perhaps more than ever, management must seriously consider system refurbishment as an integral component of cost containment and business process reengineering, and as a baseline for outsourcing, systems reengineering, and downsizing activities. This chapter presents an effective approach to maintaining and repositioning legacy systems to align them with the goal of systems that are cost-effective and competitive.

SYSTEM REFURBISHMENT AND BUSINESS PROCESS REENGINEERING

The increasing popularity of business process reengineering has placed greater pressure on IS to keep pace with similar systems reengineering projects. Companies can adopt an approach to maintain and reposition their legacy systems to make them more cost-effective and competitive so that they can support activities associated with business process reengineering.

Legacy systems share similar characteristics regardless of industry, business, or application focus. Usually, these systems are more than seven years old, may or may not be mission-critical, use outmoded or different proprietary technologies, have poorly structured program code, have ineffective reporting systems, and use system and human resources inefficiently. To further complicate these systems, the original design and development team may have changed, leaving the current support team without a complete understanding of the detailed operation of the system. In other words, legacy systems are usually the systems that everyone fears and no one wants to support.

How do companies determine the strategic contribution of their legacy systems? How do they know which systems to keep? What if the operations or development staff is outsourced? Is it possible to convert a legacy system into a more competitive tool that allows a company to provide higher-quality products and services in less time? The answers to these questions can be found in a refurbishment approach that has been successfully implemented in a variety of businesses and industries.

THE REFURBISHMENT PROCESS

The refurbishment process encompasses (encapsulates) an entire system, which may be of any size or complexity. The refurbishment process also provides IS with the ability to evaluate its functional and technical attributes and recondition the system to improve cost and maintainability.

The process comprises five key phases: preliminary inventory analysis, encapsulation, application analysis, production standardization, and design recovery. Each phase is defined briefly as follows:

1. *Preliminary inventory analysis.* This phase determines the scope of the refurbishment effort (i.e., which systems to include) and establishes the priorities of the systems to be refurbished.
2. *Encapsulation.* This phase generates an inventory of the components of a system.
3. *Application analysis.* This phase evaluates applications according to three aspects:
   a. Functional fulfillment
   b. Technical quality
   c. Fit with the IS strategic plan
4. *Production standardization.* This phase eliminates many past mistakes and provides an understanding of the functional and technical aspects of the system.
5. *Design recovery.* This phase provides detailed system documentation and positions the application software to be reverse and forward engineered.

The results of the refurbishment effort, together with other forces that influence a system's strategic direction, are used to determine the refurbishment strategy for a system. The key phases of refurbishment and the forces that influence the refurbishment strategy are illustrated in Exhibit 1. Application refurbishment improves the performance and maintainability of a system while also incorporating internal and external business forces.

PRELIMINARY INVENTORY ANALYSIS

Before jumping into the refurbishment process, a preliminary analysis of the existing systems is performed to determine the overall scope of the refurbishment effort. This analysis is an abbreviated version of the encapsulation and application analysis phases.

During this initial phase, the inventory of applications is quantified and analyzed to determine which systems should be included or excluded from the project. At this point, it is not necessary to develop a detailed inventory of each system's components. However, IS should determine the approximate number of executable jobs, procedures, and programs for each system selected.

While conducting this analysis, IS has the opportunity to determine the relative state of each system (i.e., functional and technical quality) as well as to estimate the amount of time required to complete the four remaining project phases. From this analysis, a detailed project work plan can be developed for the remaining phases of the project.

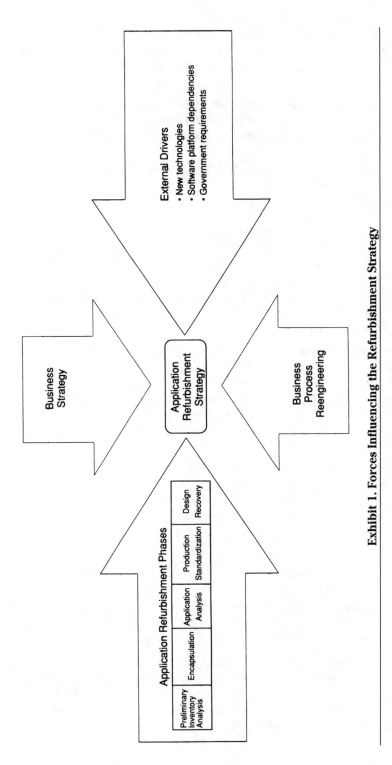

Exhibit 1. Forces Influencing the Refurbishment Strategy

ENCAPSULATION

The encapsulation process is a key aspect of refurbishment because it is this process that ensures that the system components (e.g., job control program source, load modules, copybooks) are identified. An accurate component inventory must be developed before beginning the analysis. Although it is possible to include components in the inventory after the analysis has begun, it may be costly to reproduce the analysis a number of times.

After the inventory is completed, it may be necessary to verify that modules that are executed in production are the same as those identified in the inventory. There are several ways to verify the quality and integrity of the inventory, including reviewing source edit statistics, equating source modules to load modules, and systems testing.

The extent of the effort required to develop an accurate inventory is inversely related to the quality of the controls provided within the IS change management procedures. For example, a change management procedure that incorporates excellent controls requires less inventory and verification effort than one with few controls.

Encapsulation identifies all possible system components and shakes out those that are not a part of the system. Although several software tools are available to assist in the process of defining the component inventory, the use of a combination of both manual and automated analyses provides the most accurate inventory in the least amount of time. This is accomplished by digging through the system manually (system utilities may be used) to identify libraries that contain misplaced system components and by using the automated tools to piece together the remaining components.

By completing the encapsulation process, IS establishes a definitive inventory of all system components. The inventory alone may reduce the IS cost associated with analyzing the production and departmental libraries and any other additional activities that may be required to locate the components that satisfy a user's special request. In addition, the accuracy of the systems analysis required by a new development or maintenance activity may be improved because all of the system components have been identified and are easily located.

APPLICATION ANALYSIS

Although refurbishment presents a significant opportunity for IS to effectively improve the performance, maintainability, and cost of legacy systems, it would be shortsighted not to include a more strategic review of these systems. This review should initially evaluate these systems according to three primary attributes:

- Ability to support the functional requirements of the system's users.

- System design and use of technology
- Conformance with the IS strategy

The evaluation of these three criteria provides insight into the value that the system provides to the business. A system that adequately supports the business needs of the user but employs outmoded technology is more valuable than one that provides little or no functional support to an organization but uses all the latest technology.

To complete the analysis, the functional and technical attributes of the system are mapped to the IS strategic systems plan to determine the refurbishment strategy for the system, as shown in the System Target Chart in Exhibit 2.

The forces that influence the refurbishment strategy must be considered because they may directly impact the order in which revitalization activities are performed. For example, if the business strategy is to outsource IS operations, management should focus the IS effort on those activ-

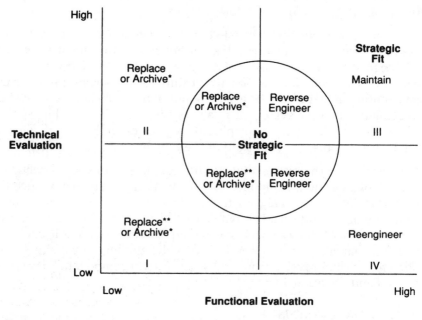

Notes:
*Functional obsolescence
**Technical obsolescence

The chart shows four quadrants (I to IV) and eight sectors (two sectors per quadrant). Sector positioning is based on the system's strategic fit. Systems whose core competencies support the IS strategy are placed outside the circle (the bull's-eye); those that do not support the IS strategy are placed inside the circle, regardless of the system's functional or technical rating.

Exhibit 2. System Target Chart

ities that will maximize resource use. This focus will achieve lower operational costs for production systems. Specific areas of focus would include central processing unit (CPU) utilization, disk and tape utilization, online performance, database efficiency, system backup and restore procedures, and documentation. The sector in which a system is placed in Exhibit 2 provides a basis for formulating a system refurbishment strategy.

Targeting the Refurbishment Strategy

The System Target Chart is a single representation of two separate charts that have been blended to communicate refurbishment alternatives for one or more systems. One chart evaluates the technical and functional attributes of the system, and the second chart evaluates the system's core competencies to determine the system's strategic importance. When combined, the charts form four quadrants (I to IV) and eight sectors (i.e., two sectors per quadrant, one that fits IS strategy and one that does not). Positioning a system within a sector provides a basis for formulating a refurbishment strategy.

The placement of a system within a quadrant represents the functional and technical capacity of the system. Within a quadrant, sector positioning is based on the system's strategic importance. Systems whose core competencies support the IS strategy are placed outside the circle (the bull's-eye) and those that do not support the IS strategy are placed inside the circle, regardless of the system's technical or functional rating.

Each system is rated on the basis of the information gathered during the preliminary inventory analysis and encapsulation phases of refurbishment. In general, systems that fall into sectors I or II provide little functional support to an organization and therefore are considered less valuable than systems that fall into sectors III or IV.

Quadrant I. Quadrant I of the Target Chart represents systems that provide little functional support to the business and use outmoded technologies or are poorly designed and constructed. Systems in this sector that provide functional support but are technically obsolete will be replaced, whereas the systems in this sector that are functionally obsolete (i.e., no longer support a business function) can be archived or deleted.

An example best illustrates this point. One organization maintained a system that relied on manual processes to collect revenue data in the form of paper receipts. It took 15 to 20 business days to enter the receipt information into the system using a data entry service bureau. The system was poorly designed, and the programs were unstructured and difficult to maintain. The users complained that the system forced them to iteratively print reports, compute adjustments on a microcomputer before entry to the system, and reprint the reports to determine the adjustment's net effect. In addition, analyzing and modifying the system reports took a great deal of time, and in many cases, the users had to resort to building a new spreadsheet or database system to produce their own reports.

Systems in a similar state of disrepair are fairly common. Quadrant I systems usually consume significant IS resources as well as increase user frustration. In the previous example, considerable time was required to create the manual receipts, audit the computerized reports to the manual receipts (what happens if a receipt is lost?), iteratively rerun and analyze reports after adjustments have been made, and develop new or maintain existing unstructured code to create or enhance reports. For this system alone, IS spent a total of one person-year responding to one-time user requests to modify or create reports. This effort was magnified by the fact that the system was supported by only three programmers. A thorough analysis would identify even more areas of cost associated with supporting such systems.

This system is currently being replaced with a new automated data collection system that uses a relational database on the mainframe. A new conversational interface is also to be written to assist users with the on-line processes, and all remaining programs are to be reengineered (using an automated program restructuring tool) to improve maintainability.

Quadrant II. Quadrant II of the Target Chart represents systems that provide little functional support to the business but use current technologies or are well designed and constructed. Technology, no matter how advanced, has little value unless it supports a business requirement. Generally speaking, systems that provide functional support to the business should be replaced; those that do not can be archived or deleted. However, for those systems that do not fulfill functional requirements, the best alternative may be to salvage and redeploy technology components to new or other existing systems.

Quadrant III. Systems that fall into Quadrant III or Quadrant IV (which is discussed in more detail in the next section) support the business functions performed by the organizations that use the system. They provide the greatest flexibility with regard to alternative system strategies because they provide more business support than Quadrant I and Quadrant II systems. Although both Quadrant III and Quadrant IV systems support the functional requirements of the business, only Quadrant III systems use current technologies, are well designed and constructed, and use IS resources efficiently.

Quadrant III represents systems that provide the best functional and technical support to the business. These systems are usually the most cost-effective users of IS resources. Supporting the strategic systems plan, Quadrant III systems are best positioned for the future and should continue to be maintained as usual. Those systems that fall within the bull's-eye are positioned to be reverse-engineered to take advantage of other technologies (e.g., hardware platform, database, or communications).

A simplified example of a Quadrant III system is an on-line purchasing system that satisfies the user's functional requirements, is well designed and coded (i.e., easy to maintain), and uses IS resources efficiently. If the system was based on an Integrated Data Management System database using the Canadian Independent Computing Services Association (CICSA) for communications that corresponded to the strategic systems plan, it would be positioned outside the Quadrant III bull's-eye and therefore would be maintained as is. If, however, the strategic systems plan called for a broad sweeping conversion to database 2 using CICSA, the system would be placed within the bull's-eye and the system would be reverse-engineered to convert the system to the new database architecture.

Quadrant IV. Quadrant IV systems satisfy the business functional requirements but do not score well on their design, code construction, or use of technology. The prognosis for systems in this sector is still positive, however. If a Quadrant IV system fits the strategic systems plan (i.e., its position is outside the bull's-eye), it would indicate that the technological components of the system support the strategy but that the system design or construction are difficult to maintain.

Systems that fall into this category are usually reengineered. In the context of the Target Chart only, computer systems reengineering differs from reverse-engineering in that reengineering operates on a system at the source-code level, whereas reverse-engineering operates on a system at a higher technical level (e.g., hardware platform, database architecture, or communication monitors). Reengineering implies improving the maintainability of a system by eliminating dead code, incorporating structured programming techniques, and adhering to IS standards for program development.

These program-level changes may be made using automated or manual methods. The use of automated tools speeds the modification process significantly. When using these tools, however, IS must review and test the regenerated source code to verify that system functionality is not altered. This method is the preferred approach for large source programs because manually converting large programs is extremely time-consuming and requires the same level of verification as the automated tools.

Quadrant IV systems that do not fit the strategic systems plan require more than just code-level modifications. These systems usually require conversion to a new database or other technical architecture. In this case, systems are usually reverse-engineered to reposition the system for the new architecture.

PRODUCTION STANDARDIZATION

The goal of production standardization is to revitalize the existing system after years of touch-up work performed by different IS personnel using different programming techniques and styles. The revitalization transforms the legacy system into one that performs better, is easier (i.e., more cost-effective) to maintain and operate, and uses resources more efficiently. Nearly every IS organization has at least one system that can benefit from this revitalization process.

The refurbishment process allows IS to approach the system from two directions simultaneously — from both a functional and technical perspective. A functional knowledge of the system is required to identify and document the business attributes that are supported by the system. The technical aspect of this two-pronged approach provides IS with detailed knowledge of the processing within the system and the information necessary to improve the maintainability and performance of the system. Obviously, the refurbishment of legacy systems and, in particular, production standardization cannot be performed in a vacuum.

To obtain an accurate functional understanding of the system, IS should meet with the system users to determine the functions performed by the organization, the information that is required by the organization, and the information that the organization currently receives from IS. The objectives are to determine the value that users place on the system and the positive and negative functional and technical attributes of the system.

Simultaneously, IS can initiate the activities that focus on analyzing and improving the technical aspects of the system. A preliminary analysis of the several systems in the inventory can be performed to determined the areas that might benefit most from the use of automated tools. A word of caution before purchasing the newest tools: it is essential to ensure that the tools perform the functions needed to perform the analysis. For example, some tools can restructure program source code to improve system maintainability, document the structure of the system, and document the system's input and output.

For one insurance company, this revitalization approach, and the use of a purchased software package, improved the monthly financial closing time from 25 days to 5 days. For another company, converting tape data sets to disk and improvements in the disaster recovery process (for one batch job) improved the processing time by nearly three hours.

When the revitalization effort is completed, IS has a system that is more cost-effective to maintain and operate and is better positioned to react to internal and external business forces, such as outsourcing, downsizing, business process reengineering, or changes in government regulations.

Production standardization provides significant benefits to IS and the business regardless of the priorities imposed by internal or external forces.

DESIGN RECOVERY

The final phase of a refurbishment effort is the design recovery phase. Design recovery captures certain elements of the current system design, incorporates these elements into a computer-aided software engineering (CASE) tool, and provides IS with the ability to accurately document the functional and technical aspects of the system. This repository of up-to-date system documentation improves systems analysis and maintenance time and cost, improves the learning curve for new IS personnel, and provides a basis for engineering these systems more competitively in a CASE environment.

The process of extracting and loading mainframe system design elements (i.e., program names and their relationships to other programs, data files and records, and data record attributes) to a microcomputer or mainframe-based CASE tool is not always straightforward. Automated analysis and documentation tools designed to pass this information to other products (e.g., CASE or data dictionary) are available; however, this is not necessarily a standard feature of these products. The element extraction process is simplified if this feature is available. Otherwise, an extraction program may be written to perform the extraction function. Currently, the extraction process applies to data elements only. The processing or logic aspect of a system cannot yet be extracted and passed to the CASE tool. Some vendors are trying to develop this logic link between the system and the CASE tool, but such products are not expected to be commercially available in the near future.

The documentation produced from this phase provides insight into the functional purpose of the system, the major components of the system, the technology used to provide system functionality, the organizations that use the system, and the interfaces to other systems. This documentation can be used to support forward engineering, downsizing, and other IS refurbishment strategies.

CONCLUSION

If IS is to play an active role in the effort to better control cost, then system refurbishment should be included as part of an overall cost-reduction plan. Although this chapter has specifically targeted legacy systems, IS can achieve substantial benefits from refurbishing newer systems that have been developed using loose standards or that have experienced several modifications.

Systems refurbishment presents IS management with an effective approach to maintenance because it reduces the operating cost of systems, improves system maintainability, and positions systems to support the IS strategy as well as activities associated with business process reengineering, outsourcing, and downsizing. Refurbishment may also avoid the cost of replacing a system with a purchased package that is in a similar state of disrepair. The approach and tools provided in this chapter were designed through experience, practice, and a few painful lessons, and they provide IS with the road map for accomplishing its performance objectives.

Section 6
Task 5: Making Money from the Supply Chain

Task 1, Designing Supply Chains for Strategic Advantage, covered the application of IT to improvement in competitive position. The authors in that section contended that "optimization" was insufficient for this task. But many, if not most, IT projects are undertaken with cost-reduction benefits as the primary goal. Justification procedures frequently demand it. Each of the chapters here focus on issues related to monetary paybacks from IT efforts. These benefits may derive from outright cuts in operating costs or improvements in top-line revenues and marketshare.

Chapter 49
Shifting to Distributed Computing

Richard Ross

Many of the top concerns of senior IS managers relate directly to the issues of distributing information technology to end users. The explosive rate at which information technology has found its way into the front office, combined with the lack of control by the IS organization (ostensibly the group chartered with managing the corporation's IT investment), has left many IS managers at a loss as to how they should best respond. The following issues are of special concern:

- Where should increasingly scarce people and monetary resources be invested?
- What skills will be required to implement and support the new environment?
- How fast should the transition from a centralized computing environment to a distributed computing environment occur?
- What will be the long-term impact of actions taken today to meet short-term needs?
- What will be the overall ability of the central IS group to deliver to new standards of service created by changing user expectations in a distributed computer environment?

The inability to resolve these issues is causing a conflict in many organizations. Particularly in large companies during the past decade, the rule of thumb for technology investment has been that the cost of not being able to respond to market needs will always outweigh the savings accrued from constraining technology deployment. This has resulted in a plethora of diverse and incompatible systems, often supported by independent IS organizations. In turn, these developments have brought to light another, even greater risk — that the opportunity cost to the corporation of not being able to act as a single entity will always outweigh the benefit of local flexibility.

0-8493-1273-6/02/$0.00+$1.50
© 2002 by CRC Press LLC

This conflict was demonstrated by a global retailer with sales and marketing organizations in many countries. To meet local market needs, each country had its own management structure with independent manufacturing, distribution, and systems organizations. The result was that the company's supply chain became clogged — raw materials sat in warehouses in one country while factories in another went idle; finished goods piled up in one country while store shelves were empty in others; costs rose as the number of basic patterns proliferated. Perhaps most important, the incompatibility of the systems prevented management from gaining an understanding of the problem and from being able to pull it all together at the points of maximum leverage, while leaving the marketing and sale functions a degree of freedom.

Another example comes from a financial service firm. The rush to place technology into the hands of traders has resulted in a total inability to effectively manage risk across the firm or to perform single-point client service or multi-product portfolio management.

WANTED — A NEW FRAMEWORK FOR MANAGING

The problem for IS managers is that a distributed computing environment cannot be managed according to the lessons learned during the last 20 years of centralized computing. First and foremost, the distributed computing environment is largely a result of the loss of control by the central IS group because of its inability to deliver appropriate levels of service to the business units. Arguments about the ever-declining cost of desktop technology are all well and good, but the fact of the matter is that managing and digesting technology is not the job function of users. If central IS could have met their needs, it is possible users would have been more inclined to forego managing their own systems.

Central IS's inability to meet those needs while stubbornly trying to deliver with centralized computing has caused users to go their own way. It is not just the technology that is at fault. The centralized computing skills themselves are not fully applicable to a distributed computing environment. For example, the underlying factors governing risk, cost, and quality of service have changed. IS managers need a new framework, one that helps them to balance the opportunity cost to the business unit against that to the company while optimizing overall service delivery.

DEFINING THE PROBLEM: A MODEL FOR DCE SERVICE DELIVERY

To help IS managers get a grip on the problem, this chapter proposes a model of service delivery for the distributed computing environment (DCE). This model focuses on three factors that have the most important influence on service as well as on the needs of the business units versus the corporation — risk, cost, and quality (Exhibit 1). Each factor is ana-lyzed to understand its cause and then to determine how best to reduce it (in the case of risk and cost) or increase it (as in quality).

Risk in any systems architecture is due primarily to the number of inde-pendent elements in the architecture (Exhibit 2). Each element carries its own risk, say for failure, and this is compounded by the risk associated with the interface between each element.

This is the reason that a distributed computing environment will have a greater operational risk than a centralized one — there are more indepen-dent elements in a DCE. However, because each element tends to be smaller and simpler to construct, a DCE tends to have a much lower project risk than a centralized environment. Thus, one point to consider in rightsizing should be how soon a system is needed. For example, a Wall Street system that is needed right away and has a useful competitive life of only a few years would be best built in a distributed computing environ-ment to ensure that it gets on-line quickly. Conversely, a manufacturing sys-tem that is not needed right away but will remain in service for years is probably better suited for centralization. One other difference between a distributed environment and a centralized environment is the impact of a particular risk. Even though a DCE is much more likely to have a system component failure, each component controls such a small portion of the overall system that the potential impact of any one failure is greatly reduced. This is important to take into account when performing disaster planning for the new environment.

Cost is largely a function of staffing levels (Exhibit 3). As the need for ser-vice increases, the number of staff members invariably increases as well. People are flexible and can provide a level of service far beyond that of automation. Particularly in a dynamic environment, in which the needs for response are ill-defined and can change from moment to moment, people are the only solution.

Unfortunately, staff is usually viewed as a variable cost, to be cut when the need for budget reductions arises. This results in a decrease in service delivered that is often disproportionately larger than the savings incurred through staff reductions.

Finally, quality is a subjective judgment, impossible to quantify, but the factor most directly related to the user's perception of service where infor-mation technology is concerned. In essence, the perception of quality is proportional to the user's response to three questions:

1. Can I accomplish my task?
2. Am I able to try new things to get the job done?
3. Am I being paid the attention I deserve?

Contributing Factor	How It Contributes
Risk	
Development methodologies	Description and rationalization of logic and points of integration
Training	Ability to design low-risk systems
Piloting	Testing of integration
Quality assurance procedures	Enforcement of testing
Use of standards	Standard integration points
Size of system	Number of integration points
Operating environment	Number of integration points
Degree of automation	Dependence on human factors
Requirements planning	Highlighting likely areas of risk
Disaster recovery planning	Highlighting likely areas of risk
Integration of help desk	Ability to view total operational environment
Number of systems	Number of integration points, amount of required knowledge
Number of architectures	Number of integration points
Volume of processing	Number of actions the system must perform in a given period of time
Dependence on network	Number of linkages between user and data or application
Rate of change in business	Rate of change of systems
Security	Introduction of unplanned conditions into system
Scalability	Number of integration points, number of architectures
Training	Ability of staff to react
Cost	
Number of personnel	Overall staff costs
Training of personnel	Price per person
Degree of automation of operational environment	Required personnel number
Standards use	Number of activities, required personnel number, economies
Number of architectures	Number of integration points
Pace of change within business	Pace of systems change
Service levels required	Personnel number, equipment levels
Degree of integration of applications	Integration points
Scalability of architecture	Number of architectures, integration points
Degree of centralization	Degree of standardization
Degree of user freedom	Number of activities, required personnel number
Performance monitoring	Proactive service
Number of business units supported	Staff numbers
Quality	
Standardization of environment	Acceptance by users
Number of personnel	Attention to users
Training of personnel	Ability to respond
Degree of user freedom	Flexibility
Applicability of service delivered to business	Responsiveness
Business process redesign	Appropriateness of application
Clearinghouse	Reduction in business unit overhead

Service Delivery

Exhibit 1. A Model of Service Delivery

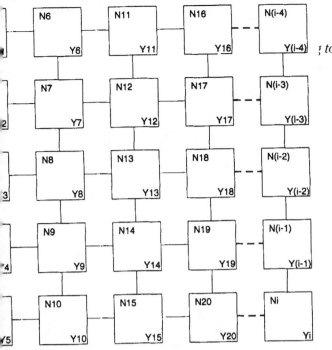

; to Distributed Computing

Component number

Component risk

ly independent components, total network risk is equivalent to the sum of
idual component risks, 1 to i. Thus, the way to minimize risk is either to mini-
e., to have a centralized computing environment) or to minimize Y for each
nt by standardizing on components with minimum risk profiles.

Exhibit 2. Optimization of Risk in a Network

One of the most important factors in the perceived quality of service
delivery is the ability of the support technology to work unnoticed.
Because of the similarities between this need and the way in which the U.S.
telephone network operates (you pick up the phone and the service is
invariably there), the term *dialtone* is used to describe such a background
level of operation.

One problem with highly functional IS environments is that users must
think about them to use them. This is not the case with the telephone system, which operates so dependably that we have integrated it into our routine working practices and use it without much conscious effort. The
phone companies maintain this level of usefulness by clearly separating
additional features from basic service and letting the customer add each
new feature as the customer desires.

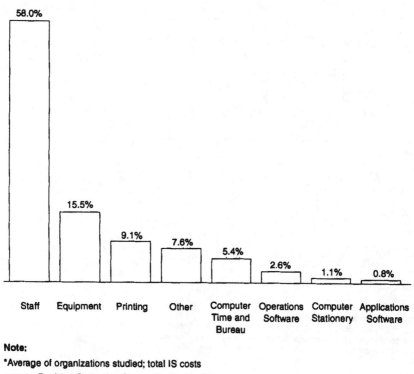

Note:

*Average of organizations studied; total IS costs

SOURCE: Decision Strategies Group, Greenwich CT

Exhibit 3. Cost Profile of the IS Function

Contrast this with the typical business system that represents an attempt to deliver a package of functions on day one and to continually increase its delivered functionality. The impact on users is that they are forced to continually adapt to changes, are not allowed to merge the use of the system into the background, and must continually stop delivering on their jobs just to cope with the technology. This coping might be as simple as looking something up in a manual or changing a printer cartridge, or it may mean not working at all while the system is rebooted.

Does anyone ever call up AT&T and congratulate it for keeping the nation's phones working that day? Of course not. Yet IS organizations are continually disappointed when users do not seem to appreciate that they have delivered 99.99 percent availability and a 24-hour help desk.

Complexity: The Barrier to Service Delivery

In general, the basic driver to each of the three service factors is complexity. Complexity increases risk by increasing the number of interfaces between system elements as well as the number of elements themselves. It increases cost by increasing the need for staff as the only way to deal with ill-defined environments. Finally, it affects quality by making it harder to provide those services upon which users base their perception of quality (i.e., dialtone and personal attention), in response to which even more staff are added.

This, then, is the paradoxical environment in which IS managers operate. To improve the quality of service, they find themselves increasing the risk and cost of the operation. Improved application delivery cycles result in more systems to manage. End-user development tools and business unit-led development increase the number of architectures and data formats. Increasing access to corporate data through networks increases the number of interfaces. Conversely, trying to improve the risk and cost aspects, typically through standardization of the environment, usually results in decreased levels of service delivered because of the constraints placed on user freedom. This paradox did not exist in the good old days of centralized computing, when the IS organization dictated the service level.

ADVICE FOR MANAGING DISTRIBUTED COMPUTING

The measure of success in a distributed computing environment is the ability to deliver service through optimizing for the factors of risk, cost, and quality while meeting the needs of both the business units and the corporation. It sounds like a tall order but it is not impossible. There are five key practices involved in corporate information processing:

1. Manage tightly, but control loosely.
2. Organize to provide on three levels.
3. Choose one standard — even a single bad one is better than none or many good ones.
4. Integrate data at the front end — don't homogenize on the back end.
5. Minimize the use of predetermined architectures.

Manage Tightly, Control Loosely

The situation for the Allied paratroopers at the Bulge was grim. Vastly outnumbered, outgunned, and in a logistically poor location, they faced a greater likelihood of total annihilation than of any sort of victory. Yet they managed to hold out for days, waiting for reinforcements and beating an orderly retreat when they finally came.

In Korea, the First Marine Division at Chosin Reservoir and the Second Infantry Division at Kanu-ri faced the Chinese backlash from the UN decision to cross the 38th parallel. The Marines retreated in good order, bringing their dead and wounded and all their equipment with them and disabling between a quarter and a third of all the Chinese troops along the way. The army in Korea, in contrast, suffered many casualties, lost most of its equipment, and escaped as a scattered bunch of desperate men.

What do these battle stories signify for the manager of a distributed computing environment? They highlight the need for flexible independence at the front lines, based on a solid foundation of rules and training and backed up with timely and appropriate levels of support. The army at the Battle of the Bulge reacted flexibly to the situation at hand; in addition, they were backed by rigorous training that reinforced standards of action as well as by a supply chain that made action possible. In contrast, the army in Korea suffered from a surfeit of central command, which clogged supply lines and rendered the front-line troops incapable of independent action.

In the distributed computing environment, the users are in the thick of battle, reacting with the best of their abilities to events moment by moment. IS can support its troops in a way that allows them to react appropriately or can make them stop and call for a different type of service while the customers get more and more frustrated.

BPR and Metrics. Two tools that are key to enabling distributed management are business process redesign (BPR) and metrics. BPR gets the business system working first, highlights the critical areas requiring support, builds consensus between the users and the IS organization as to the required level of support, and reduces the sheer number of variables that must be managed at any one time. In essence, applying BPR first allows a company to step back and get used to the new environment.

Without a good set of metrics, there is no way to tell how effective IS management has been or where effort needs to be applied moment to moment. The metrics required to manage a distributed computing environment are different from those IS is used to. With central computing, IS basically accepted that it would be unable to determine the actual support delivered to any one business. Because centralized computing environments are so large and take so long to implement, their cost and performance are spread over many functions. For this reason, indirect measurements were adopted when speaking of central systems, measures such as availability and throughput.

But these indirect measurements do not tell the real story of how much benefit a business might derive from its investment in a system. With distributed computing, it is possible to allocate expenses and effort not only to a given business unit but to an individual business function as well. IS must take advantage of this capability by moving away from the old measurements of computing performance and refocusing on business metrics, such as return on investment.

Pricing should be used as a tool to encourage users to indulge in behavior that supports the strategic direction of the company. For example, an organization used to allow any word processing package that the users desired. It then reduced the number of packages it would support to two, but still allowed the use of any package. This resulted in an incurred cost to the IS organization due to help desk calls, training problems, and system hangs. The organization eventually settled on one package as a standard, gave it free to all users, and eliminated support for any other package. The acceptance of this standard package by users was high, reducing help calls and the need for human intervention. Moreover, the company was able to negotiate an 80 percent discount over the street price from the vendor, further reducing the cost.

In addition to achieving a significant cost savings, the company was able to drastically reduce the complexity of its office automation environment, thus allowing it to deliver better levels of service.

Organize to Provide Service on Three Levels

The historical IS shop exists as a single organization to provide service to all users. Very large or progressive companies have developed a two-dimensional delivery system: part of the organization delivers business-focused service (particularly applications development), and the rest acts as a generic utility. Distributed computing environments require a three-dimensional service delivery organization. In this emerging organization model, one dimension of service is for dialtone, overseeing the technology infrastructure. A second dimension is for business-focused or value-added service, ensuring that the available technology resources are delivered and used in a way that maximizes the benefit to the business unit. The third dimension involves overseeing synergy, which means ensuring that there is maximum leverage between each business unit and the corporation.

Dialtone IS services lend themselves to automation and outsourcing. They are complex, to a degree that cannot be well managed or maintained by human activity alone. They must be stable, as this is the need of users of these services. In addition, they are nonstrategic to the business and lend themselves to economies of scale and, hence, are susceptible to outsourcing (Exhibits 4 and 5).

Value-added services should occur at the operations as well as at the development level. For example, business unit managers are responsible for overseeing the development of applications and really understanding the business. This concept should be extended to operational areas, such as training, maintenance, and the help desk. When these resources are placed in the business unit, they will be better positioned to work with the users to support their business instead of making the users take time out to deal with the technology.

The third level of service — providing maximum leverage between the business unit and the corporation — is perhaps the most difficult to main-

Common Operational Problem	Responsiveness to Automation
Equipment hangs	●
Network contention	◑
Software upgrades	●
Equipment upgrades	○
Disaster recovery	●
Backups	●
Quality assurance of new applications	●
Equipment faults (e.g., print cartridge replacement, disk crash)	○
Operator error (e.g., forgotten password, kick out plug)	○
Operator error (e.g., not understanding how to work application)	●

Responsiveness
High   ●
Medium ◑
Low   ○

SOURCE: Interviews and Decision Strategies Group analysis

Exhibit 4. Responsiveness of Operations to Automation

tain and represents the greatest change in the way IS does business today. Currently, the staff members in charge of the activities that leverage across all business units are the most removed from those businesses. Functions such as strategic planning, test beds, low-level coding, and code library development tend to be staffed by technically excellent people with little or no business knowledge. IS managers must turn this situation around and recruit senior staff with knowledge of the business functions, business process redesign, and corporate training. These skills are needed to take the best of each business unit, combine it into a central core, and deliver it back to the business.

Choose One Standard

In the immortal words of the sneaker manufacturer, "Just do it." If the key to managing a distributed computing environment is to reduce com-

Dialtone Function	Applicability
Equipment maintenance	●
Trouble calls	●
Help desk	●
Installations	●
Moves and changes	●
Billing	◑
Accounting	◑
Service level contracting	○
Procurement	○
Management	○

Applicability
High ●
Medium ◑
Low ○

SOURCE: Interviews and Decision Strategies Group analysis

Exhibit 5. Applicability of Outsourcing to Dialtone

plexity, then implementing a standard is the thing to do. Moreover, the benefits to be achieved from even a bad standard, if it helps to reduce complexity, will outweigh the risks incurred from possibly picking the wrong standard. The message is clear: there is more to be gained from taking inappropriate action now than from waiting to take perfect action later.

It should be clear that IT is moving more and more toward commodity status. The differences between one platform and another will disappear over time. Even if IS picks a truly bad standard, it will likely merge with the winner in the next few years, with little loss of investment. More important, the users are able to get on with their work. In addition, it is easier to move from one standard to the eventual winner than from many.

Even if you pick the winner, there is no guarantee that you will not suffer a discontinuity. IBM made its customers migrate from the 360 to 370 architecture. Microsoft moved from DOS to Windows to Windows NT. UNIX still is trying to decide which version it wants to be. The only thing certain about information technology is the pace of change, so there is little use in waiting for things to quiet down before making a move.

Integrate Data at the Front End

At the very core of a company's survival is the ability to access data as needed. Companies have been trying for decades to find some way to create a single data model that standardizes the way it stores data and thus allows for access by any system.

The truth of the matter is that for any sufficiently large company (i.e., one with more than one product in one market), data standardization is unrealistic. Different market centers track the same data in different ways. Different systems require different data formats. New technologies require data to be stated in new ways. To try to standardize the storage of data means ignoring these facts of life to an unreasonable extent.

The standardization approach also ignores the fact that businesses have 20 to 30 years' worth of data already. Are they to go back and recreate all this to satisfy future needs? Probably not. Such a project would immobilize the business and the creation of future systems for years to come.

Systems designed to integrate and reconcile data from multiple sources, presenting a single image to the front end, intrinsically support the client/server model of distributed computing and build flexibility into future applications. They allow data to be stored in many forms, each optimized for the application at hand. More important, they allow a company to access its data on an as-needed basis. These integration systems are an important component to successfully managing future growth.

Less Architecture Is More

To overdesign a systems architecture is to overly constrain the organization. Most architecture arises as a function of rightsizing of applications on the basis of where the data must be stored and used. Understanding this helps the IS manager size the network and associated support infrastructure.

The management of risk and impact also drives architecture by forcing redundancy of systems and, in some cases, mandating the placement of data repositories regardless of user preferences. Assessing project versus operational risk helps to determine whether a system is built for central or distributed use.

This view is one in which the business needs drive the shape of the architecture. It results in a dynamic interconnection of systems that respond flexibly to business needs. Under a centralized computing environment, it was impractical to employ such an approach. It took so long and cost so much to implement a system that investment had to come

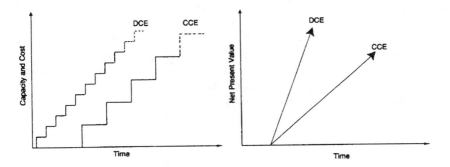

Distributed computing environment (DCE) has a higher net present value because its capacity can be used sooner relative to its marginal costs when compared with the centralized computing environment (CCE).

SOURCE: Decision Strategies Group, Greenwich CT

Exhibit 6. Net Present Value of Distributed vs. Centralized Computing

before business need. This necessitated preplanning of an architecture as an investment guide.

The economics of distributed computing are different. Systems cost much less and can be quickly implemented. This means that their use can be responsive to business needs instead of anticipative. It also results in a greater net present value, for even though their operational costs might be higher, distributed computing environments are more immediately useful for a given level of investment (Exhibit 6).

CONCLUSION

For IS managers, there indeed exists a framework for managing the new computing environment, one that in fact more directly relates to the business than their old way of managing. If you are able to master it, you enhance your opportunities to become a member of the corporate business management team instead of simply a supplier of computing services.

Success in a distributed computing environment requires a serious culture shift for IS managers. They must loosen up their management styles, learning to decentralize daily control of operations. They must provide direction to staff members so that they can recognize synergies among business units. Some jobs that were viewed as low-level support activities (e.g., value-added services such as help desk and printer maintenance) must be recognized as key to user productivity and distributed. Others, viewed as senior technical positions (e.g., dialtone functions such as network management and installations), might be outsourced, freeing scarce IS resources.

Most important, IS managers must understand the shift in power away from themselves and toward users. The IS organization is no longer the main provider of services; it now must find a role for itself as a manager of synergy, becoming a facilitator to the business units as they learn to manage their own newly found capabilities.

Chapter 50

Knowledge Management for E-Business Performance: Advancing Information Strategy to "Internet Time"

Yogesh Malhotra

Information strategy executives observed some significant transitions during the last quarter of the twentieth century: information technology (IT) as a lever of competitive advantage; the IT outsourcing bandwagon effect characterized by consideration of information as a "utility" just like electric power or the telephone; and more recently, the E-everything phenomenon with the emergence of the Internet and electronic commerce as key factors in business and IT strategy.

While some researchers suggested that same investments in information systems would yield different benefits in competitive advantage, others, such as the IT economist Paul Strassmann, concluded that there is no relationship whatsoever between computer expenditures and company performance. John Seely Brown, director of Xerox Parc, observed that despite investments of over $1 trillion in technology over two decades of this era, U.S. industry had realized little improvement in the efficiency and effectiveness of its knowledge workers. The confusion between knowledge and information has caused managers to sink billions of dollars into information technology investments that have often yielded marginal results.

The disconnect between IT expenditures and the firms' organizational performance could be attributed to an economic transition from an era of competitive advantage based on information to one based on knowledge creation. The earlier era was characterized by relatively slow and predictable change that could be deciphered and "controlled" by most formal information systems. During this period, information systems based on programmable *recipes for success* were able to deliver their promises of efficiency based on optimization for given business contexts. Discussing the case of organizations that were slow to adapt their strategy to changing business environment, Peter Drucker has argued that such organizations were hobbled by their past recipes of success.

Another way to understand the disconnect between information technology investments and organizational performance is to reflect upon the difference between *knowledge* and *information*. The intent of this chapter is not to offer another definition in terms of semantics, but to offer a more pragmatic perspective. More specifically, *knowledge* is interpreted in terms of *potential for action* and is distinguished in the following discussion from *information* in terms of its more immediate link with performance. This interpretation is consistent with what the information systems philosopher and professor Charles West Churchman observed three decades ago in his pioneering work *The Design of Inquiring Systems*: "knowledge resides in the user and not in the collection of information ... it is how the user reacts to a collection of information that matters." More recently, Nonaka and Takeuchi, the authors of the bestseller, *The Knowledge-Creating Company,* reemphasized that only human beings can take the central role in knowledge creation. They argue that computers are merely tools, however great their information-processing capabilities may be. Although information generated by computer systems is not a very rich carrier of human interpretation for potential action, knowledge resides in the user's subjective context of action based on that information.

FROM CONTINUOUS IMPROVEMENT TO RADICAL REDESIGN

In between the transitions mentioned earlier, information strategy executives participated in another significant transition during the past few years: that from Total Quality Management to Business Process Reengineering (BPR), as illustrated in Exhibit 1. In contrast to the traditional emphasis on continuous marginal improvements in existing processes, the proponents of BPR emphasized IT-intensive radical redesign of business processes. They proposed a clean-slate approach to rebuild the company's information architecture and information strategy by rethinking the company's business in terms of business processes rather than discrete func-

Exhibit 1. Transition from Incremental to Radical Change

	TQM	BPR
Level of Change	Incremental	Radical
Start from	Existing Process	Clean Slate
Frequency	One-time/Continuous	One-time
Time Required	Short	Long
Participation	Bottom-up	Top-down
Typical Scope	Narrow [within]	Cross-functional
Risk	Moderate	High
Primary Enabler	Statistical Control	IT
Type of Change	Cultural	Cultural/Structural

tions and hierarchies. An overemphasis on information technology at the cost of human involvement and commitment resulted in major implementation failures of BPR initiatives at the rate of 70 percent.

However, there were some problems with the proposed paradigm of BPR; it could not scale to the later shift to the networked paradigm enabled by the Internet and the World Wide Web. The ERP systems developed by the BPR vendors such as SAP were expected to provide lockstep regimented sharing of data across various business functions. These systems were based on a top-down model of information strategy implementation and execution, and focused primarily on the coordination of companies' internal functions. While providing for an unprecedented level of data-sharing across internal functions, these systems straitjacketed the flexibility of information processing for each of the locked-in functions. The price for the high level of integration of data related to business processes was paid in terms of the agility and flexibility required for adaptation. Earlier enterprise resource planning (ERP) models — developed by companies such as SAP — are still evolving to develop better external information flow linkages in terms of customer relationship management (CRM) and supply chain management (SCM). Meanwhile, newer companies, such as Siebel and Ariba, are offering needed external information flow functionality and information interfaces in terms of CRM and SCM. The ERP functionality, with its *internal* focus, complements the *external* focus of CRM and SCM to provide a base for creating seamless E-business applications. The continued challenge remains in terms of ensuring the adaptability and flexibility of information interfaces and information flows — both *internally* and *externally* — required for coping with dynamically changing business and competitive environments. The more recent development of E-business architectures based on software components — self-contained packages of functionality that can be snapped together to create complete business applications — seems to hold some promise for alleviating this problem.

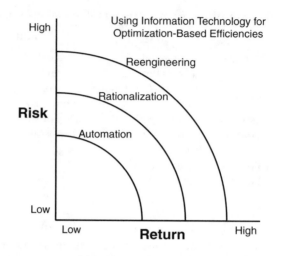

Exhibit 2. Risk and Return in the "Old World of Business"

The evolution of the information-processing paradigm during the past four decades to build intelligence and manage change in business functions and processes has generally progressed over three phases:

1. *Automation* — increased efficiency of operations
2. *Rationalization of procedures* — streamlining of procedures and eliminating obvious bottlenecks that are revealed by automation for enhanced efficiency of operations
3. *Reengineering* — radical redesign of business processes that depends on information technology-intensive radical redesign of workflows and work processes

The deployment of information technologies in all the three phases was based on a relatively predictable view of products and services as well as contributory organizational and industrial structures. Despite increase in risks and corresponding returns relevant to the three kinds of information technology-enabled organizational change, there was little, if any, emphasis on business model innovation — "rethinking the business" — as illustrated in Exhibit 2.

As demand for a company's products becomes more fickle with the increasing role of customers, suppliers, and intermediaries in dynamic pricing models (e.g., eBay, mySimon.com, priceline.com, and many other "vertical" portals), external market information plays a greater role in determining the internal logistics of the product and service lines. The ongoing shift from the "economy of atoms" to "the economy of bits," coupled with competition encountered by brick-and-mortar stores (such as Toys "R" Us) from click-and-mortar stores (such as eToys) has resulted in a reassessment of the traditional economic factors of production. Renewed emphasis on information assets or, more correctly, knowledge assets, intangible assets, and intellectual capital has fed the IPO frenzy, in which virtual companies have often achieved valuation many times over their brick-and-mortar analogues.

Most Net-based start-ups have realized that although technology is important, business model innovation is the key lever for global market share. The leading example of such new business models is Amazon.com, a relatively new entrant that is threatening traditional business models embodied in organizations such as Barnes and Noble and Borders Books. It is not that traditional brick-and-mortar companies were not leading users of information technologies; the new Net-based companies have fundamentally redefined the value equations related to their internal value chains and supply chains. Such business model innovations represent "paradigm shifts" that characterize not only transformation at the level of business processes and process workflows, but radical rethinking of the overall business model as well as the information flows between organizations and industries. Not surprisingly, many brick-and-mortar companies that are playing catch-up in the E-business game are encountering serious challenges in integrating their *physical* and *virtual* value chains and supply chains.

As noted by the business strategist Gary Hamel at an Academy of Management international meeting, the paradigm shifts characterizing the transition from the old world of business to E-world of business could account for as much as 70 percent of the *known* competitive players for many established companies. Taking this figure as a rough approximation in terms of risks and returns, one may speculate that more than 70 percent of risks and returns will depend upon companies' E-business model innovation strategies compared with the 30 percent that will depend upon use of less radical measures (see Exhibit 3).

BUSINESS PROCESS REDESIGN TO E-BUSINESS MODEL INNOVATION

Brian Arthur, the proponent of "increasing returns," working with the Santa Fe Institute, has described the new world of information-enabled business enterprises as a "world of re-everything." In this new world of business, success or failure for most enterprises depends on their ability to incessantly question and adapt their programmed logic of the way things are done. Such reality checks of the company's ways of doing business is necessary to keep up with the sustained dynamic and radical changes in the business environment. The "old world" of pre-determined and predefined recipes of success would still exist side by side with the world of re-everything in most business enterprises. However, companies' competitive survival and ongoing sustenance would depend primarily on

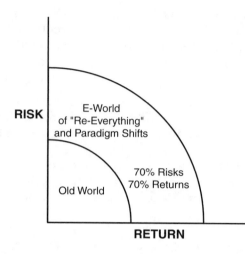

Exhibit 3. Risk and Return in the E-World of Business

their ability to continuously redefine and adapt organizational goals, purposes, and the organization's "way of doing things." Steve Kerr has described the state of business strategy for the new world in *Planning Review*: "The future is moving so quickly that you can't [predict] it ... We have put a tremendous emphasis on quick response instead of planning. We will continue to be surprised, but we won't be surprised that we are surprised. We will anticipate the surprise." Exhibit 4 provides a synopsis of the transition from the "old" world of business to the E-world of business.

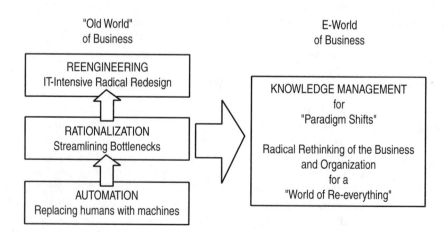

Exhibit 4. From "Old World" to E-World of Business: Knowledge Management for "Paradigm Shifts"

The new world of business puts less premium on playing by predefined rules and more on understanding and adapting as the rules of the game — as well as the game itself — keep changing. Examples of such changing business rules, conventions, and assumptions are evident in the emergence of virtual corporations and business ecosystems and are most prominently visible in dot.com enterprises living in "Internet time." Essentially, the corporate world is now encountering not only unprecedented pace of change but also radical discontinuities in such change that make yesterday's best practices tomorrow's core rigidities. In the new world of E-business, literally everything is up for grabs, including traditional concepts of industries, organizations, products, services, and channels of marketing, sales, and distribution. The new world imposes a greater need for ongoing questioning of the programmed logic and for a very high level of adaptability to incorporate dynamic changes into the business and information architecture and grow systems that can be readily adapted for the dynamically changing business environment. Organizations operating in the new business environment therefore need to be adept at the creation and application of new knowledge as well as at an ongoing renewal of existing knowledge archived in company databases.

FROM INFORMATION PROCESSING TO KNOWLEDGE CREATION

The information processing view, evident in scores of definitions of knowledge management in the trade press and academic texts, has often considered organizational memory of the past as a reliable predictor of the dynamically and discontinuously changing business environment. Most such interpretations have also made simplistic assumptions about storing *past* knowledge of individuals in the form of routinized programmable logic, rules-of-thumb, and archived best practices in databases for guiding *future* action. However, there are major problems that are attributable to the information-processing view of information systems. These problems are described in the following text as three key myths about knowledge management as it applies to the new world of E-business.

Myth 1: Knowledge management technologies can deliver the right information to the right person at the right time

This idea applies to an outdated business model. Information systems in the old industrial model mirror the notion that businesses change incrementally in an inherently stable market, and executives can foresee change by examining historical data and trends. The new business model of the Information Age, however, is marked by fundamental, not incremental, change. Businesses cannot plan for the long term; instead, they must shift to a more flexible "anticipation-of-surprise" model. Thus, for most significant decisions, it is impossible to build a system that can predefine and predict who is the right person, what is the right time, and what constitutes the right information.

Myth 2: Knowledge management technologies can store human intelligence and experience

Technologies such as databases and groupware applications store bits and pixels of data, but they cannot store the rich schemas embedded in human minds that are used for making sense of bits and pixels. Moreover, information is context-sensitive. The same assemblage of data can evoke different responses from different people at different points in time or in a different context in terms of decisions, action, and performance. Hence, storing a static representation of the explicit representation of a person's knowledge in a technology database or a computer algorithm — assuming the willingness and the ability to part with it — is not tantamount to storing human intelligence and experience.

Myth 3: Knowledge management technologies can distribute human intelligence

Again, this assertion presupposes that companies can predict the right information to distribute and the right people to distribute it to. As noted earlier, for most important business decisions, technologies cannot communicate the meaning embedded in complex data as it is constructed by human minds. This does not preclude the use of information technologies for rich exchange between humans to make sense about bits and pixels. However, dialog that surfaces meaning embedded in information is an intrinsic human property, not the property of the technology that may facilitate the process. Often, it is assumed that compilation of data in a central repository would somehow ensure that everyone who has access to that repository is capable and willing to use the information stored therein. Past research on this issue has shown that despite the availability of comprehensive reports and databases, most executives make decisions based on their interactions with others who they think are knowledgeable about the issues. Furthermore, the assumption of singular meaning of information, though desirable for seeking efficiencies, precludes creative abrasion and creative conflict that is necessary for business model innovation. In contrast, data archived in technological "knowledge repositories" does not allow for renewal of existing knowledge and creation of new knowledge.

TOWARD KNOWLEDGE MANAGEMENT THAT MAKES SENSE

Given the dangerous perception about knowledge management as seamlessly entwined with technology, "its true critical success factors will be lost in the pleasing hum of servers, software and pipes" as observed in a recent *CIO Magazine* interview. A few years ago, technologies such as intra-

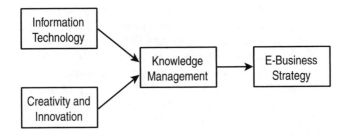

Exhibit 5. Knowledge Management and E-Business Strategy

nets, Lotus Notes, and MS-Exchange were being considered as enablers of knowledge management. The more recent interest is in technologies related to knowledge portals, artificial agents, and push-based technologies. Despite significant advancement in technologies and substantial investment by companies in such technologies, most organizations are still trying to find answers to such simple questions as how to capture, store, and transfer knowledge and how to ensure that knowledge workers share their knowledge. Given the quest for answers to such questions, it becomes imperative for organizations to clearly understand the strategic distinction between knowledge and information. This strategic difference is not a matter of semantics; rather, it has critical implications for managing and surviving in an economy of information overabundance and information overload. As most new media and Net executives competing for "eyeballs," "mindshare," and virtual communities would realize, in the new world of E-business, the scarce resource is not information, but human attention.

Based on the above arguments, it seems logical to account for the human attention, innovation, and creativity needed for the renewal of archived knowledge, the creation of new knowledge, and innovative applications of knowledge in new products and services that build market share. In the context of enabling E-business strategy, the proposed conceptualization of knowledge management is depicted in Exhibit 5.

Related to the foregoing schematic, a working definition of knowledge management is proposed here. Knowledge management caters to the critical issues of organizational adaptation, survival, and competence in face of increasingly discontinuous environmental change. Essentially, it embodies organizational processes that seek synergistic combination of data and information-processing capacity of information technologies, and the creative and innovative capacity of human beings.

Unlike most conceptions of knowledge management proposed in information systems research and in the trade press, the foregoing conception is better related to the new model of business strategy and business model innovation. Its primary focus is on outcomes in terms of performance rather than on the specification of inputs. With rapid advancements and availability of technologies, there would be multiple choices in terms of technologies that could facilitate a specific E-business strategy, such as customer relationship management (CRM), supply chain management (SCM), or selling chain management. However, the agility of the organization in being able to mesh the evolving business model with technological and structural changes on an ongoing basis will put a premium on creativity and innovation. This view relates more closely to the dynamic view of business strategy as driver of corporate information strategy. The strategic distinction between knowledge and information explained previously is relevant to the key emphasis on performance and outcomes.

RECONCILING KNOWLEDGE MANAGEMENT AND E-BUSINESS STRATEGY

It was suggested that many current interpretations of knowledge management are based on an outdated model of business strategy and may have adverse implications for E-business performance. The following discussion provides a more detailed explanation of the fundamental changes or "paradigm shifts" that have driven their underlying business model into obsolescence.

The arguments made in the discussion also made a case for reanalyzing key assumptions based on the new perspective of knowledge management that is better suited to the "new world" of E-business. These transitions are labeled as paradigm shifts as they represent changes of unprecedented proportions that are turning the tried and tested management theories and assumptions on their head. As depicted in Exhibit 6, these shifts are explained in terms of business strategy, information technology, role of senior management, organizational knowledge processes, corporate assets, and organizational design. These are interrelated issues, inasmuch as each of them has implications for other issues.

Paradigm Shift in Business Strategy

The new world of business imposes the need for variety and complexity of interpretations of information outputs generated by computer systems. Instead of long-term prediction, the emphasis is on understanding the multiple future world views by using techniques such as scenario planning. An example is the strategic planning process facilitated by Arie de Geus, the author of *Living Company*, while he was the strategy chief at Royal Dutch Shell. He facilitated strategy sessions that were not driven

Exhibit 6. Transitions to the World of E-Business

	Industrial Business	E-Business
Strategy	Prediction	"Anticipation of Surprise"
Technology	Convergence	Divergence
Management	Compliance	Self-Control
Knowledge	Utilization	Creation and Renewal
Assets	Tangibles	Intangibles
Organizations	Structure	Edge of Chaos

toward finding common ground for a shared strategy; rather, the emphasis was on understanding the differences in perspectives of various managers so that there was appreciation of the multiple world views of the future. As evident in this perspective, organizational planning activities are not eliminated. However, instead of embodying a set of instructions for what should be done, such activities are used as ideological devices for building constituency and defining the limits of responsible opinion. The organization plans for its future, but does not rely on its plans! This observation is more representative of several Internet-based start-ups that question their business logic everyday while competing in Internet time. Acute attention and response to market needs is a key determinant for most business organizations; however, for Net enterprises such as Yahoo! and eBay, it resulted in market leadership, stellar business performance, and multibillion dollar IPOs.

The process of creative abrasion illustrated previously enables a faster cycle of knowledge creation and application through detection and correction of any discrepancies between the "theory of business" and the dynamically changing business environment. In this model, access to an organizational information base, authority to take decisive action, and the requisite skills are embedded at the front lines where real action takes place so that strategy is devised and implemented in real-time.

Paradigm Shift in Design and Use of Technology

With increasing computerization in organizations, organizational routines originally embedded in standard operating procedures and policies often become embedded in the firm's programmed logic. Often, they take the form of congealed "best practices" embedded in computer programs and databases. The resulting information systems tend to be inflexible as they store a static representation of a dynamically changing business environment. With increasingly rapid, dynamic, and nonlinear changes in the business environment, static assumptions embedded in such systems become vulnerable. The growing awareness of such vulnerabilities is behind the increasing interest in designing information systems that can take dynamically changing information into account. Dynamic pricing models, and comparison-shopping agents such as mySimon.com (acquired by c|net) do take into consideration dynamically changing market data. However, such systems are still based on concrete representations of data and relatively routine and structured information. Regardless of the decision to build or buy, the challenge of walking the tightrope between adoption of the latest technologies and remaining up to speed with ongoing business and technology developments is becoming more acute in the E-world of business.

Brook Manville, while with McKinsey, viewed the implementation of these issues in terms of the shift from the traditional emphasis on transaction processing, integrated logistics, and workflows to systems that support competencies for communication building, people networks, and on-the-job learning. He had suggested that such competencies are based on flexible technologies and systems that support and enable *communities of practice* — informal and semi-informal networks of internal employees and external individuals based on shared concerns and interests. Not surprisingly, developing virtual communities of consumers and users is among the key priorities of vertical portals and specialized industry portals such as those being developed by Ford and General Motors.

Paradigm Shift in the Role of Senior Management

Scholars and practitioners are de-emphasizing the adherence to the "way things have always been done" so that prevailing practices may be continuously assessed from multiple perspectives. As noted by Chris Argyris, the explicit bias of command and control systems for seeking compliance makes such systems inadequate for motivating divergence-oriented interpretations necessary for ill-structured and complex environments. Knowledge management systems designed to ensure compliance might ensure obedience to given rules; still, they do not facilitate the detection and correction of errors. Hence, it has been suggested that the role of the senior management needs to change from *command and control* to *sense and respond.* Furthermore, if knowledge, unlike information, is about beliefs and commitment, as noted by Nonaka and Takeuchi, the new emphasis should be on building commitment to organizational vision rather than compliance to rules and prespecified best practices.

Senior managers need to view the organization as a human community capable of providing diverse meanings to information outputs generated by technological systems. They also need to make the organizational information base accessible to organization members. This is important, given the increasingly fast-paced and dynamic business environment that creates disconnects between the process of decision-making at the top and implementation of such decisions at the grassroots. Emphasis on multiple and diverse interpretations of information also helps in the development of a large repertory of responses needed for deciphering the complexity inherent in dynamic changes of the business environment.

Paradigm Shift in Organizational Knowledge Processes

Institutionalization of "best practices" by embedding them in IT might facilitate efficient handling of routine and predictable situations. However, greater proactive involvement of human imagination and creativity is needed to facilitate greater internal diversity to match the variety and complexity of the "wicked environment." Often, effective knowledge management in such an environment may need imaginative suggestions more than it does concrete, documented answers. The earlier emphasis of information systems log on defining the optimal programmed logic and then executing that logic to squeeze the highest efficiencies. However, increasing dynamics of the business environment mandate greater emphasis on ensuring *doing the right thing* than on *doing the thing right*. With ongoing reassessment of key assumptions, the emphasis is more on the ongoing renewal of existing knowledge, the creation of new knowledge, and its application in business practices. This contrasts with the "old world" model of archiving the knowledge in organizational databases devoid of human reinterpretation of its context.

The traditional information-processing model for the old world of business assumes a problem as given, and the solution is based on prespecified understanding of the business environment. In contrast, the proposed model constructs the definition of the problem from the knowledge available at a certain point in time based on its context. While individual autonomy in the proposed model facilitates divergence of meaning, the organizational vision facilitates the various views to converge in a given direction. This process avoids premature closure or convergence to surface multiple possibilities, opportunities, and threats that could lie within the fog of unknowingness enveloping the company's future.

The two interpretations of knowledge management may be highlighted by the contrast between two U.S. companies covered in the trade press. One of them, a U.S.-based global communications company, had indicated its preference for the information-processing model of knowledge management. Its knowledge management strategy could be summed up in the words of a top executive: "What's important is to find useful knowledge, bottle it, and pass it around." The other firm, a U.S.-based global pharmaceutical firm, in contrast, focused more on empowering the individuals to create and share knowledge "There's a great big river of data out there. Rather than building dams to try and bottle it all up into discrete little entities, we just give people canoes and compasses." As is evident from the foregoing discussion, the latter approach matches the knowledge management model proposed in this chapter.

PARADIGM SHIFT IN ECONOMICS OF ORGANIZATIONAL ASSETS

Peter Drucker has argued that in the emerging economy, knowledge is the primary resource for individuals and for the economy overall; land, labor, and capital — the economist's traditional factors of production — do not disappear, but they become secondary.

Similar observations are unraveling traditional accounting procedures that cannot account for new factors of production such as knowledge capital, intellectual capital, and intangible assets. The successes of Net companies and other information-centric companies such as Microsoft are attributed by some to "increasing returns." Traditional factors of production are limited by threshold of scale and scope as every marginal increase in land, labor, or capital results in diminishing returns on the production outcomes. In contrast, information assets and knowledge capital seem to be governed by a different law of economic returns: investment in every additional unit of information or knowledge created and used results in a higher return. This is often attributed to *externalities*: as more people become members of the network and use its services, greater value is added to the network.

Paradigm Shift in Organizational Design

The information-processing model of knowledge management is constrained by its overemphasis on consistency institutionalized in the form of best practices. The proposed model of knowledge management is expected to break this cycle of reinforcement of institutionalized knowledge. While the traditional business logic was based on a high level of structure and control, the dynamics of the new business environment demand a different model of organization design. Often characterized as "living on the edge of chaos," this model is characterized by its relative lack of structure and lack of external controls, as described by Kevin Kelly in *Out of Control*. It is based on only a few rules, some specific information, and a lot of freedom. In the proposed model, designers of organizational knowledge management systems can, at best, facilitate the organization's "self-designing." Not only do the organization's members define problems for themselves and generate their own solutions, they would also evaluate and revise their solution-generating processes. By explicitly encouraging experimentation and the rethinking of premises, this process promotes reflection-in-action and creation of new knowledge.

It is being increasingly realized that differences in perspectives may have a very positive role in the innovation needed for new product and service definitions. Characterized by some management thinkers as "creative abrasion," this view encourages the promotion of individual autonomy in experimentation and learning. Going beyond the NIH ("not invented here") and the "NIH yet I did it" syndromes, it encourages the questioning of all given assumptions — regardless of their legitimacy — for their ongoing and continual reassessment. Instead of emphasizing best practices archived in databases, this model encourages continuous pursuit of *better* practices that are aligned with the dynamically changing business environment.

CONCLUSION

During the past few years, the corporate world has seen the emergence of interest in knowledge management and adoption of the term by information technology vendors and industry solution providers. However, despite the popularity of the buzzword, most such implementations have been based on an outdated business model and related information-processing view. It may even be argued that in several cases, it is difficult to justify why specific information technology solutions fall in the realm of "knowledge management" rather than within the scope of good old "information management" or "data management." This ambiguity has led some consultants to assert that knowledge management is a fad.

There is a need for developing a better and more accurate understanding of knowledge management as enabler of information strategy for the E-world of business. Departing from the information-processing perspective that was relevant to the industrial world of business, a new perspective of knowledge management was explained and discussed. The proposed conceptualization is based on the need for synergy between the capabilities of advanced information technologies and human creativity and innovation to realize the agility demanded by emerging business environment. A clear explanation of the "strategic" notion of knowledge and knowledge management is offered to distinguish the proposed model from the outdated perspective.

A number of examples from the world of Net businesses and more traditional companies were presented to illustrate the key arguments of the chapter. The discussion explained the transition from the old world of business to the new world of E-business in terms of fundamental transitions or paradigm shifts. It was also explained how and why information executives should rethink fundamental assumptions about business strategy, the design and use of information technology, the role of senior management, organizational knowledge processes, the economics of organizational assets, and organization design for business model innovation. Better and accurate understanding of the strategic relevance of knowledge and knowledge management is expected to contribute to more effective E-business strategies that result in sustained business performance.

TASK 5: MAKING MONEY FROM THE SUPPLY CHAIN

References

1. Arthur, W. B., "Increasing Returns and the New World of Business," *Harvard Business Review,* July–August 1996, 74(4), pp. 100–109.
2. Drucker, P. F., "The Theory of Business," *Harvard Business Review*, September–October 1994, pp. 95–104.
3. Hagel, J. and Armstrong, A. G., *Net Gain: Expanding Markets Through Virtual Communities*, Harvard Business School Press, Boston, MA, 1997.
4. Hildebrand, C. "Does KM = IT?" *CIO Enterprise*, Sep. 15, 1999. [URL: http://www.cio.com/archive/enterprise/091599_ic.html].
5. Kalakota, R. and Robinson, M., *e-Business: Roadmap for Success*, Addison-Wesley, Reading, MA, 1999.
6. Nonaka, I. and Takeuchi, H., *The Knowledge-Creating Company*, Oxford University Press, New York, NY, 1995.
7. Strassmann, P. A., *The Squandered Computer: Evaluating the Business Alignment of Information Technologies*, Information Economics Press, New Canaan, CT, 1997.
8. Tapscott, D., Lowy, A., and Ticoll, D. (Eds.), *Blueprint to the Digital Economy: Wealth Creation in the Era of E-Business,* McGraw-Hill, New York, 1998.

Chapter 51
Supply Chain Prestudies

James B. Ayers

Identifying supply chains in a complex operation is something of an art. Many operations overlap. Many departments support multiple products. Products are sold to a variety of customers in different market segments, each of which has different objectives.

Because of this complexity, many companies evolve to functional organizations with "one-size-fits-all" supply chains. These are seldom efficient in terms of cost, service, or speed in meeting the competitive demands of customers. Newcomers, with little investment in outmoded structures, take over markets with superior supply chains. Extracting and evaluating the underlying supply chains embedded in the organization is the beginning of the improvement effort. The prestudy starts to "disassemble" functional processes and to catalog the differences among customers that can lead to tailored, competitive supply chains.

The prestudy should last no longer than one or two weeks. One or two analysts are sufficient for the effort. The conclusions of the prestudy should focus on the best opportunities for improving competitive position through supply chain redesign. The effort may reform an existing chain, create new ones, or combine multiple chains into one. In many cases, the information gathered in a prestudy will be preliminary — that is, management's best guess as to the situation. Judgment should determine whether further verification of an assumption is warranted. If so, the plan should include this work.

ORGANIZE END USERS

The prestudy should begin with end users. These may not be direct customers for an organization, but they ultimately determine the success or failure of the product. To understand what will make the supply chain more effective, one has to understand the motivations of these users.

Exhibit 1. Sample Table of Customer Groups

Customer group 1	Customer group 2	Customer group 3	Customer group 4

Exhibit 2. Sample Table of Customer Groups Combined into Segments

Segment 1 (Customer groups 1 & 2)	Segment 2 (Customer group 3)	Segment 3 (Customer group 4)

Define Market Segments

The prestudy team should list user groups. Groupings may be by application of the product, location, volume, supply chain to reach the user, or other characteristics. Exhibit 1 depicts the possible result.

Next, form segments from the customer groups. One or more groups may make up a segment. Combinations of groups into segments are particularly valid when they share supply chains. Therefore, one might have a revised chart that looks like Exhibit 2.

Four customer groups have been combined into three segments for the purpose of supply chain design. This could be due to commonality in the supply chains that reach them plus the belief that they have common requirements in terms of supply chain design.

Map Products to Segments

Next, list products or product lines. A line may be a group of products produced in the same facilities, or it may include different products that serve common markets. A common supply chain could also define a product line. An example would be "all products sold in Asia" or "all products sold through distributors." Map the product lines to segments. The resulting table might look like Exhibit 3. In the table, the dollar signs indicate product profit by segment. It shows that product C is the most profitable by virtue of sales to segment 2. Product line B is the least profitable, with sales to Segment 3.

Identify Supply Chains

Identify the supply chains supporting the customer segments. In the preceding example, three supply chain types may be distinguished. These include

- One supply chain for all three segments. This is most common in smaller companies.

Exhibit 3. Sample Table with Product Lines Mapped to Segments

	Segment 1 (Customer groups 1 & 2)	Segment 2 (Customer group 3)	Segment 3 (Customer group 4)
Product line A	$$$	$	
Product line B			$
Product line C		$$$$$	
Product line D	$$		

Exhibit 4. Sample Table with Two Supply Chains

Supply Chains		Segment 1 (Customer groups 1 & 2)	Segment 2 (Customer group 3)	Segment 3 (Customer group 4)
SC1	Product line A	$$$	$	
SC1	Product line B			$
SC2	Product line C		$$$$$	
SC2	Product line D	$$		

- A separate supply chain for each product line. This is often the case when each product is made by a different profit center. This is most common in larger companies.
- Supply chains organized by customer segment.

Seldom do we see supply chains organized around customer segments.

If two supply chains are distinguished, they might appear as Exhibit 4. In this case, we show two supply chains (bearing the prefix SC). As commonly found, they are product oriented. SC1 serves product lines A and B. SC2 serves C and D.

DESCRIBE THE SUPPLY CHAIN(S)

With the supply chains identified, their configuration should be documented with flowcharts and supporting data. These need not be elaborate given the time limitations of a prestudy but they should convey an understanding of the basic structure of the chains. Accompanying the flowcharts should be metrics and other information that characterizes current performance.

Document Physical Flow

Fundamental to most supply chain representations is physical flow. The prestudy flowchart should show the following:

- Echelons of the supply chain, including major suppliers, manufacturing centers, distribution centers, warehouses, and customer segments
- Methods of transport between echelons
- Volumes of product flow in dollars, units, or volume
- Cycle time for moving material in the chain, preferably broken out by echelon
- Inventory levels along the chain, including those at suppliers and customers

Document Information Flow

Information flow is an increasingly important component of the supply chain. A great deal of competitive advantage can be gained by improving information flow. Among the elements needed to describe information flow are the following:

- An information flowchart that shows where sales information is generated
- Decision points along the chain, including the people responsible for the decisions
- An inventory of information systems tools used to plan and control the process
- A listing of formal and informal contracts between supply chain participants

Document Financial Flow

A similar process should include financial flows. This is particularly true if there are any innovations in the way this flow is handled. Among the topics to include are the following:

- Cash-to-cash cycle — this shows how long it takes from the first expenditures to the time money is collected from the end user
- Balance sheet figures including inventories, accounts payable, and accounts receivable
- Estimated activity costs across the chain; use end user purchase price to "allocate" funds to supply chain activities

Document New Product Flow

New products can often upset existing supply chains. To the extent new products are contemplated, the processes should be examined. This should include

- Expectations for new product introductions and supply chain implications
- An understanding of how the new product process incorporates supply chain participation, if it does

- Special supply chain requirements for supporting new product development. (e.g., example is finding reliable sources for components requiring special features)

DOCUMENT MANAGEMENT PROCESSES

Time should be spent on understanding basic planning processes and recent initiatives. This will help frame management's approach to process improvement, strategic planning, and capital investment. The processes described here are usually available in document form.

- Understand strategic plans that affect the supply chain. Review strategic initiatives and competitive evaluations.
- List recently completed and ongoing improvement projects. This includes facilities, equipment, and systems. Trace back at least three years and forward over the company's planning horizon.
- Explain the justification process for capital investments. If a procedure exists, review how it is applied. If possible, review candidate projects falling within the most recently completed capital budgeting cycle.

INTERVIEW EXECUTIVES

The prestudy should include interviews in one-on-one meetings, group settings, or workshops. These should draw out the following information.

Describe Customer Requirements by Segment

Understand what customers demand by segment. Use interviews, market surveys, or direct input from key customers.

Assess Relative Strengths and Weaknesses by Segment

Gain an understanding of current position. This can be based on opinions of management, marketshare data, and financial reports.

Understand barriers

Any organization has constraints on its ability to act. Here is a list of possible constraints or barriers that should be considered in planning supply chain changes.

- *Human resources.* Considerations for employee relations and constraints on talent
- *Financial.* Constraints on capital availability and objectives for profitability
- *Capacity.* Limitations on the ability to increase or decrease capacity

- *Product lines and customers.* Products and customers, whether they are profitable or not, that must be supplied; the source of the constraint
- *Past capital investments.* Infrastructure that must be included in future plans

PREPARE CONCLUSIONS

The conclusions condense the data into recommendations for proceeding. They should set the direction for guiding supply chain changes. Among areas for comment in the conclusions are the following:

- Effectiveness of current supply chains and their appropriateness in light of customer expectations
- New supply chain proposals that would more effectively serve a customer segment
- Recommendations for dealing with constraints
- Comments on the role of systems and needs for systems upgrades
- Opportunities for improving profits and cash flow in the supply chain
- Questionable product lines and market segments in terms of profit and the supply chain capability to serve them
- Requirements, schedule(s), and program plan(s) for a multi-phase supply chain improvement project

Chapter 52

Improving Supply Chain Management for the Mining and Metals Industry

Paul Held
Karl Kelton

The mining and metals sector is among the last significant industrial area to begin to move forward aggressively with the use of integrated computer systems to renew and improve all areas of the enterprise. These areas include financial management, materials management, maintenance, processing/production, and the supply chain. Momentum began to build in the mid-1990s, to embrace the information technologies available off-the-shelf to significantly renew these and other business processes across the value chain that, in many cases, have remained unchanged for decades. The impetus for this movement is rooted in the belief, on the part of early adopters, that there is a solid business case for change, a business case which helps to significantly address executives' long-term business concerns about maximally leveraging corporate assets and stakeholder/shareholder value.

In prior years, the business case for change enabled by integrated systems was questionable. Today, each company and sector situation is different, and unique economic or operational complexities greatly can influence whether major investments in information technology (IT) truly make sense given investment constraints. The very recent advent of powerful, flexible and more cost-effective integrated system platforms from reputable vendors has changed the dynamic and created a new window of opportunity that merits a business, not technology-driven, analysis.

It is important to start by examining three key issues facing mining and metallurgy companies today.

0-8493-1273-6/02/$0.00+$1.50
© 2002 by CRC Press LLC

1. *Volatility of commodity prices.* Predictability of the factors affecting the balance between supply and demand is becoming increasingly complex. Witness the impacts of recent events such as the Asian flu, major banks selling off massive amounts of their gold reserves, and copper prices in the recent past.
2. *Operating efficiencies and cost control.* In today's competitive global economy, base metals producers continue to be price takers. Pressure will continue to build on producers' abilities to provide superior customer service, with the necessary speed and agility, at the lowest possible cost structures.
3. *Management information systems and technology.* The past several years have produced an explosion in the power and availability of tools to provide strategic, tactical, and operational decision support to companies.

Our surveys also provide some insights. For example, in the contexts of operating efficiency, process changes, and decision support, 66 percent of CIOs surveyed expect an increase in business process reengineering (BPR) activity, including supply chains. Today, of all the drivers of organizational change, one of the largest is supply chain reengineering. And almost invariably, the results of that process mean significant pressures on IT. Remarkably though, a surprising number of BPR projects still take place without IT involvement, approximately one in four, either because IT is out of touch with the business or simply is excluded.

Still the question remains: how can a company achieve its business objectives without IT involvement? Or similarly: how can IT deliver value when it inherits other people's systems or decisions?

Analysis of the survey shows that in the context of IT expenditures, companies have four areas they must evaluate if they are to improve their supply chain operations.

1. Control the duplication of technology. Simplicity is better. Conversely, complexity is expensive.
2. Manage build versus buy decisions for technology solutions. With the availability of new and powerful packaged solutions, companies need a compelling reason to justify building their own systems.
3. Deploy technology strategically. Before buying, first build a clear business case. The alternative is a technological Tower of Babel; more to support, more confusion, more to go wrong.
4. Manage the human resources aspect of technology. Poor IT supply chain decisions manifest as unfavorable human symptoms: increased training needs, stress on the job, recruiting problems, unchecked outsourcing, and so on.

Supply chain management encompasses a number of key business processes. These include managing the flow of materials, funds, and information from suppliers through manufacturing, transportation, and distribution to customers. It also supports the revenue-generating activities of the company.

Our survey highlights a major challenge in supply chain management today: leveraging advances in technology and systems to manage the flow of information within the supply chain. Managing this complex network requires timely access to information to facilitate rapid decision making.

Production must be optimized to realize maximum efficiency, responsiveness, and throughput. Inventories need to be reduced to the minimum levels necessary to support customer service objectives. Distribution must be planned carefully to ensure product is delivered at the right place, on time. The supply chain manager must be able to see everything, change anything, and to consider all aspects of the supply chain when making major decisions.

In 1999 almost 200 North American manufacturers representing a broad spectrum of industry segments participated in our annual survey, which focused on supply chain systems and technologies. Insights provided include:

- Senior management's perspectives on the overall business environment for North American companies
- Development of supply chain management in North America, including current industry dynamics and their impacts on the supply chain
- Current and planned use of supply chain systems and supporting technologies to improve supply chain operations
- Increasing focus on formal partnerships with customers and suppliers
- Challenges of information sharing among all supply chain entities through the Internet or other means

The supply chain is a key area of executive management focus. Ninety-seven percent of respondents rated efficient supply chain management as critical to the long-term success of their business. However, only 33 percent believe that their supply chain capabilities are above average for the industry. Accordingly, 80 percent of respondents have supply chain improvement initiatives either planned or currently underway. Additionally, 80 percent of respondents plan to increase their supply chain technology budget significantly to support these initiatives and to attain competitive advantage.

To enable a company to make quick and confident decisions, a supply chain management system must be built on the following fundamental principles:

- *Constraint management.* Businesses require feasible solutions. Plans that fail to consider real-world constraints are of limited use. Effective management means recognizing and minimizing the impact of constraints such as materials, capacity, manpower, transportation, warehousing, suppliers, management policies, customer and channel allocations, and others.

- *Concurrent versus serial planning.* Traditional planning is done sequentially, with separate plans for manufacturing, procurement, transportation, sourcing, allocation, and distribution, which results in unsynchronized plans. Intelligent systems are capable of concurrent planning across the supply chain, resulting in faster plan generation and a synchronized, responsive supply chain.
- *Global insight.* With constraint management and concurrent planning, mining and petroleum companies can grasp the global impact of local changes on all aspects of the supply chain and, thus, can make globally good decisions.
- *Advanced warning.* When a local change occurs, whether it is a material shortage, unscheduled equipment downtime, or a supplier failure to meet expectations, intelligent systems instantly rely on advanced warning to all stakeholders. This warning defines the change in terms of its effects on sales, inventory and work-in-progress (WIP) levels, lead times, due dates, and other key business drivers.
- *Built-in business optimization.* Because business scenarios change constantly, intelligent systems must recommend new operational solutions rapidly that maximize quantifiable business objectives such as return on assets (ROA), profit contribution, and cash flow. The decision support logic available with many tools today accommodates different business optimization criteria.

The goal of intelligent supply chain management is to achieve maximum customer responsiveness at the least possible cost.

Many processes now can be integrated across inter- and intracompany supply chains using new, powerful tools:

- *Forecasting.* Off-the-shelf packages work with forecasts at various levels of abstraction in aggregate, plant-by-plant, or process and perform accurate variance calculations for finished goods, work-in-progress, and raw materials. Impacts of forecast changes on distribution plans and procurement can be calculated instantly.
- *Available to promise.* Concurrent planning and constraint management functionality makes accurate available-to-promise and real-time order quotation possible. Tools now can consider, simultaneously, materials, capacity, transportation, customer allocations, supplier allocations, and related business constraints.
- *Distribution planning.* Technology now can support "what-if" and "can do" analysis associated with both upstream and downstream impacts of demand. Traditional distribution requirements planning tools only have been able to communicate demand to upstream operations.

Tools now provide for simultaneous planning for transportation, plant and warehouse sourcing, refining and purchasing, although recommending optimal solutions for lead times, replenishments, consolidation routines, and synchronization of deliveries.

- *Sourcing.* Available technology now can integrate efficiently both outside and inside suppliers within the demand/fulfillment formula. User-defined algorithms determine the optimal supplier, whether it is another plant, custom-feed operation, third-party vendor, or a warehouse in another country, and automatically computes transportation and processing costs, materials and capacity availability, and service performance.
- *Allocations.* Decisions can be supported quickly now regarding whether raw materials and finished goods available in one country can be allocated to warehouses and facilities in another.
- *Inventory planning.* Effective management also means modeling different inventory policies at different nodes in the supply chain. Tools now can accommodate varying reorder triggers, days of supply levels, and service levels — individually and in aggregate.
- *Plant operations: planning and scheduling.* Traditional MRPII systems are transactional tools that calculate requirements based on local demand. Historically, MRPII has been used to compute a "best guess" master production schedule that translates that data into a materials requirements plan, which in turn creates a capacity requirements plan. Such sequential planning typically requires hours or days to complete and, when generated, is often out of date and ignores constraints on capacity. Tools are now available that generate plans for all requirements and resources, looking both upstream and downstream to refining and distribution processes — in real-time.
- *Procurement.* Tools now available can model supplier capacities and provide information required for mining and metallurgical companies to make more prudent outsourcing and procurement decisions.
- *Electronic commerce.* With the advent of the Internet, EDI, intranet, and extranets, suppliers, manufacturers, and customers now can be linked by a single electronic system. Nodes in the supply chain can plan their business based on the delivery constraints of their key suppliers. Customers can be appraised of critical supply status and lead times before issuing an order.

Collectively, these are the functions that give an organization the ability to respond swiftly to change and to optimize assets across the supply chain. However, as anyone who has fought for a budget knows, there is nothing more sensitive or contentious than spending, which leads to the final and probably most important point of this discussion.

Information technology (IT) is or should be a strategic resource. This means in turn that IT professionals, along with their other business colleagues, must think and act the part, move beyond the day-to-day and the bewitchments of technology, and ultimately link information concerning the company's supply chain performance to its business objectives.

Developing a business case is critical for the project not only to secure initial funding, but also to help manage change throughout the project and to ensure that business benefits are achieved. To match integrated computer solutions to supply chain needs, a company first must identify the primary areas of the supply chain, which need improvement by asking questions such as the following:

- Is it important to improve manufacturing operations?
- Would the greatest benefit be gained by focusing on logistics?
- Is it more important to focus on the entire supply chain from a strategic perspective?

These questions do not always have obvious answers. A common mistake made by companies implementing packages is to attack the most visible supply chain problem first, without conducting a diagnostic study to identify where the largest potential benefit truly lies. For example, if a company has massive, visible amounts of raw materials, it may determine that an advanced materials requirements planning application will offer the greatest benefits. However, a well-executed diagnostic study might reveal that raw material storage costs are minimal when compared to transportation and distribution costs for work-in-process and finished goods. In this case, the company might benefit most by focusing initial implementation efforts on the strategic and tactical aspects of distribution planning.

Because many software packages offer a wide variety of applications to support different areas of the supply chain, it is important that companies identify where they expect to see benefits, prior to beginning implementation, and what the criteria for success will be. The business case should rely heavily on the supply chain diagnostic to tie expected benefits to areas of the supply chain in which the greatest gains are expected.

When assessing software package requirements, companies must specify what they want the tool to perform, what functionality is required, what type of reporting is needed, how the package needs to work with other applications currently in use at the company, if the package works within the hardware/network constraints of the company, and how customizable the application is. If certain key features are critical to a company, it should define clearly what these are and make every attempt to identify a software vendor that supports them. All these considerations should be built into the business case.

Implementation costs for companies installing either enterprisewide solutions, such as SAP, Oracle, Baan, and PeopleSoft, or tailored solutions, such as i2, Manugistics, Numertrix, Indus, Maximo, and others, vary widely. Key factors that ultimately determine the cost are

- Degree of external resources used
- Investment required for technical infrastructure
- Scope and scale of the business benefits targeted
- Overall strategy for implementing the software, including the costs of training and users

Again, these factors need to be built into the business case.

Just as different packages and applications offer different features, different software vendors work with their clients in different ways. Before deciding whom to work with, a company should agree on specific requirements it has for the software company itself. What type of consulting is needed? What guarantees are required? What experience in specific industries or planning functions are desired? A company planning to implement enterprise requirements planning (ERP), advanced planning and scheduling (APS) packages, or other logistics software should conduct an analysis of vendor capabilities similar to the software requirements process described earlier. By identifying which issues are most important, a company can approach software selection with a clear understanding of what to look for and build these considerations into the business case. Other business case considerations should include vendor demonstrations of a product, site visits where the software has been implemented successfully, and reference checks.

The package selection decision will affect the entire implementation effort. Consequently, provisions should be made in the business case for the use of outside assistance to foster more effective decision making and help assure that the best application is chosen. Qualified third-party system integrators can offer extensive experience in implementing multiple packages, experience in selecting among multiple packages, and knowledge of the types of features offered by the different applications. They also provide significant industry and planning process expertise to help gauge the applicability of a software application to a company's planning environment. This can speed the selection process and help ensure that the company makes its selection decision with as much information as possible.

Finally, does the business case reinforce the following requirements for a successful implementation?

- Active, visible and strong top management involvement
- A serious appreciation for the change management requirements
- Rigorous project and partner management
- Accelerated decision-making processes

- Creative project team incentives
- Plenty of training, education, support, and communication
- Focused alignment of the organization, team, and scope
- Reengineering in the correct doses at the correct times
- Strategic and tangible benefits and a program to measure progress toward stated goals

The business case is a critical tool that helps to manage change throughout the project, to keep people focused, aligned, and moving in the right direction, and to make sure that the expected benefits are achieved.

A question often asked is whether or not it is possible to attribute benefits to the software or to improvements in supply chain processes and whether it might not be possible to achieve the benefits simply with improvements to logistics. The answer to both is yes, in some cases; in most cases, however, the two are linked tightly, and it is not only difficult but also unproductive to try to separate the benefits of each. One company executive explained it this way, "We might have been able to make the process improvements, but we never would have been able to sustain them without enabling software."

In closing, the following points summarize the key concepts of this chapter:

- Supply chain management and the need to enable improvements through technology is "top of mind" with executive management.
- Integrated and bolt-on solutions with extensive functionality are available off-the-shelf, eliminating the need in many cases for customized solutions that are costly, take a lot of time to develop and implement, lack the necessary support for end users, and fail to cover the supply chain spectrum.
- Executive management continues to be concerned about the levels of spending on technology and the returns for every dollar invested.
- Objective business cases that support the strategic, tactical, and operational goals associated with technology-enabled supply chain initiatives are critical.

Chapter 53
Enhancing Manufacturing Performance with ERP Systems

Rajagopal Palaniswamy
Tyler Frank

Manufacturing processes are changing, becoming intellectually stimulating and challenging rather than physically exhausting. The various advanced technologies used in manufacturing, collectively known as advanced manufacturing technology (AMT), would not have been possible without rapid applications of IT. These computer-based AMTs allow firms to produce a variety of parts and end products of even small volumes by changing the software instead of replacing the hardware.

As much as technology has enabled improvements in manufacturing such as higher productivity, it has also made the process of manufacturing highly complex because of the many different computer software systems used within manufacturing and in other functions. Within local manufacturing facilities, there are discrepancies encountered in fully integrating the automated equipment. Without integration, a plant may have various "islands of automation," and such isolation results in lack of integration and coordination, preventing firms from utilizing the full potential of technology and equipment. Under such circumstances, the investments made in automation may not be fully justified (Vonderembse et al., 1996; Oliff et al., 1996).

At the global level, the effort required to integrate the various production facilities is higher, owing to differences in technology in various countries. Many manufacturers depend on technology to assist them in their efforts to cope with the increasing demands for product innovation, faster delivery, and better quality. For example, to meet customer demands in an Asian country, production capacity at an Australian subsidiary may have to be increased, which may depend on receiving materials supplied from countries in Europe or from Canada. Sometimes, there may be machine breakdowns or other such major incidents that may stop or reduce production capacity in one facility and, in order to fulfill customer demand, production capacity in another facility in another location may need to be changed.

To overcome problems associated with incompatible and nonuniform systems in an organization, especially in the manufacturing function, many companies have been implementing enterprise resource planning (ERP) systems in recent years. The ERP systems, by providing end-to-end connectivity, have enabled these companies to enhance their manufacturing performance. Based on case analysis carried out in five manufacturing firms located in Ohio, Michigan, Wisconsin, and Illinois, this study aims to understand and explain the enhanced manufacturing performance due to ERP implementation and explain how ERP implementation has enabled organizations overcome the problems associated with using disparate systems.

PROBLEMS WITH DISPARATE SYSTEMS OR ANTECEDENTS FOR AN INTEGRATED SYSTEM

Rockart and Short (1994) mention that, in the current global economy, in order to capture global levels of manufacturing efficiency, to innovate for global markets, and to understand international marketing and world markets, a firm requires increased knowledge and coordination of the firm's operations throughout the geographically dispersed subunits. Kerr (1988) reports about the "islands of automation" with reference to various individual units and their respective headquarters, each having a different platform of information systems. A standard of protocol and platforms would alleviate such problems and enable the smooth transfer of data among various units. Gullo (1988), based on interviews with executives from RJR Nabisco, stresses that even if a company's businesses are not centralized, the IS department needs to move to a view of data that is as global as possible to attain competitive advantage. Nearly half of the 75,000-person workforce of RJR Nabisco work outside the United States. If various units use different types of computer hardware and software systems, managers will have only a partial view of data and net information gain will be less. With such lack of accurate information, the decision-making process will not gain significantly from the tremendous investments made in building the information technology.

Alavi and Keen (1991) mention that the higher the communication and interaction among the various team members, the higher will be the performance of the team. In carrying out a project, the members of the product design team should communicate and coordinate with the product engineers and process engineers and the marketing professionals as well as the suppliers.

If a company uses different kinds of computers in different countries, transmitting information among these disparate systems often requires expensive interfaces and, most of the time, organizational members waste time and effort in duplication of data entry. In addition, as the organization grows and expands, the number of different computer hardware and software systems increases exponentially. Since the 1980s, the business environment has seen many mergers and acquisitions, and such activities have given rise to fragmented information systems within an organization. Rockart and Short (1994) define time to market as the firm's ability to develop new products quickly and to deliver existing products effectively. These authors contend that reducing time to market necessitates increasing coordination among various functional units in an organization, such as design, engineering, manufacturing, purchasing, distribution, and service.

Gumaer (1996) quotes Rybeck, president of Benchmarking Partners, an industrial analyst group in Massachusetts: "In the present customer driven markets, manufacturers must be able to continuously revise their schedules based upon unplanned events. To accomplish this, their process and data models, information systems and communication infrastructure must operate seamlessly in real-time." To bring about such compatibility among the systems, firms are implementing integrated systems that ensure smooth data flow. Such integrated systems, collectively known as enterprise resource planning (ERP) systems, are enabling organizations to enhance their performance, manufacturing performance in particular.

ENTERPRISE RESOURCE PLANNING SYSTEMS — AN IT INNOVATION TO INTEGRATE DISPARATE SYSTEMS

Davenport and Short (1991) explained how business processes were developed before modern computers and communications even existed; whenever technology was applied in the organizations, it was to automate or to just speed up the isolated components of the existing process. Such IT applications enabled organizations to achieve higher productivity, but it did not give them sustainable competitive advantage of any kind. There were "islands of fragmented automation," which did not allow the organization as a whole to perform better. The emergence of ERP systems has been changing this situation by providing a mechanism for the organizations to achieve "end-to-end connectivity," thus making the various computer systems compatible with one another.

ERP software is the backbone of the manufacturing systems for production scheduling, materials management, and logistics planning (Saccomano, 1998). Sales of ERP systems were expected to be around $20 billion by 2001 and to reach around $1 trillion by 2010 (Bingi, 1999). Such demand is due to the following features of ERP (Saccomano, 1998):

- Less emphasis on functional silos
- Emergence of a new class of user and a new meaning of decision support
- Real-time integration of transactional, analytical, and knowledge-based applications
- New paradigms for business simulation and optimization
- Increased importance of knowledge and computer-based applications that connect directly to the customer.

EVOLUTION OF ERP SYSTEMS

ERP evolved from the famous material requirements planning (MRP) systems. The MRP systems evolved into Manufacturing Resource Planning (MRP II) by incorporating a few important aspects of business. MRP II is a sequential technique that is used for converting the master production schedule (MPS) of the end products into a detailed schedule for raw materials and components. It starts with sales and operation planning and demand management and ends with a detailed schedule for components to be made in-house as well as purchased from vendors. MRP II is a tool for planning the engineering, operational, and financial resources of an organization. The vital part of MRP II is the MRP system; around this MRP system other resources are planned and controlled. MRP II deals with sales, production, inventory, schedules, and cash flows, which are the fundamentals of planning and controlling the manufacturing or distribution process.

MRP II systems are the predecessors of today's ERP systems and generally include fewer enterprisewide functions than ERP packages. MRP II systems often run on proprietary midrange platforms. The ERP system is an advanced information technology that overcomes the limitations of the MRP II; in other words, ERP systems are capable of integrating the data from all of the functional units, thus improving manufacturing performance. The marketplace has been changing continuously since the past decade. An integrated system such as ERP is necessary given current market conditions because customers, having more choices, are becoming more demanding and product life cycles have become shorter. New technologies are changing the way organizations are organized and business processes are designed. A manufacturing planning and control system such as MRP II is becoming less relevant in today's context because of the following important changes:

- Manufacturing is moving toward a "make to order" environment rather than a "make to stock" environment. The various products sold are customized rather than standardized, thus making the planning process complex.

636

- Quality and cost have become qualifiers or minimum requirements for the firms who wish to compete in the marketplace. Competition is now based on delivery, lead times, flexibility, greater integration with the customers and suppliers, and higher levels of product differentiation.

Gumaer (1996) has written about MRPII and how ERP has overcome the drawbacks of the MRPII systems. MRP systems focus only on the materials requirements using an infinite capacity-planning model, and these are not in real-time. In the current market environment, there is a need to plan and direct manufacturing processes in real-time, taking into account various environmental and organizational issues that affect the business and the process of manufacturing. The MRP II systems overcame only some of the drawbacks of the original MRP systems through application of Finite Capacity scheduling and manufacturing execution systems (MES), and the ERP systems have overcome the drawbacks of the MRP II systems by providing an organizationwide integration.

The ERP applications encompass the philosophy of MES and, at the same time, provide organizationwide information that touches all of the functions. In other words, ERP systems affect everything in an organization from order capturing to accounting and procurement to warehousing. Such systems are especially useful when an organization has discrete manufacturing environments and there is a need to plan, coordinate, and manage these facilities to achieve optimal sourcing and production (Laughlin, 1999).

Laughlin also mentions that as companies integrate business units through consolidation, shared services, or global operations, their information technology's ability to support these changes is often stretched. But because of the ERP applications' broad functionality, a company typically can replace much of its legacy systems (*Omnibus Lexicon* defines "legacy systems" as technically obsolescent components of the infrastructure), thus providing better support for these new business structures and strategies.

Davenport (1998) stated that an organization collects, generates, and stores vast amounts of data and these data are spread across the entire organizations stored in dozens or even hundreds of different computer systems, and each of these systems is housed in various offices, factories, or divisions. Each of these is based on legacy mainframe systems and may provide automation and enable a particular functional unit to perform more efficiently. But, in combination, these individual units only impede an organization's ability to grow and expand. Dhar and Stein (1998) discuss the benefits of integrating various computer hardware and software systems in order to bring out the latent information hidden in various functions of the organization. Davenport (1998) explains that if the company's sales and ordering systems cannot talk with its production scheduling systems, then its manufacturing productivity and customer responsiveness will suffer. Similarly, if the sales and marketing systems are incompatible with the financial reporting systems, then management is left to make important decisions by instinct rather than according to a detailed understanding of product and customer profitability.

At Owens Corning, a leading manufacturer of fiberglass-based housing materials and composites, where the authors conducted their case study, there were about 200 different systems running on the legacy systems, and all of these were working in isolation from one another. Such a fragmented IT infrastructure impeded the organization in its growth and expansion. The IT structure it had prior to ERP implementation did not fit its business strategy — that is, it would not enable the company to realize the vision of its CEO.

Eastman Kodak Company is another example of IT architecture characterized by multiple fragmented information systems. There were 2,600 different software applications, more than 4,000 system interfaces, and about 100 different programming languages. They all ran on aging mainframe-based computers before the company switched to an enterprise resource planning system (Stevens, 1997). Kodak found during the business process reengineering that information systems presented not just an opportunity but also an obstacle if not designed properly. In the words of Davenport (1998) "if the systems are fragmented in an organization then the business is fragmented." When the business is fragmented, an organization is unable to achieve success in the marketplace.

RESEARCH METHODOLOGY

In order to understand the enhanced manufacturing performance of an ERP system and its potential to overcome the drawbacks of fragmented systems, the authors carried out their case analysis in five manufacturing firms. A case study was used because of its inherent advantages in providing information. Because there exists no sound theory base yet in this area, case analysis is a strong means for conducting descriptive research and helps to gain insights into areas that have not been explored previously in the literature.

Open-ended questions were asked, and the responses of the IS executives were audiotaped, thus improving the reliability of the study. The interviews were conducted with the MIS directors, chief information officers, or ERP implementation project leaders, because these individuals have a comprehensive overview of both the technical and business aspects of the system.

RESULTS AND DISCUSSION

Exhibit 1 details some of the salient features of the companies that were studied to understand the enhanced manufacturing performance resulting from implementation of ERP systems. Owens Corning and Viskase use SAP as their ERP system; Valenite and Diebold have Baan, and Leeson has Oracle as ERP systems. The reasons for choosing a particular type of ERP are also given in the table. The SAP Company most often preferred to offer its products and services to larger firms, and some of the modules of Baan systems (e.g., Product Configurator) made it the system of choice for global companies such as Diebold. The Oracle ERP was chosen by Leeson because of its ability to meet its needs and because of the Web-based network computing architecture (NCA) of Oracle. All of the companies prior to ERP implementation had legacy mainframes, and all of these firms realized that such disparate legacy systems would not enable them to achieve competitive superiority in the coming years. The details of the case studies of each of the companies are reported elsewhere (Rajagopal et al., 1999a; Tyler and Rajagopal, 1999).

Problems with Disparate Systems

There was a common problem found in all of the firms studied — incompatibility among the systems and the corresponding poor manufacturing performance. Various work processes and transfer and access of information among the functional units and divisions were a time-consuming process prior to ERP implementation. For example, at Owens Corning, order processing and the subsequent dispatch of materials used to take three days. The paperwork associated with the order-taking process was voluminous, and various documents were circulated from office to office. In every office, copies of the same documents were made and filed. Diebold had problems in manufacturing automated teller machines (ATMs) for its global customers that required incorporating differences in currency, language, and technology in various countries. Diebold also had problems in coordinating its internal supply chain in order to practice JIT. Leeson wanted to get rid of its obsolete legacy systems and enhance manufacturing performance. At Viskase, there was no integration of any sort among the production facilities, resulting in poor manufacturing practices. Valenite realized the need to change from aging mainframe-based systems to new systems to cope with the changing business environment. All of the respondents agreed that they cannot progress and go anywhere with their existing legacy systems, and it was more than inevitable for them to switch to a system such as ERP to obtain an organizationwide integration in order to achieve a smooth flow of information. Especially for internationally active companies, a system such ERP is necessary to compete in the current and coming years. Exhibit 2 summarizes the antecedents and issues of the ERP implementation process in the five firms studied.

Exhibit 1. Demographics of the Companies Studied for Their Implementation of ERP Systems

S. No	Salient Points	Valenite	Diebold	Leeson	Owens Corning	Viskase
1	Industry	Metal Cutting	Financial Services	Electric Motors	Fiberglass	Food Packaging
2	Annual Sales	$500M	$1.2B	$180M	$5B	$800M
3	Business Description	Valenite offers the metalworking industry a complete line of standardized and special indexable-insert turning, boring, milling, drilling, and high-speed steel products.	Manufactures ATMs and other products for the financial industry. Diebold is a leading global supplier of ATMs, and holds the primary market position in many other countries.	Maker of variety of electric motors. Leeson motors can be found on material handling equipment, pumps, fans and blowers, machine tools, power transmission products, agricultural applications, treadmills, and other commercial products.	Make of fiberglass-based building materials and composites. Active in sales in 30 countries around the world and have production facilities in approximately 20 countries. The top three foreign sales areas are the U.K., Germany, and France.	Products used by companies such as Sara Lee. Viskase is a holding company with subsidiaries that produce cellulosic casings used in preparing and packaging processed meat products; heat shrinkable, oxygen barrier plastic bags, specialty films for packaging food products; polyvinyl chloride films and related products.

4	Systems Before ERP	Mainframe based	Mainframe based	Mainframe based	Mainframe based	Mainframe based
5	Problems	Incompatibility Nonuniformity	Incompatibility Global product configuration	Incompatibility	Incompatibility Impeding growth	Incompatibility Poor manufacturing
6	Type of ERP Application	Baan	Baan	Oracle	SAP	SAP
	Reason for choosing this system	SAP mentioned that the company was not large enough for them. Oracle did not have some of the modules required.	Needed a good global product configurator.	SAP mentioned that the company's ERP budget was not large enough. Oracle was found to be most suitable. Network computing architecture (NCA0 which is Web based	SAF was found to be the best ERP. SAP was found to be ideal for this large organization.	SAP was found to be ideal to solve the manufacturing problems.

Exhibit 2. Summary of the Case Findings

S. No	Company	Description
1	Owens Corning	The CEO wanted a system that would help the company better compete because of the expected growth in sales. The information system was expected not to be an impediment in the growth and development of the organization. The MIS department was required to integrate the disparate systems and bring about uniformity in the computer hardware and software platforms. Through SAP implementation the company has reduced the number of different systems from 211 to about 12 resulting in savings that amount to millions of dollars because of integrated IT.
2	Viskase	To overcome the problems in manufacturing and in various other areas such as sales, senior management wanted to reengineer the business processes. SAP was chosen to integrate computer hardware and software. The company is able to better perform, especially in manufacturing, owing to the implementation of SAP.
3	Valenite	This company in the machine tool industry wanted to make changes in its organizations to cope with changes in the budiness environment. The Baan system was pilot-tested in their facility located in Canada. They realized better performance in this facility because of Baan implementation. The performance is far superior to their other facilities in the United States. The integrated information systems is enabling them to retrieve and disseminate data in real-time.
4	Diebold, Inc.	This company in the banking industry is positioned to grow and expand in global markets. It wanted a system that would enable it to manufacture products for international customers, taking into consideration differences in language and currency.
5	Leeson Electric	This company is one of the world leaders in manufacturing electric motors. To cope with the changes in the business environment, it wanted an IS that would perform better in the current and coming years. The company implemented Oracle ERP and is realizing the benefits of the system. The salient point to note here in this company is that it uses NCA or Network Computing Architecture that llows it to use the Internet to access its databases, thus resulting in high scalability.

Issues in ERP Implementation

A salient aspect noticed during the interviews and analysis is that ERP implementation requires a business process reengineering (BPR) or some kind of discovery process before implementing the system. Such an understanding of the existing process enables the organizations to redesign their organizational processes in order to get the most out of the ERP implementation. Unless the various business processes are redesigned to suit the design of the modules of ERP, the system implementation may not yield the expected success. ERP is not just an office automation software that can be bought off the shelf and installed but a business transformation process that requires some fundamental changes in the way various business processes are designed and conducted. In addition, the organization's members need to have a good understanding of how the system works before actually putting it into use. Valenite, for example, conducted several simulation studies before putting the systems to use in its Canadian facility. Because data entered in one place connects with many areas or databases of an organization, an error made in one place is multiplied and, if left unnoticed, will result in catastrophe, which may take much time and effort to reconcile. Bingi (1999) provides examples of such situations.

An issue of concern in implementing ERP is employee turnover. Because personnel with ERP experience is much sought after in the market, many companies experienced employee turnover through and after ERP implementation. The companies also needed to revamp their IT architectures in order to implement an ERP system. Most of the companies switched to client/server architecture from mainframe-based systems in order to implement an ERP system. Dow Chemicals, after investing $500M in implementing mainframe-based SAP R/2 system, is now starting over to implement a client/server-based SAP R/3 system.

Enhanced Manufacturing Performance of ERP systems

All the companies studied realized enhanced manufacturing performance from the implementation of ERP systems. At Owens Corning, an executive from the corporate headquarters in Ohio can monitor and affect the production planning and logistics activities of a plant in the U.K., if so desired, with no delay other than the milliseconds of transmittal time. Thus, there is a centralized coordination of activities across various functions, divisions, and countries. The production managers in various factories do not have to worry about order-taking from the customers, tracking logistics, or after-sales service. While the production managers focus on getting the best output from their facilities, the corporate headquarters office takes the responsibility for the remainder of the process from advertising to after-the-sale customer service. The implementation has demonstrated significant contributions to cost savings and performance measures at Owens Corning. Inventory levels have been reduced significantly. Lot sizes and machine allocations have become efficient. Inter-facility coordination has grown significantly. Rather than physical assets being stored as inventory, it is now information access and dissemination that is the vital source of production planning and control that can now be accomplished globally and optimally because of the uniformity of systems. Before the integration of functions and divisions accomplished through ERP, the data collection process was slow and repetitive. Now, the customer can call one location to place an order — unlike the previous system which made it necessary to call two or more different locations. Information about product availability can be retrieved from any linked terminal in the organization, because the system is standardized and uniform across the entire organization. The manufacturing executives of Owens Corning, during this interview, acknowledged that the SAP systems have significantly improved the performance of the manufacturing function, and the chief information officer mentioned that without ERP, the company would not be able to compete in the global arena. (This discussion about the enhanced manufacturing performance is also reported by the same author in detail elsewhere, Rajagopal and Tyler, 1999a). Exhibit 3 details the enhanced performance due to SAP implementation at Owens Corning and Viskase.

At Viskase, another firm with SAP, some of the salient benefits realized through implementing SAP include reductions in lead time and inventory, enhanced visibility in inventory planning, reduction in head count, and an integration of information. In any manufacturing organization, the forecast and actual sales orders are converted to plant orders, which are changed into production orders. Prior to SAP implementation, this process was apparent to only a few persons, and only these few were able to comprehend the information and develop plans for production and purchasing. Through SAP implementation, such complex business processes have become available to others in the organization, thus not only connecting the entire organization end to end but also providing related functions with information that they require to work efficiently. Production-based decisions are tied to sales-based decisions in a more timely and efficient manner, and the various complex factory-level processes are becoming transparent to others in the organization. Decision-making times are therefore reduced significantly, and the organization is better enabled to meet customer demands.

At Valenite, the profitability of the Canadian facility definitely increased after the Baan implementation, but actual dollar figures were not provided. The increase was primarily attributed to lower levels of inventory and improved customer satisfaction. Prior to the Baan implementation, order-taking was a time-consuming and tedious process in which the customer service representatives first wrote the information on paper and then keyed it into the system. With the Baan system in place, this task is accomplished without the translation errors involved in moving from paper to digital mode. The data is entered directly onto the screen, and once such data has been entered, the system is automatically updated and current. The users of the system know that the changes and the actions relating to them have been taken. The statistical and daily updates are automatically

**Exhibit 3. Summary of SAP Implementation and Performance
in the Sample Firms**

	Owens Corning	**Viskase**
Driving Forces	1. Needed a system to cope with increasing sales 2. Needed a system to enable it perform better rather than being an impediment to growth and expansion	1. Needed change 2. Needed to enhance manufacturing performance
Issues in Implementation	1. Outsourced maintenance of previous system to H-P 2. Employee turnover	1. Employee turnover 2. Resistance to change because some modules of the previous systems were better than ERP
Performance	1. Reduction in inventory 2. Centralized coordination among various functions, divisions, and countries 3. Efficient lot sizes and machine allocation	1. Enhanced manufacturing performance 2. Better coordination among the various facilities 3. Enhanced ability to serve the customers.
Cost	$100 M	$15 M
Modules Used	Manufacturing	Manufacturing
Consulting Services	SAP	SAP and PricewaterhouseCoopers
Number of SAP Users	1200	35
Technology Profile	Sun Solaris server Microsoft Office products WAN connecting the various facilities	The data center has been outsourced to IBM Global Services. AT&T manages the Wide Area Networks. Switched from the AS 400 to a RISC 6000 with 14 servers, a number of LANs, routers, back-office tools, and MS Office products

and immediately made, and the financial and inventory books are always current. When the month-end closings occur, the U.S. facilities, which still have legacy mainframe systems in their facilities, take four days to retrieve the appropriate data and make the required entries. In the Canadian facilities with Baan ERP in place, the bookkeeping, journal-entry, and other such financial and accounting processes are automatic and the information is available in real-time. Month-end closings take hours to accomplish, not days. Exhibit 4 details the enhanced manufacturing performance due to Baan implementation at Valenite and Diebold Incorporated.

Prior to ERP implementation, Diebold was operating in batch mode, in which the databases were updated nightly. The desired data was available,

Exhibit 4. Summary of Baan Implementation and Performance in the Sample Firms

	Valenite	Diebold, Inc.
Driving Forces	1. Need to change the IT for competitive reasons 2. Need to enhance manufacturing performance	1. Need for a better product configurator 2. Need to enhance performance of manufacturing function 3. The old system based on mainframe was not useful for the changed environment
Issues in Implementation	1. Need to change all of the old systems into Baan 2. Need to shift to client/server environment 3. Increased workload in order entry	1. Loss of staff 2. Overrun of estimated budget 3. Increased work load in order entry function 4. Need to convert the various processes into Baan
Performance	1. Low inventory 2. Increased availability of information 3. Alleviation of Y2K problems 4. Information diffusion across the firm 5. Increased profitability	1. Alleviation of Y2K problems 2. Better manufacturing cycles 3. Reduced inventory 4. Information diffusion across the entire organization 5. Better global positioning using the Baan Product Configurator 6. Better internal supply chain management
Cost	$2.5 M	$34 M
Modules Used	Manufacturing, Finance, and Sales	Manufacturing, Sales, Finance, and Product Configurator
Consulting Services	Baan only	Arthur Andersen and Baan
Number of Baan Users	35	350

but the "age" of the data made its reliability questionable. Now the data is in real-time across the entire organization. Diebold has overcome its Y2K issues in all of the areas in which Baan is implemented. Before Baan implementation, Diebold had some proprietary interfaces between the various modules to transfer data from the disparate database types. These interfaces were minimal, and there existed no organizationwide level of integration. Since Baan implementation, there are integrated interfaces between all of the modules and data entered in one place automatically triggers changes in all the related databases. Diebold has an internal supply chain, in which the end product from one facility becomes the subassembly for the next facility. The coordination of the facilities thus reduces stockpiling and ensures supplies. Any lack of subassemblies in the process will have an effect on the downstream production processes and profitability. The coordination among the facilities in Diebold thus becomes vital for continued success. With Diebold's size and complexity, an ERP system is required to alleviate problems in coordinating and controlling their manufacturing processes. Baan enables Diebold to more readily do product configuration for the global customers. Given Diebold's expected growth in international markets, a system such as Baan is more than essential to meet customer expectations. (The enhanced manufacturing performance at Valenite and Diebold is discussed in detail in Tyler and Rajagopal, 1999).

At Leeson, after implementing Oracle, the number of phone calls and paperwork related to order processing has been reduced greatly. Order processing is streamlined and smooth. With Oracle, there is greater coordination, and the organization as a whole works together — unlike earlier times, when departments were working in functional silos independent of one another. Order levels and inventory, which were done manually before, are all automated. Before Oracle implementation, the field officers used to fax orders that generated lots of paperwork; with Oracle in place, they do it automatically and directly into the system and various order forms are available in the Oracle system. The order process itself is automatic, all the databases in manufacturing are kept current, and the data is available in real-time. Exhibit 5 shows the changes in manufacturing performance due to Oracle implementation at Leeson.

Before Oracle, when MRP II was used, only a few were able to see the various business processes. More often than not, various functional staff were calling others and the MIS department for data and reports. But the Oracle systems have opened up the information in the company and put the information needed to the end users in a readily accessible form. The finance, inventory, and transactions are all clean, and the information is available to the decision-makers without limitation.

Y2K problems have been totally alleviated. On the factory floors, large packets of paper, that contained special instructions and product revisions, had been distributed. By putting more PCs on the shop floor and using Oracle Front Page, such paper-based instructions were eliminated. The Front Page has all the needed information in it; previously that information circulated manually. Of all the IT innovations seen so far, the respondent agreed that the Oracle ERP systems have made the greatest impact in the organization. It is the authors' belief that E-commerce or conducting business over the Internet will be another IT innovation that is capable of impinging upon many functions of an organization.

As can be seen from Table 6, various criteria to measure performance, especially in manufacturing, such as global optimal procurement, coordi-

**Exhibit 5. Summary of Oracle Implementation and Performance
in the Sample Firms**

	Leeson Electric Company
Driving Forces	1. Need to change
	2. Utilize internet capabilities
	3. Increasing functionalities
Issues in Implementation	1. Data translation
	2. Beta testing
	3. User resistance
	4. Employee training
Performance	1. Integration
	2. Connectivity
	3. Less paperwork
	4. Less manual work
	5. Organizational visibility
	6. Reduction in inventory
Cost	$3.5 M
Modules Used	Oracle Manufacturing, Oracle Financials, and Oracle Human Resources (only to some extent)
Consulting Services	None
Number of Oracle Users	300
Hardware	Sun Enterprise 6000 and 3000 Servers running on Sun Solaris
Facilities Connected	31 Product Warehouses, 6 Manufacturing Facilities and 1700 authorized service centers worldwide

nation in manufacturing, manufacturing knowledge about the markets, marketing knowledge about manufacturing, customer satisfaction, paperwork associated with order processing, time to process orders and deliver, information availability for logistics for optimization, uniformity of the systems in various production units, forecasting accuracy, positioning for global markets, supply chain management activities, and monitoring of performance in various subsidiaries are all enhanced to some or great extent as a result of the implementation of ERP systems. This shows the wide variety of advantages the manufacturing function is able to achieve from ERP implementation. So far there has been no single IT innovation comparable to ERP systems for affecting the various functional units of an organization simultaneously, resulting in enhanced manufacturing performance.

CONCLUSION

Many organizations have successfully automated their business processes by implementing many different kinds of computer hardware and software systems during the past few decades. What appeared to be making the various business processes easy and simple ended up making them

Exhibit 6. Comparison of Performance Before and After Implementation of ERP Systems

	Performance Measures	Owens Corning Before[a]	Owens Corning After	Viskase Before	Viskase After	Valenite Before	Valenite After	Diebold Before	Diebold After	Leeson Before	Leeson After
1	Number of different computer systems	211	1	3	1	N/A	N/A	40	20	1	1
2	Degree of Incompatibility among the systems	Very High	Low	High	Low	High	Low	High	Low	N/A	N/A
3	End-to-End connectivity	None	High	Low	High	Low	High	Low	Very High	Avg	High
4	Global optimal procurement	Very Low	High	Low	Avg	None	Avg	Low	High	Avg	High
5	Coordination in manufacturing	Low	Very High	Above Avg	High	Avg	High	Above Avg	Very High	Avg	High
6	Manufacturing knowledge about markets	Low	Very High	Above Avg	High	Avg	Above Avg	Avg	High	Low	Above Avg
7	Marketing knowledge about manufacturing	Low	High	Low	Above Avg	Above Avg	Same	Avg	High	Low	Above Avg
8	Customer satisfaction	Avg	High	Above Avg	Same	Low	High	High	Same	Avg	High
9	Paperwork associated with order processing	High	Low	High	Above Avg	High	Low	Very High	Above Avg	Very High	Low
10	Time to process order and deliver	High	Low	High	Above Avg	Avg	Same	Avg	Same	High	Low
11	Information availability for logistics for optimization	Low	Very High	Low	High	N/A	N/A	High	Same	Above Avg	High
12	Uniformity of systems in various production units	Low	High	Avg	High	Low	High	High	Very High	Avg	High
13	Forecasting accuracy	Low	High	Low	Same	Very Low	High	Above Avg	Same	N/A	N/A

Exhibit 6. Comparison of Performance Before and After Implementation of ERP Systems *(Continued)*

	Owens Corning[a]		Viskase		Valenite		Diebold		Leeson	
Performance Measures	Before	After	Before	After	Before	After	Before	After	Before	After
14 Information availability for decision making	Low	Very High	Above Avg	High	Low	High	High	Same	Avg	Very High
15 Y2K problems	Many	None	Yes	No	Many	None	Very High	Avg	Yes	None
16 Positioning for global competition	Low	Very High	Avg	Above Avg	Very Low	High	Low	Very High	Avg	Very High
17 Supply chain management	Low	Very High	Low	Above Avg	Low	High	Avg	High	N/A	N/A
18 Monitoring of performance in subsidiaries	Poor	Very Good	Avg	Same	Low	High	Above Avg	High	Avg	High

[a] Before and after refer to the manufacturing characteristics before and after implementation of ERP systems.

complex and difficult to handle because of the wide variety of systems that were accumulating in individual functional units and divisions in the organizations over the years. With the increasingly intense international competition, shorter product life cycles in the market and ever-increasing niches, there is a need for the organizations to be able to digest the vast amount of information from the environment and make fast decisions to respond to dynamic and changing global markets. There is also a need for the organization as a whole to work together and sometimes to work with other organizations as a virtual corporation to make strategic decisions and achieve competitive gains. Toward integrating organizations to reach these goals, information technology has once again proved to be a vital tool by providing "end-to-end" connectivity in an organization through implementation of ERP systems.

This chapter has shown the benefits of implementing an ERP system in enhancing the performance of an organization — manufacturing performance in particular. For global organizations, an ERP system may prove to be a vital tool for coordinating the production at a global level, thus achieving optimal production and sales. With many vendors entering the ERP industry, it will definitely be interesting to see the various types of future information technology integration systems and their capabilities. With such systems providing information at the fingertips of the decision-makers at the right time and right place, the competitive tool in an organization will be the ability of the personnel to focus and develop core capabilities and conceive high degrees of innovation to achieve competitive gains. As much as ERP systems integrate information technology, they are also making organizations understand their core capabilities, reengineer their business processes, and make any changes needed in the business processes to become a market leader. The cost associated with ERP implementation is meager compared with the benefits offered by the integration; at the same time, ERP is proving to be a vital tool for future survival in the global marketplace.

ACKNOWLEDGEMENT

The authors wish to thank the Information Systems and Operations Management Department of The College of Business Administration at The University of Toledo for providing financial support through an Academic Challenge Grant, and the respondents from Owens Corning, Valenite, Leeson, Diebold, and Viskase for giving hours of their valuable time to explain their ERP systems.

Notes

1. Alavi, M. and Keen, P., 1989, "Business Teams in the Information Age," *Information Society*, v. 4, p. 179.

2. Beatty, C. and Gordon, J., 1988, "Barriers to the Implementation of CAD/CAM Systems," *Sloan Management Review,* SUMMER, V. 29(4), P. 25.
3. Beatty, C., 1992, "Implementing Advanced Manufacturing Technologies: Rules of the Road," *Sloan Management Review,* Summer, p. 49.
4. Benbasat, I., Goldstein, D.K., and Mead, M., The Case Research Strategy in Studies of Information Systems, *MIS Quarterly,* 11(3), Sep., 1987, p. 369.
5. Chen, I.J. and Small, M.H., Implementing Advanced Manufacturing Technology: An Integrated Planning Model, *OMEGA, International Journal of Management Science,* 22(1), 1994, p. 91.
6. Davenport, T., Putting the Enterprise into the Enterprise System, *Harvard Business Review,* July/August, 1998, pp. 121–131.
7. Gillenwater, et al, 1995, "Distributed Manufacturing Support Systems: The Integration of Distributed Group Support Systems with Manufacturing Support Systems, OMEGA, v. 23(6), Dec, p. 653.
8. Glaser, B. and Strauss, A., 1967, *The Discovery of Grounded Theory: Strategies in Qualitative Theory,* Wiedenfeld and Nicholson, London.
9. Gullo, K., 1988, "SQL: The New Universal Language," *Datamation,* Mar. 1, p. 60.
10. Green, J. and Kiran, A., 1996, "Manufacturers Meet Global Market Demands with FCS Software," *IIE Solutions.* v. 28n8, Aug 1996. p. 26.
11. Kerr, S., 1988, "Islands of Automation: Networks Emerge to Connect Them," *Datamation,* Mar. 1, p. 57.
12. Kogut, B., 1984, "International Value Added Chain and Strategic Groups," *Journal of International Business Studies,* v. 15(2), p. 151.
13. Meredith, J.R. and McCutcheon, D., 1989, "Conducting Case Study Research in Operations Management," *Journal of Operations Management,* v. 11 (3), Sep, p. 239.
14. Rajagopal, P. and Tyler, F., "A Comparative Case Analysis of Enterprise Resource Planning Systems Implementation and Performance — SAP," Submitted to *OMEGA, The International Journal of Management Science.*
15. Rockart, J.F. and Short, F.E., "Information Technology in the 1990s: Managing Organizational Interdependence," ch. 16 in *Strategic Information Management,* Edited by Galliers, R.D. and Baker, B.S.H., Butterworth-Heinemann Ltd., Oxford, 1994.
16. Saccomano, A., "More than Manufacturing," *Traffic World,* v. 256, no. 5, Nov. 2, 1998, p. 46.
17. Tyler, F. and Rajagopal, P., "A Comparative Case Analysis of Enterprise Resource Planning Systems Implementation and Performance — SAP," Submitted to *Information Systems Management.*
18. Vonderembse, M., Raghunathan, T.S., and Rao, S., 1996, "A Post Industrial Paradigm: To Integrate and Automate Manufacturing," *International Journal of Production Resources,* v. 35 (9), p. 2579.

Chapter 54
Technology, Inventory, and the Supply Chain: Roles in Business Model Building

James B. Ayers

An effective supply chain is essential to many organizations. This chapter sorts through the myths and realities of creating and maintaining one.

INTRODUCTION

Technology, inventory, and a supply chain are important elements of many companies' business models. These companies spend heavily on technology to ensure that their supply chains function well. Yet few do. This chapter explains why these companies fail and how other companies can avoid their mistakes.

TECHNOLOGY'S ROLE

The technology element, in particular, has come in for criticism lately. When Marshall Fisher wrote the quotation, he cited EDI and point-of-sale systems, now considered "old hat" in technology circles, as examples of "technology and brainpower."

As it often does, technology advances faster than the readiness of users to put it to work. Along with the recent implosion of the "dot.coms," the claims of technology purveyors are more likely to be met with well-deserved skepticism. Monday morning quarterbacks have discovered that, although the dot.coms had products and technology, the inventory and supply chain management components of the business model were not. The result was "hot" companies wasting a lot of investor money.

On the other hand, no company can long ignore the promise inherent in the technology. How can an organization do a better job in planning its evolution from "here" to "there"? What should "there" look like? The latest wave of supply chain "solutions" brings exhortations to implement ever more advanced generations of software. These include an alphabet soup of application package categories including ERP, MES, APS, WMS, CRM, and many others. The Internet is an enabler of this "connectivity" and enhances "collaboration" along the supply chain. Another enabler is the commodity exchange, also likely to be Internet based. Here, the exchange takes a fee to "automate" the marketplace for the commodity.

One dot.com lesson is that a successful business model requires balanced application of all three elements to make money. For this chapter, the three business model elements are defined as:

1. *Technology:* as in computer hardware, applications, and the Internet
2. *Inventory:* includes material selection, purchasing, distribution, and sourcing; encompasses decisions regarding service levels and the deployment of inventory to meet customer needs
3. *Supply chain:* encompasses end-to-end product, financial and information flows along with related transactions, partnerships, and collaborations

THE BALANCE PROBLEM

The three elements are frequently supportive and frequently in conflict. Perhaps the most important conclusion is that each is a necessary, but not sufficient, element in achieving a lasting competitive position. Strategy makers should understand the choices they have in striking the right balance among the three.

Exhibit 1 illustrates three situations that commonly take shape in an organization. In situation A, the three elements are considered separately. They are addressed with roughly equally weighted efforts. Their separation implies that cross-talk is minimal; the efforts are justified, administered, and measured independently; and the plans for each are not coordinated. This is particularly true for the business that has been around for a while. Starting with a blank sheet of paper can be an advantage.

In situation B, one element dominates the others. This case is typical where resources or management attention is limited to "one problem at a time."

Situation C is more desirable. The efforts are balanced and overlap where appropriate. This is accomplished by formulating the components as parts

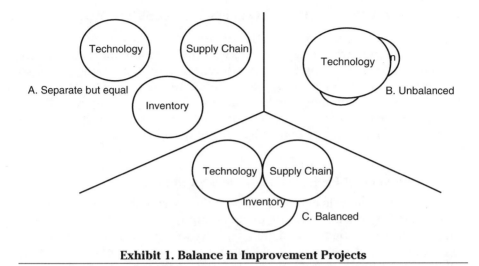

Exhibit 1. Balance in Improvement Projects

of a single strategy. A sure way to evolve into a faulty business model is not to do this. As we proceed, we need to keep the "the balance problem" in mind and fight to find ways to restore balance where it is missing.

THE COST REDUCTION PROMISE

The ongoing business will likely argue for technology and other initiatives in cost reduction terms. For example, the exchanges mentioned above claim buyers will lower the prices they pay by using their Web sites as marketplaces. The Internet exchange, so the thinking goes, provides a wide world of suppliers from which to choose. No longer will a single supplier or a cartel hold the buyer hostage with exorbitant prices. A second payoff from the exchange is reduced transaction cost. Doing away with messy paperwork cuts overhead associated with buying and selling.

A third often-cited technology benefit is inventory reduction. This saving occurs in the inbound (from suppliers to the company) and outbound (from the company to its customer) pipelines. The assumption is that the Internet and the latest application software will improve visibility along the chain. This, in turn, produces better decisions regarding what to produce, how much is needed, and when to produce it. It will also help buyers and sellers communicate progress in filling orders.

These claims are sometimes true — at least to an extent. Often, however, savings fall short. A principal reason is that the claims are based on traditional, arm's length, or even adversarial relationships between buyers and sellers. As the supply chain model of collaboration takes root, these relationships are changing. This in turn expands alternatives to solve problems, lower costs, and improve customer service.

MYTHS: COMMON OBSTACLES TO EFFECTIVE BUSINESS MODELS

To identify these alternatives, the technology manager should understand the reasons why things are the way they are and all the available alternatives for improving the status quo, not only technology but also basic structural change. One way to understand the multiple paths available is to explore common perceptions that stand in the way of building competitive business models. If the reader believes his or her organization has embraced any of the myths listed here, consider the alternatives described.

Myth: Improvement Projects Constitute a Strategy

A common mistake is confusion of activity with results. For example, an IT manager may have a full slate of small improvement projects, one that can pack his or her budget and staff capacity for years. However, virtually all of it falls into the category of "continuous improvement" or maintenance projects. Few are really the kind of project that changes the business model and improves competitive position. The result might look like situation B in Exhibit 1.

An example is a company in which executives charged a newly hired manager and a task team to make supply chain "breakthroughs." This company is a contract manufacturer with a leading market share and depends on supply chain dominance to stay competitive.

However, the team found that the company had to clean up supply chain data in the wake of a recent ERP implementation. As long as the new system spewed out inaccurate information, little in the way of real benefit would be enjoyed. And top management was anxious for a payback from their ERP investment. The team's efforts became, in reality, completion of the ERP project, a task that diverts them from their original mission.

The purpose of this story is not to belittle the real needs that are filled by projects like this one. In fact, most companies need at least two types of projects: ones that pursue continuous improvements and ones that change competitive position. Companies that want to move ahead must find the resources for both continuous improvement and strategic projects.

In the *Handbook of Supply Chain Management*, the author of this chapter presents a method for categorizing a supply chain project.[1] That framework is shown as Exhibit 2. The exhibit shows six project categories. On the vertical axis, projects are either "strategic" or "non-strategic." A strategic project changes the basis for competition. Along the horizontal axis, there are three categories that measure the breadth in the project. The categories are department level, business unit level, and supply chain level. Department level projects are confined to just one department. A business unit project involves more than one department but remains within the

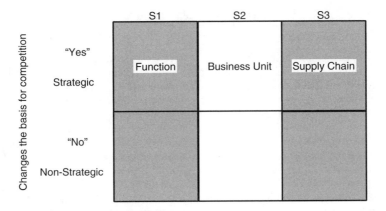

Exhibit 2. Model for Competing through Supply Chain Management

walls of the company. A supply chain project extends its reach to multiple enterprises beyond the immediate business unit.

A company should classify its projects using this framework. An honest assessment will likely place the majority of projects in the lower left-hand box — department level, non-strategic projects that do not change the basis for competition. Situation A from Exhibit 1 likely reflects this condition.

Myth: You Can "Control" Costs

You might get arguments on this one from the company controller. Financial statements "keep score," reporting costs against budgets; hence, they are "under control" from an accountant's viewpoint. Marching orders for improving the score often boil down to reducing costs, cutting items on the balance sheet inventory, and otherwise improving the bottom line.

This mindset reflects the view that cost is an *independent* variable, or one that is controllable. When managers treat costs as independent variables, they overlook the fact that the costs of operations mirror many factors. They fail to understand the root causes, which lie in the way the supply chain works. In fact, inventory levels and costs are a consequence of many supply chain "features." This means they are dependent, not independent, variables. As independent variables, you cannot achieve cost reductions without changing the way you conduct business.

Myth: Time Is Not Important

Those deeply in involved in supply chain issues often forget the role of time as a determinant of competitive position. This issue rose in a team working under the auspices of the Supply-Chain Council (or SCC). The team was deciding whether and how to explain the difference between the

Exhibit 3. Definitions of Lead-Time and Cycle Time

Lead-Time	Cycle Time
Lead-time is associated with a product or service delivered by the supply chain. It is "imposed" on the supply chain by the competitive environment. It is driven by customer expectations, supply chain innovations, and competitive pressure. All these factors are in constant motion, moving toward "faster, cheaper, better." Competitors that cannot deliver products and services within the established lead-time will likely perish. Competitors that achieve the shortest lead-times have an advantage.	Cycle time is a property of processes along the supply chain. The minimum theoretical cycle time for a product's supply chain is the sum of individual process cycle times. Cycle time reduction is achieved through process reengineering, including the introduction of technology along the chain. An example is sharing information about final demand, introducing postponement[a] through product design, and automation in production processes. A competitor that works to reduce cycle time can end up with the shortest lead-time.

[a] "Postponement" refers to product and supply chain design that allow for last-minute customizing of a product for delivery. It is often achieved by creating projects built on standard modules.

terms, *lead-time* and *cycle time*. The effort was part of an update of the SCOR model, maintained by the SCC. SCOR stands for "supply chain reference model." The model contains a standard set of supply chain activities and practices and includes a glossary. SCOR has widespread application in benchmarking, defining activities, measuring performance, and cataloging best practices.

Some participants in the effort felt that *lead-time* and *cycle time* are identical terms and that only one definition is required. Others felt the terms should have different definitions. The ensuing discussions lead to a distinction between the two terms including the author's contribution shown in Exhibit 3.

The distinction between the terms is important. The root cause for inventory and its related costs lies in the mismatch between "lead-time" and "cycle time." When the lead-time demanded by the market is less than the corresponding cycle time, inventories are required. Also, the greater the mismatch is, the greater the inventory requirement. For this reason, leading competitors strive for synchronous operations and lean on manufacturing to reduce the difference.

For example, the grocery shopper who wants a gallon of milk does not expect to wait until the cow is milked, the product is pasteurized and packaged in a processing plant, and then is delivered to the supermarket. She or he anticipates finding the milk on the shelf at any hour of the day, creating the need for inventory on the grocer's shelf. The inventory, in turn, creates needs for management and technological baggage to store it, finance it, account for it, and track it.

Likewise, there is more milk inventory back up the chain all the way to the cow. In the case of a perishable good such as milk, inventories are likely to be low as measured by the number of days of inventory. The "sell it or smell it" reality is a reason. However, for more durable goods, inventory in the supply chain can be weeks, months, or even years of requirements.

Some products operate quite differently. In these cases, the lead-time is longer than the cycle time. For example, airlines and aircraft leasing companies place orders for aircraft far in advance of their need, essentially reserving space on the assembly line. In contrast to the milk example, the customer is willing to put in his order and then wait while the airplane is built.

Dell has a short lead-time for customized computers and a positive cash-to-cash cycle. Dell receives payment from the customer before it pays its suppliers and has short lead-times for delivering customized products. When an order comes in, Dell customizes its products for the order. Dell, however, has only eliminated its own inventory; inventory is still required to support its business model. Its suppliers must carry now carry it.

Returning to our milk example, Exhibit 4 shows us at least four alternatives for designing the supply chain and their impact on the business model.

Before embarking on any technology investment — moving from Model A in Exhibit 4 to Model B for example, the company needs to understand whether there is a better way as represented by Models C and D.

Myth: The Lower the Inventory, the Better

Our opening quotation came from an article that imparted an important insight. Marshall Fisher, the author, argues there are essentially two types of products to consider in supply chain design. These are the *functional* and the *innovative* product. The supply chain for the functional product, according to Fisher, will be designed for low cost. The supply chain for the innovative product will be designed for responsiveness.

This concept also extends to the product life cycle. Early in life, the product is, by definition, new. The market is likely to be growing fast. There is ample demand and plenty of business for all competitors. This defines the innovative product. However, no good thing lasts forever. As the product ages, demand flattens and competition stiffens. The product is now functional.

How many companies make the distinction between innovative and functional products? Often, where a company sells both types of product,

Exhibit 4. Alternative Ways of Designing a Supply Chain

	Alternatives	Description
A	"Low-tech" information sharing (status quo business model)	Signal the need for restocking with manual or other less technical solutions. Includes Kanbans, shelf restocking, faxes, etc. This is the common practice today with the dairy distributor making frequent stops at the supermarket and replacing what has been sold. Empty space on the shelves is the replacement signal. This signal ripples sequentially back through the chain.
B	"High-tech" information sharing (Internet model)	Use information technology at the store level to let the distribution company, milk processing company, and the dairy farmer know a transaction has occurred. The replacement signal is electronically transmitted to interested parties. Their responses are preplanned.
C	Cycle time shortening ("lean" business model)	Move the cow and processing plant into the store to cut overall cycle time. This tight supply chain also uses the empty shelf as a replenishment signal. While not practical for milk, it is a technique finding wider use in automotive supply chains.
D	Structural business model change	Provide delayed delivery direct to the customer's home. This saves a customer trip to the store. Use the Internet or a call center to gather orders.

there is just one supply chain. That supply chain is usually designed for low cost. This includes minimizing inventory, using low-cost shipping companies, and cutting back on stocking points in the chain. Suppliers are also likely to be chosen on the basis of cost.

Such a policy overlooks the costs of being out of stock. These costs take the form of lost sales and the associated profit; these are costs not included on most financial statements.

Myth: Visibility Is the Solution

There are two types of errors one can commit in opening the supply chain to increased visibility through the Internet or other means. The first is an error of doing something just because technology makes it possible. Exhibit 4 showed a choice between a low-tech (A) and a high-tech solution (B). In the absence of loud protestations by customers or suppliers, there may not be a "visibility problem." Low tech is good enough — particularly if supply chain activities are well executed.

The second type of error is one of implementation. Unless the data made visible is timely and accurate, it may be better to keep it hidden. It is also necessary to define the expected responses in situations likely to be revealed by the flow of new data.

A case illustrates the point. A company with a widespread, global supplier base instructed its suppliers to maintain a two-week inventory at its production facility in the United States. The original purpose was to move this inventory off the company's balance sheet and onto the suppliers'. Each supplier received a weekly forecast from the ERP system defining the number of units they were expected to have on hand.

The procedure had several flaws. The ERP forecasts were not frozen and shifted significantly from week to week. For example, the week of July 15, forecasted in mid-June, might require 1000 units; a couple of weeks later, the requirement may have changed to 2000.

It was also difficult for suppliers to make the adjustments in time. The ERP reports covered only the current quarter. Near the end of the quarter, there were no forecasts to define the needs within the time it took the suppliers to respond. Thus, suppliers were "flying blind" at this time.

The lesson is that sometimes no information is better than bad information. Also, one must critically examine what information is available, when, and what has to be done with it.

Myth: Technology Is Efficient

A tendency of many is to underestimate the complexity and decision-making content in seemingly routine transactions. *The Wall Street Journal* headlined a story that defies the notion technology is the solution for "routine" transactions.[2] It tells the story of the Grant J. Hunt Co., a distributor of potatoes and other produce, and the experience of its president, Grant Hunt.

The Hunt company buys from farmers and sells their products to supermarket chains, wholesalers, and restaurant-supply companies. The article describes Hunt's experience in trying to move its low-tech, non-Internet business to a Web exchange. Exhibit 5 summarizes the claimed advantages for the exchanges and the lessons learned from tests of the technology.

Companies contemplating providing increased visibility into their supply chains should understand the Hunt experience. Any proposals should be reviewed with the lessons learned in mind.

CONCLUSION

The basis of competition has shifted from the individual company to the supply chain. Companies must continuously review and adjust their business models to stay in the game. The penalties for making mistakes like the ones we described here can be severe. The intent of this chapter has been to aid the reader in avoiding the pitfalls. Unfortunately, many will repeat

Exhibit 5. Transactions on Exchanges: Promises and Reality

The Promise	The Reality
Joining an exchange would bring new customers.	• The exchanges were seen to attract customers with marginal credit ratings. • An exchange-posted offer to sell cherries produced no bidders in four days.
The exchange would streamline transactions bringing "incalculable efficiencies."	• The exchange could handle only routine transactions. • The existing infrastructure (faxes, phones, etc.) is not that inefficient. • The exchange systems would not link to home-grown systems. The result was duplication.
The exchange would increase business.	• The best way to get business is to hit the phones and call suppliers and customers. The exchange did not attract incremental business. • The service provided by Hunt buyers includes advising suppliers and customers on market conditions. It is difficult to automate this function.
Big customers would require exchange-based transactions.	• The large customers wanted to shift business to the exchanges but were not able — as of the date of the article — to follow through. In fact, some transactions were done both the old and new ways bringing duplication.
The exchange would improve visibility along the supply chain.	• This was true. However, it was important to keep some prices and transactions confidential; the exchange opened the terms of these transactions to too many parties.
The exchange fee was competitive.	• The fee of 1–2 percent was a steep price in a narrow margin business like distribution.
The software would work.	• The software was not ready for use. Hunt became a beta test site for some of the exchanges. • Several of the early exchange providers left the business.
The software was flexible.	• The exchanges would not allow Hunt to changes prices quickly in response to market conditions. • The software had difficulty processing abnormal transactions like returns. It failed on four of nine common transactions selected for a test. • The software had difficulty classifying different types of potatoes. Different distributors used different codes for the same potato.
The Hunt systems were outmoded.	• They worked, and the supply chain had grown accustomed to using them.

the errors of the past under pressure for quick solutions or out of fear of being left behind.

Notes

1. Ayers, James B., *Handbook of Supply Chain Management*, St. Lucie Press and APICS, Boca Raton, FL, 2001.
2. Gomes, Lee, How Lower Tech Gear Beat Web "Exchange" at Their Own Game, *The Wall Street Journal*, March 16, 2001, p. A1.

Chapter 55
Managing Customer Expectations
Holmes Miller

Why are some information systems (IS) customers dissatisfied with systems that seem to meet specifications? The answer may lie in how satisfaction is defined. Service quality researchers have studied customer expectations and have found that the perceived "quality" of the service experience depends on the gap between expectations and measured performance. Because the same may be true for information systems, IS professionals should manage customer expectations to promote favorable outcomes.

TYPES OF EXPECTATIONS

Information systems expectations are both explicit and implicit. *Explicit expectations* represent what the customer expects to happen, and they are measured against specifications or targets. Explicit expectations involve static performance, dynamic performance, technology, and interpersonal interactions. They reflect expressed needs and the dynamic business, technological, and interpersonal environments that surround systems development and implementation.

Static performance expectations concern how performance and quality for a specific application are defined. Although each system's performance measures are unique, general expectations relate to quality of outcome and include accessibility, customization, dependability, timeliness, accuracy, tangible cues that augment the application, options, cutting-edge technology, flexibility, and user-friendly interfaces. Static performance expectations are the visible part of the iceberg; they are the ones we see and — often erroneously — assume are all that exist.

Dynamic performance expectations concern how the IS application evolves over time and include the support and enhancements needed to meet changing business and technological environments. As with static performance, customers define dynamic performance expectations and may even revise existing performance measures. Dynamic elements are similar to those mentioned for static performance but also include genera-

0-8493-1273-6/02/$0.00+$1.50
© 2002 by CRC Press LLC

tion of new ideas, ongoing consulting, seamless relationships between systems personnel and systems users, and expectations related to IS personnel's knowledge of changing environments.

Technological expectations relate to how the application's technology meets the evolving state-of-the-art technology. While technology affects static and dynamic performance expectations, technology creates its own expectations because technology is a "product" people consume for reasons of status, ego, self-image, or fear of being without. Technological expectations involve maintaining or enhancing the balance between how the customer sees himself *vis-à-vis* "technology," specific technologies, and competitive forces. This may mean being on the cutting edge, or it may mean being comfortably in the middle of the pack. Technological expectations change as technology changes and require meeting positional goals regarding evolving and new technologies.

Interpersonal expectations involve developing, supporting, and enhancing IS applications. They concern the relationship between customer and service provider and include the human element as an entity in and of itself. Because people develop applications for people, interpersonal relations often can outweigh technological sophistication measured performance in evaluating an application's success. Some specific interpersonal dimensions include technical competence and how well that is communicated to customers, problem-solving and consulting skills, courtesy, helpfulness, empathy, verbal and written communication skills, and customer perceptions regarding professional image, appearance, and conduct.

While explicit expectations concern the system in question, *implicit expectations* are formed by customer experiences with other applications inside and outside the organization. They reshape views of what is and should be possible. For example, implicit expectations arise from seeing a competitor implement a new data mining technology or from using a speech recognition system when booking an airline flight. The expectations arise from experience and cause the customer to relate what happens elsewhere to the workplace. In dynamic environments, meeting static specifications no longer is enough because even when applications perform as promised, rapid environmental change changes *the real* customer expectations. Like curved mirrors at a carnival that distort images of people, implicit expectations create a "mirror of experience and knowledge," in which *real* system performance is reflected and viewed.

STRATEGIES FOR MANAGING EXPECTATIONS

Because perceived quality depends on the gap between measured and expected performance, initially one might opt for a "football coach" strategy — create very low initial expectations to make this gap as large as possible. Information systems, however, is not football, and a strategy of intentionally lowering expectations can be counterproductive. Final football scores cannot be misinterpreted — the team with the most points wins. For information systems, however, a customer's perception of quality may be linked to prior expectations. High expectations can lead to positive outcome evaluations, and low expectations may lead to a self-fulfilling prophecy of low performance evaluations — i.e., the "Pygmalion effect." For this reason, IS professionals should create high expectations that are achievable, realistic, and unambiguously communicated to customers.

How can they do this? The quality literature discusses how the PDSA cycle — Plan, Do, Study, Act — is used for continual improvement. A practitioner using the PDSA cycle plans a change, does a small experiment, studies the results, and — if improvement is possible — acts to permanently change the system. IS professionals can use a variant of this to manage customer expectations: *IDentify, Evaluate, and Act* — or *IDEA*. Step one is to *identify* what customers expect, for example, explicit facts such as a one-second response time on customer inquiries, or implicit facts about favorable experiences with other automated systems. Identifying expectations requires collecting information via informal customer contacts, formal surveys, knowledge of industry and technological trends, knowledge of what other supply chain partners are doing, and information gleaned from informal internal organizational networks.

Once identified, expectations must be *evaluated*. Some expectations may be congruent with proposed development outcomes, while others may be unrealistic and unattainable. For example, customers who experience systems that can understand a wide range of sentences may for unreasonably high expectations for a more modest application with limited speech recognition capabilities. Should the proposed system be modified? Should customers learn more about the costs and limitations of speech recognition technology? Regardless, the final step is to *act*. Actions may range from modifying plans to incorporating expectations into development efforts to educating customers about why their expectations are impractical. Even when expectations cannot be met, however, some actions should be taken, because inaction may create situations in which expectations exceed potential performance.

Understanding static and dynamic customer expectations requires involving IS professionals with customers and technology. It also requires that they understand evolving marketplace realities, including the firm's products, competitors, suppliers, and customers. Managing expectations involves customer and business knowledge, technological knowledge, interpersonal skills and an aggressive attitude toward understanding change. IS professionals can take the following six steps:

1. *Segment customers and identify value.* Customer strategies are based on the maxim, "Know your customer." This includes segmenting

customers to know their business, know how they are organized, know how they operate, know their other external IS interactions, and know how they define a "favorable" outcome. Knowing how to identify differences and knowing how the customer defines value is one outcome of segmenting customers. Business structure, organizational personality, and specific business drivers shape how customers perceive value and, thus, their expectations regarding whether value is delivered. For example, one customer may value timeliness; another may value customization; and another may value accuracy. Staying one step ahead of the customer not only will shape his expectations, but it will make you more valuable to him because you will become essential to satisfying his business needs.

2. *Shape customer perceptions of past performance.* Because how past performance is perceived can affect how future performance is evaluated, one should identify outstanding concerns, answer questions, and shape actions rather than passively accepting existing erroneous customer perceptions. Determine what the customer thinks of you. Was his assessment of past performance accurate? Was favorable performance viewed unfavorably? If so, what can be done to correct the misassessment? Was overall favorable performance unfairly shaped by an isolated unfavorable incident — for example, a system crash at a sales presentation. Was context given to genuinely unfavorable performance? This need not mean apologizing or making excuses to try to redefine reality. It does mean making sure the perception of what occurred is accurate, is viewed through the proper frame, and does not adversely affect future evaluations.

3. *Understand how environmental experiences shape expectations.* Because your customers' interactions with competitors, with vendors, with customers, or in their private lives can shape their expectations, you should know and assess your customers' experiences. This requires understanding what they are experiencing and understanding — perhaps by going through the same experiences — what types of expectations are being developed. For example, a competitor's system with a faster response time and more options is going to affect expectations for your system. Or customers doing personal investment account analysis on the Internet will change their expectations for analysis on your system. Three necessary steps include staying close to what is happening in the marketplace, knowing your customers, and constantly probing to ascertain the state of the art and where you stand relative to it in your customer's eyes.

4. *Keep current with technology and technology's impact.* Needless to say, what is technologically feasible and what is happening elsewhere shapes what customers expect from you. You cannot deliver results if you remain ignorant of opportunities. This is why it is important to keep current with technology. But knowing about technology is not

enough. You must link that knowledge to your customer's needs. This link allows you to add value, both in suggesting or saying "yes" to a cost-effective new application or method, and saying "no" to a customer's suggestion that will not work in your technological environment or is not cost-justified. It is easier to say "no" when you know why "no" is the right answer, rather than just being negative, or worse, promising results that you cannot deliver.

5. *Provide positive interactions.* How customers perceive past performance includes how they perceive personal interactions. The quality of past customer interactions can shape what they expect you will deliver and how well they perceive IT's ability to deliver. Interactions can shape attributes such as timeliness, knowledge of the customer's business, personality, willing to go the extra mile to address problems, and knowledge of the customer's business. Providing positive interactions also means developing a professional environment and an environment that responds to the customer's personality and organizational culture. Finally, it means attending to basic IS development details such as providing technically capable, timely, flexible, personal service and constantly communicating with customers regarding their wants and needs.

6. *Create processes to manage expectations.* Use a process, such as *IDEA,* to manage expectations. This process need not be highly structured or rigorous, but it should ensure that the proper "bases" are touched. IS professionals should be concerned with managing expectations. This may mean managing all aspects of the process themselves or delegating pieces of the process to specialists. For example, one person may keep up with technological trends, another may focus on business trends, and another may tend to specific interactions with customers. Facts should be freely communicated and analyzed so managers can anticipate what customers expect.

CONCLUSION

Social, technological, and interpersonal factors affect how information systems are developed, implemented, maintained, and enhanced. Social factors arise from individual and group dynamics and include more user-friendly application interfaces, more interpersonal connectivity, more visual and verbal input and output, and more use of groupware to facilitate real-time communication with co-workers and on-line communities. Using these new capabilities has changed customers' experiences and has shaped their expectations for all IS applications.

Technological change also creates expectations at each end of the skill spectrum. Technologically savvy customers expect appropriate state-of-the-art technology in all applications. Their knowledge and capabilities create a frame of reference used to critically evaluate all technologies and potentially discard those found wanting. "Low competence" customers also have high expectations because technological advances have allowed them to use heretofore inaccessible applications. These advances have created new demands for simple user interfaces and raised expectations for all IS applications to be as accessible as the "most assessable" application used elsewhere.

Interpersonal experiences with other service providers affect expectations for the system. Because many organizations view customer service as a competitive weapon, service levels have become more timely, customized, and personalized. Customer experiences in other settings have raised expectations for IS product and service quality.

All of these factors create a need to understand customer needs, understand what customers expect, and use that knowledge to reshape or address expectations. Managing expectations means honestly confronting and reshaping expectations in the context of IS providers and customers achieving mutually beneficial outcomes. Managing expectations does not mean trying to create an artificial reality, but rather calls for a conscious effort to monitor, identify, understand, and react to expectations in the world. It is the difference between looking ahead with eyes open and traveling blindfolded. Although organizational culture and environment define the specific process to be followed, some process should be used to avoid a situation in which expectations spin out of control and IS customers expect something far more or far different than what can be delivered.

Managing expectations makes sense because dynamic environments change and reshape the reality held by those experiencing change. No IS professional would build an application ignoring customer needs. Managing expectations is the dynamic component of assessing customer needs. Monitoring and responding to dynamic expectations is as critical to success as initially defining and responding to customer needs. Information systems have opened Pandora's box by creating new capabilities and standards for processing, analyzing, and visually presenting massive amounts of information. Now, IS professionals should incorporate into their methodologies management strategies to meet the changes resulting from their own success.

Chapter 56
ERP, One Letter at a Time

Bill Jeffery
Jim Morrison

Are you planning on transforming your enterprise and supply chain? Better get the business case down, goal markers set up, and everyone on board to make it happen.

When Juan Sanchez took over as CIO of Delphi Automotive Systems Europe in September 1998, the company was in the midst of an ERP project with straightforward targets and a dizzying array of challenges. The European operations are a major component of Delphi Automotive Systems, the world's largest automotive supplier, headquartered in Troy, Michigan. As the project got underway, the stakes for a successful implementation increased. At the end of the day, Sanchez and his team learned that such a project took a lot more than careful planning. It took vigilant monitoring of detailed goals, the committed involvement of executives and workers alike, a focus on customer needs, and the careful building of a business case for the endeavor (see Exhibit 1).

At the time, Delphi was organized on a geographic basis with different systems in each European country. Where divisions crossed geographic borders, systems support was not consistent. A major implementation of enterprise resource planning (ERP) software, with a planned expenditure of more than $50 million, had begun more than three years previously when Delphi was still part of General Motors. The project's ambitious goal: to replace dozens of aging — and incompatible — manufacturing and distribution legacy systems scattered throughout the 69 Delphi sites in eight European countries with a single enterprisewide system.

It wasn't simply the technical aspects of the ERP implementation that made the work difficult. It was the complex business scenario at Delphi that made the new system an imperative and heightened the risk of failure. Possible complications included:

TASK 5: MAKING MONEY FROM THE SUPPLY CHAIN

Exhibit 1. Diamonds in the Rough

In retrospect, the most interesting part of this experience was that many of the reasons for the project's value couldn't have been articulated at the time the project was jump-started. You could even go so far as to say that Delphi would be a less viable company today if it had not begun putting in the ERP system. Examples of how valuable the project has been to Delphi, a company in transition, include:

- *The ability to serve more customers* — The ability to serve multiple competing customers in an open market, each having unique EDI procedures, forecast requirements, master schedules, and shipping needs. To do that with the old system would have been very difficult and costly, if not impossible.
- *Plants working in sync* — The ability to work in tandem among 69 sites to fill complex orders that spanned multiple customer sites throughout multiple countries. As but one example, plants in Delphi's U.K. operation are now able to share plant resources with plants in Portugal, which was previously difficult to do.
- *A workforce that is technologically up to speed* — Previously, some employees had never touched a PC. According to Sanchez, "The technical education alone was worth it; we pushed the latest technology throughout the entire company."

Delphi has built upon the European experience as it implements its global ERP strategy in North America and beyond.

- *Systems across borders.* The new ERP system needed to cross multiple geographic, cultural, and linguistic boundaries. More than 3,500 employees were going to depend on it to get their daily jobs done. Each country had developed business practices independently, and some could not be reconciled because of the varying legal and regulatory requirements, despite the efforts of the European Union to resolve cross-border inconsistencies.
- *Date-rollovers.* Delphi was using the project to help solve its Year 2000 compliance issues. The project also had to help the company support the new Euro currency; managers wanted the project to provide Delphi's various country locations a single conversion from one system, rather than one conversion for each different system.
- *Changes at the corporate level.* The May 1999 spin-off of Delphi Europe from its parent company, General Motors, occurred in the middle of the project.

More than two years into the project (at the end of 1997) Delphi enlisted A.T. Kearney to ensure on-time/on-budget completion of the project and a tangible ROI, while EDS took responsibility for the technical aspects of the rollout of the new SAP R/3 system.

A.T. Kearney viewed this as an opportunity to drive the implementation from a financial and operational perspective, something we felt other companies implementing ERP projects had not done. You don't have to go far to bump into lots of evidence that shows how ERP software has not delivered on the promises of vendors. Some recent cases where ERP has had publicly disastrous results include Whirlpool, where an ERP implementation crippled the shipping system, leaving appliances stacked on loading docks — and therefore not delivered to paying customers — for a full eight weeks in 1999. Hershey Foods (also in 1999) claimed that a 19 percent drop in earnings was caused by an incompetent ERP implementation that wreaked distribution havoc for one of its traditionally most profitable seasons: Halloween. While these high-profile failures were not top-of-mind when Delphi made its decision to implement ERP, they later served as reminders that such projects can easily go out of control.

Attempting a large-scale ERP implementation (including both implementation and operations) is an expensive proposition for any organization. The total cost of an average system over the course of the project runs approximately $15 million, according to Benchmarking Partners. Our 1998 survey of more than 100 SAP implementations found a whopping average cost per user of $53,000 and a 31-month implementation average.

A recent Meta Group report measuring the net present value of ERP implementation projects found that approximately 60 percent of respondents indicated a negative return on investment. That number climbed as high as 80 percent, depending on the specific software implemented. And because many of these first-generation implementations were internally focused with no associated business case (i.e., emphasizing cost reductions, technology, and process improvements rather than external benefits like extending ERP systems to players in the supply chain), quantifiable benefits were virtually nonexistent.

A HIGHLY STRUCTURED IMPLEMENTATION

The process we employed on Delphi's behalf focused on six major initiatives:

1. *Developing a quantifiable business case.* Delphi first established concrete goals for the business processes they wanted to improve, such as increasing service levels, and calculated the expected benefits to be realized from these improvements.
2. *Defining best practices.* Functional teams defined best practices, such as standardizing accounting procedures across Europe and standardizing logistics processes. These teams, composed of key Delphi executives from affected areas (in this case, logistics and finance), included representatives from a broad range of nationalities and cultures. These executives identified "key migration points," and the precise type and timing of a change were identified.
3. *Planning prior to implementation.* Planning for actual rollout of the new system at each site began very early in the project cycle. An "im-

plementation readiness" assessment was used to determine whether the necessary IT infrastructure was in place and to make sure each site was capable of handling the transition to the new ERP system.

4. *Strict monitoring of implementation schedules and costs.* Once the actual rollout began, a strict deliverable plan was imposed on each local site. All milestones were carefully tracked, measured, and rechecked to ensure that scheduled changes were made on time and on budget.

5. *Cross-cultural training.* To make sure that all affected people (targeted users of the new system as well as consultants and managers) were on the same page in terms of goals and priorities, a project "university" was established in a central location (Paris) to provide training to everyone involved in the project.

6. *Rigorous tracking of deliverables.* Identifying and then relentlessly tracking the complex web of incremental milestones were critical to the success of the project. The methods used were grounded in A.T. Kearney's deliverables philosophy and capitalized on the company's strength and experience in managing large-scale programs.

LESSONS LEARNED

After Delphi established its goals and expected benefits when the program was initiated, A.T. Kearney used its benefit assessment framework, *Implementation Value Capture,* to strictly monitor all deliverables and identify additional revenue-generating or cost-cutting opportunities that Delphi could achieve as a result of implementing the new system.

This highly structured implementation plan set the stage for success. Some of the valuable lessons learned along the way included:

- Define the business value you hope to receive, such as reduction in lead times, in concrete and easily measurable terms.
- Set up regular review measures to make sure you are achieving your goals.
- Don't underestimate the art of "change management." Establishing a training hub (e.g., Delphi's "university" in Paris) helps ensure that all participants in the project — no matter where they are or what language they speak — understand the goals of the project.
- When more than one company is involved, make sure that each one has "skin in the game," sharing in the risk of the venture. In the case of Delphi, both consulting partners — A.T. Kearney and EDS — agreed to share in the risk that the project might not succeed by adhering to a fixed timeframe at a fixed price. Any cost or time overruns would thus be the responsibility of the consulting partners, not Delphi. A.T. Kearney had to excel at planning the program, managing risk, and delivering results.

- Don't lose sight of the impact on the customer. During any major transformation of a company's core business processes, all changes must be absolutely "transparent" to customers. In Delphi's case, with a technically sophisticated clientele such as GM, Ford, Volkswagen, DaimlerChrysler, BMW, among others, the slightest hiccup in manufacturing plans could have had an enormous financial impact on a customer's business. Notes Sanchez, "We not only had to make many more changes than we had originally planned but also had to change how we had originally planned them."

Conventional wisdom says that business is changing so fast that a single Internet year is worth four calendar years; this means that the formerly standard five-year corporate strategic plan needs to take into account the equivalent of 20 years of radical change in a given industry. It's the challenge that many companies face these days. Although the business case for Delphi's ERP project was originally completed in 1996, Delphi's earlier decision to implement SAP clearly helped the company achieve specific strategic objectives such as establishing common systems and standardized internal processes; creating fast, accurate information flows across the supply chain that are customer-driven and supplier-supported; enabling the swift integration of any acquisitions; improving productivity of the finance function and working capital utilization; and reducing the cost of legacy systems by more than 30 percent.

About the decisions made so long ago, in a different business climate, Sanchez agrees it was the right thing to do at the right time. "The team made a number of very wise decisions early on in the process. We are a completely different company now," he says.

Chapter 57
Whether to Outsource and Downsize

Douglas B. Hoyt

This chapter discusses the first step in the outsourcing or downsizing process: deciding whether to outsource or simplify some of the systems and what functions can be performed advantageously or otherwise made more efficient by vendor organizations. This chapter reviews trends in the use of outside services and conditions that make outsourcing favorable. Computer operations managers must consider their organization's many functions, the pros and cons of contracting systems work, ways to downsize without outsourcing, sources for guidance and assistance, and finally an example of outsourced computer work that has proven beneficial in a large organization.

THE CHALLENGE

It has been estimated that 73 percent of leading companies contract out part of their information system (IS) functions, that $6 billion of client/server work was outsourced in 1996, and that 80 percent of IS activities would be performed by contractors as of 2000.

Organizations are finding that outsourcing can cut costs, sharpen management's focus, get access to expertise, and foster global expansion. Computer operations managers should help lead the way in finding improvement opportunities via outsourcing and downsizing and help to support exploratory studies initiated by the managements of their companies. This chapter reviews the ways to analyze and decide whether to and what to outsource and downsize.

Outsourcing Trend Statistics

Outsourcing and downsizing are being done with increasing frequency by large and small organizations to stay competitive and increase profitability. Global competition has added impetus to these steps, which are often tied to the reengineering movement whereby organizations redefine their goals and the processes for achieving them.

The Outsourcing Institute's studies have produced data that give measured perspective to outsourcing trends:

> ... over $40 million will be spent on IT [information technology] outsourcing in 1996 ... IT outsourcing represents 40 percent of the $100 billion U.S. companies will spend on all types of outsourcing in 1996.
>
> Seventy percent of companies that outsource IT, outsource less than 50 percent of their total IT budget.
>
> Areas of outsourcing that are increasing the fastest are the desktop environment and networks which now represent 40 percent of the total outsourcing expenditures.
>
> On average, companies realize a 9 percent annual cost reduction through outsourcing.
>
> Companies surveyed by the Institute report that improving their company's focus and gaining access to the provider's world-class capabilities are equally important reasons for outsourcing as are costs savings.

Need to Study and Weigh Issues

Because so many are using these tools to improve, it behooves each organization to ask itself whether to initiate outsourcing and downsizing steps to stay ahead in its field. Increasingly, service companies have grown that can provide many functions cheaper and more reliably than has been done at their client companies. (Downsizing is usually a by-product of outsourcing; however, downsizing is often done without outsourcing by eliminating "fat" that has grown from inattention, by designing simpler methods for doing the work, by eliminating an unwanted part of the business, or by reducing organizational levels.)

Computer Operations Manager's Role

Computer operations managers should play a leading role in deciding whether, and what, to outsource and downsize. By examining the options and the potential benefits from these actions, the managers who take the initiative in proposing improvements in these areas will be appreciated by their managements for pointing the way to accomplishing the organizations' goals. Also, those who propose outsourcing or downsizing are the persons most likely to be selected to manage the transition and be in charge of overseeing the work of the vendors who end up providing the services.

If senior management has initiated a study to determine whether and what computer operations to outsource or downsize, the computer operations manager should participate in that study, and this chapter should be helpful in pointing out the issues to consider in such an analysis.

Some computer operations managers may see the option of contracting out some of their work as a threat. However, when outsourcing can make for lower costs or other improvements, the managers can demonstrate their leadership by suggesting and promoting that option and should continue their control of the functions involved by being responsible for managing the contractors' work.

TRENDS IN OUTSOURCING

Several recent trends in business structure and relationships with vendors have made some companies more effective and enabled significant cost reductions. One trend is for managements to focus more heavily on the core businesses, contracting out less essential functions. Another is to establish more friendly relationships with other organizations, considering vendors and contractors as "partners" in alliances pursuing common goals. In seeking better ways, sometimes as part of reengineering processes, management questions traditional approaches, keeping an open mind in seeking alternatives that might improve their operations.

Although the organization's philosophy, goals, and strategic directions properly influence the decision whether to and what work to contract out, the organization should also apply the tried-and-true concepts relating to make-or-buy decisions. Outsourcing a computer function involves the same type of considerations that pertain to whether to make or buy a product part such as spark plugs and transmissions, janitorial and guard services, legal work, and vehicle maintenance. In all these matters, management must weigh the decision's effects on costs involved, control, flexibility, reliability, management's ability and time, and the product's or service's criticality to the business.

CONDITIONS THAT MAKE OUTSIDE COMPUTER WORK DESIRABLE

In this day and age of dynamic management and changing conditions, the computer operations manager should periodically review the IS activities to evaluate which might be done to better advantage by an outside organization. In performing such reviews, the computer operations manager should consider several factors as benefits that might be achieved by outsourcing.

Saving Money

Cost saving is a major purpose in many outsourcing decisions these days. Usually, savings can be easily demonstrated when a service provider invests in technology and hardware, the costs of which can be spread among a number of clients. Unless there is some such synergism opportunity, cost savings may be more difficult to prove, even considering all the overhead and administrative costs of doing the work internally, such as fringe benefits, office space, and phone and other services. If cost reduction is the objective, computer operations managers would do well to consider first whether internal costs might be cut before looking to outsourcing as the only way to achieve that objective.

In addition, many outsourcing arrangements provide for vendors to purchase the computer hardware, giving clients the cash resources to use more beneficially elsewhere.

Taking Advantage of Expertise: "Do Not Reinvent the Wheel"

A survey of chief information officers (CIOs) and chief executive officers (CEOs) at 365 companies showed that the need for expertise was the major reason for outsourcing decisions in their organizations.

American Airlines pioneered reservations systems and subsequently let other airlines use the system for a fee. Hyatt is doing the same with its hotel and motel reservation system. Many truckers have fought fiercely for competitive advantage with their computerized shipment tracking systems. These are all cases in which a competitor can benefit by not reinventing the wheel, rather buying a system from a vendor who has developed a practical system.

Free Management for More Critical Functions

For several years, Xerox Corp. outsourced its information systems to Electronic Data Systems Corp. (EDS) for $4.1 billion to permit Xerox's management to direct its energies more fully to strategic matters, in addition to achieving more flexibility, gaining financial advantages, and benefitting from advanced technology.

The freeing up of management's attention is akin to the concept that some systems can be regarded as "commodities." A trucking company would not design and build trucks; it would buy them as commodities. Other companies regard common systems as commodities, such as payroll or even order processing. Rather than design and run a payroll system, for example, a company might prefer to buy its payroll system and operation from a supplier such as Automated Data Processing Corp. (ADP), which specializes in payroll, and free its management's time for more strategic activities related to the organization's prime product or service.

Job Is of Short Duration

Using outside sources for information systems work is clearly advantageous when the tasks at hand are of short duration, when the alternative would be to hire specialists for a short period and then release them.

No Security or Confidentiality Vulnerability

Using outside contractors is sensible only when there is no resulting significant danger likely from the lessening of security or revealing important trade secrets or information to outsiders.

But Not When Internal IS Can Provide a Competitive Edge

If an organization is developing, or can create, a system that gives it an edge over its competitors, as did American Airlines with its Sabre reservation system, it is probably best not to subcontract the work to outsiders.

COMPUTER FUNCTIONS TO CONSIDER FOR OUTSOURCING

When evaluating what computer operations activities might be more advantageously contracted out, computer operations managers should review the systems functions and applications and weigh the types of contractor services available that might be used beneficially.

Most major companies contract out portions of their information technology functions. However, an outsourcing pioneer, Kodak, outsourced its entire data center operations in 1988.

Systems Activities

The traditional systems activities involved started with an organization that had no computers, evaluating what could be computerized, designing the systems for doing so, selecting the equipment, programming the applications, testing, and training the users. These traditional activities continue with new organizations and new functions.

However, most organizations today have gone through the traditional systems development period. Their systems efforts are now directed at maintaining and improving the systems processes for the following purposes:

1. To meet changing business plans, such as new products and new markets, and to meet competitive challenges
2. To take advantage of new technologies such as client/servers and the Internet
3. To fulfill new management goals for reengineering and restructuring business processes, including cost reduction

Each of these three challenges to computer management requires evaluating what new approaches can be adopted, how the changes can be designed and implemented, what equipment should be secured, and where and how it will be operated. The use of outside expertise and services are options to be evaluated in each phase of the reevaluation and redesign process.

The following examples of outsourced systems activities provide a picture of how some have worked well, to the advantage of the client and the contractor.

Programming. Programming assistance can be obtained from consultants, temporary help agencies, and brokers. Work can be done at the client's premises or the vendor's venue. A major trend has been to secure programming from India, the Philippines, Ireland, and other places at costs that can save up to and more than half the cost of using American programmers. These outsourcing sources can be worthwhile when the size and timing of a project make it feasible. An American retail company developed a warehousing program for $500,000 using offshore programmers, which would have cost three times that if done domestically.

Applications Development. Applications development is one of the most frequently outsourced activities. Southern Pacific and Air Canada are two companies that have sought applications development as a main part of their outsourcing plans. Southern Pacific Lines entered into a $415 million, ten-year contract with IBM's Integrated Systems Solutions Corp. (ISSC) to manage its information systems, including applications development, with the employment of new technologies. The development of applications with new technologies and client/servers was a major feature of Air Canada's request for bids to take over its information systems, for $1 billion over seven to ten years.

PCs. PC contractors can provide a variety of services to ease a client's chores, including purchasing, installation, training, cabling, asset management, parts inventory, virus safeguards, and the help desk function. For example, Chemical Bank contracted its PC support activities to Unisys.

Legacy Systems. Developing new systems while maintaining legacy systems can create a manpower and management burden that can be overcome by outside services. Some have retained outsiders to maintain legacy systems while internal staff work on new systems. Others have contracted out new systems development and used existing personnel for legacy maintenance.

LAN and WAN Management. Organizations that cannot afford to keep a network expert at each location have found it beneficial to use local area network (LAN) and wide area network (WAN) outside management services. IBM, Digital Equipment Corp. (DEC), and EDS are among the firms that provide LAN management services. Netsolve Outsourcing Service provides remote WAN service in addition to selling related equipment.

Help Desk. A survey by the Help Desk Institute indicated that most of its 4700 members outsourced the help desk function in 1994. Hewlett Packard (HP), Novell, and EDS are among those providing help desk services. Companies using help desk services find value in their vendors' staff's technical knowledge, phone capabilities, and documentation. Help desk services often involve substantial assistance to users, at widespread locations.

Some organizations maintain an in-house help service and contract out certain types of questions and peak loads.

Applications, or Business Functions

Computer operations managers should consider applications and functions that can be and have been contracted out beneficially. The following examples of outsourced systems applications provide a picture of how some have worked well, to the advantage of the client *and* the contractor.

Reengineering. Amtrak outsourced much of its IS function to IBM's ISSC as part of the organization's reengineering program; ISSC has proposed new ways to perform accounting, reservations, and collection systems as well as help desk, network, and disaster recovery services. HP, Computer Sciences Corp. (CSC), EDS, and Accenture Consulting all provide services in reengineering as well as outsourcing of IS. (Some IT outsourcing firms such as Accenture, EDS, Pricewaterhouse, and KPMG Peat Marwick have broadened their services to include business process outsourcing; that is, actually performing accounting, personnel, order processing, and such operating functions for their clients.)

Sales Effectiveness. Accenture Consulting started a sales effectiveness service, launched in collaboration with Siebel Systems.

Payroll and Human Services. ADP has been a leader in furnishing full-service payroll processing for its clients. ADP, which at one time paid 17 million employees for more than 300,000 clients, branched out to provide related human resources software developed by PeopleSoft, and client/service software with its payroll systems.

E-Mail. The outsourcing of electronic mail systems continues to increase in an effort to free up management's time for other activities and avoid switch installation difficulties. In addition, one expects that e-mail will change with the complexities of client/servers and the World Wide Web.

Traffic Functions. The systems for managing traffic departments, just-in-time material controls, and other logistics activities have similar requirements in varying industries, making it feasible to adopt or adapt a smooth-working system in one place at other organizations. Federal Express, Airborne Express, and others have established consulting services to help clients with their shipment and material control systems. Inchcape Shipping Services furnishes back-office services to shipping companies worldwide.

Electronic Data Interchange (EDI). Blue Cross/Blue Shield of Maryland contracted with EDS to develop an EDI system for processing medical claims connecting patients, insurers, and medical services. The Association of American Railroads requested bids for computer systems incorporating EDI and other features to improve delivery time, customer service, and transactions among the railroads, in an effort to compete better with the trucking industry. IBM's Health Care Network (HCN) connects clinical and benefits information among hospitals, pharmacies, insurers, and 30,000 doctors in eight states.

Healthcare. Kaiser Permanente Health Plan Inc. contracted with ISSC for $70 million of services. Many feel that the health field is a ripe source of outsourcing, being in a dramatic period of change and increased competition, and without advanced information systems in place for many of the organizations in the industry.

Types of Contractor Services

Outsourcing services are available to perform almost all computer functions that might otherwise be done internally — analysis of alternative approaches and recommendation of optimum new directions, equipment evaluation, systems design, programming, training, and running a help desk — and can include running the full range of computer operations and even managing the input and output, either at the vendor's venue or the client's.

Some organizations have outsourced their computer work from soup to nuts, 0.3 percent according to one survey. Several examples of outsourced systems work provide a picture of how some have worked well, to the advantage of the client *and* the contractor.

Training. Accenture Consulting added the training of users to the services it is prepared to furnish its clients.

Transportation Joint Venture. In an unusual arrangement, Delta Airlines subcontracted important information services to AT&T Global Information Solutions. Delta and AT&T formed a company, equally owned, to manage Delta's communications and data processing, in a ten-year $2.8 billion deal that was expected to save Delta $400 million. AT&T indicated its intention to become a leading information technology supplier in competition with major service vendors such as EDS, CSC, and ISSC.

Disaster Recovery. Many firms provide disaster recovery services, such as backup facilities and housing of backup information. Assistance in planning disaster protection measures is a service these companies usually furnish, as do some consulting firms. Disaster protection may be bundled with other information outsourcing services. One survey indicated that disaster recovery was one of the functions most frequently contracted to outsiders.

Open Systems. When Northrop Grumman formed a commercial aircraft division, it decided to establish a computer system separate from that of the parent organization, based on open systems. Cambridge Technology

Partners assisted the division in developing an Open Enterprise Plan, using packaged software tailored by its vendors to work with others through a communal database. In another situation, Telogy, a supplier of electronic test equipment, retained HCL America, a subsidiary of a company in India, to design and program Telogy's reengineering project. Using many vendors' software, HCL and Telogy completed the open system reengineering project in half the time and cost compared to what could have been done by an American firm.

Business Processes via the Internet. Accenture Consulting joined forces with BBN Corp. to provide a turnkey system structure for clients that do not wish to establish their own Internet operations. The joint venture furnished business operations such as billing and order processing on an around-the-clock basis, using the Web and supported by Internet security.

PROS OF OUTSOURCING

In weighing whether or not to contract out any particular function or group of functions, the computer operations manager can analyze the advantages and disadvantages by listing the pros and cons, weighting their relative importance, and applying some numbers to indicate their relative value or disadvantage, The following summary of pros and cons should aid computer operations managers in making such an analysis. This type of methodical appraisal can also be used in preparing a recommendation to management, thus reinforcing the thoroughness and objectivity of the analysis and supporting information.

Availability of Expertise

An outsourcing service or consulting firm may have acquired experience and expertise in an area which a client may need. It is then often faster and cheaper to retain the firm than to develop the experience and expertise in-house. Using the outside service may be the best way to acquire state-of-the-art benefits quickly. For example, some colleges find that firms specializing in college systems can serve their needs better than by developing their systems from scratch.

Economies of Scale, and Shared Costs

The Association of American Railroads developed EDI and other systems to be used by its members more cheaply and effectively than for each member to create its own systems and coordinate them with other members with which it deals. When Hyatt sells its reservation system to other chains, in effect it spreads the development cost among its many customers. Similarly, when ADP furnishes payroll services to its hundreds of clients, it is sharing the costs of developing the common features of its complex and diverse payroll systems among its many customers.

Management Focus on Prime Strategies

When functions are not key to the competitive success of a company, management can often direct more of its time and energies to its essential tasks by contracting work to other organizations that can be depended on to perform those activities reliably and with a minimum of oversight from the client's management. For example, in a company that depends on its logistics systems for its success, the information management may contract out its payroll system to help devote more of its attention to the critical logistics procedures.

Cut Costs

Cost saving may be a prime reason for considering contracting out systems work. It is always one of the important issues to be analyzed. In making a cost comparison, it is important to weigh the full cost of outsourcing — including management's time in overseeing the work — and the full costs of doing the work internally (e.g., fringe benefits, office space, and overhead and administrative costs, including supervision, human resources, and similar costs). Offshore programming, which can save 50 percent or more of programming costs, is a prime example of cost-saving opportunities.

Save Cash

In situations in which an outsourcing service undertakes the operation and management of the computer operations, the service may buy the equipment from the client, providing the client with cash that can be used more advantageously elsewhere. Similarly, when a new function is outsourced rather than done internally, it saves the investment capital — cash — that would otherwise be spent on equipment and start-up costs. When cash availability is a problem, such outsourcing arrangements can be a significant benefit.

Avoid Internal Delays

Telephone companies are anxious to move rapidly to client/server billing and customer service systems. A major reason several telephone companies are outsourcing the design and development of those systems has been to avoid internal delays they would anticipate without the outside help.

Vendors Can Be Good Employers

Countering the disadvantage of disrupting employee morale by letting employees go when a function is contracted out, some have found that employees whom a contractor employs from its client's staff often fare better. With the trend toward outsourcing, outsourcing vendors have become a growing industry, and relocated employees may end up with benefits and security superior to those they had before.

Easier to Terminate or Change

When it becomes necessary to discontinue or revise a function, it may be easier to accomplish if the work has been contracted out. Then the necessity for dropping employees and equipment, hiring new specialists or retraining existing staff, and installing new gear can be avoided.

CONS OF OUTSOURCING

A checklist describes the potential disadvantages of outsourcing. These are matters a computer operations manager should evaluate as they apply to any outsourcing plan that is being considered.

Lessened Direct Control. Control is less direct. Information about outsourced functions is slower to get and less complete than it would be if the activities were done in-house. To make a change in the process involves working with people in another business entity and may require discussions about the terms of the agreement.

Higher Costs. Lower costs of outside work are likely if there are good reasons; for example, a vendor spreading development costs among many clients, or using overseas programmers at a fraction of domestic pay rates. However, without those saving potentials, it is likely to cost more to outsource because vendors must cover their advertising and selling costs, risks, and profit. Unless the contract pricing terms are fixed costs, which many are not, it is likely that the ultimate costs may be impossible to forecast with accuracy. Another danger is that a long-term contract may lock a client into current costs, whereas technology improvements later allow the vendor to reduce its operating costs, with the savings not passed on to the client. Thus, the manager must give a great deal of care and thought to cost projection (e.g., by estimating the best possible outcome, the worst possible outcome, and the most likely outcome). This cost analysis may be the trickiest and most debated part of the thinking-through process.

Exposure of Confidential Information. Contracting work out can often, if not usually, let outsiders know about a client's business plans, customer lists, product plans, and other information that could benefit competitors. Although contract terms may forbid misuse of such information, leaks are more likely when processes are performed by outside organizations.

Dropping Employees Lowers Morale of Remaining Employees. Although openness and considerate termination arrangements can lessen morale damage, the effect of outsourcing on departing and remaining employees must be considered. Some downsized employees have sued and won. At one company, outsourced data capture annoyed its IT staff, which then caused the system to crash. These possible detrimental effects must be anticipated and evaluated in the decision-making process.

Limits a Company's Effectiveness. As one writer has put it, "Outsourcing can only make a company as functional and economically efficient as its competitors."

Inflexibility. Some vendors are unable or unwilling to tailor their services to a client's needs or desires. Also, when a contract is signed, the client is locked into the arrangement and may be less able to maneuver as conditions change.

DOWNSIZING WITHOUT OUTSOURCING

Downsizing — eliminating employees — is usually one result and sometimes the primary objective of outsourcing. The outsourcing vendor performs a needed function previously done by the client's employees. Often, the service vendor hires all or many of the employees let go by the client.

But downsizing can sometimes be effected without outsourcing in four ways: (1) identifying and cutting out "fat," (2) designing a more efficient system, (3) eliminating an unprofitable or unwanted part of the business, and (4) reducing the number of organizational levels.

Cutting Fat. Over time, without tight supervision, workers slow their pace, ineffective people are retained, and jobs that are not essential are perpetuated. The excess staffing is often reduced by arbitrary budget cuts, say 15 or 30 percent. Some work measurement studies can determine the time really necessary to do the work and identify the excess hours or people to eliminate.

Designing a More Efficient System. Creative imagination and analysis can often discover simpler ways to do a job. For example, a manually prepared interdepartmental invoice system was replaced by a simple Lotus spreadsheet design, cutting the time from five to two days to perform. Or, in the programming area, work time can sometimes be reduced by using off-the-shelf software instead of tailor-made systems, or by applying techniques such as CASE (computer-aided software engineering).

Eliminating Less Essential Businesses. Many large banks provided payroll services to clients on the theory that they could run their expensive hardware on the idle shifts and thereby save by spreading their computer equipment costs. However, these banks discovered that doing payrolls for other companies also diverted their managements' efforts, and encountered other problems that drained their sideline profits, which led them to abandon their payroll service outside businesses.

Horizontal versus Hierarchical Organization. Some organizations have reduced staff considerably by eliminating several levels in their hierarchical organization structures. A major electric company is said to have reduced the number of levels by more than 50 percent, cutting thousands of middle-management positions. The simpler structures are made feasible by spreading decision-making powers to the lower levels and by making information available to remaining management staff through more open network systems.

CONCLUSION

What author Tom Peters has said, "Do what you do best and outsource the rest," expresses the general terms of the concept of why and how organizations should decide what work should be contracted. Outsourcing has become fashionable — almost a fad — in recent years, tied in to the trend of reengineering.

Outsourcing is contrary to the traditional instincts of many leaders in business and elsewhere. The leadership type of person enjoys increasing power and control, usually measured by numbers of employees and sizes of buildings and plants. Those instincts have been tempered by examples of organizations that have found that smaller can often be better in terms of meeting goals, profits, and global competition. An extreme example is a successful $20 million consumer product concern that operates with only three employees; all other workers perform as outside contracted services.

Computer operations managers should seek out and support outsourcing and downsizing projects that can help their organizations reach their goals. Tempering normal tendencies to "build empires," managers should perform thorough analyses and evaluations of the multitude of issues involved, many of them old-fashioned make-or-buy considerations, such as the effect on costs, employees, control, reliability, and flexibility.

About the Editor

James B. Ayers is a principal with CGR Management Consultants, Los Angeles, California (e-mail: jimayers@cgrmc.com). He has consulted to management in multiple industries in a 30-year career. His work has brought him into contact with numerous supply chain improvement projects. All have involved large or small changes for the information systems used to manage the supply chain. All also involved process and organization change.

Jim has authored numerous articles on strategy, process improvement, and product development. He is active with the Supply-Chain Council in the development of its reference model for supply chain management.

Jim holds a BS with distinction from the U.S. Naval Academy and MBA and MS Industrial Engineering degrees from Stanford University. As a naval officer, he served on nuclear submarines. He is also a member of the Society of Manufacturing Engineers and Council of Logistics Management. He is a Management Consultant (CMC) certified by the Institute of Management Consultants.

Index